Studying Public Policy

PRINCIPLES AND PROCESSES

Michael Howlett
M. Ramesh
Anthony Perl

FOURTH EDITION

OXFORD
UNIVERSITY PRESS

OXFORD
UNIVERSITY PRESS

Oxford University Press is a department of the University of Oxford.
It furthers the University's objective of excellence in research, scholarship,
and education by publishing worldwide. Oxford is a registered trade mark of
Oxford University Press in the UK and in certain other countries.

Published in Canada by
Oxford University Press
8 Sampson Mews, Suite 204,
Don Mills, Ontario M3C 0H5 Canada

www.oupcanada.com

Library and Archives Canada Cataloguing in Publication

Title: Studying public policy : policy cycles and policy subsystems / Michael Howlett,
M. Ramesh, and Anthony Perl.
Names: Howlett, Michael, 1955- author. | Ramesh, M., 1960- author. | Perl, Anthony,
1962- author of screenplay.
Description: Fourth edition. | Includes bibliographical references and index.
Identifiers: Canadiana (print) 20190194170 | Canadiana (ebook) 20190194189 | ISBN 9780199026142
(softcover) | ISBN 9780199039104 (looseleaf) | ISBN 9780199026159 (EPUB)
Subjects: LCSH: Policy sciences—Textbooks. | LCGFT: Textbooks.
Classification: LCC H97 .H69 2020 | DDC 320.6—dc23

Cover image: © GraphicDealer/Shutterstock.com
Cover design: Sherill Chapman
Interior design: Sherill Chapman

Oxford University Press is committed to our environment.
This book is printed on Forest Stewardship Council® certified paper
and comes from responsible sources.

FSC
www.fsc.org
FSC® C008955

MIX
Paper from
responsible sources

Printed and bound in the United States of America

1 2 3 4 — 23 22 21 20

Contents

Acknowledgements   *viii*

II ❖ The Policy Cycle   100

III ❖ Long-Term Policy Dynamics   273

Acknowledgements

Many individuals contributed to this book. In addition to the many authors and investigators whose empirical and conceptual work provides the foundation for the summaries and discussions contained herein, we are also grateful for the comments and criticisms received from the reviewers of the book's first three editions and from the many students and instructors who have used the book and took the time to tell us about their experiences.

This edition includes a considerable amount of new material, elements of which have appeared in conference papers, journal articles, and book chapters. We would like to thank all of the publication teams, reviewers, and conference participants who have constructively engaged with this material and helped us refine our thoughts and arguments.

While the list of those to thank is far too numerous to include here, we would like to express our gratitude to some of our closest colleagues and collaborators, whose personal interventions at critical junctures very much helped to shape the direction of our thinking on the subject of "studying public policy." And, of course, we all owe much to our families for their sympathy and understanding over the years. Special thanks to Rebecca Raglon, Alex and Anna Howlett, and Andrea Banks, and Sandy and Nikisha for keeping us grounded during the writing process.

Chapter 1

Studying Public Policy
Why and How

Public Policy Defined

Nearly every experience in our life, from cradle to grave, is shaped by public policy. There are policies that create or shape the hospitals where we are born, the schools where we study, the organizations for which we work, and the homes in which we live. All the income that we will earn (legally) is taxed according to public policy, and pensions that extend that income into our retirement are both regulated and partly funded by the public treasury. And after our demise, our funeral formalities and estates, of whatever size, will be governed by public policy, too. Public policy is, however, much easier to experience than define, as is evident in the wide range of interpretations that have been offered by scholars.

While these many definitions offer substantial areas of agreement, they also differ considerably in detail (Birkland, 2001: Ch. 1). Two widely used definitions illustrate the diverse meanings ascribed to public policy by different authors, even when they agree on the fundamental motives behind policy-making and the processes that translate these ideas into action.

In probably the best-known and simplest definition, Thomas Dye describes public policy as "anything a government chooses to do or not to do" (Dye, 1972: 2). This is, of course, too simple, as it would apply equally to every governmental activity, from either purchasing or deferring the acquisition of paper clips to firing off nuclear missiles or aborting their launch. Such generality provides no means of differentiating between the trivial and the significant aspects of government activities. Nevertheless, this definition has merits.

First, Dye's definition specifies that the primary agent of public policy-making is a government. This clarifies that private decisions by businesses, social groups, or individuals are not in themselves public policies. Only governments can make *authoritative* decisions on behalf of citizens, that is, ones backed up by legitimate sanctions for transgressors in the event of noncompliance. Although the activities of non-governmental actors can often influence governments' policy decisions, and governments sometimes delegate implementation of policy to non-governmental organizations (NGOs), the efforts and initiatives of such actors do not in themselves constitute public policy. Thus, for example, how the medical profession understands the cause of lung cancer and the solutions it proposes for preventing and curing that disease may influence what a government eventually does about the public health problem caused by smoking. However, physician-recommended solutions are not in themselves public policies; only measures that a government adopts and enforces to this end—such as restricting the sale or use of tobacco—actually constitute *public* policy.

Second, Dye highlights the fact that public policy-making involves a fundamental choice on the part of governments to either do something or to do nothing about a problem and that this decision is made by elected politicians and other government officials. As Dye notes, public policy is, at its simplest, a choice made by government to undertake some course of action. This highlights that a "negative" or "non-decision," that is, a government's decision to do nothing and simply maintain the current course of action or status quo (Crenson, 1971; R.A. Smith, 1979) is just as much a policy decision as a choice to attempt to alter some part of the status quo. Such "negative" decisions, however, like more "positive" ones, must be *deliberate*, such as when a government decides not to increase taxes or declines to make funding available for arts, health care, or some other policy area rather than, for example, simply failing to address a new problem that may not have attained a position on the government's radar.

Third, and relatedly, Dye's definition also highlights the fact that a public policy is a *conscious* choice by government. That is, government actions and decisions often yield *unintended consequences*, such as when an effort to regulate tobacco consumption or some other vice results in the activity "going underground" and operating illegally as a "black market." Unless this subsequent activity or consequence was specifically anticipated and intended by government (such as occurs when governments increase gasoline taxes to discourage automobile use and thus promote the use of public transit), an unintended consequence of policy should not be equated with public policy but rather recognized as its unexpected by-product, which sometimes may be beneficial (such as when regulation spurs innovation in alternative products) and sometimes not (as in the smuggling case above).

These three points are central to understanding public policy as an applied problem-solving process, and Dye's definition highlights the need to carefully examine conscious, deliberate government decisions in order to further develop that understanding. Other definitions add additional layers of complexity, as they attempt to separate the trivial from the significant elements of policy. William Jenkins, for example, offered a much more precise conceptualization of public policy than Dye's definition provides, while illustrating many of the same themes.

Jenkins (1978) defined public policy as "a set of interrelated decisions taken by a political actor or group of actors concerning the selection of goals and the means of achieving them within a specified situation where those decisions should, in principle, be within the power of those actors to achieve." This definition is very helpful in clarifying many components of policy that were only implicit in Dye's definition. One is to clearly specify that policy-making comprises a "set of inter-related decisions," while Dye's model could be misconstrued as limiting policy-making to a single choice opportunity and result. While Dye's definition presumes that an underlying process exists behind decision-making, it does not state so explicitly. Jenkins, however, presents policy-making as an inherently *dynamic* process and explicitly acknowledges that governments rarely address problems with a single decision. Policies, rather, usually involve a *series of decisions* that cumulatively contribute to an outcome. Thus, a health policy, for example, consists of a series of decisions on building health facilities, certifying personnel and treatment, and financing healthcare provision, among many other related items (Tuohy, 1999). These interrelated decisions are often made by different individuals and agencies within government resulting in a much more complex policy-making process than a quick reading of Dye's definition might suggest. These varied actors interact within "policy subsystems" and shape many elements of the policy-making process. They are the first major topic covered by this book, and are discussed in Chapters 2 and 3.

Jenkins also improves upon Dye's definition by recognizing that a government's *capacity* to formulate and implement its decisions exerts a significant influence on public policy-making and policy outputs and is a major consideration in assessing the types of actions governments consider. Jenkins's definition recognizes, in a way that Dye's does not, that limitations on a government's ability to think and act can constrain the decision options being considered and can advance or undermine the success of policy-making efforts. A government's policy choices may be limited, for instance, by lack of financial, personnel, or informational resources required for certain programs, by international treaty obligations, or by domestic resistance to certain options. Understanding governments' actions also requires an increasingly detailed awareness of the limits and opportunities provided by international agreements, treaties, and conventions (Milner & Keohane, 1996; Doern et al., 1996a). And, to continue the above example, we will not understand health policy in many countries without realizing the powerful, self-serving opposition that the medical profession can mount against any government effort to control healthcare costs by reducing professionals' income (Alford, 1972). Such external and internal structural constraints complicate the analysis of policy-making much more than might be assumed from Dye's definition, which could be read as suggesting any decision or choice is as likely as any other. The ways in which organizational structures within and beyond government impact public policy capacity forms a second major topic of this book and is also explored in Chapters 2 and 3, as well as in subsequent chapters.

Third, Jenkins also introduces the idea of public policy-making as goal-oriented behaviour since, in his definition, public policies are decisions taken by governments that define a goal and set out a means to achieve it. This specifies that the *content* of a policy decision is composed of the "selection of goals and means." Although this says nothing about the nature of the goals (or the means involved), viewing policy as the pursuit of conscious goals raises the importance of ideas and knowledge in influencing policy-making and the need to understand both these and how they are linked to the policy tools or instruments that are the means used by governments to deliver on those goals. Ideas about goals shape actors' understanding of policy problems and the "appropriateness" of potential solutions, while the choices made about tools affects the likelihood of whether or not programs can achieve them.

This process of matching goals and means in policy-making has two dimensions: technical and political. The *technical* dimension seeks to identify an optimal relationship between goals and tools, since some tools are better suited to address the core causes of particular problems than others, and is often thought about and treated as an instance of policy *design* (Howlett, 2019). However, there is rarely agreement on what constitutes a policy problem or an appropriate "solution," which also makes the "design" process in the policy realm unavoidably *political*. Moreover, the analysis of both problems and solutions is further constrained by the existing state of knowledge about social and economic problems, as well as policy actors' ideas, norms, and principles with respect to what they consider to be appropriate courses of action to follow. These ideational and knowledge-based or epistemological assumptions shape both actors' understandings about what constitutes a "problem" as well as the kinds of policy actions that they feel are "feasible" and "acceptable" (May, 2005; Majone, 1975; Melstner, 1972; Huitt, 1968).

Methodological Considerations for Studying Public Policy

Taken together, definitions like those of Dye and Jenkins provided above give us a general sense and outline of what a public policy is. Their emphasis on the contributions that actors, structures, and ideas bring to making policy help highlight some methodological concerns that arise when studying public policy.

First, these definitions reveal that public policy cannot be studied simply by analyzing the official records of government such as laws, acts, regulations, and official reports. Although these are a vital source of information, public policies extend beyond the record of formal investigation and official decisions to encompass the realm of potential choices, or choices not made (Howlett, 1986) and who it is that influences both kinds of choices. That is, the analysis of such choices necessarily involves considering the array of state and societal actors involved in decision-making processes and their capacities for influence and action. Policy decisions do not reflect the unencumbered will of government decision-makers so much as evidence about how that will interacts with and is constrained by the actors, structure, and ideas active in a policy-making exercise at any given political and social conjuncture or point in time (Sharkansky, 1971).

Moreover, if we looked at only policy decisions per se, then describing government policy would be both straightforward and easy compared to the effort required to understand in more general terms *why* a state adopts the policy it does. Sometimes a government may officially announce the reasons behind its decision, and these reasons may even be true. However, it is also common for a government not to give any reason for making a decision, or for the publicly stated reason not to be the actual reason that a decision was taken. In such situations it is left to analysts to determine why a particular alternative was chosen and, very often, why some other seemingly more attractive option was not.

In dealing with this complexity, an oft-noted distinction is made between *policy analysis* and *policy studies* as modes of inquiry. *Policy analysis* tends to pursue formal evaluation or estimation of "policy impacts" or outcomes, usually by applying quantitative techniques such as cost–benefit analysis (CBA) or risk assessment and management (Weimer & Vining, 1992). It seeks to explicitly measure the direct and indirect effects of specific policies, using techniques of statistical inference to explore the links between, for example, specific government programs and various measures of policy "outcomes," such as indicators of social change and progress. Economists, for example, have applied policy analysis to a wide range of topics in easily quantifiable realms, yielding detailed investigations on, for example, the relationship between government expenditures and corporate investment activity or labour migration. *Policy analysis* thus focuses mainly on the effects of policy outputs, however, and says very little about the policy processes that created those outputs (Lynn, 1987).

Policy studies, on the other hand, are broader in scope, examining not just individual programs and their effects, but also their causes and presuppositions, and the processes that led to their adoption. One common type of policy study, for example, has attempted to associate particular types of policies with the attributes of political regimes—defined loosely as the organizational features of a political system (Wolfe, 1989; Przeworski & Limongi, 1997). It has often been argued, by B. Guy Peters (Peters et al., 1977) and Frances Castles (1998; Castles & McKinlay, 1997), for example, that both the policy content and the form of public policy-making vary according to the nature of a political system and the links their decision-makers have with civil society. Much effort has gone into classifying and differentiating between regime types, with the expectation that properly identifying the regime will generate insights into the policies they adopt (Steinberger, 1980).

Another approach to policy studies has sought to identify causal variables in public policy-making, which are sometimes referred to as "policy determinants" (Munns, 1975; Hancock, 1983). Analyses in this tradition, such as those carried out by Harold Wilensky (1975; Wilensky et al., 1985; Wilensky & Turner, 1987) in the mid-1970s, attempted to resolve the question of whether public policies are determined by macro-level socio-economic factors or by micro-level behaviour through the cross-national comparative analysis of policy-making in sectors such as health and welfare (Rakoff & Schaefer, 1970).

Yet another strand of the policy studies literature focuses on understanding "policy content" as a predictor of policy processes. This approach builds from the idea that the nature of a policy problem and the solutions devised to address it often determine how policy will be processed by the political system. In this approach, problems are expected to trigger different attempts to resolve them depending on whether they are regulatory, distributive, redistributive, or constitutive in character. Hence, as Theodore Lowi (1972) put it, ultimately "policy may determine politics" and not the other way around, as most analysts commonly suppose. In a similar vein, James Q. Wilson (1974) argued that the degree of concentration of costs and benefits imposed on political actors by a particular policy shapes the type of policy processes that will accompany it. Lester Salamon (1981), taking this insight to heart, argued that focusing on the attributes of the policy tools or instruments governments have at their disposal to implement public policies is therefore the best mode of analysis for understanding public policy.

These different literatures and analytical traditions have existed, in part, as a result of the diverse analytical communities working on public policy. Governments themselves, of course, have always been involved in policy analysis, both within (Meltsner, 1976; Rogers et al., 1981) and beyond their borders (Rose, 1991). However, many analysts work for NGOs such as corporations, religious orders, labour unions, and think tanks or research institutes, as well as within the university system (Pal, 1992; Cohn, 2004; Gormley, 2007). Analysts working for governments and for groups directly affected by public policies tend to focus their research on policy evaluation. They often have a direct interest in condemning or condoning specific policies on the basis of the projected or actual impact on their client organization. Private think tanks and research institutes usually enjoy more autonomy, though some may be influenced by the preferences of their funders. Nevertheless, they remain interested in the "practical" side of policy and tend to concentrate either on policy outcomes or on the instruments and techniques that generate those outcomes.

Academics, on the other hand, have greater independence and usually have no direct personal stake in the outcome of specific policies, except to the extent they are working within or are committed to a particular ideological stance. Academics can therefore examine public policies more abstractly than can other analysts and tend to grapple with the theoretical, conceptual, and methodological issues surrounding public policy-making through the lens of policy studies. Academic investigation tends to look at the entire policy process and take into account many factors, including policy regimes, policy determinants, policy instruments, and policy content in the resulting explanations (Gordon et al., 1977).

How these analysts explain specific public policy outcomes is influenced by the frameworks they employ and the aspects of policy-making these frameworks emphasize or downplay (Danziger, 1995; Yanow, 1992; Phillips, 1996). These models and techniques orient analysts toward either of two broad approaches to the subject. On the one hand, there are those who believe that a reasonably *objective* analysis of policy goals and outcomes is possible and that these subjects can be explored with standard social science methodologies for collecting data about policy choices and actions and analyzing them to determine causation or correlation (Bobrow & Dryzek, 1987; Radin, 2000; Lynn, 1999). In this *"positivist"* view, students of public policy must be skilled in evaluating policy outcomes and processes and understanding, for example, why a policy was not implemented as intended and failed, or why it may have succeeded despite poor implementation (Bovens et al., 2001; Bovens & t'Hart, 1995, 1996). This view of the nature of policy reality is one generally shared by policy analysts.

Other analysts and many adherents of policy studies, however, embrace more subjective, interpretive or what are sometimes referred to as *"post-positivist"* techniques, which they argue better help them discern and critique government aims, intentions, and actions. An example of this approach would be examining the way decision-makers' assumptions about human behaviour influence their decisions to use certain policy implementation techniques or how gender, ethnic, or other social prejudices and biases affect the choices made (Torgerson, 1996; Thompson, 2001; Yanow, 1999; Dryzek, 2005). Although the differences between positive and post-positive approaches should not be overstated (Howlett & Ramesh, 1998), they serve to underscore how orientations toward policy-making as a social phenomenon affect both the choice of analytical techniques and the outcomes of analysis.

In recent years, there has also been a growing disquiet among both positivist and post-positivist scholars and practitioners that developments in the "co-creation" of public facts may have breached both established norms of democracy and expertise and undermined both approaches to policy analysis (Jasanoff & Simmet, 2017). The ongoing transgression of evidence and expertise found in many countries in the present era threatens not only the governmental institutions that undergird both democratic politics and successful policy-making in the public interest but also the positivist need for accurate and uncontested data and the post-positivist desire to move public policy in the opposite direction, highlighting biases in order to remove or minimize, not strengthen, them (Kim et al., 2008). Undermining the public acceptance of expertise and the willingness to defer to facts and evidence is a critical element of many contemporary populist regimes and has served as a tool to negate policy efforts in areas such as climate change remediation or gender and racial equality, instead promoting, for example, climate change denial and immigrant scapegoating (Lewandowsky et al., 2015; Ley 2018).

These challenges have been devastating for efforts on the part of both positivist and post-positivist policy scholars to promote greater evidence-based policy-making and have led to questions about whether rigorous policy analysis can survive this challenge as it did earlier threats, such as the faith-based attacks of previous eras that equated careful study and rigour with an attack on religion and a denial of the significance of faith-based moral and other ideals (Hula et. al., 2007; Kissane, 2007).

These problems have several dimensions and implications. At the individual level, for example, the credibility of professional analysts who incorporate influential, but unsubstantiated, "alternative facts" into policy assessments and recommendations may see their claims to expertise compromised. Such analytical malpractice can spread among policy professionals who intentionally adopt or reproduce misinformation in order to press the priority of their claims on government action. And if the incorporation of erroneous facts and evidence into policy deliberations reaches a critical mass among either the public or experts, then the integrity of policy-making institutions themselves can also be diminished, as happened in the past with fascist and totalitarian regimes that attempted to control the truth.

It is precisely because the stakes are so high that the model for studying public policy presented in this book offers a valuable framework to guide researchers and practitioners in navigating these troubled waters. We will demonstrate how existing policy frameworks continue to remain very useful and require little change in their organization in order to continue to reveal valuable insights about influences on policy-making behaviour, outputs, and outcomes. Overall, the models set out in the book help us to understand the challenges to policy learning, the temptation to embrace placebos and empty symbols, the increased policy churn, the loss of direction, and the sources of failed policies in the contemporary world (Del Vicario, 2017).

The Policy Cycle Framework: A Problem-Solving Model of the Policy Process

All of the definitions provided above rest upon the understanding that public policy is a "process." That is, as both Jenkins and Dye noted, it is a complex phenomenon consisting of numerous decisions made by many individuals and organizations inside government, while these decisions are influenced by others operating within and outside of the state. Policy outcomes are seen as being shaped both by the structures within which these actors operate and the ideas they hold—forces that also have affected earlier policies and related decisions in previous iterations of policy-making. As such, the procedural and substantive complexity of studying public policy is considerable, posing many analytical challenges for those seeking insight.

Historically, one of the most popular means of simplifying public policy-making for analytical purposes has been to conceive of it not just as a process, but as a specific kind of process consisting of interrelated stages through which policy issues flow in a more or less sequential fashion from "inputs" (problem recognition) to "outputs" (policies). This sequence of stages is often referred to as a *"policy cycle"* (Werner & Wegrich, 2007).

This simplification has its origins in the earliest works on public policy analysis, but has received disparate treatment in the hands of different authors. The idea of advancing public policy studies by breaking the process down into a number of discrete stages was first broached in the early policy studies of Harold Lasswell (1956), one of the pioneers and promoters of what he termed "the policy science" (Farr et al., 2006). This model views policy-making in essentially pragmatic terms, as the embodiment of efforts to improve the human condition through harnessing reason to guide human activities, in this case, in the process of governing (Hawkesworth, 1992; Clemons & McBeth, 2001; Dunn, 2019). Improvements are not, however, a matter of forcing reality to fit within the confines of a theory. Rather, theory and practice reinforce each other as theory is fine-tuned in the light of practice, while practice is altered by the application of theory. This relationship is based upon *learning*, and a pragmatic approach to policy-making views policy development as a process of policy learning, in which policy-makers struggle through an incremental trial-and-error process of choosing a policy, monitoring its results, and then amending their action in subsequent policy-making rounds while pursuing their original goals or modified ones (Dunn, 2019). The policy cycle, therefore, goes beyond merely input and output stages, but also extends to monitoring and evaluative activities once outputs have emerged.

In his own work, Lasswell (1971) divided the policy process into seven stages, which, in his view, described not only how public policies were actually made but also how they should be made: (1) intelligence, (2) promotion, (3) prescription, (4) invocation, (5) application, (6) termination, and (7) appraisal. In this construct, the policy process begins with intelligence-gathering, that is, the collection, processing, and dissemination of information by policy-makers. It then moves to the promotion of particular options by those involved in making the policy decision. In the third stage the decision-makers prescribe a course of action. In the fourth stage the prescribed course of action is invoked alongside a set of sanctions to penalize those who fail to comply with these prescriptions. The policy is then applied by the courts and the bureaucracy and runs its course until it is terminated or cancelled. Finally, the results of the policy are appraised or evaluated against the original aims and goals.

Lasswell's analysis of the policy-making process was focused, like Dye's, on decision-making within government and said little about external influences on the state. It simply assumed that policy-making was pursued by a small number of officials within the government. Another shortcoming of this early model was its placing of policy appraisal after termination, since policies would logically be evaluated prior to being wound down rather than afterwards. Nevertheless, this model was highly influential in the development of policy studies (deLeon, 1999). Although not entirely accurate, it managed the complexity of studying public policy by allowing each stage to be isolated and examined before putting the process back together to ascertain the whole picture.

Lasswell's formulation inspired many other process-oriented models (Lyden et al., 1968; Simmons et al., 1974). Typical of these was a simpler version of the policy cycle developed by Gary Brewer (1974). According to Brewer, the policy process is composed of only six stages: (1) invention/initiation, (2) estimation, (3) selection, (4) implementation, (5) evaluation, and (6) termination. In Brewer's view, invention or initiation referred to the earliest stage in the sequence when a problem would be initially sensed. This stage, he argued, would be characterized by an ill-conceived definition of the problem and suggested solutions to it. The second stage of estimation concerns calculation of the risks, costs, and benefits associated with each of the various solutions raised in the earlier stage. This would involve both technical evaluation and normative choices. The object of this stage is to narrow the range of plausible choices by excluding the unfeasible ones and, somehow, to rank the remaining options in terms of desirability. The third stage consists of adopting or rejecting some combination of the solutions remaining at the end of the estimation stage. The remaining three stages comprise implementing the selected option, evaluating the results of the entire process, and terminating the policy according to the conclusions reached by its evaluation.

Brewer's version of the policy process improved on Lasswell's pioneering work by expanding beyond the confines of government in exploring how problems are recognized. It also clarified the terminology for describing the various stages of the process. Moreover, it introduced the notion of the policy process as an ongoing cycle. It recognized that most policies do not have a fixed life cycle—moving from birth to death—but rather seem to recur, in slightly different guises, as one policy succeeds another with minor or major modification (Brewer and deLeon, 1983). Brewer's insights inspired several other versions of the policy cycle to be developed in the 1970s and 1980s, the best known of which were set out in textbooks by Charles O. Jones (1984) and James Anderson (1984). Each contained slightly different interpretations of the names, number, and order of stages in the cycle.

Highlighting the logic behind the cycle model helps avoid the plethora of similar yet slightly different models of policy stages (Hupe & Hill, 2006). In the works of Brewer, Jones, and others the operative principle justifying the focus on a policy cycle is the logic of applied problem-solving, even though this logic remains implicit. The stages in applied problem-solving and the corresponding stages in the policy process are depicted in Figure 1.1.

In this model, *agenda-setting* refers to the process by which problems come to the attention of governments; *policy formulation* refers to how policy options are formulated within government; *decision-making* is the process by which governments adopt a particular course of action or non-action; *policy implementation* relates to how governments put policies into effect; and *policy evaluation* refers to the processes by which the results of policies are monitored and judged by both state and societal actors, the outcome of which may be reconceptualization of policy problems and solutions. This model will be used throughout the book and forms the basis for separate chapters on each stage found in Chapters 4–8.

This model is useful not only because of the way it separates out distinct tasks conducted in the process of public policy-making, but also because it helps clarify the different, though interactive, roles played in the process by policy actors, institutions, and ideas (Sobeck, 2003; Parag, 2006, 2008). In this view, agenda-setting is a stage in which virtually any (and all) policy actors might be involved in decrying problems and demanding government action. These policy actors—whether all, many, or few—can be termed the *policy universe*. At the next stage, formulation, only a subset of the policy universe—the *policy subsystem*—is involved in discussing options to deal with problems recognized as requiring some government action. The subsystem is composed of only those actors with sufficient knowledge of a problem area, or a resource at stake, to allow them to participate in the process of developing possible alternative courses of action to address the issues raised at the agenda-setting stage. When a decision is being taken on one or more, or none, of these options to implement, the number of actors is reduced even further, to only the subset of the policy subsystem composed of *authoritative government decision-makers*, whether elected officials, judges, or bureaucrats. Once implementation begins, however, the number of actors increases once again to the relevant *subsystem* and then, finally, with the evaluation of the results of that implementation, expands once again to encompass the entire *policy universe* (see Figure 1.2).

Figure 1.1 Stages of the Policy Cycle and Applied Problem-Solving

Applied Problem-Solving	Stages in Policy Cycle
Problem Recognition	1. Agenda-Setting
Proposal of Solution	2. Policy Formulation
Choice of Solution	3. Decision-Making
Putting Solution into Effect	4. Policy Implementation
Monitoring Results	5. Policy Evaluation

Figure 1.2 The Policy Cycle–Actor Hourglass

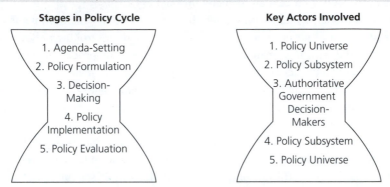

It is important to note that the policy cycle model has both advantages and disadvantages as a framework for analysis of public policy processes. The most important advantage is that it facilitates an understanding of a multi-dimensional process by disaggregating the complexity of the process into any number of stages and sub-stages, each of which can be investigated alone or in terms of its relationship to any or all the other stages of the cycle. This aids theory-building by allowing the results of numerous case studies and comparative studies of different stages to be synthesized. Second, the approach can be used at all socio-legal or spatial levels of policy-making, from that of local governments to those operating in the international sphere (Fowler & Siegel, 2002; Bogason, 2000; Billings & Hermann, 1998). Also, as discussed above, this model permits examination of the intertwined role of all actors, ideas, and institutions involved in policy creation, not just those governmental agencies formally charged with the task.

The principal disadvantage of this model is that it can be misinterpreted as suggesting that policy-makers go about solving public problems in a very systematic and more or less linear fashion (Jenkins-Smith & Sabatier, 1993; Howard, 2005). This, obviously, is not the case in reality, as the identification of problems and the development and implementation of solutions are often very ad hoc and idiosyncratic processes (Beland & Howlett, 2016). Frequently, decision-makers merely react to circumstances, and do so in terms of their interests and pre-set ideological dispositions (Stone, 1988; Tribe, 1972). Similarly, while the logic of systematic problem-solving may be elegant in principle, in practice the stages are often compressed or skipped, or are followed in an order unlike that specified by the model (Timmermans & Bleiklie, 1999). The cycle may not be a single iterative loop, for example, but rather a series of smaller loops in which, to cite just one possibility, the results of past implementation decisions may have a major impact on future policy formulation, regardless of the specifics of the agenda-setting process in the case concerned. Or, as some analysts have noted, policy formulation can sometimes precede agenda-setting as "solutions seek problems" to which they can be applied

(Kingdon, 1984; Salamon & Lund, 1989; Beland & Howlett, 2016). In other words, there is often no linear progression of policy-making as implied by the model.

Second, it is unclear exactly at which level and with what unit of government the policy cycle model should be used. Should the model be applied to all types of governmental activity, from the legislative to the judicial? Or is it only applicable to specific kinds of decisions taken by particular organizations such as bureaucracies (Schlager, 1999)? Third, and perhaps most importantly, the model in itself lacks any notion of causation. It offers no pointers as to what, or who, drives a policy from one stage to another, and seems to assume that policy development must inevitably continue to move from stage to stage, rather than stall or end at a particular point in the cycle, without explaining why this should be the case (Sabatier, 1992). Fourth, it does not say anything at all about the content of a policy (Everett, 2003).

The weaknesses of the framework underscore the need to develop better ideas to advance its understanding. While the simple five-stage cycle model helps analysis by disaggregating the policy process into a series of distinct stages, it does not illuminate the nuances and complexities of public policy-making within each stage or over the cycle as a whole. A better model is needed that delineates in greater detail the actors and institutions involved in the policy process, helps identify the instruments available to policy-makers, and points out the factors that lead to certain policy outcomes rather than others (Mazmanian & Sabatier, 1980). This improved model of the policy process is set out in Part II of this book.

The Need for Public Policy Capacity

Regardless of how policy-making unfolds, however, it is an activity that draws heavily upon the resources or capabilities of governments. That is, how a government addresses public problems and the extent to which it succeeds are not abstract issues but rather depend heavily on its *policy capacity*. This has become especially critical as governments are called upon to address increasingly varied and thus often more resource-intensive problems, such as climate change and global warming or mass migrations of populations. The increasing complexity of many contemporary policy problems coupled with rising expectations of the public for effective action present extraordinary challenges to governments in making and implementing policies. The global financial crisis of 2008, for example, starkly underscored the inability of industrialized countries to effectively control the global financial sector, not to mention developing countries where this and other capacity deficits are clearly visible and stubbornly persistent in many other areas of social and economic life.

Most scholars define policy capacity from the perspective of the government, although the capacity of non-governmental actors is also critical. It is important to note that understanding policy capacity requires extending examination beyond the government itself, recognizing that a wide range of organizations, such as political parties, NGOs, private businesses, and international organizations, as well as multiple government agencies, are involved in policy processes and thus their capacities affect government's performance. That is, the skills and resources of governments have counterparts in policy-oriented NGOs that need to be nurtured so that government can be effective. Therefore, while the policy capacity of a government plays the key role in determining policy outcomes, the capacity of other stakeholders in policy-making is also an important contributing factor to what will get accomplished.

In particular, most studies have focused on aspects of a government's ability to make and execute choices (see Peters, 1996; Bakvis, 2000; Savoie 2003; Parsons, 2004; Howlett & Lindquist 2004; Painter & Pierre, 2005). Painter & Pierre (2005), for example, define policy capacity as ". . . the ability to marshal the necessary resources to make intelligent collective choices, in particular to set strategic directions, for the allocation of scarce resources to public ends." Others have retained this governmental focus but included additional skills and resources such as those involved in the acquisition and utilization of policy-relevant knowledge, the ability to frame options, the application of both qualitative and quantitative research methods to policy problems, the effective use of communications, and stakeholder management strategies (Howlett, 2009; Oliphant & Howlett, 2010).

Following on Moore's (1995) analysis of government needs, key skills or competences that compose policy capacity can be categorized into three types: analytical, operational, and political. Each of these three competences involves resources or capabilities at three different levels—individual, organizational, and systemic—generating nine basic types of policy-relevant capacity (see Figure 1.3).

This highlights that capacity is not restricted to a particular function, stage, or task in a policy process, but rather covers all policy activities and processes. The challenges facing government in performing these various policy tasks are different, and adequate capacity in carrying out one task does not guarantee the effective performance of other tasks. At the same time, it allows for the possibility that there are often skills and resources that can be shared across task environments.

Figure 1.3 Policy Capacity: Skills and Resources

		Skills and Competences		
		Analytical	Operational	Political
Levels of Resources and Capabilities	Individual	Individual Analytical Capacity	Individual Operational Capacity	Individual Political Capacity
	Organizational	Organizational-Analytical Capacity	Organizational Operational Capacity	Organizational-Political Capacity
	Systemic	Systemic Analytical Capacity	Systemic Operational Capacity	Systemic-Political Capacity

At the systemic level, capabilities such as the level of support and trust that a public agency enjoys from its political masters and from the society at large (Blind, 2006), as well as the nature of the economic and security systems within which policy-makers operate, are key components of policy capacity. Factors such as trust and available personnel and financial resources are critical determinants of organizational capabilities and thus of public managers' and analysts' ability to work on policy. Political support both from above and below is vital because agencies and managers must be considered legitimate by citizens and policy subjects in order to obtain and retain resources and support from their authorizing institutions and constituencies (Painter & Pierre, 2005).

Capacity also depends on the skills and competences of individual actors and organizations that perform key policy functions. At the individual level, policy professionals—such as policy-makers, public managers, and policy analysts—determine how well various tasks and functions in the policy process are conducted, and their capacity in turn depends upon knowledge about policy processes, skills in policy analysis and evaluation, managerial expertise, and political judgment. However, high levels of individual policy capacity may not guarantee policy effectiveness because further resources and capacities are also required at the organizational level as well as at the system level. At the organizational level, availability and effectiveness of information infrastructure, human and financial resource management systems, and political support will enhance individual capabilities, just as their absence will detract from it. Organizations that unduly circumscribe individual decision-making responsibility or undermine morale among policy professionals, for example, can undermine an agency's ability to function effectively (Tiernan & Wanna, 2006; Gleeson et al., 2011). These and other aspects of capacity are addressed in subsequent chapters of the book.

Identifying and Studying Policy Styles and Policy Regimes

Finally, it should also be noted that while in theory the kinds of alternatives and ideas that governments could have about what actions they should take are virtually limitless, in practice the range of options and alternatives is often much smaller and the amount of change in policies over time is much less than might be expected. Numerous case studies, for example, have highlighted how existing ideological and institutional factors insulate policies from change.

Explaining why this should be the case is challenging. By as early as the mid-1970s, for example, it was apparent to many observers that actors in the policy processes, as Simmons, Davis, Chapman, and Sager (1974: 461) put it, tended to "take on, over a period of time, a distinctive style which affects . . . policy decisions, i.e., they develop tradition and history which constrains and refines their actions and concerns." The concept of a policy style they and others developed is useful not only for describing such patterned approaches to policy but also for capturing an important aspect of policy dynamics, that is, the relatively enduring nature of these arrangements (Larsen et al., 2006).

In this sense, a policy "style" can be thought of as existing within a larger "policy regime" that emerges over time after many policy cycle iterations unfold. Such a regime influences not only how policy deliberations take place but also the kinds of actors and ideas that present themselves within a subsystem. In his comparative work on social policy, for example, Gosta Esping-Andersen found different countries to have "specific institutional arrangements adopted by societies in the pursuit of work and welfare." He argued that "a given organization of state–economy relations is associated with a particular social policy logic" (Rein et al., 1987). Eisner, similarly, defined a regime as a "historically specific configuration of policies and institutions which establishes certain broad goals that transcend the problems" specific to particular sectors (Eisner, 1993: xv; see also Eisner, 1994a). In their work on US policy-making, Harris and Milkis (1989: 25) argued that regimes in many sectors developed as a "constellation" of (1) ideas justifying governmental activity, (2) institutions that structure policy-making, and (3) a set of policies themselves.

A policy regime, hence, can be thought of as integrating a common set of policy ideas (what we will discuss in subsequent chapters as a policy "paradigm"), a long-lasting governance arrangement (or what we will refer to later in the book as a policy "mix"), a more or less fixed set of policy actors (what has already been described above as a policy "subsystem"), all of which combine and result in a common or typical policy process or "policy style." The general idea is that policy-making tends to develop in such a way that the same actors, institutions, instruments, and governing ideas tend to dominate the articulation of policy problems and solutions—or goals and means—for extended periods, infusing a policy sector with both a consistent content and a set of typical policy processes or procedures. Understanding how styles and regimes form, how they are maintained, and how they change over time are important aspects of policy studies that are stressed throughout the book (Kuks, 2004; de Vries, 2005b; Howlett & Tosun, 2019).

Overview of the Book

The book begins, in Part I, with an overview of previous efforts to understand public policy-making and outline the different stages of the policy-making cycle that can be examined for insights into policy process. Chapter 1 has briefly charted the development of public policy as an academic discipline and explained what is generally meant by the term. It has outlined a five-stage model of the policy cycle and framed research questions relevant to the analysis of each stage and to the workings of the overall model. We then move to consider the elements and patterns of policy dynamics that influence organizational and political behaviour and lead to policy change before discussing the factors that entrench elements of inertia that generate policy stability. The discussion will demonstrate how insights into policy contents and processes are produced through studying the interplay of actors, intuition, and ideas at a particular stage of the policy cycle.

Chapter 2 examines in more detail several of the most commonly used approaches to studying public policy, emphasizing those employed by economists, political scientists, sociologists, and others who focus on the nature of public policy processes. The potential and limitations of each approach are discussed, as is the particular manner in which theorizing about policy-making has developed over the past several decades.

Chapter 3 then describes the institutional parameters within which policies are made, the nature of the actors who make them, and the ideas that guide the actors. It uses the concept of a policy subsystem to capture the intricate links between actors and structures involved in public policy-making.

As Chapter 2 will demonstrate, policy studies theories have always focused on these three analytical dimensions—actors, institutions, and ideas—although the emphasis on these elements in different theories has varied over time. While understandable, the existence of such separate approaches to public policy has often led to conflicting conclusions. In this volume we draw upon decades of research into policy subsystems, institutional regimes, and policy paradigms to develop a coherent conceptual framework for studying policy-making. Three important conceptual elements in this model—*subsystems, regimes, and paradigms*—are developed in Chapter 3, where we see how their use can help students interpret the apparent disarray of actors, structures, and ideas composing the policy-making "universe" and provide the basis for the identification and understanding of both policy regimes and policy styles. This allows an integrated and coherent framework to be developed that can account for both policy change and stability

Analyzing these policy dynamics is the focus of Part II, which uses the model of the policy cycle to set out the postulated steps through which policy processes unfold and examines each in turn. As noted above, this stylized model of the *policy cycle* sees public policy-making as a socio-political process involving characteristic stages from the articulation of public problems to the adoption and implementation of expected solutions to them. Examining these activities individually allows us to highlight the operative factors and forces at work in each distinct stage of the cycle, from *agenda-setting, formulation, decision-making, and implementation to evaluation* and then back through the same process once again in successive iterations of the cycle. Each of Chapters 4 to 8 examines a critical component or stage of the public policy process. How and why do public concerns make their way onto the government's agenda, and what consequences ensue for future policy-making? How and why do some individuals and groups enjoy privileged input into the formulation of governmental policy options, and what impact does this have? How and why do governments typically decide on a specific course of action and with what results? Why do governments select the types of policy instruments they do, and how do these choices affect policy outcomes? How are government actions and choices typically evaluated, and to what extent does this contribute to policy learning and improved policy-making? These and other questions are posed and answered in each chapter in this section.

Finally, Chapter 9 sets out conclusions about studying policy, drawing on the general relationships among actors, structures, and ideas outlined in the book. It presents the general pattern of the evolution of policy-making in multiple policy sectors, and discusses the reasons why policies often develop and change through an increasingly constrained or "path-dependent" process resulting in sporadic episodes of disruptive policy change through upheavals in established policy orders (Gersick, 1991; Baumgartner & Jones, 1993). The representation of policy-making as a cycle of problem-solving attempts, which results in *"policy learning"* through the repeated analysis of problems and experimentation with solutions, is a central approach and insight of the book.

Study Questions

1. What ideas about policy do different conceptions of public policy-making share in common?

2. What is the difference between policy studies and policy analysis? How do positivist and post-positivist assumptions and methodologies colour and inform these activities?

3. How useful is the policy cycle model for understanding public policy? What are its strengths and limits?

4. What are the three main components of policy capacity that governments, organizations, and policy managers need? How are they related to each other?

5. What is a policy style? What is a policy regime? How are they related, and why are they important?

Further Readings

Fischer, Frank. 2007. "Policy Analysis in Critical Perspective: The Epistemics of Discursive Practices," *Critical Policy Analysis* 1, no. 1: 97–109.

Garson, G. David. 1986. "From Policy Science to Policy Analysis: A Quarter Century of Progress," in W.N. Dunn, ed., *Policy Analysis: Perspectives, Concepts, and Methods*. Greenwich, CT: JAI Press, 3–22.

Howlett, Michael, and Jale Tosun, eds. 2019. *Policy Styles and Policy-Making: Exploring the Linkages*. London: Routledge.

Lasswell, Harold D. 1951. "The Policy Orientation," in D. Lerner and H.D. Lasswell, eds, *The Policy Sciences: Recent Developments in Scope and Method*. Stanford, CT: Stanford University Press, 3–15.

May, Peter J. 2005. "Policy Maps and Political Feasibility," in I. Geva-May, ed., *Thinking Like a Policy Analyst: Policy Analysis as a Clinical Profession*. London: Palgrave Macmillan.

Perl, Anthony, Michael Howlett, and M. Ramesh. 2018. "Policy-Making and Truthiness: Can Existing Policy Models Cope with Politicized Evidence and Willful Ignorance in a 'Post-Fact' World?" *Policy Sciences* 51, no. 4 (December): 581–600.

Rein, M., G. Esping-Andersen, and L. Rainwater. 1987. *Stagnation and Renewal in Social Policy: The Rise and Fall of Policy Regimes*. Armonk: M.E. Sharpe.

Sabatier, Paul A. 1999. The Need for Better Theories. In P.A. Sabatier, ed., *Theories of the Policy Process*. Boulder, CO: Westview Press.

Wu, X., M. Ramesh, and M. Howlett. 2015. "Policy Capacity: A Conceptual Framework for Understanding Policy Competences and Capabilities," *Policy and Society* 34, no. 3–4 (September 1): 165–71.

Chapter 2

Understanding Public Policy
Theoretical Approaches

Peter DeLeon's observation that policy studies have a long history and a short past is an apt point of departure for exploring theories found in the discipline about how public policy is made. As he points out, while the actions of government have been a focus of examination over many centuries, their systematic analysis using the conceptual frameworks of the policy sciences dates back less than one century (deLeon, 1994; Peters, 1999). Even in the short time period that the discipline has existed, however, the policy sciences have been characterized by a surprisingly large number of overlapping, yet distinct, perspectives and approaches (Sabatier, 1999b; Schlager, 1999). In this chapter we outline the main perspectives on studying public policy found in the literature, point out their strengths and weaknesses, and suggest how they may be synthesized for a better understanding of the subject.

Evolution of the Policy Sciences

Policy science emerged in North America and Europe following World War II as scholars sought new understandings of the relationship between governments and citizens that could better explain the tremendous growth of public-sector activity involved in creating increasingly ambitious economic and social programs (deLeon & Martell, 2006; deLeon, 2006). Before the era of big and active governments, studies of political life tended to focus either on the normative and moral dimensions of governing, or on the minutiae of how specific legal and political institutions functioned.

At one end of this analytical spectrum, scholars concerned with the normative or moral dimensions of government studied the great texts of political philosophy, seeking insights into the purpose of governing and the actions that those holding power should take to enable citizens to attain the good life. These inquiries generated rich discussions on the nature of the society, the role of the state, and the rights and responsibilities of citizens and governments. However, the gap between prescriptive political theory and the political practices of modern states that emerged during and after World War II led to a search for new methods of examining politics that could reconcile political theory and practice through systematic evaluation of government outputs and outcomes (Torgerson, 1990; Smith, 1982).

At the other end of the spectrum, scholars interested in the institutions of government had been conducting detailed empirical examinations of legislatures, courts, and bureaucracies while generally ignoring the normative aspects of these institutions. Such studies of formal political institutions excelled in attention to detail and procedure but remained mostly descriptive, failing to generate the basis for evaluating their strengths and weaknesses in the new era of large public programs, or their effects on policy deliberations and choices. In the immediate post-war decades of decolonization and Cold War rivalry between capitalism and communism, when the reconstruction and restructuring of defeated states such as Germany and Japan occurred and new institutions of international governance were established, students of politics sought an approach that would connect their examination of governmental processes and structures more directly with substantive questions of justice, equity, and the pursuit of social, economic, and political development (Mead, 1985).

In this context of change and reassessment, several new approaches to studying politics appeared. Some focused on the micro level of human behaviour and the psychology of citizens, electors, leaders, and followers, while others concentrated on the characteristics of national societies and cultures, or on the attributes of national and global political systems. Interest in most of these approaches—behaviouralism, elite studies, studies of political culture, and political cybernetics—waned as scholars struggled with their limitations (Cairns, 1974; Schaefer, 1974). Only the policy science perspective has continued to develop as an application to understand public policy.

Contemporary studies in public policy focus less on the structure of governments or the behaviour of political actors, or on what governments should or should not do, and more on what governments actually do. This approach focuses on the development of generalizations and laws about public policies and public policy-making, or, as its originators deemed it, *policy science*. It is cross-disciplinary, involving economists in the evaluation of market mechanisms, political scientists, and others interested in governance and a range of others from transportation engineers to criminologists interested in government activities in their sectors.

Pioneered by Harold Lasswell and others in the United States and the United Kingdom, policy science was intended to reintegrate the study of political theory and political practice without falling into the sterility of formal, legal studies (Lasswell, 1951; Torgerson, 1990).

Lasswell proposed that policy science had three distinct characteristics that would set it apart from earlier approaches. In his view, it was *multi-disciplinary, problem-solving, and explicitly normative.* By multi-disciplinary, Lasswell meant that policy science should break away from the narrow study of political institutions and structures and embrace the work and findings of such fields as sociology and economics, law and politics. By problem-solving, he referred to a vision of policy science adhering strictly to the canon of relevance, orienting itself toward the solution of real-world problems and not engaging in esoteric academic debates. By explicitly normative, Lasswell meant that policy science should not be cloaked in the guise of "scientific objectivity," but should recognize the impossibility of separating goals and means, or values and techniques, in the study of government actions (Torgerson, 1983). He expected policy analysts to clearly identify their preferred solution when multiple options were being considered.

This conceptual orientation toward government activities and their consequences remains with us and shapes the focus of this book. However, the passage of time has changed three specific components of the policy orientation that Lasswell first identified (Garson, 1986; deLeon, 1986, 1988; Hansen, 1983). First, over the past half century the principal concern of many policy scholars with concrete problem-solving has waned. At the outset, it was hoped that studying public policy-making and its outcomes would yield conclusions and recommendations directly applicable to existing social problems. Although laudable, this hope foundered on adversarial dynamics of the policy process in which governments often proved resistant to "expert" advice on subjects with which they were dealing (Wildavsky, 1979; Ascher, 1986; Sharpe, 1975). In the real world of public policy, technically superior analysis was often subordinated to political concerns and preferences (Fischer, 2007a; Weiss, 1983).

Second, and relatedly, while the emphasis on multi-disciplinarity remains, a large body of literature now focuses on explaining policy in its own terms. Policy science has become very much of a discipline in itself, with a unique set of concepts and concerns and a vocabulary and terminology all its own (Fishman, 1991). Although many of these concepts have been borrowed from other disciplines, they have acquired a particular meaning when used in the context of studying public policy. Furthermore, the concept of multi-disciplinarity has changed in the sense that policy scholars now take it for granted that they must borrow from other disciplines and must be experts in at least two fields: the concepts and concerns of policy science, and the history and issues present in the substantive area of policy, or the "policy field," from health policy to energy policy and beyond, that they wish to understand (Anderson, 1979a).

Finally, the calls for the policy sciences to remain explicitly normative have also changed over time, although to a lesser extent than the other founding principles. For the most part, policy scholars have refused to exclude values from their analyses and have insisted on evaluating both the goals and the means of policy, as well as the process of policy-making itself. This is very clear, for example, in post-positivist approaches. However, analysts' desire to prescribe specific goals and norms declined with an increasing realization of the intractability of many public problems. Hence, many investigators now either evaluate policies in terms of simple measures such as efficiency or effectiveness, or use the record of policy efforts to assess if they were directed at achievement of the stated goals, in either case without considering the desirability or rationality of the goals themselves (Greenberg et al., 1977; deLeon, 1994; Yanow, 2007).

As these changes occurred, some observers began to castigate the notion of a policy "science" and to equate its promotion with that of similarly ambitious endeavours in an era of unrealized hopes and expectations such as social engineering and government planning (Tribe, 1972; Pielke, 2004; Wedel et al., 2005). Although sometimes justified by the inflated claims of individual policy studies, this criticism should serve as a warning against premature or ill-founded prescriptions or excessive conceptual sophistry, rather than as a rejection of the need to undertake the systematic study of government actions. To the extent that the policy sciences have developed a significant body of empirical and theoretical studies of the activities of numerous governments around the globe, the early efforts and dicta of Lasswell remain valuable and continue to provide the foundation upon which the study of public policy is conducted (Wagner et al., 1991; Torgerson, 1983; Levin-Waldman, 2005).

In general, contemporary policy studies rely on one of two broad *methods of analysis*: deductive and inductive. Some analysts rely on a *deductive* method in which understanding is developed largely on the basis of applying general presuppositions, concepts, or principles to specific phenomena. This is true, for example, of many economic approaches that postulate certain psychological motivations and mechanisms through which policy actors arrive at their choices and that inform their decisions. Other approaches are less grounded in predetermined principles and apply *inductive* methods that develop generalizations on the basis of careful observation of empirical phenomena and subsequent testing of these generalizations against other cases (Lundquist, 1987; Przeworski, 1987; Hawkesworth, 1992).

Public choice, Marxist, and some economic institutionalist theories are examples of deductive theories whereas group theories like pluralism and corporatism, most feminist and gender-based analyses and historical and sociological neo-institutionalist and statist theories are examples of inductive theories. Although neither analytical method guarantees a clearer insight into the contingent and idiosyncratic circumstances of policy development than the other, the deductive and inductive methods each rely upon depict different attributes of policy-making and highlights distinctive policy dynamics (see Almond & Genco, 1977). Each of these approaches is discussed in detail below. First, however, the issue of whether or not it is possible to arrive at lawlike scientific findings in the area of policy studies needs to be considered.

Approaches to Public Policy Analysis: Positivism and Post-Positivism Revisited

Unlike the sciences for studying physical phenomena, there is no universally recognized and accepted methodology for analyzing policy problems. Instead, a range of skills and techniques—drawn from, for example, law, economics, statistical methods, organizational analysis, budgeting, etc.—are used to study policy problems and solutions. The education of policy analysts during the post-war decades focused on generic analytical tools, along with cases, workshops, and simulations to illustrate how to choose analytical tools appropriate to specific circumstances and contexts that can be considered to be largely "positive." Although the idea was often to demonstrate how the "art and craft" of policy analysis was based on inductive as opposed to deductive reasoning and proceeded through matching tools with context (Wildavsky, 1979; Vining & Weimer, 2002; Guess & Franham, 1989; Weimer, 1992; Bardach, 2000; Geva-May & Wildavsky, 1997), it retained many aspects of traditional "positivist" social inquiry geared to the use of "neutral" analytical techniques expected to reveal replicable and lawlike patterns of policy behaviour.

However, while practitioners and those who trained them concentrated on acquiring insights into which analytical approaches and applications would "work" in a given context and reveal these patterns, other policy scholars sought to discern broader general patterns of policy analysis, influence, and effectiveness. In so doing, they adopted "post-positivist" methods that allowed for more contingent findings and observations about the difficulties or impossibility of neutral or dispassionate analysis of social and political phenomenon such as government decision-making and resource allocation (Thissen & Twaalfhoven, 2001). Empirical studies of the ways in which policy analysis is generated, interpreted, and utilized taken by such scholars revealed how these processes were constructed and affected by the needs and beliefs of ultimate users, the delicacy of political relations, cooperation, and conflicts among decision-makers, the history of previous policy reforms, individual personalities and agendas, organizational routines, and other similar factors (Weiss, 1977a, 1977b; Sabatier, 1987; Shulock, 1999). These studies showed, on the one hand, that "one size does not fit all": that is, that analytic opportunities are often idiosyncratic, requiring pragmatic judgment of the appropriate techniques to apply in specific circumstances. On the other hand, they also showed that governments tended to develop long-term preferences for specific types of analysis and outputs.

One corollary of this post-positivist project was to show that successful modes of policy analysis and policy formulation are not simply a matter of the choice and skill of policy analysts and managers, but are conditioned by contextual elements that favour particular techniques and preferences (Shulock, 1999; Radin, 2000). These can include a penchant for the use of traditional "technical" tools such as cost–benefit analysis, for example, but can also involve the use of alternate or complementary techniques such as the frequent use of public consultation or stakeholder participation, or simply an entrenched preference for specific policy instruments (Richardson et al., 1982; Van Waarden, 1995; Howlett, 2000).

Taken together, both sets of studies showed how public policy is, above all, a practical discipline whose explicit purpose is to advise policy-makers on how best to address public problems, however it is that "best" is defined.

Positivist Approaches to Policy Analysis

The mainstream in prescriptive policy analysis consists of applying principles from economics, especially welfare economics, to public problems. While various approaches exist to examine public problems and propose solutions to them, the vast majority of formal analyses rely on ideas and techniques drawn from economics. The proponents of this approach usually describe themselves as "policy analysts," although their critics refer to them as *"positivist"* or "rationalist," in reference to their scientific leanings and claims to objectivity and neutrality. Positivist approaches to studying policy embrace scientific rationality and view policy analysis as part of the quest to uncover objective knowledge, in this case about government decision-making and its causes and consequences.

Indeed, much of what is identified as policy analysis research is often only very thinly veiled applied welfare economics, even though this is rarely stated explicitly (Weimer & Vining, 1999). The proponents of welfare economics, similar to other mainstream economists, accept *a priori* that the market is the most efficient mechanism for allocating society's resources, but unlike many traditional or "classical" economists also admit that markets do not work properly under all circumstances. In such special instances, referred to as *market failures*, they argue that political institutions should act to supplement or replace markets to produce better overall social welfare outcomes. This gives them a reason to carefully investigate government actions rather than dismiss them as inherently distortionary or inefficient as do many of their classical counterparts.

The principles of welfare economics were first worked out by the British economist Alfred Pigou (1932) during World War I. Although he identified only a small number of specific market failures—mainly natural monopoly and public goods—later theorists argued the existence of many more instances of such failures (Bator, 1958; Zerbe & McCurdy, 1999). The market failures on which there is broad agreement among welfare economists include *public goods, natural monopolies, externalities, imperfect information,* and *the tragedy of the commons.* Others exist but are more contested, such as moral hazard or informational asymmetries.

These problematic types of social activities are identified by noting that all goods and services in society can be divided into a relatively small number of types. A popular scheme for doing so identifies four ideal types according to the transactional criteria of "exclusivity" and "exhaustiveness" (Ostrom, 2003). "Exclusivity" (also known as non-rival consumption) refers to transactions involving a good or service limited to the consumption or use by a single consumer, while "exhaustiveness" refers to goods and services whose consumption diminishes their availability to others. These criteria of exclusivity and exhaustiveness generate four types of goods and services, as listed in Figure 2.1, and are used by welfare economists and many policy analysts to determine the need for government action.

In this view, *pure private goods* make up the bulk of goods and services produced in society. These goods or services, such as food, can be divided up for exclusive sale and are no longer available to others after their consumption and can usually be delivered effectively through the market mechanism. At the other extreme are *pure public goods* or services, such as street lighting, which cannot be parcelled out and are consumed by numerous users without diminishing the sum of the good available. These, it is argued, will not generate profits for suppliers and therefore must be supplied by non-market actors, such as governments, who can fund their supply through the tax system. Between the two are *toll goods* and *common-pool goods*. The former include semi-public goods such as bridges or highways, which do not diminish in quantity after use but for whose use it is possible to charge. These can be provided by either market or non-market means. Common-pool goods are those, like fish in the ocean, whose usage cannot be directly charged to individuals but whose quantity is reduced by consumption. These require a non-market organization, like a government, to ration their supply, which will otherwise be quickly exhausted by competitive market firms.

Market Failures
Natural monopoly refers to toll goods, which can be negatively affected by economic (and sometimes political) behaviour in certain industries with large capital requirements and disproportionate returns to scale that tend to promote a single firm over its competitors. In industries such as telecommunications, utilities,

Figure 2.1 Taxonomy of Goods and Services in Welfare Economics

		Exhaustiveness	
		High	*Low*
Exclusivity	*High*	Private Good	Toll Good
	Low	Common-Pool Good	Public Good

Source: Adapted from E.S. Savas, *Alternatives for Delivering Public Services: Toward Improved Performance* (Boulder, Colo.: Westview Press, 1977).

electricity, and railways, the first company to establish the necessary infrastructure, if unregulated, enjoys cost advantages that make it difficult for other firms to compete using the same technology. The lack of competition, when it occurs, can lead to a reduction in the society's economic welfare if monopoly prices are charged for these goods or services. Governments can correct this problem by regulating prices and other aspects of the good or service provided in order to prevent the exercise of monopoly market power by early entrant firms.

Imperfect information affects private and toll goods and occurs when consumers and/or producers lack the information necessary to make rational decisions. Unregulated pharmaceutical firms, for instance, have no incentive to reveal adverse side effects of their products, nor do consumers have the expertise required to evaluate such products prior to their use. As a result, consumption and investment decisions may be taken that do not serve the private (and thus public) interest, justifying government action to mandate information disclosure.

In the presence of *externalities*, too, the market is deemed to fail. These involve situations in all types of goods in which production costs are not borne by producers ("internalized") but rather passed on to others outside (external to) the production process. The most often cited example of an externality relates to the costs of air, water, or land pollution that a company in pursuit of reduced costs and increased profits imposes on the society as a whole or on specific segments of it. This occurs, for instance, when a pulp mill discharges pollutants into a nearby waterway and affects the environment or a fishery. In this context, the costs of dealing with the pollution are externalized to fishers or the public who pay the cost of the pollution. There may also be positive externalities, as when a person getting immunization improves others' health by reducing the instance of epidemics, or when a person benefits from public education to become a better employee, although the beneficiaries do not incur any price or cost for that advantage. In either case, government action is seen to be justified to ensure that producers bear all the costs accruing to, and/or reap all the benefits stemming from, their activities.

The tragedy of the commons is a market failure that occurs when common-pool resources, such as fisheries, pastures, or forests, are exploited without a requirement to maintain the resource for future use. In these circumstances, individual users, whether farmers pasturing their cattle on the local common land or multinational seafood or forestry corporations, often benefit from increasing their use of the resource in the short term, although all users will suffer in the long term following depletion of the resource. This destruction of the commons' ecosystem is said to justify government action to ration production among resource users.

Destructive competition is a controversial market failure that is deemed to exist when aggressive competition between firms causes negative side effects on workers and society (Utton, 1986). This usually involves private goods, although it can involve tool goods (such as when too many ferries serve a community, drive down prices, and then go out of business as a result) and can also involve common-pool goods, as the "tragedy of the commons" example provided above illustrates. It is argued that excessive competition can drive down profit margins and lead to the unnecessary reduction of safety and working conditions, adversely affecting overall social welfare. Local mobility around the world is now experiencing such dynamics because of the relative ease with which drivers can enter the market to offer paid rides using platforms like Uber, Lyft, and Didi. These services can undercut existing taxi firms and one another other until fares crash, negatively affecting many producers and consumers. Like tragedies of the commons and the situation with common-pool goods, this instability is said to support government regulation of market entry in order to prevent over-competition.

Government Failure

Sustained criticisms of the vague criteria used to define market failures led many welfare economists to attempt to reconceptualize the original notion. One way this was done was to argue that market failures are, in fact, only one side of an equation and that there are also inherent limitations to the government's ability to correct market failures, which can make such rescue efforts backfire or render them ineffective. They posit that in several specific instances—*government failures*—the state cannot improve on the market, despite the latter's failings (Le Grand & Robinson, 1984; Mayntz, 1993a; Dollery & Worthington, 1996; Bozeman, 2002).

One such failure is seen to result from the inherent gap that exists between legislative or political intent and administrative practice. This principal–agent problem was frequently held up as a major reason for the shortcomings associated with government failure (see Kerr, 1976; Ingram & Mann, 1980b; Mulford, 1978). In this policy-specific use of *principal–agent* theory, these gaps were viewed as the inevitable results of the structure of political and administrative institutions in modern states in which decision-makers must delegate responsibility for implementation to officials whose subsequent behaviour they only indirectly control.

The existence of structural discretion on the part of the administrative "agents" of political "principals" provided a powerful explanation for inefficient or in effective administrative implementation of government policy, stemming as it did from the common practice in government whereby laws passed by the political branches of government are put into effect through regulations developed by administrative agencies responsible for implementing the laws. This legal framework establishes a particular kind of principal–agent relationship between politicians and administrators in which there is an inherent problem of securing the latter's compliance (see Cook & Wood, 1989; Gormley, 1989). Administrators have their own understanding, ambitions, and fiscal and knowledge resources that may take policies a long way from the objectives originally conceived by decision-makers.

This structural problem is compounded by the complex relationships existing among policies and policy actors. For example, many policies demand action by multiple government agencies. This requires another administrative layer of inter-organizational coordination by specialized administrative entities, such as interdepartmental or intergovernmental committees, or so-called "staff" or "central agencies," which can further exacerbate principal–agent dilemmas by adding additional layers of ideas and interests between the policy objective and its realization (see Smith et al., 1993; Campbell & Szablowski, 1979; Mayntz, 1993b; Rogers & Whetton, 1982). And in many cases, these efforts occur at different levels of government—local, state, national, regional, or international—which furthers this complexity. Given this diversity of actors and interests involved in addressing problems, the possibility increases that multiple, and not necessarily commensurable, analytical frameworks will have been applied to a policy issue. Four specific instances of such common government failure are frequently cited: organizational displacement, rising costs, derived externalities, and the principal–agent problem.

Organizational displacement is the situation in which an administrative agency charged with producing a particular good or service eventually displaces publicly sanctioned goals with its own private or organizational ones. These may extend to maximizing its budget or power or whatever else the organization values. In such circumstances, government action to correct market failure such as a natural monopoly with a governmental one may simply increase inefficiency. Thus, it is argued that they should refrain from doing so over the long term and intervene only for a shorter period of time, after which the determination of activities should be returned to the market where possible (Weimer & Vining, 1992).

Rising costs are another instance of government failure. Governments receive tax revenues and, unlike their private counterparts, are not under pressure to generate revenues by competing in the marketplace. Without the fear of going bankrupt, a real possibility for private producers, it is argued that governments do not have the same incentive to control expenses and instead may allow them to grow continually. Again, it is argued that because of this limitation, a government must carefully weigh the costs and benefits of altering market relations, and that in some cases allowing "minor" market failures to persist may be cheaper than engineering a government takeover of that activity (Le Grand & Robinson, 1984).

Derived externalities are a third frequently cited such failure. These "are side effects that are not realized by the agency responsible for creating them, and hence do not affect the agency's calculations or behaviour" (Wolf, 1988: 77). Certain government actions, such as healthcare provision, have a broad impact on society and the economy and can have the effect of excluding viable market-produced goods and services, negatively affecting overall levels of social welfare (Wolf, 1979; Le Grand, 1991; Weimer & Vining, 1999: 194). Again, this suggests that government replacement of market-based goods and service production should be carefully assessed, and that the "opportunity costs" associated with such actions should be factored into the government decision-making calculus.

The exact status and causes of government and market failures remain controversial and largely inductively derived but, nevertheless, welfare economists advanced a theory of public policy-making built on these concepts. They argued that governments have a responsibility to try to correct market failures because if they do not, society will be left with suboptimal social outcomes. In this view, governments facing a demand for action should first determine if a market failure is causing a social problem; only if one is found should the government intervene to correct it (Stokey & Zeckhauser, 1978). However, even then, in order to avoid government failures, policy-makers must carefully evaluate their own capacity to correct the identified market failure before acting, taking into account both common government failings and inherent principal–agent problems (Vining & Weimer, 1990; Weimer & Vining, 1992).

Elegant and logical as the welfare economist's conception of public policy-making appears, it rarely reflects real-world policy-making, as governments almost never make their policies in the manner assumed by this theory. Even if one could identify the most efficient and effective policy, which is difficult given the limitations innate to the social sciences, the actual policy is commonly chosen in response to political pressures, ideologies, and self-interests, among other factors unrelated to market or government failures. As such, the technical analyses generated by welfare economists are often merely another political resource used by proponents of one or another option for government action or inaction to further their claims (Weiss, 1977b).

Only in very specific circumstances when welfare economists happen to be policy-makers—as happens at times in some countries' policy sectors, such as taxation or fiscal management—would one expect political decisions to be based largely on the criteria defined by welfare economists (Markoff & Montecinos, 1993). The neglect of political variables by welfare economics has led its critics to describe it as "a myth, a theoretical illusion" that promotes "a false and naive view of the policy process" (Minogue, 1983: 76; Hogwood & Gunn, 1984: 50–1) and to propose a more politically informed, alternative, view.

Post-Positivist Approaches to Policy Analysis

This alternative view has been labelled many things but can usefully be described as "post-positivist" in the sense that it claims to have moved beyond or transcended the limits of earlier "positivist" thinking. Post-positivism and the associated "argumentative turn" in public policy emerged in the early 1990s following widespread dissatisfaction with the technocratic direction the discipline had taken in the preceding decades following "positivist" welfare economics maxims. Many of the critics of mainstream public policy analysis based on the welfare economics approach described in the preceding section banded together under the label of "post-positivism" with the explicit objective of going beyond techno-cratic positivism, which is a strong version of the *empiricism* they felt incorrectly informed welfare economic analysis.

Unlike welfare economists, however, post-positivists are a disparate collec-tion of scholars bound mainly by their common purpose of generating usable policy analysis through reliance on political and social analysis of public prob-lems and policy-making processes and outcomes. They include many feminist and gender policy scholars, "interpretive policy analysts," narratologists, "dis-course theorists," and others. Indeed, any effort to draw up a single blueprint for post-positivist analysis would be anathema for its proponents because of the importance attributed to contextual socio-political factors, which by definition vary across sectors, issues, and cases and which discourage any kind of method-ological hegemony or uniformity (Dryzek, 1990; Fischer, 2003, 1998; Forester, 1993; Morcöl, 2002; Hajer & Wagenaar, 2003; Majone, 1989; Stone, 1988).

Post-positivists do, however, generally argue that mainstream policy analysts informed by welfare economics and other similar approaches are misguided in their obsession with quantitative methods, the objective separation of facts and values, and generalizable findings independent of particular social contexts—all hallmarks of "positivist" thinking. They embrace subjective reflection, normative analysis, and the study of argumentation and policy narratives and discourses as more fruitful tools for understanding public policies and policy-making. Although post-positivists are influenced by general social philosophies and methods such as critical theory, post-structuralism, postmodernism, and social constructivism, which tend to deny the existence of an objective realm of facts independent of the observer, they are often not against objectivity and empirical analysis, per se. Rather, they believe that in the policy realm, (positivist) empirical analysis needs to be combined with (post-positivist) normative or interpretive analysis because the two are inseparable in policy-making, a position that was also argued explic-itly by founders of the policy sciences such as Harold Lasswell (see above).

Post-positivists believe that the almost exclusive emphasis on empirical evidence found in positivist analyses is seriously misguided on both method-ological and ethical grounds. The instrumental, ends–means calculations on which welfare economics-inspired policy analysts spend so much effort, they argue, are mistaken because policies rarely have unambiguous goals, and rarely do policy-makers choose the most efficient means of achieving them. Instead, they suggest, policy goals and means are products of constant conflict and ne-gotiation among policy-makers guided by their values and interests and shaped by a variety of contingent circumstances. By ignoring or downplaying partisan politics and value conflicts among policy-makers, post-positivists accuse positiv-ists of failing to highlight or investigate the most vital elements that shape policy (Dryzek, 2002).

Many post-positivists not only find positivist policy analysis to be lacking in comprehending reality, but also object to it on ethical grounds, arguing it promotes "top-down" bureaucratic policy management and stifles democracy and participation (Heineman et al., 1990). By emphasizing efficiency and effectiveness in their assessment and design of the means to achieve goals, positivist analysis, they argue, promotes a "technocratic form" of governance characterized by efforts to promote experts to decision-making roles and to lead to a general disdain for politics in policy-making. As Frank Fischer (2007a: 97) noted with respect to many traditional positivist policy analysts and scholars, "If pluralist politics and competing interests don't fit into the methodological scheme, then politics is the problem. Some have gone so far as to argue that the political system itself must be rearranged to better suit the requirements of policy analysis."

However, unlike the model of market governance failure inspired by welfare economics and used by positivist policy analysts, there is no set formula for post-positivist analysis because post-positivism is not a formal theory. Rather, it is more appropriate to describe it as an "orientation" whose proponents are bound by some core common beliefs. They start from the assumption that there is no incontrovertible or "objective" understanding of policy problems or solutions, as positivists claim. Instead, they explicitly recognize that all knowledge is contestable and that this contestation takes place throughout the policy process (Fischer, 2007b: 224). Post-positivists make no pretense of analytical objectivity and political neutrality but take on the role of "deliberative practitioners operating within a clear value framework that promotes greater social and political equity" (Burton, 2006: 174). In the present era, that often involves post-positivists in debates around intersectionality or the manner in which concerns around power, diversity, and biases toward citizens based on race, class, or gender are manifested (Hankivsky & Cormier, 2011; Collins, 2016).

The need to promote democracy and public participation occupies a central place in post-positivist thinking in the same way that a faith in market inspires most positivist approaches (Dryzek, 2002). As we have seen, traditional policy analysis is criticized for its technocratic and pro-market orientation, which excludes ordinary citizens from the policy process and often reduces them to the status of consumers (Durning, 1999; Hajer & Wagenaar, 2003). To address the lacunae, post-positivists ascribe central importance to providing "access and explanation of data to all parties, to empower the public to understand analyses, and to promote serious public discourse" (Fischer, 2003: 15). In this approach, the policy analyst is more a facilitator than an arbiter or a designer. In their role as facilitator, policy analysts can promote policy deliberations by reducing inequalities among participants "so that a consensus around policy is achieved more by the inherent power of argument than by the status of the person advancing it" (Burton, 2006: 182).

Understandably, then, post-positivists place a great deal of emphasis on giving citizens the information they need to participate meaningfully in the policy process. From this viewpoint, participatory policy analysis is desirable not only because it is more democratic but also because it is seen to lead to better policies and more effective implementation by enhancing diversity and bringing more viewpoints to bear on a policy problem than is the case with a top-down, technocratic orientation (Johnson, 2017). According to Dryzek (2002: 35),

> A more participatory policy process helps to create more effective and competent citizens, who are also more effective problem solvers, within the policy process and beyond. They are also more capable of constructing productive relationships with others concerned with different facets of complex problems.

Public participation in the policy process has the additional benefit of generating social capital, which not only helps solve immediate problems but also strengthens the government and society's overall capacity for addressing public problems in the future (Dryzek, 2002). This is especially germane, it is argued, since many policies are increasingly made not by politicians responding to voters' sentiments but by unelected officials influenced by powerful special interest groups and far removed from the concerns of the general public. Only an organized dialogue between the bureaucracy and the public, it is argued, can allow generation of alternatives that effectively address the latter's needs (Hajer & Wagenaar, 2003).

Arguments, therefore, are the basic unit of analysis in post-positivism and interpretive discourse or discursive analysis its primary methodology. As Majone (1989: 7) explains, "the job of policy analyst consists in large part of producing evidence and arguments to be used in the course of public debate." In the post-positivist view, persuasion through argumentation plays a vital role at every stage of the policy process. From agenda-setting to policy evaluation, the policy process is essentially a "rhetorical and interpretative" exercise in which protagonists engage in discourses intended to both define and further their ideas and interests. As Fischer (2007b: 227) puts it, "In politics, politicians and policy decision-makers put forth proposals about what to do based on normative arguments. Empirical analysis comes into play but only when there are reasons to question or explore the factual aspects of the argument."

Legal argumentation, in which different protagonists prepare arguments for and against particular policy positions, offers a template for what post-positivist analysis and policy formulation look like. The opposing analyses take the form of a debate in which participants not only present arguments but also disclose their norms, values, and circumstances. Fischer (2007b) explains:

> In such a policy debate, each party would confront the others with counterproposals based on varying perceptions of the facts. The participants

would organize the established data and fit them into the world views that underline their own arguments. The criteria for rejecting or accepting a proposal would be the same grounds as those for accepting or rejecting a counterproposal.

Rules of evidence as used in courts are proposed as a means of assessing the conflicting arguments and choosing among them. Such a strategy would allow analysts to combine empirical and normative examinations, making their efforts pragmatic yet analytically rigorous.

Fischer (2007b: 230) offers "practical reasoning" as a way to deal with conflicting arguments. Unlike mathematical or logical proof, which is either true or false,

practical arguments are only more or less convincing, more or less plausible to a particular audience. What is more, there is no unique way to construct a practical argument: data and evidence can be chosen in a wide variety of ways from the available information, and there are various methods of analysis and ways of ordering values.

All of these allow policy-makers considerable room to use their judgment in making a final choice both among the sorts of problems to be addressed and among the tools and techniques available to address them.

Post-positivist analysis combining empirical and normative analyses proceeds at two levels (Fischer, 2007: 232–4). At the micro level, study focuses on issues concerning the actual programs in place, the problems they are directed at, and those involved in making and implementing the program. Typical questions at this level include the following: (1) Does the program fulfill its stated objective(s)? (2) Does the program fulfill these objectives more efficiently than alternative means available? and (3) Is the program objective(s) relevant to the problem? At the macro level, post-positivist analysis is concerned with abstract goals and contexts. Questions at this level include (1) Does the policy goal "contribute value for the society as a whole?" and (2) Does the policy goal result in unanticipated problems with important societal consequences? Finally, the analyst must address the broader values underpinning the conceptualization of public problems and efforts to address them.

The greatest strength of post-positivist analyses is that they are sensitive to the messy realities of the public policy process, unlike their positivist counterparts who tend to have an orderly, even mechanistic, conception of the policy realm. For positivists, policy problems are primarily technical issues that can be addressed effectively once the right solution is found through rigorous technical analysis. Post-positivists correctly point out that technical analysis needs to be complemented by the study of other factors, including conflicts based on different values and interests.

One of the limitations of post-positivism, however, is the lack of accepted criteria for evaluating competing arguments. The absence of such criteria promotes "relativism in which a commitment to avoid the privileging of any one viewpoint becomes a tolerance of anything" (Burton, 2006: 186). A second limitation is that the deliberative process on which post-positivists place so much emphasis may be hijacked by those who gain from the status quo. The potential losers in any change situation are likely to be the most active participants in such processes, and they will have an overwhelming interest in scuttling any process that negatively affects them through protracted deliberation. Third, while post-positivists correctly point out the importance of value-based discourse, they unwittingly underestimate the importance of the material interests in which the discourse is grounded. As Burton (2006: 187) warns, "in believing that discourse is everything and that material inequalities can be overcome by discourse alone, it may appear not only that words are deeds but that they are sufficient to change society for the better."

The lack of a clear research method—a guide, as it were—also severely handicaps those trying to include post-positivism in their teaching curriculum and may at least partially explain why it receives scant attention in public policy syllabi. Although Dryzek (2002: 32) has argued that "most of its proponents would say that the whole point is to replace the illusion of certainty with recognition of the reality of contention and so avoid simplistic recipes," it does raise the level of difficulty for those trying to teach or practise the post-positivist mode of policy analysis—unlike the systematically presented welfare economics-inspired "positivist" analysis it condemns.

Reconciling the Positivist and Post-Positivist Approaches

Recent empirical work has identified several of the basic parameters of the range of analytical styles found in different locales, which fall between the rational positivist analyst of the 1960s and 1970s, focused on the quantification of economic costs and benefits, and the post-positivist analyst of the 1980s and 1990s, concerned with the social construction of policy problems, policy discourses, and the politics of the policy process (Radin, 2000). Many observers have denounced the penchant of positivists to assert infallible certainty in their analyses (Manski, 2011, 2013) and looked for a method and way of thinking about policy-making that fell between that and the vague precepts of interpretive post-positivism.

Drawing on European experience, Mayer, Van Daalen, and Bots (2001) provided a finer-grained dissection of the policy analysis functions that served this aim. They noted how both positivist and post-positivist analyses may coexist within a given polity or policy sector, and argued that policy analysis in practice embraces distinct tasks of research, clarification, design, advice, mediation, and democratization.

Using pairs of these activities, they produced six distinct, but not mutually exclusive, styles of policy analysis:

1. *Rational.* In the traditional positivistic style, researchers apply mainly economic and other empirical methods to specific cases. Here, the generation of new knowledge is the main task of the analyst.
2. *Client advice.* The analyst provides political and strategic advice to clients.
3. *Argumentative.* The analyst is actively involved in debate and policy discourse as a distinct independent act or both within and outside governments.
4. *Interactive.* The analyst serves as a facilitator in consultations in which key players and participants define their preferred outcome.
5. *Participative.* The researcher/analyst is an advocate, aggregating and articulating the interests of silent players in the policy process: the poor, the general interest, or any other actor not represented in the policy process.
6. *Process.* The analyst acts as a "network manager," steering the policy process toward a preferred outcome defined as part of the analytic task.

This framework helped break out of the often sterile debate between positivist and post-positivist policy analysis and emphasizes the extent to which all types of policy analysis are often present in policy-making and how all are also subordinated to larger concerns and analyses in the policy studies tradition around knowledge generation and use (Knoepfel et al., 2007).

Approaches to Public Policy Studies: Multi-Level, Multi-Disciplinary

This high-level meta-dispute between positivists and post-positivists over the nature of policy knowledge and methods of "formal" policy analysis has affected the general approaches taken to explain policy-making and the methods used to evaluate or critique public policies within policy studies. However, these disputes have had little effect on policy studies per se, because virtually all theories developed to explain the public policy process and its outcomes from a policy studies—as opposed to a policy analysis—perspective already assumed that they were heavily politicized.

In practice a great many theories, both positivist and post-positivist in nature, generated in fields as diverse as geography, history, economics, sociology, and political science, inform work in the policy studies tradition. These theories can be differentiated according to the basic *unit of analysis* used in their investigations. *Public choice* theory, for example, focuses on the micro-level behaviour of individuals using many concepts and assumptions from classical and neo-classical economics, while *group and class* theories from political science and sociology look at the interaction of organized interests that often mediate between individuals and the state. And adopting the broadest perspective on the subject, *institutional analysis* from these three fields as well as studies of law and society and others look to the structure of political and economic arrangements, such as the role of the bureaucracy, legislatures, and courts, in affecting the policy process and policy outputs. These three perspectives (see Figure 2.2) embrace the range of focuses found in policy studies. Like the visual variety found in a good movie, however, superior policy studies combine wide-angle, mid-range, and close-up shots of policy-making in action to highlight different elements of the process. In other words, the best policy analyses from a policy studies perspective combine elements of these macro-, meso-, and micro-level approaches.

The Welfare Economics approach has already been described in depth above. In the following discussion, each of the other approaches is defined and its key principles and assumptions are set out. We then assess the strengths and weaknesses of each approach in terms of its ability to help understand policy-making, including formal policy analysis, and explain the nature of policy outcomes.

Public Choice

Public choice theory is another economistic approach to policy-making and social theory more generally that rests on a firm foundation of rationality and draws on the values of neo-classical economics to try and explain virtually all aspects of human behaviour. It is a deductive theory in that it is based on a rational choice framework, which is taken as a given and from which various deductions are made concerning policy-relevant and other kinds of activity. The framework within which it resides has informed theoretical applications in political science, psychology (Tversky & Kahneman, 1986), and sociology (Hechter & Kanazawa, 1997; Kiser & Hechter, 1991), as well as being a mainstay of economics. The primary assumption in this perspective is that political actors, like their market economic counterparts, act in a "rational" (that is, calculating) fashion to maximize their "utility" or "satisfaction."

Figure 2.2 Levels of Analysis and Examples of Relevant Theories

*Unit of Analysis	Deductive Approach	Inductive Approach
Individual	• Public Choice	• Welfare Economics
Collectivity	• Class Analysis	• Group Analysis: Pluralism and Corporatism
Structures	• Institutionalism and Neo-Institutionalism	• Statism

In this model, political and policy processes and outcomes are understood as interactions among actors pursuing their individual self-interest (McLean, 1987; Van Winden, 1988; Buchanan, 1980; Kreuger, 1974). Thus, for example, voters are deemed to vote for parties and candidates that will best serve their interest (Downs, 1957). Politicians are seen as constantly vying for election in order to promote their interests in the income, power, and prestige derived from holding office, and thus offer policies that will win them voters' support (Becker, 1958; Coase, 1960). Political parties are seen to operate in much the same way as politicians, devising policy packages that will appeal to voters (Riker, 1962). Bureaucrats' self-interest leads them to maximize their budgets because larger budgets are a source of power, prestige, perks, and higher salaries (Niskanen, 1971). Democratic governments are seen to operate in a perpetual campaign mode, buying votes with public money according to the timing of the electoral cycle. There is a sizable *political business cycle* literature built on the proposition that decisions that dispense benefits are taken before election while unpopular ones, attributing costs, are made soon afterwards (Boddy & Crotty, 1975; Frey, 1978; Locksley, 1980; Tufte, 1978).

The challenge, following this line of thinking, is to design a political order that will channel the self-serving behaviour of participants toward the common good along the lines once described by Adam Smith (Buchanan et al., 1978: 17). Put simply, for public choice theorists, the same individual utility maximization that promotes the general good in the market takes on a decidedly harmful form when combined with the ability to compel action available in the political arena. This leads public choice theorists to reject most policy analyses and prescriptions generated by researchers who tend to see government activity as more benign (Rowley, 1983). Instead, they seek to restrain and redirect government intervention to supplementing the market by enforcing and creating property rights so that economic forces can operate at a safe distance from political authority and allocate resources to benefit the whole society.

The simplicity and logical elegance of public choice, along with the impressive mathematical presentations found in many studies, mask its shortcomings (Jones, 2001; Green & Shapiro, 1994). First of all, the theory is based on an oversimplification of human psychology and behaviour that does not accord with reality. Many political activities, for example, are undertaken for symbolic or ritualistic reasons and to view them in terms of utility maximization is likely to lead to misleading conclusions (Zey, 1992).

Second, public choice theory's oversimplifications regarding human behaviour makes for poor predictive capacity. There is no empirical proof, for example, that government functions and spending grow inexorably because of competition for votes. Many governments around the world have gone to elections, and been elected, seeking to cut spending on popular social programs. The actual fluctuations in government growth patterns are also not new and bear little relationship to the electoral cycle. How and why this variation in government size and programming occurs is virtually inexplicable within a public choice framework (Dunleavy, 1986).

A third reason for empirical shortcomings can be found in public choice perspective's heavy reliance on the US experience. By presuming a pattern of electoral competition between two parties that requires voters to make "either/or" choices on contending alternatives, the political reality of multi-party democracies is distorted. The legislative coalitions that are common under multi-party representation do not present voters with the clear-cut bidding for support between "in" and "out" parties found in the US or the UK, since electoral promises may be overridden by post-election legislative deal-making (Warwick, 2000). Needless to say, the theory has nothing to say about policy-making in nondemocratic systems that do not rely on free and competitive elections, a central assumption of the model.

Fourth, the theory is explicitly normative, despite its proponents' insistence that their analysis is "positive" and "value-free." The notion that only markets produce wealth and that the state is a kind of parasite extracting rents from the marketplace ignores the important role played by the state in establishing the economy's foundation through property rights and public security and in organizing key economic activities as education and technological innovation (Dosi et al., 1988). Thus, public choice theory seeks, in effect, to promote a particular vision of orthodox liberalism (also called Neo-conservatism or Neoliberalism) that would advance markets wherever possible and severely restrict the scope for government activity without empirical justification for doing so (Hood, 1991, 1995, 1998).

Finally, the theory disregards or underestimates the effects of institutional factors in shaping actors' preferences, despite its pretensions toward institutional design (Ostrom, 1986a, 1986b). Pioneering public choice theorists tended to regard institutions themselves as malleable according to actors' preferences and were unwilling to fully recognize the durability of institutions and the pervasive impact they have on individual behaviour. Indeed, realization of the effects of institutional structures on individual choices has moved many rational choice theorists to embrace a more subtle and supple approach centred on economistic "neo-institutionalism" or "actor-centred institutionalism," which will be discussed in more detail below.

Class Analysis

Class and group theories accord primacy to collective entities, the organized interests and associations that seek to influence policy agendas, policy options, and policy outputs. These are thought to exist above and beyond the individuals who compose them and thus are not amenable to individual-level analysis. The deductive variant of this mid-range collective actor perspective is class theory, which ascribes group membership according to certain observable social characteristics, whether or not the individuals involved see themselves in those terms. While there are several types of class analysis, we will concentrate on the "Marxist" variant, which is by far the best known and theoretically developed. In this approach, class membership is determined by the presence or absence of certain characteristics, usually, but not always, related to the nature and structure of the economy (Ossowski, 1963).

The mid-nineteenth-century *Manifesto of the Communist Party* (1848), written by Karl Marx and Friedrich Engels, is the best-known articulation of this class theory. It grew out of the same political economy tradition as contemporary economics but parted ways in the late nineteenth century as more "orthodox" economics dropped its concerns for groups and collective actors and instead focused on individual behaviour. Marx and Engels conceptualized society as being composed of two classes contesting political and economic powers whose character changed throughout history. Society was said to have passed through a number of distinct stages ("modes of production"), each of which had particular technological conditions of production ("means of production") and a distinct manner in which the various actors in the production process related to each other ("class structure" or "relations of production") (Cohen, 1978). In the logic of this model, a pure mode of production develops a dichotomous class system consisting of those who own the means of production and those who must work for the owners, and the relationship between the two groups is inherently adversarial.

Thus, over the course of history slaves battled their owners in slave-holding societies; serfs contended with landlords in feudal society; and workers struggle with owners in capitalist society. Continued class struggle combined with technological changes in the means of production lead to eventual collapse of modes of production and their replacement by another mode, which in turn is eventually replaced by yet another system. Marxist class theory interprets public policies in capitalist societies as reflecting the interests of the capitalist class, which has superseded the landlord class present in feudal society and the slave-owning class of antiquity. The "ruling class" dominance of the economy affords them control over the state and what it does. Indeed, according to Marx, the state is merely an instrument in the hands of capitalists, who use it for the purposes of maintaining the capitalist system and increasing profits ("surplus value"), necessarily at the expense of labour. This included at various times, for example, developing imperial systems and colonies.

While this instrumentalist view proved a popular approach to studying public policy in many countries and colonies during the 1930s and 1940s, following its adoption by the communist government of the Soviet Union after 1917 and its dissemination throughout European colonial empires after World War II, by the late 1960s in Western Europe it was beginning to be seen as problematic by Marxists on two counts. First, even if a policy did serve the interest of capital, it was not necessarily true that the policy had been enacted at the behest of capital.

To show this, one would have to demonstrate that capitalists issued instructions that were faithfully carried out by state officials, proof of which is usually lacking. Second, and more importantly, this approach could not explain policies adopted over the opposition of capitalists. In most capitalist states, for instance, the adoption of social welfare policies was vehemently opposed by many capitalists, something that cannot be explained if the state is merely an instrument of capital. Similarly, the proliferation of Keynesian policies in the 1950s and 1960s in many countries (Hall, 1989) occurred over the opposition of entrenched business interests and cannot be understood without reference to ideological factors influencing state behaviour, just as policies promoting privatization and deregulation in many of the same countries in the 1980s (Ikenberry, 1990) cannot be traced entirely or directly to the interests of capitalists (Amariglio et al., 1988).

Recognizing this problem forced a reappraisal of the role of the state in Marxist theory (Block, 1980; Foley, 1978; Gough, 1975; Poulantzas, 1978; Therborn, 1977, 1986).

The traditional Marxist view had to address a broader range of causal factors than class analysis. As a result, increased emphasis began to be placed on institutional or structural factors to account for state activities and behaviour in the 1960s and 1970s (McLennan, 1989: 117–19). It was recognized that the state not only reflects but also plays a crucial role in organizing the economy and shaping the mode of production (Cox, 1987). To account for the state devising policies opposed by capital, for example, the notion of the *relative autonomy* of the state was developed (Poulantzas, 1973a; Althusser & Balibar, 1977). Nicos Poulantzas, for example, argued that conflicts among the various fractions of capital, coupled with the existence of a bureaucracy staffed by individuals drawn from noncapitalist classes, permitted the state to have some autonomy from capital. This autonomy, in turn, allowed the state to adopt measures favourable to the subordinate classes if such policies were found to be politically unavoidable or necessary for promoting the long-term interests of capital in social stability.

Hence, in this "structural" version of neo-Marxism, policy-making was still viewed as serving the interest of capital, but not in the same instrumental sense previously articulated (Thompson, 1978). The rise of the welfare state, for example, is explained not as a direct response to the needs of capital, but as the result of political pressures exerted by the working class on the state (Esping-Andersen, 1981, 1985; Esping-Andersen & Korpi, 1984). The structural imperatives of capitalism are not ignored, however, because they impose limits on what the state can do in response to working-class demands. Thus, for example, it is argued the welfare state, established by capitalist governments in response to working-class demands, was designed in a manner that did not undermine fundamental property rights or profits. By introducing a structural component to class analysis, however, this version of neo-Marxist social theory, as occurred with public choice theory, shifted toward more institutional types of analysis (see below).

Pluralism

One of the most prominent group-level approaches to studying the middle ranges of policy-making is "pluralism," which originated in the United States in the early twentieth century and continues, in one form or another, to dominate American political science perspectives on studying politics and policy. "Corporatism," discussed below, is a parallel group theory developed in Europe around the same time that shares many of the same precepts and principles.

While pluralist thinking can be found in the principles that James Madison articulated to justify the 1789 United States Constitution (Madison & Hamilton, 1961), the doctrine received its first formal expression by Arthur Bentley in 1908. The theory has been considerably refined since then, but the fundamental tenets remain. Prominent pluralist thinkers include Robert Dahl (1956, 1961), Nelson Polsby (1963), and especially David Truman (1964). Many feminist, gender, and identity/diversity studies adopt a similar method and were in fact heavily influenced by pluralist thinking about the nature of groups in society and how they interact in political and policy processes (Mazur, 2002; Young, 2011; Eisenberg & Kymlicka, 2012)

Pluralism is based on the assumption that interest groups are the political actors that matter most in shaping public policy. In *The Process of Government*, Bentley argued that societal interests found their concrete manifestation in different groups consisting of individuals with similar concerns and, ultimately, that "society itself is nothing other than the complex of the groups that compose it." Truman expanded on Bentley's notion of a one-to-one correspondence between interests and groups and argued that two kinds of interests—"latent" and "manifest"—resulted in the creation of two kinds of groups—potential and organized (Truman, 1964; also see Jordan, 2000). For Truman, latent interests in the process of emerging provided the underpinnings for potential groups, which over time led to the emergence of organized groups, allowing politics to be seen as a more dynamic process than Bentley seemed to depict.

Groups in pluralist theory are not only many and free-forming, they are also characterized by overlapping membership and a lack of representational monopoly (Schmitter, 1977). That is, the same individual may belong to a number of groups for pursuing his or her different interests; a person, for instance, may belong at the same time to Greenpeace, the local Chamber of Commerce, and Ducks Unlimited. Overlapping membership is said to be a key mechanism for reconciling conflicts and promoting cooperation among groups. In addition, the same interest may be represented by more than one group. Environmental causes, for example, are espoused by a large number of groups in every industrialized country. Politics, in the pluralist perspective, is the process by which various competing interests and groups are reconciled. Public policies are thus a result of competition and collaboration among groups working to further their members' collective interests (Self, 1985).

Contrary to many critics of this approach, pluralists do not believe that all groups are equally influential or that they have equal access to government (Smith, 1990: 303–4). In fact, pluralists recognize that groups vary in terms of the financial or organizational (personnel, legitimacy, members' loyalty, or internal unity) resources they possess and their access to government (Lindblom, 1968; Lowi, 1969; McConnell, 1966; Schattschneider, 1960). Nevertheless, pluralism does not have a sufficiently developed notion of groups' varying capacity to determine or influence government decision-making.

A more significant problem with the pluralist theory is its inadequate understanding of the government's role in the policy process (Smith, 1990). The government was often thought of not actually as an entity but as a place, an "arena" where competing groups met and bargained (Dahl, 1967). A more nuanced reformulation subsequently presented government as a "referee" or "umpire" of the group struggle. In this view, the state was still ultimately a place where competing groups met to work out their differences, but this time the government was considered a kind of neutral official setting out the rules of group conflict and ensuring that groups did not violate them with impunity (Berle, 1959).

This remains an overly simplistic view of how government works, however, as public choice scholars such as Mancur Olson (1965) have pointed out, because it assumes that public officials do not seek to realize their own interests and ambitions through the control they exert over governmental machinery. It also neglects the fact that states often maintain special ties with certain groups and may even sponsor establishment of groups where there are none or if those in existence are found to be difficult to co-opt or accommodate (Pal, 1993a).

The pluralist notion of the government responding to group pressure is also misconceived because it assumes both that pressure is not exerted in the opposite direction and that there is a unity of purpose and action by government. Indeed, with respect to the latter point, it has been noted that "bureaucratic politics" is a pervasive phenomenon that can have a decisive impact on public policies (Allison & Halperin, 1972). That is, different departments and agencies often have different interests and conflicting interpretations of the same problem. How these differences are resolved has an impact on what policies are adopted and how they are implemented.

Recognition of these problems with early forms of pluralism (Connolly, 1969) led to the emergence of what is sometimes described as "neo-pluralism" within the American political science community (McFarland, 2004, 2007). The reformulation retained the significance attributed to competition among groups, but modified the idea of approximate equality among groups and explicitly acknowledged that some groups are more powerful than others. Charles Lindblom, for example, argued that business is often the most powerful interest group in liberal-democratic societies for two closely related reasons. First, these types of governments are invariably located in a capitalist economy and need a prosperous economy in order to have an adequate basis of tax revenues required to spend on programs that enable their own re-election. To avoid a capital strike where businesses scale back their investment and operations, governments must maintain business confidence, which often means paying special heed to the demands of the business community. Second, in capitalist societies there is a division between public and private sectors, the former under the control of the state and the latter dominated by business. The private sector's dominance by business gives it a privileged position in comparison to other groups in that much employment and associated social and economic activity ultimately depend on private-sector investment behaviour (Lindblom, 1977).

Unlike the classical pluralists, who seemed only to acknowledge but not incorporate the observation that some groups may be more powerful than others because of their superior organization and resources, Lindblom argued that the strength of business lay in the nature and structures of capitalism and democracy itself. Business need not, though it may, exert pressure on the government to realize its interests; the government, in accordance with the imperatives of capitalism and the pursuit of its own self-interest, will itself ensure that business interests are not adversely affected by its actions.

Neo-pluralist studies revealed that groups form for a variety of reasons, and pointed to the role patrons played in providing startup funding and organizational assistance to groups, either directly through the provision of state funds or indirectly through favourable treatment afforded foundations and other funding groups by specific tax, estate, and charities laws (Nownes & Neeley, 1996; Nownes, 1995; Nownes & Cigler, 1995). Such studies highlighted another problem with pluralist theory: its excessive concentration on the role of interest groups themselves and its relative neglect of other equally important factors in the political and policy-making processes that influence their creation, operation, and activities.

While neo-pluralism was a significant improvement on its immediate past predecessor, it did not resolve all the problems inherent in a focus on groups as driving forces behind policy. Neo-pluralism, for example, continued to overlook the role of the international system in shaping public policies and their implementation (Grande, 1996; Schafer, 2006). The role of ideology was also unjustifiably neglected in the pluralist explanations of politics and public policy. The liberal tradition pre-eminent in Anglo-Saxon countries (including Canada, the US, and Australia), for example, has had a significant impact on their governments' hesitant and often contradictory intervention in the economy.

The applicability of pluralism to countries besides the United States has also been found to be problematic because of differences in underlying political institutions and processes that challenge pluralist assumptions and precepts derived only from examination of the US experience (Zeigler, 1964). British parliamentary institutions found in Australia, Canada, the United Kingdom, Japan, and

Sweden, for example, do not lend themselves to the kind of open access that groups enjoy in relation to legislatures in the US and other countries with similar republican systems of government (Presthus, 1973). And many authoritarian countries simply lack the kinds of groups conceived by pluralists as being the basic building blocks of political analysis. Even if groups have the freedom to organize, the numbers actually formed are fewer than in the US and tend to be much more permanent and formalized. This finding led some group theorists, such as Phillipe Schmitter, to speculate that pluralism was only one form in which group systems could develop. Schmitter (1977) argued that, depending on a range of variables and historical factors, a *corporatist* form of political organization was much more likely than a pluralist one to emerge in many countries outside the US.

Corporatism

In Europe, theories treating groups as their primary unit of analysis have tended to take a corporatist rather than a pluralist form. The roots of corporatist theory are also much older than pluralist ones, extending back to the Middle Ages when there were concerns about protecting the "intermediate strata" of autonomous associations between the state and the family (Gierke, 1958a, 1958b). These included, notably, guilds and other forms of trade associations as well as, most importantly, religious organizations and churches.

Corporatist theory argued that these intermediate strata had a life of their own above and beyond their constituting individuals, and that their existence was part of the "organic" or "natural order" of society. Much of political life and conflict in Europe in the fifteenth and sixteenth centuries concerned efforts by emerging national states to control the operations of these "autonomous strata"— especially religious bodies—and the latter's efforts to resist state control (Cawson, 1986; Mann, 1984; Winkler, 1976).

As a group theory, corporatism can be best understood, as Schmitter (1977) has observed, in contrast to pluralism. As we have seen, the latter proposes that multiple groups exist to represent their respective members' interests, with membership being voluntary and groups being autonomous of the state. Corporatist groups, in contrast, are not free-forming, voluntary, autonomous, or competitive, as they depend on the state for recognition and support to play their role in policy-making. Corporatism thus explicitly takes into account two problems endemic to pluralism: its neglect of the role of the state in group formation and activities, and its failure to recognize institutionalized patterns of relationships between the state and groups.

In corporatist theory, public policy is shaped by interaction between the state and the interest group or groups recognized by the state (McLennan, 1989: 245). Public policy formation toward a declining industry, for instance, would take the form of negotiations between and among the state and relevant industry associations and trade unions as to how best to rationalize or streamline the industry and make it competitive. In France and Germany, for example, corporatist bargaining was a key element in passenger train development, providing commercially successful high-speed transportation between cities (Dunn & Perl, 1994). The making of social welfare policies similarly involves negotiations with business associations, social welfare groups, and possibly trade unions—if the proposed policies affect their members. The outcome of these negotiations depends not only on the organizational characteristics of the groups but on the closeness of their relationship with the state. The state itself is viewed as a powerful actor, although characterized by significant internal fissures.

Although this conception accords fairly well with political practices in many European countries, there are still problems with corporatism as an approach to politics and public policy. First, it is a descriptive category of a particular kind of political arrangement between states and societies (such as in Sweden or Austria), not a general explanation of what governments do, especially those in non-corporatist countries. Thus, it has little to say about how policies are made in countries such as Australia, Canada, and the United States, except to point out that the lack of institutionalized cooperation between the state and groups in these countries often leads to fragmented and inconsistent policies (Panitch, 1977, 1979).

Second, the theory does little to further our understanding of public policy processes, even in ostensibly corporatist countries. The close links between governments and certain groups highlighted by corporatism are certainly important, but these are also only one among many factors shaping policies and policy-making, and these relationships may vary significantly by policy sector or issue area (Castles & Merrill, 1989; Keman & Pennings, 1995).

Third, the theory does not contain a clear notion of even its own fundamental unit of analysis, the "interest" group. Contemporary societies contain myriad interests, as pluralists have noted, and it is not clear which ones are or should be represented by the state. In some cases, the relevant groups are defined in terms of ethnicity, language, or religion (Lijphart, 1969), while in others they are defined with reference to their economic activities. The bulk of corporatist literature concentrates somewhat arbitrarily on producer groups, such as industry associations and trade unions, and on their role in specific economic sectors, such as labour market policy and wage bargaining (Siaroff, 1999).

Fourth, the theory is vague about the relative significance of different groups in politics. Are we to treat all groups as equally influential? If not, then what determines their influence? Some argue that corporatism is a manifestation of an autonomous state desiring to manage social change or ensure social stability (Cawson, 1978). Others suggest it is a system sought by the major corporate actors and thus is simply put into place by the state at their behest (Schmitter, 1985).

Despite its shortcomings, corporatist theory has played a significant role in the analysis of public policy, especially in Europe and Latin America, but also to a certain extent in China and in the former socialist countries, many of which were organized along corporatist lines, albeit with a very powerful central state apparatus. By highlighting the autonomous role of the state in politics, it paved the way for more sophisticated explanations of public policy-making than those provided by group theories such as pluralism (Smith, 1997). More significantly, by emphasizing the importance of institutionalized patterns of relationships between states and societies, it fostered the emergence of new institutional approaches such as "statism," which focus on the macro level of social and political structures to draw their insights about public policy-making and serve to correct some of the oversights not only of pluralism and corporatism, but also of class and public choice theories (Blom-Hansen, 2001).

Neo-Institutionalism

The broadest perspective on the forces that drive the policy process can be found in neo-institutionalism and statist theories. These theories seek to overcome the limits of individual and group-based theories to explain the full range of social behaviour and organizational activity behind policy-making by focusing attention as well on organizations and institutions (Peters, 1999; Hall & Taylor, 1996; Kato, 1996).

Neo-institutionalism began in the late 1970s and early 1980s with the intention of bringing institutions back into explanation of politics. It built upon, rather than rejected, the focus of the "old institutionalism" on formal institutions of government (Schmidt 2009). Unlike the institutionalism of the past, which dwelled on formal organizations such as legislatures, courts, and bureaucracy, the newer variant focuses on the regular patterns of political behaviour, and on the rules, norms, practices and relationships that influence such behaviour (Cairney, undated). There are many variants of neo-institutionalism, of which three are particularly notable: rational choice, historical, and sociological (Hall & Taylor, 1996).

Historical institutionalism considers the extent to which events and decisions made in the past shape existing institutions that, in turn, influence current practices. Following the logic of path dependence, institutions and practices are "sticky" qualities in that it is increasingly costly to choose a different path. The timing of the original decision—the "critical juncture"—is crucial, because it sets institutional development on a particular path that endures far beyond the original purpose of its establishment. *Rational choice* focuses on individuals, whose (rational) actions are shaped by the particular institutional environment within which they exist. Institutions—defined as formal or informal rules—incentivize some actions deter others. In *sociological institutionalism,* norms and values within organizations are said to influence behaviour by conditioning actors' notions of appropriate behaviour. The shared understandings of appropriate behaviour emerge as a result of "socialization" and are "followed because they are seen as natural, rightful, expected and legitimate" (March & Olson, 1995: 30–31).[1]

There are other variants of neo-institutionalism under titles such as the "New Economics of Organization" (Moe, 1984; Yarbrough & Yarbrough, 1990; Williamson, 1996) or the *Institutional Analysis and Development* (IAD) framework (Kiser & Ostrom, 1982; Ostrom et al., 1993). What all these approaches share in common is that they use a form of what Fritz Scharpf (1977) calls *"actor-centred institutionalism,"* in which the focus is on individuals, albeit those whose behaviour is shaped by the socio-economic environment in which they exist (Cooney, 2007).

Neo-institutionalism seeks to identify how rules, norms, and symbols affect political behaviour; how the configuration of governmental institutions affects what the state does; and how unique patterns of historical development can constrain subsequent choices about public problem-solving (Scharpf, 2000). Institutions are defined to include not only formal organizations, such as bureaucracies and markets, but also legal and cultural codes and rules that affect how individuals and groups calculate optimal strategies and courses of action (Ostrom, 1999).[2]

Transaction cost analysis is an example of a neo-institutionalist approach to policy studies that expands the concerns of welfare economics about how governments and markets can fall short of optimal outcomes into a broader search for the historical legacies, social structures, and political approaches that lie behind these shortcomings (North, 1990; Williamson, 1985).This approach suggests that institutions constitute an essential element of political life, because they can overcome impediments caused by information asymmetries and other barriers to "perfect" exchange in society. The basic unit of analysis in this approach is related to the "transactions" among individuals within the confines of an institutional order (Coase, 1937). Institutions of various kinds are significant to the extent that they can increase or lower the costs of transactions. In this perspective institutions are "the products of human design, the outcomes of purposive actions by instrumentally oriented individuals" (Powell & DiMaggio, 1991: 8) that also influence human behaviour.

In neo-institutionalist approaches, the argument is not that institutions *cause* an action, per se. Rather, they are said to *affect* actions by shaping the interpretation of problems and possible solutions by policy actors, and by constraining the choice of solutions and the way and extent to which they can be implemented. In the political realm, for example, institutions are significant because they "constitute and legitimize individual and collective political actors and provide them with consistent behavioural rules, conceptions of reality, standards of assessment, affective ties, and endowments, and thereby with a capacity for purposeful action" (March & Olsen, 1994: 5). That is, while individuals, groups, classes, and states have their specific interests, they pursue them in the context of existing formal organizations and rules and norms that shape expectations and affect the possibilities of their realization (Williamson, 1985; Searle, 2005). This approach is open-ended and eclectic in the sense that it directs attention to a wide range of international and local norms, rules, and behaviour that potentially affect actors' calculations of actual and perceived transaction costs of particular policy actions (Putnam, 1988; Atkinson & Harrison, 1978).[3]

A more serious problem for actor-centred neo-institutionalism, however, lies with its inability to provide a plausible coherent explanation of the origin of institutions, or their alteration, without resorting to functionalism (Blyth, 2007). That is, since this approach argues that individual and collective preferences are shaped by institutions, it is unclear how institutions or rules themselves are created and, once in place, how they would change (Cammack, 1992; March et al., 2000; Peters, 1999; Gorges, 2001; Dimitrakopoulos, 2005). Actor-centred institutionalism, for example, tends to provide an excellent discussion of the constraints placed by structures on policy actors and to show how what is "rational" for them to do in specific circumstances is affected by such institutions. But it has little to say on what causes those constraints to move in any particular direction (Bromley, 1989: Ch. 1; Ruiter, 2004). Studies that compare policy-making over time have noted an "institutional durability" in which some social and political structures endure much longer than others (Perl, 1991), an observation that is difficult to explain within the deductive logic of institutions orienting individual behaviour found in neo-institutionalism (Clemens & Cook, 1999; Greif & Laitin, 2004). This has led many students of policy studies to turn away from it and toward a more sociologically or historically informed version of institutionalism, which we shall term "statism," in order to build a deeper and more rigorous base to support their interpretation of public policy-making.

Statism

"Statism" is the term employed to describe inductive institutional studies of policy-making that focus on the state. This approach addresses both the neo-institutionalist lacunae regarding institutional origins and change as well as the neglect of the state in pluralist, corporatist, class, and public choice theories.

Statist interpretations have their origin in the works of late nineteenth- and early twentieth-century German historical sociologists and legal theorists who highlighted how establishing modern state institutions influenced the development of society. Rather than argue that the state reflected the character of a nation's populace or social structure, theorists such as Max Weber and Otto Hintze noted how the state's monopoly on the use of force allowed it to reorder and structure social relations and institutions (Hintze, 1975; Nettl, 1968; Weber, 1978).

The statist perspective on policy-making explicitly acknowledges that policy preferences and capacities are best understood in the context of the society in which the state is embedded (Nettl, 1968; Przeworski, 1990; Therborn, 1986).

There are, however, variations in the relative emphasis on state and society in such studies. Many statist policy studies focus solely on formal state structures, seeing government as the leading institution in society and the key agent in the political process. Others also attribute explanatory significance to organized social actors in addition to the state.

Like actor-centred neo-institutionalists, statists focus on the impact of large-scale structures on individuals and vice versa (Hall, 1986: 19). At the same time, the statist perspective differs from neo-institutional approaches in important aspects. First, no effort is made to reduce institutions to less organized forms of social interaction, such as norms, rules, or conventions. Second, there is no attempt to bring institutions down to the level of individuals and individual activities, such as economic or social transactions, as is the case with more actor-centred neo-institutional thinking. And, third, institutions are simply taken as "givens," that is, as observable historical social entities in themselves, with little effort made to derive the reasons for their origins from *a priori* principles of human cognition or existence (March & Olsen, 1994).

Using such a line of analysis yields, to use Theda Skocpol's terms, a "state-centric" as opposed to "society-centric" explanation of political life, including public policy-making (Skocpol, 1985). In a "strong" version of the statist approach, as Adam Przeworski (1990: 47–8) put it in a pioneering book:

> States create, organize and regulate societies. States dominate other organizations within a particular territory, they mould the culture and shape the economy. Thus, the problem of the autonomy of the state with regard to society has no sense within this perspective. It should not even appear. The concept of "autonomy" is a useful instrument of analysis only if the domination by the state over society is a contingent situation, that is, if the state derives its efficacy from private property, societal values, or some other sources located outside it. Within a true "state-centric" approach this concept has nothing to contribute.

It is problematic to accept statism in the strong form described above, however, because it has difficulty accounting for the existence of social liberties and freedoms or explaining why states cannot always enforce their will, such as in times of rebellion or civil disobedience. In fact, even the most autocratic governments make some attempt to respond to what they believe to be popular preferences. It is, of course, impossible for a democratic state to be entirely autonomous from a society with voting rights. And, as Lindblom and others have pointed out, capitalist states, both democratic and autocratic, must not only make efforts to maintain and nurture support for the regime among the population but also need to accommodate the imperatives of the marketplace in their policies. Second, the statist view suggests implicitly that all "strong" states should respond to the same problem in the same manner because of their similar organizational features.

This is obviously not the case, as different states (both "strong" and "weak") often have different policies dealing with the same problem. To explain the differences, we need to take into account factors other than the features of the state (Przeworski, 1990).

To be fair, however, few subscribe to statism in the "strong" form described above. Instead of replacing the pluralist notion of the societal direction of the state with the statist notion of the state's direction of society, most inductively oriented institutionalist theorists merely point out the need to take both sets of factors into consideration in their analyses of political phenomena (Hall & Ikenberry, 1989; McLennan, 1989; Levy, 2006). As Skocpol has conceded:

> In this perspective, the state certainly does not become everything. Other organizations and agents also pattern social relationships and politics, and the analyst must explore the state's structure in relation to them. But this Weberian view of the state does require us to see it as much more than a mere arena in which social groups make demands and engage in political struggles or compromises. (Skocpol, 1985: 7–8)

In this view, the state does not necessarily just respond to pressure from dominant social groups or classes but is rather an autonomous actor with the capacity to devise and implement its own objectives. Its autonomy and capacity derive from its staffing by officials with personal ambitions and agency interests, as well as from the fact that it is a sovereign organization with unparalleled financial, personnel, and—in the final instance—coercive resources. Proponents of this perspective claim that emphasizing state centrality as an explanatory variable enables statism to offer more plausible explanations of policy development patterns in many countries than do other political theory perspectives (Krasner, 1984; Skowronek, 1982; Orren & Skowronek, 1998–9).

This milder version of statism thus concentrates on the links between the state and society in the context of the latter's pre-eminence in pluralist group theory. To that extent, Statism complements rather than replaces society-centredness and restores some balance to social and political theorizing, which, it can be argued, had lost its equilibrium (Orren & Skowronek, 1993; Almond, 1988; Cortell & Peterson, 2001; Thelen & Steinmo, 1992; March & Olsen, 1996; Keman, 1997). This view and approach to policy studies informs the analysis of policy processes found in the remainder of this volume.

Conclusion

In considering a range of deductive and inductive perspectives on public policy-making across individual, group, and societal scales, we have encountered different and often contradictory ways to approach the study of public policy. An extensive literature exists on policy analysis from both positivist and post-positivist orientations, both promoting and denouncing the origins, assumptions, and application of each approach to the subject. Nevertheless, a few general conclusions can be offered.

In each of the theoretical frameworks that seek to make sense of policy, we can find three essential elements that are addressed, albeit differently. First, understanding policy requires some knowledge about the *actors* who raise issues, assess options, decide on those options, and implement them. These actors can be seen as subjects trying to advance their own interests, or as objects influenced by the circumstances of their surrounding environment. Second, policy insights also call for an appreciation of the *ideas* that shape policy deliberations. These ideas can range from the most particular and self-interested points of view to widely held belief systems that endure through the ages. And third, policy-making takes place within a set of social and political *structures* that affect the deliberations about what is to be done. Those structures can be seen as arenas that set the "rules of the game" for the competition among different interests and the clash of distinctive ideas. These structures can also be seen as the subjects of political initiative—providing a focus for debate over how to better govern a society, how to better sustain an economy, or how to better express a culture.

Actors, ideas, and structures form the common ground where all policy theories converge—from different directions, and with distinctive points of view. It is in adopting, and adapting, these conceptual particularities that the potential for greater insight into policy-making and policy outcomes can be realized. We turn to elaborating that context in Chapter 3.

Study Questions

1. How should the unit of analysis be selected for understanding policy attributes?

2. What are the advantages and disadvantages of using the individual as a basic unit of analysis in policy studies? Groups? Institutions?

3. Can deductive and inductive approaches to analysis be used in conjunction to study public policy, or must one choose between their competing logic of inquiry?

4. How is the emergence of women's, LGBTQ+, and other similar identities dealt with by policy theory?

5. What is the advantage of comparative policy analyses for the advancement of policy theory and knowledge?

Further Readings

Cairney, Paul. 2013. "Standing on The Shoulders of Giants: How Do We Combine the Insights of Multiple Theories in Public Policy Studies?" *Policy Studies Journal* 41, no. 1: 1–21.

Carey, Gemma, Helen Dickinson, and Sue Olney. 2019. "What Can Feminist Theory Offer Policy Implementation Challenges?" *Evidence & Policy: A Journal of Research, Debate and Practice* 15, no. 1 (February 1): 143–59.

Fischer, Frank. 2007. "Deliberative Policy Analysis as Practical Reason: Integrating Empirical and Normative Arguments," in Frank Fischer, Gerald Miller, and Mara Sidney, eds, *Handbook of Public Policy Analysis: Theory, Politics, and Methods*. Boca Raton, FL: CRC Press, 223–36.

Howlett, Michael, Allan McConnell, and Anthony Perl. 2016. "Weaving the Fabric of Public Policies: Comparing and Integrating Contemporary Frameworks for the Study of Policy Processes," *Journal of Comparative Policy Analysis: Research and Practice* 18, no. 3: 273–89.

Kiser, Larry, and Elinor Ostrom. 1982. "The Three Worlds of Action," in Ostrom, ed., *Strategies of Political Inquiry*. Beverly Hills, CA: Sage, 179–222.

Le Grand, Julian. 1991. "The Theory of Government Failure," *British Journal of Political Science* 21, no. 4: 423–42.

McLennan, Gregor. 1989. *Marxism, Pluralism and Beyond: Classic Debates and New Departures*. Cambridge: Polity Press.

March, James G., and Johan P. Olsen. 1984. "The New Institutionalism: Organizational Factors in Political Life," *American Political Science Review* 78: 734–49.

Schmitter, Phillipe C. 1977. "Modes of Interest Intermediation and Models of Societal Change in Western Europe," *Comparative Political Studies* 10, no. 1: 7–38.

Skocpol, Theda. 1985. "Bringing the State Back In: Strategies of Analysis in Current Research," in Peter B. Evans, Dietrich Rueschemeyer, and Theda Skocpol, eds, *Bringing the State Back In*. New York: Cambridge University Press, 3–43.

Tribe, L. H. 1972. "Policy Science: Analysis or Ideology?" *Philosophy and Public Affairs* 2, no. 1: 66–110.

Van Winden, Frans A.A.M. 1988. "The Economic Theory of Political Decision-Making," in Julien van den Broeck, ed., *Public Choice*. Dordrecht: Kluwer, 9–57.

Chapter 3

The Policy Context
States and Societies

Institutions, Ideas, and Actors in Public Policy

The extensive accumulation of policy studies published over the past six decades provide a rich, though complex, picture of the myriad factors shaping public policy. Contemporary research findings about influences on policy continue to fuel a debate over where to focus the examination of policy-making, which has lost none of its vitality since Harold Lasswell urged connecting the technical analysis of policies to their social and political context.

Those who seek a universal theory of policy-making might question whether policy science has made much progress from its post-war origins, given the resulting absence of consensus over what merits attention in explaining policy-making and policy outcomes. But those who accept Lasswell's claim that the policy researcher needs to understand the specific context of a policy initiative in order to gain effective insight into its design and prospects will discover advances in teasing out the intricate relationships between those generally accepted critical factors affecting policy development, namely, actors, institutions, and ideas.

With respect to actors, studies of political or administrative leadership, chronicles of policy entrepreneurs' efforts, and examinations of the way that "street-level" bureaucrats or private contractors and consultants work through the many details of delivering policy offer insight into the ways that both individual and organized actors influence policy development. Such studies indicate where, when, and how, to investigate the people behind policies for answers as to why policy turns out one way instead of another. What could be a purely behavioural focus, however, is tempered by the fact that what actors seek and do depends on their sociology: the political, economic, and social structures that surround them. And, finally, a growing number of studies also seek to explain the content of policy based on both the ideas that actors subscribe to and their beliefs regarding the appropriate role of government in resolving social problems and issues.

As the survey in Chapter 2 revealed, many of the analytical approaches to studying public policy itemized in Figure 2.2 are either too high-pitched or too idiosyncratic and fail to adequately take into account many of the different actors, institutions, and ideas that affect public policy. Welfare economics and public choice theory, for example, treat individual and group actors as key explanatory variables and would thus suggest that policy context should be examined through the activity of these entities but tend to ignore policy processes and institutions. This is very obvious in the case of theories that focus on individual behaviour, but theories built upon group and class theory, such as pluralism, feminism and diversity studies, and Marxism, which attribute influence to organized groups of actors affected by social, economic, and political structures, also consider actors to be the primary focus of analytical and theoretical attention and other factors such as structures and ideas to be secondary or peripheral.

And, as we also have seen in Chapter 2, even among the most successful syntheses that place a great deal of weight on the impact of institutions on personal and group behaviour, and vice versa, the varieties of neo-institutional models set out in the chapter typically fail to consider policy processes and how these interact with the other variables to affect policy *content* (Goldmann, 2005; Kato, 1996; Scharpf, 1991, 1997).

Building on critiques of long-established theories focusing on actors and structures, these more recently elaborated analytical frameworks for studying policy—statism and the different variants of neo-institutionalism—do attempt to account for both actor-oriented and organizational and structural variables. Although their assumptions differ, these approaches do treat state and social institutions as important entities affecting the preferences and behaviour of policy actors and hence represent an advance over purely individual- or group-level thinking. They attempt to explain public policy as the product of the interdependent interaction between state capacity and social activity.

The Role of Policy Ideas: Paradigms, Public Sentiments, Symbolic Frames, and Program Ideas

While ever more accurately describing policy-making institutions and actors, however, none of these analytical frameworks provides much insight into policy substance or *content*. In many early theories of policy-making, for example, the actual content of policy outputs was often simply assumed to be determined by, for instance, the manifestation of the "self-interest" of policy actors in any given policy choice context (Flathman, 1966; Heclo, 1994; Braun, 1999), tempered by the nature of the conflicts and the compromises policy-makers made during policy formation (Sabatier, 1988, 1993). This could be predicted by correctly mapping the nature of policy "stakeholders" and decision-makers and identifying their "interests," whether this was done empirically through recourse to interviews and documentation or deductively based on abstract models of personality and group priorities.

More contemporary neo-institutional theories, however, embrace a more sophisticated conception of the role of ideas in the policy process. They note that the presence of particular actors in the policy process and the interests they pursue are often largely determined not just by their environment but also by the nature of the organization within which they operate. Moreover, they also note that many of the ideas that participating policy actors articulate have been shaped by past policy choices and the ideas embodied in those choices and that these form an important institutional and ideational substrate affecting contemporary positions and choices.

As John Campbell has noted, it is possible to distinguish a number of distinct kinds of idea or "idea sets" that go into public policy-making: *program ideas*, *symbolic frames*, *policy paradigms*, and *public sentiments* (see Figure 3.1). Symbolic frames and public sentiments, for example, are those that tend to affect the perception of the legitimacy or "correctness" of certain courses of action; policy paradigms, on the other hand, represent a "set of cognitive background assumptions that constrain action by limiting the range of alternatives that policy-making elites are likely to perceive as useful and worth considering" (Campbell, 1998: 385; also Surel, 2000). "Program ideas," largely represent the selection of specific solutions from among the set designated as acceptable within a particular paradigm.

This notion that a distinctive policy paradigm works to filter reality and shape actors' understanding of what problems to address, and how to address them, helps to sharpen our focus on how ideas shape policy content.

Developed originally to describe enduring sets of ideas that are present in the natural sciences, the term *paradigm* was later applied to long-lasting points of view on "the way the world works" that are found in the social sciences (Kuhn, 1962, 1974; Hall, 1990, 1992, 1993). The concept is closely related to traditional philosophical notions of "ideologies" as overarching frameworks of ideas influencing action and to more recent sociological notions of "discourses" or "frames" (Goffman, 1974; Surel, 2000). The paradigm notion is compatible with the basic elements

Figure 3.1 Ideational Components of Policy Contents

		Level of Policy Debate Affected	
		Foreground	*Background*
Level of Ideas Affected	*Cognitive (Causal)*	Program Ideas	Policy Paradigms
	Normative (Value)	Symbolic Frames	Public Sentiments

Source: Adapted from John L. Campbell, "Institutional Analysis and the Role of Ideas in Political Economy," *Theory and Society* 27, 5 (1998): 385.

of a neo-institutional approach to policy studies since it captures the idea that established beliefs, values, and attitudes support understandings of public problems and paradigms also inspire notions of how *feasible* proposed policy solutions could be. These ideas correspond with, and indeed shape, actor self-interest, as well as being, correspondingly, significant determinants of policy content (Hall, 1990: 59; also, Edelman, 1988; Hilgartner & Bosk, 1981; Schneider, 1985). The implicit power of embedded ideas is clearly evident in how policy-makers understand both problems and potential solutions to them.

Much recent theorizing reflects this understanding that actors, institutions, and the ideas they represent all play a meaningful role and interactive role in affecting the unfolding and outcome of policy processes. Individuals, groups, and classes engaged in the policy process certainly have their own interests, but how they interpret and pursue their interests and the outcomes of their efforts are shaped by institutional and ideational attributes (Lundquist, 1987).[1]

As noted in Chapter 2, in this book we adopt the statist tendency to define institutions quite narrowly as comprising only the actual structures or organizations of the state, society, and the international system. Following this approach, we are less preoccupied than many scholars with the origins of these institutions, which can be taken as given without limiting our insight into specific episodes of policy-making. While not monolithic, omnipresent, or immutable, these institutions can only rarely be avoided, modified, or replaced without a considerable degree of effort. And the structural disruptions that accompany institutional change are hard to miss, and thus will become obvious to those examining an episode of policy-making.

If such disruption does not rise to the level of breaking down institutional arrangements, the forces that create and destroy institutions can safely remain in the background of policy studies. As a result, we focus on the way institutions are organized internally and in relation to each other and how this affects actor behaviour (March & Olsen, 1998b). In addition to their formal organizational characteristics—membership, rules, and operating procedures—we emphasize the principles, norms, and ideas they embody. These principles, in the shape of formal or informal rules and conventions, as well as ethical, ideological, and epistemic concerns, further help to shape actors' behaviour by conditioning their perception of their interests and the probability that these interests will be realized in policy outcomes (March et al., 2000; Timmermans & Bleiklie, 1999).

The Political-Economic Context

Two meta-institutions—*capitalism* and *democracy*—inform the structures within which the public policy process unfolds in most modern societies. These overarching institutions deserve particular attention, not only because they are influential among policy-makers, but also because they are not intrinsically compatible and hence must be somehow constantly reconciled, leading to unstable compromises that generate ongoing political challenges in liberal-democratic countries. In this chapter, these two important contextual aspects of the policy-making process and outcomes will be explored.

Capitalism

Capitalism refers to both a market-oriented political economy or system of production and exchange and to a society in which control over the property required for production (capital) is concentrated in the hands of a small section of the populace, while most of the rest of the population sells their time for wage labour.

Under capitalism, production is undertaken not for direct consumption by the producer but for purposes of sale or exchange so the producer can use the money thus derived to purchase other goods for consumption. This differs from pre-capitalist societies in which producers directly consumed much of what they produced, except for a small portion exchanged through barter or taxed for military protection. In capitalism, exchange takes place through markets among individuals usually unknown to each other.

Capitalism is a socio-economic system that was first produced by the breakdown of agricultural societies, which operated on quite different principles—lacking, for the most part, markets, capital, and wage labour. In Europe, these societies underwent industrialization toward the end of the eighteenth century. This system of organizing social and economic relations spread rapidly to North America and most of the rest of the world during the nineteenth century, often through its direct imposition on colonies in Africa, North and South America, Australasia, and Asia by European and other imperial states, but also through its emulation by many developing countries in Europe, Asia, and elsewhere.

In the twentieth century, many nations rejected capitalism and adopted socialism—a state-oriented political economy in which "capital" is publicly owned and allocated—with the expressed intention of working toward the establishment of a communist political economy, in which "capital" would be communally owned and wage labour abolished. But by the end of the twentieth century, as economic growth stagnated in socialist countries, most embraced capitalism with renewed enthusiasm. Now almost all countries in the world are capitalist, though, as discussed below, they vary a great deal in terms of their specific political arrangements (Coates, 2005; Lehne, 2001; Howell, 2003; Hall & Soskice, 2001b).

The hallmark of capitalism is that ownership of production inputs—e.g., raw materials, machinery, factory buildings—is largely in private hands. This implies that the owners of the means of production have the exclusive right to decide on the use of those means of production. This right is guaranteed by the state, with certain restrictions required to ensure the effective reproduction of the capitalist order such as avoiding fraud or the mistreatment of workers or, more recently, the environment. Capitalism thus entitles owners to decide what will be produced, in what manner, and in what quantities, a power that also establishes the capitalists as the dominant social class since other classes and strata in society—workers, peasants, small shop owners, religious authorities, intellectuals, and the like—all rely on capitalists for their incomes and well-being. To earn a livelihood, those who do not own the means of production must work for those who do. In many capitalist societies, their own labour and skill are often the only productive inputs non-capitalists own. In order to survive, these must be sold to capitalists for salaries and wages.

This underpins a critical feature of capitalism: the need for firms to make profits, or accumulate capital, in order for both producers and the economy as a whole to survive. Profit is to capitalism what motion is to bicycles: capitalism, like bicycles, cannot properly function by standing still. If an adequate return on investment is not forthcoming, capitalists will withhold their investment or invest it somewhere else. The result can be a decline in economic activity in a society and a general lowering of a society's living standards. This imposes an enormous pressure on states to ensure hospitable conditions for continued, and expanded, capital investment, often in a competitive environment with other states seeking the same investment.

Businesses and firms in such societies not surprisingly attempt to influence governments directly and through their membership in various forms of business associations, and indirectly (Coleman, 1988; Jacek, 1986). Business associations, among the many interest groups found in capitalist societies, enjoy an unmatched capacity to affect public policy, given the reliance of states in capitalist societies on businesses for their revenues and for overall levels of social well-being (Lindblom, 1977). The increasing speed and scale of globalization in production, distribution, and financial services has further reinforced this power of capital. It is now much easier than it was in the past for investors and managers to respond, if they so choose, to an unwanted government action by moving capital to another location. Although this theoretical mobility can be tempered by various practical considerations, such as the availability of resources or trained labour, the potential loss of employment and revenues is a threat that every state must take seriously in making policy decisions. Because of their potential to affect state revenues negatively, capitalists—both domestic and foreign—have the ability to "punish" the state for any actions of which they disapprove (Hayes, 1978).

Even in democratic states where power and influence lie in electoral and legislative systems that empower non-capitalist majorities in the population, the financial contributions of businesses to political parties and campaigns, for example, continue to afford them an important resource for influencing policy-makers. Modern elections can sometimes turn on sensationalized issues and personalities, which necessitate large budgets to influence voters through extensive traditional and social media advertising campaigns. In such situations, political parties and third parties supported by contributions from business are in a strong position to run successful campaigns and thus influence voting behaviour. This can lead political parties and candidates seeking office to accommodate business interests more than they would other agendas. Similarly, the financial support that businesses offer to public policy research institutions and individual researchers serve to further entrench their power. The organizations and individuals receiving funds tend to be sympathetic toward business interests and can provide business with the intellectual wherewithal and access to decision-makers often required to prevail in policy debates (McGann & Weaver, 1999; Abelson, 1999; Rich, 2004). Hence, for all these reasons, business actors and their behaviour deserve close scrutiny in the study of public policy.

Liberalism

Another distinctive feature of capitalism, as it has emerged historically, is its inextricable link with the theory and ideology of liberalism, which refers to a set of more or less well-organized and institutionalized beliefs and practices that serve to maintain and promote the capitalist system and way of life (Macpherson, 1978). Liberalism emerged in tandem with capitalism in the eighteenth century as a political ideology dedicated to justifying and reinforcing the increasingly important capitalist mode of production mainly by pursuing "free trade," "free speech," and other forms of liberal rights that supported capital in its struggle against landlords and aristocracies to control investment and production. This highly adaptive social theory has changed substantially since its origin in order to accommodate evolving economic and political circumstances, without departing very far from its fundamental belief in the righteousness and appropriateness of private ownership of the means of production as the key to the attainment of human progress and freedom (Howlett et al., 1999).

Liberalism is centred on the assumption of the primacy of the individual in society and thus does not directly exclude non-capitalists from its purview. Rather, it views individuals as having inalienable natural rights, including the right to own property and to enter into contracts with other individuals concerning the disposition of that property. These rights have to be protected from intrusion by collective social organizations such as the state, churches, or trade unions. A good society in liberal theory is one that guarantees individuals freedom to pursue their interests and realize their potential. This freedom should be restricted only when one person's freedom erodes that of another, for example, through theft or violence (Macpherson, 1962).

Freedom to pursue the livelihood of one's choice and to accumulate wealth is sacrosanct in liberalism and is generally very popular. It potentially benefits many groups and individuals at least in theory, if not always in practice. This is because not everyone has the same resources or background or privileges that allow them to compete equally "on a level playing field."

While this inequality of opportunity and condition has often spurred demands for state action to correct the situation—from affirmative action hiring policies to free tuition or subsidized student debt loads—liberalism's preferred mechanism for individuals to pursue their interests in an unencumbered fashion is the market, not the state. At least in theory, in a market all individuals selfishly seek to advance their own interests according to their own abilities and preferences. Liberals thus see exchange in the marketplace as natural, as an efficient rationing and allocation device, and as benefiting everyone who engages in it, with the net result of this activity being the enhancement of society's overall welfare. This tenet links liberalism closely to capitalism, as a system of market-based exchange based on individual property rights.

Liberalism is thus in practice essentially a theory of the market that has had to include the state on grounds of contingency to perform necessary functions that would not otherwise be performed: to both level the playing field and correct market failures.

Liberal political economy contains two slightly different formulations concerning the state. The first is the idea of the *supplementary* or *residual state*: the notion contained in neo-classical and neo-conservative liberal political economy that the state should only undertake those activities—such as the provision of pure public goods—that markets cannot perform. The second is the notion of the *corrective state*: the idea found in later so-called Keynesian and post-Keynesian analyses, which asserted that the state can act in a variety of other areas of market activity to correct the host micro- or macro-level market failures described in Chapter 2, as well as ensure that at least equality of opportunity is preserved in theory, if not always in practice (Dunleavy & O'Leary, 1987).

Significantly, both variants of liberal thinking under-theorize the state and, in so doing, public policy-making. This is because they treat the state as an entity whose very existence poses a threat to markets and individual freedoms, on the one hand, but whose threat can be mitigated, on the other hand, by embracing liberal tenets and doing only whatever it is that the market cannot do. And, moreover, the state is generally not considered to be constrained by the society in which it exists or by its organizational capacity in its pursuit of either of these two contradictory goals (Schott, 1984: 60). In fact, the capacity of the state to act and the forces that act upon the state are usually not considered at all in liberal theory, which tends to focus on questions of the sources, basis, and content of individual rights and freedoms and urges the adoption of a limited state on purely ethical or ideological grounds (Sandel, 1984). Or, in slightly more sophisticated analyses, it is usually just assumed that the state can and will act either to provide goods and services or to correct market failures out of a concern for economic growth and efficiency without ever considering why this should or can be a government goal. Neither of these analyses does justice to the full measure of values, principles, and doctrines behind state action and public policy-making in the contemporary world, as the subsequent discussion of these processes in this book will attest.

Democracy

The second major meta-institution affecting states and policy-making is democracy. Democracy is one of the most contentious concepts in the study of politics. One survey in the late 1980s, for example, found 311 definitions of "democracy" present in the literature on the subject (Cunningham, 1987: 25). It is not our objective to resolve this definitional debate. For our purposes, it is sufficient to regard democracy as a plan of political organization, a meta-political decision-making system, which involves structuring the mechanisms of day-to-day control of the state through representative institutions staffed through periodic elections (Bealey, 1988: 1). Thus, Göran Therborn (1977: 3) succinctly defines modern democracy as comprising the following:

> (1) a representative government elected by (2) an electorate consisting of the entire adult population, (3) whose votes carry equal weight, and (4) who are allowed to vote for any opinion without intimidation by the state apparatus.

Democracy confers entitlements on citizens to choose their representatives in government and can also, in the form of referenda or plebiscites, provide a mechanism for political decision-making or advice. The method of election varies among nations, but the primary purpose is always to declare the candidate with the largest number of votes as the winner in periodic competitions to staff legislative and executive branches of governments, as well as the judiciary in certain jurisdictions. This condition establishes that the government is to be formed by the representatives of the largest number of citizens and, depending on the type of electoral system used, of which there are many distinct types and permutations, that through those representatives it is to be held directly or indirectly accountable to the citizens. Elections as a means of removing a government and replacing it with another were virtually unheard of until the nineteenth century, and even today some otherwise democratic governments find ingenious excuses and means to avoid submitting themselves too often to the judgment of the electorate.

Although it is sometimes referred to as "liberal democracy," it was only toward the end of the nineteenth century that Western nations began to establish democratic institutions in that sense of the term, and it is not necessary for democracies to be liberal (Doorenspleet, 2000). This democratization process occurred in waves, and the process was not completed until well after World War II when the modern state system emerged from the wreckage of former colonial empires and the franchise, or right to vote, was made universal for most adults in most nation-states. The intent of earlier restrictions on voting, so that, for example, only white male property owners could vote, as was the case in the US, UK, Canada, Australia, and many other countries, was to limit the privilege of voting to social and economic elites and ensure their rule.

The removal of these barriers to the franchise represented a major milestone in promoting social equality and reducing or offsetting the direct power of capitalists over state actions in capitalist countries. This is because, from a political-economic perspective, insofar as democracy is based on the principle of the secret ballot and majority rule, those who do not own the means of production can, in principle, exercise their numerical superiority in elections to vote-in governments that can then use state authority to temper the adverse effects of capitalist ownership of the means of production. And this does occur, but often in the face of stiff opposition from business and other less numerous but still powerful groups and actors such as, in many countries, the military (Przeworski, 1985).

By requiring that governments be elected, democracy permits the weaker sections of the society some degree of control over the state and thus helps to shape not only the internal functioning of the state but also, through the use of state authority, how markets for particular goods and services will function. As Adam Przeworski (1985: 11) points out: "Political democracy constitutes the opportunity for workers to pursue some of their interests. Electoral politics constitutes the mechanism through which anyone can as a citizen express claims to goods and services. . . . Moreover . . . they can intervene in the very organization of production and allocation of profit." Influenced by democratic politics, for example, in most countries the state has introduced income redistribution measures, defying one of the basic capitalist tenets that the market alone ought to determine the distribution of income (Przeworski, 1991). Similarly, in many countries, states have replaced private ownership of some means of production with public, or state, ownership: all countries have some state-owned or -controlled enterprises producing a variety of goods and services; from those related to national security and defence to finance, shipping, transportation, and telecommunications activities, to the production of various kinds of small-scale consumer items.

Democracy thus offers a political mechanism that can moderate the economic effects of capitalism and often co-occurs with liberalism as its prevailing ideology in liberal capitalist democracies. The degree of harmony achieved between these meta-institutions and philosophies can be a major contributor to social cohesion and can reduce the need for coercive authority (e.g., police and prisons) to maintain domestic order. This potential for symbiosis between capitalism and democracy is realized through specific policy options and their outcomes. As will be shown in the following section, however, attaining an effective balance between capitalism and democracy is a difficult task that is by no means automatic or inevitable.

Policy-Making in the Liberal-Democratic Capitalist State

To the extent liberalism and its corollary, capitalism, are about individual rights while democracy is about collective rights, the two are fundamentally contradictory, notwithstanding the common term *liberal democracy*, often used to describe countries with both systems in place. The opportunities for political control that democracy offers economically weak but numerous groups thus sit uneasily with the basic tenets of liberalism. As early liberal eighteenth- and nineteenth-century thinkers understood all too well, democracy can pose a fundamental threat to a liberal order because it gives the majority the capacity to erode individual rights; including especially the rights of capitalists to dispose of their property, and labour, however they see fit. Liberals faced challenges not only from landowners but also from religious and ethnic groups that attempted to curtail aspects of capitalism they found onerous or unjust. Although they were often able to coexist with religious parties, they struggled with right-wing nationalist and fascist parties and with communist and other left parties that desired to replace owner control of production and capital with more state-driven forms. Although fascist and authoritarian parties often denounced liberalism as alienating and undermining the nation-state and threatening its existence, they left many aspects of the capitalist order intact. The liberals' worst fears were only realized in the twentieth century when left-leaning socialist and social democratic or labour- or worker-based parties in many parts of the world formed governments that often used their powers to nationalize industries, raise taxes, enforce worker rights, and redistribute income. While the advent of liberal democracy thus did not lead to the extermination of capitalism, as some had hoped and others had feared, it did mean that democratic governments could no longer ignore the interests of the majority of non-elites to the extent that they had in the past (Korpi, 1983).

Thus, the presence of democracy complicates policy-making and implementation tasks in a capitalist society because it means policy-makers can no longer concentrate on serving only state interests and the interests of their business allies in accordance with the tenets of a pure liberal policy paradigm (Swank, 2000; deLeon, 1997; Gourevitch, 1993). Political violence is particularly detrimental to economic growth (Butkiewicz & Yanikkaya, 2005), and democracy is often needed to defuse the tensions generated by capitalism and avoid revolution and rebellions. In democracies, policy-makers have to at least appear to be heeding the concerns of farmers and workers, children and seniors, men and women, and religious, ethnic, and racial sections of the populace who have different and often contradictory interests that need to be constantly juggled or are inherently unstable. Such conflicts make policy-making challenging and often lie at the heart of the sometimes very ad hoc and somewhat contradictory policy choices that governments regularly make in order to retain social peace and, if not harmony, at least legitimacy.

Along with liberalism, capitalism and democracy thus form an important part of the meta-institutional and macro-ideational, or "political-economic," context of policy-making in many modern countries. Taken together, they greatly influence the actors and ideas in most policy-making processes. However, a government's capacity to act autonomously or relatively autonomously within this context is shaped not just by the existence of capitalism and democracy and the ideas and interests they generate, but also by the manner in which the government and the various more or less empowered actors under liberal capitalism found in each country or issue area are organized.

Political-Economic Structures and Public Policy-Making

In order to make and implement policies effectively in a capitalist democracy, as discussed in Chapter 1, the state needs to be well organized and supported by prominent social actors: that is, it needs a fairly high level of *capacity*. The extent to which these actors are able to offer the necessary support for state action depends, among other things, on their own internal organization and their relationships with the state and with other similarly powerful social actors.

These are complex relationships. Fragmentation within and among prominent social groups, for example, can simultaneously strengthen the state's level of *policy autonomy* or its ability to develop and articulate a wide range of policy options, while undermining its *policy capacity* by limiting its ability to mobilize social actors toward its preferred method of resolving societal problems. If the societal conflicts are particularly severe, for example, despite enjoying a great deal of autonomy, the state may find its functioning paralyzed. Conversely, unity within and among social groups makes for a stable policy environment that facilitates policy-making and promotes effective implementation (Painter & Pierre, 2005) but can lead to significant opposition to state plans.

Thus, strong social cohesion can either constrain or facilitate the state's ability to change policy in a significant or large-scale way. Strong organizations can bargain more effectively and need not make unreasonable demands for the sake of maintaining their members' support. And when they agree to a measure, they can enforce it upon their membership, through sanctions if necessary. Mancur Olson has argued that in societies characterized by "encompassing" groups (that is, umbrella groups consisting of a variety of similar interests) rather than "narrow" interest groups, the groups "internalize much of the cost of inefficient policies and accordingly have an incentive to redistribute income to themselves with the least possible social cost, and to give some weight to economic growth and to the interests of society as a whole" (Olson, 1982: 92). The existence of numerous narrow interest groups, in contrast, promotes competition among groups that pressure the state to serve their members' interests only, regardless of the effects on others. The cumulative result of policy-making led by these kinds of interest groups thus often can be contradictory and ineffective policies that leave everyone worse off.

The most desirable situation for the state, insofar as effective policy-making and implementation are concerned, is for both state and society to be strong, with close partnership between the two, thereby maximizing and balancing both state policy capacity and autonomy. Peter Evans (1992) calls this institutional arrangement "embedded autonomy." In contrast, policy effectiveness is lowest when the state is weak and the society fragmented. In the former scenario, states in partnership with social groups can be expected to devise cohesive and long-term policies. In the latter, the state can be expected to produce only short-term and, usually, ineffective or difficult-to-implement policies.

Political Systems and Public Policy

Political systems also have a crucial impact on state policy capacity and on how states make and implement policies and their outcomes (Fabbrini & Sicurelli, 2008). One of the most significant aspects of the political system affecting public policy is whether or not state authority is fragmented, that is, whether it is federal or unitary. In *unitary* systems, like China, the existence of a clear chain of command or hierarchy linking the different levels of government together in a superordinate/subordinate relationship reduces the complexity of multi-level governance and policy-making. Thus, in countries like China, but also in France, Japan, Singapore, Korea, and Thailand, the national government retains all decision-making powers. It can choose to delegate these powers to lower levels of government or dictate to them, but the role of the central, national government is legally unchallenged.

The salient feature of *federal* political systems with respect to public policy is the existence of at least two autonomous levels or orders of government within a country. These two levels of government—found in such countries as Australia, Mexico, India, Brazil, Nigeria, Malaysia, and the United States, among others (Burgess & Gagnon, 1993; Duchacek, 1970)—are not bound together in a superordinate/subordinate relationship but, rather, enjoy more or less complete discretion in matters under their jurisdiction guaranteed by the constitution. This is distinct from the multi-level systems of government found in unitary systems, where the local bodies (for example, regional districts, counties, or municipalities) owe their existence to the national government but are not constitutionally distinct from it.

Federalism has been cited as a major reason for the weak policy capacity of governments in many policy sectors in countries such as the US and Canada (Howlett, 1999; McRoberts, 1993). In federal countries, governments find it difficult to develop consistent and coherent policies because national policies in most areas require intergovernmental agreement, which involves complex, extensive, and time-consuming negotiations among governments that do not always succeed in resolving jurisdictional disputes (Banting, 1982; Schultz & Alexandroff, 1985; Atkinson & Coleman, 1989b). Furthermore, both levels of government are subject to somewhat unpredictable judicial review of their measures, which further restricts governments, ability to realize their objectives and can draw out policy-making over decades.

Federalism thus makes public policy-making a longer, more drawn-out, and often more rancorous affair than in unitary governments as the different orders of governments wrangle over jurisdictional issues or are involved in extensive intergovernmental negotiations or constitutional litigation. Different governments within the same country may also make contradictory decisions that may weaken or nullify the effects of an erstwhile national policy (see Grande, 1996; McRoberts, 1993).

Another domestic institutional variable affecting public policy concerns the links between the executive, legislature, and judiciary provided under a country's constitution. In *parliamentary* systems, like Britain or Sweden, the executive is chosen by the legislature from among its members and remains in office only as long as it enjoys majority support from legislators. In *presidential and semi-presidential* systems such as the US, Mexico, and France, the executive is separate from the legislature, is usually elected directly by the voters, and need not enjoy majority support in the legislature (Stewart, 1974). The United States is the archetype of the presidential system, and many countries in Latin America, Africa, and Asia have copied its model; most of the rest of the world has some version of a parliamentary system; other countries, such as France, have a hybrid of the two systems.

The separation between the executive and legislative branches of the government in presidential systems and the role of the judiciary in mediating disputes between the two branches, and the fusion of the two in parliamentary ones, has important consequences for the policy process (Weaver & Rockman, 1993a). The division of powers in presidential systems, for example, promotes difficulties for policy-makers in enacting laws. The executive and legislatures are elected in separate contests, and individual members and committees of the legislature play an active role in designing policies, including those proposed by the president who cannot assume his or her proposals will be accepted and passed into law. It matters if the party of the president's affiliation forms the majority in both houses of the legislature, but local concerns often motivate legislators and can and do override partisan loyalties. To ensure majority support for policy measures requiring legislative approval, in such systems it is common for the president to have to bargain with the members of the legislature, offering administrative and budgetary concessions in return for support, and thereby often changing the original intent of a policy proposal. The active involvement of the members of the legislature in drafting bills also promotes multiple points of conflict with the executive and opens up greater opportunities for interest groups and voters to influence the policy process, the result of which may be diluted or even conflicting policies (Besley & Case, 2003).

In parliamentary systems, in contrast, the executive is elected at the same time as the parliament and controls the legislature through the party system. Hence, it can more often than not take legislative support for its measures for granted, thanks to the strict party discipline enforced on individual members of the parliament, who may lose their party nomination and support if they ever vote or speak out against the government. While there may be some bargaining over a policy within a party caucus, there is little chance of changing a bill once it has been introduced in parliament, as the executive controls the timing and content of votes. The only time when this may not be the case is when the governing party does not have an outright majority in the legislature and governs in a minority coalition with other parties, either formal or informal, who often can demand modification to the policy in return for their continued support. In many countries, especially those with proportional systems of representation that allow for a proliferation of minor parties, coalition governments are routine. This complicates policy-making through the need to construct and retain often very elaborate multi-party legislative coalitions, though not as much as in the presidential system, as the executive still must control a majority of legislator support in a parliamentary system if it is to retain its status as a government (Warwick, 2000).

Generally speaking, policy-making in parliamentary systems is centralized in the executive, which usually enables the government to take decisive action if it so chooses (Bernier et al., 2005). While sometimes decried as overly concentrating power and decision-making (Savoie, 1999), this is not entirely undesirable from a policy-making perspective, insofar as a state's policy capability is concerned, because the adversarial politics, legislative bargaining, and log-rolling characteristic of legislatures in presidential systems reduces the likelihood of generating coherent policies.

Domestic Policy Actors

As this discussion shows, flowing from the nature of a country's political economy and its political system, the following sets of policy actors exist in most liberal-democratic capitalist countries and exercise some influence over policy processes and outcomes.

Elected Politicians

As set out above, the elected officials participating in the policy process may be divided into two categories: members of the executive and legislators. The *executive*, also referred to in many countries as the cabinet or, simply, the government, is a key player in any policy subsystem. Its central role derives from its constitutional authority to govern the country. While other actors also are involved in the process, the authority to make and implement policies rests ultimately with the executive. As we have seen, there are indeed few checks on the executive in parliamentary systems (such as Japan, Canada, Australia, and Britain) as long as the government enjoys majority support in the legislature. It is somewhat different in presidential systems (as in the United States or Brazil), where the executive often faces an adversarial legislature with different policy preferences and priorities. But even here, the executive usually has a wide area of discretion beyond legislative control in financial and regulatory matters, as well as in defence, national security, and issues related to international treaty obligations of different kinds.

In addition to its prerogative in policy matters, the executive possesses a range of other resources that strengthen its position. Control over information is one such critical resource. The executive has unmatched information that it withholds, releases, and manipulates with the intention of bolstering its preferences and weakening the opponents' case. Control over fiscal resources is another asset favouring the executive because legislative approval of the budget usually permits wide areas of discretion for the executive. The executive also has unparalleled access to mass media in publicizing its positions—the "bully pulpit," as it is called in the US—and undermining those of its opponents. Moreover, the executive has the bureaucracy at its disposal to provide advice and to carry out its preferences. It can, and does, use these resources to control and influence societal actors such as interest groups, mass media, businesses, non-governmental organizations of all types, and think tanks. In many countries, as pointed out above, the government has important powers allowing it to control the timing of the introduction and passage of laws in the legislature. This gives the executive a great deal of control over the political agenda (Bakvis & MacDonald, 1993).

Counterbalancing the executive's immense constitutional, informational, financial, and personnel resources are conditions that make their task difficult. The tremendous growth in the size, scope, and complexity of government functions over the years, for example, prevents generalist politicians from controlling, or often even being aware of, the many specific activities of government nominally under their control and transfers much control over administration and policy development to lower levels of the bureaucracy (Adie & Thomas, 1987; Kernaghan, 1979, 1985a). Moreover, in democratic governments, ministers are constantly bombarded with many societal demands, many of which are mutually contradictory but which they often cannot ignore because of the need to maintain voters' support, hamstringing their ability to develop clear and effective policies (Canes-Wrone et al., 2001). Finally, and perhaps most importantly, a government may simply not have the organizational capacity to make coherent policies and implement them effectively, lacking trained and experienced personnel, relevant knowledge and data, or both.

Members of the *legislature* play a very different role in policy-making. In parliamentary systems the task of the legislature is to publicize government actions and hence help hold them accountable to the public rather than to make or implement policies. But the performance of this function still permits some opportunities for influencing policies. Legislatures are crucial forums where social problems are highlighted and policies to address them are demanded. Legislators also get to have their say during the process of approving government bills and governmental budgets to fund policy implementation. In return for their consent, they are sometimes able to demand changes to the policies in question. Legislators may also raise and discuss problems of implementation and request changes.

However, a legislature's policy potential often may not be realized in practice. This is because of the dominance enjoyed by the executive in parliamentary systems and its effects on the internal organization of the legislature and on the role played by legislative committees (Olson & Mezey, 1991). Most laws are proposed by the executive and more often than not subsequently adopted by the legislature. This is especially so in parliamentary systems, where the majority party forms the government and therefore is generally expected to support the passage of bills proposed by the executive. In presidential systems, on the other hand, the legislature is autonomous of the government constitutionally as well as in practice, which explains why presidents, irrespective of whether their party holds a legislative majority, must strike bargains with the legislature or risk defeat of their policy proposals.

The internal organization of the legislature is thus a significant determinant of its role in the policy process. Legislatures where the membership is tightly organized along party lines, and marked by a high degree of cohesion and discipline, permit little opportunity for legislators to take an independent stand. This is particularly true in parliamentary systems where the legislators belonging to the governing party are always expected to support the government except, infrequently, when contentious social issues of a moral nature are brought to a (so-called "free") vote. Similarly, the role of individual legislators is lower in parliaments in which one party has a clear majority; the existence of several minor parties in coalition governments, on the other hand, permitting them a greater opportunity to express their opinion and force the government to deal with them.

Also, in most contemporary legislatures, both parliamentary and presidential, most important policy functions are performed not on the floor of the legislature, as they would have been in the nineteenth century and earlier, but in the committees established along functional or sectoral lines to review proposed legislation. Committees often build considerable expertise in the area with which they deal, and the extent to which this happens enables the legislature to exercise influence over making and implementing policies. But to build expertise, the members need to serve on the committees over a relatively long period of time. Committee members must also not necessarily vote along party lines if their influence is to be maintained.

The nature of the problem being considered also affects legislative involvement in the policy process. Technical issues are unlikely to involve legislators because they may not fully understand the problems or solutions, or they may see little political benefit in pursuing the matter. National security issues and foreign policy-making are also usually conducted in a shroud of secrecy and outside the legislature. Similarly, policies dealing with a problem perceived to be a crisis are unlikely to involve the legislature very much because of the time it takes to introduce, debate, and pass a bill. Policies dealing with allocation or redistribution of resources or income among components of the public generate the highest degree of passion and debate in legislatures, but usually do not have much effect on a government's overall policy orientation. However, other policies related to the propagation and maintenance of certain symbolic values—such as the choice of a national flag, immigration, multiculturalism, prayers in schools, or the elimination of racism and sexism—are often so divisive that the executive may be somewhat more willing to take the legislators' views into account in forming legislation.

As a result of these limitations, legislatures generally play only a small role in the policy process in parliamentary systems. While individual legislators, on the basis of their expertise or special interest in a particular issue, can become engaged as individual policy actors, especially if they are appointed to cabinet or other executive positions, legislatures as a whole are not very significant actors in policy-making or implementation. In congressional or republican systems, on the other hand, where the legislative agenda is less tightly controlled by the executive, individual legislators can and do play a much more influential role in policy processes, and legislative committees and coalitions are often significant policy actors in their own right (Warwick, 2000; Laver & Hunt, 1992; Laver & Budge, 1992).

The Public
Surprising as it may appear, the *public* plays a rather small direct role in the public policy process in liberal-democratic capitalist countries. This is not to say that its role is inconsequential, as it provides the backdrop of norms, attitudes, and values against which the policy process unfolds. However, in most democratic states, policy decisions are taken by representative institutions that empower specialized representative actors to determine the scope and content of public policies, but these institutions do not, as a matter of course, provide mechanisms through which the public can directly determine policy such as plebiscites or referenda.

One important role played by members of the public in a democratic polity, of course, is as voters. On the one hand, voting offers the most basic and fundamental means of public participation in democratic politics and, by implication, policy processes. It not only affords citizens the opportunity to express their choice of government, but also empowers them to insist that political parties and candidates seeking their votes provide (or at least propose) attractive policy packages. On the other hand, the voters' capacity to direct the course of policy usually cannot be realized, at least not directly, for at least three reasons (Hibbing & Theiss-Morse, 2002).

First, most democracies delegate policy-making to political representatives who, once elected by the voters, are not required to heed constituent preferences on every issue (Birch, 1972). Second, as was discussed above, most legislators participate very little in the policy process, which tends to be dominated by executive members and government and experts in specific sectoral areas rather than by legislative generalists (Edwards & Sharkansky, 1978: 23). Third, candidates and political parties often do not run in elections on the basis of their policy platforms; and even when they do, voters often do not vote on the basis of proposed policies alone but may follow ethnic or geographic principles or other more idiosyncratic preferences for specific candidates or government composition. Having said that, it is true that politicians in democratic societies do pay very close attention to public opinion in a general sense while devising policies, even though they do not always respond to or accommodate it (Soroka, 2002).

The impact of public opinion on policy processes is more frequent and pervasive, although even less direct than voting. Despite many works over the past decades that have consistently found the relationship between public opinion and public policy-making in democratic societies to be a tenuous, complex one, there persists a tendency to view this relationship as simple, direct, and linear (see Luttbeg, 1981; Shapiro & Jacobs, 1989). From at least the time of the early works on the subject by scholars such as V.O. Key (1967), E.E. Schattschneider (1960), and Bernard Berelson (1952), prominent political scientists and others have repeatedly found little or no direct linkage between public opinion and policy outcomes. Nevertheless, in study after study this finding has been made and remade, as investigators appear dissatisfied with it (Monroe, 1979; Page & Shapiro, 1992). As Schattschneider suggested, this is no doubt due to the sincere but sometimes simplistic notion of democracy held by many investigators that privileges "government by the people" over "government for the people." But the reality is more complex (Soroka, 2002): democracy is more than mob rule (Birch, 1972). While a concern for popular sovereignty is laudable, theoretical speculations must be tempered by empirical reality if the relationship between public opinion and public policy is to be effectively analyzed and understood.[2]

The simplest model of the relationship between public opinion and public policy-making views government as a policy-making machine—directly processing popular sentiments into public policy decisions and implementation strategies. This is a highly problematic perception as it assumes that public opinion has a unified, concrete, and quasi-permanent character that can be easily aggregated into coherent policy positions (Erikson et al., 1980; Erikson et al., 1989). Numerous studies have underlined the vague, abstract, and transitory nature of public opinion, however, and have emphasized the difficulties encountered in aggregating the "babble of the collective will," as Rousseau put it, into universally endorsed policy prescriptions (Rousseau, 1973; also see Lowell, 1926). This phenomenon has become more pronounced in recent years as authoritative sources of knowledge about politics and policy-making in the traditional media have declined and been replaced by the chaotic and harder to authenticate stories found in social media sources, from Facebook to Twitter and beyond (Anspach et al., 2019; Wooley & Howard, 2018). Moreover, many opinion researchers and policy scholars have noted how these difficulties have multiplied as scientific and complex legal issues have come to dominate policy-making in contemporary societies, further divorcing policy discourses from more general and less well-informed public ones (see Pollock et al., 1989; Torgerson, 1996; Hibbing & Theiss-Morse, 2002).

The public's role in policy-making should thus not be taken for granted as either straightforward or decisive. But neither should it be ignored, especially in relation to other elements of the policy context. Even if elections rarely provide focused public input on specific policy options, they can often introduce real change to policy agendas even if the exact nature and specification of these changes remain something of a wild card.

Bureaucracy

The appointed officials dealing with public policy and administration are often collectively referred to as the "bureaucracy." Their function is to assist the executive in the performance of its tasks, as is suggested by the terms "civil servants" and "public servants." However, the reality of modern government is such that their role goes well beyond what one would expect of a "servant." Indeed, given the limitations of legislatures and the public highlighted above, bureaucrats are very often the keystone in the policy process and the central figures in many policy subsystems (Kaufman, 2001).

Most of the policy-making and implementation functions once conducted directly by legislatures and the political executive are now performed by the bureaucracy because the responsibilities of modern government are too complex and numerous to be performed by the cabinet alone (see Bourgault & Dion, 1989; Cairns, 1990b; Priest & Wohl, 1980). Certain important policies have indeed even been "automated" so that routine actions can be taken without human intervention. Indexing public pensions to the rate of inflation is an example of such "automatic government" (Weaver, 1988). The most exceptional policy decisions can also be removed from the deliberation of men and women, as with the case of The US "Mutually Assured Destruction" (MAD) security policy during the height of the Cold War, which mandated an immediate counterstrike in the event of nuclear attack—in this instance, because of the presumption that there would be no time for a deliberative reaction to a nuclear attack from the Soviet Union.

In general, the bureaucracy's power and influence are based on its command of a wide range of important policy resources (see Hill, 1992: 1–11). First, laws themselves often provide for certain crucial functions to be performed by the bureaucracy, and may confer wide discretion on individual bureaucrats to make decisions on behalf of the executive, the legislature, or the state. Second, bureaucracies have unmatched access to material resources for pursuing their own organizational, even personal, objectives if they so wish. The government is the largest single spender in most countries, a situation that gives its officials a powerful voice in many policy areas. Third, the bureaucracy is a repository of a wide range of skills and expertise, resources that make it one of the premier organizations in society, often rivalling or exceeding that of the private sector. It employs large numbers of just about every kind of professional, hired for their specialized expertise and dealing with similar issues on a continuing basis endows these experts with unique insights into many problems and potential solutions to them. Fourth, modern bureaucracies have access to vast quantities of information about society. At times the information is deliberately gathered, but at other times the information comes to it simply as a part of its central location in the government. Fifth, the permanence of the bureaucracy and the long tenure of its members often give it an edge over its nominal superiors, the elected executive who, on the contrary, come and go with much less predictability because of elections and scandals, among other things. Finally, the fact that policy deliberations for the most part occur in secret within the bureaucracy often denies other policy actors the chance to effectively oppose its plans.

For all these reasons, bureaucrats can thus exert a prominent influence on the shape of the policy context. The structure of the bureaucracy, however, has perhaps the strongest effect on public policy processes, especially at the sectoral level (Atkinson & Coleman, 1989a). Concentration of power in only a few agencies, for example, reduces occasions for conflict and permits long-term policy planning. Diffusion of power, in contrast, fosters interagency conflicts and lack of coordination; decisions may be made on the basis of their acceptability to all concerned agencies rather than their intrinsic merit. The bureaucracy's autonomy from politicians and societal groups also contributes to its strength and effectiveness in policy-making. But to be strong, a bureaucracy must have a clear mandate, have a professional ethos, and enjoy strong support, but not interference, from politicians in its day-to-day activities. Close ties with client groups are also to be avoided if a bureaucracy is to be effective in circumstances when such client's interests may be challenged. An ability to generate and process its own information is also important if reliance on interest groups is to be avoided.

Countries like France, Korea, Singapore, and Japan have historically had bureaucracies that enjoy a somewhat exalted status in government and society (Katzenstein, 1977). They are said to constitute a homogeneous elite grouping that plays the most important role in the policy process. They undergo long professional training and pursue service in the government as a lifelong career. In other societies, such as Russia and Nigeria, bureaucracies enjoy relatively low status and lack the capacity to resist pressures from legislators or social groups, which often promotes incoherence and short-sightedness in policies. At the extreme, bureaucrats can become so marginalized that corruption becomes the norm, either to supplement meagre salaries or because ethics and the rule of law are not deemed to matter, as has happened in many countries in years past and continues to occur today.

The effective mobilization of bureaucratic expertise is thus somewhat rarer than commonly believed (Evans, 1992). Despite the massive expansion in bureaucracies throughout the world over the last several decades, weak bureaucracies in the sense understood here are the norm rather than the exception (Evans, 1995). In many developing countries with corruption, low wages, and poor working conditions, for example, bureaucracies often do not have the capability to deal with the complex problems they are asked to address. If these conditions exist in a country, then it is quite likely that the state will have difficulty devising effective policies and implementing them in the manner intended (Halligan, 2003; Burns & Bowornwathana, 2001; Bekke & van der Meer, 2000; Verheijen, 1999; Bekke et al., 1996). In many other countries, even if bureaucratic expertise exists in a particular area, problems of organization and leadership may prevent its effective marshalling (Desveaux et al., 1994).

Thus, while it can be tempting to view bureaucrats as the most influential policy actors, either through their grasp of the levers of power or because their ineffectiveness constrains many policy initiatives, we must avoid exaggerating the bureaucracy's role. The political executive is ultimately responsible for all policies, an authority it does assert at times, as do legislators and electorates. High-profile political issues are also more likely to involve higher levels of executive control and public interest. Executive control is also likely to be higher if the bureaucracy consistently opposes a policy option preferred by politicians. Moreover, the bureaucracy itself is not a homogeneous organization but rather a collection of organizations, each with its own interests, perspectives, and standard operating procedures, which can make arriving at a unified position difficult. Even within the same department, there are often divisions along functional, personal, political, and technical lines. Thus, it is not uncommon for the executive to have to intervene to resolve intra- and inter-bureaucratic conflicts, and bureaucrats in democratic countries require the continued support of elected officials if they are to exercise their influence in any meaningful way (Sutherland, 1993).

Political Parties

Political parties connect people and their government in ways that affect policy. Parties operate along the boundary between state and societal actors, sometimes acting as gatekeepers through which actors gain access to political power. They tend to influence public policy indirectly, however, primarily through their role in staffing the executive and, to a lesser degree, the legislature. Indeed, once in office, it is not uncommon for party members in government to ignore their official party platform while designing policies (Thomson, 2001).

Political parties' impact on policy outcomes has been the subject of much empirical research and commentary (Blais et al., 1996; Castles, 1982; Imbeau & Lachapelle, 1993; McAllister, 1989). Findings concerning the role of parties in public policy-making, for example, have included evidence that, historically, European governments led by Christian democratic and social democratic parties have been related positively to the development of welfare state programs (Wilensky, 1975; Korpi, 1983), and that "left-wing" and "right-wing" governments have had different fiscal policy orientations toward, respectively, unemployment and inflation reduction (Hibbs, 1977). Partisan differences have also been linked to different characteristic preferences for certain types of policy tools, such as public enterprises or market-based instruments (Chandler & Chandler, 1979; Chandler, 1982, 1983).

The idea that political parties play a major role in public policy processes, of course, stems from their undeniable influence on elections and electoral outcomes in democratic states. While vote-seeking political parties and candidates attempt to offer packages of policies they hope will appeal to voters, the electoral system is not structured to allow voters a choice on specific policies. Likewise, as discussed above, the representational system also limits the public's ability to ensure that electorally salient policy issues actually move onto official government agendas (King, 1981; Butler et al., 1981). The official agenda of governments is, in fact, usually dominated by routine or institutionalized agenda-setting opportunities rather than by partisan political activity (Kingdon, 1984; Walker, 1977; Howlett, 1997a).

The contemporary significance of parties has also been challenged by those who argue that government has become too complex for influence by partisan generalists, with day-to-day influence stemming more from policy specialists in government and those in the employ of interest groups and specialized policy research institutes (King & Laver, 1993; Pross, 1992). Similarly, other studies focusing on the extent of policy learning and emulation occurring between states or subnational units (Lutz, 1989; Poel, 1976; Erikson et al., 1989) and those examining the impact of international influences on domestic policy-making have argued the case for the reduced importance of parties in contemporary policy processes (Johnson & Stritch, 1997; Doern et al., 1996a).

Even when parties do manage to raise an issue and move it from the public to the official agenda, they cannot control its evolution past that point. As Richard Rose (1980: 153) has put it,

> A party can create movement on a given issue, but it cannot ensure the direction it will lead. Just as defenders of the status quo may find it difficult to defend their position without adapting it, so too proponents of change face the need to modify their demands. Modifications are

necessary to secure the agreement of diverse interests within a party. They will also be important in securing support, or at least grudging acceptance, by affected pressure groups. Finally, a governing party will also need to make changes to meet the weaknesses spotted by civil service advisors and parliamentary draftsmen responsible for turning a statement of intent into a bill to present to Parliament.

While political parties' direct influence on policy may be muted, however, their indirect influence is not. The role played by political parties in staffing political executives and legislatures allows them considerable influence on the content of policy decisions taken by those individuals, including those related to the staffing of the senior public service. However, this power should not be overestimated. In modern governments, as we have seen, the degree of freedom enjoyed by each decision-maker is circumscribed by a host of factors that limit the conduct of each office and constrain the actions of each office-holder. These range from limitations imposed by the country's constitution to the specific mandate conferred on individual decision-makers by various laws and regulations (Pal, 1988; Axworthy, 1988). Various rules set out not only which decisions can be made by which government agency or official, but also the procedures they must follow in doing so and often attempt to insulate decision-makers and administrators from direct partisan influence—by, for example, making it difficult to remove administrators from office or forcing disclosure of party contacts and contracts.

Political parties thus tend to have only a diffuse, indirect effect on policy-making through their role in determining who actually staffs legislative, executive, and judicial institutions. Their role in agenda-setting is very weak, while they play a stronger, but still indirect, role in policy formulation and decision-making because of the strong role played in these two stages of the policy cycle by members of the political executive. Their role in policy implementation is virtually nil, while they can have a more direct effect on policy evaluation undertaken by legislators and legislative committees (Minkenberg, 2001).

The fact that the influence of parties on particular stages of the policy process may be muted, or that any such influence may be waning, does not necessarily lead to the conclusion that "parties don't matter." Richard Rose's perspective on the influence of twentieth-century political parties in governing Britain remains valid today:

Parties do make a difference in the way [a country] is governed—but the differences are not as expected. The differences in office between one party and another are less likely to arise from contrasting intentions than from the exigencies of government. Much of a party's record in office will be stamped upon it from forces outside its control . . . (Rose, 1980: 141; also see Hockin, 1977)

Interest or Pressure Groups

Another policy actor that has received a great deal of attention, thanks in part to the significant role attributed to it by pluralist and neo-pluralist theorists, is the interest group. While policy decisions are taken by government and implemented by the executive and bureaucracy, organized groups that advocate the economic interests or social values of their members can exert considerable influence on policy (Walker, 1991).

One valuable resource that such interest groups deploy is knowledge, specifically information that may be unavailable or less available to others. The members of specialized groups often have unique knowledge about the policy issue that concerns them. Since policy-making is an information-intensive process, those who possess information hold something of value. Politicians and bureaucrats often find the information provided by interest groups indispensable. Government and opposition politicians are thus inclined to assist such groups to obtain information that can improve policy-making or undermine their opponents. Bureaucrats will also solicit groups' help in developing and implementing many policies (Hayes, 1978; Baumgartner & Leech, 1998).

Interest groups also possess other important organizational and political resources besides information. These groups often make financial contributions to political campaigns. They also campaign for and deliver votes to sympathetic candidates who would support their cause in the government. However, interest groups' political impacts on the formulation and implementation of public policies vary considerably according to their differing levels of organizational resources and whether they represent business interests or any of various "altruistic" civil society causes (Pross, 1992; Baumgartner & Leech, 2001; Halpin & Binderkrantz, 2011). First, interest groups come in all sizes. All other things being equal, larger groups can be expected to be taken more seriously by the government. Second, some groups may form a "peak association" working in concert with business or labour groups that share similar interests (Coleman, 1988). A coherent peak association may exert greater influence on policy than even a large interest group operating on its own. Third, some groups are well funded, which enables them to hire more staff, including those with expertise in the "black arts" of political campaigning and elections (Nownes, 2004; Nownes & Cigler, 1995; Halpin & Thomas, 2012).

While the policy impact of interest-group campaign expenditures and political engagement on behalf of (or against) political parties and candidates is contentious, there is no doubt that differences in financial resources matter (Nownes & Neeley, 1996; Nownes, 1995, 2000; Nownes & Cigler, 1995). In democratic political systems, these information and power resources make interest groups key members of policy subsystems. While this does not guarantee that their interests will be accommodated, they are unlikely to be ignored except in rare circumstances when government leaders deliberately decide to approve a policy despite opposition from concerned groups (Thatcher & Rein, 2004).

Among interest groups, the role of business is particularly salient, as was mentioned earlier. The structural strength of business has the potential to both promote and erode social welfare. Erosion is more likely when business lacks organizational coherence. If "successful," the ability of individual firms and capitalists to pressure governments to serve their particular interests can lead to incoherent and short-sighted policies. Endemic conflicts among competing business groups only aggravate such situations. The problem may be offset if business has a central cohesive organization—or *peak association*—able to resolve internal differences and come up with coherent policy proposals.

The strength or weakness of business and the varying patterns of government–industry relations found in a country are usually shaped by historical factors (Wilson, 1990a). One political legacy that can yield powerful business organizations is a period of strong, persistent challenges from trade unions or socialist parties. The stronger the unions, the more cohesive will be the private sector's organized advocacy. The threat does not necessarily have to be continuing, so long as workers and socialist parties exerted power in the past. Another political characteristic that encourages strong business organizations is the presence of a strong (i.e., autonomous) state. Business must be well organized to have policy influence in countries with strong states. A strong state may also nurture a strong business association in order to avoid the problems arising from too many groups making conflicting demands on the same issue. Strong business associations can simplify the management of policy-making by presenting government with an aggregation of private-sector demands in place of a cacophony of disparate pleas (Halpin et al., 2017).

Another factor affecting the organizational strength of business is a nation's economic structure. In national economies characterized by low industrial concentration or high levels of foreign ownership, it is difficult for the disparate business firms to organize and devise a common position. Political culture also has an important bearing on the extent and nature of business involvement in politics. Where cultures are highly supportive of free enterprise, such as in the US and Canada, corporations have seen fewer reasons to invest in costly political organizations. Moreover, the degree to which social norms approve of functional representation affects the strength of business. Americans, and, to a lesser extent, citizens of Britain, Canada, Australia, and other Anglo-American democracies, are distrustful of companies pursuing their interests with government on a regular basis behind closed doors. In the corporatist countries, on the other hand, functional representation is accepted and, indeed, is seen as an appropriate behaviour of responsible groups (Siaroff, 1999).

Labour, too, occupies a somewhat unusual position among interest groups in that it is stronger than most, though considerably weaker than business. Unlike business, which enjoys considerable weight with policy-makers even at the level of the firm, labour needs a collective organization, a trade union, to have much influence on policy-making. In addition to their primary function of bargaining with employers regarding members' wages and working conditions, trade unions engage in political activities to shape government policies (Taylor, 1989: 1). The origin of trade unions' efforts to influence public policy is rooted in late nineteenth-century democratization, which enabled workers, who form a majority in every industrial society, to have some say in the functioning of the government. Given the clout that their members' votes could produce in democratic elections, it was sometimes easier for unions to pressure government to meet their needs than to bargain with their employers. The organization of labour or social democratic parties, which eventually formed governments in many countries, further reinforced labour's political power (Qualter, 1985).

The nature and effectiveness of trade unions' participation in the policy process depend on a variety of institutional and contextual factors. As with business, the structure of the state itself is an important determinant of union participation in policy-making. A weak and fragmented state will not be able to secure effective participation by unions, because the latter would see little certainty that the government would be able to keep its side of any bargain. Weak businesses can also inhibit the organization of a powerful trade union movement because the need appears less immediate.

However, the most important determinant of labour's capacity to influence policy-making is its own internal organization. The level of union membership affects the extent to which states seek or even accept union participation in the policy process. The same is true for the structure of bargaining units: decentralized collective bargaining promotes a fragmented articulation of labour demands. Britain, Canada, and the United States, for example, have decentralized bargaining structures, whereas in Australia, Austria, and the Scandinavian countries bargaining takes place at the industry or even country-wide level (Esping-Andersen & Korpi, 1984; Hibbs, 1987). A union movement that is fragmented along regional, linguistic, ethnic, or religious lines, or by industrial versus craft unions, foreign versus domestic unions, or import-contesting versus export-oriented labour organizations, will also experience difficulties in influencing policy. Fragmentation within the ranks of labour tends to promote local and sporadic industrial strife and yields an incoherent articulation of labour interests in the policy process (Hibbs, 1978; Lacroix, 1986).

To realize its policy potential, labour needs a central organization even more than does business. Such peak labour associations include the Australian or British Trade Union Congress (TUC), the Canadian Labour Congress (CLC), and the American Federation of Labor–Congress of Industrial Organizations (AFL–CIO). Collective action is the principal tool that labour has to influence the employers' or the government's behaviour, so the extent to which labour is able to present a united front determines to a great extent its success in the policy arena. To be effective, the trade union central needs to enjoy comprehensive membership and have the organizational capacity to maintain unity by dealing with conflicts among its members. The role of trade unions in policy-making ranges from most influential in corporatist political systems, such as in the Scandinavian countries, Austria, and the Netherlands, where the state encourages the formation and maintenance of strong trade union centrals, to least influential in pluralist political systems such as the United States and Canada, where there is no encouragement of strong central unions.

Think Tanks and Research Organizations

Another set of societal actors who influence the policy process are the researchers working at universities, institutes, and think tanks on particular policy issues and issue areas. University researchers often have theoretical and philosophical interests in public problems that can be translated directly into policy analysis. To the extent academics contribute their research to policy debates, they function in the same manner as research experts employed by think tanks. Indeed, in many instances academics undertaking relevant policy research are sponsored by think tanks (Ricci, 1993; Stone et al., 1998; Cohn, 2007). The following discussion will therefore concentrate on the role of these private organizations and the way that they interpret policy options through particular ideological and interest-based perspectives.

A think-tank can be defined as "an independent organization engaged in multi-disciplinary research intended to influence public policy" (James, 1993: 492). Such organizations maintain an interest in a broad range of policy problems and employ, either full-time or on a contract basis, experts on various issue areas in order to present thorough recommendations on their areas of concern. Their research tends to be directed at proposing practical solutions to public problems or, in the case of some think tanks, justifying their ideological or interest-driven positions. This sets them apart somewhat from academic researchers at universities, whose interests are more specialized, who do not necessarily seek practical solutions to policy problems, and who often are not so ideologically motivated. Explicitly partisan research is also generally frowned upon in academia.

However, while think tanks are generally more partisan than their academic counterparts, they, too, must maintain an image of intellectual autonomy from governments, private corporations, or any political party if policy-makers are to take them seriously. Large prominent think tanks in the United States include the Brookings Institution, the American Enterprise Institute, and the Urban Institute. Similar organizations in Canada include the C.D. Howe Institute, the Fraser Institute, the Canadian Centre for Policy Alternatives, and the Institute for Research on Public Policy. Major think tanks in Britain include the Policy Studies Institute and the National Institute for Economic and Social Research (McGann, 2008). Literally hundreds of such institutes are active in the Western, developed countries, some with broad policy mandates, others that are more limited in their purview, such as the Canadian Environmental Law Association (Lindquist, 1993; Abelson, 1996). In the developing world, think tanks tend to be financed by and linked to governments, which raises questions about their autonomy.

Think tanks target their research and recommendations to those politicians who may be favourably disposed to the ideas being espoused (Abelson, 2002). They also seek originality in their ideas and, unlike government and university-based researchers, they spend a great deal of effort publicizing their findings (Dobuzinskis, 2000; Stone, 1996; Weaver, 1989). The need for a quick response to policy "crises" has led many think tanks to develop new "product lines." Short, pithy reports and policy briefs that can be quickly read and digested have replaced lengthy studies as the primary output of many think tanks. A premium now exists on writing articles and op-ed pieces for newspapers and making appearances on radio and television programs. This new brand of research and analysis is dependent on "the public policy food chain," which includes a range of knowledge- and policy-oriented institutions. Over the last few decades, much of the work of think tanks has been devoted to promoting economic efficiency, since this has been an important preoccupation of the governments across the industrialized world (Fraussen et al., 2019).

A number of policy trends have influenced the way that think tanks function in recent years. Some of these dynamics and their effects include think tanks devoted to actors or issue areas affecting women, families (e.g., in Canada, the Vanier Institute of the Family), and indigenous groups. In addition, NGOs are now playing a central role in developing and implementing foreign and domestic policies and programs. These new entrants to the policy debates have created many new specialized think tanks and public policy research organizations, which in turn has fostered enhanced competition among them (see Rich, 2004; Abelson, 2007; Stone, 2007; McGann & Johnson, 2005). Globalization and the associated growth of transnational problems such as pandemics, hunger, and climate change require a global response, and this has affected the activities of think tanks. Some think tanks have responded by developing transnational linkages and partnerships, or by becoming multinational organizations themselves, in the effort to bridge the chasm between north/south and east/west. In addition, the emergence of regional or continental economic alliances such as the EU and North American Free Trade Agreement (NAFTA) has created new networks of regionally oriented policy institutions (Stone, 2008).

The proliferation of think tanks, however, has been accompanied by cutbacks in public funds available for research, which in turn has led to increasing competition among think tanks for funding (t'Hart & Vromen, 2008). In many countries, the cutback in government funding for policy research happened at the same time as policy units in governments were downsized or eliminated in budget-cutting exercises in the 1990s. At the same time, events such as the end of the Cold War had a profound impact on the funding of research organizations focused on areas such as international and security affairs, since donors and governments no longer saw the need for such research.

As a result, think tanks have had to devote considerable resources to raising funds at the expense of research and dissemination of findings (McGann & Weaver, 1999). This has led to "over-specialization" and to destructive competition in this aspect of the political marketplace of ideas (Stone, 2007).

Mass Media

The media constitutes another set of policy actors with an important indirect influence on public policy-making. Some suggest that the mass media plays a pivotal role in the policy process (Herman & Chomsky, 1988; Parenti, 1986), while others describe it as marginal (Kingdon, 1984). There is no denying that the mass media are crucial links between the state and society, a position that allows for significant influence on public and private preferences regarding the identification of public problems and their solutions. Yet, like political parties, the media's direct role in the various stages of the policy process is often sporadic and often quite marginal.

The role of the media in the policy process originates from the function of reporting on problems, which often leads to analyzing what went wrong and sometimes extends into advocating particular solutions. Journalists frequently go beyond identifying obvious problems to defining their nature and scope, and suggesting or implying solutions. The media's role in agenda-setting is thus particularly significant (Spitzer, 1993; Pritchard, 1992). Media portrayal of public problems and proposed solutions often conditions how they are understood by the public and many members of government, thereby shutting out some alternatives and making the choice of others more likely. Questions in parliamentary question periods or at presidential press conferences are often based on stories in the day's television news or newspapers.

This is particularly significant considering that news reporting is not an objective mirror of reality, undistorted by bias or inaccuracy. News organizations are gatekeepers in the sense that they define what is worthy of reporting and the aspects of a situation that should be highlighted. Thus, policy issues that can be translated into an interesting story tend to be viewed by the public as more important than those that do not lend themselves so easily to narrative structures, first-person accounts, and sound bites. This partially explains why, for example, crime stories receive so much prominence in television news and, as a corollary, the public puts pressure on governments to appear to act tough on crime. Similarly, groups and individuals able to present problems to the media in a packaged form are more likely than their less succinct counterparts to have their views projected (Callaghan & Schnell, 2001; Erbring & Goldenberg, 1980; Herman & Chomsky, 1988; Parenti, 1986).

We must not, however, exaggerate the mass media's role in the policy process. In the first place, traditional electronic and print media have encountered severe disruption in recent years and have found their readership and viewers shrinking as they have been undermined or replaced by newer social media sites (Hong & Nadler, 2016; Wukich & Mergel, 2016; Perl et al., 2019). But even without this development, other policy actors have resources enabling them to counteract media influence, and policy-makers are for the most part intelligent and resourceful individuals who understand their own interests and have their own ideas about appropriate or feasible policy options. As a rule, they are not easily swayed by media portrayals of issues and preferred policy solutions or by the mere fact of media attention. Indeed, they often use the media to their own advantage. It is not uncommon for public officials and successful interest groups to provide selective information to the media to bolster their case (Lee, 2001). Indeed, very often the media are led by government officials' opinions rather than vice versa (Howlett, 1997a, 1997b).

Academic Policy Experts and Consultants

As noted above, analysts working in universities or government tend to research policy problems determined by the public's or the government's interest, or by their own personal curiosity about a particular subject. Although academic policy findings tend to receive far less attention than the output from think tanks, the scholar's opportunity for sustained analysis and critique can make up for the lack of an immediate "buzz" (Cohn, 2004, 2006; Whitley et al., 2007). Carol Weiss has termed this dynamic of scholarly impact on public policy the "enlightenment function" to highlight the long-term ability to inform policy actors' understanding (Weiss, 1977a, 1977b; Bryman, 1988).

This role of introducing new findings about policy issues can also be undertaken by consultants, often the same people, who can carry the ideas and results of policy research directly to governments (Lapsley & Oldfield, 2001). There has been an explosion in the growth and use of consultants for policy analysis and implementation in governments in recent years, a development whose impact and implications are yet to be fully recognized and which policy scholars are only just beginning to explore (Speers, 2007; Perl & White, 2002; Howlett & Migone, 2014; van den Berg et al., 2020).

As van den Berg et al. (2020) point out, while the role of consultants in the policy process has long been a concern for scholars of public administration, public management, and political science, empirical studies of policy-related consulting are scarce, with little quantitative data. As they argue, several underresearched questions exist in this area of policy-making. The first is the "actual extent of the use of government consulting in a number of countries, and what have been cross-time developments." In other words, to what extent has the use of consultants grown over time, and what are the factors that explain greater or lesser growth in a particular country or sector? The second is the question of what role(s) consultants play in the public sector and "how large is the share of these consultants in various kinds of policy work (policy analysis, policy advice, implementation and evaluation)." A third is how large is the portion of consultancy work that is management consultancy, or other types of consulting, such as ICT architects, legal advisers, or accountants. The fourth is how much of consultants' work is concerned with substantive policy advice, and how much is procedurally oriented, i.e., organizing policy support, collecting input from external stakeholders, communicating the policy, and so on.

The evidence gathered to date suggests that policy consultancy has been a problematic blind spot for scholars, politicians, and other commentators and is a far more important and sizable component of the work that happens within government than the literature currently acknowledges. But it also suggests that the use of policy consultants is unevenly distributed across types of policy organizations and policy sectors, countries, and governments (van den Berg et al., 2020).

The International System and Public Policy

Policy-making is very much a domestic concern involving national governments and their citizens: in liberal-democratic countries with a capitalist economy organized along the lines set out above. However, the international system also is increasingly vital in shaping domestic public policy choices and policy developments. Its effects are manifested through individuals working as advisors or consultants to national governments or as members of international organizations with the authority under international agreements to regulate their members' behaviour.

Assessing the effects of international institutions on both global and national public policy-making is more difficult than assessing those in the domestic arena. For one thing, states are sovereign entities with, in theory, the legal authority to close their borders to any and all foreign influences as and when they choose. In reality, however, it is nearly impossible for states to stop foreign influences at the border because of constraints rooted in the international system (Held & McGrew, 1993; Walsh, 1994). The extent to which a state is able to assert its sovereignty depends on the severity of international pressures and the nature of the issue in question, as well as features innate to the state itself (Knill & Lehmkuhl, 2002; March & Olsen, 1998b).

The international system not only influences policy sectors that are obviously international—trade and defence, for example—but also sectors with no immediately apparent international connection, such as health care and old-age pensions (Brooks, 2007, 2005). The sources of influence lie in the overall structure of the international system, and a nation's place in it, and the specific "regimes" that exist in many policy areas.

International Actors, Regimes, and Non-Regimes

International actors vary considerably in their ability to influence domestic policies, and this, to a significant extent, is the result of differences in their resource endowments. One of the strongest resources determining their influence is whether an *international regime* facilitates their involvement (Krasner, 1982; Haggard & Simmons, 1987). International regimes have been defined by Robert Keohane and Joseph Nye (1989: 19) as "sets of governing arrangements" or "networks of rules, norms, and procedures that regularize behaviour and control its effects." Such regimes vary considerably in form, scope of coverage, level of adherence, and the instruments through which they are put into practice (Haggard & Simmons, 1987). Some are based on explicit treaties whereas others are based simply on conventions that develop as a result of repeated international behaviour. Some cover a variety of related issues while others are quite narrow in coverage. Some are closely adhered to and others often are flouted. Some are enforced through formal or informal penalties whereas others make no such provision. Some regimes are administered by formal organizations with large budgets and staffs, while some are more akin to moral codes (see Rittberger & Mayer, 1993).

Like other more formal institutions, international regimes affect public policy by promoting certain options and constraining others. More than that, they shape actors' preferences and the ease with which they can be realized (Doern et al., 1996b). Thus, a government willing to assist domestic producers by offering export subsidies, for example, may not be able to do so because of formal or informal international constraints. Regimes of varying scope and depth can be found in most, though not all, prominent policy areas.

International actors find it easier to intervene in policy sectors in which an international regime sanctioning their intervention already exists (Risse-Kappen, 1995: 6; Coleman & Perl, 1999). The central place occupied by the International Monetary Fund (IMF) in the international monetary regime, for example, enables its officers to intervene in the intimate details of public policy-making in many nations facing serious financial or fiscal problems.

An even more significant resource at the international level is the actor's theoretical and practical expertise in a policy sector (Barnett & Finnemore, 1999). Many international organizations—for example, the World Bank, the IMF, the Organisation for Economic Co-operation and Development (OECD), and the World Health Organization (WHO)—are vast repositories of established expertise in policy issues, and governments often rely on this expertise when making policies, thus giving such international actors significant influence in the policy process. The financial resources that international organizations can dispense to governments are another source of influence. The different levels of expertise and finance that international organizations can deploy often turn out to be crucial determinants of the impact that international actors can have on domestic policies (Finnemore & Sikkink, 1998).

However, the nature of the national policy subsystems also affects the international actors' role in the policy process. International actors can be expected to be influential in sectors with fragmented subsystems, because such fragmentation allows them greater opportunity for intervention. For example, the International Civil Aviation Organization—a UN agency responsible for the air transport sector—develops common design standards for airports that are widely adopted around the world. Since many of the world's airports are locally owned or operated, they would be hard-pressed to develop compatible design among themselves.

Conversely, international actors find it difficult to influence policies where the associated subsystem is coherent and united in opposition to external intervention (Risse-Kappen, 1995: 25; Sabatier & Jenkins-Smith, 1993b). The oil industry's resistance to the Kyoto Protocol's plan for reducing greenhouse gas emissions has undermined United Nations efforts to limit climate change by scaling back greenhouse gas emissions among many affluent nations, including Australia, Canada, and the United States. The most conducive situation for international actors is, of course, when the subsystem is coherent and in favour of external involvement, as occurs, for example, in many free trade negotiations where strong business communities support international trade regimes—in such instances the international actors can be expected to be an integral part of the domestic policy process (Pappi & Henning, 1999).

But establishing strong international regimes is problematic in many policy areas. Negotiating treaties in areas such as resource and environmental management, for example, has proved challenging. On the one hand, most states regard the disposition of natural resources within their jurisdiction (including those found in and under oceans) as purely domestic policy questions. As such, they often resent the effort to create international regimes in areas such as forestry and fisheries, which attempt to deal with transnational problems in these sectors and treat them as an affront to national sovereignty. This is also true of other areas, such as migration, where states are reticent to engage in binding agreements that interfere with or affect their ability to control movements of people in and out of their jurisdiction and areas of responsibility (Bierman et al., 2009).

Current global governance arrangements in these areas vary substantially. Thus, many sectors currently lack either or both of the binding international agreements and institutions, or the common sets of norms and expectations that form the basis of traditional "strong" treaty-based regimes. They may have instead either no regime (a "non-regime") or a kind of "weak" regime with some institutions and no treaty, or the reverse situation of a treaty with no institutions to back it up and adjudicate disputes (Dimitrov et al., 2007). Yet, as the scope and ambition of global governance have increased over the past three decades, weak international regimes now must deal with complex policy problems such as climate change, biodiversity conservation, refugees and movements of populations, transformational technologies, and deforestation, all of which require or demand extensive international collaboration and coordination (Howlett & Shivakoti, 2018).

Not all international actors work for public entities or private agencies, of course. An influential niche has been carved out by international NGOs that advocate policy issues and options. At one end of the spectrum, advocacy NGOs such as Greenpeace and Amnesty International draw attention to environmental and human rights concerns in particular national contexts. These NGOs can capture public attention, both within and beyond national borders, and exert leverage on policy options through calling for boycotts or other sanctions. At the other extreme, NGOs like the World Business Council on Sustainable Development can support international corporations trying to pre-empt the kinds of criticism launched by advocacy NGOs (Sell & Prakesh, 2004; Woodward, 2004; Mathiason, 2007).

Recognition of the international system's influence on domestic public policy is one of the more exciting recent developments in the discipline. While the international system has probably always affected public policy to some extent, its scope and intensity have increased greatly in recent times. This is the result of what is described as *globalization* or, more precisely, *internationalization* (Hirst & Thompson, 1996). Although initially conceived in somewhat simplistic terms, the recent literature recognizes the highly complex character of internationalization, the different forms it takes across space and time, and the varying effects it has on different policy sectors and states (Bernstein & Cashore, 2000; Bennett, 1997; Brenner, 1999; Hobson & Ramesh, 2002; Weiss, 1999). This recognition has led researchers to investigate more carefully the means, manner, and mechanisms through which domestic policy processes are linked to the international system (Coleman & Perl, 1999; Risse-Kappen, 1995; Finnemore & Sikkink, 1998; Keck & Sikkink, 1998).

The challenge before scholars in such studies is to incorporate changes induced by internationalization into existing conceptions of domestic policy processes and their outcomes (Hollingsworth, 1998; Lee & McBride, 2007; Cohen & McBride, 2003). However, several key trends can still be identified.

First, the internationalization of the world economy has accelerated the speed with which the effects of events elsewhere (natural calamities, wars, terrorist actions, financial crises, stock market gyrations, etc.) spread via the telecommunications media (Rosenau, 1969). This has expanded the scope for *policy spillovers* as previously isolated sectors converge, overlap, and collide.

What were in the past seen as discrete sectors—such as telecommunications and computers, or agriculture and trade—are now increasingly viewed as elements of a single sector. Any international effort to reduce agricultural subsidies, for instance, has an effect on rural development, social welfare, and environment policies and, ultimately, overall government fiscal policy. Traditional social policy areas such as social security and health care have thus become a part of economic and trade policy-making as a result (Unger & van Waarden, 1995; Coleman & Grant, 1998).

Second, internationalization also creates new opportunities for learning from the policy experiences of others. This is the theme of much recent work on policy transfers, which especially highlights the role of transnational epistemic (knowledge-based) communities and NGOs in promoting learning activities (Haas, 1992; Evans & Davies, 1999; King, 2005; Levi-Faur & Vigoda-Gadot, 2006). The lessons of privatizing telecommunications in Britain and deregulating airlines in the United States in the 1980s rapidly spread around the world and across policy sectors because of the active role played by the associated policy communities (Ikenberry, 1990; Ramesh & Howlett, 2006; Eisner, 1994b). Although these ideas are often reinterpreted in the transfer process and are the adapted to fit into particular policy-making processes (Dobbin et al., 2007), there is no doubt that opportunities for drawing on ideas that originated beyond a nation's boundary have increased in recent years as internationalization has proceeded apace (Coleman & Perl, 1999; de Jong & Edelenbos, 2007; Pedersen, 2007).

Moreover, internationalization promotes new patterns of policy-making (Rittberger & Mayer, 1993). When a domestic policy actor loses out in a domestic setting, it now may seek to have the policy transferred to the arena of international organizations if it expects its position to receive a more favourable reception in that venue. Powerful new international organizations and regimes such as the EU, the World Trade Organization (WTO), and NAFTA have opened up new action channels for domestic policy actors pursuing their interests (Howlett & Ramesh, 2002; Richardson, 1999; Cortell & Davis, 1996; Demaret, 1997).

Mapping the myriad effects of international regimes and non-regimes on domestic policy-making is beyond the scope of this book. Here we outline only the regimes prominent in the areas of trade, finance, and production to illustrate how they affect actors and institutions.

The edifice on which the contemporary international trade regime is based is the General Agreement on Tariffs and Trade (GATT), signed in 1947 and succeeded by the WTO in 1995. Its membership includes almost all states in the world and the vast majority of world exports are governed by its provisions.

The WTO requires members to work toward lowering trade barriers by according "national treatment"[3] to imports and not subsidizing exports. These requirements are intended to assist internationally competitive producers, at the expense of producers who are not competitive. The agreement restricts governments' ability to support domestic industries, either through protection against imports or subsidy for exports, although tenacious governments do find ways of getting around the restrictions. The difficulties involved in protecting against imports create opportunities and wealth for successful exporters, and by implication the whole economy, but at the same time impose costs on uncompetitive industries and firms. Some of these costs are then borne by society in the form of higher unemployment that triggers greater public expenditure on social welfare programs (see Hoekman & Kostecki, 1995).

The international monetary regime has an even greater impact on public policy, especially since the adoption of a flexible exchange rate system in 1976. The fact that exchange rates of currencies are determined by financial markets according to the demand and supply of a country's currency—instead of being fixed by international agreement, as was the case under the Bretton Woods agreement of 1944—exposes governments to significant international financial pressures. Since the financial markets are influenced by currency traders' interpretation of a country's present economic conditions and their expectations for the future, this system often encourages fluctuations in the value of national currencies. Governments are therefore under constant pressure not to do anything that may, rightly or wrongly, attract the attention of speculators who seek to bet against their currency on the foreign exchange market.

Even more important than the flexible exchange rate system are the effects of financial deregulation and technological improvements that enable the transfer of money around the globe at the speed of light. By the late 1990s, foreign exchange trading around the world amounted to more than $2 trillion per *day*. With such huge volumes at stake, international money markets have the ability to cause havoc for a country whose policies are presented unfavourably in the 24-hour news cycle and on social media. States must now be extremely careful about how their policies will be received by financial markets, as these affect exchange rates, which in turn affect interest rates and export competitiveness, the repercussions of which are felt by the entire economy. A government's decision to increase expenditure on social welfare, for instance, could be presented unfavourably in financial media, leading currency traders to sell off their holdings, thereby depreciating the value of the currency, which might in turn necessitate increasing interest rates to shore up the value of that currency. The net result of such manoeuvring could yield an economic slowdown and higher unemployment. The cumulative effect of all these actions and reactions would thus negate the original decision to increase spending. Anticipation of negative market reaction to budget deficits also limits the scope for using this vital fiscal policy instrument to boost economic activity and lower unemployment (Huber & Stephens, 1998). The rapid fall in the US dollar's value in 2008 following years of budget and current accounts deficits suggests that even a superpower is not immune to the forces propagated in deregulated global financial markets.

Similarly, the liberalization of rules restricting foreign investment, particularly since the 1980s, has led to a massive expansion of foreign direct investment and proliferation of transnational corporations (TNCs), which in turn have affected states' policy options. In 2016, the total assets of TNCs' foreign affiliates stood at over $112 trillion, they employed over 82 million workers, and their annual sales exceeded $37 trillion (F, 2017: 26).

TNCs not only control large pools of capital, but they are also major players in international trade—they account for over two-thirds of world trade—and control much of the world's leading technology and management skills. Since their primary interest is profits, the TNCs have a motive to locate production where they see the greatest opportunity for maximizing the bottom line. But with the rise of electronic commerce and digitalization, a subset of TNCs has been increasing their international sales without much expansion of productive assets outside their home countries. This so-called light footprint approach to transnational commerce is found mainly in technology companies whose outputs rely on a high degree of digitalization (Casella & Formenti, 2018).

Given their size, strength, and influence TNCs are major players in the world economy and, by implication, in politics and public policy. They can cause serious disruption to a country's economy by withholding investment or deciding to take their investment elsewhere, possibilities that policy-makers can ignore only at their peril. There is also now a competition among countries to attract TNCs by offering conditions the latter would find appealing. This often takes the form of a state commitment to control labour costs, maintain tax levels comparable to those in other similar nations, and relax restrictions on international trade and investment. Such pledges can also be elicited by transnational financial companies such as banks and bond rating agencies, which can downgrade public debt, increasing the costs governments must pay to borrow money abroad. All these pressures create severe constraints on states' policy options, not just in economic matters but in non-economic domains as well.

However, international regimes do not affect all nations equally. The more powerful nations enjoy greater policy autonomy within the international system than their less powerful counterparts. This is not only because the powerful states have the capacity to force other nations to change their behaviour, but also because others often voluntarily alter their behaviour to match the expectations of the dominant powers (Hobson & Ramesh, 2002). Thus, for example, any international trade or investment agreement opposed by a predominant trade and investment nation such as the United States is unlikely to be fully realized, and whatever might be achieved against the wishes of trading superpower is unlikely to be of much significance. The Chinese government is similarly able, for example, to negotiate terms with TNCs desiring access to its gigantic domestic market that are unlikely to be made available to most other nations. By leveraging their economic and military power in the international arena, some countries can operate as policy-*makers* while others that have a modest hand to play have to adopt the role of policy-*takers*. The more powerful countries and actors—for instance, China, the EU, and the United States—exercise leverage on other nations to conform to their preferred policy options. Policy-takers—which include most countries in the world—are nations that give up their capacity to pursue preferred policy options in exchange for guaranteed access to financial and product markets and/or security alliances.

Policy Subsystems and Policy Regimes: Integrating Institutions, Ideas, and Actors

The actors we have identified above originate from the political-economic structure and institutions of contemporary society and exercise their influence on policy-making through interacting with government, with one another, and with society at both the national and international levels. These interactions are imbued with meaning from the ideas that actors invoke in supporting or opposing particular policy options.

Given this mutually defining relationship among actors, institutions, and ideas, it is useful to have analytical concepts that can encompass these fundamental elements of policy relationships. We have already discussed the concept of a *policy paradigm*, or a set of high-level ideas that structure policy debates. Identifying the key actors in policy-making, what brings them together, how they interact, and what effect their interaction has on policy-making and policy outcomes has attracted the attention of many students of public policy-making and policy formulation (Timmermans & Bleiklie, 1999). The notion of a *policy subsystem* has emerged from these studies as a concept that captures the interplay of actors, institutions, and ideas in policy-making (McCool, 1998).

Policy Subsystems

The policy universe can be thought of as an encompassing aggregation of all possible international, state, and social actors and institutions that directly or indirectly affect a specific policy area. The actors and institutions found in each sector or issue area can be understood to constitute a *policy subsystem* (Freeman, 1955; Cater, 1964; Freeman & Stevens, 1987; McCool, 1998) within the larger political-economic system of the policy universe (Knoke, 1993; Laumann & Knoke, 1987; Sabatier & Jenkins-Smith, 1993b).

This is not to say that all actors and institutions play the same role in every subsystem. Some actors are engaged mainly in the struggle over ideas, as members of knowledge- or idea-based discourse or "epistemic" communities (Hajer, 1993; Fischer, 1993; Kisby, 2007), while only a subset of that group—a policy network—is engaged in the active and ongoing formulation and consideration of policy options and alternatives (Marier, 2008) In the banking sector, for example, numerous academics, think tanks, journalists, consultants, and others specialize in monitoring the sector and recommending policy alternatives. This subset of the

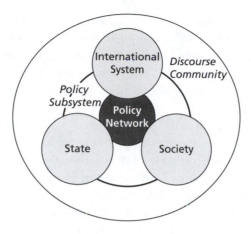

Figure 3.2 The Policy Universe and Policy Subsystems

entire possible universe of policy actors constitutes an epistemic or discourse community. The group of government regulators, decision-makers, and bankers who actually make government policy, constitute the policy network (see Figure 3.2).

Over the years scholars have developed a variety of models to try to capture the manner in which ideas, actors, and institutions interact in the policy process. The oldest conception of a policy subsystem was developed in the United States by early critics of pluralism who developed the notion of the *"sub-government,"* understood as groupings of societal and state actors who engaged in routinized patterns of interaction, and thus formed a key entity in policy development (de-Haven-Smith & Van Horn, 1984). This concept was based on the observation that interest groups, congressional committees, and government agencies in the United States developed systems of mutual support in the course of ongoing interaction over legislative and regulatory matters. The three-sided relationships found in areas such as agriculture, transportation, and education were often dubbed *iron triangles* to capture the essence of their structure as well as their iron-clad control over many aspects of policy-making (Cater, 1964).

Such groupings were usually condemned for having "captured" the policy process, thus subverting the principles of popular democracy by ensuring that their own self-interests prevailed over those of the general public (Bernstein, 1955; Huntington, 1952; Lowi, 1969). However, in the 1960s and 1970s, further research into the American case revealed that many sub-governments were not all-powerful, and that in fact their influence on policy-making varied across issues and over time (Hayes, 1978; Riker & Franklin, 1980). Soon a more flexible and less rigid notion of a policy subsystem evolved, called the *"issue network"* by Hugh Heclo (1978). He argued that while some areas of American political life were organized in an institutionalized system of interest representation, others were not (Heclo, 1974). The membership and functioning of "iron triangles," he suggested, were often not as closed or rigid as they were depicted to be. Heclo conceived of policy subsystems as existing on a spectrum, with iron triangles at one end and issue networks at the other. Issue networks were thus larger, less stable, experienced a regular turnover of participants, and were much less institutionalized than iron triangles.

Subsequent studies led to the identification of a large variety of subsystems, which in turn necessitated the development of alternative taxonomies to Heclo's simple spectrum of issue networks and iron triangles. Thus, R.A.W. Rhodes (1984) argued that interactions within and among government agencies and social organizations constituted policy networks that were instrumental in formulating and developing policy. He argued that networks varied according to their level of "integration," which was a function of their stability of membership, restrictiveness of membership, degree of insulation from other networks and the public, and the nature of the resources they controlled. In the US, similar attributes were specified by Hamm (1983), who argued that sub-governments could be differentiated according to their internal complexity, functional autonomy, and levels of internal and external cooperation.

In a major study of European industrial policy-making, Wilks and Wright (1987) endorsed Rhodes's typology, arguing that networks varied along five key dimensions: "the interests of the members of the network, the membership, the extent of members' interdependence, the extent to which the network is isolated from other networks, and the variations in the distribution of resources between the members." Refining the iron triangle–issue network spectrum developed by Heclo, they argued that this conception allowed a "high–low" scale to be developed in which highly integrated networks would be characterized by stability of memberships and inter-membership relations, interdependence within the network, and insulation from other networks. At the other extreme, weakly integrated networks would be large and loosely structured, with multiple and often inchoate links with other groups and actors.

In the US, empirical efforts to clarify and reformulate the concept of policy networks were also undertaken. Salisbury, Heinz, Laumann, and Nelson (1987; see also Heinz et al., 1990), for example, argued that networks tended to have "hollow cores" in that even the most institutionalized networks appeared to have no clear leadership. Others argued that networks could be classified according to whether or not state and societal members shared the same goals and agreed on the same means to achieve those goals. Still others argued that the number of discernible interests participating in the network was the crucial variable defining different types of networks (McFarland, 1987).

The insight that a policy subsystem might consist of a number of sub-components was developed at length in the 1980s in the works of Paul Sabatier and his colleagues. In their work, an *advocacy coalition* refers to a particular subset of actors within the policy subsystem (Sabatier & Jenkins-Smith, 1993b). An advocacy coalition consists of actors from a variety of public and private institutions at all levels of government who share a set of basic beliefs (policy goals plus causal and other perceptions) and who seek to manipulate the rules, budgets and personnel of governmental institutions in order to achieve these goals over time (1993b: 215).

Jenkins-Smith and Sabatier argued that advocacy coalitions include both state and societal actors at all levels of government. Their scheme cleverly combined the role of knowledge and interest in the policy process, as policy actors are seen to come together for reasons of common beliefs, often based on their shared knowledge of a public problem and their common interest in pursuing certain solutions to it. The core of their belief system, consisting of views on the nature of humankind and the ultimate desired state of affairs, is quite stable and holds the coalition together. All those in an advocacy coalition participate in the policy process in order to use the government machinery to pursue their (self-serving) goals.

While belief systems and interests determine the policies an advocacy coalition will seek to have adopted, their chances of success are affected by a host of factors. These include the coalition's resources, such as money, expertise, number of supporters, and legal authority (Sabatier, 1987). External factors also affect what the coalition can achieve by making some objectives easier to accomplish than others (Jenkins-Smith & Sabatier, 1993). Some of these external factors—such as the nature of the problem, natural resource endowments, cultural values, and constitutional provisions—are relatively stable over long periods of time, and are therefore quite predictable. Others are subject to a greater degree of change, including public opinion, technology, level of inflation or unemployment, and change of political party in government (Kim & Roh, 2008).

By the end of the 1980s, it was clear from these works and others in many different countries that a variety of different types of subsystems existed, depending on the structural interrelationships among their component parts. Efforts then turned to developing a more consistent method of classifying these components so that the different types of subsystems could be better understood (Atkinson & Coleman, 1989; McCool, 1989; Ouimet & Lemieux, 2000).

A useful distinction can be drawn between communities in which there is a dominant knowledge base and those in which there is not. A second critical dimension of policy community structure is the number of relatively distinct "idea sets" (Schulman, 1988; MacRae, 1993; Smith, 1993) in the community and if, and to what extent, a consensus exists on any particular set. Using these two dimensions allows us to construct a simple matrix of common discourse community types (see Figure 3.3).

In a situation where one idea set is dominant and unchallenged—such as is presently the case in the area of fiscal policy, where there is

Figure 3.3 A Taxonomy of Discourse Communities

		Number of Idea Sets	
		Few	Many
Dominant Idea Set	Yes	Hegemonic Community	Fractious Community
	No	Contested Community	Chaotic Community

Source: Adapted from Michael Howlett and M. Ramesh, "Policy Subsystem Configurations and Policy Change: Operationalizing the Post-positivist Analysis of the Politics of the Policy Process," *Policy Studies Journal* 26, 3 (1998): 466–82.

virtually no opposition to balanced-budget orthodoxy—a form of monopolistic or "hegemonic" community may develop. On the other hand, where multiple sets of ideas circulate, with no single idea in a dominant position, a more chaotic community will exist. A good example of this at present is biogenetics policy, where ideas ranging from the "pure science" of genome research to ethical, religious, and conspiratorial theories coexist in the subsystem (Howlett & Laycock, 2012). When several major idea sets contest dominance, as Sabatier and Jenkins-Smith noted, a third type of contested community may form, as is the case in many countries' debates over environmental protection where ideas such as biodiversity and sustainable development contest equally well-entrenched concepts of resource exploitation and utilitarianism. Finally, where one idea set is dominant but faces challenges from less popular ideas, a fractious community is likely to be found. This is a type of community found at present in trade and development policy subsystems, for example, where a dominant global neoliberalism faces a challenge from nationalist inspired idea sets promoting more local or national control over migration, economic exchange and development (Coleman et al., 1996).

With respect to policy networks, or more structured forms of subsystem interactions, many observers have highlighted the significance of two key variables in shaping the structure and behaviour of policy networks: the number and type of their membership and the question of whether state or societal members dominate their activities and interactions (Smith, 1993; Coleman & Perl, 1999). With these variables, a reasonable classification of issue networks can be developed (see Figure 3.4) (Coleman & Skogstad, 1990).

In this model, small (state corporatist) networks dominated by government actors, as are commonly found in highly technical issue areas such as nuclear, chemical, or toxic substance regulation, can be distinguished from those (state pluralist) in which many societal actors are included, as might be the case with education or other areas of state-led social policy-making. Other distinct network types exist where a few societal actors dominate a small (social corporatist)

Figure 3.4 A Taxonomy of Policy Networks

		Number of Members	
		Few	Many
Dominant	*State*	State Corporatist Networks	State Pluralist Networks
Actor	*Societal*	Social Corporatist Networks	Social Pluralist Networks

Source: Adapted from Michael Howlett and M. Ramesh, "Policy Subsystem Configurations and Policy Change: Operationalizing the Post-positivist Analysis of the Politics of the Policy Process," Policy Studies Journal 26, 3 (1998): 466–82.

network—as in many areas of industrial policy—or where they dominate large networks (social pluralist), as is the case in many countries in areas such as transportation or healthcare delivery.

These types of classification schemes help to clarify the possible structure of discourse communities and interest networks in policy subsystems and give us a general mechanism through which to organize the complex reality of multiple actors and institutions found in the policy-making process. Combining policy paradigms and policy subsystems, as discussed below, helps to further clarify policy-making complexity by linking those two components together into specific, relatively long-lasting policy frameworks or *policy regimes*, as discussed in Chapter 1 (Richardson, 1995).

Conclusion

The policy context is the setting in which the drama of disputing and responding to public problems unfolds. While policy-making can extend to cover issues ranging from local to global, it is not a uniform backdrop. The policy universe is filled with distinctive constellations of actors, ideas, and institutions or "policy subsystems" that constitute the space where actual problems are engaged and responses get crafted.

Policy processes draw upon actors from this subsystem, increasingly at both the domestic and international levels, and involve both state and societal actors in complex systems of mutual interaction. Political-economic, constitutional, and legal provisions are important determinants of subsystem participation, while the power and knowledge resources of subsystem actors critically affect the nature of their activities and interactions. The ideas invoked to justify some actions and to disparage others are both introduced by these actors and embedded in the institutions that structure subsystem creation.

In liberal-democratic capitalist societies, most subsystems, given their central location and access to abundant organizational resources, feature a minister(s) and bureaucrats in charge of a policy sector who are usually the key governmental actors in policy processes, with the legislators (particularly in parliamentary systems) playing a secondary role. Their societal counterparts are drawn mainly from among interest groups, research organizations, and business and labour. These non-state participants bring expertise, information, and interest in the issues under consideration, and seek influence over the policy outcomes through subsystem membership and participation in the policy process. The media often play an intermediating role in publicizing issues connected to the subsystem and identifying possible solutions to those issues.

Studying regime interactions within different stages of the policy cycle thus enables researchers to reveal not only a static "snapshot" of the policy-making process in particular areas of government activity, but also the *dynamics* of policy stability and policy change. The distinctive problem-solving dynamics in which subsystem actors participate is the policy process, which will be elaborated in subsequent chapters focusing on the idea of a *policy cycle*. When policy subsystems and paradigms are connected to appropriate stages of the policy cycle, it is possible to uncover how policy issues get on the agenda; how choices for addressing those issues are selected; how decisions on pursuing courses of action are taken; how efforts to implement the policy are organized and managed, and how assessments of what is working and what is not are produced and fed back into subsequent rounds or cycles of policy-making.

This analytical framework offers much greater depth than the intuition, hearsay, and educated guessing of many of the "informed sources" and media pundits that bolster many generally held beliefs about policy-making processes in liberal-democratic and other states. Mastering the configuration and application of policy subsystems and policy paradigms within different stages of the policy cycle is what this book intends to teach its readers and is the subject of the next five chapters.

Study Questions

1. How are different policy actors empowered, or disempowered, in a liberal-democratic capitalist system?

2. In the context of a particular policy sector, identify the range of policy actors that compose the policy universe and the policy subsystem. Why are some actors found in one group and not the other?

3. Is the policy universe expanding or contracting with the advent of internationalization? What difference would this make for policy-makers?

4. Identify examples of "strong," well-organized policy subsystems; "weak," disorganized ones; and policy "regimes" and "non-regimes."

5. What are the salient features of policy subsystems? How can these be identified in practice?

Further Readings

Casella, Bruno, and Lorenzo Formenti. 2018. "UNCTAD Insights," *Transnational Corporations* 25, no. 1: 101.

Chari, Raj, Gary Murphy, and John Hogan. 2007. "Regulating Lobbyists: A Comparative Analysis of the United States, Canada, Germany and the European Union," *The Political Quarterly* 78, no. 3: 422–38.

Dimitrov, Radoslav S., Detlef Sprinz, Gerald M. DiGiusto, and Alexander Kelle. 2007. "International Nonregimes: A Research Agenda," *The International Studies Review* 9: 230–58.

Fraussen, Bert, and Darren Halpin. 2018. "How Do Interest Groups Legitimate Their Policy Advocacy? Reconsidering Linkage and Internal Democracy in Times of Digital Disruption," *Public Administration* 96, no. 1: 23–35.

Guess, Andrew, Jonathan Nagler, and Joshua Tucker. 2019. "Less than You Think: Prevalence and Predictors of Fake News Dissemination on Facebook," *Science Advances* 5, no. 1 (January 1).

Haggard, Stephen, and Beth A. Simmons. 1987. "Theories of International Regimes," *International Organization* 41, no. 3: 491–517.

Held, David. 1991. "Democracy, the Nation-State and the Global System," in D. Held, ed., *Political Theory Today*. Oxford: Polity Press, 197–235.

Kaufman, Herbert. 2001. "Major Players: Bureaucracies in American Government," *Public Administration Review* 61, no. 1: 18–42.

King, Anthony. 1981. "What Do Elections Decide?" in D. Butler, H.R. Penniman, and A. Ranney, eds, *Democracy at the Polls: A Comparative Study of Competitive National Elections*. Washington: American Enterprise Institute for Public Policy Research.

Olson, David M., and Michael L. Mezey, eds. 1991. *Legislatures in the Policy Process: The Dilemmas of Economic Policy*. Cambridge: Cambridge University Press.

Weaver, R. Kent, and Bert A. Rockman. 1993. "Assessing the Effects of Institutions," in Weaver and Rockman, eds, *Do Institutions Matter? Government Capabilities in the United States and Abroad*. Washington: Brookings Institution, 1–41.

Chapter 4

Agenda-Setting
Definition and Problematics

What Is Agenda-Setting?

Why are some issues addressed by governments and not others? And why are they addressed at a particular moment in time and not at another instant? These are key questions in the study of public policy dynamics that scholars, practitioners and the public have sought to understand for some time.

Agenda-setting is concerned with the way policy problems emerge, or not, as candidates for government's attention. Agenda-setting is a label for the process by which governments decide which issues need their attention and prioritize among them. It involves, among other things:

- the determination and definition of what constitutes the "problems" that subsequent policy actions are intended to resolve;
- preliminary exploration of the possible solutions to such issues;
- assessment of the extent and nature of political support for any kind of action to resolve them (Dery, 2000; Kingdon, 1984; Mukherjee & Howlett, 2014).

John Kingdon, in his path-breaking 1984 inquiry into agenda-setting practices in the United States, provided the following concise definition of this crucial first stage of the policy cycle:

> The agenda, as I conceive of it, is the list of subjects or problems to which governmental officials, and people outside of government closely associated with those officials, are paying some serious attention at any given time. . . Out of the set of all conceivable subjects or problems to which officials could be paying attention, they do in fact seriously attend to some rather than others. So, the agenda-setting process narrows this set of conceivable subjects to the set that actually becomes the focus of attention. (Kingdon, 1984: 3–4)

It is perhaps the most critical stage of the policy cycle because what happens at this early stage of the policy process has a decisive impact on the entire subsequent policy cycle and its outcomes. As Cobb & Elder (1972: 12) put it a half-century ago, "Pre-political, or at least pre-decisional, processes often play the most critical role in determining what issues and alternatives are to be considered by the polity and the probable choices that will be made."

The manner and form in which problems are recognized, if they are recognized at all, are thus important determinants of whether, and how, they will be ultimately addressed by policy-makers. Although sometimes taken for granted, the means and mechanisms by which issues and concerns are identified as needing government action are not simple. Many issues remain on the public radar for some time before they are addressed by government, while others rise quickly to the forefront of government attention (Kingdon, 1984). And it has long been observed that some are never or only rarely addressed (Bachrach & Baretz, 1962, 1970) while others receive periodic treatment but are never actually solved or permanently go away (Downs, 1972). Fortunately, explaining what causes these patterns has preoccupied students of policy-making for some time and some progress has been made in understanding why these different issue trajectories occur.

Issue Initiation

Initial demands for government action can come from inside and/or outside governments, described as *inside initiation* and *outside initiation*, respectively (Cobb et al., 1976). In the case of *inside initiation*, the government controls many aspects of problem definition, framing and issue articulation. Under these circumstances, officials can often place an issue onto the formal agenda of the government even in the absence of any public pressure, or even any publicly recognized grievance. There may be considerable debate within a government over the issue, but the public may well be unaware of it until its formal announcement. In some cases, such as with certain highly technical issues or security-related policies, no formal announcement of the policy change may be forthcoming at all. A good example of inside initiation is pension reforms, which are often tied to demographic changes that alter actuarial projections of financial performance. They thus reflect present-day and future fiscal pressures as opposed to popular clamour to work longer (admittedly an unlikely proposition) or to increase contributions.

Inside initiation also includes situations in which influential groups with special access to the government initiate a policy without the general public's involvement (Fischer, 2003). The wish to exclude public scrutiny may reflect special characteristics of the sector involved (such as with national security issues) but may also stem from political considerations (such as government's fear that an issue might be hijacked or stalled by opponents). Many aspects of banking and financial regulation as well as trade negotiations—areas in which narrow but well mobilized and well-resourced actors have much to gain or lose—have been linked to such agenda dynamics at least in part due to concerns over stability or instability in financial and capital markets.

In *outside initiation*, on the other hand, issues appear on the government agenda as a result of "pressure" or lobbying from individuals, groups, and organizations outside government (Jones, 1994). In this better-known pattern, issues arise first within a societal space, and then—if non-governmental actors play their cards well and circumstances are propitious—issues expand sufficiently in the public realm so as to find space within the government's informal, and eventually its formal, policy agenda.

How common such a pattern is varies by country and jurisdiction. Some systems of government are more open to outside agenda-setting than others (Cobb et al., 1976). California and Switzerland, for example, experience frequent citizens' initiatives that are put to vote by the entire electorate due to constitutional provisions for referenda. Other countries, such as Belarus, Brunei, and China, discourage or informally suppress the formation of interest groups not controlled by the government. In others, such as North Korea, such groups are generally illegal. In yet other cases, such as Singapore and Rwanda, state actors may, because of constitutional design, capacity or tradition, so dominate the public sphere that most interest-group activity, if internalized, and outside initiation remain relatively rare phenomena.

Issue Articulation

There are multiple ways to frame a particular policy issue in a given context, and the ways in which problems are defined and (re)framed dictates how they are treated in subsequent policy activities (Felstiner et al., 1980). For example, if the problem of low school enrolment rate for girls in many countries is defined merely as an education problem, it might not receive adequate attention in a country where gender inequality is the cultural norm. But if it is framed as a developmental problem affecting a population's health, housing, labour productivity, economic growth and poverty levels, it may receive a rather different reaction and a higher priority, motivating swifter public investment in female education.

Both state and non-state actors attempt to construct "policy monopolies" that control the definition and image of a problem in the way they prefer it to be framed. That is, policy actors and managers encourage the framing of problems in ways that expand the constituency in support of their issue prioritization and, ultimately, resolution (Cobb & Edler, 1972). Government-sponsored activities such as education and information campaigns, for example, can affect the kinds of issues perceived by the public as problems and how they are defined in the public imagination.

A sudden crisis that foists a problem onto the public agenda can help to break down an existing image "monopoly," allowing different views of policy problems and solutions to compete in public and government discourses. This loss of agenda control by state actors can happen when government communication efforts are weak, fragmented, and/or generally unconvincing, allowing other state and societal actors to rally support for their own naming and framing of issues. This was the case, for example, in 2006 when the issue of US involvement in war in the Middle East was predominantly framed within the US media not as "how to achieve victory" and "whether" to withdraw troops (frames that the government of the day would have preferred), but as "how to cut losses" and "why" troops were still deployed at all.

Issue Expansion

Regardless of how popular a policy initiative may be, or how strong its internal champions are, however, its induction on to the formal agenda of government can be problematic. Outside actors encounter more difficulty in seizing control of the agenda than do their internal government counterparts, and must be backed by expensive and time-consuming public campaigns and lobbying for their issues to make it onto the agenda (Dion, 1973; Hansford, 2004). The mobilization of support can occur through a range of activities, from organizing letter-writing or social and traditional media campaigns to picketing and civil disobedience. Good examples of such processes found recently in many countries include campaigns:

- against drunk driving, led by groups such as Mothers Against Drunk Driving (MADD);
- for the legalization of certain drugs such as marijuana; and
- for gay, lesbian, and transgender rights.

In all of these cases, groups engaged in sustained and ultimately successful public education and lobbying efforts and not only managed to get their concerns and demands on to the government agenda but ultimately were successful in changing policies in their preferred direction.

While inside actors may be able to skip the "social mobilization" phase as they seek to push their issue onto the government's informal agenda, their task is not that much easier. In order to move their issue onto the formal agenda, they must compete in a crowded agenda field with other issues being promoted inside governments (by other inside initiators) and by outsider initiators who are meeting with success in their own efforts.

And, of course, the formal agenda of government and the informal public agenda are not independent of each other. Government activities (such as government-sponsored public education and information campaigns), as well as more direct measures (such as the funding of specific public works projects), have an effect on the kinds of issues defined by the public as "problems," providing a kind of "feedback loop" between government action and public problem perception and definition (Fischer, 2003; Hammond, 1986).

Also, of course, not every issue promoted for attention by inside or outside initiators is seriously advanced for policy adoption or impact. For example, actors in any political arena may attempt to use issue framing as a means to position themselves favourably among their supporters, or to deflect attention from defeats in other areas. Such phenomena—which underscore that "[b]ecause politics is driven by how people interpret information, much political activity is an effort to control interpretations" (Stone, 2002)—are a reminder that the process of agenda-setting, like much else in the policy-making process, is not as "rational" and technical as it is sometimes made out to be.

Agenda-Entrance

Timing is critical in agenda-setting. The concept of a "policy window" or "opportunity opening" through which an issue may be placed onto a government agenda drives home the point that the agenda-setting process is sometimes driven by random and unpredictable events that move problems suddenly to the forefront of public consciousness and concern (Kingdon, 1984). We see this, for example, when an airliner crashes and forces changes to safety practices or when an election produces a new government with different priorities. The year 2016 saw several such examples—for instance, the multi-dimensional shockwaves emanating from the British electorate's decision to exit the EU, and Donald Trump's victory in the 2016 US presidential election. However, many policy windows are not random but quite predictable. The high-profile nature of random windows might lead to the impression that agenda-setting is uncontrollable; but most policy windows open quite predictably. Legislation comes up for renewal on schedule, for instance, creating opportunities to change, expand, or abolish certain programs; policy actors and managers neglect such predictable action points at their own peril.

In fact, studies have found that four types of policy windows are common, and at least one is very routine and common:

- routinized windows: in which regularly scheduled procedural events such as budget cycles dictate agenda openings;
- discretionary windows: where individual political preferences on the part of decision-makers dictate window openings;
- random windows: where unforeseen events, such as disasters or scandals, open agenda windows; and
- spillover windows: where related issues are drawn into already opened windows in other sectors or issue areas, such as when railway safety issues arise because of the increased attention paid to airline or automobile safety after some crisis or accident (Howlett, 1998).

Given this predictability, policy actors often prepare well in advance in order to be able to seize a chance to push their concerns forward when a window opening occurs. In order to use window openings, policy actors need the capacity to identify and act upon the kinds of windows likely to be present in their areas of interest. Regardless of their source, however, open windows are scarce and often short-lived; actors must be prepared for them. Opportunities come, but they also pass. Windows do not stay open long, and if a chance is missed, another must be awaited, sometimes for a very long time. The strategies of agenda control that policy actors and managers employ, then, should include the ability to prepare for the different kinds of windows that may open, a subject that requires the analytical capacity to predict events and take advantage of them.

The Problematics of Agenda-Setting: Issue-Attention Dynamics

Issue-Attention in Governments and Society

At its most basic, agenda-setting is about the recognition of some subject as a problem requiring further government attention (Jones & Baumgartner, 2005). Attention to problematic issues originate in a variety of ways and most undergo intense scrutiny from both the public and officials before they are seriously considered for resolution by government. This recognition does not guarantee that the problem will ultimately be addressed, but merely that it has been singled out for the government's consideration from among the mass of problems existing in a society at any given time. That is, it has been raised from its status as a subject of *concern* to that of a private or social *problem* and finally to that of a *public issue*, potentially amenable to government action. While threats and challenges to existing programs and policies are frequently the forces that motivate issue definition in policy agenda-setting, there are also times when policy agendas are set by the attraction of an opportunity, such as an airplane or train crash promoting concerns for more action on public safety.

Understanding the processes through which a subject of concern comes to become interpreted as a public issue susceptible to further government action raises deep questions about the nature of human knowledge and the social construction of that knowledge (Berger & Luckmann, 1966; Holzner & Marx, 1979). The policy sciences literature has gone through significant changes over the last several decades in its understanding of what constitutes such problems and how they are constructed.

Early works in the policy sciences in the immediate post-WWII period, for example, often assumed that problems had an "objective" existence and were, in a sense, waiting to be "recognized" by governments who would do so as their knowledge and understanding of natural and social processes increased and as their capacity for action progressed. Hence mental illness could not be dealt with until knowledge and understanding of human psychology advanced to the point of recognizing conditions and proposing solutions, and until governments had absorbed this knowledge in public health departments and other agencies and were capable of proposing solutions that might address these conditions.

Later works in a more "post-positivist" direction, however, acknowledged that problem recognition is very much a socially and politically constructed process that involves the creation of accepted definitions of normalcy and of what constitutes an undesirable deviation from that status quo (McRobbie & Thornton, 1995). Hence, in this view, problem recognition is not a simple mechanical process of recognizing challenges and opportunities as knowledge and capacities increase; rather, it is a sociological one in which the "frames" or sets of ideas within which governments and non-governmental actors operate and think, and how they shift and develop, are of critical significance (Goffman, 1974; Haider-Markel & Joslyn, 2001; Schon & Rein, 1994).

In the abstract, a successful agenda-setting process is one that is able to prioritize and assess the root causes of problems, and to focus the lion's share of attention onto those problems with a fighting chance of resolution within a reasonable time period, utilizing an available amount of government resources. However, this is often not the case. Rather governments typically have a great deal of trouble understanding the sources of problems, estimating what is feasible and what is not, and controlling the sequencing in which issues that will be dealt with (Skodvin et al., 2010). In many cases, they are unable to exercise control over the issues that appear on their agendas; issues may be driven instead by factors such as natural calamities, partisan political manoeuvring and fickle public concerns driven by media headlines (Levin et al., 2012). Dealing with these process- and substance-related problems is essential both to agenda management and to understanding why policy actors act the way they do.

Problems versus Conditions

The difficulties governments face in agenda-setting begin with the very definition of what is a policy "problem" needing action. As Kingdon (1984) noted, a "problem" is not the same as a "condition," which is some aspect of social life that may or may not be amenable to correction by government (even though it may be a source of public or government concern). A good example of a condition is human aging, broadly considered to be inevitable and outside the bounds of government control. While aspects of aging—such as elderly poverty or elderly care—may involve related issues that *may* be amenable to policy intervention and thus become "policy problems," aging in itself is a condition of life that governments cannot alter, not a problem per se.

A problem, then, is the undesirable effect of a condition that is amenable to government action (Peters, 2005). Hence the fact that airplanes crash, for example, is a condition linked to gravity, which makes some accidents inevitable. But air traffic safety and aircraft maintenance are problems that can be addressed through, for example, the development of air traffic control systems and standards or, in the case of aircraft maintenance, regular inspections and maintenance standards and protocols (Rochefort & Cobb, 1994).

Problem Tractability

Problems vary in their "tractability"—the degree of difficulty involved in developing and implementing solutions to them (Hisschemoller & Hoppe, 1995). A problem such as deaths from car collisions might be effectively and affordably mitigated by, for example: mandating seat belt installation and use; better traffic law enforcement; increasing fines for speeding and drunk driving; and so on. In contrast, problems such as eliminating homelessness may be less tractable, as they might involve a staggering array of issues, such as individual lifestyle; family life; job preparation and employment trends; housing markets; mental health, drug, alcohol, and sexual abuse; and many other factors. Some problems deeply rooted in human behaviour such as cigarette smoking and drug and sexual abuse are especially pernicious and difficult to root out or correct, making them, highly intractable although, as the example of cigarette smoking highlights, not impossible to address (Cnossen, 2005).

Notwithstanding newspaper columnists, pundits, and media commentators who typically present the causes and nature of policy problems and the solutions to them as simple and self-evident, and hence the failure to attain a correct outcome as being the fault of venal, unintelligent or ideologically blinkered politicians and civil servants (Rose & Parsons, 2015), in reality the opposite is often true. Problems with tractable characteristics—sometimes referred to as "well-structured" or "tame" problems (Simon, 1973)—are quite rare in the real world of public policy, not least because easily tractable issues are "low-hanging fruit" that typically have already been the subject of earlier policy activity and in many cases greatly mitigated (at least as compared with initially very high levels).

Even for problems deemed to be relatively tractable, policy efforts take place in a complex, dynamic environment. This is even more true in the case of "ill-structured" or "wicked" problems. These problems have

- boundaries subject to dispute;
- causes that may be unknown or poorly understood; and
- potential solutions that are highly uncertain and/or subject to deep disagreement among technical experts and social and political actors (Rittel & Webber, 1973; Churchman, 1967).

Such problems are occurring more frequently on government agendas as citizens, NGOs and government agencies search for or demand ameliorative action on a wider range of problems linked to boundary-crossing conditions such as global warming.

Highly intractable issues can appear and disappear from policy agendas in a pattern that Anthony Downs (1972) called an "issue-attention" cycle. In it, immediate concerns and calls for action run up against the difficulties and costs involved in correcting or altering relevant policy behaviour. Government and public attention drifts elsewhere until the issue is again raised by some event and/ or interest group. The public outcry against gun violence following periodic mass shooting events in the United States is a good example of this process. Efforts to limit or control access to weaponry in many countries that have proved effective in preventing such massacres are stymied by constitutional and interest-group impediments in the US (Erbing et al., 1980).

Other Dilemmas of Policy Problems

Governments face other challenges in agenda-setting, beyond issues of agenda control and the tractability of issues. Consider two. First, the poor framing of public problems often leads to government and public preoccupation with ineffective and wasteful solutions—preoccupation that may crowd out attention to more feasible solutions. Certainly, many social media and media commentators and pundits (but also politicians more interested in constituency building than problem-solving) contribute to this dysfunction.

Second, many critical public problems fail to reach official policy agendas, while relatively minor concerns—or concerns affecting narrow interest groups—frequently do so. A prominent cause for this is the nature of the interest articulation and aggregation systems present in a country or jurisdiction; these can favour the concerns of minor groups of "special" interests over more general or "public" ones. The attention paid by many governments to tax breaks for the richest and wealthiest group of citizens and businesses—those capable of hiring lobbyists and public relations firms to press their claims for exemptions and special treatment— for example, is far greater than that paid to issues such as gender inequality or child poverty. This is the case despite the fact that the latter issues affect many more people in much more serious ways than a lower capital gains tax. But issues such as poverty and inequality are also much less amenable to clear solutions or to sustained and focused public pressure, given their diffuse character and the voluntary nature of groups and individuals concerned with their elimination.

NGOs and other non-governmental actors can and do take these processes and potential outcomes into account as they attempt to make their voices heard in policy-making circles. And governments and policy managers are well positioned to facilitate or hinder such efforts by, for example, easing the process of agenda access for broadly constituted public interest groups or making the same more difficult for narrow groups (Cobb & Ross, 1997a; Rochefort & Cobb, 1994). While public agencies are well positioned to tackle these and other defects in agenda-setting and thus improve policy processes and outcomes, this potential remains largely untapped. This is not least due to the widespread misperception that public managers' responsibility is confined to implementation of a given mandate handed down from above (Rosenbloom, 2008).

The Substance of Agenda-Setting: Problem Construction

Given the different configurations of conditions, institutions and actors found in different jurisdictions, it is not surprising that the actual content of policy agendas differs across governments and time periods. That is to say, agenda items differ greatly between countries and jurisdictions in terms of the substance or content of agenda issues and the timing of their entrance into the process (Dowding et al., 2015).

In general, agenda formation depends on the nature of the economic and social circumstances in which people live and governments operate. In China, for example, the government's top agenda items in the late-twentieth century focused on spurring economic growth and addressing chronic problems in social service delivery. In the twenty-first century, China's economic policy agenda shifted away from production and supply concerns toward more consumption- and safety-oriented concerns, including threats to food safety and growing air pollution. In France and Japan, on the other hand, priorities in the later period included the reform of the pension system for public-sector employees, and on health and immigration concerns—with both issues spurred largely by shifting demographics and the aging of their populations (Pritchard, 1992). These are phenomena that China too will face, but at a later date given the structure of its population demographics.

As discussed in Chapter 3, policy subsystems—actors involved in defining and interpreting a problem and identifying solutions to it—play a significant role in bridging the gap between the formal, government agenda and the informal, public one. The "image" that a policy problem has within a policy community— how it is named, claimed, blamed, and framed by different policy actors—heavily influences a problem's articulation, deliberation, and resolution (Baumgartner & Jones, 1993).

Hence, as mentioned above, when a problem such as unemployment is portrayed as a technical and economic issue rather than a social one, economic experts in the policy community may dominate policy-making, and solutions can be discussed within a frame of immigration targets, apprenticeship quotas, or tax burdens. When the ethical, social, or political aspects of the problem assume the centre stage, however, a much broader range of policy community participants might be involved. For example, if the problem of unemployment is framed as being the result of unequal and unjust distributions of income, wealth, or opportunities, then actors such as political parties, trade unions, religious organizations, and social justice activists may rise in salience.

Furthermore, the nature of the issue at hand may influence the ability of any actor to affect the timing and entrance of a problem onto a societal or government agenda. Some issues—for example, adjusting resource allocation across industrial or social welfare portfolios—afford public managers greater opportunity and discretion for deciding on the time and circumstance of their entrance onto a policy-making agenda. In other cases, critical events—such as the 9-11 attack on the World Trade Center in 2001—force an agenda item onto the front burner of government attention and compel action whether or not they are prepared to do so (Birkland, 1998; Levin et al., 2012). The great majority of issues, however, afford more discretion and leeway to the gatekeepers of government agendas. The construction of a new highway or hospital, for instance, may well be left for consideration until immediately prior to an election for reasons that are explained below.

Objective Construction: Convergence Theory and Political Business Cycles

Most early works on the subject of agenda-setting began with the assumption that relatively long-term socio-economic conditions—such as demographic changes, urbanization, and changes in wealth and occupations—led to the emergence of particular sets of problems to which governments eventually responded. These models often posited that the issues facing all modern governments were converging toward a common pattern because of similar social, economic, and demographic processes, which in turn elicit similar response from governments. Other models postulate that the interplay of economic and political activity affects the nature and timing of issues that make it onto the agenda, leading to much more idiosyncratic pattern of agenda-setting.

The idea that public policy problems and issues originate in the level of "development" of a society, and that particular sets of problems are common to states at similar levels of development, was first broached by early observers of comparative public policy-making. In the mid-1960s, observers began to conclude that cultural, political, and other factors were less significant for explaining the mix of public policies than were factors related to the level of economic development of the society (Dye, 1966; Sharkansky, 1971). Subsequently, authors such as Harold Wilensky (1975), Philip Cutright (1965), Henry Aaron (1967), and Frederick Pryor (1968) all developed the idea that the structure of a nation's economy determined the types of public policies adopted by the government. This line of analysis led scholars to develop the *convergence thesis*, which suggests that as countries industrialize, they tend to converge toward the same policy mix (Bennett, 1991; Kerr, 1983; Seeliger, 1996). The emergence of similar welfare states in industrialized countries was presented as evidence for the trend (Wilensky, 1975). Agenda-setting in this perspective was thus seen as a virtually automatic process occurring as a result of the stresses and strains placed on governments by social and economic dislocations and the requisites of industrialization and economic modernization.

The convergence thesis was disputed by critics who argued that it oversimplified actual policy development processes, ignoring significant variations in the substance and timing across countries (Heidenheimer et al., 1975). By the mid-1980s a second, less deterministic explanation of agenda-setting behaviour had emerged, which treated political and economic factors as an integral whole. This *power-dependency model* argued that industrialization creates both a need for programs such as social security (because of the aging of the population and processes of urbanization that usually accompany economic modernization) and also generates the economic resources (increased tax revenues because of increased productivity) to allow states to address these needs through programs such as public pension plans, unemployment insurance, and the like (Korpi, 1980, 1983). More importantly, in this view, industrialization also creates a working and middle class with a need for social security and the political resources (because of the number of voters in these groups and their ability to disrupt production through work stoppages and other forms of industrial protests) to exert pressure on the state to meet those needs. The ideology of the government in power and the political threats it faces are thus seen as important factors affecting the extent to which the state is willing to meet the demand for social welfare, the types of programs it is willing to utilize to do so, and when these initiatives might occur (Esping-Anderson & Korpi, 1984; Therborn, 1989).

While some issues, such as the role of international economic forces in driving domestic policy agendas in these and other areas are still debated (Cameron, 1984; Katzenstein, 1985), this power resource-dependency view offered a reasonable alternative to convergence-inspired explanations of public policy agenda-setting. However, it remained at a fairly high level of abstraction and was difficult to apply to specific instances of policy-making (see Uusitalo, 1984).

One way that scholars sought to overcome this problem was by reintegrating political, specifically electoral variables with economic ones in a new "political economy of public policy" (Hancock, 1983). Here it was argued that both electoral and economic factors are important determinants of agenda-setting and should therefore be studied together, especially insofar as political electoral-economic events can affect the *timing and content* of specific policy initiatives.

One of the most important versions of this line of argument posited the idea of a *political business cycle*. The notion of a political business cycle grew out of the literature on business cycles, which found that the economy grew in fits and starts according to periodic flurries of investment and consumption behaviour (see Schneider & Frey, 1988; Frey, 1978; Locksley, 1980). When applied to public policy-making, it was argued that modern governments often intervened in markets to smooth out fluctuations in the business cycle with an eye on elections (Tufte, 1978: 71). Policies that caused difficulties for voters and hence could affect the electoral prospects of the ruling party were more likely to be placed on the government's agenda when an election did not loom on the immediate horizon.

While few disagreed that partisan ideology could have an impact on the nature of the types and extent of government efforts to influence the economy, this approach was criticized for its limited application to democratic countries, and only to a subset of these such as the United States, where electoral cycles were fixed. In many other countries, elections either do not exist or are not competitive, or their timing is indeterminate and depends on events in parliaments or other branches of government, making it difficult if not impossible for governments to make very precise calculations about policy timing (Foot, 1979; Johnston, 1986). It was also argued that the concept of the business cycle itself was fundamentally flawed and that the model simply pointed out the interdependence of politics and economics already acknowledged by most analysts (see McCallum, 1978; Nordhaus, 1975; Schneider & Frey, 1988; Boddy & Crotty, 1975). Nevertheless, such thinking moved policy scholars away from purely objective notions of agenda-setting behaviour to take more seriously the social and political construction of this policy activity.

Subjective Construction: Ideas and Discourses

In the alternative view of the nature of policy problems set out above, the "problems" that are the subject of agenda-setting are considered to be constructed in the realm of public and private ideas, detached from economic conditions or other macro-social processes (Berger & Luckmann, 1966; Hilgartner & Bosk, 1981; Holzner & Marx, 1979; Rochefort & Cobb, 1993; Spector & Kitsuse, 1987). In this view, the idea that agenda-setting proceeds in a mechanistic fashion or through rational analysis of objective conditions by social and political actors is considered to be deceptive, if not completely misleading. Rather, policy-makers are a part of the same discourses as the public and, in Edelman's metaphor of the "political spectacle" (Edelman, 1988), are involved in manipulating the signs, sets, and scenes of a political drama. According to the script of these discourses, which is written as the play is underway, different groups of policy actors are involved, and different outcomes prescribed, in agenda-setting (Muntigl, 2002;

Schmidt & Radaelli, 2005; Johnson, 2007). As both the volume and the influence of misinformation, agnotology, and spin expands in the global reverberation of social media, it is not surprising to find multiple and incommensurate policy agendas being composed about discourses on climate change, trade, and human rights (Perl et al., 2018).

Of course, as noted in earlier chapters, it had long been noted in policy studies that the ideas policy actors hold have a significant effect on the kinds of decisions they make. Although efforts have been made by economists, psychologists, and others to reduce these sets of ideas to rational calculations of self-interest, it is apparent that, even in this limiting case, traditions, beliefs, and attitudes about the world and society held by policy-makers and in the general public affect how individuals interpret their interests, including policy-makers (Flathman, 1966).

As discussed in Chapters 2 and 3, specific policy-relevant sets of ideas— ideologies or paradigms—can exert a significant influence over public policy-making. For it is through these ideational prisms that individuals conceive of social or other problems that inspire their demands for government action and through which they design proposed solutions to these problems (Chadwick, 2000; George, 1969). As Murray Edelman (1988: 12–13) argued, in this view policy issues arise largely on their own within social discourses, often as functions of pre-existing ideological constructs applied to specific day-to-day circumstances. Social media work to expand the scope of circumstances that can trigger ideological reactions as information moves globally, and almost any policy problem or issue around the world can now go "viral" in distant places and with unpredictable consequences.

Different types of ideas have different effects on policy-making, especially agenda-setting. As Goldstein and Keohane (1993b) and Campbell (1998) have noted, at least three types of ideas are relevant to policy: world views, principled beliefs, and causal ideas (see Braun, 1999; Campbell, 1998). These ideas influence policy-making by serving as "road maps" for action, defining problems, affecting the strategic interactions between policy actors, and constraining the range of policy options that are proposed.

World views or *ideologies* have long been recognized as helping people make sense of complex realities by identifying general policy problems and the motivations of actors involved in politics and policy. These sets of ideas, however, tend to be very diffuse and do not easily translate into specific views on particular policy problems. While scholars recognized that the general *policy mood* or *policy sentiment* found in a jurisdiction can be an important component of a general macro-policy environment, for example by influencing voting for representatives and yielding a certain political orientation in government (Durr, 1993; Stimson, 1991; Stimson et al., 1995; Lewis-Beck, 1988; Suzuki, 1992; Adams, 1997), the links of these kind of beliefs to agenda-setting remain quite indirect (Stevenson, 2001; Elliott & Ewoh, 2000).

Principled beliefs and causal stories, on the other hand, can exercise a much more direct influence on the recognition of policy problems and on subsequent policy content (see George, 1969). In the policy sciences, this notion of ideas creating claims or demands on governments was taken up by Frank Fischer and John Forester (1993) and Paul Sabatier (1987, 1988), among others writing in the 1980s and 1990s. As originally presented by the French social philosopher Michel Foucault (1972), the concept of a political discourse was a tool for understanding the historical evolution of society. Foucault believed that historical analysis should contribute to social theory by explaining the origin, evolution, and influence of discourses over time, and by situating current discourses into this framework.

In a policy context this means that policy issues can be seen as arising from pre-existing social and political discourses that establish both what a problem or policy opportunity is and who is capable of articulating it. The effect of causal stories, in particular, on agenda-setting was explored by Deborah Stone (1988, 1989). As she noted, policy-making often features a clash of frames and a struggle among policy actors over the "naming" of problems, the "blaming" of conditions and actors for their existence, and the "claiming" of specific vantage points or perspectives for their resolution (Felstiner et al., 1980–1; Bleich, 2002). The resolution of this conflict and the elevation of a private or social grievance to the status of a public problem, therefore, is often related more to the abilities and resources of competing actors than to the elegance or influence of their ideas, although these ideas remain critical in determining the specific content of that problem (Surel, 2000; Snow & Benford, 1992; Steinberg, 1998, Dostal, 2004).

In this view, then, the policy-making agenda is created out of the history, traditions, attitudes, and beliefs of central policy actors encapsulated and codified in the discourses they construct (Jenson, 1991; Stark, 1992). These discourses are not always "positive" but can involve racist, misogynist, and other kinds of malevolent discourses that can, in turn, exacerbate ethnic, religious, and other kinds of societal tensions (Htun & Weldon, 2012). In this view, symbols and statistics, both real and fabricated, are used to back up one's preferred understanding of the causes and solutions of a problem. Symbols are discovered from the past or created anew to make one's case. And even when using statistics, policy-makers and analysts know how to find what they are looking for and use this data less to convince others of the correctness of their positions and claims, but in order to support their claims and undermine those of rivals (Howlett & Cuenca, 2016; Schaffrin et al., 2014; Lehtonen et al., 2016).

Thus, in this post-positivist view, understanding agenda-setting requires both a knowledge of contextual factors related to the dynamics of the economy and society, as positivists would have it, and also an understanding of how individuals and/or groups make demands for a policy in ways that will influence government, and vice versa.

In short, in this view policy researchers need to identify the conditions under which these demands emerge and are articulated in prevailing policy discourses (Spector & Kitsuse, 1987: 75–6; McBeth et al., 2005). Definitively explaining how the material interests of social and state actors are filtered through, and reflect, their institutional and ideological contexts to influence the specific timing and content of agenda-setting has proved elusive (Thompson, 1990).

Gauging Problem Severity: Indicators and Measures

Whether it is thought to be objective or "only" a subjective construct, determining how extensive or important a problem is forms a key component of agenda-setting and indicators play a powerful but under-investigated role in shaping this process (Kingdon, 1984). This is because no government has the resources or capacity to allow it to address all problems at all times, and choices have to be made to prioritize some rather than others. One way to do this is to look at the severity of a problem, especially whether or not that severity has been increasing or growing over time. In order to accomplish this, most governments attempt to measure problems and develop metrics that allow them to monitor changes over time. Although these measures and indicators are typically used in an effort to promote "objective" policy-making, the existing scholarship on the subject has emphasized that indicators offer political advantages of focusing public attention on a problem that enhance value to policy-makers well beyond their technical merits.

The role played by indicators and measures in agenda-setting and policy appraisal and evaluation activity has been highlighted by many scholars as a significant factor directly influencing both how public policy issues get on a government agenda and how they are addressed (Kingdon, 1984; Lehtonen, 2013). Kingdon (1984), for example, noted how quantitative indicators such as unemployment rates and GDP growth figures often trigger governments to pay more attention to specific kinds of problems than they might otherwise have done. And Lehtonen (2009) noted that research on the role of indicators in policy-making has shown that "presenting information in the form of social statistics enhances its use" in assessing the severity and dimensions of a problem and the ability of certain kinds of solutions to address it.

Studies of how policy research is used by government have shown expert technical knowledge often exerts an indirect, rather than a direct, influence on policy-makers and other stakeholders by shaping their frameworks of thought, promoting individual and collective learning, and "serving as 'ammunition' in political battles for power and influence" (Weiss, 1977, 1986; Whiteman, 1985; Landry et al., 2003; Head et al., 2014). And Lehtonen (2009), for example, has argued that policy-makers' direct and instrumental use of indicators, as is the case with these other sources of knowledge, may well be "an exception [rather] than a rule."

The construction and use of indicators are affected by individual and collective beliefs which in turn affect argumentation and dialogue among actors, ultimately influencing policy decisions and outcomes. As such, indicators can be expected to be used in identifying and monitoring policy problems, assessing performance, and fostering accountability. However, little attention has been paid to how specific indicators emerge and especially to how disputes between conflicting indicators are resolved (Rapport & Friend, 1979).

Actors and Tasks in Agenda-Setting

Agenda-setting is concerned with the following question: "What makes people in and around government attend, at any given time, to some subject and not to others?" (Kingdon, 2011: 1). But who are these "people" in the agenda-setting process?

As McCool (1998) pointed out, the subsystem family of concepts was developed beginning in the late 1950s in order to better understand the role of interests and discourses in the policy process by allowing for complex formal and informal interactions to occur between both state and non-state actors. Proliferation of scholarship on the subject in the 1970s to 1990s generated a wide variety of competing concepts—such as iron triangles, sub-governments, cozy triangles, power triads, policy networks, issue communities, issue networks, advocacy coalitions, and policy communities, among others—all alluding to the tendency of policy actors to form substantive issue alliances that cross institutional boundaries and include both governmental and non-governmental actors (McCool, 1998; Freeman, 1997; Arts & van Tatenhove, 2006).

The relationship between ideas, interests, institutions, and actors found in subsystem theory was something that previous policy theory had largely ignored, as its focus had usually been upon formal institutional procedures and relationships between governmental and non-governmental agents active in policy-making, such as interest groups and lobbyists (McCool, 1998; Howlett & Ramesh, 2009). The more nuanced subsystem concept merging actors, ideas, and institutions together, however, enables students of the policy sciences to distinguish more precisely who are the key actors in a policy process, what unites them, how they engage one another, and what effect their dealings would have on policy outcomes as compared to analysis using a more formal institutional lens (Howlett et al., 2009).

In general, the subsystem was an appropriate unit of analysis for distinguishing the different actors involved in the politics, process, and problem aspects of policy-making activities such as agenda-setting, in which informal interactions are just as important as formal engagements when it comes to explaining the timing and content of issue-attention. However, it is useful to examine several specific subsets of subsystem actors who play especially important roles in agenda-setting and other stages of the policy cycle.

Epistemic Communities

Epistemic communities, is a term originally developed in the international relations literature to describe groups of scientists and government officials involved in articulating and delimiting problem spaces in areas such as oceans policy and climate change (Haas, 1989, 1992; Zito, 2001; Gough & Shackley, 2001). It can also be used as an effective descriptor of the array of actors involved in problem definition.

That is, knowledge regarding a policy problem is the "glue" that unites actors within an epistemic community, differentiating it from those actors involved in political negotiations and practices around policy goals and solutions, as well as those who specialize in the development, design and articulation of policy tools or solutions (Biddle & Koontz, 2014), discussed in the following chapter.

Haas described the "epistemic communities" involved in environment policy deliberations as a diverse collection of policy actors including scientists, academic experts, public-sector officials, and other government agents who are united by a common interest in or a shared interpretation of the science behind a dilemma, in his case an environmental one (Haas, 1992; Gough & Shackley, 2002). These "epistemic communities," influence "policy innovation not only through their ability to frame issues and define state interests but also through their influence on the setting of standards and the development of regulations" (Adler & Haas, 1992). Epistemic communities are crucial in leading and informing the activities of other policy actors with respect to problem severity and causation defining the main direction that policy-making will subsequently follow.

Several studies exist supporting this view on the perceptions of epistemic community members and the problem-framing role they play in policy-making. In his studies of global oceans research and policy, for example, Rudd (2014, 2015) provides important empirical findings illuminating the influence of scientists in framing environmental dilemmas at the science-policy interface.

Instrument Constituencies

Epistemic communities active in problem definition and framing are conceptually separate and distinct from the activities of a second group of subsystem actors who focus much less on policy problems than they do on the ways and means of solving policy problems. *Instrument constituencies* is a term used in the comparative public policy field to describe this set of actors involved in solution articulation, often *independently of the nature of the problem to be addressed* (Voss & Simons, 2014). Such constituencies typically advocate for particular tools or combinations of tools to address a range of problem areas and hence are active in proposing policy alternatives and instruments both at the agenda-setting stage and at other points in policy-making, such as formulation, discussed in Chapter 5.

Through the instrument constituency focus, the policy instruments that are devised or revised and considered and assessed in the effort to match problems with solutions (see also Chapter 5) can usefully be viewed as the constructs of these subsets of policy actors who embrace specific means of policy-making over all others. These actors are united by their adherence to the design and promotion of specific policy instruments as the solutions to multiple and varied policy problems, usually in the abstract, which can then be operationalized under real-world conditions. Voss and Simons (2014), for example, highlighted the role played by instrument constituencies who, albeit originating from a multitude of backgrounds and organizations, came together in support of particular types of policy instruments in European environmental policy-making; forming a distinct "policy" stream to promote climate change–linked emissions trading.

Just as epistemic communities perpetuate ideas about the nature of policy problems, members of instrument constituencies are drawn to collaborate in policy-making by their promotion of a particular policy tool or a specific combination of policy tools. The members of such constituencies are not necessarily inspired by the same definition of a policy problem or by shared beliefs. They are "networks of heterogeneous actors from academia, policy consulting, public policy and administration, business, and civil society, who become entangled as they engage with the articulation, development, implementation and dissemination of a particular technical model of governance" (Voss & Simons, 2014). As Voss and Simons put it, the practices of such actors "constitute and are constituted by the instrument" and develop "a discourse of how the instrument may best be retained, developed, promoted and expanded" (Voss & Simons, 2014).

Advocacy Coalitions

The "politics" side of agenda-setting can also be thought of as being the milieu where a specific subset of policy subsystem actors are active. The term *advocacy coalition* was coined by students of American policy-making to describe the action of those involved in political contests over matching problem definitions with policy tools (Sabatier & Weible, 2007; Schlager & Blomquist, 1996) and can be used to capture this notion. These sets of actors often compete with other coalitions to get their preferred match between problem definitions and potential solutions adopted at all stages of the policy process, including at agenda-setting.

Within advocacy coalitions, politically active members, such as elected officials, are usually more publicly visible than the substantive experts who collaborate in formulating policy options and alternatives, and constitute an often "hidden cluster" of coalition members' actors. More visible actors of the politics stream include, for example in the case of the US policy-making, "the President and his high-level appointees, prominent members of the Congress, the media and such elections-related actors as political parties and campaigns"

(Kingdon, 2011, p. 64), while less visible actors include lobbyists, political party brokers and fixers, and many other behind-the-scenes advisors and analysts.

Advocacy coalition actors aggregate and coordinate their actions based on shared policy core beliefs, and several coalitions with competing views can vie for space, and dominance within a subsystem. Led by their primary interest in forwarding their ideas and beliefs, coalitions compete with one another to transform these into policies (Weishaar, 2015).

These beliefs, as well as coalition membership, stay consistent over time, and the relative success of a coalition in furthering its policies depends on a number of elements, including external factors like their resource endowments and the nature of policy problems, both of which remain relatively constant over time (Sabatier, 2007). These internal factors include the coalition's own financial resources, its level of expertise, and number of supporters. Coalition members employ their knowledge about the positions and behaviour of other policy actors to advance a "variety of uses from argumentation with opponents to mobilization of supporters" (Weible et al., 2011).

Policy Entrepreneurs and Policy Brokers

Much attention has been paid in the literature to the role played by policy entrepreneurs in moving agenda items forward into the formal policy process (Kingdon, 1984). Entrepreneurs in this area are seen as being intimately involved in struggles over problem framing and linking together actors and solutions competing for policy attention. Policy entrepreneurs can be organizations or individuals, can be either heavily interlinked or quite distinct and separate, and also, most importantly, can take on different roles depending on their problem, policy, or politics orientation (Cairney, 2012; Cairney & Jones, 2015; Mintrom & Norman, 2009; Meijerink & Huitema, 2010; Jordan & Huitema, 2014; Skok, 1995).

However, the "elbow room" available to these individuals for investing time, energy, and resources toward a desired policy end is often constrained if they are outside a policy subsystem. Cairney and Jones (2015) thus concluded that entrepreneurs "are best understood as well-informed and well-connected insiders who provide the knowledge and tenacity to help" agenda items develop and move between unofficial, or public, and official, or governmental, status. Yet, they also noted that such actors cannot do more than their environments allow. They are "'surfers waiting for the big wave,' not Poseidon-like masters of the seas" (Cairney & Jones, 2015).

Echoing these observations, other scholars have also pointed out the shortcomings of relying exclusively on individual policy entrepreneurial activity to understand agenda-setting behaviour absent an appreciation of the other communities and constituencies involved in this stage of policy-making (Knaggård, 2015; Herweg et al., 2015). Knaggård (2015), for example, has argued that a single notion of entrepreneurship is misplaced; and sees the need for a second related actor—a *"problem broker"*—emerging out of the epistemic community. This kind of actor, she argues, has a primary interest in framing policy problems and having policy-makers accept these frames, thereby conceptually distinguishing problem framing as a separate process and "enabling a study of actors that frame problems without making policy suggestions," unlike traditional notions of policy entrepreneurs (Knaggård, 2015).

As Ackrill, Kay, and Zahariadis (2013) note, this means "no entrepreneur alone will ever be enough to cause policy reform; we always require an account of the context or configuration of the various other actors in the subsystem." Regardless of their names, however, both brokers and entrepreneurs are actors dedicated to the framing of policy problems and matching them to solutions and political currents (Zahariadis, 2007) and hence play a key role in agenda-setting alongside epistemic communities, instrument constituencies, and advocacy coalitions.

Theories of Agenda-Setting: Ideas, Actors, and Structures

Given this complex array of actors, it is difficult to settle upon a single source of the factors driving public policy agenda-setting. This has led to the development of more complex models that attempt to systematically combine the macro-variables identified in early studies with elements of agenda-setting behaviour in subsystems into comprehensive, and empirically accurate, multivariate theory of agenda-setting.

Funnels of Causality

One early multivariate model was advanced through parallel efforts by Anthony King (1973) in Great Britain, Richard Hofferbert (1974) in the United States, and Richard Simeon (1976a) in Canada. Each author developed a model of policy formation that sought to capture the relationships existing among social, institutional, ideational, political, and economic conditions in the policy process writ large, including the agenda-setting process. These models tried to consider many possible variables as important and focused on the nature of their interactions. These authors situated each variable within a *funnel of causality*, in which each set of factors was "nested" among the others.

That is, rather than considering structural, ideational, and actor-related behaviour in agenda-setting as contradictory or zero-sum, the funnel-of-causality conception suggested the substance of government's agenda is shaped not only by the socio-economic and physical environment but also by the distribution of power in society, the prevailing ideas and ideologies found both in society and among policy-makers, the institutional frameworks of government, and the process of decision-making within governments that brought these ideas to bear on policy-making (King, 1973). These variables were said to be intertwined in a nested pattern of interaction whereby policy-making occurs within institutions, institutions exist within prevailing sets of ideas, ideas operate within relations of power in society, and the relations of power in turn arise from the overall social and material environment. Thus, large-scale macro-variables could be said to determine policy behaviour and government issue-attention, but only indirectly, as filtered through ideational and institutional variables, much as was argued in Chapter 3 with respect to the manner in which democratic practices were embedded in the economy and vice versa.

This synthetic model pointed to the significance of both material and ideational variables to the policy context without bogging down in attempts to specify their exact relationship or causal significance at any given moment in time. Such causal diversity is the model's greatest strength because it allows different views on agenda influences to be explored empirically so that specific relationships among the variables can be established, such as how demographic change affects social policy ideas and content. This approach is also a weakness, though, because it does not explain the precise configuration of these variables in specific circumstances, and hence the reasons for these factors influencing agendas in different ways. Why the place of pensions on the public agenda might be influenced by certain ideas in one location and not another when faced with the same problem is not broached or resolved. The funnel-of-causality model also says very little about how multi-dimensional influences on policy agendas, such as the environmental context, ideas, and economic interests, actually create a particular effect on policy actors to move the agenda-setting process forward at specific points in time and not others (Mazmanian & Sabatier, 1980; Green-Pedersen, 2004). That is, the *mechanisms* of agenda-setting are underspecified in this model.

Issue-Attention Cycles

Another early example of an agenda-setting model, built on the premise that this stage of the policy process involved the interaction of institutions, actors, and ideas, was put forward by Anthony Downs in 1972 and does address this concern for mechanisms. Based on his observations of several policy fields, most notably around environmental protection, Downs proposed that agenda-setting often followed what he termed an *"issue-attention cycle,"* much like the media "news cycle."

In a short but influential article focusing on the emergence of environmental policy in the United States in the early 1960s, Downs (1972) noted that public policy-making often focused on issues that momentarily capture public attention and trigger demands for government action. However, he also noted that many of these problems soon fade from view as their complexity or intractability becomes apparent and the public loses patience with the attendant complications.

Downs identified an institutional mechanism of agenda-setting that was lacking in the funnel-of-causality model. He emphasized that, in a democracy, politicians ignore public demands at their electoral peril, meaning waxing and waning public attention to policy problems generates a cyclical pattern of agenda-setting as politicians respond to urgent calls for action and then slacken off their efforts when public interest in the issue dies down. As he noted, this is often due to the mistaken belief that the actions taken earlier have resolved the issue, but also occurs when the cost of a real resolution becomes apparent or when interest shifts to another topic (Harring et al., 2011; Daw et al., 2013).

In 1985 Peters and Hogwood made an effort to operationalize their own version of Downs's cycle, attempting to assess the relationship between waves of public interest as measured in Gallup polls and periodic waves of organizational change or institution-building in the US federal government. Although they found evidence of major periods of administrative consolidation and change over the course of recent US history, they noted that only 7 of 12 instances of administrative reorganization met the expectations of the Downsian model, when dramatic administrative changes occurred during the same decade as the peak of public interest as measured by Gallup survey questions. However, they were also careful to note that there appeared to be at least two other patterns or cycles at work in the issue-attention process. In the first type, cycles were initiated by external or exogenous events such as war or an energy crisis and then were mediated by public attention. In this type of crisis cycle, the problem would not fade away as Downs hypothesized. In the second type of political cycle, issue initiation originated from the political leadership and then caught the public's attention (Peters & Hogwood, 1985: 252; see also Hogwood, 1992).

Peters and Hogwood's work emphasized the key role played by state actors in socially constructed agenda-setting processes, a factor that Downs had either downplayed or reduced to a reaction to a purely electoral calculation (Sharp, 1994b; Yishai, 1993). They noted that officially scheduled political events, such as annual budgets, speeches from the throne, or presidential press conferences, can spark media coverage and thus draw public attention, reversing the purely reactive causal linkages attributed to political actors by Downs (Cook et al., 1983; Howlett, 1997; Erbring et al., 1980; Flemming et al., 1999). Evidence from other case studies revealed that interest groups' success or failure in gaining agenda access depended on state institutional structures and the access points, or policy venues, they created from which societal groups could gain the attention of government officials and decision-makers (Baumgartner & Jones, 1993; Pross, 1992; Newig, 2004). These insights and others were soon accumulated in new models in order to more accurately model agenda-setting behaviour.

Modes of Agenda-Setting

A major breakthrough in agenda-setting studies occurred in the early 1970s when Cobb, Ross, and Ross developed a clear rationale for identifying several distinct patterns or "modes" of agenda-setting. In so doing, they followed the insight of Cobb's earlier work with Elder, which distinguished between the *systemic* or "informal" public agenda and the *institutional* or "formal" state agenda, and used this distinction to identify several modes of state-led, societally led, and other kinds of agenda-setting behaviour.

In Cobb and Elder's view, the systemic agenda "consists of all issues that are commonly perceived by members of the political community as meriting public attention and as involving matters within the legitimate jurisdiction of existing governmental authority" (Cobb & Elder, 1972: 85). This is essentially a society's agenda for discussion of *individual and social* problems, such as crime and health care. Each society, of course, has literally thousands of issues that some citizens find to be matters of concern and expect the government to do something about. Only after a government has accepted that something needs to be done about a problem can the issue be said to have entered the institutional agenda. In other words, the informal agenda is for *discussion*, while the institutional agenda is primed for *action*.

For Cobb and his colleagues, issues are first *initiated*, their solutions are *specified*, support for the issue is *expanded*, and, if successful, the issue *enters* the institutional agenda (Cobb et al., 1976: 127). However, this can occur in several distinct ways.

Cobb, Ross, and Ross (1976) went on to propose three basic patterns or modes of agenda-setting. Each of these modes is associated with the different manner and sequence in which issue initiation, specification, expansion, and entrance occur. In a further step, they identified or linked each mode with a specific type of political regime.

The first mode they identified was what they termed the *outside initiation model*. This model was associated in their minds with liberal pluralist societies. In this model, "issues arise in non-governmental groups and are then expanded sufficiently to reach, first, the public [systemic] agenda and, finally, the formal [institutional] agenda." Here, social groups play the key role by articulating a grievance and demanding its resolution by the government. These groups lobby, contest, and join with others in attempting to get the expanded issue onto the formal agenda. If they have the requisite political resources and skills and can out-manoeuvre their opponents or advocates of competing issues and actions, they will succeed in having their issue enter the formal agenda (Cobb et al., 1976). Successful entry on the formal agenda does not necessarily mean a favourable government decision will ultimately result. It simply means that the item has been singled out from among many others for more thorough consideration.

The second, *mobilization,* model is quite different. It is a mode attributed by Cobb and his colleagues to "totalitarian" regimes. This model describes "decision-makers trying to expand an issue from a formal [institutional] to a public [systemic] agenda" (1976: 134.) In the mobilization model, issues are simply placed on the formal agenda by the government with no necessary preliminary expansion from a publicly recognized grievance. There may be considerable debate within government over the issue, but the public may well be kept in the dark until an official announcement. Gaining support for the new policy is important, however, since successful implementation will depend on public acceptance. Toward this end, government leaders hold meetings and engage in public relations campaigns, but only once the issue is on the institutional agenda. As the authors put it, "The mobilization model describes the process of agenda building in situations where political leaders initiate a policy but require the support of the mass public for its implementation. . . . [T]he crucial problem is to move the issue from the formal agenda to the public agenda" (1976: 135).

Finally, in the third model, the *inside initiation* model, influential groups with special access to decision-makers can launch a policy and often do not want public attention. This can be due to technical as well as political reasons and is an agenda-setting pattern one would expect to find in corporatist regimes. In this model, initiation and specification occur simultaneously as a group or government agency enunciates a grievance and specifies some potential solution. Deliberation is restricted to specialized groups or agencies with some knowledge of or interest in the subject. Entrance on the agenda is virtually automatic due to the privileged place of those desiring a decision (Cobb et al., 1976: 136). Unlike the mobilization model, however, no outside or public legitimation of the proposed activity is needed, and activity remains firmly situated in the internal institutional workings of government.

This line of analysis was very useful in not only identifying several typical agenda-setting modes but also linking expectations for such modes of activity and actor behaviour with regime type, simultaneously identifying key sources of policy ideas and discourses associated with each mode.

In its original formulation, Cobb, Ross, and Ross (1976) suggested that the type of agenda-setting process followed in any particular circumstance is ultimately determined by the nature of the political system, with outside initiation being typical of liberal democracies, mobilization characteristic of one-party states, and inside initiation reflective of authoritarian bureaucratic regimes. However, it was subsequently recognized that these different styles of agenda-setting varied not so much by political regime as by policy sector, as examples of each type of agenda-setting behaviour could be found within each regime type (Princen, 2007).

Further investigations and efforts at model building thus sought to specify exactly what processes were followed within these different kinds of political regimes, especially in complex democratic polities like the United States with multiple quasi-autonomous policy subsystems. The results of these studies led to more nuanced understandings of how agenda-setting modes are linked to actors, structures, and ideas and, ultimately, as set out below, to how the actual content of the problems and issues are likely to emerge in specific instances of agenda-setting and why this occurs when it does, rather than at some other possible moment in history.

The Multiple Streams Model and Its Evolution

In the 1980s, John Kingdon (1984) developed an analytical framework for agenda-setting that drew upon this earlier work, coupled with his own investigations of policy initiation in the US Congress. His book *Agendas, Alternatives and Public Policies* was a major breakthrough in this area of public policy research and now constitutes the orthodoxy in contemporary agenda-setting studies (Cairney & Jones, 2016; Beland, 2016; Beland & Howlett, 2016).

Kingdon's model examined state and non-state influences on agenda-setting by exploring the role played by *policy entrepreneurs* both inside and outside of government in constructing and utilizing agenda-setting opportunities—labelled *policy windows*—to bring issues onto government agendas (Mintrom, 1997; Mintrom & Norman, 2009; Copeland & James, 2014). His model suggested that policy agenda windows open and close based on the dynamic interaction of political institutions, policy actors, and the articulation of ideas—what he termed "*policy streams*"—in the form of proposed policy solutions. These forces can open, or close, policy windows, thus creating the chance for policy entrepreneurs to construct or leverage these opportunities to shape the policy agenda (Copeland & James, 2014).

In Kingdon's study of agenda-setting in the United States, three sets of variables—distinct *streams* of problems, policies, and politics—are said to interact. The *problem stream* refers to the perceptions of problems as public issues requiring government action. The *problem stream* is filled with concerns about what to do that typically attract policy-makers' attention either because of dramatic crises, or through feedback from the operation of existing programs (1984: 20). The *policy stream* contains solutions created by experts and analysts who examine problems and propose options to address them. In this stream, the various possibilities are explored and narrowed down. Finally, the *political stream* "is composed of such factors as swings of national mood, administrative or legislative turnover, and interest group pressure campaigns" (1984: 21). In Kingdon's view, these three streams operate along different paths and pursue courses more or less independent of one another until specific points in time, or during *policy windows*, when their paths intersect or are brought together by the activities of entrepreneurs linking problems, solutions, and opportunities.

Thus, in the right circumstances, policy windows can be seized upon by key players in the political process to place issues on the agenda. Policy entrepreneurs play the key role in this process by linking, or "coupling," policy solutions and policy problems together with political opportunities (Kingdon, 1984; Roberts & King, 1991; Mintrom, 1997; Tepper, 2004).

As Kingdon argues, "The separate streams of problems, policies, and politics come together at certain critical times. Solutions become joined to problems, and both of them are connected to favourable political forces." At that point, an item enters the official (or institutional) agenda and the public policy process begins. Kingdon suggests that window openings can result from fortuitous happenings, including seemingly unrelated external "focusing events," crises, or accidents; scandals; or the presence or absence of policy entrepreneurs both within and outside of governments. At other times, policy windows can be opened by institutionalized events such as periodic elections or budgetary cycles (Birkland, 1997, 1998; Tumber & Waisbord, 2004; Nohrstedt, 2005; Mertha & Lowry, 2006).

Kingdon's model was used to assess the nature of US foreign policy agenda-setting (Woods & Peake, 1998); the politics of privatization in Britain, France, and Germany (Zahariadis, 1995; Zahariadis & Allen, 1995); the nature of US domestic anti-drug policy (Sharp, 1994a); the collaborative behaviour of business and environmental groups in certain anti-pollution initiatives in the US and Europe (Lober, 1997; Clark, 2004); and the overall nature of the reform process in Eastern Europe (Keeler, 1993). While a major improvement on earlier models, it has been criticized for presenting a view of the agenda-setting process that is too contingent on unforeseen circumstances, ignoring the fact that in most policy sectors, as Downs had noted, action tends to produce bursts of change that are followed by lengthy periods of inertia (Dodge & Hood, 2002).

In this model, the level of institutionalization of a window type determines its frequency of appearance and hence its predictability (Boin & Otten, 1996; Howlett, 1997b). One way that policies "congeal" into lengthy periods of program stability, for example, is that policy windows can be designed to stay closed for extended periods—as occurs, for example, in the multi-year funding authorizations of transportation and military programs that reduce the opportunities available to discuss issues and adjust priorities. Windows can even be locked through fiscal devices such as trust funds and revenue bonding that commit spending and taxing for many years into the future (French & Phillips, 2004).

The idea of agenda-setting following this pattern of fairly stable policy-making interrupted by periods of change was developed further by Baumgartner and Jones in their works on "punctuated equilibrium" processes in policy-making during the 1990s and afterward.

Punctuated Equilibrium and Agenda-Setting

In Kingdon's framework, the construction of a stable policy subsystem or "policy monopoly" serves as a key mechanism that provides stability in agenda-setting, through its control over the policy discourse. Such a subsystem entrenches the core idea set, many of the actors, and the institutional order in which policy development occurs, "locking in" a policy frame. Frank Baumgartner and Bryan Jones (1991, 1993, 1994; Jones & Baumgartner, 2005), in a landmark series of studies, examined the causes and implications of the forces behind this policy stasis and when it changed, thus extending Kingdon's insight and helping to explain the likely content of the agenda-setting behaviour identified earlier by Cobb and his colleagues.

The key element that differentiates modes of agenda-setting, Baumgartner and Jones argue, revolves around the manner in which specific subsystems gain the ability to control the interpretation of a problem and thus how it is conceived and discussed within epistemic communities, instrument constituencies, and advocacy coalitions. For Baumgartner and Jones, the "image" of a policy problem is significant because

> [w]hen they are portrayed as technical problems rather than as social questions, experts can dominate the decision-making process. When the ethical, social or political implications of such policies assume centre stage, a much broader range of participants can suddenly become involved. (Baumgartner & Jones, 1991: 1047)

The primary relationship that affects agenda-setting dynamics, in Baumgartner and Jones's view, is that between individuals and groups who control an existing subsystem compared to those who are seeking to impact that subsystem by leveraging outside influences. In their model, policy monopolies construct hegemonic images of policy problems that allow influential actors in a subsystem to practise *agenda denial*—that is, preventing alternate images and ideas from penetrating and thus influencing governments (Yanow, 1992; Bachrach & Baratz, 1962; Debnam, 1975; Frey, 1971; R.A. Smith, 1979; Cobb & Ross, 1997b). Subsystem members opposed to prevailing conditions and government responses, however, seek to alter policy images through a number of tactics related to altering the venue of policy debate or other aspects of the prevailing policy discourse, thus undermining the complacency or stability of an existing policy subsystem and allowing new ideas about problems and solutions to enter into policy debates (Sheingate, 2000).

Baumgartner and Jones posited that actors attempting to alter the official agenda of government typically adopt either of two strategies to make subsystems more "competitive." In the "Downsian" strategy of drawing attention to an issue, groups can publicize a problem in order to alter its venue through mobilizing public demands for government to resolve it (Baumgartner & Jones, 1993: 88). In a second typical approach, which they term a *"Schattschneider"* mobilization (after an early American scholar of pressure group behaviour), groups involved in the policy subsystem dissatisfied with the policies being developed or discussed "counter-mobilize" to alter the institutional arrangements within which the subsystem operates in order to expand or contract its membership (1993: 89; for examples of these strategies in practice, see Maurer & Parkes, 2007; Daugbjerg & Studsgaard, 2005; Hansford, 2004; Pralle, 2003).

The key change that results if either strategy succeeds is the breaking open of a policy monopoly into a more competitive situation where new actors and new discourses, and thus new issues, can enter into policy subsystems and debates, causing a "policy punctuation" (van Assche, 2011; John & Bevan, 2012; Jones & Baumgartner, 2002). A good example of this can be found in the transformation of smoking from a personal consumption issue to one of social health and welfare. This reframing led, ultimately, to the articulation and subsequent implementation of alternative options for tobacco control related to sales, advertising, and workplace bans and other restrictions, which had previously been unthinkable as restrictions on personal freedoms (Studlar, 2002).

In subsequent work, Baumgartner and Jones suggested these kinds of processes result in a consistent policy dynamic where incremental changes to the status quo dominate agendas until major turning points when "institutional friction" is overcome and new problem understandings enter the official agenda. Such recognition is a relatively rare occurrence, but not as infrequent as might be expected, leading to a pattern of "punctuated equilibrium" in policy outputs and deliberations (John & Margetts, 2003; Epp & Baumgartner, 2016; Jones et al., 2009).

Four ideal typical modes of agenda-setting that flow from the analysis of Baumgartner and Jones are shown in Figure 4.1.

In this model, the chance for new problems or options to emerge on government agendas depends on whether policy subsystems are monopolistic or

Figure 4.1 Typical Agenda-Setting Modes

	Subsystem Type	
	Monopolistic	**Competitive**
Old Ideas	**Status Quo** Character: static/hegemonic (agenda denial)	**Contested** Character: contested variations on the status quo
New Ideas	**Redefining** Character: internal discursive reframing	**Innovative** Character: unpredictable/chaotic

competitive and whether new ideas about the nature of a policy problem and its solution can be found in the subsystem. Where a well-established monopoly exists with no new ideas present, agenda denial and a status quo orientation are likely to result. When that same monopoly has some new ideas, these are likely to result in partial reframing of issues within the subsystem.

When a more competitive subsystem exists but no new ideas have been developed, contested variations on the status quo are likely to be features of agenda-setting. When the established ideas predominate, however, nothing more than proposals for incremental changes to the status quo is likely to be raised to the institutional agenda. Only when both situations exist—that is, both a competitive subsystem and the presence of new ideas—are more profound (and potentially paradigmatic) innovative changes in problem definition and identification likely to proceed onto the formal agenda of governments and advance new options into the next stage of the policy cycle: policy formulation.

Conclusion: A Policy Subsystem Conception of Agenda-Setting

This overview of agenda-setting studies has shown how investigations have moved from simple univariate models focused on "objective" or "subjective" constructions of policy problems to more sophisticated examinations that link a considerable number of variables and actors together in complex multivariate relationships, resulting in a punctuated equilibrium pattern of agenda-setting. It has also shown how contemporary studies have shown this stage of the policy process to be influenced by key actors in prevailing policy subsystems, the dominant sets of ideas about policy problems they espouse, and the kinds of institutions within which they operate. These models address many of the shortcomings of earlier works and give us a good sense of how the agenda-setting process unfolds, the types of agenda-setting that can occur, the timing of agenda appearance, and the likely content of an agenda, given the nature of the policy subsystem at work in this issue area.

The most significant variables influencing patterns of agenda-setting in this view turn out to have less to do with automatically responding to changes in the nature of the economy (as Dye, Wilensky, and Sharkansky argued) or with the nature of the political regime involved (as Cobb, Ross, and Ross had claimed). Instead, as Kingdon points out, agenda-setting processes are contingent, but very often still predictable, involving the complex interrelationships of ideas, actors, and structures carried forward through multiple streams that span stages of policy-making. And, as Baumgartner and Jones have suggested, the nature of the actors initiating policy discussions and whether the structures in which they operate allow new ideas to come forward are the most important determinants of the movement of public problems from the informal agenda to the state's institutional agenda (Daugbjerg & Pedersen, 2004).

While the exact timing of the emergence of an issue onto the systemic or formal policy agenda depends, as Kingdon showed, on the existence of a policy window and of the capacity and ability of policy entrepreneurs to take advantage of it, the content of the problems identified in the agenda-setting process depends very much on the nature of the policy subsystem in the area concerned and the members' policy ideas (Haider-Markel & Joslyn, 2001; Jeon & Haider-Markel, 2001).

Research on agenda-setting remains vibrant and continues to generate new findings (Pump, 2011). Recent studies have addressed questions concerning the existence of national styles in this area (Bonafant, et al., 2015; John et al., 2013; Dowding et al., 2010; Marsh, 2013); the influence of the media (Vliegenthart et al., 2016; Walgrave & Vliegenthart, 2010; Birkland & Lawrence, 2009; Boswell, 2012) and new social media (Wukich & Mergel, 2016; Greenwood 2016; Halpern & Gibbs, 2013); and questions related to the average size of an agenda, the extent to which issues compete for attention (Green-Pedersen & Mortensen, 2010; Mortensen & Seeberg, 2015), and the impact of Big Data (Russell et al., 2014).

How governments strategize to control the agenda and realize their own rather than someone else's agenda items (Wu et al., 2017; Princen, 2009; Graziano & Percoco, 2016) and the specific mechanisms through which they announce their intentions (John & Jennings, 2010; Dowding, 2015) are also subjects of investigation in policy studies.

Study Questions

1. How do problems get recognized as public problems and make it on to the official policy agenda?

2. What is the difference between informal and formal, or systemic and official, policy agendas?

3. How do different agenda-setting modes reflect the presence or absence of policy monopolies?

4. Why and how is access to the policy agenda denied to certain problems? What are the implications of this for action on public problems?

5. Who are the main sets of actors involved in agenda-setting, and what do they do?

Further Readings

Baumgartner, Frank R., and Bryan D. Jones. 1993. *Agendas and Instability in American Politics*. Chicago: University of Chicago Press.

Cobb, Roger W., J.K. Ross, and M.H. Ross. 1976. "Agenda Building as a Comparative Political Process," *American Political Science Review* 70, no. 1: 126–38.

Downs, Anthony. 1972. "Up and Down with Ecology—the 'Issue-Attention Cycle,'" *The Public Interest 28*: 38–50.

Greenwood, Molly M., Mary E. Sorenson, and Benjamin R. Warner. 2016. "Ferguson on Face-book: Political Persuasion in a New Era of Media Effects," *Computers in Human Behavior* 57 (April): 1–10. doi:10.1016/j.chb.2015.12.003.

Halpin, Darren R., Bert Fraussen, and Anthony J. Nownes. 2018. "The Balancing Act of Establishing a Policy Agenda: Conceptualizing and Measuring Drivers of Issue Prioritization within Interest Groups," *Governance* 31, no. 2 (April 1): 215–37. doi:10.1111/gove.12284.

Kingdon, John W. 1995 [1984]. *Agendas, Alternatives and Public Policies*. Boston: HarperCollins.

Simons, Arno, and Jan-Peter Voss. 2018. "The Concept of Instrument Constituencies: Accounting for Dynamics and Practices of Knowing Governance," *Policy and Society* 37, no. 1: 14–35.

Spector, Malcolm, and John I. Kitsuse. 1987. *Constructing Social Problems*. New York: Aldine de Gruyter.

Weible, Christopher M., Karin Ingold, Daniel Nohrstedt, Adam Douglas Henry, and Hank C. Jenkins-Smith. 2019. "Sharpening Advocacy Coalitions," *Policy Studies Journal*. Accessed July 3, 2019.

Wu, Xun, M. Ramesh, Michael Howlett, and Scott Fritzen. 2018. *The Public Policy Primer: Managing Public Policy*. Shanghai: Truth & Wisdom Press.

Yanow, Dvora. 1992. "Silences in Public Policy Discourse: Organizational and Policy Myths," *Journal of Public Administration Research and Theory* 2, no. 4: 399–423.

Zito, Anthony R. 2001. "Epistemic Communities, Collective Entrepreneurship and European Integration," *Journal of European Public Policy* 8, no. 4 (January 1): 585–603. doi: 10.1080/13501760110064401.

Chapter 5

Policy Formulation
Identifying and Assessing Policy Alternatives

What Is Policy Formulation?

Policy formulation refers to the process of generating options on what to do about a publicly recognized problem. In this phase of policy-making, options that might help resolve issues and problems emerging from the agenda-setting process are identified, refined, and formalized. This often occurs after a problem has been recognized and placed on the official agenda, but can also occur prior to this in discussions of "informal" public agenda items (Beland & Howlett, 2016). In this effort, sometimes in a systematic way and more often in a less thorough fashion, an initial feasibility assessment of policy options is conducted and decisions are reached as to which alternatives might be more suitable to adopt than others. Although they involve "decisions," these formulation efforts and dynamics are distinct from public policy decision-making (discussed in Chapter 6), where a specific course of action is approved by authoritative decision-makers in government and often passed into law or regulation bound for implementation (Keyes, 1996).

As Charles Jones (1984: 7) has observed, the distinguishing characteristic of policy formulation is simply that means are proposed to resolve perceived societal needs. Once a government has acknowledged the existence of a public problem and the need to do something about it—that is, once it has entered onto the formal agenda of government—policy-makers must decide either to ignore it or to arrive at some course of action to deal with it. Developing or "formulating" what this course of action will entail is the second major activity of the policy cycle.

Policy formulation involves identifying and assessing possible solutions to problems, or, to put it another way, exploring the various options or alternative courses of action available for addressing a problem. These are activities that occur both in theory, when possible alternatives are invented or proposed, and in practice as their number is reduced through deliberations and actions of policy actors. These proposals may originate in the agenda-setting process itself when, as often occurs, a problem and its possible solution(s) are placed simultaneously on the government agenda (Kingdon, 1984), or options may be developed only after an item has moved onto the official agenda. In all cases, the main work of policy formulation is to narrow down the range of all possible options to those that are available and that decision-makers might accept. It is this short list that reaches the formal deliberations of decision-makers themselves in the next phase of policy-making.

Defining and weighing the merits and risks of various options thus characterizes the policy cycle's formulation stage, and some degree of formal policy analysis is typically, but not necessarily, a substantive component of formulation activity. Drawing up policy options can be a demanding activity that involves defining and weighing the merits and risks of various possible alternative courses of action or "policy appraisal." In its modern guise, this typically involves formal *ex ante* policy analysis; that is, analytical work undertaken to generate and evaluate policy options in order to address problems or issues on a policy agenda (Howlett et al., 2009; Turnpenny et al., 2013; Kingdon, 1984). Policy appraisal in this sense is a type of policy formulation activity that involves the use of both formal and informal analytical methods to develop policy-relevant knowledge or evidence, engage policy-makers and analysts in dialogue about the nature of policy problems and solutions, and identify and assess the impacts of different policy options (Jordan & Turnpenny, 2014; Turnpenny et al., 2009; Hertin et al., 2009).

As Turnpenny et al. (2013) note, policy appraisal is concerned with "how evidence is collected, marshalled, communicated, digested and used." But what kinds of knowledge or evidence are used, how, and by whom in this process is unclear *a priori* (Feldman, 1989; Pawson, 2002; Sanderson, 2009; Nutley et al., 2007; Howlett et al., 2014).

Jones (1984: 78) described several other broad characteristics of policy formulation, including the following:

- Formulation need not be limited to one set of actors. Thus, there may well be two or more formulation groups producing competing (or complementary) proposals.
- Formulation may proceed without clear definition of the problem, or without formulators ever having much contact with the affected groups.
- There is no necessary coincidence between formulation and particular organizations, though it is a frequent activity of bureaucratic agencies.
- Formulation and reformulation may occur over a long period of time without ever contributing to sufficient support to act on any one proposal.
- There are often multiple appeal points for those who lose in any one component of the formulation process.
- The process itself never has neutral effects. Somebody wins and somebody loses even in the workings of science.

This picture presents policy formulation as a highly diffuse, politicized, and disjointed process that varies from case to case, which is no doubt accurate. However, it is possible to say something about the general nature of how authority ebbs and flows during the formulation process, the activities it involves, and its likely outcomes despite the idiosyncratic nature of many formulation activities.

One such generalization is that policy formulation is a process, which can be subdivided into temporal phases. In his detailed study of Lithuanian education policy formulation, for example, Harold Thomas (2001) identified four key phases in policy formulation: appraisal, dialogue, formulation, and consolidation. These phases clarify how various options are considered and highlight how only some options are carried forward while others are set aside.

In the *appraisal* phase, data and evidence on various policy alternatives proposed by different groups and actors, both in the public and in government, are identified and considered. Appraisals can take many forms, for example research reports, expert testimony, stakeholder input, or public consultation on an identified policy problem. Here, government agencies and officials both generate and receive input about policy problems and possible solutions.

This appraisal phase accompanies or is followed by a *dialogue* phase in which policy actors communicate both among themselves and externally their perspectives on the issue and their preferred potential solution. Sometimes, open meetings are held where presenters can discuss and debate proposed policy options. In other cases, the dialogue is closed or more circumscribed, with experts and societal representatives from business and labour organizations invited to speak for or against potential solutions in a variety of forums.

The choice and structure of these dialogic modes matter. As Hajer (2005) notes, the structure used for engaging input about policy options can make a considerable difference in the effects of that participation, both on the policy process and on the participants themselves. Formal consultations and formalized public hearings, for example, tend to privilege expert input and legalistic and technical analysis, which can frustrate new participants; while techniques that engage participants from less established organizations and points of view can add energy and enthusiasm to the dialogue over policy options but often do so at the expense of expertise and experience.

At the core of these deliberations, the aptly named *formulation* phase sees public officials responsible for developing a fully fledged policy alternative or set of alternatives weighing the evidence and opinions put forward on various policy options and drafting some form of proposal that identifies which of these options, if any, should advance to the ratification stage. Such feedback can take the form of draft legislation or regulations, or may identify the framework for subsequent public and private policy actors to negotiate a more developed plan of action.

Making these recommendations about which policy options to pursue will often provoke dissent by those who have seen their preferred strategies and instruments set aside during formulation activity. These objections and others are addressed during the *consolidation* phase, when formulators try to legitimize or justify their choices and win over converts from the ranks of the disaffected.

Policy actors often have an opportunity to provide more or less formal feedback on the recommended option(s), but also may lobby or undertake less formal kinds of activity to express their views and shape policy. Some actors who advocated alternative options may come around to joining the consensus simply so that they can stay connected to official policy development efforts. "Staying in the game" is often important, since supporting the policy solutions that are being recommended for further action may provide the opportunity to subsequently influence the policy during the decision-making and implementation stages. Other policy actors will register their continued dissent from specific policy options, hoping to leverage future developments from outside the consensus that has emerged over what is to be done. Sometimes this is done by undertaking direct action such as protests and strikes; other times, it is done more indirectly through legal and administrative challenges to the options being proposed for action.

Note once again that the limitations that lead policy actors to reject certain types of options need not be based on facts (Merton, 1948). If a significant number of influential actors in the policy subsystem believe that something is unworkable or unacceptable, this is often sufficient for its exclusion from further consideration in the policy process, regardless of its technical merits (Carlsson, 2000). Just as we have seen with the discussion of agenda-setting in the previous chapter, perception can be as real as reality itself in this phase of policy-making activity.

The Problematics of Policy Formulation

Procedural and Substantive Capacity Limits

A prominent characteristic of most policy formulation processes is that they share a concern for effectively outlining and anticipating constraints on government action. Policy appraisal, for example, often involves formal policy analysis, which is all about identifying the potential technical and political constraints a policy might face (Jordan et al., 2014). It also involves recognizing limitations on government capacities and competence, which uncover what is infeasible and, by implication, what is possible (Wu et al., 2015).

This may seem obvious, but it is not reflected in the literature, which often fails to acknowledge the need to clearly understand the practical limitations to a proposed course of action, including constitutional and resource constraints (Wellstead et al., 2013a, 2013b). For instance, the public choice theorists' key assumption—that politicians choose policies that best promote their electoral appeal—presumes politicians have more room for manoeuvre than is often actually available to them (Majone, 1989: 76). Neither politicians nor any other governmental actor can do anything they would like, whether or not they think it might appeal to voters or interest groups or their supporters and funders.

Constraints also arise from the limits of the state's administrative and financial capacity, for example, which can block alternatives that are expensive or labour intensive to implement. Of course, in some cases capacities may be higher than in others, and this can expand the range of possible policy options open to the government. Governments that have an ownership stake in economic sectors such as energy, finance, and transportation, for example, may have more policy options open to them than where the private sector exclusively delivers these goods and services and may resist initiatives they feel, justifiably or not, may adversely affect their profits and bottom lines.

Policy-makers also typically face numerous other substantive or procedural constraints when considering policy options beyond their own finances and resources. *Substantive* constraints are innate to the nature of the problem itself and linked to its "tractability," or ease of solution. Thus, policy-makers wishing to eliminate poverty do not have the option of printing money and distributing it to the poor because inflation will offset any gains, and so they must necessarily address the problem in more indirect ways. Similarly, the goal of promoting excellence in arts or sports cannot be accomplished simply by ordering people to be the best artists or sportswomen in the world. Problems such as global warming, for instance, cannot be entirely eliminated because there is no known effective solution that can be deployed without causing tremendous economic and social dislocations, which leaves policy-makers to tinker with options that barely scratch the surface of the problem (Howlett, 2014).

Substantive problems are thus "objective" in the sense that redefining them does not make them go away, and their resolution or partial resolution requires the use of state resources and capacities such as money, information, personnel, and/or the exercise of state authority. *Procedural* constraints, on the other hand have to do with limitations placed on governments by the process that is required to adopt an option and carry it out. These constraints may be either institutional or tactical. Institutional constraints, as discussed in Chapter 3, can include constitutional provisions, the nature of the organization of the state and society, and established patterns of ideas and beliefs that can prevent consideration of some options or promote others (Yee, 1996).

Efforts to control handguns in the United States, for example, run up against constraints imposed by the constitutional right to bear arms. Federalism imposes similar constraints on German, American, Mexican, and Australian policy-makers, among others, in areas of public policy from healthcare to energy where two levels of government must agree or share funding before anything can be done (Montpetit, 2002; Falkner, 2000).

How the main social groups are organized internally and are linked with the state also affects what governments can and cannot do. This is especially the case with the nature of political party and electoral systems, which can create "policy horizons" or limited sets of acceptable choices for specific actors in the policy process (Warwick, 2000; Bradford, 1999) beyond which they cannot move without losing support to opposition parties and candidates. This can centre on positions on specific issues such as abortion, for instance, which can spill over into areas such as limits on genomic and other kinds of DNA research or issues related to assisted suicide or euthanasia. In a similar vein, the predominance of specific sets of philosophical or religious ideas in many societies can lead to difficulties with potential policy solutions that might seem routine in others (deLeon, 1992), such as the assisted suicide and abortion cases cited above, which are considered acceptable in more secular countries but generally encounter resistance from churches and other religious groups in more devout ones.

Even if a positive design space exists, a government may not have the capacity required to carry out formulation or implement policy effectively. Such concerns about formulation and implementation capacity gaps have sparked a renewed interest among both practitioners and scholars in the nature, definition, and composition of policy capacity in the contemporary era (Fukuyama, 2013; Savoia & Sen, 2014; OECD, 2006).

It bears repeating in this context that, as was pointed out in Chapter 1, policy capacity results from the *combination* of skills and resources found at each of the individual, organizational, and systemic levels. At each of these levels, analytical capacities help to ensure policy actions are *technically sound* in the sense they can contribute to attainment of policy goals if carried out. Operational capacity allows the alignment of resources with policy actions so that they can be *implement*ed in practice. And political capacity helps to obtain and sustain *political support* for policy implementation (Wu et al., 2010; Tiernan & Wanna, 2006; Gleeson et al., 2009; Gleeson et al., 2011; Fukuyama, 2013; Rotberg, 2014).

At a minimum, then, formulation requires governments with a significant number of officials to possess a modicum of analytical capacity, defined as the ability to access and apply technical and scientific knowledge and analytical techniques (Howlett, 2015). This is especially important in light of the growing emphasis on evidence-based policy-making, which requires officials involved in policy work to absorb and process information in all aspects of policy formulation, decision-making, implementation, and evaluation. Many studies of knowledge utilization in government point out that governments do not often use evidence even when it is available because they lack the skills to do so. This discussion suggests that governments, as a whole, exhibit an uneven distribution of capacities, technical capabilities, and utilization practices across different organizational and thematic venues, and that this can be problematic for policy-making.

An efficient information system for collecting and disseminating knowledge within and across public-sector agencies is especially important in the context of the present-day emphasis on evidence-based policy-making, which requires not only the ability to analyse data but also the channels to make it available in a timely and systematic manner (Davies et al., 2000). Governments may need to build and enhance their evaluation capacity and ultimately their organization-al-analytical capacity if these are lacking.

Systemic-information capacity, defined as the general state of scientific, sta-tistical, and educational facilities in a society, allows policy-makers and workers to access high-quality information to carry on their analytical and managerial functions. The state of education in general, and of public policy education and training in particular, along with diligent collection and widespread dissemina-tion of data on public affairs, has a strong impact on governments' capacity to ad-dress policy problems. Varied policy analytical capacity within a policy subsystem may necessitate the participation of new institutions and actors if capabilities and competences are to be enhanced.

While most attention has been paid to the individual analytical level, the political capability of policy formulators should not be neglected. Political knowl-edge and experience build skills that support "policy acumen" (Wu et al., 2011). A keen nose for politics not only within but also relating to the broader poli-cy-making environment is essential for effective formulation. Identifying and understanding the interests and ideologies of other policy actors, as well as the relationships among them, are essential traits of successful public managers, as is understanding the political trade-offs necessary to broker deals among contend-ing actors and interests.

At the organizational-political level, a key challenge for formulation lies in developing learning relationships with governance partners and the public. To succeed, governments need to be able to define an issue and draw the public into focusing on it and actively contributing to its resolution (Post, Salmon, & Raile, 2008). Two-way communication through traditional policy dialogues and newer social media can allow citizens to monitor states' activities, enter into dialogue with state actors on issues that matter to them, and influence political outcomes. (Haider, Mcloughlin, & Scott, 2011).

Systemic-political capacity is the most all-encompassing of all capacity types and is important since it embodies the potential to shape all the other variants. Insofar as it influences the broad environment that frames governmental activi-ties, systemic-political capacity concerns the level of trust in the political, social, economic, and security spheres of policy action, which is an important determi-nant of the nature of formulation processes.

Context in Policy Formulation: Design and Non-Design Orientations

In the policy sciences, the concept of policy "design" has been increasingly linked to policy formulation. Policies are seen as the result of efforts made by governments to alter aspects of their own or public behaviour in order to pursue some end or purpose they consider important. In recent years, studies of formulation have evolved from an earlier focus on achieving singular purposes such as social protection, provision of health and education, or increasing civil society engagement. Policies are seen to be increasingly integrated and engaged in multiple levels of public administration spanning multiple sectors. They are also viewed as dynamic and context-specific in that they comprise complex arrangements of policy goals and means that have arisen at different times and in different locations through processes of policy formulation unique to each jurisdiction and government (Howlett & Cashore, 2009).

Several processes of policy formulation have been revealed by empirical studies, ranging from bargaining to partisan electoral manoeuvring to more design-oriented approaches. "Design" is usually thought to exist at one end of a spectrum ranging from contingent "non-design" to more precise instrument selection to match problems and solutions (Howlett & Mukherjee, 2014). Policy design is thus an approach to formulation that is used to examine and assess the policy instruments that are proposed in strategies for problem-solving projects and programs, as well as their use during policy implementation (May, 2003; Howlett, 2014; Linder & Peters, 1988; Schon, 1988, 1992). In this view, policy design involves the effort to more or less systematically develop efficient and effective policies through applying knowledge about policy means gained from experience and reason.

Policy design, in this sense, is a specific mode of formulation based on the gathering of knowledge about the effects of policy instruments and tools on policy targets. Applying that knowledge to developing and implementing policies to attain desired policy objectives represents the essence of the design process (Bobrow, 2006; Bobrow & Dryzek, 1987; Montpetit, 2003; Weaver, 2009, 2010). This involves the deliberate and conscious attempt to define policy goals and connect them in an instrumental fashion to tools expected to realize those objectives (Gilabert & Lawford-Smith, 2012; Majone, 1975; May, 2003; Linder & Peters, 1988; Wintges, 2007; Bason, 2014; Brown & Wyatt 2010).

Problem-centred policy design consists of considering alternative arrangements deemed potentially capable of resolving or addressing some aspect of a policy problem, one or more of which is ultimately put into practice. Much existing work on policy design adopts this orientation uncritically and advocates or desires policy-making to take on this technique (Tribe, 1972).

Such a problem-centred policy-making process is, of course, only one possible orientation or set of practices that can be followed (Colebatch, 1998; Tribe,

1972). In contrast to those scholars who view policy-making as intentional and instrumentally rational, for example, many commentators, pundits, and jaded and cynical members of the public often assume that all policy-making is driven by politics and hence is more or less irrational and involved in various processes of non-design. That is, policy formulators may base their analyses on logic, knowledge, and experience, but also upon purely political calculations that can also serve to generate alternatives (Bendor, Kumar, & Siegel, 2009; Sidney, 2007).

Indeed, *politically centred policy design* is a staple of policy-making in democracies and non-democracies alike. Although instances of politics driving policy are well known in political science, they have not been examined as deeply in the policy sciences, and the extent to which such considerations as political gain or blame avoidance calculations outweigh instrumental factors in policy formulation poses a key question (Hood, 2010) that empirical studies have begun to illuminate.

Indeed, politics has always been one of the primary determinants of social policy choices, especially in democracies, as governments increasingly realized that they needed popular support in order to retain office (Flora & Heidenheimer, 1981; Overbye, 1994). Bismarck, for example, established health and pension programs in the German Empire in the 1870s primarily to undercut the growing support for socialist parties among the working class (Rimlinger, 1971) and only secondarily to perfect a solution to the problem of income during old age. Similarly, the spread of democratization has deepened the role of politics in policy-making, especially in the area of social security (Amenta & Carruthers, 1988; Myles, 1989). Governments throughout the world, from Europe to Latin America, heightened their social welfare efforts in response to the spread of trade unions and the electoral success of the political parties affiliated with them (Korpi, 1980; Shalev, 1983; Myles, 1989). Thus, politics has always been an integral part, and a primary determinant, of policy formulation, particularly in social policies.

There are also situations in which policy formulation is driven by neither instrumental problem-solving nor socio-political concerns, a phenomenon and process of policy formulation that can be described as "non-design." This includes a variety of contexts in which social policy formulators or decision-makers engage in interest-driven trade-offs or log-rolling between different values or resource uses, often in response to concerns about legislative expediency.

Or, in other circumstances, the same non-design situation can emerge when policy-makers engage in venal or corrupt behaviour in which personal gain from a decision may trump other evaluative and decision-making criteria (Cohen et al., 1979; Dryzek, 1983; Kingdon, 1984; Eijlander, 2005; Franchino & Hoyland, 2009). In such formulation and decision processes, design considerations may be more or less absent, and the quality of the logical or empirical relations between policy components as solutions to problems may be incorrect or ignored

(Cohen, March, & Olsen, 1979; Dryzek, 1983; Eijlander, 2005; Franchino & Hoyland, 2009; Kingdon, 1984; Sager & Rielle, 2013).

The high level of contingency found in some decision-making contexts, identified in the previous section, for example, has led some critical observers of policy efforts to suggest that policies cannot be "designed" in the sense that a house or a piece of furniture is (Dryzek & Ripley, 1988; deLeon, 1988) and suggest that non-design processes dominate policy formulation (Cohen et al., 1972 to 1979). However, this opinion is not universally shared or endorsed (Mucciaroni, 1992). On the contrary, it is often suggested that most if not all policies are carefully crafted to ensure that policy means are capable of achieving policy goals in a relatively cost-efficient manner and that exceptions to this rule are rare (Packwood, 2002; Kay, 2011).

Some of this disagreement is philosophical in nature (Tribe, 1972; Nelson, 1977, Forester, 1983; Dery, 1984), but to a very great extent many of these disagreements are the result of a poor record of empirical studies uncovering the motives and techniques of policy design and formulation (Junginger, 2013). This observation is true of policy formulation in general, but is especially acute in the design of major policy areas such as social policies, which are major areas of government spending and action with a long history dating back over several centuries which is difficult to trace and assess (Esping-Anderson, 1990; Chindarkar et al., 2017).

Understanding which kind of formulation process is likely to unfold or has unfolded is the key to understanding this phase of policy-making. That is, the design of successful policies requires thinking about policy-making in such a way as to fully take into account the dual purposes—both technical/problem and political—that polices serve and the extent to which efforts to attain those ends are adequately resourced and capable. An effective study of policy formulation will thus seek to understand its "design space" (Hillier, Musgrove, & O'Sullivan, 1972; Hillier & Leaman, 1974; Gero, 1990).

An optimal situation in public policy formulation is one wherein the interests and aims of both politicians and technical analysts and advisors are congruent and policy-makers seek to attain both policy and political objectives through the same tools. While policy-makers both within and outside the government are multi-dimensional creatures with varied needs, political survival is a major concern that leads them to make policies to garner political support for their election or re-election as well as to solve public problems (Mukherjee & Howlett, 2015). The health insurance program launched by the Thaksin government in Thailand in 2001 is an example of such a policy: it extended insurance coverage to the entire population while reducing total health expenditures at the same time, and won the government the subsequent election (Ramesh, 2008).

As Figure 5.1 shows, other kinds of policy design spaces are also very possible. In those other spaces, either one or the other goal is missing or contested. As a result, policy processes other than the effective and legitimated ones found in an optimal design space are likely to occur. The pursuit of political objectives

Figure 5.1 Policy Design Spaces and Process Implications

		Political Goals	
		Very Important	*Less Important*
Technical/Problem-Centred Concerns	*Very Important*	*Optimal Design Space* High-profile policy-making encompassing both technical and political considerations. Effective policy-making	*Technical Design Space* Legal-technical policy-making that may consider politically infeasible options. Technocratic policy-making
	Less Important	*Political Design Space* Valence/electorally driven policy-making that may consider technically infeasible options. Populist policy-making	*Suboptimal Design Space* Excels at neither political nor technical analysis. Contested and ineffective policy-making

unaccompanied by the intention to solve a policy problem, for example, may be described as "populist" policy-making that focuses on "valence" issues, which may or may not be susceptible to effective action (such as fighting crime). Measures that seek to address problems regardless of political implications may be described as "technocratic" policy-making, which can easily generate politically infeasible options (such as raising taxes to increase welfare budgets to deal with homelessness). In situations where neither political nor technical concerns are perceived to be legitimate, or when policy-makers are pressured to adopt contradictory positions because of conflicting political and/or technical demands, policy-making may be paralyzed or result in ineffective or damaging policies.

The Substance of Policy Formulation: Selecting Policy Tools

All of this discussion raises the questions of what, exactly, is being designed or formulated. Policy formulation in this sense is primarily about assessing and arriving at the mixture of policy tools or instruments to be used to achieve policy goals. As pointed out in earlier chapters, policies have different components but it is instruments that give them effect. Hence policy tools retain a special place in formulation activity.

A typical policy involves abstract general aims or goals (such as, in the cases of criminal justice or education policy, attaining a just or prosperous society), along with a set of less abstract objectives such as reducing crime or providing better educational opportunities. Further, those objectives themselves must be concretized in a set of specific targets that allow policy resources to be directed toward goal attainment, such as reducing specific types of crimes to specific levels within specified periods of time or increasing post-secondary educational attendance within some set temporal period (Stavins, 2008; Kooiman, 2008).

Similarly, the means or techniques for achieving these goals also exist on several levels. Highly abstract preferences for specific forms of policy implementation, such as a preference for the use of market, government, or non-profit forms of organization can inform the implementation of policy goals in areas such as healthcare, or crime prevention. A more concrete focus on the use of specific governing tools or mechanisms can lead policy-makers to focus on regulation, information campaigns, public enterprises, or government subsidies to alter actor behaviour, for example, in promoting or increasing wellness or preventing crime. At the most specific level of deciding or determining exactly how policy tools should be "calibrated" during implementation in order to achieve policy targets, policy actors can attempt to set a specific number of additional police on the streets within a specified period of time, or a specific level of subsidy to non-profit groups that provide additional hospital beds or other types of health services within a set period of time (Howlett, 2005; Stavins, 2008)

Thus, while formulating a policy to tackle traffic congestion, for example, policy-makers must simultaneously consider whether to build more roads, improve public transit, restrict automobile usage, or use some combination of these, as well as the tools by which the policy will actually be implemented. These *policy tools*, also known as *policy instruments* and *governing instruments*, are the actual means or devices that governments put to use when implementing policies. Proposals that emanate from the formulation stage, therefore, will specify not only whether or not to act on a policy issue, but also how best to address the problem and implement a solution. For example, in a case such as that of deteriorating water quality, policy options could emphasize public educational campaigns that urge people to refrain from polluting activities; they could embrace regulations that prohibit all activities causing the pollution; they could propose a subsidy to the polluting firms encouraging them to switch to safer technologies; or they could advance some combination of these or other means (Gunningham et al., 1998; Gunningham & Young, 1997).

When policy actors are exploring policy options, they consider not only what to do but also how to do it. Conceptually, an instrumentally oriented policy formulation process begins with an assessment of the abilities of different policy tools to affect policy outputs and outcomes and the kinds of resources required to allow them to operate as intended (Hood, 1986; Salamon, 2002). Such instrumental knowledge is required to understand how the use of specific instruments affects target group behaviour and compliance with government aims (Weaver, 2009a, 2009b, 2013, 2015). It thus includes knowledge and consideration of many constraints on tool use originating in the limits of existing knowledge, prevailing governance structures, and other arrangements and behaviours that may preclude consideration of certain options and promote others (Howlett, 2009a,

2011). It requires both analytical and evidentiary capacity on the part of the government as well as the intention to exercise such skills (Wu et al., 2015).

The variety of instruments available to policy-makers is limited only by their imaginations. Rather than attempt to construct exhaustive lists, which had already produced arcane inventories (such as the scheme for at least 64 general types of instruments in European economic policy produced by Kirschen and his colleagues [1964]), policy researchers have sought ways to group roughly similar types of instruments into a few categories whose merits and demerits could then be analyzed more easily. Scholars have made numerous attempts to identify such instruments and classify them into meaningful categories (see Salamon & Lund, 1989: 32–3; Lowi, 1985; Bemelmans et al., 1998; Balch, 1980).

A simple and powerful taxonomy, the "NATO model," was developed by Christopher Hood (1986a), who noted that all policy tools used one of four broad categories of governing resources and thus could be classified according to their primary resource use. Thus, Hood argued that governments confront public problems through the use of the information in their possession as a central policy actor ("*nodality*"), their legal powers ("*authority*"), their money ("*treasure*"), or the formal organizations available to them ("*organization*"), or "NATO."

The idea is that governments can use these resources to manipulate policy actors, for example, by withdrawing or making available information or money, by using their coercive powers to force other actors to undertake activities they desire, or simply by undertaking the activity themselves using their own personnel and expertise.

Using Hood's idea of governing resources, a basic taxonomy of instrument categories can be set out. Figure 5.2 presents such a classification scheme with illustrative examples of the types of policy tools found in each category.

Figure 5.2 Policy Tools, by Principal Governing Resource

	Nodality	*Authority*	*Treasure*	*Organizations*
Substantive Tools	Information Campaign Exhortation Benchmarking and Performance Indicators Commission and Inquires Nudging	Regulation Delegated and Self-Regulation Standard Setting	Grants and Loans Tax Expenditures Taxes User Charges	Direct Provision Public Enterprises, Quangos, and Partnerships Co-production Family, Community, and Voluntary Organizations
Procedural Tools	Commissions and Inquiries	Advisory Committees	Creating and Funding Interest Groups and Think Tanks	Market Creation Government Reorganization

(Cells provide examples of instruments in each category.)

Source: Adapted from Christopher Hood, *The Tools of Government* (Chatham, NJ: Chatham House, 1986), 124–5.

These substantive tools have their *procedural* counterparts—that is, instruments designed mainly to affect or alter aspects of policy *processes* rather than social or economic behaviour per se (Riker, 1983, 1986; Dunsire, 1986, 1993a), often in order to support or bolster the effectiveness of substantive tools.

In the following discussion, we offer examples of common policy tools that are included in policy designs using Hood's schema along with a discussion of their strengths and weaknesses, factors that condition their appearance in proposals emerging from the policy formulation process, however it is undertaken.

Nodality, or Information-Based Policy Tools

The first category of policy tools that Hood identified involve the use of information resources at government's disposal. There are many such tools, as the possibilities outlined below demonstrate.

Public Information Campaigns

Governments chronicle a great deal about societal activities through both routine reporting and special studies. It is not uncommon, therefore, for government to disseminate information with the expectation that individuals and firms and other organizations and actors will change their behaviour in response to it. This information is often fairly general, intended to make societal actors more knowledgeable so that they can make informed choices. For instance, data on tourism, trade, and economic and social trends can be disseminated by the government through public service advertising, leaving it to the population to draw conclusions and respond accordingly (Salmon, 1989b).

Public information may also be more precisely targeted to elicit a particular response, as in the case of publicizing information on the ill effects of smoking (Weiss & Tschirhart, 1994; Vedung & van der Doelen, 1998). In either case, there is no obligation on the public to respond in a particular manner (Adler & Pittle, 1984). In many countries, this passive release of information may be mandated or facilitated by freedom of information laws (Relyea, 1977; Bennett, 1990, 1992a); Qualter, 1985).

Findings on the impact of public information campaigns suggest that disclosure will not automatically lead to policy change. Other conditions must be present, such as an ability to calculate the impact of data on (and by) societal actors (Cohen & Santhakumar, 2007). The public's capacity to interpret information has also been shown to vary by socio-economic status, by the quantity of information presented, and by the ways in which this information is presented (Howells, 2005).

Exhortation

Exhortation, or "suasion," as it is also called, involves slightly more government activity than pure dissemination of information (Stanbury & Fulton, 1984). Here, public effort is devoted to influencing the preferences and actions of societal members, rather than just by informing the public about a situation with the hope that behaviour will spontaneously change in a desired manner (Salmon, 1989a, 1989b). Rather, public advertisements urge people to undertake certain kinds of behaviour such as keeping fit and healthy, not to waste water or energy, or to use public transportation (Firestone, 1970). Agency spokespersons can play an important in both delivering and shaping these messages (Lee, 2001). Consultations between government officials and financial, industry, or labour representatives are another form of exhortation because government officials often use these meetings to try to alter target group behaviour in the direction they would prefer it to go.

Ultimately, government exhortation can only go so far. As Stanbury and Fulton (1984) conclude, "In the absence of positive or negative inducements (or more bluntly, leverage), most efforts at suasion probably have either a low probability of success or have a relatively short shelf life." At best, it should be used in conjunction with other instruments when they are available. Complex problems, such as influencing private corporations to make their industrial production more sustainable, require policy packages that also include other components of the NATO tool kit (Norberg-Bohm, 1999).

Benchmarking and Performance Indicators

Benchmarking is increasingly used as a process-oriented information-gathering technique in the public sector (Papaioannou et al., 2006). In theory, it enables structured comparison and, when successful, enhances the opportunity for policy learning by presenting relevant information in ways that can generate policy insight (Johnsen, 2005). The standardization of benchmarks promotes coordination of policy across jurisdictions, as seen in the EU's use of an "open method of coordination" in sharing information on employment and labour market policies (de la Porte et al., 2001). Performance management schemes can also work to redefine the problems addressed by public agencies such as hospitals or universities (Adcroft & Willis, 2005).

Previous chapters have already discussed the strengths and weaknesses of measures and indicators. Such measures often can improve policy delivery but are also susceptible to gaming and evasion, making it unclear what their actual impact on target behaviour will be.

Commissions and Inquiries

Governments often employ temporary bodies to gather information about an issue or sometimes just to procrastinate in making a decision, hoping that public pressure for action will fade by the time a report is prepared. Foremost among the techniques they utilize to do so is the ad hoc inquiry, commission, or task force. These agencies exist in many forms and are often established to deal with notorious and particularly troubling policy problems. They attempt to provide a forum that combines specialized academic research and general public input into the diagnosis and potential resolution of policy problems, generating information that becomes available to all participants in the policy process and altering their knowledge base as a result (Sheriff, 1983; Wraith & Lamb, 1971: 302–23; Chapman, 1973; Elliott and McGuinness, 2001; Resodihardjo, 2006; McDowall Robinson, 1969; Cairns, 1990a; d'Ombrain, 1997).

In many jurisdictions, a system of formal reviews of ongoing policy areas is also evident. These reviews serve as "institutionalized" task forces or investigations into ongoing issues and the efforts made by government bodies to deal with them (Bellehumeur, 1997; de la Mothe, 1996; Raboy, 1995; Banting, 1995). These reviews are usually done in-house but sometimes also involve the use of outside experts (Owens & Rayner, 1999).

Such reviews can serve an important purpose in making policies more flexible or agile. However, they can also introduce uncertainties into policy formulation and can fall prey to the vagaries of who takes part in them and what ideas they put forward.

Nudging

Behavioural policy instruments—commonly known as nudging—are new types of tools for promoting behavioural change and policy compliance that also rely upon the manipulation of the information available to consumers and other policy targets. These behavioural instruments rely upon what Herbert Simon termed the "bounded rationality" (Simon, 1955, 1957, 1976) of individuals. That is, actual human behaviour frequently falls short of objective rationality because of difficulties associated with anticipating the future and a lack of complete knowledge of all possible alternative and consequences (1976). Over time, predictable behavioural departures from the predicted utilitarian model have been documented so as to identify a number of behavioural patterns that influence individual decision-making. An example of this is the use of "heuristics," or mental shortcuts that reduce the cognitive burden associated with decision-making (Shah & Oppenheimer, 2008; Ariely 2010).

In their pioneering work, Amos Tversky and Daniel Kahneman identified three central heuristic principles affecting behaviour in less than rational but nevertheless predictable ways—availability, representativeness, and anchoring (1974). In later work they demonstrated the influence of other traits such as framing (of acts, contingencies, and outcomes) on preferences and the characteristic nonlinearities of values and decision weights (Kahneman & Tversky, 1979; Tversky & Kahneman, 1981; 2000). Following Kahneman and Tversky, a number of other behavioural patterns that influence decision-making have since been noted, such as "overconfidence" (Moore & Healy, 2008), "present bias," (O'Donoghue & Rabin, 1999) and the tendency to gravitate toward the default option (Lunn, 2014). Such patterns of behaviour have been explained by drawing on concepts from psychology which speak of two systems of thinking that humans employ—system I and system II. While system I is more intuitive and automatic (adopts a narrower frame and employs little or no effort), system II is reflective and deliberate (adopts a wider frame and employs more effort) (Kahneman, 2013) Nudges such as painting footsteps on floors to lead subway riders to take the stairs versus an escalator and hence improve their health deploy the automatic system (Kahneman, 2003).

An increasing awareness and recognition of these behavioural processes has contributed toward the use of behavioural policy tools that aim to reduce "behavioural market failures" (Thaler & Sunstein, 2008). Such behaviourally premised policy instruments as organ donor opt-out defaults and drawing flies or targets on urinals to discourage unwanted splashing and janitorial expenses make use of insights drawn from behavioural sciences so as to secure better compliance with government aims and policies. Below, we briefly describe some of these nudge instruments: information disclosure, invoking social norms, changing defaults, goal setting, and framing.

Information Disclosure
Provision of information that is comprehensible, simple, and accessible, can be used to shift individual behaviour in a desired direction. This may take the form of providing individuals with information regarding the otherwise hidden consequence or costs of certain actions, or it may take the form of informing them about their own past choices and its consequences—i.e., "smart disclosure" (Sunstein, 2014). For example, the deployment of smart meters that provided real-time as well as historic-consumption information was shown to contribute more to energy savings than other forms of information (AECOM, 2011). Similarly, a randomized controlled trial testing the effect of energy labelling (providing information on the monetary lifetime running cost of the electric appliance) provided robust evidence that labelling resulted in purchase of more energy-efficient appliances (Department of Energy and Climate Change, 2014). Other studies have found similar effects regarding the influence of targeted information (see for instance Codagnone et al., 2013; Delmas et al., 2013; Kallbekken & Sælen, 2011). Estonia, South Africa, and the UK (OECD, 2017) are providing simplified information to consumers on energy consumption with the expectation of changing their behaviour in a desired direction.

Invoking Social Norms
Social psychologists regard social norms—defined as the broadly shared beliefs about what group members are likely to do and ought to do—as an important dimension affecting human behaviour (McKirnan, 1980; Staub, 1972) and these norms can be invoked to nudge behaviour in a preferred direction. Highlighting what most people think others should do, for example, acts as a nudge toward

changing behaviour from dog-walking to traffic control (Sunstein 2014). For instance, an energy conservation program in the US provided utility consumers with information about how their energy usage compared to that of their neighbours, which resulted in a subsequent reduction in energy consumption (Allcott, 2011). In the context of climate change, social norms have been successfully invoked across countries in the energy sector (see Ayres et al., 2013; Dolan & Metcalfe, 2012), water sector (Datta et al., 2015; Ferraro & Price, 2013; Ferraro et al., 2011), and others to engender pro-environmental behavioural changes (Goldstein et al., 2008; Kuhfuss et al., 2016). Social norms may also be applied to organizations to overcome their reluctance to invest in energy-saving technologies (Hall et al., 2012), given the strong effects exerted by normative and mimetic behaviour (Perez-Batres et al., 2011). Social norms also operate on policy-makers, wherein the actions of neighbouring jurisdictions can influence policy choice, for example in the case of carbon taxes (Krause, 2011).

Goal Setting

Getting people to commit to certain strategies ahead of implementation may be used as a policy tool to motivate action, counteract lack of willpower, and overcome the tendency to procrastinate (Sunstein, 2014). The greater the perceived cost of breaking such a commitment, the more effective it is in achieving behaviour change (Dolan & Metcalfe, 2012). This can be done, for example, with registered retirement saving plan contributions by making it appear difficult or costly to withdraw funds once they are "locked in." Another related mechanism to nudge behaviour in the desired direction is to make the commitment public. Individuals' desire to maintain a consistent and positive self-image (Cialdini, 2008) makes them likely to uphold commitments in order to avoid reputational damage or cognitive dissonance (Festinger, 1962). In Costa Rica a randomized controlled trial involving 5,626 households tested three behavioural treatments, one of which was plan-making (establishing personal goals for water use reduction). It was found that plan-making was the most effective in reducing household water consumption (Datta et al., 2015).

Changing Defaults

Defaults establish goals in policy settings, including outcomes that apply when individuals do not meet these standards (Brown & Krishna, 2004; Johnson & Goldstein, 2003). Since governments normally define policy settings, designing defaults such as automatic opt-ins and opt-outs for certain government programs can have a profound impact on individuals' choices and the resulting outcomes (Barr et al., 2011). According to Sunstein & Reisch (2013), three principal factors contribute to the large effect of defaults on outcomes: (1) suggestion and endorsement—i.e., people who consider themselves non-specialists think that the default was chosen with good reason (see McKenzie, 2006); (2) the tendency to procrastinate and the power of inertia, which lead people to continue with the status quo (see Sethi-Iyengar et al., 2004); and (3) defaults provide a reference point relative to which changes can be evaluated. Examples of "climate-friendly defaults" (Sunstein & Reisch, 2016) can be found in Southern Germany, where they resulted in a significantly higher percentage of customers buying green electricity (Pichert & Katsikopoulos, 2008). Another study exploring consumer uptake of an energy-efficient but costly compact fluorescent light bulb (CFLB) versus an inefficient but inexpensive incandescent light bulb (ILB) found a lower preference for the ICB when the energy-efficient CFLB was established as the de-fault standard (Dinner et al., 2011). Defaults have also made their way to several municipal electricity utilities in Switzerland that have changed the default elec-tricity tariff to include a greener mix of energy sources (Sousa Lourenço et al., 2016).

Framing

Framing is a cognitive bias in which individuals tend to make decisions influ-enced by how information is presented or framed (Tversky & Kahneman, 1981). Presenting the same information in different formats can affect people's deci-sions: behaviour is directed toward mental representations of the world (rather than its actual state), and these mental representations may not "necessarily constitute a faithful rendition of actual circumstances" (Zaval & Cornwell, 2016; Mullainathan & Shafir, 2013). Information that is vivid and salient usually has a larger impact on behaviour than information that is abstract (Sunstein, 2014).

Research has demonstrated that differences in the way environmental issues are framed affects individuals' engagement with the issue (Gifford & Comeau, 2011). Another study, related to the fuel efficiency of vehicles, found that manip-ulating information on the fuel economy labels shifted preferences toward more fuel-efficient choices (Camilleri & Larrick, 2014). Similarly, even a seemingly minor change in terminology, such as the use of the term "carbon tax" instead of "carbon offset," was found to have a strong influence on the level of support and preference for a certain policy (Hardisty et al., 2010).

Authority-Based Policy Tools

Regulation

Regulation is a prescription by the government that must be complied with by the intended targets; failure to do so usually involves a penalty. This type of in-strument is often referred to as "rule-making" or "command-and-control" regu-lation (Kerwin, 1994, 1999). Regulations take various forms and include rules, standards, permits, prohibitions, laws, and executive orders (Keyes, 1996). Some regulations, such as proscribing criminal behaviour, take the form of laws en-forced by police and the judicial system (Rosenbloom, 2007). Most regulations, however, are written and promulgated by civil servants working under the delegated authority of enabling legislation. These regulations are then administered by a government department or a specialized, quasi-judicial government agency (first called independent regulatory commissions in the US) that is more or less autonomous of government control in its day-to-day operations.

The nature of regulations varies somewhat depending on whether they are targeted at economic or social problems. Economic regulations have been the traditional form of regulation and their purpose has been to control specific aspects of the market economy, such as the prices and volumes of production, or return on investment, or the entry into or exit of firms from an industry (Salamon, 2002b). A good example of this type of regulation is that carried out by various kinds of marketing boards, regulatory bodies that are particularly prominent in the agricultural sector. The intent of such boards is to restrict the supply of agricultural output to keep farm commodity prices at or above a certain threshold of income deemed acceptable for farmers. Their objective is to correct perceived imbalances or inequities in economic relationships that may emerge as a result of the operation of market forces.

Social regulations are of more recent origin and refer to controls in matters of health, safety, and societal behaviour such as civil rights and discrimination of various sorts. They have more to do with our physical and moral well-being than with our pocketbooks, though the costs to business of certain regulatory measures, such as environmental protection, often are passed on to the consumer. Examples of social regulation include rules regarding liquor consumption and sales, gambling, consumer product safety, occupational hazards, water-related hazards, air and noise pollution, discrimination on the basis of religion, race, gender, or ethnicity, and pornography (Padberg, 1992). With a proliferation of industry-developed norms and standards for ethical and environmentally sustainable business practices, government's regulatory role can sometimes involve enforcing compliance with these private codes of practice (Baksi & Bose, 2007).

There are several advantages of regulation as a policy instrument (see Mitnick, 1980: 401–4). First, the information needed to establish regulation is often less compared to other tools. Second, where the concerned activity is deemed entirely undesirable, as is the case with films and videos depicting pedophilia, it is easier to establish regulations prohibiting the possession of such products than to devise ways of encouraging the production and distribution of other types of more benign materials. Third, regulations allow for better coordination of government efforts and planning because of the greater predictability they entail. Fourth, their predictability makes them a more suitable instrument in times of crisis when an immediate response is needed or desired. Fifth, regulations may be less costly than other instruments, such as subsidies or tax incentives.

The disadvantages of regulation are equally telling (see Anderson, 1976). First, regulations, whether technical or not, are set politically and hence quite often distort voluntary or private-sector activities and can promote economic inefficiencies (Wilson, 1974). Price regulations and direct allocation restrict the operation of the forces of demand and supply and affect the price mechanism in capitalist societies, raising the potential for economic windfalls through distortions in the market. These tendencies create powerful incentives for regulated firms to try to "capture" the organizations that supervise them, to yield ongoing economic advantages through regulation. To avoid such capture, the regulatory body can nurture working relationships with other societal actors who will keep up the pressure to regulate in the public interest (Sabatier, 1975, 1977). Second, regulations can, at times, inhibit innovation and technological progress because of the market security they afford existing firms and the limited opportunities for experimentation they permit. Third, regulations are often inflexible and do not permit the consideration of individual circumstances, resulting in decisions and outcomes not intended by the regulation (Dyerson & Mueller, 1993). Such instances annoy the subject population and often create easy targets for the government's critics.

The early 1980s saw a turning point in the debate on regulations, as the idea that regulations were conceived and executed solely in the public interest came under heavy attack from a wide range of critics.[1] Understanding why *deregulation* occurred has proven to be a challenge to regulatory theorists, however. In Libecap's view, five conjectures regarding the forces animating deregulation are offered: (1) dissatisfied incumbent firms join with consumers in lobbying for deregulation and seek to capture quasi-rents during the transition to a more competitive environment; (2) stockholders, dismayed at poor firm performance, pressure management to jettison regulation; (3) management chafes at government restrictions; (4) regulators lose enthusiasm for regulatory controls; and (5) exogenous forces, such as changes in regulatory policies in other jurisdictions, force adoption of more competitive arrangements (Libecap, 1986). Often, all five reasons underlie deregulation efforts.

Delegated or Self-Regulation

Unlike command-and-control regulation, delegated regulation, or self-regulation, involves governments allowing non-governmental actors to regulate themselves. However, while non-governmental entities may, in effect, regulate themselves, they typically do so with the implicit or explicit permission of governments (Gunningham & Rees, 1997; Donahue & Nye, 2001). These delegations can be explicit and direct, for example, when governments allow professions such as doctors, lawyers, or teachers to regulate themselves through the grant of a licensing monopoly (see Sinclair, 1997; Tuohy & Wolfson, 1978). However, they can also be less explicit, as occurs in situations where manufacturing companies develop standards for products or where independent certification firms or associations certify that certain standards have been met in various kinds of private practices (see Andrews, 1998; Gunningham & Rees, 1997; Iannuzzi, 2001).

While many standards are invoked by government command-and-control regulation, others can be developed in the private sphere. As long as these are not replaced by government-enforced standards, they represent the acquiescence of a government to the private rules, a form of delegated regulation (see Haufler, 2000, 2001; Knill, 2001).

A major advantage of the use of voluntary standard setting should be in cost savings, since governments do not have to pay for the creation, administration, and renewal of such standards, as would be the case with traditional command-and-control regulation. While these attributes offer a powerful general incentive toward delegated regulation, empirical findings of negotiated environmental rule-making in the US show that both time and cost savings turned out to be minimal compared to command-and-control processes (Coglianese, 1997). The potential cost savings of delegation can be highest in professional areas such as medicine or law, where information asymmetries between those being regulated and regulators mean that public administration of standards is especially expensive and time consuming. Such programs can also be effective in international settings, where establishing effective governmental regimes, such as sustainable forestry practices, can be especially difficult (Elliott & Schlaepfer, 2001). However, possible administrative cost savings must again be balanced against additional costs to society that might result from ineffective or inefficient administration of voluntary standards, especially those related to noncompliance.

Advisory Committees

A long-established procedural tool based on authority is the *advisory committee* (Smith, 1977; Gill, 1940). Some of these are formalized and more or less permanent, while others tend to be more informal and temporary (Brown, 1955, 1972; Balla & Wright, 2001). Both involve governments selecting representatives to sit on these committees and the extension to those representatives of some special rights within the policy process. Many countries have created permanent bodies to provide advice to governments on particular ongoing issue areas, such as the economy, science and technology, and the environment (for Canada, see Phidd, 1975; Doern, 1971; Howlett, 1990). However, many other ad hoc bodies can be found in almost every policy area. These range from general advisory committees and specialized clientele advisory committees to specific task-oriented committees and others (see Peters & Barker, 1993; Barker & Peters, 1993).

Advisory bodies are often situated closer to societal actors than the formal governments they report to. They are usually quite specific in their focus and conduct different types of hearings and "stakeholder" consultations to receive input and, at times, to engage in dialogues that seek to build consensus with, and among, societal actors (van de Kerkof, 2006; Flitner, 1986; Chapman, 1973). These advisory bodies should not be confused with the more open-ended, research-oriented organizations created under these same titles (Sheriff, 1983).

Ad hoc task forces and similar bodies are not intended to develop new knowledge or promulgate current know-how, but rather to provide a venue for organized and unorganized interests to present their views and analyses on pressing contemporary problems, or to frame or reframe issues in such a way that they can be dealt with by governments (Owens & Rayner, 1999; Jenson, 1994; Barker et al., 1993; Peters & Barker, 1993).

Exactly who should be on such committees, how often they should meet, what powers they have, and other design factors heavily influence their legitimacy and effectiveness.

Treasure-Based Policy Tools

A third general category of policy instrument relies not so much on government personnel or governmental authority for its effectiveness, but rather on public financial resources and the government's ability to raise and disburse funds. This refers to all forms of financial transfers to individuals, firms, and organizations from governments or from other individuals, firms, or organizations under government direction. These transfers can serve as incentives or disincentives for private actors to follow government's wishes. The transfer rewards or penalizes and thus encourages or discourages a desired activity, thereby affecting social actors' estimates of costs and benefits of the various alternatives. While the final choice is left to individuals and firms, the likelihood of the desired choice being made is enhanced because of the financial subsidy it draws (Beam & Conlan, 2002; Cordes, 2002). Several key types of such tools are set out below.

Financial Incentives

One of the most prominent forms of treasure-based instrument is *grants*, which are "expenditures made in support of some end worthy in itself, almost as a form of recognition, reward or encouragement, but not closely calibrated to the costs of achieving that end" (Pal, 1992: 152; Haider, 1989). Grants are usually offered to producers, with the objective of making them provide more of a desired good or service than they would otherwise. The expenditure comes out of the government's general revenues, which requires legislative approval. Examples of grants include government funds provided to schools, universities, and public transportation operators.

Another prominent form of subsidy is the *tax incentive* involving "remission of taxes in some form, such as deferrals, deductions, credits, exclusions, or preferred rates, contingent on some act (or the omission of some act)" (Mitnick, 1980: 365). Tax incentives or tax expenditures involve taxes or other forms of government revenues, such as royalties or licence fees, which are forgone. That is, a subsidy is provided since revenues that would normally have been collected are not. Governments find tax incentives appealing, not least because they are hidden in complex tax codes and so escape outside scrutiny, which makes their establishment and continuation relatively easy (McDaniel, 1989; Leeuw, 1998; Howard, 1997). Moreover, in most countries they do not need legislative budgetary approval, for no money is actually spent; rather, revenues are forgone (Maslove, 1994). Nor is their use constrained by availability of funds, because they involve no direct expenditure. They are also easier to administer and enforce because no special bureaucracy needs to be created to administer them, as would be the case with many other instruments (Brunori, 1997). The existing taxation bureaucracy is usually entrusted with the task. The amounts "spent" in this manner are huge. For example, Christopher Howard has estimated that US federal tax expenditures alone accounted for $744.5 billion or 42 per cent of total federal direct expenditures in the year 2000 (Howard, 2002: 417).

Loans from the government at an interest rate below the market rate are also a form of subsidy. However, the entire amount of the loan should not be treated as a subsidy, only the difference between the interest charged and the market rate (Lund, 1989).[2]

Subsidies offer numerous advantages as policy instruments (see Mitnick, 1980: 350–3; Howard, 1993, 1995). First, they are easy to establish if government and an organization share a preference for doing a particular activity. Second, subsidies are flexible to administer because participants decide for themselves how to respond to the subsidy in the light of changing circumstances. Likewise, they take local and sectoral circumstances into account, since only individuals and firms seeing a benefit would take up the subsidy. Third, by allowing individuals and firms to devise appropriate responses, subsidies may encourage innovation. Fourth, the costs of administering and enforcing subsidies may be low because it is up to potential recipients to claim benefits. Finally, subsidies are often politically more acceptable because the benefits are concentrated on a few whereas the costs are spread across the population, with the result that they tend to be supported strongly by the beneficiaries and opposed less intensely by their opponents, if they are noticed at all (Wilson, 1974).

There are also disadvantages to using subsidies. Since subsidies (except tax incentives) need financing, which must come from new or existing sources of revenues, their establishment through the formal budgetary process is often difficult. They must compete for funding with other government programs, each backed by its own network of societal groups, politicians, and bureaucrats. Second, the cost of gathering information on how much subsidy would be required to induce a desired behaviour[3] may also be high. Arriving at a correct amount of subsidy by trial and error can be an expensive way of implementing policy. Third, since subsidies work indirectly, there is also often a time lag before the desired effects are discernible. This makes them an inappropriate instrument to use in a time of crisis. Fourth, subsidies may be redundant in cases where the activity would have occurred even without the subsidy, thus causing a windfall for the recipients.

At the same time, they are hard to eliminate because of the opposition from existing beneficiaries. Fifth, subsidies may be banned by international agreements, as they are in export-oriented sectors because of the pernicious effects that subsidized imports can have on local industries and employment.

Financial Disincentives

A *tax* is a legally prescribed compulsory payment to government by a person or firm (Trebilcock et al., 1982: 53). The main purpose of a tax is normally to raise revenues for the government expenditures. However, it can also be used as a policy instrument to induce a desired behaviour[4] or discourage an undesirable behaviour.

In contrast to a subsidy, which is a positive incentive and works by rewarding a desired behaviour, taxes can be applied as a negative incentive (or sanction) that penalizes an undesired behaviour. By taxing a good, a service, or an activity, the government indirectly discourages its consumption or performance by making it more expensive to purchase or produce. Many governments' policy objectives of reducing smoking, drinking, and gambling because of their ill effects, for example, can be partially achieved through exceptionally high taxes on cigarettes, alcohol, and gambling revenues (Cnossen, 2005; Studlar, 2002; OECD, 2006).

A relatively recent innovation in the use of a tax as a policy instrument is the *user charge*. Instead of motivating behaviour by rewarding it through subsidy or requiring it through regulations, the government imposes a "price" on certain behaviours that those undertaking them must pay. The price may be seen as a financial penalty intended to discourage the targeted behaviour. User charges are most commonly used to control negative externalities. An example from the area of pollution control is that of user charges on pollution, known as effluent charges (Sproule-Jones, 1994; Zeckhauser, 1981). Reducing pollution has costs, the marginal rate of which tends to increase with each additional unit of reduction. If a charge is levied on effluent discharge, the polluter will keep reducing its level of pollution to the point at which it becomes more expensive to reduce pollution than simply to pay the effluent charge. In theory at least, the polluter will thus be constantly seeking ways to minimize its charges by cutting back on the level of pollution it discharges.[5]

Taxes and user charges offer numerous advantages as policy instruments. First, they are easy to establish from an administrative standpoint. Second, taxes and user charges provide continuing financial incentives to reduce undesirable activities. Third, user charges promote innovation by motivating a search for cheaper alternatives. Fourth, they are flexible, since the government can adjust rates until the desired amount of the target activity occurs. Finally, they are desirable on administrative grounds because the responsibility for reducing the target activities is left to individuals and firms, which reduces the need for bureaucratic enforcement machinery.

These opportunities must be weighed against the disadvantages of employing taxes and user charges. First, they require precise and accurate information in order to set the correct level of taxes or charges to elicit desired behaviour. Second, during the process of experimentation to arrive at optimum charges, resources may be misallocated. Third, they are not effective in times of crisis when an immediate response is required. Finally, they can involve cumbersome and possibly damaging administration costs if their rates are not set properly and they encourage evasive behaviour (e.g., smuggling) on the part of their targets, as occurred in the smoking example cited above.

Funding for Advocacy, Interest Groups, and Think Tanks

A prominent procedural tool in this category is *advocacy funding*. As public choice theorists have pointed out, interest groups do not arise spontaneously to press for certain policy solutions to ongoing problems, but rather require active personnel, organizational competence, and, above all, funding if they are to exert influence in the policy subsystem. While different countries have different patterns and sources of advocacy funding, governments play a large role in this activity in all democratic states (Maloney et al., 1994).

In some countries, including the US, funding for interest group creation and ongoing expenses tends to come from private-sector actors, especially philanthropic trust funds and private companies, but governments facilitate this through favourable tax treatment for estates, charitable trusts, and corporate donations (Nownes & Neeley, 1996; Nownes, 1995). These private foundations then partner with governments in certain policy areas, such as social service delivery (Knott & McCarthy, 2007). The magnitude of public funding can influence non-profit organization governance, insulating their policies from societal preferences when these diverge from those of government (Guo, 2007). Similar dynamics have been noted for research and communication grants made by governments to interest groups and think tanks (Rich, 2004; Lowry, 1999).

In other countries, including Canada and Australia, the state plays a much greater role in providing direct financing for interest groups in specific areas where the government wishes to see such groups operate, or become more active (Pal, 1993a; Phillips, 1991a; Pross & Stewart, 1993; Finkle et al., 1994). And, of course, in corporatist countries in continental Europe, states not only facilitate interest group activities through financial means, but also through the extension of special recognition and associational rights to specific industry and labour groups, providing them with a monopoly or near-monopoly on representation. (Jordan & Maloney, 1998; Schmitter, 1977, 1985).

Like many other procedural instruments, alteration of the advocacy system through the use of financial or treasure-based instruments involves some risks. Although it may be useful for government to build social capacity in these areas of interest group activity in order to obtain better information on social needs and wants, this kind of "boundary-spanning" activity also can result in the co-optation or even emasculation of bona fide interests (Young & Everitt, 2004). In addition, it can bring about a significant distortion of the overall system of interest articulation if only certain groups receive funding (Saward, 1990, 1992; Cardozo, 1996).

Organization-Based Policy Tools

Direct Provision

In analyzing the more exotic instruments employed by governments, we tend to forget the basic and widely used public policy instrument of direct action by the public sector. Most public policy involves bureaucratic action, a reality that can be overshadowed by the rhetoric on government reinvention whereby governments are expected to rely on private initiative and public–private partnerships (Olsen, 2005; Mayntz, 1979). Instead of waiting for the private sector to do something or regulating non-governmental performance, government often performs the task itself, delivering goods and services directly through government employees, funded from the public treasury (Leman, 1989: 54; Leman, 2002; Mayntz, 1979; Devas et al., 2001). Much of the policy output of government is delivered by government and its bureaucracy, including national defence, diplomatic relations, policing, firefighting, social security, education, management of public lands, maintenance of parks and roads, public health services, and census and geological surveys.

Direct provision offers three main advantages (Leman, 1989: 60). First, direct provision is easy to establish because of its low information requirements—there is no need to ascertain the preferences of non-government actors. Second, the large size of public agencies usually involved in direct provision enables them to enlist established resources, skills, and information to offer cost-effective project delivery. Adding a new task to a bureaucracy with existing know-how can often be done for far less than contracting outside provision. Third, direct provision avoids many problems associated with indirect provision—discussion, negotiations, and regulatory concerns with noncompliance—that can lead governments to pay more attention to enforcing terms of grants and contracts than to results.

The disadvantages of direct provision also can be significant. While in theory a government can do everything that the private sector can, in practice this may not be the case. Bureaucratic program delivery is often characterized by inflexibility, something that is unavoidable in liberal democracies, which value accountability and the rule of law, meaning that governments must follow time-consuming budgeting and appointment requirements. Second, political control over the agencies and officials involved in providing goods and services may, and often does, promote political meddling to strengthen a government's re-election prospects or address other political needs of the moment rather than to serve the public as a whole. Political control also may lead to incoherent directives to agencies delivering goods and services because of the contradictory pressures that beset governments. Third, since bureaucratic agencies are not subject to competition, they are often not sufficiently cost-conscious, for which the taxpayers ultimately pay. Fourth, the delivery of programs may suffer because of inter- and intra-agency conflicts within the government (Bovens et al., 2001).

Public Enterprises

Also known as state-owned enterprises, Crown corporations, or parastatal organizations, public enterprises are entities totally or partially owned by the state but yet enjoying some degree of autonomy from the government. There is no universally accepted definition of a public enterprise, which explains why governments often do not maintain a list of the enterprises they own. The main problem is determining how public an enterprise must be in order to qualify as a "public" enterprise. At one extreme, with only a small government share of ownership, a firm may resemble a private enterprise, and at the other, with close to 100 per cent government equity ownership, an enterprise may appear no different from a bureaucratic agency (Stanton & Moe, 2002). Examples of such confusion can be found in Amtrak, the United States' national passenger rail service provider, which was incorporated as a for-profit corporation in the District of Columbia but has received well over $30 billion in federal grants to cover the difference between its revenues and costs since 1971 (Perl & Dunn, 1997). The US Corporation for Public Broadcasting's motto, "A private corporation funded by the American people," echoes this ambiguity.

However, three broad generalizations can be made about public enterprises (Ahroni, 1986: 6). First, they involve a large degree of public ownership. Analysts often use a minimum 51 per cent government ownership threshold to classify a firm as being a public enterprise, since this ensures government control of the company's board of directors. However, in large corporations with widely held stock, a much smaller percentage would be sufficient to appoint the controlling interest on a board. The term "mixed enterprise" is used to describe a category of firms owned jointly by government and the private sector. Second, public enterprises entail some control over management by the government. Passive public ownership of an enterprise that operates entirely free from government control does not constitute a public enterprise. Hybrid "special operating agencies" or "public authorities" created in many countries in recent years to operate specific services such as airports, harbours, and water or electrical power utilities are not traditional public enterprises in that governments usually do not directly control their boards of directors (Advani & Borins, 2001; Kickert, 2001; Walsh, 1978). Third, public enterprises produce goods and services that are sold, unlike public goods such as defence or street lighting for which those receiving the services do not pay directly but rather through taxation.

Public enterprises provide governments with four advantages among organization-based policy instruments (Mitnick, 1980: 407). First, they are an efficient economic development tool in situations where a good or service necessary to productive activity is not being provided by the private sector because of high capital costs or low expected profits. Examples include rural electrification and internet access to smaller communities. Second, as with direct provision, the information threshold required to launch public enterprises is often lower than that required by other means, such as voluntary instruments or regulation. It does not require information on the target activity or the goals and preferences of the targeted firms, because the government can act directly through the enterprise it owns. Third, public enterprises can simplify public management of a policy domain if extensive regulation already exists. Instead of building additional layers of regulation to enforce compliance with government aims, for instance, it might be desirable simply to establish a company that does so without the costs of further regulation. Finally, profits from public enterprises may accrue to the public treasury, supporting public expenditures in other areas. A significant proportion of government revenue in Singapore, for example, comes from the profits of its public enterprises.

The disadvantages of public enterprises are no less significant. First, governments often find them difficult to control because managers can evade government directives. Moreover, the ultimate shareholders (the voters themselves) are too diffuse, and their personal interest too distant, to exercise effective control over the company. Second, public enterprise can be inefficient in operation because continued losses do not lead to bankruptcy, as would occur in the private sector. Indeed, a large number consistently lose money, which is a major reason underlying recent efforts to privatize them in many countries (see Howlett & Ramesh, 1993; Ikenberry, 1988). Without this market discipline, politicians find it hard to resist pressure from beneficiaries to keep public enterprise subsidies (and the below-cost goods and services they yield) flowing. Finally, many public enterprises, such as those delivering electricity and water, exercise a monopoly that enables passing the costs of their inefficiency on to consumers, just as a private firm would do under such circumstances (Musolf, 1989).

Quangos

In recent years governments have been leery of creating new "traditional" forms of public enterprises and instead have turned to a variety of forms of what are known in Britain as "quasi-autonomous non-government organizations," or *quangos* (Flinders & McConnel, 1999; Hood, 1986). Quangos share many of the same characteristics as public enterprises but usually are more at arm's length from government, functioning as quasi-independent, self-organizing actors (Christensen & Laegreid, 2003). They are only quasi-independent, however, because they often enjoy a government-granted monopoly—for example, over an airport's operation or delivery of a scholarship program (Advani & Borins, 2001; Aucoin, 2006)—and their licence to do so can be revoked by the government.

Quangos have advantages for governments by making it possible to offload expensive or controversial areas of government activity to "local" authorities. This is also a disadvantage in that the ability of governments to control their activities becomes limited by such delegation, even though any resulting policy failure could cause significant expenses—politically as well as financially—for governments (Kickert, 2001; Koppell, 2003).

Partnerships

A hybrid form of market and governmental reorganization, the public–private partnership (PPP), has recently gained momentum despite, and in some cases spurred by, political conflicts over privatization and outsourcing of public services (Linder, 1999). There are numerous different types of such partnerships. One trajectory for PPPs takes the form of contracting out the delivery of goods and services. However, some of these partnerships exist primarily to enhance the capacity of private-sector actors. NGOs, for instance, are sometimes delegated minor government tasks in order to receive funding, though the main purpose is to maintain their availability for consultation (Armstrong & Lenihan, 1999; Kernaghan, 1993).

Using partnerships to promote engagement between state and societal organizations raises questions of procedural and substantive equity. The criteria for including or excluding organizations in a partnership—the breadth of interests represented, and how specific individuals are designated as "representative"—can all affect the resulting partnership and its policy implications (Edelenbos & Klijn, 2006; Cook, 2002). It is also common for partnerships to include provisions that attribute profits to the private partner while the government assumes most of the risks.

Family, Community, and Voluntary Organizations

In all societies, relatives, friends, and neighbours, or family and community organizations, such as churches and charities, provide numerous goods and services, and the government may take measures to expand their role in ways that serve its policy goals. The characteristic feature of this instrument type is that it entails no or little government involvement. Instead, the desired task is performed on a voluntary basis by non-governmental actors. In some cases, however, governments must create the conditions under which voluntary actors operate (Phillips et al., 2001). In others, governments deliberately decide to do nothing (a "non-decision," which will be discussed in Chapter 6) about a recognized public problem because they believe a solution is already being provided, or will be, by some societal actor. These services are often provided by NGOs operating on a voluntary basis in that their members are not compelled to perform a task by the government. If they do something that serves public policy goals, it is for reasons of self-interest, ethics, or emotional gratification (Salamon, 1995; Salamon, 1987; Salamon, 2002c; Dollery et al., 2003).[6]

Voluntary organizations produce "activities that are indeed voluntary in the dual sense of being free of [state] coercion and being free of the economic constraints of profitability and the distribution of profits" (Wuthnow, 1991: 7). Voluntary organizations providing health services, education, and food to the poor and temporary shelter for battered women and runaway children are prime examples of policy delivery that relies on voluntary choice. Voluntary groups that form to clean up beaches, riverbanks, and highways are other examples. Charitable, not-for-profit groups, often faith-based, used to be the primary means of fulfilling the basic needs of those who could not provide for themselves, but over the last century the expansion of the welfare state gradually diminished their importance.

Even so, they are still a widely used means of addressing social problems today. In fact, in the US, often seen as the archetype of an individualist materialistic society, the non-profit voluntary sector delivers more services than the government itself (Salamon, 1987: 31). In recent years, the US government has encouraged faith-based organizations to play a larger role in program delivery, with implications for the relationship between governments, markets, and religion that are yet to be well understood (Hula et al., 2007).[7]

In theory, voluntary organizations are an efficient means of delivering most economic and social services. If it were feasible, it would obviously be cost efficient to provide social security or health and education services or build dams and roads on the basis of voluntary efforts of individuals. For example, local communities supplied volunteer labour to maintain the roads of eighteenth-century France and nineteenth-century America (Cavaillès, 1946: 70–1; Lane, 1950). Voluntary organizations also offer flexibility, speedy response time, and the opportunity for experimentation that are rarely matched by government departments (Johnson, 1987: 114). They often beat government to the scene of natural disasters, providing initial assistance to the victims (Mitchell, 2001). Another beneficial spillover is their positive contribution to promoting community spirit, social solidarity or cohesion, and political participation (Putnam, 1995a, 1995b, 1996, 2000, 2001).

However, practical circumstances severely limit the usefulness of voluntary organizations. Because they often lack the hierarchy of a formal bureaucracy, voluntary organizations demand considerable time and energy to keep their deliberative processes functioning. Oscar Wilde famously pinpointed the draw-back of such arrangements when he said that "[t]he only problem with socialism is that it takes up too many evenings" (Sampson, 1991: 16). But when voluntary groups emulate bureaucracy's administrative specialization and chain of command, they can easily lose their democratic character and function as unaccountable oligarchies (Jonsson & Zakrisson, 2005). Furthermore, voluntary efforts are largely inapplicable to many economic problems, such as the promotion of technological innovation and enhanced productivity. Financing arrangements can exacerbate the administrative challenges faced by voluntary associations. Government contracts impose heavy performance and reporting burdens that strain administrative capacity, and can erode program delivery as resources are reallocated to meet these managerial imperatives (Phillips & Levasseur, 2004)

Using the family as a policy tool has some additional disadvantages. It may be inequitable because many individuals do not have anyone, or anyone with the financial resources, physical ability, or emotional commitment, to look after them. It is similarly inequitable for the caregivers. In most societies, women tend to be the main care providers, a role increasingly difficult to perform because of increasing female participation in the workforce. As such, family and community instruments can often be relied on only as adjuncts to other instruments needed to address the pressing social problems of our times.

Co-Production

A similar tool to voluntary provision is "co-production." Co-production is intimately linked with the idea of "self-service" provision (Mizrahi, 2012) or the use of combinations of state and non-state actors to produce or inform public service delivery (Alford, 1998; Pestoff, 2006; Osborne, 2006; Voorberg et al., 2014). The idea of co-production can be traced back to Elinor Ostrom's (1973) study of the Chicago police force and her theory on polycentric governance (Ostrom, 1996). In the US, these ideas generated interest among public administration scholars in the 1970s and the 1980s (Parks et al., 1999; Brandsen & Pestoff, 2006) and experienced a revival in the decades after the turn of the century (Pestoff et al., 2012). The idea has, since, been picked up and studied by some scholars around the world (e.g., Whitaker, 1980; Parks et al., 1981; Ostrom, 1996; Alford, 2002; Brandsen & Pestoff, 2006; Prentice 2006; Bovaird 2007; Pestoff & Brandsen 2009; Pestoff, Brandsen, & Verschuere 2012).

Originally, co-production was narrowly defined as the "involvement of citizens, clients, consumers, volunteers and/or community organizations in producing public services as well as consuming or otherwise benefiting from them" (Alford, 1998: 128). In early studies of activities such as parent–teacher interactions in childhood education in Scandinavia, this involvement in co-production activity was typically voluntary, meaning it existed as a positive externality reducing production and delivery costs of public services. This made it very attractive to governments seeking cost reductions in public service delivery, especially ones favourable to notions of "social enterprise" and enhanced community participation as ends or goods in themselves (Parks et al., 1981; Salamon, 1981, 1987).

Although co-production emerged as a concept that emphasized citizens' engagement in policy design and delivery, its meaning has evolved in recent years to include both individuals (i.e., citizens and quasi-professionals) and organizations (citizen groups, associations, non-profit organizations) collaborating with government agencies (Alford, 1998; Poocharoen & Ting, 2015).

This broader and more complex definition of co-production is now common. Co-production can be thought of and empirically traced as both a managerial device that enriches provision of public or private services, and also as a set of policy tools that can offset or replace the use of other means such as public organizations (i.e., the state) or private contracts (i.e., the market) in goods and service delivery through enhancing and facilitating citizen-based provision of those goods and services.

Market Creation

By far the most important, and contentious, type of policy instrument is the market organization. The voluntary interaction between consumers and producers, with the former seeking to buy as much as they can with their limited funds and the latter searching for highest possible profits, can usually be expected to yield outcomes that satisfy both. In theory at least, while the primary motive on the part of both sides is self-interest, the society as a whole gains from their interaction because whatever is wanted (backed by the ability to pay) by the society is provided at the lowest price. Theoretically, then, those wanting even such critical goods as health care or education can simply buy the services from hospitals and schools operating for profit.

Markets exist when there is both scarcity of and a demand for particular goods or services. But government action is required both to create and to support market exchange. This is accomplished by securing the rights of buyers and sellers to receive and exchange property through the establishment and maintenance of property rights and contracts through the courts, police, and quasi-judicial systems of consumer and investor protection. Even so-called "black," "grey," or other types of illegal or quasi-legal markets for commodities or services, such as illegal drugs or prostitution, owe their existence to governments that ban the production and sale of these goods or services, thereby creating shortages that produce high rates of return for those willing to risk punishment for their provision. Governments can use a variety of regulatory, financial, and information-based tools to affect market activities. However, they use their organizational resources to create markets (Averch, 1990; Cantor et al., 1992).

One way this can be done is by creating property rights through government licensing schemes. Based on the assumption that the market is often the most efficient means of allocating resources, property-rights auctions by the government establish markets in situations where they do not exist. The market is created by setting a fixed quantity of transferable rights to consume a designated resource, which has the effect of creating an artificial scarcity of a public good and enabling the price mechanism to work. The resource can be communal radio, television, or cellphone frequencies, oil wells, or fish stocks—anything that would not be scarce in the short term unless the government acted to limit its supply (Sunnevag, 2000).

Many countries have proposed controlling dangerous pollutants in this manner (Bolom, 2000), and market creation has been a feature of international environmental agreements, such as the Kyoto Protocol on greenhouse gases. In these schemes, the government is expected to set the total amount of the pollutant that will be permitted and then, through periodic auctions, sell rights to discharge amounts below this level. This means that firms intending to use or generate a pollutant in their activities must buy the right to do so. Those with cheaper alternatives will avoid using or generating the pollutant because of the extra cost. Manufacturers for whom there is no cheap alternative will pay for pollution rights. However, they remain under cost pressure to search for alternatives.

The advantage of auctioning such rights is that it restricts the use of specific goods while still making them available to those without alternatives. If the same goal were pursued through regulation, the government would have to determine access rules, a difficult task because of the high information costs involved. In the case of auctions, in theory the decision will be made by the market according to the forces of demand and (government-controlled) supply.

One advantage of auctions of property rights to establish markets is that they are easy to conduct (Cantor et al., 1992). The government, based on what it considers the maximum amount of a good or service that should be permitted, fixes the ceiling and then lets the market do the rest. Second, they are flexible, allowing the government discretion to vary the ceiling whenever it wants. Property-rights auctions also allow the subjects to adjust their behaviour according to changes in their circumstances, such as with respect to development of cost-saving technology, without requiring a corresponding change in the government's policy or instrument. Third, auctions offer the certainty that only a fixed amount of a particular activity occurs, something not possible with other voluntary or mixed instruments. Moreover, auctions are, of course, a highly lucrative source of revenue for the government.

One of the disadvantages of auctions is that they may encourage speculation, with speculators inflating prices and hoarding all rights by bidding high, thereby erecting entry barriers to small firms or consumers. Second, it is often the case that those who cannot buy the rights, because none may be available for sale, will be forced to cheat, whereas in the case of user charges or subsidies they would have an alternative, albeit often at a high price. This can result in high enforcement costs if grey or black markets are to be avoided (Marion & Muehlegger, 2007). Third, auctions are inequitable to the extent that they allocate resources according to ability to pay, rather than need, and can generate fierce opposition from those affected because of the extra costs they must bear in buying the right (Woerdman, 2000; Kagel & Levin, 2002). Thus, rich families in Singapore buy more than one car, while those who really need one, for example to start up a business or take children to school, may not be able to buy a vehicle if they do not have the additional money required to purchase the Certificate of Entitlement.

Another way that governments can create or enhance markets is through the privatization of public enterprises, especially if those enterprises had previously exercised a state-sponsored monopoly or near-monopoly on the production or distribution, or both, of a particular good or service. Privatization can be carried out in numerous ways, from issuing shares to all citizens, to the simple transfer of state shares to community organizations or their sale on public exchanges. In all cases, this amounts to the transfer of a public enterprise to the private sector and the transformation of the goal of the enterprise from public service provision to maximization of shareholder value. In addition, it usually involves the signal, either overt or covert, that new firms will be able to enter into the market formerly served by the state-owned company, allowing for the creation of a competitive market for that particular good or service (Starr, 1989).

Although some scholars see privatization as a panacea, capable at one stroke of eliminating corrupt or inefficient public-sector providers and replacing them with more efficient private-sector ones, others point out that this is not always the case (Donahue, 1989). In many Eastern European post-socialist countries, for example, large-scale and largely uncontrolled privatizations resulted in many instances of massive layoffs and plant closures, with severe economic consequences for affected families, communities, and regions. In others, such as Russia, where securities markets were not well developed, plants were simply transferred to their managers, who in many cases were able to reap windfall profits from their sale. It is also the case, as welfare economists have argued, that some industries have economies of scale that allow large firms to maintain their monopolistic position, regardless of whether they are owned by governments or private investors. Privatization of such firms merely transfers monopoly profits from the public sector, where they can be used to finance additional public services, to the private sector, where they are often used for personal luxury consumption (Beesley, 1992; Bos, 1991; Donahue, 1989; Le Grand & Robinson, 1984; MacAvoy et al., 1989; Starr, 1990a).

In Western countries with much smaller numbers of public enterprises, a more common form of privatization has involved *contracting out government services*, that is, the transfer of various kinds of goods and services formerly provided "in-house" by government employees to "outsourced" private firms (Kelman, 2002; DeHoog & Salamon, 2002). Again, while some see any transfer of service provision from the state to the private sector as an inherent welfare gain, others note that in many cases the same employees end up being hired by the new service provider to provide the same service, but at less pay, while others have noted that the costs to administrators of establishing, monitoring, and enforcing contracts often cancels out any cost savings (see Lane, 2001; Ascher, 1987; Grimshaw et al., 2001; Donahue & Zeckhauser, 2006; Zarco-Jasso, 2005).

A much discussed but little used form of government market creation relies on *vouchers*. These government-issued certificates have a monetary face value that consumers can use to acquire a particular good or service from their preferred supplier, who in turn presents the voucher for redemption. Vouchers allow consumers to exercise relatively free choice in the marketplace, but only for specific types or quantities of goods. They are common in wartime as a means to ration supplies of various goods, and have also been used in peacetime in schemes such as food stamps for the poor. This promotes competition among suppliers, which arguably improves quality and reduces costs to the government. However, vouchers can also disrupt established patterns of public service provision. Their proposed use in education, for example, may force schools to compete against each other for students, which can lead to greater inequities in service provision between wealthy and impoverished school districts (Valkama & Bailey, 2001; Steuerle & Twombly, 2002). Vouchers can also be issued to producers to ration access to limited natural resources (e.g., fish stocks) by market mechanisms (Townsend et al., 2006). Other similar instruments exist, such as the provision of government insurance, which allows some activities to take place that otherwise might not occur because of the costs associated with failure or because of their risky nature (Feldman, 2002; Katzman, 1988; Moss, 2002; Stanton, 2002).

Establishing markets can be a highly recommended instrument in certain circumstances (Averch, 1990; OECD, 1993; Hula, 1988). It is an effective and efficient means of providing most private goods and can ensure that resources are devoted only to those goods and services valued by the society, as reflected in the individual's willingness to pay. It also ensures that if there is meaningful competition among suppliers, then valued goods and services are supplied at the lowest possible price. Since most goods and services sought by the population are of a private nature, governments in capitalist societies rely extensively on the market instrument.

In many situations, however, the market may be an inappropriate instrument (Kuttner, 1997). As we saw in Chapter 2, markets cannot adequately provide public goods, precisely the sort of things most public policies involve. Thus, markets cannot be used for providing defence, policing, street lights, and other similar goods and services valued by society. Markets also experience difficulties in providing various kinds of toll goods and common-pool goods[8] because of difficulties involved in charging consumers for these kinds of products. The market is also a highly inequitable instrument because it meets the needs of only those with the ability to pay. In a purely market-based system of health care delivery, for example, a rich person with money can have a wish for cosmetic surgery fulfilled, while a poor person suffering from kidney failure will not receive treatment. It is not surprising that the market, in such situations, faces tough political opposition in democratic societies otherwise structured along more egalitarian principles.

A "free market" in the true sense of the term is therefore almost never used as a policy instrument in practice. When a government does resort to this instrument to address a public problem, it is usually accompanied by other instruments, such as regulation to protect consumers, investors, and workers; it is also accompanied frequently by subsidies intended to further promote the desired activity (Cantor et al., 1992). Thus, the voluntarism embodied by markets is relative rather than absolute.

Government (Re)organizations

The foremost example of such an instrument in a procedural sense is institutional reorganization whereby governments seek to affect policy processes by reorganizing the structures or processes through which they perform a function (Peters, 1992b; Carver, 2001). Reorganizations can involve the creation of new agencies or the reconfiguration of existing ones. One popular technique for such purposes is ministerial reorganization. Some of these alterations can occur accidentally or as a by-product of organizational changes in government machinery brought about for other reasons, such as electoral or partisan ones. Since "there is no agreed normative basis for organizing government," the political, policy, and administrative priorities and pressures of the day provide disparate points of departure for prime ministers and presidents considering what, if anything, to do about their government's organization (Davis et al., 1999: 42).

Intentional organizational change to the basic structures or personnel of government departments and agencies has become an increasingly significant aspect of modern policy-making (Lindquist, 1992; Aucoin, 1997; Bertelli & Feldmann, 2007; March & Olson, 1996). This can involve changes in the relationships between departments and central coordinating agencies, or between departments, or within ministries. In the first instance, ministries can be given greater autonomy and capacity to set their own direction, or they can be brought into tighter control by central executive agencies (Smith et al., 1993). Proposals over how far, and in what direction, to go with government reorganization can depend on how those pursuing a particular policy agenda judge the existing organizational arrangements will serve their substantive preferences, as compared to some organizational alternative (McCubbins et al., 1987, 1989).

However, there are limits to such reorganizations. First, they can be expensive and time consuming. Second, if they occur too frequently, their impact can be much dissipated. Third, constitutional or jurisdictional factors may limit the kinds of activities that specific governments can take and the fashion in which they can do so (Gilmore & Krantz, 1991).

The Formulation Challenge: Mixing and Bundling Policy Tools

Most older literature on policy tools focused on single instrument choices and designs (Tupper & Doern, 1981; Salamon, 1989; Trebilcock & Prichard, 1983), and these studies provide only limited insights into the complex arrangements of multiple policy instruments that are commonly found in all contemporary policy fields (Jordan et al., 2011 and 2012; Givoni, 2013). Many significant issues related to how tools are bundled and evolve over time affect the propensity for designs to avoid the twin shoals of over- and under-reacting to problems (Maor, 2012; Howlett & Rayner, 2007) while incorporating better knowledge (del Rio, 2010; LePlay & Thoyer, 2011; Grabosky, 1995; Justen et al., 2013b).

Choosing and advocating policy tools becomes more complex when multiple goals and multiple policies are involved, as is very common in many policy-making situations (Doremus, 2003; Jordan et al., 2012; Howlett et al., 2009). These latter kinds of multi-policy, multi-goal and multi-instrument mixes—what Milkman et al. (2012) call "policy bundles," Chapman (2003) and Hennicke (2004) call a "policy mix" and Givoni et al. (2012) call "policy packages"—are examples of complex portfolios of tools. These mixes typically involve much more than functional logics linking tools to a goal but also deal with ideological or even "aesthetic" preferences in tool choices and goal articulation (Beland & Wadden, 2012; Williams & Balaz, 1999). This makes their design especially problematic (Peters, 2005; Givoni, 2013; Givoni et al., 2012). Ideally, the focus should move from the design of specific instruments to the appropriate design of instrument mixes, but this is difficult when instruments belong to different territorial/administrative levels, adding a "vertical" dimension to policy (see Figure 5.3).

In this model, mixes can be seen to range from the simplest type, when multiple tools are an issue (Type I), to the most complex multi-level, multi-policy, multi-goal type (Type VIII). Four of these eight types are *"instrument mixes,"* which involve single policy contexts (Types I, II, V, and VI) and therefore are less complex than their multi-policy counterparts (Types III, VII, and VIII), which can be termed *"policy mixes."*

Figure 5.3 Basic Typology of Portfolio Designs

Dimension				Types of Policy Tools				
	I	II	III	IV	V	VI	VII	VIII
Multi-Level	No	No	No	No	Yes	Yes	Yes	Yes
Multi-Policy	No	No	Yes	Yes	No	No	Yes	Yes
Multi-Goal	No	Yes	No	Yes	No	Yes	No	Yes
	Simple Single-Level Tools Mix	Complex Single-Level Tools Mix	Simple Single-Level Policy Mix	Complex Single-Level Policy Mix	Simple Multi-Level Tools Mix	Complex Multi-Level Tools Mix	Simple Multi-Level Policy Mix	Complex Multi-Level Policy Mix

Are all these eight types equally likely to occur? Although much of the literature seems to suggest that Type I situations are the norm, empirical studies suggest this is not the case (Howlett et al., 2006; Hosseus & Pal, 1997) and that more complex design spaces and hence policy portfolios are both commonplace and growing. Factors such as the administrative and legislative arrangements present in federal and non-federal systems affect the likelihood of appearance of multi-governmental mixes (Howlett, 1999; Bolleyer & Borzel, 2010), while increasing efforts to promote collaborative or horizontal governance arrangements, for example, will affect the number of multi-sectoral and multi-policy situations that exist (Peters, 1998; Koppenjan et al., 2009).

Actors in Policy Formulation

Another analytical focus on this stage of policy-making examines the actors involved in policy formulation, how they are organized and how they operate. The style and substance of advice provided to decision-makers turns out to be connected to the experts employed to advise governments, and the ways that their work is organized.

Policy Advisors and Policy Advisory Systems

Given the range of actors who participate in policy formulation, it is not surprising that it is a highly diffuse and disjointed process that is hard to track. Nevertheless, most policy formulation processes do share certain characteristics that emerge in empirical case studies and help to illuminate the role of actors behind policy design. First, formulation is not usually limited to one set of actors (Sabatier & Jenkins-Smith, 1993). Formulation may also proceed without a clear definition of the problem to be addressed (Weber & Khademian, 2008) and may occur over a long period of time in "rounds" of formulation and reformulation of policy problems and solutions (Teisman, 2000). And while formulators often search for win-win solutions, it is often the case that the costs and benefits of different options fall disproportionately on different actors (Wilson, 1974). This implies, as Linder and Peters, among others, have suggested, that the capability of policy designs to be realized in practice depends upon many political as well as technical variables. However, this does not imply that policy design is impossible or a fruitless effort, simply that it must be recognized that some designs may prove impossible to adopt under particular political contexts and that the adoption of any design will be a fraught and contingent process as various types of policy actors attempt to construct and champion their preferred policy alternatives (Dryzek 1983).

Politicians situated in authoritative decision-making positions ultimately "make" public policy. However, they do so most often by following the advice provided to them by civil servants and others whom they trust or rely upon to provide expert opinion on the merits and demerits of the proposals put before them (Heinrichs, 2005;

MacRae, & Whittington, 1997). It is useful to think of advisors as being arranged in an overall "policy advisory system" that will differ slightly across subsystems.

Recent studies of advice systems in countries such as New Zealand, Israel, Canada, and Australia have developed the idea that government decision-makers sit at the centre of a complex web of policy advisors (Dobuzinskis, Howlett, & Laycock, 2007; Maley, 2000; Peled, 2002; Eichbaum & Shaw, 2007) that includes both "traditional" political advisors in government as well as non-governmental actors in NGOs, think tanks, and other similar organizations; this also includes less formal or professional forms of advice from colleagues, friends and relatives, members of the public, and political parties, among others. As Anderson (1996) noted, "a healthy policy research community outside government can play a vital role in enriching public understanding and debate of policy issues, and it serves as a natural complement to policy capacity within government."

Understanding the nature of policy formulation and design activities in different analytical contexts involves discerning how the policy advice system is structured and operated in the specific sector of policy activity under examination (Brint, 1990; Page, 2010). At their most basic, policy advice systems can be thought of as part of the knowledge utilization system of government, itself a kind of marketplace for policy ideas and information, comprising three separate components: a supply of policy advice, its demand on the part of decision-makers, and a set of brokers whose role it is to match supply and demand in any given conjuncture (Lindquist, 1998; Brint, 1990). That is, these systems can be thought of as arrayed into three general "sets" of analytical activities and participants linked to the positions actors hold in the "market" for policy advice.

The first set of actors is composed of "proximate decision-makers" who act as consumers of policy analysis and advice—that is, those with actual authority to make policy decisions, including cabinets and executives as well as parliaments, legislatures and congresses, and senior administrators and officials delegated decision-making powers by those other bodies. The second set is composed of those "knowledge producers" located in academia, statistical agencies, and research institutes who provide the basic scientific, economic, and social scientific data upon which analyses are often based and decisions made. The third set is composed of those "knowledge brokers" who serve as intermediaries between the knowledge generators and proximate decision-makers, repackaging data and information into usable form (Page, 2010; Lindvall, 2009). These include, among others, permanent specialized research staff inside government as well as their temporary equivalents in commissions and task forces, and a large group of non-governmental specialists associated with think tanks and interest groups. Although often thought of as "knowledge suppliers," policy advisors almost by definition operate in the brokerage space of the subsystem (Verschuere, 2009; Lindvall, 2009; Howlett & Newman 2010).

The exact configuration of an advisory system can vary not only temporally, but also spatially, by jurisdiction, especially by nation-state, and, somewhat less so, by policy issue or sector (Prince, 1983; Wollman, 1989; Hawke, 1983; Rochet 2004). This helps to explain why different styles of policy analysis and formulation can be found in different policy fields (Mayer, Bots, & van Daalen, 2004; Thissen & Twaalfhoven, 2001), since these can be linked to larger patterns of institutional structures that condition the behaviour of political actors and knowledge suppliers that, in turn, influence how policy advice is generated and deployed (Peled, 2002; Howlett & Lindquist, 2004; Bevir & Rhodes, 2001; Bevir, Rhodes, & Weller, 2003; Aberbach & Rockman, 1989; Bennett & McPhail, 1992).

In general, four distinct "communities" of policy advisors can be identified within any policy advice system depending on their location inside or outside of government, and by how closely they operate to decision-makers: core actors, public-sector insiders, private-sector insiders, and outsiders (see Figure 5.4).

Instrument Constituencies

While it is debatable whether a strict separation of political and technical advice was ever the case in most policy subsystems, it is now clear that the supply of technical advice is no longer, if it ever was, a monopoly of governments. Multiple sources of policy advice exist across the different policy activities in which governments are engaged. When it comes to policy formulation, however, these actors often engage in coalitions that allow them to participate in policy-making collectively rather than individually.

Figure 5.4 Four Communities of Policy Advisors

	Proximate Actors	**Peripheral Actors**
	Core Actors	*Public-Sector Insiders*
Public/Governmental Sector	Central Agencies Executive Staff Professional Governmental Policy Analysts	Commissions, Committees, and Task Forces Research Councils/Scientists International Organizations
	Private-Sector Insiders	*Outsiders*
Non-Governmental Sector	Consultants Political Party Staff Pollsters Donors	Public Interest Groups Business Associations Trade Unions Academics Think Tanks Media International Non-Governmental Organizations

As pointed out in the previous chapter on agenda-setting, Voss and Simons and their colleagues identified specific groups of advisors advocating for specific kinds of options acting together as an "instrument constituency" in order to better promote their preferred means of public problem-solving (Voss & Simons, 2014; Mann & Simons, 2014; Palier, 2007). In a series of studies on the emergence of various trading schemes in the area of environmental policy (Voss & Simons, 2014; Mann & Simons 2014), they observed that members of instrument constituencies were distinct and stayed united because of their common "fidelity" not to a political agenda or problem definition but rather to promoting a particular instrument or combination of instruments as a superior technique of public governance.

Instrument constituencies are defined as "networks of heterogeneous actors" from across the worlds of academia, policy consulting, public policy and administration, business, and civil society. Connections between these practices evolve from interactions in articulating, developing, disseminating, and implementing a particular policy instrument. As Voss and Simons note, "As actors reflexively pursue the management of interdependencies emerging from their joint engagement with an instrument, they mutually enrol each other for the realization of particular versions of the instrument according to the specific expectations that they attach to it" (Voss & Simons, 2014). Understanding the ideas and experiences that members of instrument constituencies bring to policy formulation, and the contexts within which they operate, can help explain why some options gain considerable attention while others are ignored although, again, it must be stressed that this will vary from context to context.

Modelling Policy Formulation

The multi-element composition of a policy, the multi-dimensional nature of policy mixes and the multiple nature and sources of policy advice are phenomena that make policy formulation challenging, both in theory and in practice (Leutz, 1999; Justen et al., 2013a, 2013b). Even in simple circumstances the situation is more complex and nuanced than is normally depicted in the existing policy literature (Howlett et al., 2018; Mandell, 2008; Howlett & Rayner, 2013; del Rio, 2014).

These intricate policy mixes inherently involve interactions between the different instruments of which they are composed, in the form of either conflicts or synergies. Mitigating the conflicts and encouraging synergies within these instrument mixes through effective policy design is a fundamental challenge for policy designers, one that is not always overcome in policy formulation processes in which political imperatives can prove to be as significant as technical ones, if not more so.

What type of regime exists in a given sector or issue area is of major significance in understanding the dynamics of policy formulation within that subsystem (Thompson, 2003), from structuring policy advice to informing considerations and determinations of what is feasible and what is not. Which policy options on the institutional

Figure 5.5 A Model of Policy Formulation Modes

		Entrance of New Actors	
		No	Yes
Availability of New Ideas	Yes	*Open policy subsystem:* policy renewal; inclusion of alternative instruments	*Contested policy subsystem:* program reform within existing range of policy instruments
	No	*Resistant policy subsystem:* policy experimentation, working with new instruments within existing paradigm	*Closed policy subsystem:* program instrument tinkering, with instrument settings within existing paradigm

agenda will be considered seriously for adoption, the types of solutions or options thought to be feasible for resolving policy problems, and the kinds of instruments selected to address them are largely a function of the nature and motivation of key actors arrayed in policy subsystems and the ideas that they hold (Howlett, 2002).

Similarly, capacity is important. High levels of capacity are linked to superior policy outputs and outcomes while capacity deficits are viewed as a major cause of policy failure and suboptimal outcomes (Bullock, 2001; Canadian Government, 1996; Fukuyama, 2014).

Conclusion: Policy Formulation— Opening up the Black Box

Studies of policy formulation in the policy sciences are not as advanced as those of agenda-setting or, as we shall see in subsequent chapters, as they are in studies of decision-making, policy implementation or policy evaluation. In most cases, this is because much of the actual work in policy formulation takes place behind the scenes in the confines of the bureaucracy and executive offices often with strict measures in place to ensure secrecy and confidentiality.

While this is beginning to change, and new studies and handbooks have emerged that grapple with these issues (Howlett & Mukherjee, 2017), there is still work to do before this area of the policy process is as well known and modelled as effectively as the other stages of the policy process. This is an urgent need in policy studies, since it is clear that this is a highly significant part of policy-making: the types of policy designs and alternatives generated at this stage of the policy process are central to subsequent activities involved in approving them and putting them into practice.

It is to these two tasks we now turn in Chapters 6 and 7.

Study Questions

1. Think of a policy instrument not mentioned in the text. How would you classify it using Hood's NATO model?

2. Are there limits to what can be accomplished through nudging? Why or why not? If so, what are they?

3. How does understanding the nature of a policy subsystem help us understand the kinds of policy alternatives considered during policy formulation?

4. Choose a policy sector. Outline the tools used in it and describe the nature of the policy portfolio used to address it.

5. How do different countries and sectors vary in terms of the nature of their policy advice and formulation systems?

Further Readings

Adcroft, A., and R. Willis. 2005. "The (Un)Intended Outcome of Public Sector Performance Measurement," *International Journal of Public-Sector Management* 18, no. 5: 386–400.

Craft, Jonathan, and Michael Howlett. 2012. "Policy Formulation, Governance Shifts and Policy Influence: Location and Content in Policy Advisory Systems," *Journal of Public Policy* 32, no. 02: 79–98.

Craft, Jonathan, and Michael Howlett. 2013. "The Dual Dynamics of Policy Advisory Systems: The Impact of Externalization and Politicization on Policy Advice," *Policy and Society* 32, no. 3: 187–97.

DeLeon, Peter. 1992. "Policy Formulation: Where Ignorant Armies Clash by Night," *Policy Studies Review* 11, nos. 3 and 4: 389–405.

Hajer, M.A. 2005. "Setting the Stage: A Dramaturgy of Policy Deliberation," *Administration and Society* 36, no. 6: 624–47.

Hall, Peter A. 1993. "Policy Paradigms, Social Learning and the State: The Case of Economic Policy-Making in Britain," *Comparative Politics* 25, no. 3: 275–96.

Howlett, Michael, and Jeremy Rayner. 2013. "Patching vs Packaging in Policy Formulation: Assessing Policy Portfolio Design," *Politics and Governance* 1, no. 2: 170–82.

Howlett, Michael, and Ishani Mukherjee, eds. 2017. *Handbook of Policy Formulation*. Cheltenham: Edward Elgar.

Howlett, Michael. 2019. "Comparing Policy Advisory Systems beyond the OECD: Models, Dynamics and the Second-Generation Research Agenda." *Policy Studies* 40, nos. 3–4 (July 4): 241–59.

Hula, Richard, Cynthia Jackson-Elmoore, and Laura Reese. 2007. "Mixing God's Work and the Public Business: A Framework for the Analysis of Faith-Based Service Delivery," *Review of Policy Research* 24, no. 1: 67–89.

Majone, Giandomenico. 1975. "On the Notion of Political Feasibility," *European Journal of Political Research* 3: 259–74.

Milward, H. Brinton, and Gary L. Walmsley. 1984. "Policy Subsystems, Networks and the Tools of Public Management," in Robert Eyestone, ed., *Public Policy Formation*. Greenwich, Conn.: JAI Press, 3–25.

Olsen, J.P. 2005. "Maybe It Is Time to Rediscover Bureaucracy," *Journal of Public Administration Research and Theory* 16, no. 1: 1–24.

Sunstein, Cass R. 2014. "Nudging: A Very Short Guide." *Journal of Consumer Policy* 37, no. 4 (December 1): 583–88.

Chapter 6

Decision-Making in Public Policy
Policy Selection and Choice

What Is Decision-Making in the Public Sector?

The public policy process, as Thomas Dye pointed out in Chapter 1 is all about decision-making. Decisions, large and small, are made throughout the process by individuals, groups and organizations: decisions to deal with a problem, to analyze it in certain ways, to engage the public or not, and so on. However, the subject of this chapter is about making an authoritative decision to commit government resources and prestige to a certain course of action expected to attain some desired end. It is about "policy choice," selecting a policy from among whatever options are available and moving it forward to implementation.

The decision-making stage of the policy process is thus when one or more, or none, of the multiple definitions of policy problems and solution options that have been identified, debated, and examined during the previous two stages of the policy cycle are approved and become an official course of action. Such policy decisions usually produce some kind of a formal or informal statement of intent on the part of authorized public actors to take, or not to take, some action. These statements can take the form of a law passed by the legislature, an administrative regulation, or even just a speech or a policy statement from an elected or appointed government official (O'Sullivan & Down, 2001). Acting on this decision and putting in place practices and procedures to give it effect is the subject of the next stage of the policy cycle, policy implementation, discussed in the following chapter.

Gary Brewer and Peter DeLeon (1983: 179) characterized the decision-making stage of the public policy process as a choice process. It is one that happens once:

> the choice among policy alternatives that have been generated and their likely effects on the problem estimated. . . . It is the most overtly political stage insofar as the many potential solutions to a given problem must somehow be winnowed down and but one or a select few picked and

readied for use. Obviously most possible choices will not be realized and deciding not to take particular courses of action is as much a part of selection as finally settling on the best course.

This definition makes several important points about the decision-making stage of the policy cycle. First, decision-making is not a self-contained activity, but neither is it synonymous with the decisions that take place over the course of the entire public policy-making process. Rather, it is a specific activity rooted firmly in the previous stages of the policy cycle and involves choosing or selecting from among a relatively small number of alternative policy options identified, systematically or otherwise, in the process of policy formulation. This is done typically with the expectation that the action will resolve a public problem either in reality or symbolically, placating societal demands for action.

Second, this definition highlights the fact that different kinds of decisions can result from a decision-making process. That is, decisions can be *"positive"* in the sense that they are intended, once implemented, to alter the status quo in some way, or they can be *"negative"* in the sense that the government declares that it will do nothing new about a public problem but will retain the status quo.

Third, this definition underlines the point that public policy decision-making is not a technical exercise but an inherently political process. It recognizes that public policy decisions create "winners" and "losers," even if the decision is a negative one.

Brewer and deLeon's definition, of course, says nothing about the actors involved in this process, or the desirability, likely direction, or scope of public decision-making. To deal with these issues, different theories and models have been developed to describe how decisions are made in government as well as to prescribe how decisions ought to be made. The nature of public policy decision-makers, the different types of decisions that they make, and the development and evolution of decision-making models designed to help understand the relationship between the two are described below.

Problematics of Decision-Making: An Unknown Future and Risks of Failure

Over- and Under-Reactions

In an ideal world, governments would choose only the most efficient and effective policies, spending the exactly appropriate amount of time, effort, and resources to match the severity of a problem. This assumes, however, that a government's policy efforts can be "perfectly calibrated," seamlessly leading to the minimum appropriate amount of effort being used to maximize the solution to a policy problem. This simple "proportionality" between problem severity and reaction, unfortunately, is not backed up by empirical evidence (deLeon, 1999; Hargrove, 1975). Rather, studies of policy success and failure suggest more complex patterns in which relatively few efforts are very well calibrated, with most either under- or over-reacting to problems, on either a one-off or a sustained basis (Maor, 2012, 2014a; de Vries, 2010).

In general, there are four possible ideal scenarios for the relationship between policy efforts and policy solutions. In two cases, there is "proportionate response," either when a severe problem generates a large response or when a small problem encounters a similarly small expenditure of government resources. The two other cases are "disproportionate" in nature: when policy reactions either over- or under-shoot the severity of the problem and thus do not adequately match the nature of the underlying problem. Poorly calibrated responses often persist over sustained periods of over- and under-reaction in which either government resources are wasted or unresolved problems persist (de Vries, 2010).

Scholarly attention on this mismatch has mostly focused on studying the reasons for sustained over-reactions (Maor, 2012, 2014a; Jones et al., 2014), and the phenomenon of sustained under-reactions is both less well examined and less well understood (Maor, 2014b). Examples of the former over-reactions range from studies of over-regulation in food and environmental safety standards (Tosun, 2013), to excessive reforms in social or health policies (Kemmerling & Makszin, 2018), and to over-reactions against terrorist threats or crime (e.g., Desch, 2007).

Part of this problem has to do with the underlying valuation difficulties in determining the nature and impact of policy problems (e.g., Zuckerman, 2012), difficulties that always leave room for political controversy and disagreement in assessing the exact nature of the problem at hand and therefore what is a reasonable or proportionate response to it. Such actions are often linked to well known "credit-claiming" motives on the part of decision-makers anxious to be seen by the public, electorates, or affected parties to be "doing something" about a problem (Twight, 1991; Marsh & Tilley, 2010). In these dynamics, more action is usually equated with better results, whether or not the extra effort and cost are worth any additional results achieved.

The literature on under-reactions is less well developed (Maor, 2014b). One can find cases that have been recognized, but in which the decisions behind under-reaction remain unexplained: for instance, problems of harmful international tax competition (e.g., Genschel et al., 2011), epidemics (e.g., Oosterveer, 2002), or continued deforestation and soil erosion (e.g., Blaikie and Brookfield, 1987; Ostrom, 1999). Identified causes of under-reaction include the role of institutions and veto players (e.g., Tsebelis, 2002), and problems of collective action such as the famous "tragedy of the commons" discussed in Chapter 2 (Ostrom et al., 1999), which can lead to the extent of a problem "creeping up" on decision-makers who may not be aware of its potential significance from initial reports. Organizational studies have also highlighted how standard operating routines and default modes of operation may block change (Baumgartner & Jones, 2002), and how under-reactions may also be the consequence of cognitive biases if issues are invisible or their costs and benefits are difficult to calculate, such as problems with unequal treatment of races, ethnic groups, or women in healthcare systems. Both subjects are well studied in social and organizational psychology and policy evaluation (e.g., Kahneman, 2003; Slovic, 1992). And mechanisms of diffusion and cross-border learning could lead governments to believe that no action is necessary if other (major) governments have not initiated action in response to the same or similar problem.

Uncertainty, Ambiguity, Ignorance, and Incompetence

These problems highlight a critical challenge that decision-makers and policy-makers more generally must deal with in responding to a problem, which is that they face an unknown future and must attempt in some way to estimate anticipated problem severity and solution potential without ever being 100 per cent certain that they have either correctly diagnosed a problem or that their proposed solution will work. This is a problem in policy formulation and implementation, but is especially acute in policy choice where it is expected that some choice will be made. As such, problems cannot always be put off or solutions phased in order to assess their effectiveness as this process unfolds. Decision-makers trying to deal with issues on their agendas must cope with conditions of uncertainty and ambiguity as they try to ensure their efforts will prove effective (Simon, 1991; Morgan & Henrion, 1990; Swanson et al., 2010).

Failing to correctly identify the bounds and range of these uncertainties is a major cause of policy over- and under-reaction (Maor, 2012a, 2012b) and over- and under-design, and uncertainties and ambiguities must be correctly understood and diagnosed by policy-makers in specific circumstances if policy failures are to be avoided both in the short and long term. Some of these uncertainties stem from a lack of knowledge of cause-and-effect relationships between policy interventions and outcomes, and may be overcome through better research and information, assuming that time exists in which to design and gather this data. Not all problem characteristics and environments change as rapidly as others, however, and not all uncertainties demand the same response.

The concept of uncertainty has been widely interpreted and studied in diverse disciplines that influence public policy, such as the physical sciences, social sciences, mathematical sciences, engineering, economics, philosophy, and psychology, and some guidelines are available there (Walker et al., 2012). A key distinction drawn in this literature distinguishes between situations in which uncertainty is represented by known probability distributions in which parameter estimates may be difficult to make or error-prone ("Knightian risk") and those in which the overall distributions themselves are unknown ("Knightian uncertainty") (Knight, 1921).

Schrader et al., for example, argue that uncertainty and ambiguity are two very different concepts that should not be confused or improperly juxtaposed but rather can be combined to illustrate the fundamental problematics or aspects of a design or policy-making "space." They suggest two further levels of ambiguity: Level 1, where the variables are given but not their functional relationships, and Level 2, where both the variables and their functional relationships are unknown.

The more recent uncertainty classifications by Walker et al. (2003), Kwakkel et al. (2010), and Walker et al. (2010) utilize these insights and distinctions to develop a set of propositions for policy-making dealing with a range of levels of ambiguity between "shallow" and "deep uncertainty." Walker et al. (2010) usefully identify four common situations of relative ignorance. These are "Level 1," shallow or parameter uncertainty where multiple alternative states representing the system with specific probabilities are present; "Level 2," medium or fuzzy uncertainty where multiple alternatives can be ranked based on the "perceived likelihood" of their occurrence are present; "Level 3," deep uncertainty where multiple alternatives are present but these cannot be ranked in terms of their likelihood of occurrence; and "Level 4," complete ignorance, where there is an inability to present multiple alternatives and the "possibility of being surprised" is real (see Figure 6.1).

Figure 6.1 Levels of Uncertainty

		Level 1	Level 2	Level 3	Level 4
				Deep Uncertainty	
Determinism	Context	A clear enough future	Alternative futures (with probabilities)	A multiplicity of plausible futures	Unknown future
	System model	A single system model	A single system model with a probabilistic parameterization	Several system models, with different structures	Unknown system model; know we don't know
	System outcomes	A point estimate and confidence interval for each outcome	Several sets of point estimates and confidence intervals for the outcomes, with a probability attached to each set	A known range of outcomes	Unknown outcomes; know we don't know
	Weights on outcomes	A single estimate of the weights	Several sets of weights, with a probability attached to each set	A known range of weights	Unknown weights; know we don't know

Source: Adapted from Walker et al., 2010.

These distinctions are useful in assessing how decision-makers can deal with different levels of uncertainty in making their policy choices. That is, different policy problems correspond to these different levels of uncertainty and their policy treatment should vary accordingly. Policy problems characterized by Level I uncertainty, for example, are at least in theory not very difficult and are thus likely to be resolved by standard treatments with the expectation that a proportional response is likely to result. Hence, for example, controlling housing markets though interest (mortgage) rate manipulations or traffic through stoplights and traffic "calming" are well known problems and solutions and offer only a very limited risk of failure. Level II uncertainty is slightly more complex, and policy decisions may produce some unexpected results—such as when tobacco price hikes trigger problems with smuggling and black markets—and may generate some level of disproportionality as a result.

Day and Klein (1989) note that while most government policies are crafted in response to events that are "reasonably predictable," however, policy events can also be (1) unpredictable, "unforeseen" and "unprojectable," (2) catastrophic, and (3) events where interpretation of uncertainty is obscured by moral and social controversy. That is, even in Level I and II scenarios there can be unexpected events or "wild-cards" (Wardekker et al., 2010) that can impact policy decisions with significant social and political implications. In these cases, circumstances offer limited scope for the decision-maker to draw upon history or experience (Walker et al., 2010; Lempert et al., 2003).

The final two scenarios, however, are likely to involve a much higher ratio of ambiguity to uncertainty, are much more likely to lead to disproportionate responses and under- and over-design of solutions and thus require a different type of policy response. These level III and IV situations often arise in dealing with problems that persist over the long run as fuzzy parameter estimates accumulate and multiply. Level III problems, such as green transport initiatives (for example, when planners try to increase the share of walkers and cyclists at the expense of car drivers), require applying a number of policy tools to uncertain expectations about rider behaviour, yielding scenarios where the uncertainty of outcomes climbs dramatically and changes over time (Taeihagh et al., 2013). A common response is to select policies that either over-design or over-manage expectations, or the reverse. Policies designed to address such issues should, then, be both more flexible and adaptable than those dealing with problems accompanying Level I or II uncertainty, but this is rarely the case.

Finally, there are Level IV problems. These create the worst-case scenarios for decision-makers, as they entail competing perspectives about the nature of the problem as well as multiple potential solutions whose prospects for success are unknown (Rittel & Weber, 1973). Uncertainties can arise from many sources, including lack of data or lack of agreement on results, statistical methods, error of measurement, use of approximations, subjectivity in judgment, uncertainty in human behaviour, errors in model structure, errors in values of parameters, likelihood of change in parameters from historical values, differences in concepts and terminology, choice of spatial/ temporal units, and assumptions taken. Levin et al. (2012) argue that policies dealing with climate change, for example, fall into this category, as delays in action toward addressing climate change only make the problem more difficult to address. In such circumstances, attaining some level of disproportionality with standard policy packages is almost certain, and highly flexible arrangements that can be altered as implementation unfolds are called for.

The Substance of Decision-Making: Seeking Advice and Evidence about Policy Choices

In addition to simply receiving input on a proposed course of action from policy formulators about how to deal with a problem, decision-makers can and do seek their own counsel in arriving at their choices. As we have seen in Chapter 5, in contemporary governments, a great deal of this advice is available in most societies through participants in policy advisory systems. Much of this advice is internal, with executive agencies and staff available to provide a counterpoint to advice received from subject matter experts in the bureaucracy. But external advice is also available from think tanks, universities, and policy research institutes among others, and is increasingly drawn upon (Craft & Howlett, 2014).

The exact role of these advisors, however, varies. Maley (2000: 453), for example, summarizes evidence for various roles played by political advisors who offer input on decision options beyond their "in-house" policy work; Dunn suggests an important brokering role within the executive; Ryan detects a significant role in setting policy agendas; Halligan and Power (1992) refer to advisors as "managing networks of political interaction." And additional studies have also noted the role political advisors can play in the brokerage, coordination, and integration of various endogenous and exogenous sources of policy advice to decision-makers (Dunn, 1997: 93-97; Maley, 2011; Gains & Stoker, 2011; OECD, 2011).

To better understand the content of policy advice, Connaughton (2010a, 2010b) has developed a set of "role perceptions"—*Expert, Partisan, Coordinator,* and *Minder*—for classifying the advisory roles played by important actors in policy advice systems such as political staffers and advisors. Distinguishing between the substantive and procedural dimensions of content also helps assess the politics of policy advice (see Eichbaum & Shaw, 2008).

Policy Analysis

One important source of advice in many contemporary governments comes from policy analysts. Paid professional policy analysts in government and the private sector play an increasingly important role in policy choice, although their precise role is somewhat hard to fathom. As Gill and Saunders (1992) put it, policy analysis at its heart is "a method for structuring information and providing opportunities for the development of alternative choices for the policymaker" (pp. 6–7). Analysts provide information or advice on the relative advantages and disadvantages of different policy choices (Wildavsky, 1969; Mushkin, 1977) and in addition to their role in formulating policy options, also affect their selection.

While there has always been a range of methodologies used in the provision of policy advice, the policy analysis movement (Mintrom, 2007) has remained firmly centred until recently on positivist methodologies. That is, they have only recently begun to encourage public participation and activities such as co-design (Blomkamp, 2018; Trischler et al., 2019), and rather have focused on the use and promotion of an analytic toolkit grounded in micro-economics, quantitative methods, and organizational analysis (Weimer & Vining, 1999). Policy education and training has for many years been largely a matter of familiarization with these tools of technical policy analysis such as supply demand, cost-effectiveness, and cost–benefit analysis (Wildavsky, 1979; Jann, 1991; Geva-May & Maslove, 2007; Gow & Sutherland, 2004).

This way of thinking about the general nature of professional policy work in government has flowed from both a set of empirical studies describing what analysts do in practice and another set of normative arguments about what they should do in order to improve their practices and generate optimal outcomes. Either directly or indirectly, many contemporary policy analysts have built upon Arnold Meltsner's path-breaking 1970s-era studies of a small set of Washington, DC, policy analysts (Meltsner, 1975, 1976) for their empirical referents to the kinds of analysis being practised in government.

In his valuable early work on bureaucratic policy analysis, Meltsner (1975, 1976) compressed and highlighted several variables in defining four specific kinds of analysts according to their level of competence and skill in dealing with either or both of the technical or political elements that he uncovered in the analytical tasks they faced: classifying analysts as "technicians" or "politicians" if they focused on one of these items; as "entrepreneurs" if they combined both talents; and, finally, as "pretenders" (a sub-type of which Meltsner actually found no examples in his interviews), if they lacked both sets of skills.

While astute, however, Melstner's observations are now almost 50 years old and were based on only 116 interviews conducted at the federal level in the US in 1970 and 1971 (Meltsner, 1975: 14). While the number of studies proposing, applying, and validating the use of such a micro-economic tool-kit is legion, the number of empirical studies into the day-to-day practices of policy analysts is much smaller and, in many cases, evidence that such practices are followed in government is either non-existent or outdated (Cole-batch, 2006).

More recent empirical research has sought to revalidate and adapt these categories to advance pedagogy, recruitment, and training of policy analysts (Cole-batch & Radin, 2006). These studies have found that analysts tend to do the following:

1. Practise some combination of as many as nine different policy-related activities, including those related to tasks such as data acquisition and legal issues often neglected in previous studies.
2. Fall into one of four general types—appraisers, implementers, strategists, and evaluators—when categorized by task.
3. Practise one of four common sets of analytical techniques, ranging from consultation to mathematical modelling that are a very different set of techniques than those usually taught in policy schools (Morcul & Iva-nova, 2010; Geva-May & Maslove, 2007).
4. Address at least three different issue types that vary not only in terms of their technical complexity and consultative or "political" nature, as Meltsner argued, but also by their routine versus innovative character.
5. Have very different sets of contacts with actors either within or external to governments (Mintrom, 2003).

While this work has helped illuminate the world of internal governmental policy advice and its impact on decision-making, little is known about the non-governmental components of policy advisory systems (Hird, 2005; Smith, 1977; Stone & Denham, 2004; McGann & Johnson, 2005; Abelson, 2007; Stritch, 2007; Cross, 2007; Murray, 2007). And even less is known about aspects such as the growing legion of consultants who work for governments in the "invisible public service" (Speers, 2007; Boston, 1994).

Moreover, the personal and professional components of the policy advice supply system, along with their internal and external sourcing, can be expected to be combined in different ratios in different policy-making situations (Prince, 1983; Wollman, 1989; Hawke, 1983; Rochet, 2004). Figure 6.2. sets out the kinds of policy advice decision-makers now commonly receive in their work.

Figure 6.2 Policy Advice and Advisors Organized by Policy Content

	Short-Term/Reactive	Long-Term/Anticipatory
Procedural	***"Pure" Political and Policy Process Advice*** Political parties, parliaments and legislative committees; regulatory agencies	***Medium to Long-term Policy Steering Advice*** Deputy ministers, central agencies/executives; royal commissions; judicial bodies
	As well as	As well as
	Internal as well as external political advisors, interest groups; lobbyists; mid-level public service policy analysts and policy managers; pollsters	Agencies, boards and commissions; Crown corporations; international organizations (e.g., OECD, ILO, UN)
Substantive	***Short-Term Crisis and Firefighting Advice*** Political peers (e.g., cabinet); executive office political staffs	***Evidence-Based Policy-Making*** Statistical agencies; senior departmental policy advisors; strategic policy unit; royal commissions
	As well as	As well as
	Expanded ministerial, legislative staffs; cabinet committees; external consultants; political strategists; pollsters; community organizations/NGOs; lobbyists, media	Think tanks; scientific & academic advisors; open data citizen engagement driven policy initiatives/web 2.0; blue ribbon panels

Evidence-Based Decision-Making

One way in which it is expected that policy choices can be made more scientific and effective, regardless of the methods used to analyze them, is to enhance the amount and type of evidence or data used to support their formulation and choice. The "evidence-based policy-making" movement represents a contemporary effort to reform or restructure policy processes in order to prioritize evidentiary or data-based input over other influences on decision-making with the expectation that better and more proportional decisions will result than when choices are made purely on the basis of personal experience, intuition, or partisan or ideological sensibilities. Like earlier efforts in the policy analysis movement, its aim is to avoid or minimize policy failures caused by uncertainty and a mismatch between government expectations and efforts and actual, on-the-ground conditions and results. Toward this end, evidence-based or "evidence-informed" policy-making is an attempt to improve the amount and type of information processed in public policy decision-making as well as the methods used to assess it (Morgan & Henrion, 1990; Nilsson et al., 2008).

This movement is based on the idea that better decisions are those that incorporate the best available information, which is expected to result in policy decisions with the best chance of attaining government expectations, even if this does not necessarily occur 100 per cent of the time because of factors such as failure to incorporate new knowledge or including incorrect information in policy advice and decision-making rationales. It is expected, though, that iterative monitoring and evaluation of results will allow errors to be caught and corrected and new evidence to be incorporated in policy reviews and reforms. Such uses of evidence is expected to enhance policy learning, avoid policy failures, and increase the potential for greater success and proportionality in designs, efforts, and outcomes (March, 1981, 1994).

A significant variable influencing policy-makers' ability to pursue evidence-based policy-making, however, is both governmental and non-governmental "policy analytical capacity." That is, governments require a high level of policy analytical capacity in order to effectively manage informational inputs and pursue evidence-based policy-making. Recent studies, unfortunately, suggest that even in advanced countries the level of policy analytical capacity found in many governments and non-governmental actors is low, potentially contributing to a failure of evidence-based policy-making as well as limiting capacity to deal with complex policy challenges and contributing to policy over and under-reactions and over and under-designs (Howlett, 2009).

Exactly what constitutes "evidence-based policy-making" and whether analytical efforts in this regard actually result in better or improved policies also are subjects that remain contentious in the literature on the subject (Boaz et al., 2008; Jackson, 2007; Packwood, 2002; Pawson, 2002). A spate of studies has questioned the value of simply assuming collecting and analyzing large amounts of data is a route to better policy outcomes (Tenbensel, 2004).

Several concerns have been raised. First, evidence is only one factor required for successful policy-making and is not necessarily able to overcome other factors such as constitutional divisions of powers or jurisdictions that can arbitrarily assign policy responsibilities to specific levels or institutions of government and diminish the rationality of policy-making (Davies, 2004; Radin & Boase, 2000; Young et al., 2002). Second, data collection and analytical techniques employed in its gathering and analysis by specially trained policy technicians may not be necessarily superior to the experiential judgments of politicians and other key decision-makers in all cases, especially when there is a high level of uncertainty and issues around political feasibility and social acceptance are involved (Jackson, 2007; Majone, 1989). Third, the kinds of "high-quality" and universally acknowledged evidence initially proposed when evidence-based policy-making first entered the lexicon of policy analysts in the healthcare field—especially the "systematic review" of clinical findings—often has no analogue in many policy sectors where generating evidence using the "gold standard" of random clinical trial methodologies may not be possible (Innvaer et al., 2002; Pawson et al., 2005). And, fourth, as mentioned above, an increased emphasis on evidence-based policy-making can stretch the analytical resources of participating organizations to the breaking point (Hammersley, 2005). That is, government and especially non-governmental organization efforts in this area may have adverse consequences in terms of requiring greater expenditures on analytical activities at the expense of operational ones, meaning organizations of all kinds may be forced to divert financial, personnel, and other scarce resources from implementation or membership service activities to policy-making (Laforest & Orsini, 2005).

The Nature of Policy Choices: Negative, Positive, and Non-Decisions

Regardless of who makes a policy selection, and on what grounds, from a large group of legislators in a partisan arena to a civil servant working alone in a bureaucracy, the results will fit into one of just a few categories. That is, although the actual substance or content of a decision can be infinitely varied, its effect will be to either perpetuate the policy *status quo* or alter it. Traditional *"positive" decisions* that alter the status quo receive considerable attention in the decision-making and policy choice literature and are therefore accorded most attention in this chapter.

However, it is important to note that other decisions uphold the status quo. Here we can distinguish between *"negative"* decisions, in which a deliberate choice is made to uphold the status quo, and what are sometimes termed *"non-decisions,"* where options to deviate from the status quo are avoided at the policy formulation or agenda-setting stages (see Zelditch et al., 1983; R.A. Smith, 1979). *Non-decisions* have been the subject of many inquiries and studies by scholars interested in tracing the effects of ideologies, religions, gender, racial, ethnic, and other similar factors that blind decision-makers to the need to act on a public problem; similarly, power allows decision-makers to ignore certain issues despite public clamour for change as has happened in many jurisdictions around climate change policy in recent years, for example (see Bachrach & Baratz, 1962, 1970 [Ch. 3]; Debnam, 1975; Bachrach & Baratz, 1975; Zelditch & Ford, 1994; Spranca et al., 1991; Oliviera et al., 2005).

Very little research into negative decisions, however, exists. This is partly due to the difficulties associated with identifying when policy changes are explicitly rejected in favour of maintaining the status quo (see Howlett, 1986). Nevertheless, these decisions are important and can be examined from their effect on the policy cycle's function. That is, negative decisions are instances of *arrested* policy cycles in which plans and options move up to the stage of policy choice but then fail to move forward from there to implementation on the ground. This is unlike non-decisions, in which certain options are filtered out at earlier stages of the policy process and may thus never reach decision-makers. When a negative decision is made, policy deliberations stop, at least for a time (van der Eijk & Kok, 1975).

While negative and non-decisions pose problems to observers, a useful way to assess the nature of a positive decision is simply to measure the extent to which adopted solutions depart from the policy status quo. Some choices call for new, substantial, or dramatic policy change, while others only tinker slightly with existing policies and programs (Majone, 1991).

In his work on macroeconomic policy change in Britain, Peter Hall identified three different possible types of policy change that are observable outcomes of positive decision-making: *first-order* change, in which only the settings (or calibrations) of policy instruments varied; *second-order* change, in which the types or categories of instruments used to effect policy were alternated; and *third-order* change, in which the goals of policy were substituted (Hall, 1993). While useful, the logic of the model suggests there should be four basic types of change, not three, however. These can be described as changes related to abstract *policy goals* or more concrete *program specifications*, referring to the ends of policy-making; and to basic policy *instrument type* or genus, as opposed to alterations of existing *instrument components*, when discussing changes in policy means.

Decisions to transform policy goals and instrument types require the injection of new ideas and thinking into policy deliberations. Narrower options for change that target program specifications and instrument "settings" or components are less disruptive, often creating relatively minor alterations to existing policies. Proposals for policy goal and program substitution tend to arise after new actors have joined existing policy processes, including deliberations on policy choices, while instrument adjustments and component changes tend to develop among existing actors when their preferences change (Krause, 1997; Berridge, 2005; Chari & McMahon, 2003; Boyer & Cremieux, 1999). This general situation is set out in Figure 6.3.

In practice, there is often a tendency to develop incremental adjustments in policy formulation, that is, to propose changing instrument settings. This occurs because, as we saw in earlier chapters, policy regimes tend to form in most policy areas, and these regimes entrench both policy subsystems (the configuration of actors involved in decision-making) and policy paradigms (the ideas they carry into the policy process), limiting the ability of new actors and new ideas to penetrate these processes.

Figure 6.3 Effects of New Actors and Ideas on Policy Choices

	Presence of New Actors	*Continuity of Old Actors*
Presence of New Ideas	Choices relating to changes in policy goals	Choices relating to changes in program specifications
Continuity of Old Ideas	Choices relating to changes in instrument types	Choices relating to changes in instrument components

Actors in the Decision-Making Process

Executive, Legislators, Judges, and Administrative Officials

With the exception of usually infrequent exercises in direct democracy, such as referendums (Wagschal, 1997; Butler & Ranney, 1994), the number of influential policy actors decreases substantially when the public policy process reaches the decision-making stage. Such concentrated engagement is not found at the agenda-setting stage, where virtually any actor in the policy universe could, theoretically at least, become involved. The policy formulation stage is also open to numerous actors, though in practice only members of policy subsystems with specific knowledge and/or an interest tend to participate. But when it comes time to decide on adopting a policy, the relevant group of actors is almost invariably restricted to those very few in government with the authority to make binding decisions.

In other words, decision-making in public policy normally falls to those occupying formal offices in government. Excluded are virtually all non-state actors, including those from other levels of governments, both domestically and internationally, although these other actors may influence authoritative decision-makers through activities such as lobbying or agitation, or in some cases bribery and corruption (Wedel, 2012; Heller et al., 2016; Kasekende et al., 2016).

This is not to say that non-state actors, including ones associated with other governments, are not active during policy decision-making. These actors can lobby and advocate to persuade, encourage, and sometimes even coerce public officials to adopt preferred options and avoid objectionable ones (Woll, 2007). However, unlike office-holders, those other actors have, at best, a "voice" in the decision-making process, not a "vote" (see Pal, 1993b; Richardson et al., 1978; Sarpkaya, 1988). That is, despite vigorous participation within a subsystem, only those politicians, judges, and government officials actually empowered to make authoritative decisions about the policy in question can engage in decision-making by exercising both "voice" and "vote" (Aberbach et al., 1981).

However, this formal authority does not mean that decision-makers can adopt whatever policy they wish. As discussed earlier, decision-makers' freedom is constrained by rules and structures governing political and administrative offices, as well as by actors' ideas or paradigms and their social, economic, and political circumstances. As we have seen, rules and structures that affect political power and resources available to both state and non-state actors range from the country's constitution to the specific mandates conferred on decision-makers by elections or legislation. Administrative decision-makers, such as judges and civil servants, must act within specific sets of laws, conventions, and regulations governing their behaviour and fields of competence (Markoff, 1975; Page, 1985a; Atkinson & Coleman, 1989a). The different actors who contend to influence these decisions were discussed in Chapter 3.

There is a great deal of variation among the specific officials—both appointed and elected—who make a policy decision. As was shown in earlier chapters, some political systems concentrate decision-making authority in the elected executive and the bureaucracy, while others assign the legislature and judiciary a greater role in policy-making. Parliamentary systems tend to fall in the former category and presidential systems in the latter. Thus, in Australia, Britain, Canada, and other parliamentary democracies, the cabinet and bureaucracy are often solely responsible for making many policy decisions. They may have decisions imposed on them by the legislature in situations when the government does not enjoy a parliamentary majority, or by the judiciary in its role as interpreter of the constitution, but in Latin America, the Philippines and elsewhere these are not routine occurrences. In the United States and other presidential systems, although the authority to make most policy decisions rests with the executive (and the cabinet and bureaucracy acting on the executive's behalf), those decisions requiring legislative approval often involve intense negotiations with lawmakers, and both executive orders and legislation are modified or overturned on a regular basis by the judiciary on constitutional, procedural, or other grounds (Weaver & Rockman, 1993b).

At the micro level, bureaucratic rules and administrative practices and procedures set out not only which decisions can be made by which government agency or official, but also the steps that must be followed for this to occur. These range from provisions mandating that societal groups—from businesses to affected minorities—must be consulted in actions affecting them, to "notice and comment" rules that mandate specific consultation periods and information disclosure regarding a government's intent to act.

As Allison and Halperin (1972) have noted, over time such rules and operating procedures often provide decision-makers with "action channels"—a regularized set of *standard operating procedures*—for producing decisions. These rules and standard operating procedures help explain why so much of government's decision-making is routine and repetitive in nature. Nevertheless, while rules and normal procedures circumscribe the freedom available to some decision-makers (especially those in administrative or judicial positions), others (especially elected officials) nevertheless retain considerable discretion to judge the "best" course of action to follow in specific circumstances.

Since decision-makers themselves vary greatly in terms of background, knowledge, and the beliefs that affect how they interpret a problem and its potential solutions (Huitt, 1968), different decision-makers operating in similar institutional environments can respond distinctively even when dealing with the same or similar problems. Hence, even with standard operating procedures, exactly what process is followed and which decision is considered "best" will vary according to the structural and institutional context of a decision-making situation.

Observers have also noted how policy-makers, in the course of interaction among themselves and in their day-to-day dealings with the public, tend to

Figure 6.4 Policy Subsystem Configurations That Influence Decision-Making

		Receptive to New Actors	
		No	Yes
Receptive to New Ideas	No	Closed subsystem	Resistant subsystem
	Yes	Contested open subsystem	Open subsystem

develop a common way of looking at and dealing with a problem (Kenis, 1991; Haas, 1992; Sabatier, 1988). This suggests that policy subsystems play a significant role in the process of policy formulation (Zijlstra, 1978–9; Rhodes & Marsh, 1992; Raab & Kenis, 2007). Sabatier (1988), for example, has argued that the nature of the policy subsystem responsible for policy formulation is an important element in the analysis of policy change as advocacy coalition members mediate the exchange of interests and ideas in the process of policy-making and do so in characteristic and semi-permanent ways.

Policy Networks

Some analysts have suggested that the "cohesiveness" or "closedness" of policy subsystems is thus an important factor affecting the propensity for new or innovative policy solutions to emerge from the policy formulation process (Marsh & Rhodes, 1992b; Bressers & O'Toole, 1998; Zahariadis & Allen, 1995; Jordana & Sancho, 2005). As Hanspeter Kriesi and Maya Jegen (2001: 251) put it, "to know the actor constellation is to know the parameters determining the choices among the substantive policy options."

This suggests that, as seen with agenda-setting and policy formulation, a principal factor affecting the propensity of a policy subsystem to generate policy options involving substantial changes is a subsystem structure that allows new actors and new ideas to enter into policy deliberations (Schmidt, 2001). The relevant types of policy subsystems that can influence decision-making are set out in Figure 6.4.

Theories of Decision-Making

Early Rational and Incremental Models

Whether a public policy decision is negative or positive, it involves creating an expression of intent by authoritative decision-makers to undertake or implement some course of action (or inaction). In this section we will review the different models that have been developed to help describe, conceptualize, and analyze such expressions of decision-making. We set out key elements of these models and discuss their success and failure in describing decision-making processes. Although many decision-making models can be found across fields as diverse as psychology and business management, we shall see that these literatures all suggest that a variety of different decision-making process styles exist, and that the likelihood of one being followed can be ascertained with some certainty by examining the actors making the decision and the constraints under which they operate.

The policy cycle's decision-making stage received considerable attention early on in the development of the policy sciences. At that time, analysts borrowed heavily from models and studies of decision-making in complex organizations developed by students of public administration and business organization. By the mid-1960s, these discussions about public policy decision-making had ossified into two purportedly incompatible models: rational and incremental.

The first to emerge was the *rational model*, which asserted that public policy decision-making was inherently a search for maximizing solutions to complex problems in which policy-relevant information was gathered and then used in a scientific mode of assessing policy options. The other model—often termed *the incremental model*—identified public policy decision-making as a less technical and more political activity, in which analysis played a much smaller role in determining outcomes than did bargaining, and other interactions and negotiation between decision-makers (see Mossberger, 2000: Ch. 2). The mainstream position throughout much of this period was that while the "rational" model was more preferable for showing how decisions ought to be taken to assure "maximum" results, the "incremental" model best described the *actual* practice of decision-making within government (Dror, 1968; Etzioni, 1967; Howard, 1971).

However, by the mid-1970s it was apparent that neither model accurately represented all instances of decision-making; that different decision-making opportunities featured different methods and modes of decision-making; and that the range of decision-making styles varied beyond the two "ideal types" represented by the rational and incremental models (Smith & May, 1980; Allison, 1969, 1971). This led to efforts to develop alternative models of the decision-making processes followed by complex organizations. Some attempted to synthesize the rational and incremental models (Etzioni, 1967). Others—including the so-called *"garbage can"* model of decision-making—focused on the irrational elements of organizational behaviour in order to arrive at a third path beyond rationalism and incrementalism (Cohen et al., 1972; March & Olsen, 1979a). Subsequently, efforts were made to move beyond the debates among rationalists, irrationalists, and incrementalists and develop a more nuanced understanding of public policy decision-making and the role that policy subsystems play in influencing these dynamics.

The Comprehensive and Bounded-Rationality Models

First developed to aid economic analysis, and especially the analysis of producer and consumer choices, the "rational" theory of decision-making postulated that in developing and expressing a preference for one course of action over another, decision-makers would attempt to pursue a strategy that, in theory, would maximize the expected outcomes of the choices they could make (Edwards, 1954). Decision-making in the public policy arena was seen to parallel the marketplace behaviour of buyers and sellers seeking to obtain top "utility" from their limited resources by minimizing costs and maximizing benefits.

This idealized model of rational decision-making presumed that decision-makers and policy choice would consistently and predictably undertake the following series of sequential activities leading to decision:

1. A goal for solving a problem is established.
2. All alternative strategies of achieving the goal are explored and listed.
3. All significant consequences of each alternative strategy are predicted and the probability of those consequences occurring is estimated.
4. Finally, the strategy that most nearly solves the problem or solves it at least cost is selected (Carley, 1980: 11).

Ideally, the process would involve attributing costs and benefits to each option, comparing these across widely divergent options, and estimating the probability of failure and success for each option (Edwards, 1954; March, 1994).

The rational model is "rational" in the sense that it prescribes decision-making procedures that, in theory, will consistently lead to choosing the most efficient means of achieving policy goals. Rooted in Enlightenment notions of rationality and positivist schools of thought that sought to develop scientific knowledge to improve human conditions (Jennings, 1987; Torgerson, 1986), this model assumes that maximal outcomes can be achieved through the ordered gathering of relevant information allowing the "best" alternative to be identified and selected (Weiss, 1977b). Decision-makers are assumed to operate as technicians or business managers, who collect and analyze information that allows them to adopt the most effective or efficient way of solving any problem they confront. Because of its "neutral," technical application to problem-solving, this mode is also known as the "scientific," "engineering," or "managerialist" approach (Elster, 1991: 115).

Early attempts to address organizational behaviour through a scientific mode of investigation identified the rational model of decision-making as a promising technique that would yield managerial advances in business and public administration. Elements of the model can be found in the work of early students of public administration such as Henri Fayol in France, and Luther Gulick and Lyndal Urwick in the United States. Drawing on the insights gleaned by Fayol

(1949) from his studies of the turn-of-the-century French coal industry, in the 1930s Gulick and Urwick, for example, promoted what they termed the "POS-DCORB" model of management, in which they urged organizations to maximize their performance by systematically planning, organizing, staffing, directing, co-ordinating, reporting, and budgeting their activities (Gulick, 1937). "Directing" a particular course of action, for Gulick and Urwick and the management theorists who followed in their footsteps, amounted to weighing the benefits of any decision against its expected costs and arriving at a "steady stream" of maximizing decisions required for the organization's optimal function (see, e.g., Kepner & Tregoe, 1965).

It was recognized very early on, however, that it would not always be possible to achieve "full" rationality in practice. This was because even if a decision-maker wished to adopt maximizing decisions, these might not be possible due to limited information and time. However, many analysts did not consider these to be insurmountable problems. Rather, they simply recognized the difficulties that could be found in translating decision-making theory into decision-making practice, which meant that the resulting decisions might not be perfectly rational or error-proof, but would normally be close enough to approximate "perfect" rationality.

Some analysts, however, claimed that these limitations on rationality had much more serious implications for decision-making theory and practice. Perhaps the most noted critic of the rational model was Herbert Simon, until recently the only student of public administration ever to win a Nobel Prize. Simon and others argued that the constraints on rationality previously noted were not simply "deviations" that might be overcome by more careful analysis, or that would crop up only in exceptional circumstances. Rather, these shortcomings represented the norm and were impossible to avoid and serious enough to undermine notions of "pure" rationality or outcome maximization as embodied in the classical rational model.

Simon produced a series of books and articles in the 1950s highlighting the obstacles preventing decision-makers from ever attaining "pure" rationality in their decisions and proposing an alternative notion of "bounded rationality" to replace the maximizing principle underlying rational choice theory (Simon, 1955, 1957b; Jones 2002). First, he noted that decision-making would generate maximal results only if *all* possible alternatives and their costs were assessed before a decision was made. He then demonstrated that decision-makers faced cognitive limits in considering an almost infinite number of possible options, leading them to focus on only a subset of alternatives that they deemed likely, or probable, or feasible. Simon noted that such pre-decisional choices were typically made on ideological, professional, cultural, or similar grounds, if not randomly. With efficiency implications being ignored in such initial choices, the opportunity to select a rational course of action from the resulting options was lost (see Fernandes & Simon, 1999).

Second, Simon examined the implication of the rational model's requirement for decision-makers to know the consequences of each decision in advance. He concluded that this rarely, if ever, occurred. But without accurately predicting the future, Simon noted it would be impossible to assess the costs and benefits of different options as required by the rational model. Third, Simon pointed out that most policy options yield a "bundle" of favourable and adverse consequences, and that the "costing" of each "bundle" is not straightforward, as it requires a prospective ranking of relative potential gains that, again, cannot be validated on "rational" grounds. Fourth, Simon also noted that very often the same option can be efficient or inefficient depending on other, and changing, circumstances. Hence, it is rarely possible for decision-makers to draw robust conclusions about which alternative is superior, as required by the rational model (see Einhorn & Hogarth, 1986).

Numerous efforts to modify the rational model followed these criticisms, all in the effort to preserve the principle that "maximization" could guide decision-making (Kruse et al., 1991: Ch. 1; Conlisk, 1996). Theories of *"fuzzy" decision-making*, for example, argued that even if costs and benefits associated with specific policy options could not be clearly stated or specified with great precision, probabilistic techniques could be used to illuminate the *range* of "maximized" outcomes, allowing at least an approximately rational choice to be made (Bellman & Zadeh, 1970; Whalen, 1987; Mendoza & Sprouse, 1989).

Other studies, mainly in the field of psychology, attempted to specify, on the basis of field experiments, exactly what sorts of common biases decision-makers exhibited in dealing with the uncertainties described by Simon (see Slovic et al., 1977, 1985). This is the case, for example, with models linked to *prospect theory* (see Kahneman & Tversky, 1979; Tversky & Kahneman, 1981, 1982, 1986; Haas, 2001), which postulated that humans "overweight losses relative to comparable gains, engage in risk-averse behaviour in choices but risk-acceptant behaviour in choices among losses, and respond to probabilities in a nonlinear manner" (Levy, 1997: 33). This was done in the hope that specifying the cognitive limits in decision-making that Simon had uncovered would enable the development of "second-best" maximizing rational models that would account for actual human behavioural limitations in the face of uncertainty (see Yates & Zukowski, 1976; Suedfeld & Tetlock, 1992; Einhorn, 1982; Kanner, 2005).

Simon, however, concluded that public decisions ostensibly taken in accordance with the precepts and methods outlined by the rational model would never *maximize* benefits over costs, but would instead tend only to *satisfy* whatever criteria decision-makers had set for themselves at the time of a decision. This *"satisficing"* criterion, as he put it, was a realistic one given the bounded rationality with which human beings are endowed and within which they must work when taking decisions (see March, 1978, 1994). Although he did not himself develop an alternative model of decision-making built on the notion of satisficing (see Jones, 2001: Ch. 3), his insights would later be taken up by Charles Lindblom, who would incorporate them into the best-known alternative to the rational model: the *incremental* model of decision-making based on limited analysis and political exchange or bargaining, rather than knowledge-based analysis (Thomson et al., 2003).

Incremental Model

Doubts about the usefulness of the rational model led to development of a second major school of public policy decision-making theory that sought a closer fit between theory and the actual behaviour of decision-makers in real-life situations. These efforts yielded the incremental model, which portrayed public policy decision-making as a political process characterized by bargaining and compromise among self-interested decision-makers (Braybrooke & Lindblom, 1963; Dahl & Lindblom, 1953; Lindblom, 1959). In this model, the decisions made represent what is politically feasible rather than technically desirable, and what is possible or "optimal" rather than "maximal" in the rational model's meaning of getting the most output for the least cost.

The credit for developing the incremental model of public decision-making is attributed to Yale University political scientist Charles Lindblom and his colleagues at other North American universities in the late 1950s and early 1960s (Dahl & Lindblom, 1953; Lindblom, 1955, 1958, 1959). Lindblom took to heart the ideas of bounded rationality and satisficing behaviour among decision-makers pioneered by Simon and, based on his own observations of government decision-making processes, outlined what he suggested were the common elements of "strategies of decision" actually pursued by public policy decision-makers (Jones, 2002). The model he put forward arranged these strategies into a "mutually supporting set of simplifying and focusing stratagems" and included the following elements:

a. limitation of analysis to a few somewhat familiar policy alternatives . . . differing only marginally from the status quo;
b. mixing policy goals and other values along with the empirical aspects of a problem in policy analysis (that is, no obligation to specify values first before identifying the means to promote them);
c. a greater analytical preoccupation with ills to be remedied than positive goals to be sought;
d. a sequence of trials, errors, and revised trials;
e. analysis that explores only those possible consequences of an alternative considered to be important; and
f. fragmentation of analytical work to many (partisan) participants in policy-making (each attending to their piece of the overall problem domain) (Lindblom, 1979: 517).

In Lindblom's view, decision-makers both did and should develop policies through a process of making "*successive limited comparisons*" with earlier decisions, those with which they are most familiar. As he put it in his oft-cited article "The Science of Muddling Through," decision-makers typically, and should, work through a process of "continually building out from the current situation, step-by-step and by small degrees" (Lindblom, 1959: 81). Decisions thus arrived at are usually only marginally different from those that exist. In other words, the changes from the status quo in decision-making are *incremental*.

According to Lindblom, there are two reasons why decisions typically do not stray far from the status quo. First, since bargaining requires distributing limited resources among various participants, it is easier to continue the existing pattern of distribution rather than try to negotiate the redistribution that would be required under any proposal for radical change. Since the benefits and costs of present arrangements are known to the policy actors, unlike the uncertainties surrounding new arrangements, securing agreement on major changes is more difficult. The result is typically either continuation of the status quo or agreement to make only small changes to it. Second, the standard operating procedures of bureaucracies also tend to promote continuity in practice. The methods by which bureaucrats identify options and the procedures and criteria for choice are usually long-established, inhibiting innovation and perpetuating existing arrangements (Gortner et al., 1987: 257).

Lindblom also argued that the rational model's requirement of separation between ends and means in the calculus of decision-making was unworkable in practice. This was not only because the time, information, and cognitive constraints identified by Simon and others were beyond the reach of actual decision-makers, but also because rationalism assumed policy-makers could both clearly separate means from ends in assessing policies and then agree upon their meaning. Lindblom argued that in most policy areas, discussion of ends is inseparable from the means to achieve them, since which goals are pursued often depends on whether or not viable means are available to accomplish them. The beneficial essence of incrementalism, Lindblom argued, was to try to systematize decision-making processes by stressing the need for political agreement and learning by trial and error, rather than simply stumbling into random decisions without any strategy at all, or failing to develop pseudo-maximal ones through futile application of the rational method (Lindblom & Cohen, 1979).

Some critics of incrementalism have debated the extent to which the incremental model accurately describes how many public policy decisions are actually made in practice (see Berry, 1990; Jones et al., 1997), since decisions to significantly alter the status quo do occur periodically. Others, however, found several faults with its theoretical implications (see Weiss & Woodhouse, 1992). First, the model was criticized for lacking any kind of goal orientation. As John Forester (1984: 23) put it, incrementalism "would have us cross and recross intersections without knowing where we are going." Second, the model was challenged for being inherently conservative, given its apparent suspicion of large-scale change and innovation. Third, it was censured for justifying decision-making as implicitly undemocratic, to the extent that it confined decision-making to bargaining within a select group of senior policy-makers (Gawthrop, 1971). Fourth, by discouraging systematic analysis and planning and discounting the need to search for promising new alternatives, it was said to promote short-sighted decisions that could have adverse consequences for society in the long run (Lustick, 1980).

Beyond these normative criticisms about the desirability of decisions made incrementally, the model was also criticized for its narrow analytic usefulness. Yehezkel Dror (1964), for example, noted that incrementalism can only work when there is a great deal of continuity both in the nature of problems that policies are intended to address and in the means available to address them. Such continuity is far from universal in policy-making. Incrementalism is thus more characteristic of decision-making in a relatively stable environment, rather than in unusual situations, such as a crisis or a novel policy issue (Nice, 1987; Lustick, 1980). Fifth, it was pointed out that in practice it is very difficult to know exactly what an "increment" is versus what is not a unit of measure when differentiating how a policy would move beyond the previous status quo (Bailey & O'Connor, 1975).

Lindblom countered many of these criticisms in his own writings, stating that incrementalism was neither inherently conservative nor short-sighted, since the relative size and direction of increments were not predetermined but would emerge from the deliberative bargaining process that characterized incremental policy-making (Lindblom, 1979: 517). He also suggested that the incremental method was neither inherently democratic nor undemocratic, but would simply follow the structure of representation present in different political systems and situations (Lindblom, 1968).

However, in responding to one major criticism—that incrementalism was better suited for or more likely to occur in some policy-making contexts than others—adherents of the incremental model had to accept that the nature of the decision-making process would vary according to factors such as whether a policy was new, the number of decision-makers involved, and whether or not they shared a consensus on the goals and objectives of policy-making (Bendor, 1995; Jones, 2001). This meant that the model was neither the ideal method of decision-making, as had been suggested by some adherents, nor, as Lindblom had alleged in some of his writings, the *only* possible method of policy-making. Rather, it was only one of several possible types or styles of public policy decision-making (Hayes, 2007).

By the early 1980s, it had become apparent to many observers that the continuing debate between the advocates of rationalism and those of incrementalism over the merits and demerits of their favoured models was constraining both empirical analysis and theoretical development. Rather than continue the debate, Smith and May (1980: 156) suggested that

> we require more than one account to describe the several facets of orga-
> nizational life. The problem is not to reconcile the differences between
> contrasting rational and incremental models, nor to construct some third
> alternative which combines the strongest features of each. The problem
> is to relate the two in the sense of spelling out the relationship between
> the social realities with which each is concerned.

This awareness of the limitations of both the rational and incremental models of decision-making led policy scholars to look for alternatives. These came in many forms. Despite Smith and May's admonition, some analysts attempted to synthesize the two models, an unlikely outcome but one that is not impossible to imagine. Others embraced the elements of unpredictability and capriciousness opened by the fall of incrementalism as the main alternative to the rational model. While neither of these theoretical directions proved particularly fruitful, a third effort to clarify the exact nature of alternative decision-making modes or styles, and the likely conditions under which they would be employed, generated more lasting value and continues to inform present-day work on decision-making.

Mixed-Scanning Models

The initial response of many scholars to criticisms of incrementalism as an alternative to the rational model was to attempt to "rescue" both models by combining them in a constructive synthesis. As early as 1967, for example, Amitai Etzioni proposed his *mixed-scanning* model to bridge the shortcomings of both rational and incremental models by combining elements from both.

Accepting the criticisms of the rational model as largely unworkable in practice and of the incremental model as only appropriate to certain policy environments, Etzioni suggested that combining the two models could overcome both criticisms, while providing decision-makers with a practical guide to "optimal" decision-making. Adopting a similar position to that of Simon, Etzioni, followed by many others, suggested that the decision-making process in fact consisted of two stages, a "pre-decisional" or "representative" stage of assessing a problem and "framing" it, which would utilize incremental analysis, and a second analytical phase in which specific solutions could be more carefully assessed, which would be more rational in nature (see Voss, 1998; Svenson, 1979; Alexander, 1979, 1982).

In Etzioni's "mixed-scanning" model, optimal decisions would result from a cursory search ("scanning") for alternatives, followed by a detailed probe of the most appealing alternatives. This would allow for more innovation than permitted by the incremental model, without imposing the unrealistic demands prescribed by the rational model. Etzioni argued that this was, indeed, how many decisions were made in reality, where it is not uncommon to find a series of incremental decisions followed by a substantially different decision when decision-makers are faced with a problem significantly different from those dealt with before. Thus, he presented his model as both a prescriptive and descriptive approach to decision-making that would overcome the conceptual limitations of earlier models while conforming to the actual practices of decision-makers.

In later work, students of US foreign policy decision-making developed a similar two-stage model of decision-making processes, sometimes referred to as the "*poliheuristic*" model (see Mintz & Geva, 1997; Mintz et al., 1997). In this view, decision-makers use a variety of cognitive shortcuts ("heuristics," "operational codes," or "standard operating procedures") to compensate for limitations in knowledge and to achieve some initial winnowing of alternatives to a set of "feasible" or "acceptable" ones (Fernandes & Simon, 1999; Voss & Post, 1988; George, 1969, 1979; Drezner, 2000; Allison & Halperin, 1972; Brule, 2008). These heuristics include the use of historical analogies, a preference for incremental policies, the desire for consensus among competing policy actors, and the desire to claim credit or avoid blame for potential policy outcomes (see George, 1980; Weaver, 1986; Hood, 2002; Vertzberger, 1998; Sulitzeanu-Kenan & Hood, 2005; Hood & Rothstein, 2001). In the second stage, a limited number of alternatives are subjected to a more rational, "maximizing" analysis (Mintz, 2004, 2005; Ye, 2007). As Mintzberg et al. found in their 1976 study of "strategic" or non-routine decision-making with uncertain outcomes:

> When faced with a complex, unprogrammed situation, the decision-makers seek to reduce the decision into sub-decisions to which he [sic] applies general purpose, interchangeable sets of procedures or routines. In other words, the decision-makers deal with unstructured situations by factoring them into familiar, structural elements. Furthermore, the individual decision maker uses a number of problem-solving shortcuts—satisficing instead of maximizing, not looking too far ahead, reducing a complex environment to a series of simplified conceptual "models." (Mintzberg et al., 1976: 247; see also Weiss, 1982)

It is not clear, however, exactly how these models differ from the incremental and rational ones they were ostensibly designed to replace. That is, the techniques of marginal analysis put forward by Lindblom and others already envisioned a limited search for, and selection of, alternatives, which would then be singled out for more detailed analysis. And it is also not clear how mixed-scanning would overcome the problems associated with the rational model, since without the systematic comparison of all possible alternatives, it is impossible to assure that a final decision is a maximizing one.

Nevertheless, Etzioni's call for a less overtly political type of incrementalism than that based on Lindblom's "partisan mutual adjustment" was well received by many policy practitioners. Among policy scholars, however, it was quickly by-passed in favour of other models—such as the so-called "garbage can" theory, discussed below—that purported to directly address the reality of uncertainty and ambiguity facing policy-makers in day-to-day decision-making situations (Walker & Marchau, 2004; Driedger & Eyles, 2003; Gupta et al., 2003; Morgan & Henrion, 1990; Potoski, 1999).

Garbage Can Models

In the late 1970s, a very different model asserted and, in fact, embraced the inherent lack of rationality in the decision-making process identified by Simon and others. Developed in part by one of Simon's collaborators, James March, and March's Norwegian colleague, Johan Olsen, the so-called *garbage can model* of decision-making denied to the decision-making process even the limited rationality attributed to it by incrementalism (March & Olsen, 1979b; Cohen et al., 1972).

March and Olsen, working with Michael Cohen, began by assuming that both the rational and incremental models presumed a level of intentionality, comprehension of problems, and predictability of relations among actors that simply did not correspond with reality. In their view, decision-making was a highly ambiguous and unpredictable process only distantly related to searching for means to achieve goals. Rejecting the instrumentalism that characterized most other models, Cohen, March, and Olsen (1979: 26) argued that most decision opportunities were

> a garbage can into which various problems and solutions are dumped by participants. The mix of garbage in a single can depends partly on the labels attached to the alternative cans; but it also depends on what garbage is being produced at the moment, on the mix of cans available, and on the speed with which garbage is collected and removed from the scene.

Cohen, March, and Olsen deliberately used the garbage can metaphor to strip away the aura of scientific precision attributed to the authority behind decision-making by earlier theorists. They sought to drive home the point that goals are often unknown to policy-makers, along with ignorance about causal relationships. Under these circumstances, actors define goals and choose means using idiosyncratic rationales as they proceed through a policy process that is necessarily contingent and unpredictable. As Gary Mucciaroni (1992: 461) explained, in this model

[t]here is plenty of room for chance, human creativity, and choice to influence outcomes. What gets on the agenda at given points in time is the result of a fortuitous conjunction—whatever the combination of salient problems, available solutions, and political circumstances that exist. Events, such as the opening of a window of opportunity, are often unpredictable, and participants often are unable to control events once they are set in motion. Yet, individual actors are not completely without an ability to affect outcomes. Entrepreneurs decide which problems to dramatize, choose which solutions to push, and formulate political strategies to bring their issues onto the agenda. Actors in the process develop problem definitions and solutions that are plausible and compelling, link them together, and make them congruent with existing political conditions.

March and Olsen (1979a) presented evidence from several case studies of decision-making processes in European universities to substantiate their proposition that public decisions are often made in too ad-hoc and haphazard a fashion to be considered incremental, much less rational. Others, such as Paul Anderson (1983), for example, also demonstrated that policy decisions about high-stakes strategic and military options such as those debated during the 1962 Cuban Missile Crisis, one of the most critical periods of the Cold War conflict, were made in terms of simplistic yes/no binary choices on proposals that would emerge in the course of discussion.

While the garbage can model's key tenets may well be a fairly accurate description of how organizations make decisions some of the time, in other instances it would be reasonable to expect more order. As critics such as Mucciaroni argued, albeit in a national context, rather than present a general model of decision-making, the garbage can idea represents only one type of decision-making that is characteristic of a particular political or organizational context:

> Perhaps the mode of policy-making depicted by the garbage can model is itself embedded in a particular institutional structure. Put another way, the model may be better at depicting decision-making in the United States, where the institutional structure is fragmented and permeable, participation is pluralistic and fluid, and coalitions are often temporary and ad hoc. By contrast, policy-making in other countries takes place among institutions that are more centralized and integrated, where the number of participants is limited and their participation is highly structured and predictable. (Mucciaroni, 1992: 466)

This irrational mode of decision-making is also more likely to occur at points when policy paradigms are in transition, when the coherence commonly held core beliefs typically impose upon policy-making is weak or entirely absent (Hood, 1999).

"Decision Accretion" Model

Challenging and controversial, the greatest contribution of the garbage can model was in helping to break the logjam of what had become a rather sterile debate between rationalists and incrementalists over the merits of their models, thereby allowing for more nuanced studies of decision-making within specific institutional and ideational contexts to be undertaken.

By the 1980s, most studies pointed to the significance of understanding decision-making structures and contexts in advancing the analysis of how decisions are actually taken in complex organizations. In her work on the use of knowledge in the policy process, for example, Carol Weiss noted that in many instances policy decisions are not decided in a "brisk and clear-cut style" in a single institution or setting at a single point in time. Rather, many decisions, from the momentous to the inane, are actually taken piecemeal, without any overall plan of attack or conscious deliberation; in this sense, they appear more like pearls in oysters, having been accreted in multiple layers over a relatively lengthy period of time through the actions of multiple decision-makers (Weiss, 1980).

Unlike incrementalism, which paints a similar portrait of policy-making as the buildup of previous decisions, or the garbage can model, which also describes policy emergence as largely fortuitous, notions of decision accretion do not rely on intra-organizational bargaining processes or fluid sets of participants to explain this pattern. Instead, it is said to emerge because of the nature of the decision to be made and the structure of the organizations that make them. As Weiss argued,

> [i]n large organizations, decisions on complex issues are almost never the province of one individual or one office. Many people in many offices have a say, and when the outcomes of a course of action are uncertain, many participants have opportunities to propose, plan, confer, deliberate, advise, argue, forward policy statements, reject, revise, veto, and re-write. (1980: 399)

In such situations, Weiss suggested, individuals often do not even realize when a decision has been made. Each person takes only some small step in a large process with seemingly small consequences. But over the course of time, "these many small steps foreclose alternative courses of action and limit the range of the possible. Almost imperceptibly, a decision has been made, (sometimes) without anyone's awareness that he or she was deciding" (1980: 401).

This analysis highlights the significance of *multiple arenas* and *multiple rounds* of decision-making for many modern-day public policy decisions (Howlett, 2007). That is, as Weiss and others have suggested, decision-making often tends to occur in multiple locations or venues, each with a distinct set of actors, rules of procedure, and ability to influence the outcome of a decision process in a preferred direction (see Klijn, 2001; Mintzberg et al., 1976; Timmermans, 2001). In each arena, different actors can "score points" in terms of having their definition of a problem or solution adopted. These decisions are collected in a "round" in which the results of each round are fed back into other arenas for continued discussion and debate; a process in which new actors can be activated, new arenas become involved, and new or modified decisions emerge (see Teisman, 2000; Hammond, 1986).

In addition, each venue or arena can be involved in one or more simultaneous decision-making processes, increasing the likelihood that couplings and uncouplings of issues can occur in a highly contingent fashion (see Roe, 1990; Perrow, 1984; van Bueren et al., 2001; Klijn & Teisman, 1991). Similar effects result from actor positions changing over time in lengthy multi-round decision-making processes (Klijn & Koppenjan, 2000b; Howlett, 2007).

Conclusion: Revisiting Public Policy Decision-Making Modes

Focusing on the interactions between actors both within and between organizational arenas and on the strategies used to influence outcomes allows some predictions to be made about the likely kinds of decisions that can emerge from these lengthy and complex policy processes (see Allison & Halperin, 1972; Sager, 2001; Stokman and Berveling, 1998). Moreover, it also allows for the conscious design of decision-making processes in order to clarify the roles of different actors and stages in the process and to ensure that outcomes are less "irrational" and contingent than might otherwise be the case with instances of pure "decision creep" (de Bruijn and ten Heuvelhof, 2000; Klijn & Koppenjan, 2005).

As we have seen, the early rational and incremental models suggested that disparate decision-making styles can be found animating the public policy process. Later models, such as the mixed-scanning, garbage can, and decision-round models, provide some indication of which variables are responsible for the predominance of a particular decision style in a specific circumstance: the nature of a policy problem; the number and type of actors involved; the nature of the informational, temporal, and institutional constraints within which they operate; and the pre-existing sets of ideas or "frames" and decision-making routines with and through which decision-makers approach their tasks (Ley-Borras, 2005).

The idea that there is a range of possible decision-making styles is not a new one (see Wildavsky, 1962; Scharpf, 1991). In some of his earlier writings, for example, Charles Lindblom and several of his co-authors held out the possibility that incremental decision-making could coexist with efforts to achieve more "rational" decisions. Thus, Braybrooke and Lindblom (1963), for example, argued that four different types of decision-making could be discerned, depending on the amount of knowledge at the disposal of decision-makers and the amount of change the selection involved from earlier decisions. In Braybrooke and Lindblom's view, the overwhelming majority of decisions were likely to be taken in an incremental fashion, involving minimal change in situations of low available knowledge. However, three other possibilities also existed: the rational model emerged as one possibility and two other poorly defined styles—"revolutionary" and "analytic"—also existed as infrequently utilized alternatives given specific change and knowledge configurations. Later in his career, Lindblom revisited this idea, arguing that a spectrum of decision-making styles existed according to how systematic the analysis supporting the decision was. These ranged from "synoptic" decision-making, which is similar to the rational ideal, to "blundering," that is, simply following hunches or guesses without any real effort at systematic analysis of alternative strategies, which is akin to the garbage can model.

Neither of these early taxonomies took into account the principal variables identified as significant in the selection process by more recent decision-making models. A more promising start in this direction was made by John Forester in his work on decision-making styles. Forester (1984, 1989) argued that there were at least five distinct decision-making styles associated with six key sets of conditions. According to him, "what is rational for administrators to do depends on the situations in which they work." That is, the decision-making style and the type of decision made by decision-makers would be expected to vary according to issue and institutional contexts. As he put it,

> [d]epending upon the conditions at hand, a strategy may be practical or ridiculous. With time, expertise, data, and a well-defined problem, technical calculations may be in order; without time, data, definition, and expertise, attempting those calculations could well be a waste of time. In a complex organizational environment, intelligence networks will be as, or more, important than documents when information is needed. In an environment of inter-organizational conflict, bargaining and compromise may be called for. Administrative strategies are sensible only in a political and organizational context. (Forester, 1984: 25)

Forester suggested that for decision-making to take place along the lines proposed by the rational model, the following conditions had to be met. First, the number of *agents* (decision-makers) had to be limited, possibly to as few as one person. Second, the organizational *setting* for the decision had to be simple, and insulated from the influences of other policy actors. Third, the *problem* had to be well defined; in other words, its scope, time horizon, value dimensions, and chains of consequences had to be well understood. Fourth, *information* must be as close to perfect as possible; in other words, it must be complete, accessible, and comprehensible. Finally, there must be no urgency for the decision; that is, *time* had to be infinitely available to the decision-makers to consider all possible contingencies and their present and anticipated consequences.

When these conditions are met completely, rational decision-making can be expected to prevail. However, since these five conditions are rarely met in practice, Forester argued that other styles of decision-making would be more likely to emerge. Thus, the number of agents (decision-makers) can expand and multiply almost to infinity; the setting can include many different organizations and can be more or less open to external influences (Heikkila & Isett, 2004; Hammond, 2003); the problem can be ambiguous or susceptible to multiple competing interpretations (Bozeman & Pandey, 2004); information can be incomplete, misleading, or purposefully withheld or manipulated; and time can be limited or artificially constrained and manipulated (Wright, 1974).

From this perspective, Forester suggested the existence of five possible styles of decision-making: what he termed "optimization," "satisficing," "search," "bargaining," and "organizational." *Optimization* is the strategy that obtains when the conditions (mentioned above) of the rational-comprehensive model are met. The prevalence of other styles depends on the degree to which those conditions are not met. When the limitations are cognitive, for reasons mentioned earlier, we are likely to find the *satisficing* style of decision-making. The other styles mentioned by Forester, however, are overlapping and therefore difficult to distinguish clearly. A *search* strategy is one he argued is likely to occur when the problem is vague. A *bargaining* strategy is likely to be employed when multiple actors deal with a problem facing a shortage of information and time. The *organizational* strategy involves multiple settings and actors with both time and informational resources but also multiple problems. Suffice it to say that these types involve greater numbers of actors, more complex settings, more intractable problems, incomplete or distorted information, and limited time for making decisions.

While a major improvement over earlier classifications and taxonomies, and certainly an improvement over the rational and incremental models and their "garbage can" challengers, Forester's framework was only a first step in surpassing earlier models of decision-making styles. A major problem with his particular taxonomy is that it does not actually flow very logically from his arguments. A close examination of his discussion of the factors shaping decision-making (Forester, 1984: 26) reveals that one would expect to find many more than five possible styles flowing from the cited combinations and permutations of the variables. Although many of these categories are indistinguishable in practice and would thus serve little analytical purpose, it remains unclear why one should expect only the five cited styles to emerge.

An improvement on Forester's model of decision-making styles can be made by recasting his variables to more clearly and consistently relate decision-making styles to the types of variables found to be significant in earlier investigations of public decision-making. Combining Forester's concepts of "agent" and "setting," for example, highlights the role of different kinds of policy subsystems—that is, different numbers and types of actors situated in different numbers and types of institutional settings—in the decision-making process (March, 1994; Beach &

Mitchell, 1978). The complexity of the policy subsystem affects the number of venues, the nature of dominant policy ideas and interests, and the level of agreement or opposition to an option within the subsystem and among decision-makers (see Bendor & Hammond, 1992). Some options accord with the core values of the subsystem members, while others do not, thereby structuring decisions into hard (e.g., contested and cognitively challenging) and easy (e.g., broadly understood and familiar) choices (Pollock et al., 1993).

Similarly, it is possible to combine Forester's notions of "problem," "information," and "time" resources, which can all be seen to reflect the types of decision-making constraints identified by Simon and Lindblom and others (see Payne, 1982; Simon, 1973; Maule & Svenson, 1993; Payne et al., 1988). That is, the making of decisions is constrained to varying degrees by information and time limitations (Rochefort & Cobb, 1993; Webber, 1992; Pappi & Henning, 1998), as well as by the intractability or "wickedness" of the problem (Weick, 1976; Rittel & Webber, 1973; Sharkansky, 1997: Ch. 2; Hisschemoller & Hoppe, 1995). But it is often the case that these constraints run together because part of the issue of problem tractability is related to lack of information about potential solutions and a lack of time required to gather or develop it (Radford, 1977).

Thus, two pertinent variables can be used to construct an effective taxonomy of decision-making styles: (1) the cohesion of the policy subsystem involved in the decision and, specifically, whether or not decision-makers enjoy legitimacy within the subsystem, and (2) the severity of the constraints that decision-makers face in making their choices (see Lindquist, 1988; Martin, 1998: Ch. 2). The constraints may be institutional or cognitive: political or social institutions may hinder dealing with a problem or decision-makers may simply not know how to deal with it. Figure 6.5 outlines the four basic decision-making styles that emerge on the basis of these two dimensions.

In this model, decisions made within cohesive policy subsystems are less likely to resort to adjustment strategies and, depending on the nature of the constraints they face, tend to promote either rational or negative decision-making. On the other hand, as incrementalists suggest, highly constrained policy contexts are likely to result in an incremental adjustment approach to decision-making in policy subsystems that lack cohesion (Holzmann & Rutkowski, 2003; Weyland, 2005). In situations of low constraint and low cohesion, decisions are likely to be non-linear and ad hoc, often shuttling between different alternatives over fairly short periods of time, as suggested by the garbage can model (t'Hart & Kleiboer, 1995; de Bruijn & ten Heuvelhof, 2000).

This discussion demonstrates that the essential character of the public decision-making process is very much the same as that of the other policy stages we have examined. That is, like the earlier stages of agenda-setting and policy formulation, the decision-making stage is affected by the nature of the policy subsystem involved (the number and type of actors, their institutional setting, and the kinds

Figure 6.5 Decision-Making Styles

		Cohesion of Policy Subsystem	
		Low	High
Severity of Policy Constraints	Low	Ad hoc Style (May adopt non-linear change)	Rational Style (May adopt either linear and non-linear change)
	High	Incremental Style (Will tend toward linear change)	Negative Decision Style (will tend toward status quo)

of ideas they hold), and by the constraints under which decision-makers operate (Agranoff & Yildiz, 2007; Woll, 2007). A focus on these variables can help predict the type of outcome likely to arise from the particular style of decision-making adopted in the policy process in question (Stokman & Berveling, 1998).

Ultimately, then, as John Forester (1984: 23) put it, what is rational for administrators and politicians to do

> depends on the situations in which they work. Pressed for quick recommendations, they cannot begin long studies. Faced with organizational rivalries, competition and turf struggles, they may justifiably be less than candid about their plans. What is reasonable to do depends on the context one is in, in ordinary life no less than in public administration.

Study Questions

1. How do agenda-setting and policy formulation shape policy choices?

2. What is uncertainty? What is ambiguity? Why are these important in understanding policy decision-making?

3. What is "bounded rationality"? To what extent is it possible to make rational decisions?

4. Is incrementalism the default decision-making option in public policy-making? Is that desirable?

5. What subsystem features are likely to generate non-decisions?

Further Readings

Allison, Graham T., and Morton H. Halperin. 1972. "Bureaucratic Politics: A Paradigm and Some Policy Implications," *World Politics* 24 (Suppl.): 40–79.

Cohen, M., J. March, and J. Olsen. 1972. "A Garbage Can Model of Organizational Choice," *Administrative Science Quarterly* 17, no. 1: 1–25.

Forester, John. 1984. "Bounded Rationality and the Politics of Muddling Through," *Public Administration Review* 44: 23–30.

Head, Brian W. 2016. "Toward More 'Evidence-Informed' Policy-Making?" *Public Administration Review* 76, no. 3 (May 1): 472–84.

Howlett, Michael. 2007. "Analyzing Multi-Actor, Multi-Round Public Policy Decision-Making Processes in Government: Findings from Five Canadian Cases," *Canadian Journal of Political Science* 40, no. 3: 659–84.

Jones B.D. 2002. "Bounded Rationality and Public Policy: Herbert A. Simon and the Decisional Foundation of Collective Choice," *Policy Sciences* 35: 269–84.

Lindblom, Charles. 1959. "The Science of Muddling Through," *Public Administration Review* 19: 79–88.

Meltsner, Arnold J. 1975. "Bureaucratic Policy Analysts," *Policy Analysis* 1, no. 1: 115–31.

Meltsner, Arnold J. 1979. "Creating a Policy Analysis Profession," *Society* 16, no. 6: 45–51.

Oliphant, Samuel, and Michael Howlett. 2010. "Assessing Policy Analytical Capacity: Comparative Insights from a Study of the Canadian Environmental Policy Advice System," *Journal of Comparative Policy Analysis: Research and Practice* 12, no. 4: 439.

Simon, Herbert. 1955. "A Behavioral Model of Rational Choice," *Quarterly Journal of Economics* 69, no. 1: 99–118.

Smith, Gilbert, and David May. 1980. "The Artificial Debate between Rationalist and Incrementalist Models of Decision-Making," *Policy and Politics* 8: 147–61.

Teisman, G.R. 2000. "Models for Research into Decision-Making Processes: On Phases, Streams and Decision-Making Rounds," *Public Administration* 78, no. 4: 937–56.

Walker, Warren E., Vincent A.W. J. Marchau, and Jan H. Kwakkel. 2013. "Uncertainty in the Framework of Policy Analysis." In *Public Policy Analysis: New Developments*, edited by Wil A. H. Thissen and Warren E. Walker, 215–60. New York: Springer.

Weiss, Carol H. 1980. "Knowledge Creep and Decision Accretion," *Knowledge: Creation, Diffusion, Utilization* 1, no. 3: 381–404.

Chapter 7

Policy Implementation
Putting Policies into Effect

What Is Policy Implementation?

After a public problem has reached the policy agenda, various options have been proposed to address it, and the government has decided on a course of action, it must put its choice into practice. The effort, knowledge, and resources devoted to translating policy decisions into action comprise the policy cycle's implementation stage. While most policy decisions identify the general means expected to be used to pursue their goals, subsequent choices are inevitably required to create and administer programs and attain results. In addition to other tasks, funding must be allocated, personnel assigned, and rules of procedure developed to actually make a policy work.

Implementation is the activity in the policy process in which actors attempt to convert policy intentions and resources into actions resulting in specific policy outputs and ultimately in the achievement (or not) of intended policy outcomes. In addition, the implementation stage may influence other "stages" of the process, as when it involves interpretation and negotiation of policy aims (as in the policy formulation stage), or when implementers make decisions about pursuing significantly different administrative and program design alternatives that may affect the type of policy outcomes actually produced and their reception among key players in the policy community.

Policy implementation typically relies on civil servants and administrative officials to establish and manage the necessary actions needed to put a policy into place. However, non-governmental actors who are part of the policy subsystem can also be involved in implementation activities. Some countries, like Sweden, have developed a tradition of non-governmental actors directly implementing some important social programs (Ginsburg, 1992; Johansson & Borell, 1999) or in having the state and societal groups work together to *co-produce* policies (Alford, 2009; Pestoff & Brandsen, 2009). In some countries, like the US, attempts to implement some programs through community and religious ("faith-based") groups are more recent and only partially successful (Kuo, 2006). Instead, non-governmental actors often participate in the design and evaluation of policies but not their actual administration and management.

Implementation is often a high-stakes game that exposes even well-formulated policies that have passed formal decision-making points to several acid tests around administrative feasibility and capacity, political and social acceptability, unforeseen consequences, and a wide range of other contingencies, any of which can singly or in combination block policies from achieving their intended objectives. The implementation process itself not only creates winners and losers, it is also the stage in the policy process where the stakes of winning or losing begin to manifest themselves very clearly to many participants whose interests and desires may have been unfocused in earlier stages of the process. Agencies, and even divisions within agencies, may continue to compete for resources and control over implementation activities; and tensions may arise between the public, private, and non-profit organizations as they vie for influence and funds to implement government programs (Hupe & Hill, 2009).

In policy formulation and even decision-making, conflicts between and among stakeholders and agencies may be managed by using vague language or even postponing decisions on "mission-critical" but politically or bureaucratically "sensitive" aspects of policies. This has the advantage of keeping a policy process moving forward and "buying time" for more supportive coalitions to be built. But the consequences of such conflict avoidance become unavoidable during the implementation stage, when public managers will struggle to generate, allocate, and control resources, and interpret policy intentions. While implementation can sometimes trigger a recurrence of highly visible conflict and controversy that roiled other stages of the policy cycle, many policy areas witness a decline in public attention once a policy decision has been made. This has the effect of giving greater opportunity for bureaucrats and/or well-organized special interests to vary the original intent of a decision should they so desire. As a consequence, the anticipated outputs and results of a policy may fail to materialize, while negative side effects of policies often become more evident (Wu et al., 2017).

These dynamics create not only a management challenge, but also a potential source of blame and risk for both politicians and bureaucrats who are the ones held accountable for policy failures, including those caused by poor implementation. The electoral and career stakes of policy conflict thus tend to rise during implementation. Potential problems have to be anticipated and carefully managed in program design and tool deployment. But this is a difficult task. Failure to accurately anticipate implementation problems is the most common cause of policy failure. An "optimism bias," for example, often afflicts policy-makers who assume that many problems will take care of themselves, or will never materialize at all, resulting occasionally in high-profile policy disasters and even more frequently in policies that perform far below expectation (Bovens & t'Hart, 1996).

Barriers to Policy Implementation

One way of looking at implementation challenges is to assess what it would take to achieve "perfect" implementation and then determine how the obstacles or barriers to such attainment can be overcome. When Hogwood and Gunn (1993) adopted this perspective, they identified 10 the following "preconditions for implementation success."

- circumstances external to the implementing agency do not impose crippling constraints;
- adequate time and sufficient resources are made available to the program;
- the required combination of resources is available;
- the policy to be implemented is based on a valid theory of cause and effect;
- the relationship between cause and effect is direct and that there are few, if any intervening links;
- the dependency relationships are minimal;
- there is agreement of, and understanding on, objectives;
- the tasks are fully specified in correct sequence;
- there is perfect communication and coordination; and
- those in authority can demand and obtain perfect compliance.

Examining these preconditions for success can help us categorize some of the main conditions that may typically *obstruct* an implementation process. The first broad category of conditions obstructing implementation is *mission related*. The poor design of interventions implies that policies may fail even if implemented as intended. Goals adopted in a multi-sectoral process may be too vague to meaningfully translate into operational programs and interventions (Wu et al., 2017).

A second category of difficulties involves the lack of adequate bureaucratic and political *support* for implementation. Support for policies often stop at the rhetorical level, or at the agencies or levels of government that initiated them. Lower levels of government, and grassroots actors on whom actual implementation success may hinge, may discover that they have little understanding of, or stake in, the policies they are asked to execute. Initial implementation may also trigger resistance to an integrated plan that might not have been predicted at the beginning of the process, particularly if not all relevant stakeholders have been consulted. "Political will" may begin to evaporate when difficult trade-offs need to be made in practice, not just on paper, and as constituencies negatively affected by policy trade-offs raise their voices (or even flex their political muscle) (Wu et al., 2017).

Finally, a range of *capacity*-related difficulties may have negative repercussions on implementation. Many—perhaps most—ambitious attempts at integrated planning stop at the level of paper plans. The multiple types of capacity necessary to implement these plans often go ignored, or are optimistically subsumed under the heading of "capacity building requirements." Capacity includes human and financial resources, the institutional arrangements and procedures that underpin policies and ensure consistent delivery, and even the social capacities that help determine how social groupings will respond to implementation initiatives (Wu et al., 2015, 2017).

While capacity needs may be underestimated by public managers initially and then compensated for during implementation, policy delivery is even more vulnerable to deficiencies in *network coordination capacity*—the ability of organizations to work together to achieve a co-produced outcome. Coordination across agencies and across sectors may be required in several different forms, such as sharing information, pooling resources, and (where activities fall outside the traditional gambit of any one organization) jointly implementing assigned tasks. Coordination in delivering policy must thus overcome the perceived threat agencies may feel to their autonomy from working together and the confusion or conflict over the nature of the task that stems from the inherently complicated, multi-sectoral nature of many policy goals (Agranoff & McGuire, 1999; Peters & Savoie, 1996; Peters, 2013).

Environment and Context

Long-term factors such as administrative traditions and styles of management as well as the nature of administrative recruitment and merit systems all play a role in conditioning the activities which lie behind implementation (Knill, 1999). It is important for managers, decision-makers, and others, to be aware of these structures and practices when assessing obstacles to effective implementation, and then draw appropriate conclusions for avoiding or overcoming such constraints (Howlett, 2003).

While a plethora of other contextual factors may be important to any given case, four warrant universal attention. The first is the *degree of political and policy stability* present in the policy system, and particularly the subsystems engaged in a particular implementation effort. The environment for policy implementation may be considered "enabling" if there is relatively strong political support for the program outputs that are called for, and if bureaucratic capacity for analytical and implementation tasks is relatively strong (Matland, 1995).

A second is the *degree of environmental turbulence,* or the extent to which the external political and economic environment in which policy-makers work is changing slowly and steadily or rapidly and disjointedly. When an environment is "turbulent," it may be necessary to alter bureaucratic routines and program parameters much more quickly than in stable environments (Hill & Hupe, 2002). In stable circumstances, there may be more opportunities to build network capacities that will facilitate more interdepartmental coordination, especially if managers can identify and build strong coalitions supporting integrated policy-making that builds bridges to a wide variety of potential partners and thus boosts network capacity (the "partnering" approach). But when change occurs rapidly, implementation will need to be nimbler, even "entrepreneurial," and policy-makers will need to look for actions that can serve to focus political attention onto outputs that generate a quick win.

Where the environment is not particularly facilitative, and where change (economic, social, or political) is rapid and disruptive, public managers are likely to be restricted to "damage control"—keeping open the possibility of a more integrated and effective approach to implementation when environmental conditions become more favourable. If unfavourable environmental conditions persist, public managers may be relegated to "coping" or, at best, "scheming"; that is, identifying interventions to target for implementation that can serve as stepping stones of a longer-term, more ambitious approach should circumstances change.

Where political forces are unsupportive of policy initiatives even after official adoption, implementation may have to have to "fly under the radar," keeping the initial content as low-key and technical (non-overtly political) as possible, while scanning the policy subsystem for potential allies when conditions change. Where to look for such opportunities—and how ambitious those charged with implementation can be during tough times in adverse environments—is a difficult question to answer in the abstract; but careful delineation of stakeholders and their interests, as suggested below, may offer useful cues.

A third contextual factor concerns the openness of the policy process—the degree to which implementation is influenced by diverse actors rather than restricting input to a narrow and homogeneous base of participants. For instance, in a highly pluralistic country with a strong non-governmental sector and a free press, implementation will inevitably be shaped by broader input than in a country where policy-making is controlled by an insular elite. In more democratic, open polities, conflicts at the agenda-setting, policy formulation, and decision-making stages are likely to be relatively transparent and widely recognized. This *may* imply that proponents and opponents of policies will be more likely to reach compromises that get built into the policy and carry forward into implementation. In countries where political decisions are less openly contested, the politics of implementation may instead become "hotter," as actors who were excluded from prior deliberations protest and resist policies that they oppose. The resulting implementation conflicts can, and often do, divert policy from its original objectives.

Finally, the *degree of public-sector decentralization* is another contextual element that will almost always influence policy implementation. Decentralization is one of the catchwords of public management in recent decades, with most countries implementing, or at least endorsing, the devolution of resources and authorities down to subnational and local governments (territorial decentralization) or to non-traditional, reconstituted authorities (functional decentralization). The extent to which such trends are present will affect the way decisions regarding policy adoption are reached, resources mobilized, and administrative and non-bureaucratic actors coordinated for implementation (see Table 7.3) (Wu et al., 2017).

Policy Subjects' Behaviour

Since effective implementation depends on the target groups' behaviour actually matching the anticipated influence tools upon them (May, 2004; Kaine et al., 2010; Duesberg et al., 2014), understanding the relationship between tools and targets is of great importance in studying policy implementation (Weaver, 2009a, 2009b, 2010).

Unfortunately, studies of policy implementation have traditionally focused on the use of governing resources to attain policy goals, with insufficient consideration of how the subjects of those interventions are actually affected by the deployment of policy tools. Despite the fact that "compliance" with government policy intentions has been a longstanding concern in policy studies (Feeley, 1970; Etienne, 2011; Meier & Morgan, 1982; Rodgers, 1975; Mulford & Etzioni, 1978), the links between tool selection and policy implementation have rarely been examined (Grabosky, 1995; Weaver, 2009a, 2009b, 2013, 2015; Winter & May, 2001; Nielson & Parker, 2012). A similar gap in examination exists for how settings of policy instruments are chosen during implementation (Duesberg, 2014; Corner & Randall, 2011; Taylor et al., 2013).

Typically, "policy targets" are assumed to act as rational utility maximizers who are acutely sensitive to shifts in perceived gains and losses linked to policy incentives and disincentives. Analysis of policy tools and their impact of targets is thus premised on the idea of affecting citizens' self-maximizing behaviour, which may vary considerably in practice.

But what is the best way to attain compliance during implementation is often not immediately apparent. To encourage and increase birthrates, for example, is it best to provide subsides that might tip the balance of a woman's or family's calculations of affordability of children? Or is it more effective to promote family-centred events and activities in public service announcements and movie and television placements to promote the joys of home life and the pleasures of children and family (Lichtenstein & Slovic, 2006)? Or should both approaches be pursued? Implementation choices and policy programs built around the first orientation can involve discussions around particular kinds of financial tools such as providing more subsidized daycare and better local schools rather than around how much of a direct subsidy to a parent through tax incentives or cash grants will promote higher levels of childbirth and larger families (Woodside, 1979). The second approach may involve activities such as movie theatre and TV public service advertisements and educational programs in schools and elsewhere, rather than the actual provision of new services or subsidies. And whether both work in conjunction with each other or at cross purposes would need to be known for implementation to succeed.

Under the influences of advances in behavioural economics and social psychology, scholars and practitioners have recently begun to focus more closely on better understanding when and how policy targets behave in less rational ways (Ariely, 2010; Thaler et al., 2010; Thaler & Sunstein, 2009, Mulgan, 2008, Bason, 2014). Yet, it is still the case that most mainstream implementation theory continues to conceive of policy targets rationally calculating their interests when deciding whether to comply with the demands of regulation and laws, or the incentives of subsidies (Stover & Brown, 1975; Gevrek & Uyduranoglu, 2015; Weaver, 2015; Jones et al., 2014; Duesberg, 2014; Araral, 2014; Maskin, 2008). Hence, policy analysis often focuses on "getting incentives right" through the calibration of financial tools expected to achieve expected compliance and outcomes, rather than upon examining other, more normative or culturally determined motivations behind target behaviour and the full range of policy tools available to affect it (Weaver 2009; Gunningham et al., 1998). The same applies to "disincentives". Taxes, for example, are fines established to deter non-compliers (Doern & Phidd, 1983). Utility calculations are applied to calibrating penalties for those who disregard policy obligations or seek to free-ride on compliers (Lowi, 1966; Balch, 1980).

This utilitarian way of thinking about compliance in policy implementation fits within the positivist orientation that was adopted by the policy sciences at its inception (Tribe 1972; Banfield, 1977). It continues to dominate even recent thinking about tool use for policy "nudging," even when behavioural assumptions extend beyond utilitarian concepts such as perfect information and reciprocal risk and benefit valuations (Oliver 2015; Legett, 2014; Room 2013; John et al., 2009). Although nudging strategy eschews "perfect rationality" among policy targets, it still accepts utilitarian "hedonic" principles that "subjects" will seek pleasure and avoid pain through a "cost–benefit" calculus when considering whether to comply with policy (Steg et al., 2014). Weaver (2009b, p. 5) has enumerated various "compliance problems" that originate beyond the bounds of rational calculus by targets and governments. These include the following:

- **Incentive and sanction problems** where positive and or negative incentives are insufficient to ensure compliance
- **Monitoring problems** where target compliance may be difficult or costly to monitor
- **Resource problems** where targets lack the resources to comply even if they want to
- **Autonomy problems** where targets do not have the power to make decisions that comply with policy even if they want to
- **Information problems** where targets lack information that would make compliance more likely, and
- **Attitude and objectives problems** where targets are hostile /mistrustful toward providers or programs.

Viewed in this way, it is evident that compliance presents challenges to implementation and tool deployment that a purely utilitarian focus on policy tools cannot fully resolve. Governments need to determine, for example, whether or not a target is likely to comply with policy intentions and whether that compliance will be freely given (Scholz, 1991). Subjective evaluations of the legality and normative "appropriateness" of government's actions (March & Olsen, 1989) influence both policy targets' degree of compliance, and the general public's tolerance for enforcing penalties to secure that compliance. Governments will thus have to look beyond financial tools to achieve success in implementation (Hawkins & Thomas, 1989; Hood, 1986).

In doing so, policy implementers need to understand how each category of policy tool not only depends upon a specific governing resource and its efficacy in influencing policy targets but also triggers or activates a specific behavioural response in them. Thus, the effectiveness of deploying policy tools is linked both to resource availability—a precondition of their use—and to the sensitivity of the "receptors" policy targets have that prompt them to respond. In the case of deploying information, for example, tool effectiveness relies not only upon the availability of knowledge and the means to distribute it, but also on the target's belief in the accuracy of the content, i.e., its *credibility*. Similarly, the effectiveness of authoritative tools depends on perceptions of government *legitimacy*; the effective use of treasure resources depends on target group financial need and receptivity to receive or pay for government funding, or their *cupidity*; and the effective use of organizational tools relies upon target group perceptions of government *competence* and fairness in providing services. Figure 7.1 presents a model of the behavioural attributes upon which governing tools rely for their effect.

Figure 7.1 Requirements for Influencing the Behaviour/Compliance of Policy Targets

Tool Type	Resource Applied	Target Behavioural Pre-Requisite
Nodality	Information	Credibility/Trust—willingness to believe and act on information provided by government
Authority	Coercive Power/Force	Legitimacy—willingness to be manipulated by government invoked penalties and proscriptions
Treasure	Financial	Cupidity—willingness to be manipulated by gain/losses imposed by governments
Organization	Organization	Competence—willingness to receive goods and services from government and enter into partnership arrangements

Source: Howlett 2011.

When designing for high levels of compliance during implementation, governments need to create a "compliance regime" that will link tools with commensurate behavioural attributes. Such a regime includes traditional utilitarian components, such as the following:

- positive incentives for compliance;
- negative incentives for noncompliance; and
- prohibitions and requirements with punishments attached.

But it also needs to embrace less-utilitarian precepts, including

- information about what behaviour is compliant, how to comply and the advantages of compliance;
- admonitions to comply on moral, self-interested or other grounds as well as utilitarian ones;
- resources to comply that may be targeted to those who would otherwise lack those resources; and
- options and defaults (choice architecture) without substantially affecting the payoff to individuals of so doing (Weaver, 2015).

This second set of principles is intended to boost the chances that implementation will activate motivations among policy targets that actually change behaviour.

Classifying targets according to their likelihood of compliance can enhance the efficacy of policy tools. For example, healthcare clients and citizens facing

Figure 7.2 Nature of Compliance of Policy Targets

		Likelihood of Compliance	
		High	*Low*
Willingness to Comply	*High*	*Model Subjects* Require little coercion, education, or persuasion	*Reluctant Subjects* Require education and persuasion
	Low	*Resistant Subjects* Require incentives to comply	*Combative Subjects* Require a high level of co-ercion and monitoring to compel compliance

Source: Adapted from Scholz 1991.

obesity challenges may be young or old, share some ethnic or racial character-istics, be segmented by gender and in other ways, and respond to policy out-puts based on a range of understanding of obesity science and views about food preparation and intake. Yet only some of these distinctions may be important in affecting compliance, while others may be less significant. A well-designed com-pliance regime will connect the distinctions that matter among policy targets to tools that can affect them. Figure 7.2 shows how estimations and diagnoses about likely compliance behaviour can usefully be linked to the use of specific kinds of governing instruments involved in coercive versus persuasive actions on the part of governments (Hawkins & Thomas, 1989).

As Weaver (2009a, 2009b, 2015) has pointed out, this generates a spectrum of potential compliers and non-compliers. Compliance regimes have to deal with a variety of actors and behaviours, ranging from unwilling resisters to voluntary or willing compliers. To implement effectively, governments need to know which specific kinds of actors fall into which type (Braithwaite, 2003) in order to accu-rately design their policies. How governments perceive these targets and classify groups within them is thus a critical aspect of policy implementation.

Policy Uncertainties

Better understanding the motivations underlying policy implementation can im-prove the efficacy of putting policy decisions into practice, especially when im-plementation, like other aspects of policy-making discussed in previous chapters, is marked by high levels of uncertainty and surprise (Linder & Peters, 1988; de-Leon, 1992). Implementation occurs with limited and sometimes no information about the future policy environment, and may need to adapt to changing con-ditions. Hence, they are only as good as the knowledge that informed problem recognition and shaped policy design and adoption. As Swanson et al. (2010) have argued, policy implementation is akin to gardening insofar as it is "muddy, attentive and experiential, because we really do not know what growing conditions will prevail."

"Policy surprise" describes what bureaucrats and politicians experience when unexpected challenges arise during implementation. These surprises can be tempered when best evidence is used in putting together a policy and when best practice is followed in deploying it. But knowledge that went into policy formulation and decision-making is only useful if it is carried forward into implementation (Lempert et al., 2003). Uncertainty about expected results due to incomplete information about policy targets, and the ways that such targets might respond to an intervention is quite common. Bureaucrats are thus all too familiar with surprises that emerge during "normal" policy implementation and undermine the best laid plans and program designs (Jarvis, 2011; Morgan & Henrion, 1990; Schrader et al., 1993).

Another dimension of uncertainty can be introduced when data is lacking or if there is disagreement about its accuracy. Both of these limitations can make it difficult to come up with meaningful probability estimates in the projections of how different implementation options might unfold and thus reduce confidence in the prospects for successful implementation (McInerney et al., 2012; Lempert et al., 2002; Walker et al., 2010; Jarvis, 2011).

This has been the case, historically, with scholars who compared the implementation challenges of efforts to address problems that had a very different character in terms of the availability of accepted evidence about their causes and solutions. Describing these as "wicked" versus "tame" policy problems (Churchman, 1967; Rittel & Webber, 1973), scholars differentiated the underlying uncertainty confronted during implementation into two different categories according to whether the policy problem's causes and solutions were known or unknown. In Simon's terms, this distinction was between "well-structured" and "ill-structured" problems (Simon, 1973; Head & Alford, 2013).

This is a problem throughout the policy process but also effects implementation. Thus, as Becker and Brownsen (1964) and others have pointed out, even when knowledge is plentiful, policy actors may be unaware of it and remain uninformed, thus pursuing implementation on the basis of ignorance rather than awareness. Better evidence can sometimes deal with this. But relative levels of understanding become even more critical when causal knowledge about a subject is scarce, such as occurred with AIDS in the early 1980s and climate change during the 1990s. And policy actors may be unaware of their knowledge gap and can be hubristic or overconfident, or they may be aware of this problem and function with an attitude of prudent awareness (Becker & Brownsen, 1964). These alternative approaches are presented in Figure 7.3.

Figure 7.3 Policy Actors' Knowledge and Comprehension Matrix

		Nature of Existing Knowledge of a Phenomenon	
		Aspects of the problem and possible solutions are generally known	Aspects are unknown
Nature of Decision-Makers or Implementer Awareness of Existing Knowledge of a Phenomenon	Aware	Known-Known: Key policy actors are aware of the known aspects of a phenomena (INFORMED AWARENESS)	Known-Unknown: Key policy actors are aware that certain aspects of the phenomenon are unknown (PRUDENT AWARENESS)
	Ignorant	Unknown-Known: Key policy actors are unaware of known aspects of a phenomenon (UNINFORMED IGNORANCE)	Unknown-Unknown: Key policy actors are unaware that certain aspects of the phenomenon are unknown (IMPRUDENT IGNORANCE)

As Stirling (2010) noted, the different epistemological situations in which policy-makers find themselves justifies distinctive implementation responses. For example, well-understood relationships within stable contexts may react well to routinization, although even when such a policy provides effective initial results changes in problem or policy contexts may render it ineffective over time (Nair & Howlett, 2015). And while some government policies are crafted in response to events that are "reasonably predictable"—such as cycles of commodity price swings, periods of inflation and unemployment, or longer-term demographic changes such as aging of populations or increasing urbanization—others are affected by policy events and futures that are more unpredictable, "unforeseen," and "unprojectable," or potentially "catastrophic" (Wardekker et al., 2010). In such circumstances it is prudent to design some reflexivity or robustness into policy implementation in order to foster adaptation or resilience in the face of change (Voss et al., 2006).

Implementing policy processes and programs that promote agility, however, requires care and forethought. Simply enhancing the discretion of managers or street-level administrators working in traditional bureaucratic organizations, for example, is unlikely to overcome knowledge barriers, locked-in policy routines and incentives to pursue short-term economies. Overcoming both short-term electoral and bargaining orientations that prevent or constrain adapting to change, and overcoming an emphasis in public administration toward routinization and narrowly defined considerations of efficiency, is required (Howlett & Mukherjee, 2014; Junginger, 2013; Bason, 2013; Mulgan, 2008). This in turn requires a conscious effort to design policy implementation that is capable of change and modification in order to address unexpected circumstances.

Implementation Capacity

Whether or not implementation follows the desired course, however, is a complex matter. First, governments must have the policy capacity needed to implement their preferred choices of action (Davis, 2000). Parsons (2004), for example, defined policy capacity as the "weaving" function of modern governments—the ability to join together the multiplicity of organizations and interests to form a coherent policy fabric. Holmberg and Rothstein (2010) and Rotberg (2014) similarly go well beyond policy formulation in emphasizing the systemic and structural preconditions of good governance, such as honesty, rule of law, merit appointments, social trust, and legitimacy, which serve as key components of implementation capacity (Holmberg et al., 2009, Rotberg, 2014).

The significance of capacity and governance issues can be seen in the results of numerous efforts at policy and administrative reform that have been pursued in recent decades. Many of these efforts have featured waves of management reforms and administrative restructuring, privatizations, de-regulation, and re-regulation and the like (Ramesh & Howlett, 2006), and can be characterized as efforts to shift between different modes of governing (Treib et al., 2007). For example, the sentiment behind many reform efforts and coalitions in the 1980s and 1990s favoured transitions from government service delivery and regulation to more market-based governance regimes. Recently, the trend has shifted from hierarchical and market forms of governance to more network-oriented governance relationships (Lowndes & Skelcher, 1998; Lange et al., 2013; Weber, Driessen, & Runharr, 2011).

Even more recent reforms in many countries and sectors have sought to reverse excesses in "de-governmentalization" from past initiatives, often introducing hybrid governance designs (Ramesh & Howlett, 2006; Ramesh & Fritzen, 2009). Many proponents, for example, claim "collaborative governance" combines the best of government- and market-based arrangements by sharing governance among public and private actors in a policy subsystem (Rhodes, 1997). Because of these ongoing reforms, many sectors from health to education now exhibit a multiplicity of approaches in implementation—relying upon regulation, bureaucratic oversight, and service delivery—as well as both market- and network-based hierarchical and non-hierarchical approaches such as markets, voluntary organizations, and, increasingly, co-production (Brandsen & Pestoff, 2006; Pestoff, 2006; Pestoff et al., 2012; Pestoff et al., 2006). These layers of older and newer approaches to governing policy implementation are set out in Figure 7.4.

Not all of these reforms have succeeded (Ling, 2002), not least because performance depends in large part on the capacity required to meet existing conditions (Howlett, 2009). That is, each mode of governance requires a high level of state and actor capacity in order to function effectively (Bullock et al., 2001).

Whether such capacity exists and how it is mobilized is a significant but little understood factor affecting the effectiveness and efficiency of implementation (Canadian Government, 1996).

Actors and Activities in Policy Implementation

A conspicuous aspect of implementation is the sheer number of actors involved in the process of delivering policy programs and services. Although not as expansive as agenda-setting, implementation both affects and is affected by many actors who continue to (re-)define problems and solutions in a given policy domain. These may include actors who played only marginal roles in policy formulation and decision-making deliberations but who then come to the fore as the policy is put into practice (May, 2003). Relatively minor administrative complications can then trigger efforts to reverse decisions through attacks on the goals and objectives behind the program.

Despite this plethora of players, however, the bureaucracy is always a significant actor in, and a decisive factor underpinning, policy implementation, whether it plays the role of overseeing other actors or directly delivering outputs. While politicians are indispensable actors in the decisions that enable implementation to proceed and can play an active role in subsequent oversight and evaluation efforts, most of the day-to-day activity required to deliver policy typically falls within the purview of salaried public servants. This is because of the key role played by laws codifying the results of decision-making and empowering state agencies to put those decisions into practice (Keyes, 1996; Ziller, 2005).

Different bureaucratic agencies at various levels of government (national, state or provincial, and local) are usually involved in implementing policy, each carrying particular interests, ambitions, and traditions that affect the implementation process and shape its outcomes, in a process of "multi-level" government or governance (see Bardach, 1977; Elmore, 1978; Bache & Flinders, 2004).

Implementation by public agencies is often an expensive, multi-year effort involving continued struggle for resources and support. Politicians, agencies, and other members of policy subsystems may well use the implementation process as simply another opportunity for continuing the conflicts they may have lost at earlier stages of the policy process. Such processes, of course, greatly complicate implementation and move it further away from being simply a technical exercise of decision-processing (Nicholson-Crotty, 2005).

In most countries, traditional or *civil or common laws* form a "default" or basic set of principles governing how individuals interact with each other and with the state in their daily lives. These laws are often codified in writing—as is the case in many continental European countries—but they may also be found in less systematic form in the overall record of precedents set by judicial bodies,

Figure 7.4 Governance Modes Employed in Implementation

	Traditional Public Administration	New Public Management	New Public Governance
Policy Clients	Subjects	Customers	Citizens
Main goal	Legitimacy and compliance	More effective, efficient and better-quality public service	More legitimate, inclusive, flexible and effective government
Logic of Interaction among Actors	Bureaucratic	Post-bureaucratic, competitive	Post-competitive, collaborative
Dominant Substantive Policy Tool	Direct provision by government	Contract-out to private entities	Co-production with non-government actors and citizens
Management and Policy Instrumentation	Rules and input-based management tools	Benchmarking and other output-based tools	Public participation and trust as key management tool
Accountability	Hierarchies	Market-driven	Multifaceted
Role of Government	Rowing	Steering	Facilitating

Source: By authors, with some adaptation from O'Flynn 2007.

as is the case in Britain and its former colonies. Even in these so-called common law countries, *statutory laws* are passed by parliaments to replace or supplement the civil or common law (Gall, 1983; Bogart, 2002). These statutes take the form of acts, which, among other things, usually also create a series of rules to be followed in implementing particular policies, as well as a range of offences and penalties for noncompliance with policy.

Statute law usually also designates a specific administrative agency or ministry as empowered to make whatever *regulations* or administrative rules are required to ensure the successful implementation of the goals embodied in the enabling legislation. Regulations giving effect in specific circumstances to the general principles codified in laws are then prepared by civil servants employed by public agencies, often in conjunction with target or "clientele" groups (Kagan, 1994). Regulations cover items ranging from the standards of behaviour or performance that must be met by target groups to the criteria used to administer policy. These serve as the basis for licensing or approval and, although unlegislated, provide the de facto source of direction for most implementation processes. As was discussed in Chapter 5, this approach to implementation is sometimes referred to as "*command-and-control*" regulation whereby a command is given by an authorized body and the administration is charged with controlling the target group to ensure compliance (Sinclair, 1997; Kerwin, 1994, 1999; Baldwin & Cave, 1999).

Although recent efforts have been made to supplement or replace this mode of implementation with one that relies more on collaboration or incentives (Freeman, 1997; Armstrong & Lenihan, 1999; Kernaghan, 1993), in the modern era, rules-based implementation prevails in all but the worst instances of dictatorship or personal authority. Instructions may be issued through compliant legislatures but also directly from the executive to the administration. These types of legal processes are a necessary part of adapting sometimes very general statements of intent with respect to policy choices to the actual circumstances and situations that must be engaged to advance the policy output that was ratified. Even in the case of efforts to develop more collaborative relationships with target groups, administrative actions must still be based on legal authority provided by legislatures and executives (Grimshaw et al., 2001; Klijn, 2002; Phillips & Levasseur, 2004).

The usual form of such administrative venues is the *ministry* or *department*, and the actual practice of administering policy and delivering services is performed overwhelmingly by civil servants in such agencies. However, other forms of quangos (Hood, 1986; Koppell, 2003), ranging from state-owned enterprises (Stanton, 2002; Chandler, 1983; Laux & Molot, 1988) to non-profit corporations and bodies (McMullen & Schellenberg, 2002; Advani & Borins, 2001) and public–private partnerships (English & Skellern, 2005; Hodge & Greve, 2007), as discussed in Chapter 5, can also become vehicles for service delivery.

This does not, however, exhaust the types of state agencies involved in implementation, which also include organizations designed to perform specific tasks related to service delivery without being directly or indirectly involved in its management. Among these are various kinds of tribunals, such as *independent regulatory commissions*, that exist at arm's-length from the government and develop the rules and regulations required for administration (Cushman, 1941; Braithwaite et al., 1987; Christensen & Laegreid, 2007). Other forms of implementing agencies are the administrative appeal *board* and various types of *commissions and tribunals* created by statute or regulation to perform many quasi-judicial functions, including appeals concerning licensing, certification of personnel or programs, and the issuance of permits. Appointed by government, administrative tribunals and boards usually represent, or purport to represent, some diversity of interests and expertise and are expected to monitor the public–private interface in goods and service delivery without displacing non-state actors in the production and distribution of various kinds of goods and services.

Public hearings may be statutorily defined as a component of such administrative process and operate to secure regulatory compliance. In most cases, however, such hearings are held at the discretion of a decision-making authority and are often after-the-fact public information sessions rather than true consultative devices (Talbert et al., 1995; Grima, 1985). *Specialized advisory boards and commissions* (Brown, 1955, 1972; Smith, 1977) often supplant public consultations, yielding more expert views on specific regulatory activities than open public hearings would typically provide, but also allowing some subsystem members to exercise inordinate influence on policy implementation (Dion, 1973).

Thus, while state officials remain an important force in the implementation stage of the policy process, advisory and quasi-governmental agencies allow them to be joined by members of the relevant policy subsystems, as the number and type of policy actors return to resembling those found at the formulation stage (Bennett & McPhail, 1992). Just as they do during formulation, *target groups*, that is, groups whose behaviour is intended or expected to be altered by government action, play a major role in the implementation process (Donovan, 2001; Kiviniemi, 1986; Schneider & Ingram, 1993).

The political and economic resources target groups can deploy in this process certainly have an impact on policy implementation (Montgomery, 2000). Powerful groups affected by a policy can influence the character of implementation by supporting or opposing it through lobbying and spending. Thus, regulators will commonly strike compromises with groups, or attempt to use the groups' own resources in some cases, to make the task of implementation simpler or less expensive (Giuliani, 1999). Although often done informally in some jurisdictions, such as the United States, more formal efforts have been made to develop administrative and procedural standards through negotiation between regulators and regulated (Coglianese, 1997).

Changing levels of public support for a policy can also affect implementation. Many policies witness a decline in support after a policy decision has been made, enabling administrators to vary the original intent of a decision (see Hood, 1983, 1986a). Bureaucrats thus possess considerable influence, whether they seek it or not, in shaping the policy initiatives they engage in implementing. How these influences play out depends on the mix of ideas, beliefs, and interests that flow through implementation in multiple streams.

Multiple Streams and Actors in Implementation

In seeking to understand the effort that actors will devote to implementation, it can help to build upon Kingdon's examination of policy actors during agenda-setting that led to development of his Multiple Streams Framework, discussed in the context of agenda-setting in Chapter 4. We can interpret how actors will work to deliver policy outputs by considering the influence of Kingdon's original three streams and then exploring the effect of two further streams that flow through policy implementation. Once actors begin preparing to deliver policy outputs in the formulation stage, they create a process stream that can also shape the design of implementation procedures. And the program stream that commences flowing when a positive decision to proceed with policy is taken gets filled with organizational elements that can influence both instrument choice and calibration. How these streams orient policy actors during implementation is thus worth considering.

The Problem Stream

In conveying the ideas and insights about challenges facing society, the problem stream contributes a source of impetus for action during policy implementation. Rather than relying on particularistic terminology to describe the specific meanings that subgroup of actors creates during to the implementation process, drawing upon the problem stream can reveal goal orientations that are transferable and comparable across policy subsystems. As discussed in Chapter 4, researchers can look to *"epistemic communities,"* a term developed in the international relations literature to describe groups of scientists involved in articulating and delimiting problem spaces in areas such as oceans policy and climate change (Gough & Shackley, 2001; Haas, 1992; Zito, 2001), as relevant sources of problem specification and significance that motivate efforts to deliver policy outputs.

The academic exploration of epistemic communities thus far has been dominated by examples from environmental policy, a space where science and politics often clash over understanding problems that could pose an existential challenge to human survival over time, and usually in the context of agenda-setting or policy formulation. Thus, Haas first described the "epistemic communities" involved in these deliberations as a diverse collection of policy actors including scientists, academics experts, public-sector officials, and other government agents who are united by a common interest in or a shared interpretation of the science behind an environmental dilemma (Gough & Shackley, 2001; Haas, 1992). The principal effect of these epistemic communities was to influence "policy innovation not only through their ability to frame issues and define state interests but also through their influence on the setting of standards and the development of regulations" (Adler & Haas, 1992).

These problem-defining actors who can be found in epistemic communities, from scientists to political partisans and others depending on the case, however, remain active beyond agenda-setting and into policy formulation by contributing to discourses within the problem stream that advance the definition of broad policy issues or problems that cross over into policy implementation and evaluation, the subject of Chapter 8 (Cross, 2015; Hajer, 1997, 2005; Howlett et al., 2009; Knaggård, 2015).

Knowledge regarding a policy problem is the "glue" that unites actors within an epistemic community, and connects them with those actors involved in political negotiations and practices around policy goals and solutions as well as those, discussed below, who specialize in the development, design, and articulation of policy tools used in pursuit of solutions (Biddle & Koontz, 2014).

In their contribution to agenda-setting, epistemic communities can influence the activities of other actors, thus helping to guide the subsequent direction of the policy process. This path-dependent evolution of problem definition indicates, as Adler & Haas (2009) noted, that "the effects of epistemic involvement are not easily reversed. To the extent to which multiple equilibrium points are possible . . . epistemic communities will help identify which one is selected" (Adler & Haas, 1992). This, in turn, heavily influences implementation activities by shaping the goals and outcomes that participants will strive to either advance or resist, depending on their position on the legitimacy of the problem.

The Policy Stream

As we saw in Chapter 4, the epistemic communities that can play a formative role in articulating problems on the policy agenda are separate and distinct from another group of policy actors who generate ideas about preferred solutions to the problems facing government and society.

These sources of solutions that flow through the policy stream have been labelled *"instrument constituencies"* by Voss & Simons (2014). Unlike epistemic communities that focus on translating societal challenges into clear-cut problems that policy-makers can act upon, instrument constituencies embrace particular policy tools and generate information about the design and efficacy of these tools in order to facilitate their uptake. Think tanks, for example, often act as key players in instrument constituencies, as they provide policy-makers with "basic information about the world and societies they govern, how current policies are working, possible alternatives and their likely costs and consequences" (McGann et al., 2014: 31). Universities, interest groups, industry associations, and labour unions can also be found as frequent participants in instrument constituencies, with the actual mix of actors depending on the type of instrument being endorsed.

Advocacy for particular tools or combinations of tools to address a range of problem areas are directed with the intent to shape the methods and mechanisms developed to pursue policy options during formulation, but these interests and activities also affect implementation. That is, constituencies are "networks of heterogeneous actors from academia, policy consulting, public policy and administration, business, and civil society, who become linked as they engage with the articulation, development, implementation and dissemination of a particular technical model of governance" (Voss & Simons, 2014). What unites these actors is the role they play in articulating "the set of stories, knowledge, practice and tools needed to keep an instrument alive both as model and implemented practice" (Voss & Simons, 2014).

The Politics Stream

"Advocacy coalitions," as Sabatier and others who conceptualized them (Sabatier & Weible, 2007; Schlager & Blomquist, 1996), direct their input into agenda-setting and policy formulation, but, like epistemic communities and instrument constituencies, also remain active in implementation and policy evaluation. These actors compete to get their preferred problem definitions *and* solutions adopted during each stage of the policy cycle.

Some politically influential participants in advocacy coalitions exhibit a higher profile in the policy subsystem than either the "hidden cluster" of substantive experts who explore the nature of problems in epistemic communities or the instrument constituencies that promote preferred means of solution, while others exercise their impact by working more subtly. For example, in the United States, actors contributing to implementation can include "the President and his high-level appointees, prominent members of the Congress, the media and such elections-related actors as political parties and campaigns" (Kingdon, 2011: 64), while less conspicuous actors include lobbyists, political party brokers and fixers, and other behind-the-scenes advisors and participants (Weishaar et al., 2015).

The Process Stream

Once governments get focused on solving a problem that has entered the policy agenda, a structure for the analysis and engagement of potential solutions needs to be developed. The results of such deliberation, which pick up momentum in the formulation stage, create outputs that flow into a process stream that joins Kingdon's classic three streams as a conceptual focus, revealing another locus of influence on implementation in which, as set out above, administrators and public servants play a key role. Actors in the process stream inputs offer guidance on who will do what when it comes time to deliver policy. Not only does this division and specification of labour help to clarify the relationship between different levels of government in policy delivery, but it also sets the boundaries for the working relationship between the state and civil society.

Indeed, bureaucrats typically bring the endemic intra- and inter-organizational conflicts of public agencies into their work in policy implementation (Dye, 2001), and such tensions and rivalries are usually addressed at least initially in the formulation stage when different policy options have to be developed, interpreted, and prioritized for decision-makers. But different bureaucratic agencies at various levels of government (national, state or provincial, and local) are usually involved in implementing policy, each carrying particular interests, ambitions, and traditions that affect the implementation process and shape its outcomes, in a process of "multi-level" government or governance that echoes these concerns and carries them over into implementation (see Bardach, 1977; Elmore, 1978; Bache & Flinders, 2004). The procedural principles that were initiated in formulating and presenting policy options, carry through into implementation and, provide direction in how these relationships will be navigated during the practice of implementation.

The Program Stream

As noted above, implementation follows a positive decision to proceed with policy and features the introduction of a new "program" stream. Norms, precedents, and standard operating procedures are key components in the program stream that give weight to the procedures and practices through which policy outputs are produced.

The political stream remains active, and in some countries with corrupt or highly politicized administrations political actors may be highly influential on program and policy delivery, with inputs from advocacy coalitions flowing through the politics stream tend to exert an effect on implementation. But more often, as described earlier in the chapter, policy implementation relies on civil servants and administrative officials to establish and manage the necessary actions, their organizational norms and structures generate an ongoing flow of knowledge, experience, expertise, and values that contributes to shaping the execution and evolution of policy outputs. Non-governmental actors who are part of the policy subsystem can also contribute to implementation activities, of course, and especially in various forms of collaborative governance will be similarly influential in implementation (Answell & Gash, 2008; Kekez et al., 2019).

Implementation Theories

Implementation studies have been shaped by the theoretical debates, discussed in Chapter 2, between neo-classical or public choice adherents and welfare economists on the proper role of the state in the economy. While most economists, for example, prefer voluntary instruments that allow markets to operate in the most unfettered fashion, as we have seen some welfare economists endorse the use of more authoritative instruments in order to correct market failures (Bator, 1958; Economic Council of Canada, 1979; Utton, 1986; Howse et al., 1990). In contrast, neoliberal economists accept public authority only for providing pure public goods; any other usage is viewed as distorting the market and yielding suboptimal outcomes (Breyer, 1979, 1982; Posner, 1974; Stigler, 1975; Wolf, 1987). These approaches to society and governance in general affect the kinds of tools and activities which their proponents would like to see in policy implementation.

Welfare economists' greater openness to state intervention, for example, leads them to more systematic analyses of policy instruments and implementation than many classical or neo-classical economists. However, like their neoliberal colleagues, welfare economists still treat implementation and instrument choice as a technical exercise that consists of evaluating the features of various instruments, matching them to different types of market failures, estimating their relative costs, and choosing and administering the instrument that most efficiently overcomes the market failure in question (Mitnick, 1980; Stokey & Zeckhauser, 1978; Weimer & Vining, 1992).

Other economists use public choice theory to explain the ways instruments are used and the patterns of implementation that results from their deployment. Again, as we saw in Chapter 2, it is argued that democratic politics leads states to choose instruments that provide concentrated benefits to marginal voters while spreading the costs to the entire population (see Buchanan, 1980; Trebilcock & Hartle, 1982; Wilson, 1974). Public choice theory thus argues that in a democracy the self-serving behaviour by voters, politicians, and bureaucrats promotes an increasing tendency to tax and spend, and to regulate and nationalize private activity. To gain electoral advantages, it is claimed, governments choose instruments that do not immediately reveal their costs to the voters who ultimately pay for them.

While incorporating a political calculus of instrument choices improves on earlier economic analyses, the public choice perspective does not explain systematic patterns of instrument choices very well. It is very difficult, for example, to match types of instruments with patterns of the distribution of costs and benefits (Wilson, 1974) since one must first know whether governments seek to claim credit or avoid blame for the action being undertaken (Weaver, 1986; Hood, 2002).

Economic explanations of instrument use and implementation thus tend to be overly deductive and lack a solid empirical base in actual implementation practices. Political scientists, geographers, sociologists and others, on the other hand, tend to study a wider variety of factors influencing instrument choices using more empirical evidence. To those looking for theoretical parsimony, however, they may not appear as elegant as the findings generated by economists, but the models and ideas they have developed do help to grapple with the complexity of actual policy delivery and inductively develop a plausible theory of instrument use in policy implementation (see Howlett, 1991).

One oft-cited political science approach to understanding policy instrument choice and policy implementation was developed by Bruce Doern and several Canadian associates in the early 1980s which is quite powerful (Doern, 1981; Phidd & Doern, 1983; Tupper & Doern, 1981). Assuming that all instruments are *technically substitutable*, they argued that in liberal-democratic societies governments would simply *prefer* to use the least interventionist instruments available. These, generally, would involve the least cost and effort while complying with the fundamental ideological faith in markets held by liberal-democratic governments along with constitutional and institutional constraints on government action in place in most jurisdictions. A government would only "move up the scale" toward the use of more "interventionist" or coercive instruments as necessary to overcome any societal resistance it encountered to achieving its aims. Doern and his colleagues thus suggested, contra the public choice model, that a typical pattern of instrument use was for governments to begin with minimally authoritative activities such as exhortation and information provision and move slowly, if at all, toward direct provision.

Looking beyond studies of instrument use, however, the literature on policy implementation has inherited a tradition of atheoretical work from public administration, which has been exacerbated recently by the addition of an equally descriptive set of works in public management. As a result, the study of policy implementation is fractured and largely descriptive, with several proto-theories of implementation behaviour competing for attention—from network management to principal–agent theory, game theory and others.

First Generation: Borrowing from Public Administration

Until the early 1970s, implementation was often regarded as unproblematic, despite the evidence from an accumulation of century-old literatures in public administration, organizational behaviour, and management (Wilson, 1887; Goodnow, 1900; Gaus, 1931). Many early policy researchers ignored or downplayed the political pitfalls arising at this stage of policy-making, for example, assuming that once a policy decision was made, the administrative arm of government would simply carry it out (Hargrove, 1975). However, this view began to change with the publication of Pressman and Wildavsky's (1973) now classic assessment of the complexities and challenges of program implementation. Their study of job-creation programs for unemployed inner-city residents of Oakland, California, showed that implementation was not actually being carried out in the manner anticipated by policy-makers (van Meter & van Horn, 1975; Bardach, 1977) and similar research in other countries reached similar conclusions (Hjern, 1982; Mayntz, 1979). The upshot of these findings was a more systematic effort in the 1980s to understand the factors that influenced implementation in practice (Sabatier & Mazmanian, 1981).

Second Generation: Borrowing from Organization Theory

In the second generation of implementation studies scholars drew on organization theory to rethink implementation challenges. These efforts quickly became embroiled in a dispute over the most appropriate focus for analyzing implementation: the so-called *"top-down"* versus *"bottom-up"* debate (Barrett, 2004). This was as much a debate about agency as methodology and some studies presented policy implementation to be most successful when viewed as a "top-down" process whose mechanisms ensured that implementing officials could keep to the original intent of the public officials who had ratified the policy.

This top-down perspective was opposed by a more "bottom-up" approach, which examined the actions of those affected by and engaged in the front lines of policy delivery (Sabatier, 1986). Here, effectiveness was seen to arise from the adaptive behaviour of "street-level bureaucrats" seeking to attain and sustain the means to achieve policy goals on the ground (Lipsky, 1980). Studies conducted in bottom-up fashion showed that the success or failure of many programs often depended on the commitment and skills of the actors directly involved in implementing programs (Lipsky, 1980).

While both of these approaches generated valuable insights, like many similar dichotomous debates in policy studies, they tended to ossify into hardened positions that stifled conceptual development and research, leading to calls in the late 1980s and 1990s for new approaches that would yield more "scientific" implementation research (see Lester et al., 1987; Goggin et al., 1990; deLeon, 1999a).

Third Generation: Rationalist Theories and Game Theories

Many implementation scholars subsequently moved beyond the top-down versus bottom-up debate during the 1990s, yielding what Malcolm Goggin and his colleagues labelled the "third generation" of implementation research (Lester & Goggin, 1998; O'Toole, 2000b). In addition to studies using the insights of recent models of administrative behaviour such as game theory and principal–agent models of behaviour (e.g., Scholz, 1984, 1991; Hawkins & Thomas, 1989a)—which focused on the nature of enforcement involved in traditional administrative techniques—an attention to choosing and using policy instruments emerged. Rather than studying the purely administrative concerns of putting a program into practice, this approach considered implementation as an attempt to apply the tools of government to resolving policy problems (see Salamon, 1981; Mayntz, 1983; Bobrow, 2006).

In the 1990s, authors drew upon rationalist economic theories to understand implementation. Game theories and principal–agent theories were incorporated into this line of thinking.

Game Theory

Game theory concepts were applied to studying implementation in search of explanations for the administrative behaviour involved in the promotion of policy compliance. Regulatory theorists such as Keith Hawkins (1984) and John Thomas (Hawkins & Thomas, 1989) in the UK had long noted how distinct regulatory styles could be observed in different sectors and jurisdictions (Kagan, 1994, 1996). They concluded that, broadly speaking, regulators could construct oversight systems based on either coercion or persuasion. This insight was taken up by analysts such as John Scholz (1984, 1991) to operationalize game-theoretic principles during regulatory implementation. Scholz demonstrated that the incentives and payoff for compliance and noncompliance on the part of the regulated could be matched to payoffs and incentives for regulators to pursue education or enforcement as implementation strategies.

A typical implementation strategy, therefore, would be one in which regulators initiate implementation with efforts at persuasion, yielding outputs that often would not motivate adequate compliance among the regulated. This would lead regulators to move toward more coercive rules in the next iteration of policy outputs, yielding a worse situation for both regulators and the regulated, who would face, respectively, high enforcement and high compliance costs. The strategy would then progress to an intermediate position in which coercion would be scaled back in exchange for compliance by the regulated, although this would be an unstable equilibrium requiring monitoring and periodic temporary increases in coercion on the part of regulators to maintain compliance.

This application of game theory to regulatory implementation generated interesting insights. However, it did not take into account a second key dimension of the implementation situation highlighted by the top-down versus bottom-up debates: the divisions within the state itself that affect the ability of implementation on the ground to match the aims and expectations of those decision-makers who sanctioned proceeding with a policy. This resulted in the deployment of another game theory model to the implementation analysis: that of principal–agent theory.

Principal–Agent Theory

As discussed above and in earlier chapters, administrative activity is affected by the changing social, economic, technological, and political contexts of implementation (Hutter & Manning, 1990). Changes in social conditions may affect the interpretation of a policy problem that prompts adjustment of established programs. For example, many of the challenges faced by social security programs in industrialized countries arise from the fact that they were not designed to cope with the ever-increasing lifespan, and a commensurately aging population, nor with continuous high rates of unemployment.

Changes in economic conditions can similarly impact social policy. A program targeting the poor and unemployed, for instance, is more likely to face pressures for change after an economic upturn or downturn. New technology also can be expected to change policy implementation options, such as when a more effective or cheaper pollution control technology prompts adjustments in environmental regulation. A new government may also trigger changes in the way policies are implemented. Conservative governments, for example, have been known to tighten the availability of social security programs established by labour or socialist governments without necessarily changing the policy itself (Mazmanian & Sabatier, 1983: 31).

Because of such variations, civil servants often acquire a great deal of discretionary authority in implementation, pursuing policy goals under changing environments. And as noted in earlier chapters, civil servants also tend to become more expert in an administrative area than the generalists who staff political offices. As a result, civil servants can often decide how and to whom the laws will be applied (Calvert et al., 1989; McCubbins et al., 1987, 1989), placing politicians and administrators in a particular kind of *principal–agent relationship*, such as those commonly found in associations between lawyer and client, physician and patient, or buyer–broker–seller. This is one in which the principal is dependent on the goodwill of the agent to further his or her interests when it may not be in the interests of the agent to do so (Ellig & Lavoie, 1995; Francis, 1993; Banks, 1995). The particular dynamics of this relationship affect the tenor and quality of their interactions and limits the ability of political "principals" to circumscribe effectively the behaviour of their erstwhile "agents" (Bozeman, 1993; Milward & Provan, 1998).

One principal–agent problem that has long been recognized by policy researchers, for example, is the tendency for regulators (the agents in this case), over time, to identify more with the needs of the regulated than with their erstwhile political principals. At the extreme, this tendency is thought to undermine the regulatory structure and trigger its demise and replacement (Bernstein, 1955). This theory of *regulatory capture* is based on flaws in the principal–agent relationship that encourage such behaviour. Career patterns where individuals move back and forth between the government bureaucracy and industry employment over time will consciously or unconsciously blur their interests and ambitions (Sabatier, 1975).

Principal–agent theory pointed to the implications of the design of administrative structures for effective implementation and underlined the importance of mechanisms that ensure effective oversight of administrative actors by their political "masters." This focus extended the insight of "bottom-up" implementation studies of the need for structures allowing senior officials to control street-level ones while granting those on the ground enough autonomy to perform their work effectively (McCubbins & McCubbins, 1994; McCubbins & Schwartz, 1984). However, like game theory, it primarily described the logic of structurally constrained implementation behaviour rather than implementation processes per se.

Fourth Generation Implementation Theory: Taking Capacity Seriously

In recent years, many authors studying policy implementation have focused attention on deeper capacity issues underlying effective implementation. From this perspective, the question of how to implement a policy must take account of the capacity possessed by the relevant agencies to carry out plans and programs. Based on this capacity assessment, policy-makers should either temper the goals to match the capacity or take initiative to build the requisite level of capacity (Wu et al., 2015).

As we have seen, at its heart, policy capacity is a function of three inter-active dimensions of competences or skills that affect government's ability to perform policy functions: analytical capacity to understand what needs to be done and assess different ways of doing it; operational capacity to coordinate and organize the collective efforts required to implement policies; and political ca-pacity to mobilize resources and support for the policy (Wu et al., 2010; Tiernan & Wanna, 2006; Gleeson et al., 2009; Gleeson et al., 2011; Fukuyama, 2013; Rotberg, 2014).

These three sets of skills need to exist not only in the authorized imple-menting agencies but also at the level of individual implementers as well as system-wide.

Resources or capabilities must exist at the individual level that allow indi-vidual policy workers (Colebatch, 2006; Colebatch et al., 2011) and managers (Howlett & Walker, 2012) to participate in and contribute to designing, deploy-ing, and evaluating policies. It includes not only their ability to analyse but also to learn and adapt to changes as necessary.

Resources must also be available at the level of the organization. These are aspects of the structure and makeup of policy-relevant organizations that affect their members' ability to perform policy functions. Organizational features that unduly circumscribe individual decision capabilities or sap morale among policy workers, for example, can undermine an agency's ability to acquit its functions. The organizational conditions most relevant to policy capacity include those related to information, management, and political support (Tiernan & Wanna, 2006; Gleeson et al., 2011).

Finally, system level capabilities include the level of support and trust a public agency enjoys from its political masters and from the society at large (Blind, 2006). Such factors are critical determinants of organizational capabil-ities and thus shape public managers" capability to perform their policy func-tions. Political support for both from both above and below is vital because agencies and managers must be considered legitimate in order to access re-sources from their authorizing institutions and constituencies on a continuing basis, and such resources must also be available for award in the first place (Painter & Pierre, 2005).

Not all capacities are, of course, equally necessary for all functions. Some functions may require more of one capacity than others. Monetary authorities, for example, typically require more analytical capacity while their law enforcement counterparts need more organizational capacity. A modicum of political capacity is essential for all policy tasks but is especially necessary when pursuing changes in difficult areas such as agricultural, environmental or pension reforms. If these critical capacity deficits are not taken into account then any short-term gain enjoyed by pandering to contemporary political preferences are likely to be offset later when the consequences of governance failures and poor institutional design become apparent (Hood, 2010; Weaver, 1986).

Conclusion: Implementation Styles and Long-Term Instrument Preferences

The central assumption of most approaches to policy implementation is that it is most influenced by a combination of political factors related to state capacity and the complexity of the subsystem within which the problem is embedded (Atkinson & Coleman, 1989).

The set of functions practically associated with implementation is best understood as a "continuum of strategic and operational task functions" (Brinkerhoff & Crosby, 2002: 25). Functions necessary for implementation must be addressed throughout the policy process, from high-level strategic design considerations (such as constituency building) to concurrent operational-level design and capacity-building mechanisms such as project management techniques. Failing such anticipatory development of means and methods, large gaps are likely to loom between policy intentions and actual execution. Two of the academic founders of the study of implementation, Jeffrey Pressman and Aaron Wildavsky, captured the mood of early implementation research in the subtitle to their classic text *Implementation* (Pressman & Wildavsky, 1973), "How great expectations in Washington are dashed in Oakland; Or, Why it's amazing that federal programs work at all."

There are six functional categories of implementation prerequisites that recent studies urge should be developed before a policy is implemented:

1. *Policy design.* Among the necessities for an effective policy design, we can distinguish between substantive policy content and the resources made available for producing these outputs and outcomes. Are clear, consistent statements of objectives and criteria for successful outcomes provided in the legal framework underpinning the policy? And are needed resources for realizing these results made available, or is a plan for resource mobilization in place?

2. *Inter-organizational communication and enforcement capacity.* This category of preparation recognizes the need to communicate both substantive and procedural attributes of policy among departments and levels

of government and between the state and civil society policy subsystem participants. Among the most important categories of communication is the policy's framework of accountability. Knowing who will be responsible for what outputs is crucial to effective implementation. Enforcement of those responsibilities is an essential element of implementation, which also requires inter-organizational structures to enforce accountability.

3. *Characteristics of the implementing agencies / disposition of implementers.* The institutional characteristics of agencies can have a profound effect on implementation by shaping how lower level actors delivering policy outputs perceive and act upon upper-level directives. The disposition of individual implementers is closely linked to the characteristics of agencies in which they are embedded—from the degrees of freedom that are permitted when interpreting policy on the front lines of delivering outputs to the perceptions about equity and fairness across the agency. It is also affected by other factors, such as their potential for incentives from non-agency sources. Aligning the key aspects of agency culture and accountability relationships with the tasks and expectations can smooth policy implementation, just as mismatches between who is expected to deliver policy and what these agents expect to do can derail implementation.

4. *Connecting implementation outputs to their outcomes/impacts.* The three categories above will jointly influence implementation outputs, which need to be linked to the impacts on the defined problem via their "policy logic." If outputs follow the causal relationships that were foreseen during policy formulation, then the policy logic will be valid and outcomes will begin to address the problem that policy was anticipated to address. But if that relationship does not hold up, then actors will need to assess whether the policy logic was valid to begin with, or whether causal relationships differ in practice from what was anticipated. Such early warning capacity can enable adapting implementation to avoid pitfalls and problems that lead to failure.

5. *Policy learning.* Policy evaluation, to be explored fully in Chapter 8, focuses explicitly and systematically on drawing lessons about the results from policy-making initiatives. But learning about what works when pursuing policy objectives can occur throughout the policy cycle. To facilitate ongoing policy learning, implementation designs can build in mechanisms and procedures that assess results as they unfold, from identifying and collecting key indicators of policy impact to specifying assessment tools and techniques that should be applied during policy delivery. Implementation that builds such learning features into its design

can deliver greater adaptive capacity, by providing rapid feedback on policy success, or lack of it. Having capability for continuous detection of effects and impacts allows for policy adjustment during implementation, rather than only after formal evaluation, when problems and shortcomings could spiral into a crisis. More informal and iterative adjustments enable operationalizing the incrementalist tradition of policy-making in implementation.

6. *Managing the action environment.* When policies are put into practice, bureaucrats and other participants in delivering outputs often need to deal with actions and reactions to their effort that extend beyond the target group and the causal relationships that were envisioned in the policy's design. Important elements of this action environment can include the public sector's institutional configuration, political support, and social and economic factors. This environment generates structural influences on policy development throughout the policy cycle, but during implementation it can create a reflexive dynamic wherein policy outputs either amplify conflicting forces that then generate disruptive feedback into policy delivery or those outputs can reinforce support for the established trajectory, as in the case of path-dependent policy feedback (Pierson, 2000a). Those engaged in policy implementation thus need to be ready for managing the intended and unintended consequences of policy output on the environment beyond the policy target(s). For example, unanticipated effects on the action environment could shift stakeholder alignment in ways that create new support or opposition to a policy.

Study Questions

1. Why is it common for a gap to emerge between the intentions of decision-makers and the outcomes of implementation?

2. Is it harder to implement solutions to wicked problems than it is to formulate solutions to them? Why?

3. How does the role of bureaucracy differ in implementation from that of other actors?

4. What are some common barriers to implementation? Choose a policy topic and illustrate these implementation issues and how they might be overcome.

5. Why is implementation capacity important? How can it be enhanced?

Further Readings

Bardach, Eugene. 1977. *The Implementation Game: What Happens after a Bill Becomes a Law*. Cambridge, Mass.: MIT Press.

Ellig, Jerry, and Don Lavoie. 1995. "The Principal–Agent Relationship in Organizations," in P. Foss, ed., *Economic Approaches to Organizations and Institutions: An Introduction*. Aldershot: Dartmouth.

Goggin, Malcolm L. et al., 1990. *Implementation Theory and Practice: Toward a Third Generation*. Glenview, Ill.: Scott, Foresman/Little, Brown.

Howlett, Michael. 2005. "What Is a Policy Instrument? Policy Tools, Policy Mixes and Policy Implementation Styles," in P. Eliadis, M. Hill, and M. Howlett, eds, *Designing Government: From Instruments to Governance*. Montreal and Kingston: McGill-Queen's University Press, 31–50.

Kagan, Robert A. 1991. "Adversarial Legalism and American Government," *Journal of Policy Analysis and Management* 10, no. 3: 369–406.

O'Toole, Laurence J. 2000. "Research on Policy Implementation: Assessment and Prospects," *Journal of Public Administration Research and Theory* 10, no. 2: 263–88.

Pressman, Jeffrey L., and Aaron B. Wildavsky. 1984. *Implementation: How Great Expectations in Washington Are Dashed in Oakland*, 3rd edn. Berkeley: University of California Press.

Saetren, Harald. 2014. "Implementing the Third Generation Research Paradigm in Policy Implementation Research: An Empirical Assessment," *Public Policy and Administration* 29, no. 2 (April 1): 84–105. doi:10.1177/0952076713513487.

Simon, H.A. 1946. "The Proverbs of Administration," *Public Administration Review* 6: 53–67.

Chapter 8

Policy Evaluation
Policy-Making as Learning

What Is Policy Evaluation?

Once a policy has been adopted and outputs are generated, questions arise regarding the impacts and effectiveness of those efforts. To better understand how policies work out, governments as well as other members of the relevant policy subsystem conduct informal or formal assessments of policy outputs and outcomes of varying intensity and sophistication. Such initiatives to determine how a public policy has actually fared in practice fall within the policy evaluation stage of the policy cycle framework. How evaluation is conducted and the influence that its substantive findings have on policy-making are the focus of this chapter. Once these effects are highlighted, the chapter considers the patterns of policy change that can result from different types of policy evaluation.

Definition

According to one mainstream definition, "policy evaluation assesses the effectiveness of a public policy in terms of its perceived intentions and results" (Gerston 1997: 120). Value judgment—whether a policy is effective or not—is critical to evaluation, according to this definition. One may, and indeed many do, go further and may include judgment on the worth or efficiency or equity effects of the policy in question. Thus, according to the OECD (2002), "Evaluation refers to the process of determining the worth or significance of an activity, policy, or program." This is still a narrow definition, however, because it does not cover evaluations that seek to go beyond effects or inquire into the factors that shape those effects.

This broader conception is captured in the definition by Vedung (2010), who defines policy evaluation as:

> careful retrospective assessment of public-sector interventions, their organization, content, implementation and outputs or outcomes, which is intended to play a role in future practical situations . . . .. It is not limited only to effects of interventions and activities at the outcome level (i.e. in society or nature) but also includes outputs, implementation processes, content and organization.

It is in this broad sense that we approach policy evaluation in this chapter.

The purpose of evaluation is to shed light on the actual experience of the policies on the ground. It cannot be assumed that policies will be implemented as intended, as we have seen in the preceding chapter. And even when implementation proceeds as intended, there are often many unintended effects, not to mention under- and over-achievement of set objectives.

First, evaluations seek to record what actually transpired, since implementing agents will not take on producing this type of chronicle unless they are explicitly tasked with such documentation. This dimension of evaluation seeks to explain the specific processes, inputs, and activities that were deployed to implement the policy.

Next, evaluation looks to explain whether the intended results were achieved. To what extent? To what effect? Why or why not? Do the results vary across socio-economic groups or geographic location? How were the results affected by specific activities undertaken? Finally, some evaluations seek to draw lessons from their assessment of what happened and what difference the results made. Can these lessons be used to improve the program? The scope of recommendations from evaluations can focus narrowly on components of the new policy, or range more widely to address systemic effects on policy outcomes.

The evaluation may thus focus on a single program or project, or a broader grouping of them to form a sector or theme. Governments and international organizations also conduct evaluations of particular agencies or offices delivering a program, such as when UNICEF evaluates its entire operation or one or more of its national offices.

History

Evaluation of government action is not something new, as ancient Egyptians, Chinese, and Greeks are believed to have taken regular stock of their grain and livestock production (Imas & Rist, 2009). However, evaluation as we know it today began only after the emergence of empirical methods and the associated emphasis on rationality and the measurement of carefully observed phenomena in the eighteenth century. The first systematic focus on policy evaluation emerged with the efforts to assess the quality of school systems in the United States during the nineteenth century. Heightened concerns about contagious diseases further expanded the practice of evaluation to public health programs.

Evaluation was further extended with the launch of the New Deal programs in the United States, which expanded social protection program delivery and initiated public infrastructure delivery in the wake of the Great Depression. After World War II, large-scale program expansion in the military, urban housing, job and occupational training, and health led to unprecedented interest in evaluation. The steady pace continued with the launch and expansion of social programs as a part of Lyndon Johnson's "War on Poverty" during the 1960s. Elaborate and ambitious evaluation systems followed, such as the government-wide Planning, Programming, and Budgeting System (PPBS) implemented in the US in the mid-1960s and the "monitoring for results" movement more broadly across the public sector in the 1970s and 1980s (Imas & Rist, 2009).

What these twentieth-century evaluation approaches shared in common was an unqualified faith in the potential rationality of policy-making—"radical rationalism" as it has been called (Vedung, 2010)—which peaked in the mid-1970s. The thinking inspired careful quantitative analysis of program efforts and results in the name of enhanced efficiency and effectiveness.

By the 1970s, policy evaluation had become a full-fledged profession in the US and Europe, with the formation of professional associations of evaluators and the development of handbooks and standard methods of appraisal. The enthusiasm for rationalism waned during the 1980s, following recognition of the difficulties many evaluations encountered in adhering to a strict methodology and, more importantly, the lacklustre or even negative results that flowed following the receipt of evaluation results and recommendations. In place of rationality, dialogue with stakeholders soon became a preferred approach to understanding policy impacts, later articulated as "deliberative democracy" (Vedung, 2010) and viewed as a value in itself in policy-making, regardless of the "objective" merits of various programs and tools. This change in orientation paralleled and engaged directly with the emergence of post-positivism as a perspective on policy and politics.

The spread of stakeholder engagement and deliberative evaluation was, however, eclipsed by the rise of New Public Management (NPM) during the 1990s. NPM's mission was to improve public policy and administration by introducing private-sector practices in the public sector. It sought to improve administrative performance through the introduction of market competition (privatization and deregulation) and results-based management, the success of which depended on constant monitoring of administrative practices and results and continuous improvements based on the findings (Vedung, 2010). Process monitoring and cost–benefit analysis were its principal methodological tools and re-introduced positivist methodologies into evaluation.

The of the evidence-based policy-making (EBP) movement, discussed in Chapter 6, and were also carried over into evaluation. Discovering what works and why, demonstrated through analysis of evidence, is the primary goal for EBP's proponents (Vendung, 2010) and also led policy evaluation to adopt quantitative and experimental research methods so as to isolate the specific beneficial and weak policy effects of different program components. "This [EBP] movement is working toward a rationalist dream: that hard evidence can remove the partisan wrangling from policy-making and turn it into a scientific process, guided by numbers, run like a lab, and devoted not to political ideologies but to the simple question, what works?" (Guay, 2018). In reality, however, as post-positivists had noted, even when we have the necessary information, which is often not the case, we don't know what to do with it because of political constraints (Cairney, 2016).

These developments all occurred in the context of developed countries and the evaluation movement has taken a somewhat different trajectory in developing countries, where it grew out of the audit tradition that continues to shape its practice to this day. The auditing tradition adopts a financial management and accounting orientation that "seeks to determine whether a program did what it was supposed to do and whether the money spent was done so within the rules, regulations, and requirements of the program. . . . Its emphasis is on accountability and compliance" (Imas & Rist, 2009).

In a sense, audit is a narrow form of evaluation focused on internal processes rather than outcomes. "Auditing tends to focus on compliance with requirements, while evaluation tends to focus on attributing observed changes to a policy, program, or project" (Wisler, 1996). In recent decades, evaluation in developing countries has taken the form of results-based monitoring and evaluation (RBME), which is a tool to help keep track of programs and projects' progress and impacts. This emphasis on "results" has led policy evaluation in developing countries to converge toward practices in the developed countries, though the paucity of data and analytical skills make attaining full equivalence difficult.

This brief history of policy evaluation shows that it has changed and adapted with evolving circumstances and public expectations. The changes respond to the belief that it is not sufficient for governments to formalize good intentions into laws, allocate resources, and establish processes in the hope that the desired goals will be achieved. Governments are increasingly expected to demonstrate that what they do makes a positive difference and that the resources being spent will achieve results.

However, this understandable technocratic urge has had to countenance the realities of policy-making, which include extensive uncertainty, limited information, and political conflict over incommensurable beliefs about the appropriate roles of government, society, and individuals.

Perspectives on Evaluation: Positivist and Post-Positivist

Since the instantiation of positivist and rational ideology into the heart of the policy sciences, policy evaluation has encouraged its practitioners to view such assessment methods and orientations as neutral, technical exercises in determining the success (or failure) of government efforts to deal with policy problems. David Nachmias (1979: 4), an influential figure in the field's early development, thus captured this positivist spirit well in defining policy evaluation as "the objective systematic, empirical examination of the effects ongoing policies and public programs have on their targets in terms of the goals they are meant to achieve."

The positivist premise underlying this definition is unmistakable, in that it explicitly specifies that the examination of a policy's effects should be objective, systematic, and empirical. However, as mentioned before, public policy goals are often neither clear nor explicit, necessitating subjective interpretation to determine what exactly was intended or achieved. Objective analysis is further limited by the difficulties encountered in developing neutral standards by which to evaluate government success in dealing with societal demands and socially constructed problems in a highly politicized environment.

As set out above, the emphasis on positivist evaluation found in the early years of evaluation was amplified with the increasing popularity of EBP in recent years. As we have seen, EBP represents an effort to restructure policy processes by prioritizing data-based evidentiary decision-making over more "intuitive" or experiential policy assessments in order to avoid or minimize policy failures caused by a mismatch between government expectations and on-the-ground realities. The EBP movement (Pawson, 2006) is thus the latest in a series of efforts undertaken by reformers in governments over more than half a century in the effort to enhance the efficiency and effectiveness of public policy-making through the application of rational approaches to addressing policy problems (Sanderson, 2006; Mintrom, 2007).

Exactly what constitutes "evidence-based policy-making" and whether analytical efforts in this regard actually yield better or improved policies are, not surprisingly, contentious subjects (Packwood, 2002; Pawson, 2002; Tenbensel, 2004; Jackson, 2007). Through a process of theoretically informed empirical analysis consciously directed toward promoting policy learning, proponents of this approach believe that governments can better learn from experience, avoid repeating past errors, and better apply new techniques to the resolution of old and new problems (Sanderson, 2002a, 2002b).

While policy analysts and government officials have continued to call for enhanced EBP, it has become increasingly clear that practising it is more problematic than initially understood (Anderson, 1979a; Kerr, 1976; Manzer, 1984). Astute observers noted that it was naive to believe that policy evaluation would always be intended to reveal the objective effects of a policy. In fact, evaluation is at times employed deliberately to show a policy in a better or worse light than justified by objective evidence, depending on the intention of those commissioning or conducting the evaluation.

This is accomplished through framing the terms of evaluation in such a way as to lead to conclusions that suit the sponsor's motives. Or if the government seeks to change or scrap a policy, it can adjust the terms of the evaluation accordingly. Similarly, evaluations by those outside the government are not always designed to improve a policy, but often to criticize it in order to gain partisan political advantage or to reinforce ideological postulates (Chelimsky, 1995; Bovens & t'Hart, 1995).

As a result, recent thinking tends to view policy evaluation as an inherently political activity, albeit, like the other stages of policy-making, one relying on an organized structure that influences its content and contours. In its extreme, post-positivist form, it has been argued that since the same condition can be interpreted quite differently by different evaluators, there is no definitive way of determining the "correct" evaluation mode, and all evaluations are necessarily partial and "interpretive." Which interpretation prevails, in this view, is ultimately determined by political conflicts and compromises among the various actors involved, conditioned by their political resources and influence (Ingram & Mann, 1980b: 852).

This is not to suggest that policy evaluation is an irrational or a purely political process, or always devoid of a genuine intention to assess the functioning of a policy and its effects. Rather, it serves as a warning that we must be aware that relying solely on formal evaluation for drawing conclusions about a policy's relative success or failure will undoubtedly yield unduly limited insights into policy outcomes and their assessment. To get the most out of studying policy evaluation, the limits of rationality and the political forces that shape it must also be taken into account, without going so far as to believe that the subjective nature of policy assessments allows no meaningful evaluation at all to occur.

Approaches to Evaluation: Administrative and Political

The increasing scope and complexity of programs fostered the growth of the formal policy analysis profession (Nachmias, 1979; Suchman, 1967, 1979). There has been also a proliferation of works comparing evaluation policies across nations and agencies and with private-sector counterparts (Swiss, 1991; Kernaghan et al., 2000; Triantafillou, 2007).

In the 1970s and 1980s these included such evaluatory systems as the PPBS, first developed at the Ford Motor Company and then adopted by the US Department of Defense and ultimately the entire US federal government; Zero-Based Budgeting (ZBB), a variant of PPBS developed at the Xerox Corporation and adopted by the Carter administration in the US and, later, in many other countries; and Management by Objectives (MBO), a self-reporting managerial performance system implemented in the US and Canada, among other places (Reid, 1979; Rogers, 1978; Wildavsky, 1969). These early efforts subsequently manifested in moves to "reinvent" government under the banner of "New Public Management" promoting smaller, leaner government (Aucoin, 1990; Pollitt, 2001; Osborne & Gaebler, 1992; Abma & Noordegraaf, 2003).

The increasing complexity of technical administrative evaluations like these, however, has not been matched by a similar increase in usefulness (Friedman, 2002). These efforts have all had to contend with the inherent limitations of rationalist policy analysis (Dobell & Zussman, 1981; Jordan & Sutherland, 1979), which is ill-equipped to cope with the messy rough-and-tumble and hard-to-measure world of public policy-making. Policies often do not state their objectives precisely enough to permit rigorous analysis of whether they are being achieved. Moreover, baseline data does not always exist and governments often seek to avoid having their failures publicized and dissected.

As well, the same policy may be directed at achieving a variety of objectives, without indicating their relative priority, thus making it difficult to find out if a particular objective's achievement is an essential or simply desirable policy outcome (Cahill & Overman, 1990; Formaini, 1990; McLaughlin, 1985; Palumbo, 1987; Weiss, 1977a). Social and economic problems tend to be tightly interrelated, as is the case, for example, with housing and employment, and it is virtually impossible to independently isolate and evaluate the effects of policies directed at either subsystem.

In addition, each policy has effects on problems other than those intended, which a comprehensive evaluation must consider but which may make the task of assessment unwieldy and unmanageable. The difficulties involved in gathering reliable and usable information and aggregating it into generally acceptable benchmarks further aggravate these data problems.

The limitations faced by administrative evaluation—and we have noted only a few—increase with the level of sophistication and comprehensiveness expected of such analyses. Thus, effectiveness evaluations, which look at whether or not a policy or program has accomplished its goals would clearly be of considerable use to policy-makers in their budgeting and other decisions, but are the most difficult to undertake. Although still popular in areas such as infrastructure and health care policy, significant limits on a government's ability to collect and apply relevant program-level data limit the production of meaningful effectiveness evaluations (Head, 2008; Hammersley, 2005; Laforest & Orsini, 2005; Moseley & Tierney, 2004).

To broaden administrative evaluation and attempt, somehow, to assess the question of program effectiveness, many governments have experimented with creating specialized internal audit agencies (Adair & Simmons, 1988; Good,

2003) and with promoting public participation in the evaluation process. The intention is both to better evaluate policies and to head off challenges to these policies on the grounds of a "lack of consultation" with interested or affected members of the public. But the usefulness and legitimacy of these kinds of public forums have been challenged on many grounds. There are concerns with the extent to which participants are actually representative of a range of views and ideas and with the effects of issues such as funding on the quality and quantity of representation (see Pateman, 1970; Wagle, 2000; Englehart & Trebilcock, 1981; Mitchell et al., 1997; Johnson 2007).

Frustration with the difficulties involved in such administrative evaluations, for example, led the Auditor General of Canada to conclude in his 1983 *Annual Report* that "a significant proportion of evaluation assessments did not form an adequate basis for sound advice." Ten years later, the Auditor General's review of program evaluation in the Canadian federal government again found numerous changes in form but little in substance. According to the *Report*, evaluations were still

> less likely to be an important source of information in support of pro-
> gram and policy decisions addressing questions of continued relevance
> and cost effectiveness. Evaluations are more likely to provide informa-
> tion for accountability purposes but are often partial. The most complete
> information available is related to operational effectiveness, the way a
> program is working. (Canada, Auditor General, 1993)

In contrast to administrative evaluations, which are carried out by and within government agencies, political evaluation of policies is undertaken by just about everyone with any interest in politics. They are usually neither systematic nor technically sophisticated, and are often explicitly partisan and biased. Partisan political evaluations often simply attempt to label a policy a success or failure, for example, followed by demands for continuation or change. This is true of the work of many think tanks, for example, which, like political parties, bring a specific ideological or other more or less fixed perspective or "frame" to the evaluation process (see Bovens & t'Hart, 1995; Abelson, 1996; Lindquist, 1998; Ricci, 1993; Weaver, 1989).

This does not undermine their significance, however, because their initial objective in undertaking an evaluation is rarely to improve a government's policy, but rather to either support or challenge it. Praise or criticism at this stage can lead to new iterations of the policy cycle as governments respond to criticisms, similar to what occurs with much of the more reasoned, technical evaluations.

While political evaluation is ongoing, it influences the policy process directly on specialized occasions, such as during or around elections. At election time, citizens get an opportunity to render judgment on a government's performance. Votes at elections or in referendums thus express the voters' informal evaluations of the efficiency and effectiveness of governments and their programs and policies.

However, in most democratic countries, referendums or plebiscites on particular policies are relatively rare. As was discussed in Chapter 3, while elections are held regularly, by their very nature they usually involve a range of issues, so when citizens express their preferences and sentiments through the ballot box at election time, their evaluation is usually made as an aggregate judgment on a government's overall record of activities in office rather than about the effectiveness or usefulness of a specific policy or policies. Nevertheless, public perceptions of the ineffectiveness or harmful effects of specific high-profile government activities can and do affect voting behaviour, a reality governments ignore at their peril come election day (King, 1981).

A more common type of political policy evaluation involves consulting with members of relevant policy subsystems. There are many mechanisms for such consultations, which involve the use of the procedural policy instruments discussed in Chapter 5. These include setting up administrative forums for public hearings and establishing special consultative committees, task forces, and inquiries for evaluative purposes (see Cairns, 1990a; Bulmer, 1993; Clokie & Robinson, 1969), and can range from small meetings of less than a dozen participants lasting several minutes to multi-million dollar inquiries that hear thousands of individual briefs and can take years to complete (Doern, 1967; Salter, 1981; Wilson, 1971).

In many countries, political evaluation of government action is built into the system, in the form, for example, of congressional or parliamentary oversight committees (see McCubbins & McCubbins, 1994; McCubbins & Schwartz, 1984). While in some countries, such as the US, these tend to meet on a regular basis, in others, such as Canada and Australia, the process may be less routine and undertaken in a much more ad hoc fashion (see de la Mothe, 1996; Banting, 1995).

These political mechanisms for policy evaluation are usually capable of ascertaining the views of many members of the policy subsystem and affected public on specific policy issues. However, it is not certain that the simple fact of a government hearing the public's views makes a difference to its policy, much less that this leads to change in policy outcomes. Effectiveness often depends on whether the views heard are congruent with those of the current government (Dye, 1972: 353–75), which in turn depends on the criteria government members and political officials use to assess success or failure of particular policies or programs.

Policy Evaluation as Policy Learning

One way of looking at policy evaluation, which combines elements of both the positivist and post-positivist perspectives on the subject, is to regard it as a significant part of an overall process of *policy learning* (Grin & Loeber, 2007;

Lehtonen, 2005). Perhaps the greatest benefits of policy evaluation are not the assessment reports of the success and failure of particular policies per se, but rather the educational dynamics and learning that it can stimulate among policy-makers (Pressman & Wildavsky, 1984). Whether they realize it or not, actors engaged in policy evaluation are often participating in a larger process of policy learning, in which policy improvements can be promoted through reassessment of problem definition and policy formulation and implementation processes associated with the policy (see Etheredge & Short, 1983; Sabatier, 1988; Lehtonen, 2006).

The concept of "learning" is generally associated with intentional, progressive, cognitive consequences of the education that results from policy evaluation. However, policy learning also has a broader meaning that includes better understanding both the intended and unintended (see Merton, 1936) consequences of policy-making activities, as well as both the "positive" and "negative" implications of existing policies and their alternatives on the status quo and efforts to alter it.

From a learning perspective, public policy evaluation is conceived as an iterative process of active learning about the nature of policy problems and the potential of various solutions to address them (Rist, 1994; Levitt & March, 1988). This view shares some similarities with the idea of policy-making as a trial-and-error process of policy experimentation, but with the added idea that successive "rounds" of policy-making, if carefully evaluated after each "round," can avoid repeating mistakes and move policy implementation ever closer toward the achievement of desired goals (Howlett, 2007).

Like other concepts in policy science, there are differing interpretations of what is meant by "policy learning" and whether its source and motivation are within or outside existing policy processes. Peter Hall makes the case for *"endogenous"* learning, defining the activity as a "deliberate attempt to adjust the goals or techniques of policy in the light of the consequences of past policy and new information so as to better attain the ultimate objects of governance" (Hall, 1993: 278).

Hugh Heclo, on the other hand, suggests that learning is a less conscious, *"exogenous"* activity, often occurring as a government's response to some kind of external or exogenous change in a policy environment. According to Heclo, this often takes the form of an almost automatic process, as "learning can be taken to mean a relatively enduring alteration in behaviour that results from experience; usually this alteration is conceptualized as a change in response made in reaction to some perceived stimulus" (Heclo, 1974: 306).

The two definitions describe the same relationship between policy learning and policy change, but differ substantially in their approach to the issue. For Hall, learning is a part of the normal public policy process in which policy-makers attempt to understand why certain initiatives may have succeeded while others failed. If policies change as a result of learning, the impetus for change originates within the normal policy process of the government. For Heclo, on the other hand, policy learning is seen as an activity undertaken by policy-makers largely in reaction to changes in external policy "environments." As the environment changes, policy-makers must adapt if their policies are to succeed. Regardless of its external or internal causes, however, most scholars agree that several types of learning can result from different kinds of evaluations.

It is also important to note that the number of actors—both governmental and non-governmental—involved in policy evaluation expands toward the size of the policy universe existing during agenda-setting (Bennett & Howlett, 1991; May, 1992; Sabatier, 1988; Hall, 1993; Etheredge, 1981; see also Argyris, 1992; Argyris & Schon, 1978). Some lessons are likely to concern practical suggestions about specific aspects of the policy cycle, based on the actual experience with the policy on the part of policy implementers and target groups. These include, for example, their perceptions of the lessons they have learned about which policy instruments have succeeded in which circumstances and which have failed to accomplish expected tasks or goals, or which issues have enjoyed public support in the agenda-setting process and which have not, and therefore which are likely to do so in future.

Richard Rose (1988, 1991) defined one such relatively specific and limited type of learning as *lesson-drawing*. This type of learning originates within the formal policy process and is aimed primarily at the choice of means or techniques employed by policy-makers in their efforts to achieve their goals; in Rose's formulation this often involves the analysis of, and derivation of lessons from, experiences in other sectors, issue areas, or jurisdictions.

Other lessons probe broader policy goals and their underlying ideas or paradigms, or the "frames" in which lesson-drawing takes place. This is a more fundamental type of learning, which is accompanied by changes in the thinking underlying a policy that might result in a policy being terminated or drastically revised in light of new conceptions and ideas developed through the evaluation process. Following Hall (1993), this type of learning is often referred to as *social learning*. It tends to originate outside the formal policy process and affects the policy-makers' capacity to change society.

Actors in the Policy Evaluation Process

The range of actors involved in policy evaluation is much broader than often presented in the administrative and managerial literature on evaluation, which tends to concentrate overwhelmingly on internal evaluation by agencies themselves as well as those done at their behest by external consultants or by think tanks. The range of actors also includes the judiciary, interest groups and indeed, as discussed above, the public at large. Evaluation by those inside the government—bureaucrats, politician, and regular consultants—are of a different nature and often intended for different purposes.

Internal Evaluators

Internal evaluators are usually paid and trained professionals who routinely apply formal techniques such as cost–benefit or budgetary analysis (Boardman et al., 2001; Sinden & Thampapillai, 1995) and performance measures to quantify program outputs and outcomes (see Meltsner, 1976; Friedman, 2002). These analysts can have a substantial impact on how the policy and the problem it targets are interpreted and addressed in future. They can affect the "framing" and assessment of policy success and failure by how they develop and apply various techniques, measures, and benchmarks to the program (see Davies, 1999; de la Porte et al., 2001; Levy, 2001). At other times, they may serve as "brokers" linking policy-makers to implementers, or to those outside the formal institutions of government who are generating new knowledge on social problems and the techniques for resolving these problems (see Meltsner, 1976; Guess & Farnham, 2000).

The internal evaluators within the government know the details of the program and its contexts and are hence able to ask the most relevant questions. They also have better access to information and officials who may supply it. On the other hand, they may be too closely attached to the program to ask hard questions and conduct independent evaluation. Indeed, they may have a vested interest in defending the program rather than genuinely assessing its impact. Even when they do conduct rigorous evaluation, their findings may not be viewed as credible by outsiders (Imas & Rist, 2009).

External Evaluators

External evaluators include a variety of actors directly or indirectly involved in assessing and otherwise passing formal or informal judgment on a policy's performance and its impacts. They include concerned interest groups that conduct their own, less formal, reviews of policy performance. They also include paid consultants who have been playing an increasingly important role in evaluation (Speers, 2007; Dent, 2002; Perl & White, 2002; Lapsley & Oldfield, 2001; Martin, 1998; Saint-Martin, 1998; Bakvis, 1997). Think tanks, on the other hand, once played an important role in independently evaluating policies in many countries, but their proliferation and the trend toward their identification with specific partisan positions have undermined their ability to affect policy discourses and directions through their evaluative activities, despite the exponential increase in the number of the latter (McGann & Johnson, 2005; Rich, 2004; Abelson, 2002, 2007; Ladi, 2005; Stone, 2007; Lindquist, 2004).

Judges are able to review legislative and administrative actions to determine the extent to which policies match up to larger, often constitutionally established principles of social justice and conduct (see de Smith, 1973; Edley, 1990; Humphries & Songer, 1999; Jaffe, 1965). Evaluation by the judiciary is concerned with possible conflicts between government actions and constitutional provisions or established standards of administrative conduct and individual rights (Jacobson et al., 2001). The judiciary is entitled to review government actions either on its own initiative or when asked to do so by an individual or organization filing a case against a government agency in a court of law. The grounds for judicial review differ considerably across countries but usually extend to the examination of the constitutionality of the policy being implemented, or whether its implementation or development violated laws or principles of natural rights and/or justice in democratic societies, or religious or ideological doctrines in others. In the former case, judges typically assess such factors as whether the policy was developed and implemented in a non-capricious and non-arbitrary fashion according to principles of due process and accepted administrative law (Jaffe, 1965).

In parliamentary systems—such as Australia, New Zealand, Sweden, Japan, Ireland, and Britain—judicial courts do not review the facts specific to the case, but tend to restrict their evaluation to procedural issues (Jaffe, 1969; Wade, 1965, 1966). Thus, as long as administrative agencies operate within their jurisdiction and according to principles of fundamental justice and due process, their decisions are unlikely to be overturned. In comparison, courts in republican systems with constitutionally entrenched divisions of powers, as in the US, courts enjoy more authority to question legislative and executive actions. As a result, they are much more active and willing to consider errors of fact as well as errors of law in their evaluations of administrative behaviour (Jaffe, 1965).

Members of the public can be said to have the ultimate say on a government's policy record when they vote at elections (Brewer & deLeon, 1983: 319–26) or comment to the media or pollsters about it. That their involvement is post hoc, informal, and external to the intra-governmental policy "loop" does not make them less impactful. Such evaluations may involve critiques of both the substance and process of policy that lead to policy changes of varying magnitude (see Snow & Benford, 1992). To draw on the public's collective wisdom, there are enhanced efforts to bring public views into the evaluative process through focus groups, surveys, inquiries, citizens' juries, consensus conferences, and advisory committees (see Hastak et al., 2001; Peters & Barker, 1993; Schwartz, 1997; Wraith & Lamb, 1971).

To systematize the process by which the public offers opinion on policy issues, Participatory Evaluation methods are being expanded to give the population a direct role in the process. They are intended to encourage concerned citizens to engage in regular monitoring and evaluation of public programs and projects.

Such citizen evaluators work with other internal and external evaluators to design, carry out, and interpret an evaluation (Johnson, 2007).

> Participatory evaluation represents a further and more radical step away from the model of independent evaluation. . . . [It] is a form of evaluation where the distinction between experts and layperson, researcher and researched is deemphasized and redefined. . . . Evaluators . . . [act] mainly [as] facilitators and instructors helping others to make the assessment. (Molund & Schill, 2004)

A variety of international organizations, both governmental and non-governmental, are also increasingly conducting policy evaluation. These can focus on their own activities within a policy sector or look to the efficacy of governments' initiatives. International charities such as Oxfam and the Melinda and Bill Gates Foundations are major producers of evaluation reports on social policy and public health issues, respectively. Other international NGOs such as Transparency International and World Economic Forum regularly publish reports on corruption (Dell & McDevitt, 2018) and economic policy (Schwab, 2018), making recommendations that are widely followed around the world.

Nearly every bilateral aid organization—such as AusAid, CIDA, JICA, DID, and USAid—also conducts evaluations of the projects they fund and subsequently publish the findings. Indeed, the techniques developed by the US Agency for International Development (2016) are widely used in the international development world. Large-scale evaluations by the IMF and the World Bank, such as the *Doing Business* report series (World Bank, 2019), have become frequent in recent decades, generating outputs that have a significant influence in shaping policy agendas around the world. Specialist UN agencies—UNICEF, UNESCO, UNCTAD, UNIDO, ILO, ITC, FAO, and others—play a critical role in shaping perceptions of successful and problematic approaches to delivering policy in their respective purviews. Evaluations of learning initiatives produced by international organizations (e.g., UNDP, OECD, UNESCO, the World Bank, and the EU) have been demonstrated to influence education policy decisions around the world (Neves, 2008).

The intense evaluation of aid projects by NGOs, international organizations, and aid agencies is the result of heightened concern for accountability and the need to ensure that money is being spent as intended, to the extent this intent can be clearly identified. More importantly, it is intended to ensure that they are getting the desired results. However, international evaluators are constrained by the fact that states are sovereign entities, and thus access to data and evidence used in evaluation depends on the level of cooperation and collaboration offered by host governments.

Evaluation by external actors can convey an image of independence and impartiality that leads to their findings being received more favourably. They may also have more specialized skills that may be lacking among governments that have less experience with new programs and their evaluation. All these affirmations of external expertise are, however, only expectations about potential capacity. In practice, external consultants, think tanks, and interest groups often have close professional ties to government agencies that make them accommodating to the needs of the agency under review. The agencies commissioning an evaluation may also frame the terms of reference in ways that skew the findings toward favourable outcomes as is often alleged, for example, in evaluations conducted by "outside" consultants.

Types of Policy Evaluation

The literature identifies a plethora of policy evaluation approaches, of which only a subset are useful. The commonly used classification of evaluation as quantitative or qualitative, for instance, is unhelpful because most evaluations in the real world encompass both metrics. Similarly, to classify evaluations as formative, summative, process, or impact is more confusing than clarifying, because of the overlaps among them.[1] While there are indeed multiple approaches based on different objectives and especially methodological techniques, they boil down to two broad, yet fundamental, assessment categories, process and impact, as shown in Figure 8.1.

Inputs in this framework refer to resources (funding, staffing, equipment, etc.) that go into implementing a policy, while activities refer to what is done ("provide," "promote," "facilitate," etc.) with these inputs. *Outputs* are the observable products and services produced by the inputs and activities. *Outcomes* are the changes that result from the outputs (e.g., smoking cessation, increased school attendance, etc.), whereas *impacts* are the intended and unintended medium- and long-term effects of the outcomes. To illustrate, in the case of anti-smoking programs, time and money spent on the program are inputs, anti-smoking laws and campaigns are activities, increased taxes and smoking bans are outputs, decline in smoking rate is an outcome, and decline in smoking-related mortality and reduction in lung cancer rates are impacts.

Figure 8.1 Types of Policy Evaluation

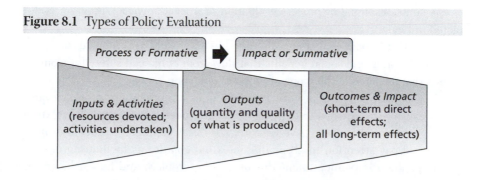

Process evaluations—also referred to as *formative* evaluation—concentrate on the inputs and activities devoted to producing outputs. In comparison, *impact* evaluation—also called *summative* evaluation—concentrates on the effects of the outputs. Process evaluations are often carried out using a logic- or theory-based framework, a conceptual construct more fully discussed below, whereas impact evaluation often follows economic or experimental approaches. The former assesses how and the extent to which a policy has worked, while the latter focuses on the policy's long-term effects. However, the distinction between the two types of evaluation is not entirely clear-cut. As the UK government's *HM Treasury* (2003) points out, it is arguable that "determining whether or not a policy has worked, or has been effective, necessarily involves asking questions about *how* it has worked, for *whom, why,* and *under what conditions* it has worked or not worked." Nevertheless, maintaining a distinction between the two assessment approaches is useful for heuristic purposes.

Process Evaluation

The "process" conception of evaluation views public policy as conversion of inputs and activities into outputs, which, in turn, cause effects on the target population. Its objective is to assess the linkages between inputs and activities on the one hand, and outputs and outcomes on the other. The intent is not only to generate information on the linkages but to draw conclusions about how to improve them. This is the reasons why it is also called "formative" evaluation.

Process evaluation occurs once a program has been in operation for some time and policy-makers seek to assess its performance so that improvements may be made if necessary. It allows them to know if the program is working as intended and reaching the target population in the desired ways. It pays particular attention to implementation processes so as to identify bottlenecks and waste. It seeks to assess the extent to which the goals are being achieved without assessing the goals themselves. For instance, a program to reduce hospital waiting time or increase high school completion will look only at whether these goals are achieved, not whether they are valid goals.

A simple example of process evaluation of a legal advocacy program is depicted in Figure 8.2.

Note that impact evaluation, discussed below, would also include the unintended economic and social benefits that flow from enhanced safety for women, results that fall outside the scope of process evaluation.

Beyond assessing the performance of a policy intervention, process evaluations explore the reasons underlying it, paying special attention to contextual and organizational factors (HM Treasury, 2003). A competent process evaluation would pay attention to all main contextual conditions facilitating or hindering program implementation—history of the problem and how it has been

Figure 8.2 Logic Model for Evaluating Domestic Violence Legal Advocacy Program

Inputs	Activities	Outputs	Outcomes
Two part-time legal advocates. Relevant law books. A volunteer attorney is on hand 5 hours per week.	Program provides legal information regarding protection orders, divorce, custody, and child visitation. Program staff assist women in completing necessary paperwork. Advocates discuss individualized safety planning with women.	100 women per week are assisted with their legal rights and options.	Women receive justice and protection from the criminal and civil legal justice systems. Women and their children are safe.

Source: Adapted from National Center on Domestic and Sexual Violence, Example Logic Model for a Fictional Domestic Violence Program, Legal Advocacy http://www.ncdsv.org/images/NRCDV_FVPSA%20 Outcomes%20APP%20A-Logic.pdf

addressed, level of cultural acceptance, interests of the key stakeholders, and so on—as these, rather than policy design, may be the main factors determining outcomes.

The success of process evaluation depends crucially on effective *monitoring* of policy implementation. Without proper monitoring and the information and data it generates, no meaningful evaluation can be expected (IOB, 2009). Monitoring requires systematic collection of data on personnel, capital, and recurrent expenditures and the quality and quantity of outputs and their effects. Indeed, it is arguable that monitoring, if done systematically and thoroughly, is a good enough form of evaluation on its own when only a quick and proximate assessment of performance is desired.

Under effective monitoring, all critical information on the program's performance and effects are collected on a routine basis. Data collected and presented systematically reveals a trend line that allows policy managers to quickly spot variations and respond accordingly. Monitoring by itself does not explain the reasons behind the trend; only evaluation can do that. But even here, experienced policy managers can find enough information to quickly gain insights into the future trajectory and the reasons underlying the trends.

The Logic Framework

Process evaluations are often conducted within the rubric of the logic framework, also called theory-based evaluation (for a brief discussion of this, see Weiss, 1997; Rogers & Weiss, 2007; Funnell & Rogers, 2011; Canada, Treasury Board, 2012). Logic-based approaches focus on "unpacking the theoretical or logical sequence by which a policy intervention is expected to bring about its desired effects . . . . [They] attempt to identify the mechanisms by which policies and/or programmes might produce their effects" (HM Treasury, 2003). The logic model typically starts with an outline of the sequence of events and results—described as "program logic"—connecting inputs to outcomes of a policy intervention. Its purpose is to explain how an intervention is expected to produce the intended results.

Beyond highlighting the logic, the framework identifies the mechanisms of change and how they are affected by the context. It thus shines light on the black box within which inputs transform into outputs and cause effects. Rather than determining causation through comparison to a counterfactual, as do the experimental methods discussed below, logic approaches explore the causal chain to develop a plausible explanation of cause and effects. Logic-based approaches seek to only offer a plausible explanation of factors, based on program logic, that shaped the outcomes in question. "Understanding *contribution*, rather than proving attribution, [is] the goal" of logic models, as a Canadian government document put it (Canada, Treasury Board, 2012). Thus, for example, the success of a program to encourage teachers to relocate to rural areas depends not only on the incentives offered, but also the overall unemployment rate among teachers, the attractiveness of the specific rural location, the personal preferences and background of the teachers. Focusing only on the program's effects would overlook many other factors that shape where teachers choose to work.

The program logic is backed by some "theory of change" explaining how the intervention is expected to bring about the desired results (Judge & Bauld, 2001). The expectation is based on knowledge and experience of the program, monitoring, and research on similar programs in other sectors and jurisdictions. It is of course possible to construct a theory of change based entirely on logical reasoning without reference to an actual program, but it would be less convincing. According to Imas and Rist (2009), the theory of change should be able to answer the following questions:

- Is the model an accurate depiction of the program?
- Are all elements well defined?
- Are there any gaps in the logical chain of events?
- Are elements necessary and sufficient?
- Are relationships plausible and consistent?
- Is it realistic to assume that the program will result in the attainment of stated goals in a meaningful manner?

Research methods used by process evaluations tend to be qualitative, which allows investigators to get into the details of the program as well as the context. As Patton (1990: 156) put it, "There is no attempt in formative evaluation to generalize findings beyond the setting in which one is working.

The purpose of the research is to improve effectiveness within that setting." Particularities of a policy and the context within which it exists are very important to the logic model.

Impact Evaluation

Impact or summative evaluation refers to assessment of the effects that flow from the program's outcomes (for a brief discussion of key issues and methods in impact evaluation, see *Better Evaluations* [undated]). It is typically undertaken after a program has been in operation for some time or has ended. Its purpose is to comprehensively understand the effects caused by the program. No less importantly, it seeks to pass judgment on the program's performance, which is the reason why it is also called "summative" evaluation. Whether the policy's goals have been achieved is of no particular concern in this mode of evaluation.

However, there are sizable differences in the understanding of the term "impact," which may be defined broadly or narrowly, and in many shades in between (Hearn & Buffardi, 2016). As the Evaluation Consultation Group (2012) put it,

> some understand "impact evaluation" to mean an assessment of the achievement of the objectives reflected in the final level of the results chain. Others interpret it to mean the project's effect on broad social and economic indicators that are not included in the results chain. For others . . . "impact evaluation" means an evaluation that establishes causality, i.e., attributes results to the project.

It is important to keep these varying objectives in mind when studying or conducting impact evaluation.

According to a widely used definition, impact is "positive and negative, primary and secondary long-term effects produced by a development intervention, directly or indirectly, intended or unintended" (OECD, 2002). This is a very broad definition, encompassing all long-term effects—economic, social, political, technical, ecological etc.—produced by a policy intervention, directly or indirectly, both intended and unintended. This is an impractical definition, however, because the cost and time needed for estimating all costs as well as benefits (direct and indirect, intended and unintended) of a policy intervention would be prohibitive, even if it were technically possible.

A more feasible and commonly used approach to impact evaluation is to estimate only the direct costs of inputs assessed against observable first-order effects (IOB, 2009). Thus, for instance, impact evaluation of poverty alleviation program in this sense would include reduction of poverty (outcome) as well as reduction of malnutrition, school absenteeism etc., but not other more distant effects such as labour productivity, political efficacy, cultural advancement, and so on. The logic methodology is sufficient for this kind of impact evaluation.

However, it is arguable that it is insufficient to merely assess all effects resulting from a policy and it is necessary to specify the causality—that is, what effect was caused by which specific program component—for evaluation to be rigorous and definitive. In this line of thinking, impact evaluation is primarily about determining causation. As the Evaluation Cooperation Group (2012) put it, impact evaluation is "[a]n evaluation that quantifies the net change in outcomes that can be attributed to a specific project or program, usually by the construction of a plausible counterfactual." Similarly, for the World Bank, impact evaluation "assesses the causal effects (impacts) attributable to specific interventions, where the outcomes of interest are compared with a counterfactual situation—that is, with what would have happened without the program" (Independent Evaluation Group, 2013: 3). The search for cause–effect relationships has led to the development of a variety of empirical methods to examine and identify which factors caused what effects.

Methods for Attributing Causality

The fundamental problem that all evaluations face is how to attribute the effects or outputs of a policy intervention to the inputs that were launched following a positive decision to initiate policy. Even when a policy achieves its goals, it cannot be concluded that the achievement was the effect of the policy in question because other factors—including other policies and broader contextual conditions—may have played an influential role. Thus, improvements in health status cannot be entirely attributed to a health policy innovation because of the corollary effects of education and housing conditions on wellness. To confirm whether the policy in question is indeed the one that was responsible for the outcome, it is necessary to assess the *counterfactual*, that is, what would have happened without the policy. Various research techniques have been developed to find out what would have happened if there had been no program (Canada, Treasury Board, 2012).

Experimental and quasi-experimental methods are commonly employed for ascertaining causation. Experimental methods, especially Randomized Control Trials (RCT), have emerged as the "gold standard" for drawing causal inference and making causal statements about a policy's effects. In RCT research, participants are randomly assigned to distinct treatment and control groups. The purpose of random assignment is to create two or more groups that are, on average, virtually identical so as to eliminate selection bias. As a result, any difference in outcomes can be attributed to the treatment rather than group characteristics. Its greatest strength is that it allows evaluators to make statements about causal effect of program and thus eliminate competing explanations. On the downside, it can be difficult to operationalize—even impossible—for complex long-term interventions dealing with, for example, pensions, industrial development or climate change. It is also expensive and time consuming, especially considering the rather marginal issues on which RCTs are often conducted.[2]

In situations when random assignment is not possible or desirable, evaluations can resort to other methods such as natural or quasi-experiments and propensity score matching. The key feature of these methods is that the groups compared are not created through random assignment. Such methods often require less time and money, and allow broader generalizations. They are particularly useful when reliable administrative data is available. However, selection bias is a major limitation of these methods. As Weiss (2010) cautioned, "Groups may self-select; Mechanism of selection may be related to outcomes; Baseline characteristics can confound."

A natural experiment involves identifying some naturally occurring or unplanned event that has an impact on the subject of study (the dependent variable) but no impact on the (independent) variable being studied (Dean, 2017). (For further discussion of experimental methods, see White and Sabarwal [2014]). In quasi-natural experiments, the change is caused not by a random event but by a political or policy decision. The natural event or policy intervention has the effect of inadvertently creating separate control and treatment groups, which in RCT are created by sampling. This allows comparison of the effects on two or more groups of subjects that are affected differently by the event. For experiments to be useful for evaluation, the two groups must be broadly comparable with regard to the characteristics relevant to the study (Dean, 2017). There are as many as 18 different types of natural and quasi-natural experiments involving different levels of complexity and rigour. There is often a trade-off between robustness and practicality, as the more robust evaluations tend to be less practical and more costly (Dean, 2017).

A key advantage of quasi-experiments is that, unlike RCTs, they occur in the real world, which makes the findings more robust and generalizable. On the other hand, since researchers cannot manipulate the treatment, it is difficult to control the conditions affecting the policy in order to definitively attribute causation. Moreover, identifying and adjusting for the differences between those exposed to the policy intervention and the rest is a major challenge and sometimes not possible (Craig, 2017). Policy experiments usually rely on administrative data, which is often either unavailable or not available in a refined enough form to conduct an effective study (Leatherdale, 2018).

The main challenge that experimental and quasi-experimental assessments face is practical: it is usually difficult to develop a counterfactual because it is not possible to manipulate the program delivery in ways needed to demonstrate attribution. Another challenge is that the resources and time required for doing these assessments may be too high. The higher or more distant the impact being assessed, the harder it is to establish a counterfactual scenario—that is, what would have happened without the program—because of the intervening effects of conditions unrelated to the policy intervention. That explains why many experimental evaluations are of programs targeted at simple behavioural changes. Moreover, and more importantly for evaluation, experiments shed little light on why and how the results occurred (Canada, Treasury Board, 2012). Whether results differ from goals due to a problem of program design or because of ineffective implementation are questions that remain hidden in the black box of experimental assessment. Logic frameworks are better at shedding light on such questions.

Propensity score matching addresses the bias in non-randomized design while maintaining much of the rigour of RCT. It does that by statistically estimating what would have happened if the people in treatment and control groups had exchanged places, that is, if those receiving treatment had not and vice versa. Since the counterfactual cannot be examined through observation, propensity score techniques do this through estimates of predicted probability of receiving or not receiving a treatment based on observed predictors (Weiss, 1997). This is useful in cases where random assignment cannot be used, such as studying a program's effects on school children at different levels, because it is not possible to randomly assign children to different levels.

The generalizability of findings from methods establishing causation is also low: a carefully tested program or initiative that works in one context may not work in another for a variety of reasons that cannot be anticipated by researchers. Such methods are also criticized for privileging interpretation by technical analysts and ignoring local knowledge of those on the ground who are directly implementing the policy. Street-level bureaucrats deal with cultural and political factors that may not be visible to researchers, making the evaluation less useful or even relevant. Jenny Lewis (2003: 253) aptly calls reliance on such evaluations "nothing more than a technocratic wish in a political world."

Policy Success and Failure

Policy-makers and the public are eager and indeed often demand that evaluations offer definitive conclusions on whether a particular policy has been a success or failure. This is more complicated than most actors realize, however. As Bovens & t'Hart (1996: 4) point out, "the absence of fixed criteria for success and failure, which apply regardless of time and place, is a serious problem" for anyone who wants to understand policy evaluation. Policies can succeed or fail in numerous ways. Sometimes an entire policy regime can fail, while more often specific programs within a policy field may be deemed as successful or unsuccessful (Mucciaroni, 1990; Moran, 2001; Gundel, 2005). And both policies and programs can fail not only in substantive terms—in the sense of not delivering the goods—but also in procedural terms, in the sense of being legitimate or illegitimate, or fair or unfair (Bovens & t'Hart, 1995; Weaver, 1986; McGraw, 1990; Hood, 2002).

"Success" is always hard to define. In some instances of an unequivocal disaster, like an airplane crash or nuclear reactor meltdown, analyses can pinpoint obvious causes such as technical failures, managerial incompetence, or corruption that have affected safety concerns or delayed needed repairs (Bovens & t'Hart, 1996; Gray & t'Hart, 1998). Evaluation can also uncover lesser known causes of breakdown such as "practical drift," in which increasingly large deviations from expected norms are allowed to occur until, finally, significant system failure occurs (Vaughan, 1996). Although some of the lessons drawn from these spectacular accidents—such as the significant potential for failure of complex organizational systems when elements are either too loosely or too tightly coupled (Perrow, 1984)—can be translated into policy studies, the causes behind more typical policy failures, such as overspending on project development or the unintended consequences of a policy initiative, are harder to pin down.

Failures can occur at any stage of the policy process (Michael, 2006). Thus, an overly ambitious government may commit to addressing intractable ("wicked") problems (Pressman & Wildavsky, 1973; Churchman, 1967) at the agenda-setting stage, a decision that can lead to failure during any subsequent stage in the policy process. Failure can also arise from a mismatch between goals and policy tools in the formulation stage (Busenberg, 2000, 2001, 2004a, 2004b), or it can result from the consequences of lapses or misjudgements at the decision-making stage (Bovens & t'Hart, 1995, 1996; Perrow, 1984; Roots, 2004; Merton, 1936). Another set of pitfalls arises through various "implementation failures" in which the aims of decision-makers fail to be properly or accurately translated into practice (Kerr, 1976; Ingram & Mann, 1980). Policy failure can also arise from a lack of effective oversight by decision-makers over those who implement policy (McCubbins & Schwartz, 1984; McCubbins & Lupia, 1994; Ellig & Lavoie, 1995). Finally, failure can stem from governments and policy-makers not effectively evaluating policy processes and learning useful lessons from past experiences (May, 1992; Scharpf, 1986; Busenberg, 2000, 2001, 2004a, 2004b).

In many circumstances, the policy process is too idiosyncratic, the actors too numerous, and the number of outcomes too small to permit clear and unambiguous post-mortems of *policy outcomes*. Nevertheless, such efforts are made by many actors with varying degrees of formality, and the results of these investigations, whether accurate or not, are fed back into the policy process, influencing the future direction and content of the policy.

As we have seen already, the role of actors is crucial to how an evaluation is carried out and the results that it produces. This is no less true of assessments of success and failure. Different types of evaluations can be undertaken by different sets of actors and can have very different impacts on subsequent policy deliberations and activities (Fischer and Forester, 1987). As Bovens & t'Hart (1995, 21) note, ultimately "judgements about the failure or success of public policies or programs are highly malleable. Failure is not inherent in policy events themselves. "Failure" is a judgement about events." These judgments about policy success and failure often depend partly on imputing notions of intentionality to government actors, assuming that there was a "method to the madness" and that policy actors meant to achieve what their actions produced. Intentionality makes it possible to assess policy-making results against expectations.

However, even with this rational assumption, assessment is not a simple task (see Sieber, 1981). First, as we have seen, government intentions may be vague and ambiguous, or even potentially contradictory or mutually exclusive. Second, labels such as "success" and "failure" are inherently relative and will be interpreted differently by different policy actors and observers. Moreover, such designations are also semantic tools used in public debates to seek political advantage. That is, policy evaluations affect considerations and consequences related to assessing blame and taking credit for government activities at all stages of the policy process, all of which can have electoral, administrative, and other consequences for policy actors (Bovens & t'Hart, 1996: 9; Brandstrom & Kuipers, 2003; Twight, 1991; Hood, 2002; Hood & Rothstein, 2001).

Such judgments, by nature, are at least partially linked to factors such as the nature of the causal theories used to frame policy problems at the agenda-setting and formulation stages and the conceptual solutions developed at the formulation stage. The expectations of decision-makers about likely program or policy results and the extent of time allowed for those results to materialize before evaluators make their assessments are other important factors (Bovens & t'Hart, 1996: 37). Policy evaluation processes, recognizing these built-in biases, often simply aim to provide enough information to make reasonably intelligent and defensible claims about policy outcomes, rather than offering definitive explanations that build airtight cases concerning their absolute level of success or failure.

Assessing the Results of Policy Evaluation

Evaluation Criteria

Value criteria for assessing the results of evaluation are numerous and broad. The OECD/DAC specifies five criteria for policy evaluation: efficiency, effectiveness, impact, relevance, and sustainability (IOB, 2009). Economists tend to focus mostly on efficiency, while effectiveness is the touchstone for numerous policy practitioners. Equity is an important criterion for many people, though little agreement on what it means and, more importantly, how to promote it. Here we will only briefly look at efficiency and effectiveness, two criteria that are widely used in policy evaluation.

Efficiency

This criterion is about allocating resources to achieve policy goals in an economical manner. It measures the relationship between input and output with the intention of maximizing outputs for a given input or minimizing costs for a given output. It considers not simply the quantity but also the quality of outputs because there are often trade-offs between the two. Efficiency evaluation is an unavoidably comparative exercise, in that it seeks to assesses the efficiency of a policy measure in comparison with alternative measures. In reality, there may not be a comparable past or current measure to use as a benchmark for assessing efficiency (IOB, 2009).

Efficiency in the policy context includes not only the material costs but also the transaction and other costs associated with rules and operating procedures. It relies heavily on cost-effectiveness analysis, which is a tool for estimating a program's outputs against its costs. A more rigorous economic evaluation would estimate and compare all costs, including opportunity costs, with all present and future benefits employing cost–benefit analytical techniques (HM Treasury, 2003).

While all economic evaluation techniques are sometimes identified as modes of efficiency evaluation (Pindyck & Rubinfedl, 2018; Hirshleifer et al., 2005), this is not entirely accurate because efficiency, technically speaking, is a much broader and multifaceted concept. Calculating costs and benefits in public policy is complicated by the intangible nature of many inputs, outputs, and outcomes. In educational policy outputs, for example, it is not easy to calculate the cost of the support for learning offered by parents and community, much less the value of all the benefits that the community derives from educating children. Be that as it may, concern about efficiency is helpful to the extent it promotes awareness of costs among program managers. Policies and programs consume scarce resources and so allocating them wisely is vital. Ideally, this would have been done at the policy formulation stage and verified again after the policy has been implemented.

Effectiveness

While efficiency receives the most attention in discussions about evaluation—perhaps reflecting the preponderant influence of economists—it is effectiveness that is the primary criteria for assessing polices. Effectiveness relates to the extent to which policy inputs and activities achieve the desired outcomes. If the main objective of public policy is to solve collective problems, an effective policy is one that helps solve the problem in question. A policy that is ineffective in achieving its primary goals is a useless policy, regardless of its performance with regard to efficiency, equity, and other criteria. Note that an effective policy may not necessarily be efficient in the sense of being the most economical means of attaining a policy goal.

A policy intervention is considered effective if it has made a demonstrable contribution to the achievement of the set objectives. Assessment of effectiveness involves three analytical steps:

- The measurement of changes in the effect variables in comparison to the situation at the start (baseline);
- Attribution of the observed changes to the intervention;
- Assessment of changes observed and attributed to the intervention in terms of the objectives (IOB, 2009).

However, it is not usually possible to clearly demonstrate that it was the policy intervention—separate from contextual factors and other policies—that was the "cause" of the desired change. That is, would the same results have been achieved without the intervention?

Dealing with the Results of Evaluation: Policy Feedback and Policy Termination

Regardless of what is concluded about the efficiency, effectiveness, and equity of a policy, there are three possible paths for what is done with the findings. First, a policy can be judged successful and continued in its present form. Second, and much more typically, a policy can be judged wanting in some respect and efforts suggested for its reform (see Patton & Sawicki, 1993). Finally, a policy can be judged a complete failure (or success), leading to the recommendation that it be terminated (see deLeon, 1978; Geva-May, 2001; Bovens & t'Hart, 1996; Bovens et al., 2001). In the first two outcomes, the policy evaluation stage serves to feed the results of the policy intervention back to some other stage of the policy process. While it is not clear to which stage the process will proceed, in many cases it returns to the agenda-setting stage, hence providing the policy cycle with its cyclical, iterative shape (see Pierson, 1993; Anglund, 1999; Coleman et al., 1996; Billings & Hermann, 1998).

The third alternative option for policy reform is, of course, simply to terminate or end a policy or program. Like more limited proposals for reform, this option involves feeding the results of the evaluation back into the policy process, usually directly to the decision-making stage. Unlike proposals for more limited reform or simply accepting the status quo, the option of policy termination envisions a complete cessation of the policy cycle, at least in its then-current form, at a point in the very near future (deLeon, 1978, 1983).

Although it is common for evaluations, especially political ones, to suggest the adoption of the termination option, observers have noted the reluctance of decision-makers to adopt this course of action and the general tendency for policies to persist even when they are considered by many to have failed to achieve their goals (Weaver, 1988). This is partially due to the inherent difficulties, mentioned above, of arriving at agreement on policy success or failure. Although, occasionally, a problem may be seen as so pernicious that no possible option can reasonably be expected to resolve it—in other words, that all options will fail—or as having been so successful that government action is no longer required, all observers note that the attainment of unified opinion on these matters among relevant policy actors is an exceedingly rare circumstance (see Daniels, 1997; Kaufman, 1976; Lewis, 2002; Franz, 2002). Much more typically, existing programs and policies will have developed established beneficiaries who will define their interests and depending on program continuation and, often, have become so institutionalized that attempts at policy cessation would trigger a costly battle involving considerable legal, bureaucratic, and political expense (Weaver, 1988; Bardach, 1976; Geva-May, 2001). Handbooks and guidelines for would-be terminators all stress the need to develop political coalitions and circumstances allowing these costs to be overcome if termination is to proceed (see Behn, 1977; Geva-May & Wildavsky, 1997).

These observations all underscore the extent to which termination represents, in effect, an effort to overcome *path dependencies* or *policy legacies* in the policy process; that is, the manner in which earlier decisions affect the course of future ones by altering the context in which future decisions can be made (Mulvale et al., 2007; Kay, 2005; Greener, 2005; Pierson, 2000a). Such legacies from the past make the achievement of termination very difficult, often requiring an ideological shift in government and society to allow the more or less uniform judgments of success or failure to emerge, and such broad consensus is most frequently required for uncontested terminations to be made (Kirkpatrick et al., 1999; deLeon, 1997).

It also bears mentioning that a successful termination in the short term does not guarantee a similar long-term result. Thus, if the perception of a problem persists, a termination will usually feed back directly into a reconceptualization of problems and policy alternatives and a new round of policy-making. If no other suitable alternative emerges in this deliberation, this can result in the reversal of a termination and the reinstatement of a terminated program or policy.

Linking Policy Evaluation and Learning: Evaluation Styles in Government

Understanding the links between the evaluation process and its outcomes requires an understanding of the reasons why learning, "non-learning," and other forms of "limited learning" occur in complex organizations. Non-learning involves failing to undertake any evaluations, while limited learning occurs when lessons of only a very restricted scope are drawn from the evaluation process (Abrahamson & Fairchild, 1999; Tamuz, 2001; May, 1999; Simon, 1991; March & Olsen, 1975). Research in the administrative and organizational sciences suggests that which type of learning will occur depends on the capacity and willingness of policy-makers to absorb new information (see Huber, 1991; Peters, 1998; Zarkin, 2008).

As Cohen and Levinthal (1990: 132; also see Lane & Lubatkin, 1998) have observed with reference to private firms,

> the ability to evaluate and utilize outside knowledge is largely a function of the level of prior related knowledge. At the most elemental level, this prior knowledge includes basic skills or even a shared language but may also include knowledge of the most recent scientific or technological developments in a given field. Thus, prior related knowledge confers an ability to recognize the value of new information, assimilate it, and apply it to commercial ends. These abilities collectively constitute what we call a firm's "absorptive capacity."

In a complex organization such as a large firm or government, this implies that learning is a cumulative process and that the existing store of knowledge largely determines what will be done with any new information that flows into the organization. That store of knowledge resides, of course, in the personnel who staff such organizations, and their training and experience on the job thus constitute a key determinant of the propensity for learning within the organizations, whether private firms or governments.

Also critical in this regard, as Aldrich and Herker (1977) note, are "boundary-spanning" links between the organization and its environment, links receptive to new information and capable of disseminating it within the organization. That is, learning requires policy elites and administrators to be open to these new inputs and not threatened by their dissemination across the organization. Hall (1993) and Sabatier (1987) have suggested that this engagement and transmission of new ideas must be found in larger sets of the policy universe. The impact of this latter form of *social learning*, as discussed above, both authors have argued, is likely to be more profound than the more limited effects generated by closed elite or insider evaluation and reflection.

Two relevant variables affect the potential for evaluations to lead to learning: (1) the capacity of government in terms of the level of training, skill, and professionalism of its employees; and (2) the nature of the policy subsystem and especially its open or closed stance to admitting new ideas and interests.

Thus, for "social learning" to take place, a state must have a high-capacity civil service operating within a relatively open and permeable policy subsystem.

When personnel are poorly trained or inexperienced and subsystems are closed, only perfunctory or limited forms of learning can be expected to result. Low-capacity civil services dealing with large and complex subsystems are likely to generate only limited forms of learning, most likely contested learning—whereby different actors draw disparate conclusions from any results obtained; while high-capacity evaluators dealing with closed subsystems are likely to focus on technical issues in the hope of making improvements that rest upon the ideas that are currently within bounds. These outcomes are set out in Figure 8.3, along with examples of each outcome drawn from the case of transportation policy-making.

Policies meant to address the problems posed by growing motor vehicle traffic, for instance, illustrate the divergent evaluations that are possible. Debates over "what is to be done about traffic" are commonplace in affluent urban areas, particularly where economic activity and population are growing. Where civil engineers, who are trained to produce road infrastructure, are primarily responsible for transportation policy, road use is evaluated through traffic counts, a simple metric that captures the volume of driving but ignores both the causes behind it and the consequences beyond transportation impacts. The typical response to such evaluations documenting growing traffic volume, and identifying the primary impact of road congestion, is to propose building new roads or removing bottlenecks. The extra road, of course, is soon choked up again as the number of cars increases, a lesson that evaluators are unlikely to learn under this mode of evaluation.

If the same transportation policy subsystem adopts a broader assessment framework, such as measuring energy efficiency and air pollution in addition to traffic volume, policy evaluation moves to the upper-right quadrant of Figure 8.3 and raises the opportunity for technical learning. Here, enabling automobile use to provide growing levels of urban mobility remains the policy goal, but by using additional assessment tools, civil engineers and other transport policy actors gain feedback on the energy and environmental challenges that also arise from auto use, in addition to the traffic congestion. This can show the value of transportation demand management options, such as road pricing or incentives to carpool, bike, or telecommute. Such feedback represents an opportunity for technical learning, and has been used to initiate road pricing in cities as diverse as Singapore, Trondheim, and London, while other cities (including New York City) are considering its imposition (Cardwell, 2008).

When a broader set of assessment techniques is applied by policy actors with a wide range of viewpoints, the result is likely to be contested learning, depicted in the lower-left quadrant of Figure 8.3. Here one set of evaluators, such as environmental groups, will evaluate the automobile's impacts in relation to goals that extend well beyond transportation performance, while another set sticks with the established mobility goals. Environmental sustainability, conservation of agricultural lands, and public health improvements will then be pitted against mobility goals. To those who

Figure 8.3 Types of Learning Outcomes Expected from Different Evaluative Modes

		Evaluation Techniques	
		Partial	Comprehensive
Subsystem Complexity	Low	Non-learning Perfunctory evaluation that validates existing policy. E.g.: Highway expansion planning	Technical learning Consideration of alternative means, same goals. E.g.: Traffic management planning
	High	Contested learning Competing/partial evaluations by different organizations. E.g.: Separate evaluation by agricultural, environmental, and road user interests of traffic patterns and use.	Social-political learning Consideration of paradigmatic alternatives. E.g.: Car-free days; reducing roads by reserving lanes for buses; taxing cars and channelling the revenues thus generated to public transportation.

assess environmental, energy, and public health impacts, the car's costs will clearly outweigh its benefits, while those who assess automobile travel in terms of mobility will not recognize these costs and dispute the conclusions for policy change that flow from them. Such contested learning is characterized by the phenomenon of "duelling experts," who often contribute to a policy stalemate where rival organizations assert their findings, which are used mainly to block changes based on each other's evaluative conclusions.

Finally, when the policy subsystem is open to comprehensive evaluation of an urban transportation policy, such as when a change in government introduces new officials to policy deliberations, and the evaluation techniques cover a broad range of assessment tools, the opportunity for a paradigmatic shift in policy exists. Here, in the lower-left quadrant of Figure 8.3, we would find transportation breakthroughs like the decision to close large sections of Bogota, Colombia, to automobiles on weekends, to restrict daily driving into the city on weekdays, and to reallocate road space away from automobiles to rapid bus services. Such policy decisions, of course, require a recognition that automobiles can never meet the demand for urban mobility in a truly sustainable manner (Ardilia & Menckoff, 2002).

Conclusion: The Role of Evaluation in Policy Cycle

Different forms of evaluation take place in the public policy process under the direction, and with the involvement, of different types of policy actors in the policy subsystem, and result in different learning outcomes. These feed back into succeeding phases or rounds of the policy cycle. Despite inherent difficulties with assessing the success or failure of policy efforts, past writings on the subject of policy evaluation have tended overwhelmingly to concentrate on developing, criticizing, and refining the techniques of formal administrative evaluations. In that process of technical refinement, the limits of rationality in the policy process were often forgotten, along with the lesson that policy evaluation is an inherently political exercise (Hellstern, 1986; Chelimsky, 1995).

Analysts who do account for the politics underlying policy evaluation see it as a continuation of the struggle over scarce resources or contested ideologies. However, they also see it part of a policy cycle in which policies develop and change on the basis of assessments of past successes and failures and conscious efforts to emulate successes and avoid failures (see Sanderson, 2002a, 2002b). This conception not only helps to make sense of policy evaluation and removes it from the narrow technocratic concerns characteristic of administrative evaluation, but also helps to identify the different learning that can emerge in the evaluative process. It highlights the significant role played by all forms of evaluation in animating the policy cycle as decisions play out over time, the subject of the final chapter of the book.

Study Questions

1. What are the potentials and limitations of different evaluation techniques?

2. What are the respective advantages and disadvantages of evaluation by internal and external experts?

3. What capacity is required to carry out effective evaluation? How can this be developed?

4. To what extent is it possible to engage the public in policy evaluation?

5. What is policy learning, and how would you promote it?

Further Readings

Better Evaluations (undated). "Impact Evaluation Series," https://www.betterevaluation.org/resources/guide/unicef_impact_evaluation_series

Canada, Treasury Board. 2012. *Theory-Based Approaches to Evaluation: Concepts and Practices*. Ottawa: Treasury Board Secretariat.

Davies, I. 1999. "Evaluation and Performance Management in Government," *Evaluation* 8, no. 2: 150–9.

HM Treasury. 2011. *The Magenta Book: Guidance for Evaluation*. https://assets.publishing.service.gov.uk/government/uploads/system/uploads/attachment_data/file/220542/magenta_book_combined.pdf

Kaufman, Sandra, Connie Ozawa, and Deborah F. Shmueli. 2013. "Evaluating Participatory Decision Processes: Which Methods Inform Reflective Practice?" *Evaluation and Program Planning*.

Marsh, David, and Allan McConnell. 2010. "Toward a Framework for Establishing Policy Success," *Public Administration* 88, no. 2: 564–83.

May, Peter J. 1999. "Fostering Policy Learning: A Challenge for Public Administration," *International Review of Public Administration* 4, no. 1: 21–31.

Meadowcroft, James, and Reinhard Steurer. 2018. "Assessment Practices in the Policy and Politics Cycles: A Contribution to Reflexive Governance for Sustainable Development?" *Journal of Environmental Policy & Planning* 20, no. 6: 734–51.

Pierson, Paul. 1993. "When Effect Becomes Cause: Policy Feedback and Political Change," *World Politics* 45: 595–628.

Preskill, Hallie, and Shanelle Boyle. 2008. "A Multidisciplinary Model of Evaluation Capacity Building," *American Journal of Evaluation* 29, no. 4: 443–59.

Rose, Richard. 1993. *Lesson-Drawing in Public Policy: A Guide to Learning across Time and Space.* Chatham, NJ: Chatham House.

Stern, Elliot. 2009. "Evaluation Policy in the European Union and Its Institutions," *New Directions for Evaluation* 123: 67–85.

Stufflebeam, Daniel L. 2001. "Evaluation Models." *New Directions for Evaluation* 89: 7–98.

Chapter 9

Patterns of Policy Change
Between Punctuations and Increments

The ideas, arguments, and evidence presented in this book have revealed that public policy-making is rarely as simple and straightforward an exercise as either analysts or policy-makers might wish for, but neither is it so complex and convoluted that it becomes impenetrable to an effective examination of what has transpired, and more importantly an understanding of why it has occurred.

Public policy arises from the activity and decisions of many actors operating under the influence of an amorphous, yet inescapable, context of ideas and institutions, employing a variety of diverse and multifaceted policy instruments to try and achieve the goals of government (Braun, 1999). This intricacy poses real challenges to those seeking to build a comprehensive and cumulative understanding of the policy-making endeavour; requiring the development of a distinct vocabulary of policy-related terms and concepts that can be integrated to generate testable hypotheses and thus build robust theories and models of policy-making processes and activities.

As the chapters in this book have shown, one of the most recognized and time-tested approaches to advancing analysis through such complexity is to break down the public policy-making process into a series of discrete but related functions that, together, form a cycle of tasks and activities that lead to policy outcomes. The key components of that cycle correspond to the five stages found in many other instances of applied problem-solving, whereby problems are recognized, possible solutions are proposed, a solution is considered and ratified, the chosen strategy is put into effect, and finally the outcomes are monitored, evaluated, and fed back into the process. In the creation of public policy, these stages are manifested as agenda-setting, policy formulation, decision-making or policy choice, policy implementation, and policy evaluation.

Of course, the public policy process is not necessarily as tightly sequential or goal-driven as the model illustrates. Policy actors, it is justifiably argued, do not go about making and implementing policies in quite the systematic manner suggested by the idealized approach in the policy cycle model. While the critique of rigidly interpreting public policy as being carried out in a series of stages is certainly valid, it is also true that such a limitation can be mitigated through diligent examination and cautious inference from the model to evidence found in reality, and vice versa.

The cycle model's greatest advantage comes from its role as a methodological heuristic: facilitating the understanding of the public policy process by subdividing it into parts that can be investigated both directly and in terms of their relationship to other stages of the cycle. This enables the accumulation of empirical insights derived from individual cases, comparative studies of multiple cases, and the aggregation of insight from stages of one or multiple cases into policy models and theories.

The policy cycle model's greatest virtue is thus its deep empirical foundation, which has supported the systematic evaluation of diverse factors driving public policy-making at each of their procedural stages. The policy studies literature is replete with these insightful perspectives on policy, including those challenging and rejecting the policy cycle model, which have been built on the conceptual foundations of, and accumulated knowledge gained from, studies that originated from focusing on all or part of the policy cycle.

While abstract conceptualization is necessary to develop a broad picture of the policy process, however, an analytical framework that offers insight into the sub-processes by revealing the dynamics that animate the mechanics of policy-making is also essential.

These animating forces considered in this book at each stage of the policy cycle have been the actors, institutions, and ideas influencing the content and processes that create the policy in question, the context in which it occurs, and the instruments employed to pursue it. These aspects of the policy-making process are intricate phenomena in their own right, and the general nature of these elements has been sketched out in the preceding chapters. Ultimately, it has been argued, policy-making can be thought of as both a process in which interests and ideas collide as actors contest and deliberate over what to do, and also a knowledge along which actors learn from past successes and mistakes as the cycle extends through successive rounds or iterations.

Studying policy-making by applying the policy cycle perspective thus highlights the dynamic forces at work in policy-making and helps to reveal the otherwise difficult-to-discern political influences among actors, ideas, institutions, and instruments that can offer meaning to these dynamics. However, while disaggregation has permitted the detailed examination of each stage of the policy process presented in Chapters 4 to 8, there remains the question of what the whole process adds up to or reveals over time. Are there typical patterns of policy development and change? And, if so, how do such patterns come into being, and how do they influence subsequent policy actions and outcomes? These issues will be examined in this concluding chapter.

The Outcomes of Policy Succession

Policy Feedback

As E.E. Schattschneider (1935: 38) noted, "new policies create new politics." That is, the outcomes of the policy process tend to "feed back" into the policy environment, thus altering important aspects of the political in which policy was created, including institutional rules and operations, the distribution of wealth and power in society, the nature of the ideas and interests relevant to policies, and even the selection of personnel assigned to deal with policy problems.

As we have shown in Chapter 8, the feedback process from formal and informal evaluation efforts can easily affect the identification and interpretation of policy problems, assessments of the feasibility of potential solutions, and target groups' responses to them, thereby altering the conditions under which policies are further developed and implemented. Policies can create new "spoils" for policy actors to contest and new ideas about "what works" and why policy actions produced particular effects, or can result in the mobilization or "countermobilization" of actors who feel threatened or disadvantaged by an existing policy or program (Pierson, 1993). Hence, it is not at all unusual—in fact, it is typical—for policy-making to reiterate the policy process following the outcome of the evaluation stage, as captured in the policy cycle's logic of recurring deliberation and iterative processing.

Exactly where or to which stage a policy process may go following any other stage, but particularly after evaluation, depends on the nature of the feedback provided and the types of actors involved. As we have seen, formal evaluations by governmental actors, for example, tend to result in limited critiques that typically might involve alterations to the policy implementation process, such as the organization, or reorganization, of agencies or regulations to deal with an issue raised in the evaluative process. However, these and other types of evaluations can also result in new ways of thinking about a problem and solutions to it, feeding back into earlier stages such as agenda-setting and policy formulation where problems and options are initially framed and assessed.

Reconsideration and revision of options, tools and techniques that were developed within some stage of the policy cycle are a typical result of evaluation processes and often yield larger or smaller reforms of existing policies and processes. It is important to note, however, that subsequent iterations of the cycle take on a distinctive form through the development of entirely new policies, since they build on an already existing policy framework or "regime."

That is, as incrementalists such as Charles Lindblom have suggested, future rounds of policy-making typically build on the results from earlier rounds and, as a result, successive rounds and their outcomes tend to incorporate many aspects of existing policies rather than develop completely new forms of policy action. Although dramatic shifts in policies could occur, typically only more minor changes actually do arise because the general configuration of existing policy processes—subsystem membership, political and other relevant policy institutions, policy ideas, discourses and frames, and state and societal capacities and constraints—do not change substantially between iterations of the cycle. Thus, typical feedback processes emerging from policy evaluation, as Paul Pierson has noted, underscore and help to explain the historical or "path-dependent" nature of policy cycle deliberations in modern states (Pierson, 2000a, 2004).

"Path dependency" in this sense is a term used by economists, sociologists, and others to capture the manner in which previous conditions affect future conditions (see Mahoney, 2000; Pierson, 2000a; Haydu, 1998); in short, the term is a kind of shorthand for the idea that, in policy-making, "history matters." That is, the continuity of policies over time because of the existence of "policy legacies" limits the nature and extent of choice policy-makers have in making subsequent decisions (see Weir, 1992; Rose, 1990; Kay, 2006).

Policy path dependence describes the situation whereby once a system is in place, policy tends to perpetuate itself by limiting the range of choices or the ability of forces both outside ("exogenous") and inside ("endogenous") the system to alter that trajectory. In other words, once a trajectory gets established it tends to "lock in" the previous state of the system and the direction of its dynamics (Arthur, 1989; Duit, 2007). Examples of this phenomenon range from how decisions on the initial locations of hospitals and schools affect their operations to that of decisions to ban nuclear power, which are much harder and more expensive to take once plants have been built than if they had never been constructed in the first place (Wilsford, 1994; Pollock et al., 1989; Rona-Tas, 1998; Davidson, 2004).[1]

While the concept of path dependency may exaggerate the extent to which policy lock-in occurs (Kay, 2005; Greener, 2002; Dobrowolsky & Saint- Martin, 2005; Howlett & Rayner, 2006; Ross, 2007), it is quite clear that policy legacies affect policy-making by creating institutional routines and procedures that can drive decision-making in particular directions—by either eliminating or distorting the range of options available to governments (see Wilsford, 1985, 1994; Pierson, 2000a; Rona-Tas, 1998).[2] Policies continue to develop through iterations of the policy cycle, and a common theme in the literature on policy dynamics is the manner in which aspects of policy subsystems and dominant ideas become institutional obstacles to change.

Policy Termination

Before we discuss the substance of these policy change patterns and their implications, however, we should recall that another course of change is possible: policy termination. That is, while many permutations of policy feedback exist and can feed back into the policy process in different ways, as was also set out in Chapter 8, one basic option for change is simply to terminate a policy or program. Like more modest reform proposals, this option involves feeding the results of an evaluative process back into the policy process, usually directly to the decision-making stage. Alternatively, policy termination invokes a complete break in the policy cycle, which rarely happens in reality (deLeon, 1978, 1983).

As we saw in Chapter 8, although it is fairly common for evaluations, especially political ones, to suggest the termination option, decision-makers find it difficult to adopt this course of action and, as a result, most policies tend to persist over long periods once they have been established (Weaver, 1988). This is partially due to the inherent difficulties of reaching agreement about a policy's success or failure (which were also noted in Chapter 8). Only rarely would a problem be seen to be so pernicious that no possible option could be expected to improve it—in other words, that all options will fail—or as having been so successful that further government action is no longer required (see Daniels, 1997; Kaufman, 1976; Lewis, 2002; Frantz, 2002; Geva-May, 2001; Behn, 1977; Geva-May & Wildavsky, 1997: Ch. 5).

Types of Policy Change

Most observers of policy dynamics recognize that two common types or patterns of change are typical of public policy-making. The more "normal" pattern involves relatively minor tinkering with policies and programs already in place through successive rounds of policy-making, which can result in new policies being "layered" on top of existing ones. Such changes are "incremental" and do not individually affect the essential substance of existing policy styles or paradigms, although collectively, as discussed below, they can affect the coherence and consistency of the elements of a policy regime. The second, more substantial pattern relates to the fundamental transformation of policy-making and involves changes in basic sets of policy ideas, institutions, interests, and processes. Termination is one such mode of transformation, but other paths to major change also are possible. Like termination, though, major changes confront the constraints of past policy legacies, making such changes difficult and rare.

Normal Policy Change

There is a surprising degree of continuity in public policy, for most policies made by governments are, for the most part and most of the time, in some way a continuation of past policies and practices. Even what are often portrayed as "new" policy initiatives are often simply variations on existing practices (Polsby, 1984; Lindblom, 1959; Hayes, 1992). This is because, as we have seen, the principal elements of policy-making—the actors, ideas, and institutions involved, and the constraints and capacities with which they operate—change very slowly, if at all, between deliberative iterations of a policy process, while periods of activity within a stage of the policy cycle occur much more frequently.

The structure of policy subsystems in particular affects the overarching sets of policy ideas that determine the recognition of policy problems, the construction of options to address those issues, and the implementation and evaluation of means to advance solutions in practice. As we have seen, subsystem structure shapes the policy discourse by conditioning the members' perception of what is desirable and possible, and affects the selection and use of policy instruments and shapes the evaluation of policy outcomes.

The sources of these ideas are varied, not to mention contentious; they range from purely ideological constructs, to manifestations of material conditions, to developments in science and the knowledge base of society, policy-makers and analysts. And more recently, the inputs to policy discourse include deliberate disinformation, misinformation and half-truths presented as alternative facts, and wishful thinking that infiltrate across borders through social networks. The disruptive influence of post-factual inputs raises challenges to both the study and practice of public policy-making that will be addressed once our consideration of normal policy change is completed.

Rhodes (1997a) and Schaap and van Twist (1997), as well as many others, have argued that policy stability is greatly enhanced by the fact that all subsystems tend to construct "policy monopolies" in which the interpretation and general approach to a subject is more or less fixed (see Baumgartner & Jones, 1991, 1993). Only when a monopoly is broken by the emergence of new members or the departure of old ones can we expect to find substantial policy change in any significant sense (see Kubler, 2001; Dudley & Richardson, 1998; de Vries, 2000, 2005a, 2005b).

These "closed networks" are a key source of policy stability, which is based largely on the ability of existing policy actors to keep new actors from entering into policy debates and discourses or to marginalize their participation (see Daugbjerg, 1997; Hammond & Knott, 2000). This can occur, for example, when governments choose not to appoint prominent critics to advisory boards or regulatory tribunals, or when funding is not made available for outside interveners to participate in public hearings. Governments can also resist creating the entities and procedures that broaden inputs into policy-making, or interest groups can cultivate specialized structures within epistemic communities creating niches that restrict participation in a policy network (Browne, 1990, 1991; Greenaway, 2007; Raphael, 2008).

Atypical Policy Change

Within a policy regime, considerable fluctuations and marginal changes can occur without altering the long-term pattern of policy procedures or contents (Hayes, 2001). Forces promoting policy stability and limited change are powerful, yet at times we can observe major breaks from the established substance and process of policy-making. This type of atypical policy change involves a substantial disruption or transformation in the components of policy regimes, including policy paradigms and styles.

Normally, policy "monopolies" retain their control over policy deliberations and outcomes through a variety of means, including denying room on policy agendas for new ideas and actors; closing membership in policy networks at the formulation stage and thus restricting the range and type of policy alternatives that can be articulated; promoting *status quo* decision-making; limiting the resources and ability of implementers to alter policies; and scoping the terms of evaluation so that only limited forms of learning can emerge from policy assessment (Greenaway et al., 2007).

All of these activities inhibit change at various stages of the policy cycle and thus promote policy stability. They help to maintain stable policy "frames," or relatively enduring sets of policy ideas, and filter out alternative visions of public policy that could inspire efforts toward more fundamental change (Schon & Rein, 1994). These procedures and practices established by policy monopolies explain why a "normal" pattern of policy change typically involves tinkering with or altering particular components of existing policies without actually changing the configuration of a policy regime. While there may be a great deal of continuity in policy succession, however, over time it is possible for the addition of new layers of complexity to result in duplication of initiatives, confusion in policy goals, and the inconsistent use of policy instruments. These factors can lead to policy failures or can make existing regimes vulnerable to the criticisms raised by actors within a policy subsystem as well as by excluded members of the policy universe. This can lead to the development of increasingly problematic policy mixes (Pierson, 2000c; Greener, 2002; Stead & Meijers, 2004; Meijers & Stead, 2004).

In their studies of institutional and policy change in Europe and elsewhere, Kathleen Thelen (2003, 2004) and Jacob Hacker (2004a, 2004b), among others, identified several common processes of policy development that tend to yield suboptimal policy outcomes over time. These paths to deficiency include layering, drift, conversion, and replacement or redesign with associated redirection of policy. Layering, as noted above, is a process in which new ends and means are simply added to existing ones without abandoning the previous ones. This is likely to promote incoherence among the policy ends as well as inconsistency with respect to policy means (Howlett & Rayner, 1995; Rayner et al., 2001). Drift is said to occur when policy ends change while policy means remain constant, thus making the means inconsistent with respect to the changed ends and hence often ineffective in achieving them (Torenvlied & Akkerman, 2004). Conversion is a process in which there is an attempt to change the mix of policy means in order to redirect results toward new goals that have (self)-evolved. (Falkenmark, 2004; Hacker, 2004a, 2004b). In policy redesign or replacement there is a conscious effort to fundamentally restructure both the means and ends of policy so that they are consistent and coherent in terms of their goals and means orientations (Eliadis et al., 2005; Gunningham et al., 1998) (see Figure 9.1).

Many established policy regimes have been developed haphazardly through layering processes in which new tools and objectives were simply piled on top of older ones, creating a palimpsest-like mixture of overwritten policy elements (Scrase & Sheate, 2002; May et al., 2007; Thomas, 2003; May et al., 2005; Lafferty & Hovden, 2003; Evers & Wintersberger, 1990; Evers, 2005). As these layers build up, however, they can result in failure to achieve goals and objectives that in turn undermine the ability of an existing policy monopoly to continue control over policy processes and outcomes, leading to a second mode of atypical policy change.

Atypical policy changes often occur as a result of the activities of specialized policy actors reacting to discordances or "anomalies"—discrepancies between events on the ground and their theorization within the dominant paradigm—which frequently occur as the layers of policy build up over multiple rounds of policy-making (Wilder & Howlett, 2014). As Sabatier (1987), Kingdon (1984), and others have argued, anomalous events and activities are those that are not expected or understandable in terms of prevalent policy discourses. These deviations from the expected policy norm perturb calculations of actor self-interest and subsystem legitimacy and allow innovative actors—"policy entrepreneurs"—to leverage changing circumstances in order to introduce new ideas into the policy milieu (Bundgaard & Vrangbaek, 2007). These new actors are often seen as engaged in a struggle with established ones, who usually resist the introduction of new ideas and defend the status quo or, at least, attempt to limit changes to those compatible with existing arrangements and understandings (see Nunan, 1999; Howlett & Rayner, 1995; Jenkins-Smith et al., 1991).

Two exogenous sources of atypical policy change have received detailed examination in the literature: systemic perturbations and policy spillovers. In his studies of policy anomalies, for example, Paul Sabatier has argued that "changes in the core aspects of a policy are usually the results of perturbations in non-cognitive factors external to the subsystem such as macroeconomic conditions or the

Figure 9.1 Relationship between Policy Means and Policy Ends in a Policy Portfolio

	Policy Means	
	Consistent	Inconsistent
Coherent	Redesign (optimal)	Drift (ineffective)
Incoherent	Conversion (redirected)	Layering (misdirected and ineffective)

Policy Ends

rise of a new systemic governing coalition" (Sabatier, 1988: 140; see also Sabatier, 1987; Sabatier & Jenkins-Smith. 1993a).

"Systemic perturbation" is thus a term used to describe one of the oldest known forces that can trigger atypical policy changes—external crises that upset established policy routines and relationships (Meyer, 1982; Brandstrom & Kuipers, 2003). These can include idiosyncratic phenomena such as wars or disasters, or recurring events such as critical elections and leadership changes (Meijerink, 2005; Birkland, 2004). The principal mechanism by which change occurs is through the introduction of new actors into policy processes, very often in the form of enhanced public attention being paid to a policy issue as a result of a perceived crisis situation (Cobb & Primo, 2003; Kindleberger, 1996).

"Subsystem spillovers" refers to exogenous change processes that occur when activities in otherwise distinct subsystems transcend old boundaries and affect the structure or behaviour of other subsystems (Dery, 1999; Lynggaard, 2001; Djelic & Quack, 2007; Kay, 2006). Examples include the collision of internet-based computing with existing telecommunications regimes and long-established natural resource policy actors dealing with Aboriginal land claims (Hoberg & Morawaski, 1997; Grant & MacNamara, 1995; Rosendal, 2000; Gehring & Oberthur, 2000; Marion, 1999; Rayner et al., 2001).

Although this particular process of regime change has received less attention than episodes of perturbation, it would appear that spillovers can either occur in specific issues without any permanent change in subsystem membership (subsystem intersection) or they can be more long-term in nature (subsystem convergence). This general process, like systemic perturbations, affects policy processes largely through the introduction of new actors into otherwise stable regimes. Unlike systemic perturbations, however, the new actors tend to be policy specialists and interested parties, rather than members of an aroused public or their newly empowered leaders (Deeg, 2007; May et al., 2007).

Two endogenous processes have also been linked to important atypical policy regime changes: venue change and policy learning. "Venue change" refers to changes in the strategies policy actors follow in pursuing their interests. In their work on policy formation in the United States, for example, Baumgartner and Jones (1993: 26, 239–41) noted several strategies employed by actors excluded from policy subsystems to gain access to policy deliberations and affect policy outcomes. They noted that venue-shifting strategies usually involved the redefinition of a policy issue or "frame" in order to facilitate alteration of the location where policy deliberations, especially formulation and decision-making, occur. The internationalization of public policy-making and its impact on policy change—often addressed in shorthand as globalization—results in policy regime change largely through the proliferation of new venues for actors to exploit (Epstein, 1997; Cerny, 2001; Doern et al., 1996a; Melo, 2004; Bleich, 2002, 2006).

Not all policy issues are susceptible to reframing or image manipulation, however, and not all political systems contain any, or as many, alternative policy venues (Perl & Dunn, 2007; Meijerink, 2005; Wood, 2006). Notable instances of policy change through venue-shifting include those when environmental groups have attempted to redefine the image of an issue like waste disposal from a technical regulatory process to either a public health threat or a property-rights conflict that would be susceptible to lawsuits and recourse to the courts (see Jordan, 1998; Hoberg, 1998; Richardson, 1999).

"Policy learning" is a second endogenous change-enhancing process. As discussed in Chapter 8, it refers to the manner in which, as Hugh Heclo (1974) has noted, a relatively enduring alteration in policy results from policy-makers and participants learning from their own and others' experience with similar policies. While some types of learning are limited to reflections on existing practices, others are much more far-reaching and can affect a wide range of policy elements (see Bennett & Howlett, 1991; May, 1992). All involve the development and diffusion of new ideas into existing policy processes. These different conceptions reveal a common tendency for policies to change following variation among the policy ideas circulating within policy subsystems, as knowledge of past experience influences actors' judgments as to the feasibility or desirability of existing courses of action (Knoepfel & Kissling-Naf, 1998; Benz & Furst, 2002; Nilsson, 2005; de Jong & Edelenbos, 2007).

Punctuated Equilibrium: Linking Normal and Atypical Policy Change

Much anecdotal and empirical evidence suggests that normal and atypical policy dynamics are connected in an overarching pattern of policy change that can be described as a "punctuated equilibrium" (Wollin, 1999). In punctuated equilibrium models, first developed in the areas of natural history and paleobiology, change occurs as an irregular, non-linear, or stepped function in which relatively long periods of policy stability are interspersed with infrequent periods of disruptive change (see Eldredge & Gould, 1972; Gould & Eldredge, 1977; Gersick, 1991).

In the policy realm this refers to normal policy-making, which involves fairly common, routine, non-innovative changes at the margin of existing policies, followed by bouts of atypical, or non-incremental, change involving new policies that represent a sharp break from how policies were previously developed and implemented leading to different outcomes (Baumgartner & Jones, 1993; Berry, 1990; Rose, 1976; True et al., 1999; Hayes, 2001). Frequently cited examples of such patterns include shifts in fiscal and monetary policy in most Western countries from a balanced-budget orthodoxy to Keynesian demand management in the late 1940s and the subsequent shift to forms of monetarism in the late

1970s (Hall, 1989, 1992). Similar shifts occurred in many resource policy sectors, as policies shifted from pure exploitation to conservation in the nineteenth century, and then from conservation to sustainable management in the twentieth (see Hays, 1959, 1987; Cashore & Howlett, 2007; Gould, 2007; Robinson, 2007; Robinson et al., 2007; Robinson & Caver, 2006; John, 2003).

While many cases of punctuated equilibrium have been well explored (Schrad, 2007; Heron & Richardson, 2008; Greer, 2008), a fully elaborated theory of when this particular policy dynamic emerges and how it establishes a new paradigm remains a work in progress. The extent to which examples from economic policy transformation can be generalized to support the assessment of change in other sectors such as security policy or environmental policy is far from settled. Among the questions remaining to be answered are the degree to which the dynamics of profound policy change transcend political systems and sectors, and the extent to which they depend on the substantive character of the policy that is changing (Mortensen, 2005; Howlett & Cashore, 2007; Kuhner, 2007; Bannink & Hoogenboom, 2007; John, 2003).

The general argument that has been proposed to explain punctuated equilibrium patterns of policy dynamics, however, is that atypical change ultimately occurs because anomalies build up between the policy regime and the reality it "regulates," causing a crisis of legitimacy within the existing regime and making it susceptible to both endogenous and exogenous forces and processes of change (Linz, 1978; Flink, 2017). The process of regime change is initially quite unstable as conflicting ideas emerge and compete for dominance when an existing paradigm or subsystem breaks down. The process becomes complete until the next upheaval, when a new set of ideas wins out over others and is accepted by most, or at least the most powerful, members of the policy subsystem then in place. The new regime's hegemony is eventually established when it is institutionalized and its legitimacy yields recognition of policy ideas and options as normal and self-evident (see Wilson, 2000; Skogstad, 1998; Jenson, 1989; Legro, 2000) (see Figure 9.2, below).

The more stable the subsystem and the more established and embedded the ideas within it are about how policy should operate, the greater the propensity to resist change. When this is combined with a stable political regime where state agents are most comfortable reacting to change (e.g., adopting a "wait-and-see" approach to dealing with anomalies), the level of policy dysfunction will have to rise quite high before delegitimation yields a "big bang" political realignment that breaks away from an established policy monopoly. The resulting change will, by its nature, appear quite innovative.

Conversely, chaotic policy subsystems can become fertile ground for debating policy change, without necessarily yielding substantial innovation (McBeth et al., 2007). In their contest over different paradigms, an unstable mix of participants will introduce diverse ideas in pursuit of disparate interests (Loughlin, 2004; Van Kersbergen & Van Waarden, 2004; Jones & Baumgartner, 2005).

Figure 9.2 Non-Linear Model of Policy Regime Change: Stage Characteristics

1. **Regime stability**. The reigning orthodoxy is institutionalized and policy adjustments are made largely by a closed group of experts and officials and other members of a closed subsystem.

2. **Accumulation of real-world anomalies**. Developments are neither anticipated nor fully explicable in terms of the reigning orthodoxy, thereby undermining its effectiveness and legitimacy.

3. **Experimentation**. Efforts are made by subsystem members to stretch the existing regime to account for the anomalies.

4. **Fragmentation of authority**. Experts and officials become discredited and new participants challenge the existing subsystem, paradigm, and regime.

5. **Contestation**. Debate spills into the public arena and involves the larger political process, including electoral and partisan considerations.

6. **Institutionalization of a new regime**. After a period of time, the advocates of a new regime secure positions of authority and alter existing organizational and decision-making arrangements in order to institutionalize the new subsystem, paradigm, and regime.

Sources: Adapted from Peter A. Hall, "Policy Paradigms, Social Learning and the State: The Case of Economic Policy-Making in Britain," Comparative Politics 25, 3 (1993): 275–96; M.S. de Vries, "Generations of Interactive Policy-Making in the Netherlands," *International Review of Administrative Sciences* 71, 4 (2005): 577–91.

While the degree of chaos in policy subsystems has yet to be precisely calibrated into a widely accepted scale of turmoil, a growing level of disruption in the established understandings of policy initiatives across many domains is a leading cause of change.

The Continued Contemporary Relevance of Studying Public Policy: Can the Policy Cycle Model Cope with Challenges from "Truthiness"?

In recent years, growing concern has been voiced about the threat posed by the increased proliferation of "post-factual" evidence. The policy sciences legacy, as embedded within established policy regimes, appears to be at risk from a new type of anomaly—the obscuring of the distinction between fact and fabrication which potentially threatens the existence of the policy cycle as a model of learning processes writ large in society.

More and more policy processes as diverse as Brexit and international trade negotiations have been disrupted by the well-publicized growth of disinformation campaigns, "alternate" facts, and the wilful desire of many politicians and members of the public to avoid recognizing and engaging with reality (Kakutani, 2018; McIntyre, 2018; Kavanagh & Rich, 2018).

This is clearly a challenge for adherents of evidence-based processes. The functions within each stage of the policy cycle thus risk being impaired by a shift away from seeking and utilizing empirically valid knowledge toward what the satirist Stephen Colbert derisively termed the embrace of "truthiness." That is, toward opinion-driven selective engagement of information or, worse, adoption of intentionally false data and the alternate realities of conspiracy-theory-driven worldviews and judgments (Dossey 2014; Proctor & Schiebinger 2008; Warnier 2013).

The explosive growth and pervasive rise of social media and internet journalism as key sources of information have been singled out as force multipliers for post-factual disruptions of policy analysis, creating politically potent weapons through a malicious compilation of deliberate misinformation, lies, and misdirection (Theocharis & van Deth, 2018; Greenwood et al., 2016). When the endogenous propagation of alternative facts overlaps with, and amplifies, the disruptive effect of exogenous campaigns to convey misinformation, the uninformed become increasingly confident in the value of their ignorance as a valid alternative to expertise (Johnson & Kaye, 2016; Kruger & Dunning, 1999; Motta et al., 2018).

While deception, misinformation, and spin have been perennial tactics in conflict over policy-making, the contemporary increase in both the volume of erroneous evidence and the willingness to avoid differentiating subjectively constructed phenomena from objectively verified evidence have raised fears that future policy regimes could be based on something completely other than evidence-based analysis and deliberations (MacAfee, 2013; Hong & Nadler, 2016).

Thus, the spread of truthiness threatens the policy sciences legacy because, as Vosoughi et al. (2018: 1146) have noted, "Foundational theories of decision-making, cooperation, communication, and markets all view some conceptualization of truth or accuracy as central to the functioning of nearly every human endeavor." Hence, if the distinction between real and imagined evidence erodes, the viability of the evidence-based policy-making paradigm is undermined, potentially derailing the results of policy studies that have been laboriously built up over the past 75 years (McIntyre, 2018; Kakutani, 2018; Mintrom, 2007; Carlsson, 2017). Such a post-factual policy future would undermine the models, frameworks, and theories of policy-making set out in this volume.

However, as has been illustrated in the preceding chapters, especially Chapter 2, the policy cycle model offers an exceptionally open-ended and supple framework in comparison with the many intellectual constructs that have been developed to interpret the policy-making process. Because it was inspired by a normative engagement with practical policy-making the policy cycle sought to understand all the functions pursued to solve public problems in their own terms. Lasswell's original model of seven discrete but related policy stages (1956, 1971), for example, was not a purely abstract conceptual construct but was informed by his own experience working for the American government during the mid-twentieth century, when ambitious measures were initiated, and coordinated, across many sectors and disciplines to win World War II, and then to conduct the Cold War. Refinement and elaboration of Lasswell's stages into an iterative dynamic of policy construction and deconstruction similarly sought to capture feedback effects and interdependence among the various policy-making functions, including how policy learning occurs through evaluation and adjustment of processes in light of past and present experiences (Brewer, 1974; Anderson, 1975; Jones, 1984).

Within the universe of conceptual tools for examining empirical policy analysis, the policy cycle model thus stands out as the longest-serving heuristic for illuminating how political actors, ideas about problems and potential solutions, and the structural influence of institutions interact to influence policy-making for good reason (Capano, 2012). The model endures, offering guidance for those seeking to understand the interplay of policy subsystem participants through their initiative at particular points of action to solve public problems, because of its practical and pragmatic character, firmly grounded in observations of policy reality.

But can such resilience, exhibited over the decades when evidence-based policy analysis was the norm, carry forward into policy processes that are increasingly influenced by falsehoods presented as alternative facts? The continued relevance of the policy cycle model will depend on its ability to understand, account for, and incorporate the utilization of alternative facts across the various functions of policy deliberation.

To that end, the policy cycle model could be accused of too easily accommodating efforts to introduce post-factual discourse and thus inhibiting the critical exposure of truthiness. Because the policy cycle embodies no inherent standard of truth, it readily allows for accommodating the misinformation that fuels truthiness. In other words, the cycle model is agnostic regarding the accuracy of the knowledge and arguments being deployed and the epistemological stances of policy actors. If falsehoods posing as alternative facts become part of policy deliberations, the policy cycle model will reflect this empirical reality just as it would if policy-making were fuelled by evidence-based factual inputs.

That is, the policy cycle model's articulation of distinctive functions in policy-making offers the opportunity to identify where and how disinformation and manipulation of evidence could influence analysis, or corrupt authority, during the course of policy deliberations. Misinformation, for example, be it malicious selective interpretations of data or the results of conspiracy theories, can be exposed in the policy cycle framework. For example, if fake news is targeted to generate a shift in the policy agenda, or when biased evaluative methods are applied to discredit the performance of an existing policy, these effects stand out in contrast to the workings of expertise and evidence found in other policy-making stages such as policy choice and implementation. The resulting contrast between political dynamics in the stages where post-factual influences have accumulated and the stages where more traditional policy deliberations remain the norm help to highlight the alternative factual manipulations of policy-making, but also advance understanding of how elements of a policy subsystem respond and might (or might not) resist the influence of such "false facts."

In recent years, the speed, volume, and intensity of information flowing through social networks has raised the potential for disruptive forces to challenge policy regimes by creating an overwhelming expansion of post-factual truthiness to subvert more traditional evidence and expertise. Processes such as policy learning and path dependence often overlap with these disruptive forces, and the resulting struggles for legitimacy among policy alternatives can lead to minor or major change. The presence or absence of exogenous conditions that enhance the opportunities for new actors and ideas to penetrate established policy regimes can make a difference between continuity and disruption in policy trajectories and traditions (see Thomas, 1999; Alink et al., 2001; Nisbet, 1972; Campbell, 1997; Studlar, 2007).

Like other mutagenic processes, the earlier that symptoms of corruption of policy-making through disinformation and willful ignorance are recognized, the easier it is to diagnose and then treat. If the policy cycle is observed carefully and consistently, then the anomalous inputs of truthiness should be easier to detect in one or two stages of deliberation. And if these anomalies are challenged and called to account for their disruption of the policy sciences' core mission of building better policy capacity out of empirical evidence and accumulated learning, the malady that truthiness creates in the body politic should remain treatable.

Conclusion

Discussion of the key roles played by policy actors, ideas, and institutions at all stages of the policy process helped us throughout this book to provide an alternative way to view the operation of a policy cycle than was typically offered by earlier literature (see deLeon & Kaufmanis, 2001). Examining the workings of actors, ideas, and institutions within policy subsystems is a way of looking at policy-making that helps to reveal the dynamics of policy deliberation within each stage of the cycle, even in a world filled with fake news and alternate facts.

Chapters 1–3 set out the basic intentions of the policy sciences and discussed the manner in which existing general theories of political life fall short in providing a satisfactory understanding of public policy-making and the roles played by actors, institutions, and instruments found in the policy process of modern liberal-democratic states. Chapters 4–8 discussed the specific stages of the policy cycle and identified the different styles in which policy deliberations proceed, but said little about how these stages fit together, or whether characteristic patterns of policy change occur in public policy processes or outputs.

This final chapter has addressed the issue of policy change and the existence of long-term patterns of relative stability in policy-making, highlighting the manner in which actors, institutions, and ideas combine to produce reasonably stable policy styles, subsystems, paradigms, and regimes. This analysis showed how policy dynamics typically involve the establishment of an equilibrium characterized by normal change—wherein policies adapt only incrementally through layering, conversion, and drift—until it is periodically interrupted by more fundamental change affecting the control exercised by policy regimes and resulting in policy replacement or redesign. These policy dynamics are complex and characterized by different forces and processes that either enhance or undermine en hancing policy stability in specific cases.

Analyzing the policy process in terms of policy cycles and policy subsystems both aids in the conceptualization of these fundamental dynamics and facilitates their analysis. Identifying the characteristic policy styles, subsystems, paradigms, and policy regimes through analysis of the stages in the policy cycle allows the establishment of a baseline against which change can be measured. Only careful observation of subsystem behaviour will clarify tendencies toward atypical policy change involving a significant, though not necessarily complete, break from the past in terms of the overall policy goals, the understanding of public problems and their solutions, and the policy instruments used to put decisions into effect (Mortensen, 2007; Liefferink, 2006; Kenis, 1991; Menahem, 1998, 2001).

The notion of fundamental policy change as synonymous with changes in policy regimes brings to the fore the insight that public policy-making is not simply a process of conflict resolution, as most past economic and political science–based theories allege, nor is it a process composed solely of policy-makers responding to external shocks or jolts. Rather, policy-making is influenced largely by the activities of policy subsystem members attempting to shape the structure and operation of policy-making through activities such as venue-shifting, image reframing, and policy learning.

Policy analysis itself is just as much a subject of interpretation and reflection as are the objects of its assessment. In contemporary policy studies, grand theories are eschewed and have been replaced by the recognition that social problems and government's response to them are affected by a range of factors whose general form, but not specific content, can be assumed in advance (see Cook, 1985; Jennings, 1987). The focus is now very much directed at considering as many factors as possible in seeking to explain the causes, consequences, and dynamics of public policy-making. Studying public policy is demanding and difficult because government decision-making is complex and nuanced. But careful conceptualization and systematic analysis along the lines set out in this volume go a long way toward bringing some light into what was seen, for many years, as the "black box" of government activity (see Roe, 1990, 2000; Bernstein et al., 2000).

The moves away from a traditional linear interpretation of the policy cycle and toward a more intricate approach to the investigation and conceptualization of the public policy process set out in the book reflect many themes in "post-positivist" modes of inquiry in policy science, but they are not synonymous with it (see Dudley et al., 2000; Howlett & Ramesh, 1998; Lynn, 1999). Rather, policy scholars of all persuasions and approaches should recognize not only that policy phenomena are shaped by highly contingent and complex processes, but that they also require an appropriate research methodology to move beyond description of their uncertainty, complexity, and context-boundness (see Hilgartner & Bosk, 1981; Holzner & Marx, 1979).

Study Questions

1. Is policy feedback an inherently conservative force that entrenches established ideas and interests? Can it be employed to promote new policy dynamics?

2. To what degree is policy knowledge unique to a specific context? How much insight into policy can be acquired from studying the experience of other sectors and events?

3. How are patterns of normal and atypical change linked together?

4. What are some of the processes that typically engender policy punctuations?

5. How does the rise of social media, false news, and "alternate facts" affect policy-making and policy analysis?

Further Readings

Capano, Giliberto, and Jun Jie Woo. 2018. "Resilience and Robustness in Policy Design: A Critical Appraisal," *Policy Sciences* 37, no. 4: 422–40.

Dunlop, Claire A., and Claudio M. Radaelli. 2018. "The Lessons of Policy Learning: Types, Triggers, Hindrances and Pathologies," *Policy & Politics* 46, no. 2: 255–72.

Perl, Anthony, Michael Howlett, and M. Ramesh. 2018. "Policy-Making and Truthiness: Can Existing Policy Models Cope with Politicized Evidence and Willful Ignorance in a 'Post-Fact' World?" *Policy Sciences* 51, no. 4 (December): 581–600.

Peters, B. Guy, Pauline Ravinet, Michael Howlett, Giliberto Capano, Ishani Mukherjee, and Meng Hsuan Chou. 2018. *Designing for Policy Effectiveness: Defining and Understanding a Concept.* Elements Series. Cambridge: Cambridge University Press.

Proctor, Robert, and Londa Schiebinger, eds. 2008. *Agnotology: The Making and Unmaking of Ignorance.* Stanford, CA: Stanford University Press.

Stevens, T.M., N. Aarts, C.J.A.M. Termeer, and A. Dewulf. 2018. "Social Media Hypes about Agro-Food Issues: Activism, Scandals and Conflicts," *Food Policy* 79: 23–34.

Weaver, Kent. 2010. "Paths and Forks or Chutes and Ladders?: Negative Feedbacks and Policy Regime Change," *Journal of Public Policy* 30, no. 02: 137–62.

Notes

Chapter 2

1. Keohane (1989: 163) described them as "persistent and connected sets of rules (formal or informal) that prescribe behavioural roles, constrain activity, and shape expectations."

2. Identifying the institutional logic of appropriate behaviour regarding economic transactions can be applied to many other areas of social and political life. Policy-relevant activities such as the negotiation of international treaties, the operation of multi-level systems of government, and issues of regulatory enforcement are subject to similar analyses in which the actions and decisions of policy actors are modelled as the outcomes of multiple, nested games occurring within the confines, costs, and payoffs established by institutional orders (Scharpf, 1997; Putnam, 1988; Scholz, 1984; Sproule-Jones, 1989).

3. See the efforts to accomplish this in the synthesis of deductive and inductive neo-institutionalisms in Aspinwall and Schneider (2000) and Hollingsworth (2000). On the limits of these efforts, see Hay and Wincott (1998).

Chapter 3

1. Even more significantly, some institutional arrangements are believed to be more conducive to effective policy-making and implementation than others (Stoker, 1989; May, 1993; Siedschlag, 2000).

2. The normative and ideological nature of much discussion on this subject is apparent in the titles and terms used to describe many findings. This can be seen in the otherwise excellent comparative and historical studies of Joel Brooks, who, finding very little relationship between public opinion and policy-making, terms this phenomenon "democratic frustration," suggesting it results from a problem with the policy system failing to react properly to the democratic one. See Brooks (1985, 1987, 1990). More recently, see Petry (1999).

3. That is to say, not discriminating against imports once they have crossed the border after meeting all legal requirements, including payment of applicable tariffs.

Chapter 5

1. Much of this criticism relied heavily on works by authors of the Chicago and Virginia schools of political economy, who showed how regulations were inefficient as well as inequitable (for examples of the former, see Becker, 1983; Peltzman, 1974; Stigler, 1971; for the latter, see Buchanan and Tollison, 1984; Landes & Posner, 1975; Posner, 1974; Tollison, 1991). Neo-conservative politicians, led by Britain's Margaret Thatcher and US President Ronald Reagan, further fanned popular sentiments against regulations, which put deregulation at the centre of the economic policy reform agenda right around the world (Eisner, 1994b; Ramesh & Howlett, 2006; Crew & Rowley, 1986; Derthick & Quirk, 1985).

2. Other policy instruments not technically considered as subsidies may involve some component of subsidy. Thus, regulations that restrict the quantity of a particular good or service produced or sold also involve subsidy to the producers because they can often artificially increase prices. Restrictive licensing, such as that received by the taxicab industry in most places, is another example of this kind of subsidy through regulation. Government procurement from local producers at a price higher than the market price is also a subsidy to these producers to the extent of the difference between the purchase price and the market price (Howard, 1997). Where government is purchasing leading-edge products and services, as can occur in defence and aerospace contracts, the way in which the uncertain costs of deploying new technology are dealt with can be critical to policy success or failure (Bajari & Tadelis, 2001). Public procurement can also be targeted

to advance policy priorities such as the promotion of minority-owned enterprises and transnational human rights (Mc-Crudden, 2004).

3. Payroll taxes of various sorts are used in most countries to fund social security programs. Under such schemes, the employer typically withholds a specified portion of the employee's salary, matches the amount by a proportion determined by the government, and then transmits both the employee's and employer's contributions to the government. Payroll taxes often build an insurance pool for designated risks such as unemployment, sickness, industrial injury, and old age pensions. When the specified contingency occurs, the insured collects from the fund. In a sense this is no different from private insurance one can buy, except that some risks are regarded as crucial to the society and hence government makes insurance against them compulsory. Compulsory participation in an insurance fund expands the number of insured and thus reduces the cost of premiums by spreading the risk for specific individual activities among the general populace (Katzman, 1988; Feldman, 2002).

4. Another innovative example of user charges is provided by the efforts of Singapore and, more recently, London to control downtown traffic congestion. During peak hours, commuters in Singapore are required to pay a set fee to enter the downtown area, which forces them to compare the costs of entering the area in their own vehicles with the cost of taking a bus or underground train, which are exempt from the charge (Lam & Toan, 2006). The charge has had a marked impact, reducing traffic inflow into the downtown area (Phang & Toh, 2004). London, England, has followed Singapore's lead in charging drivers for centre city roads, yielding a 30 per cent decrease in driving delays and an 18 per cent reduction in traffic volume (Leape, 2006). Other cities, such as New York, are now considering similar schemes.

5. All societies regard looking after the needs of family members and others close to them as an essential individual responsibility. Children, the aged, and the sick are ordinarily looked after in this manner, mainly in terms of care, but financial assistance is also common. It has been calculated that in 1978 the total cost of the transfer of cash, food, and housing within families in the United States amounted to US$86 billion (Gilbert & Gilbert, 1989: 281). Non-monetary transfers are almost impossible to estimate, however, because families provide a range of services whose value cannot be priced. It is estimated, for example, that about 80 per cent of home health-care services for the elderly in the US are provided by family members (1989: 19).

6. Initial findings suggest that as non-profit organizations funded primarily from donations shift their focus to activities that generate fees and sales revenue, they become more focused on program delivery to client group(s) and less engaged with the broader community of related organizations (Galaskiewicz et al., 2006). Despite the possibility that focusing voluntary and faith-based organizations on service delivery can have indirect costs in their ability to contribute to the broader community, budgetary pressures have prompted governments in many countries to rely more on the voluntary sector as a way to lower program costs (Brock & Banting, 2001).

7. Toll goods include semi-public goods, such as bridges or highways, which do not diminish in quantity after use but for the use of which it is possible to charge. Common-pool goods are those, like fish in the ocean, whose usage cannot be directly charged to individuals but whose quantity is reduced after use.

8. Examples of first-order changes in a health sector, for example, would include altering staffing levels in hospitals or altering physician fee schedules. Second-order changes would involve changing the type of instrument used to deliver health care, such as moving from user fees to mandatory insurance arrangements. Third-order change would involve a shift in policy goals, such as moving away from a biomedical focus on the individual to a more holistic goal of collective, social, or community well-being.

Chapter 9

1. "Path dependency" is often used simply as a synonym for the idea that "history matters" in policy studies (Pierson, 2000a). This is useful insofar as it points to the idea that "sequence matters" in terms of when and how policies develop (Abbott, 1983, 2001). However, a more specific view of path dependency includes the idea that policy development is essentially chance-like, at least insofar as initial events establishing policy trajectories are concerned. Mahoney, for example, outlines the three principal elements of a path-dependent model of historical evolution as (1) only early events in sequence matter; (2) these early events are contingent; and (3) later events are inertial (Mahoney, 2000). These elements separate this model from narrative analyses and from other historical models, such as process sequencing (see Howlett & Rayner, 2006). Identifying these "turning points" or "conjunctures" is thus critical to path-dependency analyses of historical processes, although there is significant debate in the literature over exactly what is meant by characterizing an event as "contingent" (Wilsford, 1985, 1994; Abbott, 1997). At its simplest, contingency implies that, although the particular sequence of events is not a strictly necessary one, predictable from the conditions of the starting point according to general laws, an explicable pattern nonetheless relates one point to another, especially in the early part of the sequence. While a random sequence implies that any event has an equal probability of following from any other, in a contingent sequence each turning point renders the occurrence of the next point more likely until, finally, "lock-in" occurs and a general explanatory principle, such as increasing returns, takes over the work of explanation (Mahoney & Schensul, 2006; Liebowitz & Margolis, 1995).

2. As Pierson (2000b), Weir (1992), and March and Olsen (1989: 52), among others, have argued, policy stability emerges when a problem definition or policy solution is routinized, increasing the constituency for its preservation and raising the costs and difficulty of its alteration or termination (see Haydu, 1998; Torfing, 2001; David, 2005; Goodin & Rein, 2001).

References

Chapter 1 Sources

Alford, Robert R. 1972. "The Political Economy of Health Care: Dynamics without Change," *Politics and Society* 2, no. 2: 127–64.

Anderson, James E. 1984. *Public Policy-Making: An Introduction*, 3rd edn. Boston: Houghton Mifflin.

Bakvis, Herman. 2000. "Rebuilding Policy Capacity in the Era of the Fiscal Dividend: A Report from Canada," *Governance*. 13, no. 1: 71–103.

Baumgartner, Frank R., and Bryan D. Jones. 1993. *Agendas and Instability in American Politics*. Chicago: University of Chicago Press.

Beland, Daniel, and Michael Howlett. 2016. "How Solutions Chase Problems: Instrument Constituencies in the Policy Process," *Governance* 29, no. 3: 393–409.

Billings, Robert S., and Charles F. Hermann. 1998. "Problem Identification in Sequential Policy Decision-Making: The Re-representation of Problems," in D.A. Sylvan and J.F. Voss, eds, *Problem Representation in Foreign Policy Decision-Making*. Cambridge: Cambridge University Press, 53–79.

Birkland, Thomas A. 2001. *An Introduction to the Policy Process: Theories, Concepts, and Models of Public Policy-Making*. Armonk, NY: M.E. Sharpe.

Blind, Peri K. 2006. *Building Trust in Government in the Twenty-First Century: Review of Literature and Emerging Issues*. UNDESA. https://pdfs.semanticscholar.org/f9bf/cdf4c5bb-042212b7c05c6cf695539d2ae235.pdf?_ga=2.94030237.1263274397.1569294978-480841420.1569294978

Bobrow, D. B., and Dryzek, J. S. 1987. *Policy Analysis by Design*. Pittsburgh: University of Pittsburgh Press.

Bogason, Peter. 2000. *Public Policy and Local Governance: Institutions in Postmodern Society*. Cheltenham: Edward Elgar.

Bovens, M., and P. t'Hart. 1996. *Understanding Policy Fiascos*. New Brunswick, N.J.: Transaction Press

———, and ———. 1995. "Frame Multiplicity and Policy Fiascos: Limits to Explanation," *Knowledge and Policy* 8, no. 4: 61–83.

Bovens, M., P. t'Hart, and B. G. Peters. 2001. "Analysing Governance Success and Failure in Six European States,"in *Success and Failure in Public Governance: A Comparative Analysis*, eds. M. Bovens, P. t'Hart and B. G. Peters, 12–32. Cheltenham: Edward Elgar.

Brewer, Gary, D. 1974. "The Policy Sciences Emerge: To Nurture and Structure a Discipline," *Policy Sciences* 5: 239–244.

———, and P. deLeon. *The Foundations of Policy Analysis*. Homewood: Dorsey, 1983.

Castles, Francis G. 1998. *Comparative Public Policy: Patterns of Post-War Transformation*. Cheltenham: Edward Elgar.

———, and R.D. McKinlay. 1997. "Does Politics Matter? Increasing Complexity and Renewed Challenges," *European Journal of Political Research* 31: 102–7.

Clemons, Randall S., and Mark K. McBeth. 2001. *Public Policy Praxis: Theory and Pragmatism, a Case Approach*. Upper Saddle River, NJ: Prentice-Hall.

Cohn, D. 2004. "The Best of Intentions, Potentially Harmful Policies: A Comparative Study of Scholarly Complexity and Failure," *Journal of Comparative Policy Analysis* 6, no. 1: 39–56.

Crenson, Matthew A. 1971. The Un-Politics of Air Pollution: A Study of Non-Decision-making in the Cities. Baltimore: Johns Hopkins University Press.

Danziger, Marie. 1995. "Policy Analysis Postmodernized: Some Political and Pedagogical Ramifications," *Policy Studies Journal* 23, no. 3: 435–50.

deLeon, P. 1999. "The Stages Approach to the Policy Process: What Has It Done? Where Is It Going?" in *Theories of the Policy Process*, edited by P. A. Sabatier, 19–34. Boulder: Westview.

Del Vicario, Michela, Fabiana Zollo, Guido Caldarelli, Antonio Scala, and Walter Quattrociocchi. 2017. "Mapping Social Dynamics on Facebook: The Brexit Debate," *Social Networks* 50 (July): 6–16. doi:10.1016/j.socnet.2017.02.002.

de Vries, M.S. 2005b. "Changing Policy Views at the Local Level: The Effect of Age,

Generations and Policy Periods in Five European Countries," *European Journal of Political Research* 44: 1–15.

Doern, G. Bruce, L. Pal, and B.W. Tomlin, eds. 1996a. *Border Crossings: The Internationalization of Canadian Public Policy.* Toronto: Oxford University Press.

Dunn, William N. 2019. *Pragmatism and the Origins of the Policy Sciences.* doi:10.1017/9781108676540.

Dryzek, John S. 2005. "Handle with Care: The Deadly Hermeneutics of Deliberative Instrumentalism," *Acta Politica* 40: 197–211.

Dye, Thomas R. 1972. *Understanding Public Policy.* Englewood Cliffs, NJ: Prentice-Hall.

Eisner, Marc Allen. 1993. *Regulatory Politics in Transition.* Baltimore: Johns Hopkins University Press.

———. 1994a. "Discovering Patterns in Regulatory History: Continuity, Change and Regulatory Regimes," *Journal of Policy History* 6, no. 2: 157–87.

Everett, S. 2003. "The Policy Cycle: Democratic Process of Rational Paradigm Revisited," *Australian Journal of Public Administration* 62, no. 2: 65–70.

Farr, J., J.S. Hacker, and N. Kazee. 2006. "The Policy Scientist of Democracy," *American Political Science Review* 100, no. 4: 579–87.

Fowler, Edmund P., and David Siegel, eds. 2002. *Urban Policy Issues.* Toronto: Oxford University Press.

Gersick, Connie J.G. 1991. "Revolutionary Change Theories: A Multilevel Exploration of the Punctuated Equilibrium Paradigm," *Academy of Management Review* 16, no. 1: 10–36.

Gleeson, Deborah, David Legge, Deirdre O'Neill, and Monica Pfeffer. 2011. "Negotiating Tensions in Developing Organizational Policy Capacity: Comparative Lessons to Be Drawn," *Journal of Comparative Policy Analysis: Research and Practice* 13, no. 3 (June): 237–263.

Gordon, I., J. Lewis, and K. Young. 1977. "Perspectives on Policy Analysis," *Public Administration Bulletin* 25: 26–30.

Gormley, William T. 2007. "Public Policy Analysis: Ideas and Impact," *Annual Review of Political Science* 10: 297–313.

Hancock, M. Donald. 1983. "Comparative Public Policy: An Assessment," in A.W. Finifter, ed., *Political Science: The State of the Discipline.* Washington: American Political Science Association, 283–308.

Harris, Richard, and Sidney Milkis. 1989. *The Politics of Regulatory Change.* New York: Oxford University Press.

Hawkesworth, Mary. 1992. "Epistemology and Policy Analysis," in W. Dunn and R.M. Kelly, eds, *Advances in Policy Studies.* New Brunswick, NJ: Transaction, 291–329.

Howard, Cosmo. 2005. "The Policy Cycle: A Model of Post-Machiavellian Policy Making?" *Australian Journal of Political Science* 64, no. 3: 3–13.

Howlett, Michael. 1986. "Acts of Commission and Acts of Omission: Legal-Historical Research and the Intentions of Government in a Federal State," *Canadian Journal of Political Science* 19: 363–71.

———. 2009. "Government Communication as a Policy Tool: A Framework for Analysis," *The Canadian Political Science Review* 3, no. 2. June.

———, and E. Lindquist. 2004. "Policy Analysis and Governance: Analytical and Policy Styles in Canada," *Journal of Comparative Policy Analysis* 6, no. 3: 225–249.

———, and M. Ramesh. 1998. "Policy Subsystem Configurations and Policy Change: Operationalizing the Postpositivist Analysis of the Politics of the Policy process," *Policy Studies Journal* 26: 466–481.

———, and Jale Tosun, eds. 2019. *Policy Styles and Policy-Making: Exploring the Linkages.* London: Routledge.

Huitt, Ralph K. 1968. "Political Feasibility," in A. Ranney, ed., *Political Science and Public Policy.* Chicago: Markham Publishing, 263–76.

Hula, Richard, Cynthia Jackson-Elmoore, and Laura Reese. 2007. "Mixing God's Work and the Public Business: A Framework for the Analysis of Faith-Based Service Delivery," *Review of Policy Research* 24, no. 1: 67–89.

Hupe, Peter L., and Michael J. Hill. 2006. "The Three Actions Levels of Governance: ReFraming the Policy Process beyond the Stages Model," in B. Guy Peters and Jon Pierre, eds, *Handbook of Public Policy.* London: Sage, 13–30.

Jasanoff, S., and Simmet, H. R. 2017. "No Funeral Bells: Public Reason in

A 'Post-Truth' Age," *Social Studies of Science* 47, no. 5: 751–770.

Jenkins, William I. 1978. *Policy Analysis: A Political and Organizational Perspective*. London: Martin Robertson.

Jenkins-Smith, Hank C., and Paul A. Sabatier. 1993. "The Study of Public Policy Processes," in Sabatier and Jenkins-Smith (1993a).

Jones, Charles O. 1984. *An Introduction to the Study of Public Policy*. Monterrey, California: Brooks/Cole.

Kim, Young-Jun, and Chui-Young Roh. 2008. "Beyond the Advocacy Coalition Framework in Policy Process," *International Journal of Public Administration* 31: 668–89.

Kingdon, John W. 1984. *Agendas, Alternatives and Public Policies*. Boston: Little, Brown.

Kissane, Rebecca Joyce. 2007. "How Do Faith-Based Organizations Compare to Secular Providers? Nonprofit Directors and Poor Women's Assessments of FBOs," *Journal of Poverty* 11, no. 4: 91–115.

Kuks, S. 2004. "Comparative Review and Analysis of Regime Changes in Europe," *Environmental Politics* 40, 2: 329–68.

Larsen, T.P., P. Taylor-Gooby, and J. Kananen. 2006. "New Labour's Policy Style: A Mix of Policy Approaches," *International Social Policy* 35, no. 4: 629–49.

Lasswell, Harold D. 1956. *The Decision Process: Seven Categories of Functional Analysis*. College Park: University of Maryland Press.

———. 1971. *A Pre-View of Policy Sciences*. New York: American Elsevier.

Lewandowsky, Stephan, Naomi Oreskes, James S. Risbey, Ben R. Newell, and Michael Smithson. 2015. "Seepage: Climate Change Denial and Its Effect on the Scientific Community," *Global Environmental Change* 33 (July): 1–13. doi:10.1016/j.gloenvcha.2015.02.013.

Ley, Aaron J. "Mobilizing Doubt: The Legal Mobilization of Climate Denialist Groups," *Law & Policy* 40, no. 3. Accessed May 18, 2018. doi:10.1111/lapo.12103

Lowi, Theodore J. 1972. "Four Systems of Policy, Politics and Choice," *Public Administration Review* 32, no. 4: 298–310.

Lyden, F. J., G. A. Shipman, R. W. Wilkinson, and P. P. Le Breton. 1968. "Decision-Flow Analysis: A Methodology for Studying the Public Policy-Making Process," in *Comparative Administrative Theory*, 155–168. Seattle: University of Washington Press.

Lynn, Laurence E. 1987. *Managing Public Policy*. Boston: Little, Brown.

———. 1999. "A Place at the Table: Policy Analysis, Its Postpositive Critics, and the Future of Practice," *Journal of Policy Analysis and Management* 18, no. 3: 411–424.

Majone, Giandomenico. 1975. "On the Notion of Political Feasibility," *European Journal of Political Research* 3: 259–74.

May, Peter J. 2005. "Policy Maps and Political Feasibility," in I. Geva-May, ed., *Thinking Like a Policy Analyst: Policy Analysis as a Clinical Profession*. London: Palgrave Macmillan, 127–51.

Mazmanian, Daniel A., and Paul A. Sabatier. 1980. "A Multivariate Model of Public PolicyMaking," *American Journal of Political Science* 24, no. 3: 439–68.

Meltsner, Arnold J. 1976. *Policy Analysts in the Bureaucracy*. Berkeley: University of California Press.

Milner, Helen V., and Robert O. Keohane. 1996. "Internationalization and Domestic Politics: A Conclusion," in Keohane and Milner (1996: 243–58).

Moore, Mark H. 1995. *Creating Public Value: Strategic Management in Government*. Cambridge: Harvard University Press.

Munns, Joyce M. 1975. "The Environment, Politics, and Policy Literature: A Critique and Reformulation," *Western Political Quarterly* 28, no. 4: 646–67.

Oliphant, S., and Howlett, M. 2010. "Assessing Policy Analytical Capacity: Insights from a Study of the Canadian Environmental Policy Advice System," *Journal of Comparative Policy Analysis*, 12(4), 435–441.

Painter, M., and J. Pierre. 2005. *Challenges to State Policy Capacity: Global Trends and Comparative Perspectives*. London: Palgrave Macmillan.

Pal, Leslie A. 1992. *Public Policy Analysis: An Introduction*, 2nd edn. Scarborough, ON: Nelson.

Parag, Yael. 2006. "A System Perspective for Policy Analysis and Understanding: The Policy Process Networks," *The Systemist* 28, no. 2: 212–24.

———. 2008. "Who Governs the Air We Breathe? Lessons from Israel's Industrialist Covenant," *Journal of Environmental Policy and Planning* 10, no. 2: 133–52.

Parsons, W. 2004. "Not Just Steering but Weaving: Relevant Knowledge and the Craft of Building Policy Capacity and Coherence," *Australian Journal of Public Administration* 63, no. 1: 43–57.

Peters, B. G. 1996. *The Policy Capacity of Government.* Ottawa: Canadian Centre for Management Development.

Peters, B. Guy, John C. Doughtie, and M. Kathleen McCulloch. 1977. "Types of Democratic Systems and Types of Public Policy," *Comparative Politics* 9: 327–55.

Phillips, Susan. 1996. "Discourse, Identity, and Voice: Feminist Contributions to Policy Studies," in *Policy Studies in Canada: The State of the Art*, ed. Laurent Dobuzinskis, Michael Howlett, and David Laycock, 242–65. Toronto: University of Toronto Press

Przeworski, Adam and Fernando Limongi. 1997. "Modernization: Theories and Facts," *World Politics* 49: 155–83.

Radin, B. A. 2000. *Beyond Machiavelli: Policy Analysis Comes of Age.* Washington DC: Georgetown University Press.

Rakoff, Stuart H., and Guenther F. Schaefer. 1970. "Politics, Policy, and Political Science: Theoretical Alternatives," *Politics and Society* 1, no. 1: 51–77.

Rein, Martin, Gosta Esping-Andersen, and Lee Rainwater, eds. 1987. *Stagnation and Renewal in Social Policy: The Rise and Fall of Policy Regimes.* Armonk, NY: M.E. Sharpe.

Rogers, H.G., M.A. Ulrick, and K.L. Traversy. 1981. "Evaluation in Practice: The State of the Art in Canadian Governments," *Canadian Public Administration* 24, no. 3: 371–86.

Rose, Richard. 1991. "What Is Lesson-Drawing?" *Journal of Public Policy* 11, no. 1: 3–30.

Sabatier, Paul A 1992. "Political Science and Public Policy: An Assessment," in W.N. Dunn and R.M. Kelly, eds, *Advances in Policy Studies Since 1950.* New Brunswick, NJ: Transaction, 27–58.

Salamon, Lester M. 1981. "Rethinking Public Management: Third-Party Government and the Changing Forms of Government Action," *Public Policy* 29, no. 3: 255–75.

———, and Michael S. Lund. 1989. "The Tools Approach: Basic Analytics," in Salamon (1989a: 23–50).

Savoie, Donald J. 2003. *Breaking the Bargain: Public Servants, Ministers, and Parliament.* Toronto: University of Toronto Press.

Schlager, Edella. 1999. "A Comparison of Frameworks, Theories, and Models of Policy Processes," in Sabatier (1999a: 233–60).

Sharkansky, Ira. 1971. "Constraints on Innovation in Policy Making: Economic Development and Political Routines," in Frank Marini, ed., *Toward a New Public Administration: The Minnowbrook Perspective.* Scranton, PA: Chandler.

Simmons, Robert H., et al. 1974. "Policy Flow Analysis: A Conceptual Model for Comparative Public Policy Research," *Western Political Quarterly* 27, no. 3: 457–68.

Smith, Richard A. 1979. "Decision Making and Non-Decision Making in Cities: Some Implications for Community Structural Research," *American Sociological Review* 44, no. 1: 147–61.

Sobeck, J. 2003. "Comparing Policy Process Frameworks: What Do They Tell Us about Group Membership and Participation for Policy Development?" *Administration and Society* 35, no. 3: 350–74.

Steinberger, Peter J. 1980. "Typologies of Public Policy: Meaning Construction and the Policy Process," *Social Science Quarterly* 61, 2: 185–97.

Stone, Diane A, Andrew Denham, and Mark Garnett. 1998. *Think Tanks across Nations: A Comparative Approach.* Manchester: Manchester University Press.

Thompson, W.B. 2001. "Policy Making through Thick and Thin: Thick Description as a Methodology for Communications and Democracy," *Policy Sciences* 34: 63–77.

Tiernan, A., and Wanna, J. 2006. "Competence, Capacity, Capability: Towards Conceptual Clarity in the Discourse of Declining Policy Skills," presented at the Govnet International Conference, Australian National University. Canberra: ANU.

Timmermans, Arco and Ivar Bleiklie. 1999. "Institutional Conditions for Policy Design: Types of Arenas and Rules of the Game," ECPR Joint Sessions of Workshops, Mannheim.

Torgerson, Douglas. 1996. "Power and Insight in Policy Discourse: Post-Positivism and Policy Discourse," in L. Dobuzinskis, M. Howlett, and D. Laycock, eds, *Policy Studies in Canada: The State of the Art*. Toronto: University of Toronto Press, 266–98.

Tribe, Laurence H. 1972. "Policy Science: Analysis or Ideology?" *Philosophy and Public Affairs* 2, no. 1: 66–110.

Tuohy, Caroline. 1999. *Accidental Logics: The Dynamics of Change in the Health Care Arena in the United States, Britain, and Canada*. New York: Oxford University Press.

Weimer, David L., and Aidan R. Vining. 1992. *Policy Analysis: Concepts and Practice*, 2nd edn. Englewood Cliffs, NJ: Prentice-Hall.

Werner, Jann, and Kai Wegrich. 2007. "Theories of the Policy Cycle," in Frank Fischer, Gerald J. Miller, and Mara S. Sidney, eds, *Handbook of Public Policy Analysis: Theory, Politics and Methods*. Boca Raton, FL: CRC Press, 43–62.

Wilensky, Harold L. 1975. *The Welfare State and Equality: Structural and Ideological Roots of Public Expenditures*. Berkeley: University of California Press.

——et al. 1985. *Comparative Social Policy: Theories, Methods, Findings*. Berkeley: Institute of International Studies.

——, and Lowell Turner. 1987. *Democratic Corporatism and Policy Linkages: The Interdependence of Industrial, Labor-Market, Incomes, and Social Policies in Eight Countries*. Berkeley: University of California International & Area Studies.

Wilson, James Q. 1974. "The Politics of Regulation," in J.W. McKie, ed., *Social Responsibility and the Business Predicament*. Washington: Brookings Institution, 135–68.

Wolfe, Joel D. 1989. "Democracy and Economic Adjustment: A Comparative Analysis of Political Change," in R.E. Foglesong and J.D. Wolfe, eds, *The Politics of Economic Adjustment*. New York: Greenwood Press.

Yanow, Dvora. 1992. "Silences in Public Policy Discourse: Organizational and Policy Myths," *Journal of Public Administration Research and Theory* 2, no. 4: 399–423.

——. 1999. *Conducting Interpretive Policy Analysis*. Thousand Oaks, CA: Sage.

Chapter 2 Sources

Allison, Graham and Morton H. Halperin. 1972. "Bureaucratic Politics: A Paradigm and Some Policy Implications," *World Politics* 24 (supp.): 40–79.

Almond, Gabriel A. 1988. "The Return to the State," *American Political Science Review* 82, no. 3: 853–901.

——, and Stephen J. Genco. 1977. "Clouds, Clocks and the Study of Politics," *World Politics* 29: 489–522.

Althusser, L., and E. Balibar. 1977. *Reading "Capital,"* London: New Left Books.

Amariglio, Jack L., Stephen A. Resnick, and Richard D. Wolff. 1988. "Class, Power, and Culture," in C. Nelson and L. Grossberg, eds, *Marxism and the Interpretation of Culture*. Urbana: University of Illinois Press

Anderson, Charles W. 1979a. "The Place of Principles in Policy Analysis," *American Political Science Review* 73, no. 3: 711

Ascher, William. 1986. "The Evolution of the Policy Sciences: Understanding the Rise and Avoiding the Fall," *Journal of Policy Analysis and Management* 5: 365–89.

Atkinson, A.B and A.J. Harrison. 1978. *Distribution of Personal Wealth in Britain*. New York: Cambridge University Press.

Bardach, Eugene. 2000. *A Practical Guide for Policy Analysis: The Eightfold Path to More Effective Problem Solving*. New York: Chatham House.

Bator, Francis M. 1958. "The Anatomy of Market Failure," *Quarterly Journal of Economics* 72, no. 3: 351–79.

Becker, Gary S. 1958. "Competition and Democracy," *Journal of Law and Economics* 1: 105–9.

Berle, Adolf. 1959. *Power without Property*. New York: Harcourt Brace.

Biermann, F., P. Pattberg, H. van Asselt, and F. Zelli. 2009. "The Fragmentation of Global Governance Architectures: A Framework for Analysis," *Global Environmental Politics* 9, no. 4: 14–40.

Block, Fred. 1980. "Beyond Relative Autonomy: State Managers as Historical Subjects," *Socialist Register*: 227–42.

Blom-Hansen, Jens. 2001. "Organized Interests and the State: A Disintegrating Relationship? Evidence from Denmark," *European Journal of Political Research* 39: 391–416.

Blyth, Mark M. 2007. "Powering, Puzzling or Persuading? The Mechanisms of Building Institutional Orders," *International Studies Quarterly* 51: 761–77.

Boddy, Raford, and James Crotty. 1975. "Class Conflict and Macro-Policy: The Political Business Cycle," *Review of Radical Political Economics* 7, no. 1: 1–19.

Bozeman, Barry, ed. 2002. "Public-Value Failure: When Efficient Markets May Not Do," *Public Administration Review* 62, no. 2: 145–61.

Bromley, Daniel W. 1989. *Economic Interests and Institutions: The Conceptual Foundations of Public Policy.* New York: Blackwell.

Buchanan, James. 1980. "Rent Seeking and Profit Seeking," in Buchanan et al. (1980).

———et al. 1978. *The Economics of Politics.* London: Institute of Economic Affairs.

Burton, P. 2006. "Modernising the Policy Process: Making Policy Research More Significant?" Policy Studies 27, no. 3: 172–192.

Cairney, Paul (undated). Politics & Public Policy. Institutions and New Institutionalism. https://paulcairney. wordpress.com/2014/03/28/policy-concepts-in-1000-words-institutions-and-new-institutionalism/

Cairns, Alan C. 1974. "Alternative Styles in the Study of Canadian Politics," *Canadian Journal of Political Science* 7: 102–28.

Cammack, Paul. 1992. "The New Institutionalism: Predatory Rule, Institutional Persistence, and Macro-Social Change," *Economy and Society* 21, no. 4: 397–429.

Campbell, Colin, and George J. Szablowski. 1979. *The Superbureaucrats: Structure and Behaviour in Central Agencies.* Toronto: Macmillan.

Castles, Francis G and Vance Merrill. 1989. "Towards a General Model of Public Policy Outcomes," *Journal of Theoretical Politics* 1, no. 2: 177–212.

Cawson, Alan. 1978. "Pluralism, Corporatism and the Role of the State," *Government and Opposition* 13, no. 2: 178–98.

———. 1986. *Corporatism and Political Theory.* Oxford: Blackwell.

Clemens, E.S., and J.M. Cook. 1999. "Politics and Institutionalism: Explaining Durability and Change," *Annual Review of Sociology* 25: 441–66.

Coase, R.H. 1937. "The Nature of the Firm," *Economica* 4, 13–16 (Nov.): 386–405.

———. 1960. "The Problem of Social Cost," *Journal of Law and Economics* 3: 1–44.

Cohen, G.A. 1978. *Karl Marx's Theory of History: A Defense.* Oxford: Clarendon Press.

Collins, Patricia Hill. 2016. *Intersectionality (Key Concepts).* Cambridge, UK: Polity Press.

Connolly, William E. 1969. "The Challenge to Pluralist Theory," in Connolly, ed., *The Bias of Pluralism.* New York: Atherton Press.

Cook, Brian, and B. Dan Wood. 1989. "Principal–Agent Models of Political Control of Bureaucracy," *American Political Science Review* 83: 965–78.

Cooney, Kate. 2007. "Field, Organizations, and Agency: Toward a Multilevel Theory of Institutionalization in Action," *Administration and Society* 39, no. 6: 687–18.

Cortell, Andrew P., and Susan Peterson. 2001. "Limiting the Unintended Consequences of Institutional Change," *Comparative Politics Studies* 34, no. 7: 768–799.

Cox, Robert W. 1987. *Production, Power and World Order: Social Forces in the Making of History.* New York: Columbia University Press.

Dahl, Robert A. 1956. *A Preface to Democratic Theory.* Chicago: University of Chicago Press.

———. 1961. *Who Governs? Democracy and Power in an American City.* New Haven: Yale University Press.

———. 1967. *Pluralist Democracy in the United States: Conflict and Consent.* Chicago: Rand McNally.

deLeon, Peter. 1986. "Trends in Policy Sciences Research: Determinants and Developments," *European Journal of Political Research* 14, nos. 1 and 2: 3–22.

———. 1988. *Advice and Consent: The Development of the Policy Sciences.* New York: Russell Sage Foundation.

———. 1994. "Reinventing the Policy Sciences: Three Steps Back to the Future," *Policy Sciences* 27, no. 1: 77–95.

———, and Christine R. Martell. 2006. "The Policy Sciences: Past, Present and Future," in B. Guy Peters and Jon Pierre, eds, *Handbook of Public Policy.* London: Sage, 31–48.

Dimitrakopoulos, Dionyssis G. 2005. "Norms, Interests and Institutional Change," *Political Studies* 53: 676–93.

Dimitrov, Radoslav S., Detlef F. Sprinz, Gerald M. DiGiusto, and Alexander Kelle. 2007. "International Nonregimes: A Research Agenda," *The International Studies Review* 9: 230–58.

Dollery, Brian E. and Andrew Worthington. 1996. "The Evaluation of Public Policy: Normative Economic Theories of Government Failure," *Journal of Interdisciplinary Economics* 7, no. 1: 27–39.

Dosi, G., et al., eds. 1988. *Technical Change and Economic Theory*. London: Pinter.

Downs, Anthony. 1957. *An Economic Theory of Democracy*. New York: Harper.

Dryzek, John S. 1990. *Discursive Democracy: Politics, Policy and Political Science*. Cambridge: Cambridge University Press.

———. 2002. "A Post-Positivist Policy-Analytic Travelogue," *The Good Society* 11, no. 1: 32–6.

Dunleavy, Patrick. 1986. "Explaining the Privatization Boom: Public Choice versus Radical Approaches," *Public Administration* 64, no. 1: 13–34.

Dunn, James, Jr., and Anthony Perl. 1994. "Policy Networks and Industrial Revitalization: High Speed Rail Initiatives in France and Germany," *Journal of Public Policy* 14, no. 3: 311–43.

Durning, Dan. 1999. "The Transition from Traditional to Postpositivist Policy Analysis: A Role for Q-Methodology," *Journal of Policy Analysis and Management* 18, no. 3: 389–410.

Eisenberg, Avigail, and Will Kymlicka, eds. 2012. *Identity Politics in the Public Realm: Bringing Institutions Back In*. Vancouver: UBC Press.

Esping-Andersen, Gosta. 1981. "From Welfare State to Democratic Socialism: The Politics of Economic Democracy in Denmark and Sweden," in M. Zeitlin, ed., *Political Power and Social Theory*, 111–40.

———. 1985. *Politics Against Markets: The Social Democratic Road to Power*. Princeton, NJ: Princeton University Press.

———, and Walter Korpi. 1984. "Social Policy as Class Politics in Post-War Capitalism: Scandinavia, Austria, and Germany," in J.H. Goldthorpe, ed., *Order and Conflict in Contemporary Capitalism*. Oxford: Clarendon Press.

Fischer, Frank. 1998. "Beyond Empiricism: Policy Inquiry in Postpositivist Perspective," *Policy Studies Journal* 26, no. 1: 129–46.

———. *Reframing Public Policy: Discursive Politics and Deliberative Practices*. Oxford: Oxford University Press, 2003.

———. 2007a. "Policy Analysis in Critical Perspective: The Epistemics of Discursive Practices," *Critical Policy Analysis* 1, no. 1: 97–109.

———. 2007b. "Deliberative Policy Analysis as Practical Reason: Integrating Empirical and Normative Arguments," in Fischer, Gerald Miller, and Mara Sidney, eds, *Handbook of Public Policy Analysis: Theory, Politics, and Methods*. Boca Raton, FL: CRC Press, 223–36.

Fishman, Ethan. 1991. "Political Philosophy and the Policy Studies Organization," *PS: Political Science and Politics* 24: 720–3

Foley, Duncan K. 1978. "State Expenditure from a Marxist Perspective," *Journal of Public Economics* 9, no. 2: 221–38.

Forester, John. 1993. *Critical Theory, Public Policy, and Planning: Toward a Critical Pragmatism*. New York: SUNY Press.

Frey, Bruno S. 1978. "Politico-Economic Models and Cycles," *Journal of Public Economics* 9: 203–20.

Garson, G. David. 1986. "From Policy Science to Policy Analysis: A Quarter Century of Progress," in W.N. Dunn, ed., *Policy Analysis: Perspectives, Concepts, and Methods*. Greenwich, Conn.: JAI Press, 3–22.

Geva-May, Iris, and Aaron Wildavsky. 1997. *An Operational Approach to Policy Analysis: The Craft Prescriptions for Better Analysis*. Boston: Kluwer.

Gierke, Otto von. 1958a. *Natural Law and the Theory of Society, 1500–1800*. Cambridge: Cambridge University Press.

———. 1958b. *Political Theories of the Middle Age*. Cambridge: Cambridge University Press.

Gorges, Michael J. 2001. "The New Institutionalism and the Study of the European Union: The Case of the Social Dialogue," *West European Politics* 24, no. 4: 152–68.

Gormley, William T. 1989. *Taming the Bureaucracy: Muscles, Prayers and Other Strategies*. Princeton, NJ: Princeton University Press.

Gough, Ian. 1975. "State Expenditure in Advanced Capitalism," *New Left Review* 92:

53–92. Gould, Stephen Jay. 2002. *The Structure of Evolutionary Theory*. Cambridge, MA: Harvard University Press.

Grande, E. 1996. "The State and Interest Groups in a Framework of Multi-Level Decision Making: The Case of the European Union," *Journal of European Public Policy* 3: 313–38.

Green, Donald, and Ian Shapiro. 1994. *Pathologies of Rational Choice Theory*. New Haven: Yale University Press.

Greenberg, George D., et al. 1977. "Developing Public Policy Theory: Perspectives from Empirical Research," *American Political Science Review* 71: 1532–43.

Greif, A., and D.D. Laitin. 2004. "A Theory of Endogenous Institutional Change," *American Political Science Review* 98, no. 4: 633–52.

Guess, George M. and Paul G. Farnham. 1989. *Cases in Public Policy Analysis*. New York: Longman.

Hajer, Maarten A and Hendrik Wagenaar, eds. 2003. *Deliberative Policy Analysis: Understanding Governance in the Network Society*. Cambridge: Cambridge University Press.

Hall, John A, ed. 1989. *The Political Power of Economic Ideas: Keynesianism across Nations*. Princeton, NJ: Princeton University Press.

———, and G. John Ikenberry. 1989. *The State*. Minneapolis: University of Minnesota Press.

———, and Rosemary C.R. Taylor. 1996. "Political Science and the Three New Institutionalisms," *Political Studies* 44: 936–57.

Hall, Peter A. 1986. Governing the Economy: The Politics of State Intervention in Britain and France. Cambridge: Polity Press.

Hankivsky, Olena, and Renee Cormier. 2011. "Intersectionality and Public Policy: Some Lessons from Existing Models," *Political Research Quarterly* 64, no. 1: 217–29.

Hansen, Susan B. 1983. "Public Policy Analysis: Some Recent Developments and Current Problems," *Policy Studies Journal* 12: 14–42.

Hawkesworth, Mary. 1992. "Epistemology and Policy Analysis," in W. Dunn and R.M. Kelly, eds, *Advances in Policy Studies*. New Brunswick, NJ: Transaction, 291–329.

Hechter, Michael and Satoshi Kanazawa. 1997. "Sociological Rational Choice Theory," *Annual Review of Sociology*, 23: 191–214.

Heineman, R.A. et al. 1990. The *World of the Policy Analyst: Rationality, Values and Politics*. Chatham, NJ: Chatham House.

Hintze, Otto. 1975. *The Historical Essays of Otto Hintze*. New York: Oxford University Press.

Hogwood, Brian W and Lewis A. Gunn. 1984. *Policy Analysis for the Real World*. New York: Oxford University Press.

Hood, Christopher. 1991. "A Public Management for All Seasons?" *Public Administration* 69 (Spring): 3–19.

———. 1995. "Contemporary Public Management: A New Global Paradigm?" *Public Policy and Administration* 10, no. 2: 104–17.

———. 1998. *The Art of the State: Culture, Rhetoric and Public Management*. Oxford: Clarendon Press.

Howlett, M. 2000. "Managing the "Hollow State": Procedural Policy Tools and Modern Governance," *Canadian Public Administration* 43, no. 4: 412–3.1

Howlett, Michael, and Richa Shivakoti. 2018. "Improving International Policy-Making in the Absence of Treaty Regimes: The International Forestry, Migration and Water Policy Cases," *International Journal of Public Policy* 14, no. 5/6: 303–19.

Ikenberry, G. John. 1990. "The International Spread of Privatization Policies: Inducements, Learning, and 'Policy Bandwagoning,'" in Suleiman and Waterbury (1990).

Ingram, Helen M., and Dean E. Mann, eds. 1980b. "Policy Failure: An Issue Deserving Analysis," in Ingram and Mann (1980a).

Johnson, Genevieve. 2017. "The Role of Public Participation and Deliberation in Policy Formotion," in *Handbook of Policy Formulation*, eds. Michael Howlett and Ishani Mukherjee. Cheltenham: Edward Elgar. Pp. 198–216.

Jones, Bryan D. 2001. *Politics and the Architecture of Choice: Bounded Rationality and Governance*. Chicago: University of Chicago Press.

Jordan, A. Grant. 2000. "The Process of Government and the Governmental Process," *Political Studies* 48: 788–801.

Kato, Junko. 1996. "Review Article: Institutions and Rationality in Politics—Three Varieties of Neo-Institutionalists," *British Journal of Political Science* 26: 553–82.

Keman, H. 1997. "Approaches to the Analysis of Institutions," in B. Steunenberg and F.V. Vught, eds, *Political Institutions and Public Policy: Perspectives on European Decision Making*. Dordrecht: Kluwer, 1–27.

———, and P. Pennings. 1995. "Managing Political and Societal Conflict in Democracies: Do Consensus and Corporatism Matter?" *British Journal of Political Science* 25: 271–81.

Kerr, Donna H. 1976. "The Logic of "Policy" and Successful Policies," *Policy Sciences* 7, no. 3: 351–63.

Kiser, Edward, and Michael Hechter. 1991. "The Role of General Theory in Comparative-Historical Sociology," *American Journal of Sociology*, 97(1), 1–30.

Kiser, Larry L., and Elinor Ostrom. 1982. "The Three Worlds of Action: A Meta-theoretical Synthesis of Institutional Approaches," in Ostrom, ed., *Strategies of Political Inquiry*. Beverly Hills, CA: Sage, 179–222.

Knoepfel, Peter, Corinne Larrue, Frederic Varone, and Michael Hill. 2007. *Public Policy Analysis*. Bristol, UK: Policy Press.

Krasner, Stephen D. 1984. "Approaches to the State: Alternative Conceptions and Historical Dynamics," *Comparative Politics* 16, no. 2: 223–46.

Kreuger, Anne O. 1974. "The Political Economy of the Rent-Seeking Society," *American Economic Review* 64, no. 3: 291–303.

Lasswell, Harold D. 1951. "The Policy Orientation," in Lerner and Lasswell (1951: 3–15).

Le Grand, Julian. 1991. "The Theory of Government Failure," *British Journal of Political Science* 21, no. 4: 423–42.

———, and Ray Robinson, eds. 1984. *Privatization and the Welfare State*. London: George Allen and Unwin.

Levin-Waldman, O.M. 2005. "Welfare Reform and Models of Public Policy: Why Policy Sciences Are Required," *Review of Policy Research* 22, no. 4: 519–39.

Levy, J.D. 2006. *The State after Statism: New State Activities in the Age of Liberalization*. Cambridge, MA: Harvard University Press.

Lijphart, A. 1969. "Consociational Democracy," *World Politics* 21, no. 2: 207–25.

Lindblom, Charles E. 1968. *The Policy-Making Process*. Englewood Cliffs, NJ: Prentice-Hall.

———. 1977. Politics and Markets: The World's Political Economic Systems. New York: Basic Books.

Locksley, Gareth. 1980. "The Political Business Cycle: Alternative Interpretations," in Paul Whiteley, ed., *Models of Political Economy*. London: Sage.

Lowi, Theodore J. 1969. *The End of Liberalism: Ideology, Policy and the Crisis of Public Authority*. New York: Norton.

Lundquist, Lennart J. 1987. *Implementation Steering: An Actor-Structure Approach*. Bickley, UK: Chartwell-Bratt.

Majone, Giandomenico. 1989. *Evidence, Argument, and Persuasion in the Policy Process*. New Haven: Yale University Press.

Manski, Charles F. 2011. "Policy Analysis with Incredible Certitude," *The Economic Journal* 121, no. 554 (August 1): F261–89.

———. 2013. *Public Policy in an Uncertain World: Analysis and Decisions*. Cambridge, MA: Harvard University Press.

Mazur, Amy G. 2002. *Theorizing Feminist Policy*. 1 edition. Oxford: Oxford University Press.

McConnell, Grant. 1966. *Private Power and the American Democracy*. New York: Alfred A. Knopf.

McFarland, Andrew S. 2004. *Neopluralism: The Evolution of Political Process Theory*. Lawrence: University Press of Kansas.

———. 2007. "Neopluralism," *Annual Review of Political Science* 10: 45–66.

McLean, Iain. 1987. *Public Choice: An Introduction*. Oxford: Blackwell.

McLennan, Gregor. 1989. *Marxism, Pluralism and Beyond: Classic Debates and New Departures*. Cambridge: Polity Press.

Madison, James, and Alexander Hamilton. 1961. *The Federalist Papers: A Collection of Essays Written in Support of the Constitution of the United States*. Garden City, NY: Anchor Books.

Majone, Giandomenico. 1989. *Evidence, Argument, and Persuasion in the Policy Process*. New Haven: Yale University Press.

Mann, Michael. 1984. "The Autonomous Power of the State: Its Origins, Mechanisms and

Results," *European Journal of Sociology* 25, 2: 185–213.

March, James G and Johan P. Olsen. 1994. "Institutional Perspectives on Political Institutions," paper presented to the International Political Science Association, Berlin.

———, and ———. 1995. *Democratic Governance*. New York: Free Press.

———, and ———. 1996. "Institutional Perspectives on Political Institutions," *Governance* 9, no. 3: 247–64.

March, James G, Martin Schulz, and Xueguang Zhou. 2000. *The Dynamics of Rules: Change in Organizational Codes*. Stanford, CA: Stanford University Press.

Markoff, John and Veronica Montecinos. 1993. "The Ubiquitous Rise of Economists," *Journal of Public Policy* 13, no. 1: 37–68.

Mayer, I.S., C.E. Van Daalen and P.W.G. Bots. 2001. "Perspectives on Policy Analysis: A Framework for Understanding and Design," presented at Association for Public Policy Analysis and Management Conference, 1–3 November, Washington DC.

Mayntz, Renate. 1993a. "Governing Failure and the Problem of Governability: Some Comments on a Theoretical Paradigm," in J. Kooiman, ed., *Modern Governance: New Government–Society Interactions*. London: Sage.

———. 1993b. "Modernization and the Logic of Interorganizational Networks," in J. Child et al., eds, *Societal Change between Market and Organization*. Aldershot: Avebury, 3–18.

Mead, Lawrence M. 1985. "Policy Studies and Political Science," *Policy Studies Review* 5, 2: 319–35.

Minogue, Martin. 1983. "Theory and Practice in Public Policy and Administration," *Policy and Politics* 1, no. 1.

Moe, Terry M. 1984. "The New Economics of Organization," *American Journal of Political Science* 28: 739–77.

Morcöl, Göktug. 2002. *A New Mind for Policy Analysis: Toward a Post-Newtonian and Postpositivist Epistemology and Methodology*. New York: Praeger.

Mulford, Charles L. 1978. "Why They Don't Even When They Ought To: Implications of Compliance Theory for Policymakers," in A. Etzioni, ed., *Policy Research*. Leiden: E.J. Brill, 47–62.

Nettl, J.P. 1968. "The State as a Conceptual Variable," *World Politics* 20, no. 4: 559–92.

Niskanen, William A. 1971. *Bureaucracy and Representative Government*. Chicago: University of Chicago Press.

North, Douglas C. 1990. *Institutions, Institutional Change and Economic Performance*. Cambridge: Cambridge University Press.

Nownes, Anthony J. 1995. "The Other Exchange: Public Interest Groups, Patrons, and Benefits," *Social Science Quarterly* 76, no. 2: 381–401.

———, and Allan J. Cigler. 1995. "Public Interest Groups and the Road to Survival," *Polity* 27, no. 3: 380–404.

———, and Grant Neeley. 1996. "Toward an Explanation for Public Interest Group Formation and Proliferation: "Seed Money," Disturbances, Entrepreneurship, and Patronage," *Policy Studies Journal* 24, no. 1: 74–92.

Olson, Mancur. 1965. *The Logic of Collective Action: Public Goods and the Theory of Groups*. Cambridge, MA: Harvard University Press.

Orren, Karen, and Stephen Skowronek. 1993. "Beyond the Iconography of Order: Notes for a "New Institutionalism,"" in L.C. Dodd and C. Jillson, eds, *The Dynamics of American Politics: Approaches and Interpretations*. Boulder, CO: Westview Press.

———, and ———. 1998–9. "Regimes and Regime Building in American Government: A Review of Literature on the 1940s," *Political Science Quarterly* 113, no. 4: 689–702.

Ossowski, Stanislaw. 1963. *Class Structure in the Social Consciousness*, trans. Sheila Patterson. New York: Free Press of Glencoe.

Ostrom, Elinor. 1986a. "A Method of Institutional Analysis," in Kaufman et al. (1986).

———. 1986b. "An Agenda for the Study of Institutions," *Public Choice* 48: 3–25.

———. 1999. "Institutional Rational Choice: An Assessment of the Institutional Analysis and Development Framework," in Sabatier (1999a: 35–71).

———. 2003. "How Types of Goods and Property Rights Jointly Affect Collective Action," *Journal of Theoretical Politics* 15, no. 3: 239–70.

Ostrom, Vincent, David Feeny, and Hartmut Picht, eds. 1993. *Rethinking Institutional*

Analysis and Development: Issues, Alternatives and Choices. San Francisco: Institute for Contemporary Studies Press.

Pal, Leslie A. 1993a. *Interests of State: The Politics of Language, Multiculturalism, and Feminism in Canada*. Montreal and Kingston: McGill-Queen's University Press.

Panitch, Leo. 1977. "The Development of Corporatism in Liberal Democracies," *Comparative Political Studies* 10, no. 1: 61–90.

———. 1979. "Corporatism in Canada," *Studies in Political Economy* 1, 1: 43–92.

Perl, Anthony. 1991. "Financing Transport Infrastructure: The Effects of Institutional Durability in French and American Policymaking," *Governance* 4, no. 4: 365–402.

Peters, B. Guy. 1999. *Institutional Theory in Political Science: The "New Institutionalism,"* London: Pinter.

Pielke, R.A. 2004. "What Future for the Policy Sciences?" *Policy Sciences* 37: 209–25.

Pigou, A.C. 1932. *The Economics of Welfare*, 4th edn. London: Macmillan.

Polsby, Nelson W. 1963. *Community Power and Political Theory*. New Haven: Yale University Press.

Poulantzas, Nicos. 1973a. *Political Power and Social Classes*. London: New Left Books.

———. 1978. *State, Power, Socialism*. London: New Left Books.

Powell, Walter W., and Paul J. DiMaggio, eds. 1991. *The New Institutionalism in Organizational Analysis*. Chicago: University of Chicago Press.

Presthus, Robert V. 1973. *Elite Accommodation in Canadian Politics*. Cambridge: Cambridge University Press.

Przeworski, Adam. 1987. "Methods of Cross-National Research, 1970–83: An Overview," in M. Dierkes, H.N. Weiler, and A.B. Antal, eds, *Comparative Policy Research: Learning from Experience*. Aldershot: Gower, 31–49.

———. 1990. *The State and the Economy under Capitalism*. Chur, Switzerland: Harwood.

Putnam, Robert D. 1988. "Diplomacy and Domestic Politics: The Logic of Two-Level Games," *International Organization* 42: 427–60.

Radin, B. A. *Beyond Machiavelli: Policy Analysis Comes of Age*. Washington, DC: Georgetown University Press, 2000.

Ramesh, M. and Michael Howlett, eds. 2006. *Deregulation and Its Discontents: Rewriting the Rules in Asia*. Cheltenham: Edward Elgar.

Richardson, Jeremy, Gunnel Gustafsson, and Grant Jordan. 1982. "The Concept of Policy Style," in Richardson, ed., *Policy Styles in Western Europe*. London: George Allen and Unwin, 1–16.

Riker, William H. 1962. *The Theory of Political Coalitions*. New Haven: Yale University Press.

Rogers, David L., and David A. Whetton, eds. 1982. *Interorganizational Coordination: Theory, Research and Implementation*. Ames: Iowa State University Press.

Rowley, C.K. 1983. "The Political Economy of the Public Sector," in R.J.B. Jones, ed., *Perspectives on Political Economy*. London: Pinter.

Ruiter, D.W.P. 2004. "Types of Institutions as Patterns of Regulated Behaviour," *Res Publica* 10: 207–31.

Sabatier, Paul A. 1987. "Knowledge, Policy-Oriented Learning, and Policy Change," *Knowledge: Creation, Diffusion, Utilization* 8, 4: 649–92.

———. 1999b. "The Need for Better Theories," in Sabatier (1999a: 3–17).

Schaefer, Guenther F. 1974. "A General Systems Approach to Public Policy," *Policy and Politics* 2, 4: 331–46.

Schafer, A. 2006. "Resolving Deadlock: Why International Organisations Introduce Soft Law," *European Law Journal* 12, no. 2: 194–208.

Scharpf, Fritz W. 1977. Public Organization and the Waning of the Welfare State: A Research Perspective. *European Journal of Political Research*, 5: 339–362.

———. 2000. "Institutions in Comparative Policy Research," *Comparative Political Studies* 33, nos. 6 and 7: 762–90.

Schattschneider, E.E. 1960. *The Semi-sovereign People: A Realist's View of Democracy in America*. New York: Holt, Rinehart and Winston.

Schlager, Edella. 1999. "A Comparison of Frameworks, Theories, and Models of Policy Processes," in Sabatier (1999a: 233–60).

Schmidt, Vivien A. 2009. "Comparative Institutional Analysis," in Landman, Todd, and Neil Robinson, *The SAGE*

Handbook of Comparative Politics. Sage, Chapter 7.

Schmitter, Phillipe C. 1977. "Modes of Interest Intermediation and Models of Societal Change in Western Europe," *Comparative Political Studies* 10, no. 1: 7–38.

P.C. Schmitter, eds. 1985. "Neo-corporatism and the State," in W. Grant, ed., *The Political Economy of Corporatism*. London: Macmillan.

Searle, J.R. 2005. "What Is an Institution?" *Journal of Institutional Economics* 1, no. 1: 1–22.

Self, Peter. 1985. *Political Theories of Modern Government: Its Role and Reform*. London: Allen and Unwin.

Sharpe, L.J. 1975. "The Social Scientist and Policy-Making: Some Cautionary Thoughts and Transatlantic Reflections," *Policy and Politics* 4, no. 2: 7–34.

Shulock, N. 1999. "The Paradox of Policy Analysis: If It Is Not Used, Why Do We Produce So Much of It?" *Journal of Policy Analysis and Management* 18, no. 2: 226–44.

Siaroff, Alan. 1999. "Corporatism in 24 Industrial Democracies: Meaning and Measurement," *European Journal of Political Research* 36: 175–205.

Skocpol, Theda. 1985. "Bringing the State Back In: Strategies of Analysis in Current Research," in Evans et al. (1985).

Skowronek, Stephen. 1982. *Building a New American State: The Expansion of National Administrative Capacities 1877–1920*. Cambridge: Cambridge University Press.

Smith, Martin J. 1990. "Pluralism, Reformed Pluralism and Neopluralism: The Role of Pressure Groups in Policy-Making," *Political Studies* 38 (June): 302–22.

———, David Marsh, and David Richards. 1993. "Central Government Departments and the Policy Process," *Public Administration* 71 (Winter): 567–94.

Smith, Rogers M. 1997. "Still Blowing in the Wind: The American Quest for a Democratic, Scientific Political Science," in T. Bender and C.E. Schorske, eds, *American Academic Culture in Transformation: Fifty Years, Four Disciplines*. Princeton, NJ: Princeton University Press, 271–305.

Smith, T. Alexander. 1982. "A Phenomenology of the Policy Process," *International Journal of Comparative Sociology* 23, nos. 1 and 2: 1–16.

Stokey, Edith, and Richard Zeckhauser. 1978. *A Primer for Policy Analysis*. New York: Norton.

Stone, Deborah A. 1988. *Policy Paradox and Political Reason*. Glenview, IL: Scott, Foresman.

Thelen, Kathleen and S. Steinmo. 1992. "Historical Institutionalism in Comparative Politics," in Steinmo, Thelen, and F. Longstreth, eds, *Structuring Politics: Historical Institutionalism in Comparative Analysis*. Cambridge: Cambridge University Press.

Therborn, Goran. 1977. "The Rule of Capital and the Rise of Democracy," *New Left Review* 103: 3–41.

———. 1986. "Neo-Marxist, Pluralist, Corporatist, Statist Theories and the Welfare State," in A. Kazancigil, ed., *The State in Global Perspective*. Aldershot, UK: Gower.

Thissen, W.A.H., and P.G.J. Twaalfhoven. 2001. "Toward a Conceptual Structure for Evaluating Policy Analytic Activities," *European Journal of Operational Research* 129: 627–49.

Thompson, E.P. 1978. *The Poverty of Theory and Other Essays*. London: Merlin Press.

Torgerson, Douglas. 1983. "Contextual Orientation in Policy Analysis: The Contribution of Harold D. Lasswell," *Policy Sciences* 18: 240–52.

———. 1990. "Origins of the Policy Orientation: The Aesthetic Dimension in Lasswell's Political Vision," *History of Political Thought* 11 (Summer): 340–4.

Tribe, Laurence H. 1972. "Policy Science: Analysis or Ideology?" *Philosophy and Public Affairs* 2, no. 1: 66–110.

Truman, David R. 1964. *The Governmental Process: Political Interests and Public Opinion*. New York: Knopf.

Tufte, Edward R. 1978. *Political Control of the Economy*. Princeton, NJ: Princeton University Press.

Tversky, Amos, and Daniel Kahneman. 1986. "Rational Choice and the Framing of Decisions," *Journal of Business* 59, no. 4, part 2: S251–79.

Utton, M.A. 1986. *The Economics of Regulating Industry*. Oxford: Blackwell.

Van Waarden, Frans. 1995. "Persistence of National Policy Styles: A Study of Their

Institutional Foundations," in Brigitte Unger and Frans van Waarden, eds. *Convergence or Diversity? Internationalization and Economic Policy Response*, Aldershot: Avebury, 333–372.

Van Winden, Frans A.A.M. 1988. "The Economic Theory of Political Decision-Making," in J. van den Broeck, ed., *Public Choice*. Dordrecht: Kluwer.

Vining, Aidan R., and David L. Weimer. 1990. "Government Supply and Government Production Failure: A Framework Based on Contestability," *Journal of Public Policy* 10, no. 1: 1–22.

Vining, Aidan R., and David L. Weimer. 2002. "Introducing Policy Analysis Craft: The Sheltered Workshop," *Journal of Policy Analysis and Management* 21, no. 4: 683–695

Wagner, Richard K. 1991. "Managerial Problem Solving," in R.J. Sternberg and P.A. French, eds, *Complex Problem Solving: Principles and Mechanisms*. Hillsdale, NJ: Lawrence Erlbaum Associates, 159–83.

Warwick, Paul V. 2000. "Policy Horizons in West European Parliamentary Systems," *European Journal of Political Research* 38: 37–61.

Weber, Max. 1978. *Economy and Society: An Outline of Interpretive Sociology*. Berkeley: University of California Press.

Wedel, J.R., C. Shore, G. Feldman, and S. Lathrop. 2005. "Toward an Anthropology of Public Policy," *Annals, American Academy of Political and Social Science* 600: 30–51.

Weimer, D.L. 1992. "The Craft of Policy Design: Can It Be More Than Art?" *Policy Studies Review* 11, no. 3/4: 370–88

———, and Aidan R. Vining. 1992. *Policy Analysis: Concepts and Practice*. New Jersey: Prentice Hall.

———, and Aidan R. Vining. 1999. *Policy Analysis: Concepts and Practice*. New Jersey: Prentice Hall.

Weiss, Carol H. 1977a. *Using Social Research in Public Policy Making*. Lexington, MA: Lexington Books.

———. 1977b. "Research for Policy's Sake: The Enlightenment Function of Social Science Research," *Policy Analysis* 3, no. 4: 531–45.

———. 1983. "Ideology, Interests, and Information," in Daniel Callahan and Bruce Jennings, eds, *Ethics, the Social Sciences, and Policy Analysis*. New York: Plenum Press, 213–45.

Wildavsky, Aaron. 1979. *Speaking Truth to Power: The Art and Craft of Policy Analysis*. Boston: Little, Brown.

Williamson, Oliver E. 1985. *The Economic Institutions of Capitalism: Firms, Markets, Relational Contracting*. New York: Free Press.

———. 1996. "Transaction Cost Economics and Organization Theory," in Williamson, ed., *The Mechanisms of Governance*. New York: Oxford University Press, 219–49.

Winkler, J.T. 1976. "Corporatism," *European Journal of Sociology* 17, no. 1: 100–36.

Wolf, Charles, Jr. 1979. "A Theory of Nonmarket Failure: Framework for Implementation Analysis," *Journal of Law and Economics* 22, no. 1: 107–39.

———. 1988. *Markets or Governments: Choosing between Imperfect Alternatives*. Cambridge, MA: MIT Press.

Yanow, Dvora. 2007. "Interpretation in Policy Analysis: On Methods and Practice," *Critical Policy Analysis* 1, no. 1: 110–22.

Yarbrough, Beth V., and Robert M. Yarbrough. 1990. "International Institutions and the New Economics of Organization," *International Organization* 44, no. 2: 235–59.

Young, Iris Marion. 2011. *Justice and the Politics of Difference*. Paperback reissue / with a new foreword by Danielle Allen. Princeton, NJ: Princeton University Press.

Zeigler, L. Harmon. 1964. *Interest Groups in American Society*. Englewood Cliffs, NJ: Prentice-Hall.

Zerbe, Richard O., and Howard E. McCurdy. 1999. "The Failure of Market Failure," *Journal of Policy Analysis and Management* 18, no. 4: 558–78.

Zey, Mary. 1992. "Criticisms of Rational Choice Models," in Zey, ed., *Decision Making: Alternatives to Rational Choice Models*. Newbury Park, CA: Sage, 10–31.

Chapter 3 Sources

Abelson, Donald E. 1996. *American Think Tanks and Their Role in U.S. Foreign Policy*. London: Macmillan.

Abelson, Donald E. 1999. "Public Visibility and Policy Relevance: Assessing the Impact and Influence of Canadian Policy Institutes," *Canadian Public Administration* 42, no. 2: 240–70.

———. 2002. *Do Think Tanks Matter? Assessing the Impact of Public Policy Institutes*.

Montreal and Kingston: McGill-Queen's University Press.

———. 2007. "Any Ideas? Think Tanks and Policy Analysis in Canada," in Dobuzinskis et al. (2007: 298–310).

Adie, R.F., and P.G. Thomas. 1987. *Canadian Public Administration: Problematical Perspectives*, 2nd edn. Scarborough, ON: Prentice-Hall.

Aglietta, Michel. 1979. *A Theory of Capitalist Regulation*. London: New Left Books.

Anspach, Nicolas M., Jay T. Jennings, and Kevin Arceneaux. 2019. "A Little Bit of Knowledge: Facebook's News Feed and Self-Perceptions of Knowledge," *Research & Politics* 6, no. 1 (January 1).

Atkinson, Michael M., and William D. Coleman. 1989a. "Strong States and Weak States: Sectoral Policy Networks in Advanced Capitalist Economies," *British Journal of Political Science* 19, no. 1: 47–67.

———, and ———. 1989b. *The State, Business, and Industrial Change in Canada*. Toronto: University of Toronto Press.

Axworthy, Thomas S. 1988. "Of Secretaries to Princes," *Canadian Public Administration* 31, no. 2: 247–64.

Bakvis, Herman and David MacDonald. 1993. "The Canadian Cabinet: Organization, DecisionRules, and Policy Impact," in M. Michael Atkinson, ed., *Governing Canada: Institutions and Public Policy*. Toronto: Harcourt Brace Jovanovich.

Banting, Keith G. 1982. *The Welfare State and Canadian Federalism*. Kingston, ON: Queen's University Institute of Intergovernmental Relations.

Barnett, Michael N., and Martha Finnemore. 1999. "The Politics, Power, and Pathologies of International Organizations," *International Organization* 53, no. 4: 699–732.

Baumgartner, Frank R. and Beth L. Leech. 1998. *Basic Interests: The Importance of Groups in Politics and in Political Science*. Princeton, NJ: Princeton University Press.

———, and Beth L. Leech. 2001. "Interest Niches and Policy Bandwagons: Patterns of Interest Group Involvement in National Politics," *Journal of Politics* 63, no. 4: 1191–1213.

Bealey, Frank. 1988. *Democracy in the Contemporary State*. New York: Oxford University Press, USA.

Bekke, H.A.G.M., J.L. Perry, T.A.J. Toonen. 1996. *Civil Service Systems in Comparative Perspective*. Bloomington: Indiana University Press.

———, and F.M. van der Meer. 2000. *Civil Service Systems in Western Europe*. Cheltenham: Edward Elgar.

Bennett, Colin J. 1997. "Understanding Ripple Effects: The Cross-National Adoption of Policy Instruments for Bureaucratic Accountability," *Governance* 10, no. 3: 213–33.

Berelson, Bernard. 1952. "Democratic Theory and Public Opinion," *Public Opinion Quarterly* 16 (Fall): 313–30.

Bernier, Luc, Keith Brownsey, and Michael Howlett. 2005. *Executive Styles in Canada: Cabinet Structures and Leadership Practices in Canadian Government*. Institute of Public Administration of Canada Series in Public Management and Governance. Toronto: University of Toronto Press.

Bernstein, Marver H. 1955. *Regulating Business by Independent Commission*. Princeton, NJ: Princeton University Press.

Bernstein, Steven, and Benjamin Cashore. 2000. "Globalization, Four Paths of Internationalization and Domestic Policy Change: The Case of EcoForestry in British Columbia, Canada," *Canadian Journal of Political Science* 33, no. 1: 67–100.

Besley, T., and A. Case. 2003. "Political Institutions and Policy Choices: Evidence from the United States," *Journal of Economic Literature* 41 (Mar.): 7–73.

Birch, Anthony H. 1972. *Representation*. New York: Praeger.

Blais, André, Donald Blake, and Stéphane Dion. 1996. "Do Parties Make a Difference? A Re-Appraisal," *American Journal of Political Science* 40, no. 2: 514–20.

Bourgault, Jacques, and Stéphane Dion. 1989. "Governments Come and Go, But What of Senior Civil Servants? Canadian Deputy Ministers and Transitions in Power (1867–1987)," *Governance* 2, no. 2: 124–51.

Braun, Dietmar. 1999. "Interests or Ideas? An Overview of Ideational Concepts in Public Policy Research," in D. Braun and A. Busch, eds, *Public Policy and Political Ideas*. Cheltenham: Edward Elgar, 11–29.

Brenner, Neil. 1999. "Beyond State-Centrism? Space, Territoriality, and Geographical

Scale in Globalization Studies," *Theory and Society* 28: 39–78.

Brooks, Sarah M. 2005. "Interdependent and Domestic Foundations of Policy Change: The Diffusion of Pension Privatization around the World," *International Studies Quarterly* 49: 273–94.

———. 2007. "When Does Diffusion Matter? Explaining the Spread of Structural Pension Reforms across Nations," *Journal of Politics* 69, 3: 701–15.

Bryman, Alan. 1988. *Quantity and Quality in Social Research*. London: Unwin Hyman.

Burgess, Michael, and Alain-G. Gagnon, eds. 1993. *Comparative Federalism and Federation: Competing Traditions and Future Directions*. New York: Harvester Wheatsheaf.

Burns, J.P., and B. Bowornwathana, 2001. *Civil Service Systems in Asia*. Cheltenham: Edward Elgar.

Butkiewicz, J.L., and H. Yanikkaya. 2005. "The Impact of Sociopolitical Instability on Economic Growth: Analysis and Implications," *Journal of Policy Modeling* 27, no. 5: 629–45.

Butler, David, H.R. Penniman, and Austin Ranney, eds. 1981. *Democracy at the Polls: A Comparative Study of Competitive National Elections*. Washington: American Enterprise Institute for Public Policy Research.

Cairns, Alan C. 1990b. "The Past and Future of the Canadian Administrative State," *University of Toronto Law Journal* 40: 310–61.

Callaghan, Karen, and Frauke Schnell. 2001. "Assessing the Democratic Debate: How the News Media Frame Elite Policy Discourse," *Political Communication* 18: 183–212.

Campbell, John L. 1998. "Institutional Analysis and the Role of Ideas in Political Economy," *Theory and Society* 27, 5: 377–409.

Canes-Wrone, Brandice, Michael C. Herron, and Kenneth W. Shotts. 2001. "Leadership and Pandering: A Theory of Executive Policymaking," *American Journal of Political Science* 45, 3: 532–50.

Casella, Bruno, and Lorenzo Formenti. 2019. "FDI in the Digital Economy: A Shift to Asset-light International Footprints," *Transnational Corporations* 25, no. 1: 101–130.

Castles, Francis G. 1982. "The Impact of Parties on Public Expenditure," in Castles, ed., *The Impact of Parties: Politics and Policies in Democratic Capitalist States*. London: Sage.

Cater, Douglas. 1964. *Power in Washington: A Critical Look at Today's Struggle in the Nation's Capital*. New York: Random House.

Chandler, M.A. 1982. "State Enterprise and Partisanship in Provincial Politics," *Canadian Journal of Political Science* 15: 711–40.

———. 1983. "The Politics of Public Enterprise," in Prichard (1983: 185–218).

———, and W.M. Chandler. 1979. *Public Policy and Provincial Politics*. Toronto: McGrawHill Ryerson.

Coates, David, ed. 2005. *Varieties of Capitalism, Varieties of Approaches*. New York: Palgrave Macmillan.

Cohen, M.G., and S. McBride. 2003. *Global Turbulence: Social Activists and State Responses to Globalization*. Aldershot: Ashgate.

Cohn, D. 2004. "The Best of Intentions, Potentially Harmful Policies: A Comparative Study of Scholarly Complexity and Failure," *Journal of Comparative Policy Analysis* 6, no. 1: 39–56.

———. 2006. "Jumping into the Political Fray: Academics and Policy-Making," *IRPP Policy Matters* 7, no. 3.

Cohn, Daniel. 2007. "Academics and Public Policy: Informing Policy-Analysis and Policy-Making," in *Policy Analysis in Canada*, edited by Laurent Dobuzinskis, Michael Howlett, and David Laycock, 574–98. Toronto: University of Toronto Press.

Coleman, William D. 1988. *Business and Politics: A Study of Collective Action*. Montreal and Kingston: McGill-Queen's University Press.

———, G.D. Skogstad, and M. Atkinson. 1996. "Paradigm Shifts and Policy Networks: Cumulative Change in Agriculture," *Journal of Public Policy* 16, no. 3: 73–302.

———, and Wyn P. Grant. 1998. "Policy Convergence and Policy Feedback: Agricultural Finance Policies in a Globalizing Era," *European Journal of Political Research* 34: 225–47.

———, and Anthony Perl. 1999. "Internationalized Policy Environments and Policy

Network Analysis," *Political Studies* 47: 691–709.

———, and Grace Skogstad, eds. 1990. *Policy Communities and Public Policy in Canada: A Structural Approach*. Mississauga, ON: Copp Clark Pitman.

Cortell, Andrew P., and James W. Davis. 1996. "How Do International Institutions Matter? The Domestic Impact of International Rules and Norms," *International Studies Quarterly* 40: 451–78.

Cunningham, Frank. 1987. *Democratic Theory and Socialism*. Cambridge: Cambridge University Press.

deHaven-Smith, Lance, and Carl E. Van Horn. 1984. "Subgovernment Conflict in Public Policy," *Policy Studies Journal* 12, no. 4: 627–42.

de Jong, Martin, and Jurian Edelenbos. 2007. "An Insider's Look into Policy Transfer in Transnational Expert Networks," *European Planning Studies* 15, no. 5: 687–706.

deLeon, Peter. 1997. "Afterward: The Once and Future State of Policy Termination," *International Journal of Public Administration* 20: 33–46.

Demaret, Paul. 1997. "The Reciprocal Influence of Multilateral and Regional Trade Rules: A Framework of Analysis," in Demaret, J., F. Bellis, and G.G. Jimenez, eds, *Regional and Multilateralism after the Uruguay Round: Convergence, Divergence and Interaction*. Liège: Institute d'Études Juridiques Européennes de Université Liège, 805–38.

Desveaux, James A., Evert Lindquist, and Glen Taner. 1994. "Organizing for Innovation in Public Bureaucracy: AIDS, Energy and Environment Policy in Canada," *Canadian Journal of Political Science* 27, no. 3: 493–528.

Dobbin, Frank, Beth Simmons, and Geoffrey Garrett. 2007. "The Global Diffusion of Public Policies: Social Construction, Coercion, Competition, or Learning?" *Annual Review of Sociology* 33: 449–72.

Dobuzinskis, Laurent. 2000. "Global Discord: The Confusing Discourse of Think Tanks," in T. Cohn, S. McBride, and J. Wiseman, eds, *Power in the Global Era*. London: Macmillan.

Doern, G. Bruce. 1998. "The Interplay among Regimes: Mapping Regulatory Institutions in the United Kingdom, the United States, and Canada," in Doern and Wilks (1998: 29–50).

———et al. 1999. "Canadian Regulatory Institutions: Converging and Colliding Regimes," in Doern, M.M. Hill, M.J. Prince, and R.J. Schultz, eds, *Changing the Rules: Canadian Regulatory Regimes and Institutions*. Toronto: University of Toronto Press, 3–26.

———, L. Pal, and B.W. Tomlin, eds. 1996a. *Border Crossings: The Internationalization of Canadian Public Policy*. Toronto: Oxford University Press.

———, ———, and ———. 1996b. "The Internationalization of Canadian Public Policy," in Doern, Pal, and Tomlin (1996a: 1–26).

Doorenspleet, Renske. 2000. "Reassessing the Three Waves of Democratization," *World Politics* 52, no. 3: 384–406.

Duchacek, Ivo D. 1970. *Comparative Federalism: The Territorial Dimension of Politics*. New York: Holt, Rinehart and Winston.

Dunleavy, Patrick and B. O'Leary. 1987. *Theories of the State: The Politics of Liberal Democracy*. Basingstoke: Macmillan Education.

Edelman, Murray. 1988. *Constructing the Political Spectacle*. Chicago: University of Chicago Press.

Edwards, George C., and Ira Sharkansky. 1978. *The Policy Predicament: Making and Implementing Public Policy*. San Francisco: Freeman.

Eisner, Marc Allen. 1993. *Regulatory Politics in Transition*. Baltimore: Johns Hopkins University Press.

———. 1994a. "Discovering Patterns in Regulatory History: Continuity, Change and Regulatory Regimes," *Journal of Policy History* 6, 2: 157–87.

———. 1994b. "Economic Regulatory Policies: Regulation and Deregulation in Historical Context," in Rosenbloom and Schwartz (1994: 91–116).

Erbring, Lutz, and Edie N. Goldenberg. 190. "Front-Page News and Real-World Cues: A New Look at Agenda-Setting by the Media," *American Journal of Political Science* 24: 16–49.

Erikson, Robert S., Norman R. Luttbeg, and Kent L. Tedin, eds. 1980. *American Public Opinion*. New York: John Wiley and Sons.

———, Gerald C. Wright Jr., and John P. McIver. 1989. "Political Parties, Public Opinion and State Policy in the United States," *American Political Science Review* 83, no. 3: 729–39.

Esping-Andersen, Gosta. 1990. *The Three Worlds of Welfare Capitalism*. Cambridge: Polity.

———, and Walter Korpi. 1984. "Social Policy as Class Politics in Post-War Capitalism: Scandinavia, Austria, and Germany," in J.H. Goldthorpe, ed., *Order and Conflict in Contemporary Capitalism*. Oxford: Clarendon Press.

Evans, Mark, and Jonathan Davies. 1999. "Understanding Policy Transfer: A Multi-Level, Multi-Disciplinary Perspective," *Public Administration* 77, no. 2: 361–85.

Evans, Peter. 1992. "State as Problem and Solution: Predation, Embedded Autonomy, and Structural Change," in Stephen Haggard and Robert R. Kaufman, eds, *The Politics of Economic Adjustment: International Constraints, Distributive Conflicts, and the State*. Princeton, NJ: Princeton University Press, 139–81.

———. 1995. *Embedded Autonomy: States and Industrial Transformation*. Princeton, NJ: Princeton University Press.

Fabbrini, Sergio, and Daniela Sicurelli. 2008. "Bringing Policy-Making Structure Back In: Why Are the US and the EU Pursuing Different Foreign Policies?" *International Politics* 45: 292–309.

Finnemore, Martha, and Kathryn Sikkink. 1998. "International Norm Dynamics and Political Change," *International Organization* 52, no. 4: 887–917.

Fischer, Frank. 1993. "Policy Discourses and the Politics of Washington Think Tanks," in Fischer and Forester (1993: 21–42).

Flathman, Richard E. 1966. *The Public Interest: An Essay Concerning the Normative Discourse of Politics*. New York: Wiley.

Fraussen, Bert, Timothy Graham, and Darren R. Halpin. 2018. "Assessing the Prominence of Interest Groups in Parliament: A Supervised Machine Learning Approach," Journal of Legislative Studies 24, no. 4 (November 15): 1–25. doi:10.1080/135723 34.2018.1540117.

Freeman, John Leiper. 1955. *The Political Process: Executive Bureau–Legislative Committee Relations*. New York: Random House.

———, and Judith Parris Stevens. 1987. "A Theoretical and Conceptual Reexamination of Subsystem Politics," *Public Policy and Administration* 2, 1: 9–24.

Goffman, Erving. 1974. *Frame Analysis: An Essay on the Organization of Experience*. Cambridge, MA: Harvard University Press.

Goldmann, K. 2005. "Appropriateness and Consequences: The Logic of Neo-Institutionalism," *Governance* 18, 1: 35–52.

Gormley, William T and B. Guy Peters. 1992. "National Styles of Regulation: Child Care in Three Countries," *Policy Sciences* 25: 381–99.

Gourevitch, P. 1993. "Democracy and Economic Policy: Elective Affinities and Circumstantial Conjunctures," *World Development* 21, 8: 1271–80.

Grande, E. 1996. "The State and Interest Groups in a Framework of Multi-Level Decision Making: The Case of the European Union," *Journal of European Public Policy* 3: 313–38.

Haas, Peter M. 1992. "Introduction: Epistemic Communities and International Policy Coordination," *International Organization* 46, no. 1: 1–36.

Haggard, Stephen and Beth A. Simmons. 1987. "Theories of International Regimes," *International Organization* 41, no. 3: 491–517.

Hajer, Maarten A. 1993. "Discourse Coalitions and the Institutionalization of Practice: The Case of Acid Rain in Britain," in Fischer and Forester (1993: 43–76).

Hall, Peter A. 1990. "Policy Paradigms, Experts, and the State: The Case of Macroeconomic Policy-Making in Britain," in Brooks and Gagnon (1990).

———. 1992. "The Change from Keynesianism to Monetarism: Institutional Analysis and British Economic Policy in the 1970s," in S. Steinmo et al., eds, *Structuring Politics: Historical Institutionalism in Comparative Analysis*. Cambridge: Cambridge University Press, 90–114.

———. 1993. "Policy Paradigms, Social Learning and the State: The Case of Economic Policy Making in Britain," *Comparative Politics* 25, no. 3: 275–96.

———, and David Soskice, eds. 2001b. "Varieties of Capitalism: The Institutional

Foundations of Comparative Advantage," in Hall and Soskice (2001a: 1–70).

Halligan, J. 2003. *Civil Service Systems in Anglo-American Countries*. Cheltenham: Edward Elgar.

Hamm, Keith E. 1983. "Patterns of Influence among Committees, Agencies, and Interest Groups," *Legislative Studies Quarterly* 8, no. 3: 379–426.

Halpin, Darren, and Anne Binderkrantz. 2011. "Explaining Breadth of Policy Engagement: Patterns of Interest Group Mobilization in Public Policy," *Journal of European Public Policy* 18, no. 2 (March): 201–19.

——, and H.F. Thomas. 2012. "Evaluating the Breadth of Policy Engagement by Organized Interests," *Public Administration* 90, no. 3: 582–99.

——, Bert Fraussen, and Anthony J. Nownes. 2018. "The Balancing Act of Establishing a Policy Agenda: Conceptualizing and Measuring Drivers of Issue Prioritization within Interest Groups," *Governance* 31, no. 2 (April 1): 215–37.

Harris, Richard, and Sidney Milkis. 1989. *The Politics of Regulatory Change*. New York: Oxford University Press.

Hayes, Michael T. 1978. "The Semi-Sovereign Pressure Groups: A Critique of Current Theory and an Alternative Typology," *Journal of Politics* 40, no. 1: 134–61.

Heclo, Hugh. 1974. *Modern Social Politics in Britain and Sweden: From Relief to Income Maintenance*. New Haven: Yale University Press.

——. 1978. "Issue Networks and the Executive Establishment," in A. King, ed., *The New American Political System*. Washington: American Enterprise Institute for Public Policy Research, 87–124.

——. 1994. "Ideas, Interests and Institutions," in L.C. Dodd and C. Jillson, eds, *The Dynamics of American Politics: Approaches and Interpretations*. San Francisco: Westview, 366–92.

Heinz, John P., et al. 1990. "Inner Circles or Hollow Cores," *Journal of Politics* 52, 2: 356–90.

——et al. 1993. *The Hollow Core: Private Interests in National Policy Making*. Cambridge, MA: Harvard University Press.

Held, David, and Anthony McGrew. 1993. "Globalization and the Liberal Democratic State," *Government and Opposition* 28, no. 2: 261–85.

Herman, Edward S., and Noam Chomsky. 1988. *Manufacturing Consent: The Political Economy of the Mass Media*. New York: Pantheon Books.

Hibbing, John R., and Elizabeth Theiss-Morse. 2002. *Stealth Democracy: Americans' Beliefs about How Government Should Work*. Cambridge: Cambridge University Press.

Hibbs, Douglas A., Jr. 1977. "Political Parties and Macroeconomic Policy," *American Political Science Review* 71: 1467–87.

——. 1978. "On the Political Economy of Long-run Trends in Strike Activity," *British Journal of Political Science* 8, no. 2: 153–75.

——. 1987. *The Political Economy of Industrial Democracies*. Cambridge, MA: Harvard University Press.

Hilgartner, Stephen, and Charles L. Bosk. 1981. "The Rise and Fall of Social Problems: A Public Arenas Model," *American Journal of Sociology* 94, no. 1: 53–78.

Hill, Larry B., ed. 1992. The State of Public Bureaucracy. Armonk, NY: M.E. Sharpe.

Hirst, Paul, and Grahame Thompson. 1996. *Globalization in Question*. Oxford: Polity Press.

Hobson, John, and M. Ramesh. 2002. "Globalisation Makes of States What States Make of It: Between Agency and Structure in the State/Globalisation Debate," *New Political Economy* 7, 1: 5–22.

Hockin, Thomas A. 1977. "Mass Legitimate Parties and Their Implications for Party Leaders," in Hockin, ed., *Apex of Power: The Prime Minister and Political Leadership in Canada*. Scarborough, ON: Prentice-Hall, 70–85.

Hoekman, Bernard, and Michel Kostecki. 1995. *The Political Economy of the World Trading System: From GATT to WTO*. Oxford: Oxford University Press.

Hollingsworth, J. Rogers. 1998. "New Perspectives on the Spatial Dimensions of Economic Coordination: Tensions between Globalization and Social Systems of Production," *Review of International Political Economy* 5, no. 3: 482–507.

Hong, Sounman, and Daniel Nadler. 2016. "The Unheavenly Chorus: Political Voices of Organized Interests on Social Media," *Policy & Internet* 8, no. 1 (March 1): 91–106.

Howell, Chris. 2003. "Varieties of Capitalism—and Then There Was One?" *Comparative Politics* 36, 1: 103–24.

Howlett, Michael. 1997a. "Issue-Attention and Punctuated Equilibria Models Reconsidered: An Empirical Examination of the Dynamics of Agenda-Setting in Canada," *Canadian Journal of Political Science* 30, no. 1: 3–29.

———. 1997b. "Predictable and Unpredictable Policy Windows: Issue, Institutional and Exogenous Correlates of Canadian Federal Agenda-Setting," paper presented to the annual meeting of the Canadian Political Science Association, St John's, NL.

———. 1999. "Federalism and Public Policy," in J. Bickerton and A. Gagnon, eds, *Canadian Politics*, 3rd edn. Peterborough, ON: Broadview Press.

———, and M. Ramesh. 2002. "The Policy Effects of Internationalization: A Subsystem Adjustment Analysis of Policy Change," *Journal of Comparative Policy Analysis* 4, 3: 31–50.

———, Alex Netherton, and M. Ramesh. 1999. *The Political Economy of Canada: An Introduction*, 2nd edn. Toronto: Oxford University Press.

———, and David Laycock, eds. 2012. *Regulating Next Generation Agri-Food Biotechnologies: Lessons from European, North American and Asian Experiences.* 1st ed. Abingdon, UK: Routledge.

———, and Andrea Migone. 2014. "Making the Invisible Public Service Visible? Exploring Data on the Supply of Policy and Management Consultancies in Canada," *Canadian Public Administration* 57, no. 2 (June 1): 183–216.

Huber, Evelyne, and John D. Stephens. 1998. "Internationalization and the Social Democratic Model: Crisis and Future Prospects," *Comparative Political Studies* 31, no. 3: 353–97.

Huntington, Samuel P. 1952. "The Marasmus of the ICC: The Commissions, the Railroads and the Public Interest," *Yale Law Review* 61, 4: 467–509.

Ikenberry, G. John. 1990. "The International Spread of Privatization Policies: Inducements, Learning, and "Policy Bandwagoning,"" in Suleiman and Waterbury (1990).

Imbeau, Louis M., and Guy Lachapelle. 1993. "Les Déterminants des politiques provinciales au Canada: une synthèse des études comparatives," *Revue Québécoise de Science Politique* 23: 107–41.

Jacek, H.J. 1986. "Pluralist and Corporatist Intermediation, Activities of Business Interest Associations, and Corporate Profits: Some Evidence from Canada," *Comparative Politics* 18, no. 4: 419–37.

James, Simon. 1993. "The Idea Brokers: The Impact of Think Tanks on British Government," *Public Administration* 71: 491–506.

Jenkins-Smith, Hank C., and Paul A. Sabatier. 1993. "The Study of Public Policy Processes," in Sabatier and Jenkins-Smith (1993a).

Johnson, A.F., and A. Stritch, eds. 1997. *Canadian Public Policy: Globalization and Political Parties.* Toronto: Copp Clark Pitman.

Kasza, Gregory J. 2002. "The Illusion of Welfare "Regimes,"" *Journal of Social Policy* 31, no. 2: 271–87.

Kato, Junko. 1996. "Review Article: Institutions and Rationality in Politics—Three Varieties of Neo-Institutionalists," *British Journal of Political Science* 26: 553–82.

Katzenstein, Peter J. 1977. "Conclusion: Domestic Structures and Strategies of Foreign Economic Policy," *International Organization* 31, no. 4: 879–920.

Kaufman, Herbert. 2001. "Major Players: Bureaucracies in American Government," *Public Administration Review* 61, no. 1: 18–42.

Keck, Margaret E., and Kathryn Sikkink, eds. 1998. *Activists beyond Borders: Advocacy Networks in International Politics.* Ithaca, NY: Cornell University Press.

Kelman, Steven. 1981. *Regulating America, Regulating Sweden: A Comparative Study of Occupational Safety and Health Policy.* Cambridge, MA: MIT Press.

Keohane, Robert O. and Joseph S. Nye. 1989. *Power and Interdependence.* Glenview, IL: Scott, Foresman.

Kernaghan, Kenneth. 1979. "Power, Parliament and Public Servants in Canada: Ministerial Responsibility Reexamined," *Canadian Public Policy* 5, no. 3: 383–96.

———. 1985a. "The Public and Public Servants in Canada," in Kernaghan, ed.,

Public Administration in Canada: Selected Readings. Toronto: Methuen, 323–33.

Key, V.O., Jr. 1967. Public Opinion and American Democracy. New York: Knopf.

Kim, Young-Jun, and Chui-Young Roh. 2008. "Beyond the Advocacy Coalition Framework in Policy Process," *International Journal of Public Administration* 31: 668–89.

King, Anthony. 1981. "What Do Elections Decide?" in Butler et al. (1981).

King, Gary, and Michael Laver. 1993. "Party Platforms, Mandates and Government Spending," *American Political Science Review* 87, no. 3: 744–50.

King, M.R. 2005. "Epistemic Communities and the Diffusion of Ideas: Central Bank Reform in the United Kingdom," *West European Politics* 28, no. 1: 94–123.

Kingdon, John W. 1984. *Agendas, Alternatives and Public Policies.* Boston: Little, Brown.

Kisby, Ben. 2007. "Analysing Policy Networks: Towards and Ideational Approach," *Policy Studies* 28, 1: 71–90.

Knill, Christoph and Dirk Lehmkuhl. 2002. "Private Actors and the State: Internationalization and Changing Patterns of Governance," *Governance* 15, no. 1: 41–63.

Knoke, David. 1993. "Networks as Political Glue: Explaining Public Policy-Making," in W.J. Wilson, ed., *Sociology and the Public Agenda.* London: Sage, 164–84.

Kolberg, Jon Eivind, and Gosta Esping-Andersen. 1992. "Welfare States and Employment Regimes," in Kolberg, ed, *The Study of Welfare State Regimes.* New York: M.E. Sharpe.

Korpi, Walter. 1983. *The Democratic Class Struggle.* London: Routledge & Kegan Paul.

Krasner, Stephen D. 1982. "Structural Causes and Regime Consequences: Regimes as Intervening Variables," *International Organization* 36, no. 2: 185–205.

———, ed. 1983. International Regimes. Ithaca, NY: Cornell University Press.

Kuhn, Thomas S. 1962. *The Structure of Scientific Revolutions.* Chicago: University of Chicago Press.

———. 1974. "Second Thoughts on Paradigms," in F. Suppe, ed., *The Structure of Scientific Theories.* Urbana: University of Illinois Press, 459–82.

Lacroix, L. 1986. "Strike Activity in Canada," in W.C. Riddell, ed., *Canadian Labour Relations.* Toronto: University of Toronto Press.

Lapsley, Irvine, and Rosie Oldfield. 2001. "Transforming the Public Sector: Management Consultants as Agents of Change," *European Accounting Review* 10, no. 3: 523–43.

Laumann, Edward O., and David Knoke. 1987. *The Organizational State: Social Choice in National Policy Domains.* Madison: University of Wisconsin Press.

Laver, Michael J., and Ian Budge. 1992. *Party Policy and Government Coalitions.* New York: St Martin's Press.

———, and W.B. Hunt. 1992. *Policy and Party Competition.* London: Routledge.

Lee, Mordecai. 2001. "The Agency Spokesperson: Connecting Public Administration and the Media," *Public Administration Quarterly* 25, no. 1: 101–30.

Lee, Simon, and Stephen McBride, eds. 2007. Neo-Liberalism, *State Power and Global Governance.* New York: Springer.

Lehne, Richard. 2001. *Government and Business: American Political Economy in Comparative Perspective.* New York: Chatham House.

Leman, Christopher. 1977. "Patterns of Policy Development: Social Security in the United States and Canada," *Public Policy* 25, no. 2: 261–91.

Levi-Faur, D., and E. Vigoda-Gadot. 2006. "New Public Policy, New Policy Transfers: Some Characteristics of a New Order in the Making," *International Journal of Public Administration* 29: 247–62.

Lindblom, Charles E. 1977. *Politics and Markets: The World's Political Economic Systems.* New York: Basic Books.

Lindquist, Evert A. 1993. "Think Tanks or Clubs? Assessing the Influence and Roles of Canadian Policy Institutes," *Canadian Public Administration* 36, 4: 547–79.

Lipietz, Alain. 1982. "Towards Global Fordism," *New Left Review* 132: 33–48.

Lowell, A. Lawrence. 1926. *Public Opinion and Popular Government.* New York: David McKay Company.

Lowi, Theodore J. 1966. "Distribution, Regulation, Redistribution: The Functions of Government," in R.B. Ripley, ed., *Public Policies and Their Politics: Techniques of Government Control.* New York: Norton, 27–40.

——. 1969. The *End of Liberalism: Ideology, Policy and the Crisis of Public Authority.* New York: Norton.

——. 1972. "Four Systems of Policy, Politics and Choice," *Public Administration Review* 32, no. 4: 298–310.

——. 1998. "Foreword: New Dimensions in Policy and Politics," in R. Tatalovich and B.W. Daynes, eds, *Moral Controversies in American Social Politics: Cases in Social Regulatory Policy.* Armonk, NY: M.E. Sharpe, xiii–xxvii.

Lundquist, Lennart J. 1987. *Implementation Steering: An Actor-Structure Approach.* Bickley, UK: Chartwell-Bratt.

Luttbeg, Norman R. 1981. "Where We Stand on Political Linkage," in Luttbeg, ed., *Public Opinion and Public Policy: Models of Political Linkage.* Itasca, IL: F.E. Peacock, 455–62.

Lutz, James M. 1989. "Emulation and Policy Adoptions in the Canadian Provinces," *Canadian Journal of Political Science* 22, 1: 147–54.

Macpherson, C.B. 1962. *The Political Theory of Possessive Individualism: Hobbes to Locke.* Oxford: Clarendon Press.

——. 1978. *The Life and Times of Liberal Democracy.* Oxford: Oxford University Press.

MacRae, Duncan, Jr. 1993. "Guidelines for Policy Discourse: Consensual versus Adversarial," in Fischer and Forester (1993: 291–318).

McAllister, James A. 1989. "Do Parties Make a Difference?" in A.G. Gagnon and A.B. Tanguay, eds, *Canadian Parties in Transition: Discourse, Organization, Representation.* Toronto: Nelson, 485–511.

McCool, Daniel. 1989. "Subgovernments and the Impact of Policy Fragmentation and Accommodation," *Policy Studies Review* 8, no. 2: 264–87.

——. 1998. "The Subsystem Family of Concepts: A Critique and a Proposal," *Political Research Quarterly* 51, no. 2: 551–70.

McFarland, Andrew S. 1987. "Interest Groups and Theories of Power in America," *British Journal of Political Science* 17, no. 2: 129–47.

McGann, James G. 2008. The Global "Go-To Think Tanks": *The Leading Public Policy Research Organizations in the World.* Philadelphia: stoneThink Tanks and Civil Societies Program.

——, and E.C. Johnson. 2005. *Comparative Think Tanks, Politics and Public Policy.* Cheltenham: Edward Elgar.

——, and R. Kent Weaver, eds. 1999. *Think Tanks and Civil Societies: Catalysts for Ideas and Action.* New Brunswick, NJ: Transaction

McRoberts, Kenneth. 1993. "Federal Structures and the Policy Process," in M. Michael Atkinson, ed., *Governing Canada: Institutions and Public Policy.* Toronto: Harcourt Brace Jovanovich.

March, James G., and Johan P. Olsen. 1998b. "The Institutional Dynamics of International Political Orders," *International Organization* 52: 943–69.

——, Martin Schulz, and Xueguang Zhou. 2000. *The Dynamics of Rules: Change in Organizational Codes.* Stanford, CA: Stanford University Press.

Marier, Patrik. 2008. "Empowering Epistemic Communities: Specialized Politicians, Policy Experts and Policy Reform," *West European Politics* 31, no. 3: 513–33.

Mathiason, John. 2007. *Invisible Governance: International Secretariats in Global Politics.* Bloomfield, NJ: Kumarian Press.

Minkenberg, Michael. 2001. "The Radical Right in Public Office: Agenda-Setting and Policy Effects," *West European Politics* 24, no. 4: 1–21.

Monroe, Alan D. 1979. "Consistency between Public Preferences and National Policy Decisions," *American Politics Quarterly* 7, no. 1: 3–19.

Nownes, Anthony J. 1995. "The Other Exchange: Public Interest Groups, Patrons, and Benefits," *Social Science Quarterly* 76, no. 2: 381–401.

——. 2000. "Policy Conflict and the Structure of Interest Communities," *American Politics Quarterly* 28, no. 3: 309–27.

——. 2004. "The Population Ecology of Interest Group Formation: Mobilizing for Gay and Lesbian Rights in the United States, 1950–98," *British Journal of Political Science* 34, no. 1: 49–67.

——, and Allan J. Cigler. 1995. "Public Interest Groups and the Road to Survival," *Polity* 27, no. 3: 380–404.

——, and Grant Neeley. 1996. "Toward an Explanation for Public Interest Group Formation and Proliferation: 'Seed Money,' Disturbances, Entrepreneurship, and Patronage," *Policy Studies Journal* 24, no. 1: 74–92.

Olson, David M., and Michael L. Mezey, eds. 1991. *Legislatures in the Policy Process: The Dilemmas of Economic Policy*. Cambridge: Cambridge University Press.

Olson, Mancur. 1982. *The Rise and Decline of Nations: Economic Growth, Stagflation, and Social Rigidities*. New Haven: Yale University Press.

Ouimet, Mathieu, and Vincent Lemieux. 2000. *Les Réseaux de Politique Publique: Un Bilan Critique et Une Voie de Formilization*. Québec: Université Laval Centre d'Analyse des Politiques Publiques.

Page, Benjamin I., and Robert Y. Shapiro. 1992. *The Rational Public: Fifty Years of Trends in American Policy Preferences*. Chicago: University of Chicago Press.

Painter, M., and J. Pierre. 2005. *Challenges to State Policy Capacity: Global Trends and Comparative Perspectives*. London: Palgrave Macmillan.

Pal, Leslie A. 1988. "Hands at the Helm? Leadership and Public Policy," in Pal and David Taras, eds, *Prime Ministers and Premiers: Political Leadership and Public Policy in Canada*. Scarborough, ON: Prentice-Hall, 16–26.

Pappi, Franz Urban, and Christian H.C.A. Henning. 1999. "The Organizationof Influence on the EC's Common Agricultural Policy: A Network Approach," *European Journal of Political Research* 36: 257–81.

Parenti, Michael. 1986. *Inventing Reality: The Politics of the Mass Media*. New York: St Martin's Press.

Pedersen, Lene Holm. 2007. "Ideas Are Transformed as They Transfer: A Comparative Study of Eco-Taxation in Scandinavia," *Journal of European Public Policy* 14, no. 1: 59–77.

Perl, Anthony and Donald J. White. 2002. "The Changing Role of Consultants in Canadian Policy Analysis," *Policy and Society* 21, no. 1: 49–73.

Perl, Anthony, Michael Howlett, and M. Ramesh. 2018. "Policy-Making and Truthiness: Can Existing Policy Models Cope with Politicized Evidence and Willful Ignorance in a 'Post-Fact' World?" *Policy Sciences* 51, no. 4 (December): 581–600.

Poel, Dale H. 1976. "The Diffusion of Legislation among the Canadian Provinces," *Canadian Journal of Political Science* 9: 605–26.

Pollock, Philip H., Stuart A. Lilie, and M. Elliot Vittes. 1989. "Hard Issues, Core Values and Vertical Constraint: The Case of Nuclear Power," *British Journal of Political Science* 23, no. 1: 29–50.

Preston, Lee E., and Duane Windsor. 1992. *The Rules of the Game in the Global Economy: Policy Regimes for International Business*. Boston: Kluwer.

Priest, Margot, and Aron Wohl. 1980. "The Growth of Federal and Provincial Regulation of Economic Activity 1867–1978," in W.T. Stanbury, ed., *Government Regulation: Scope, Growth, Process*. Montreal: Institute for Research on Public Policy.

Pritchard, David. 1992. "The News Media and Public Policy Agendas," in Kennamer (1992).

Pross, A. Paul. 1992. *Group Politics and Public Policy*. Toronto: Oxford University Press.

Przeworski, Adam. 1985. "Marxism and Rational Choice," *Politics & Society* 14, no. 4: 379–409.

———. 1991. *Democracy and the Market: Political and Economic Reforms in Eastern Europe and Latin America*. Cambridge: Cambridge University Press.

Qualter, Terence H. 1985. *Opinion Control in the Democracies*. London: Macmillan.

Ramesh, M. and Michael Howlett, eds. 2006. *Deregulation and Its Discontents: Rewriting the Rules in Asia*. Cheltenham: Edward Elgar.

Rein, Martin, Gosta Esping-Andersen, and Lee Rainwater, eds. 1987. *Stagnation and Renewal in Social Policy: The Rise and Fall of Policy Regimes*. Armonk, NY: M.E. Sharpe.

Rhodes, R.A.W. 1984. "Power-Dependence, Policy Communities and Intergovernmental Networks," *Public Administration Bulletin* 49: 4–31.

Ricci, David. 1993. *The Transformation of American Politics: The New Washington and the Rise of Think Tanks*. New Haven: Yale University Press.

Rich, A. 2004. *Think Tanks, Public Policy, and the Politics of Expertise*. New York: Cambridge University Press.

Richardson, Jeremy J. 1995. "EU Water Policy: Uncertain Agendas, Shifting Networks and Complex Coalitions," in H. Bressers, L.J. O'Toole, and J.

———. 1999. "Interest Groups, Multi-Arena Politics and Policy Change," in S.S. Nagel, ed., *The Policy Process*. Commack, NY: Nova Science, 65–100.

Riker, William H. and Grace A. Franklin. 1980. *Congress, the Bureaucracy, and Public Policy*, 3rd edn. Homewood, IL: Dorsey Press.

Risse-Kappen, Thomas. 1995. "Bringing Transnational Relations Back." In: *Non-State Actors, Domestic Structures and International Institutions*. Cambridge: Cambridge University Press.

Rittberger, Volker, and Peter Mayer, eds. 1993. *Regime Theory and International Relations*. Oxford: Clarendon Press.

Rose, Richard. 1980. *Do Parties Make a Difference?* London: Macmillan.

Rosenau, James N. 1969. Linkage Politics: *Essays on the Convergence of National and International Systems*. New York: Collier-Macmillan.

Rousseau, Jean-Jacques. 1973. *The Social Contract and Discourses*. London: J.M. Dent.

Sabatier, Paul A. 1987. "Knowledge, Policy-Oriented Learning, and Policy Change," *Knowledge: Creation, Diffusion, Utilization* 8, no. 4: 649–92.

———. 1988. "An Advocacy Coalition Framework of Policy Change and the Role of Policy-Oriented Learning Therein," *Policy Sciences* 21, nos. 2 and 3: 129–68.

———. 1993 "Top-down and Bottom-up Approaches to Implementation Research," in Hill (1993).

———, and Hank C. Jenkins-Smith. 1993b. "The Advocacy Coalition Framework: Assessment, Revisions, and Implications for Scholars and Practitioners," in Sabatier and Jenkins-Smith (1993a).

Salisbury, Robert H., et al. 1987. "Who Works with Whom? Interest Group Alliances and Opposition," *American Political Science Review* 81, no. 4: 1217–34.

Sandel, Michael J., ed. 1984. *Liberalism and Its Critics*. Oxford: Blackwell.

Savoie, Donald J. 1999. *Governing from the Centre: The Concentration of Power in Canadian Politics*. Toronto: University of Toronto Press.

Scharpf, Fritz W. 1991. "Political Institutions, Decision Styles, and Policy Choices," in R.M. Czada and A. Windhoff-Heritier, eds, *Political Choice: Institutions, Rules and the Limits of Rationality*. Frankfurt: Campus Verlag, 53–86.

———. 1997. *Games Real Actors Play: Actor-Centered Institutionalism in Policy Research*. Boulder, CO: Westview Press.

Schattschneider, E.E. 1960. *The Semi-sovereign People: A Realist's View of Democracy in America*. New York: Holt, Rinehart and Winston.

Schneider, Joseph W. 1985. "Social Problems Theory: The Constructionist View," *Annual Review of Sociology* 11: 209–29.

Schott, Kerry. 1984. Policy, Power and Order: *The Persistence of Economic Problems in Capitalist States*. New Haven: Yale University Press.

Schulman, Paul R. 1988. "The Politics of 'Ideational Policy,'" *Journal of Politics* 50: 263–91.

Schultz, Richard, and Alan Alexandroff. 1985. *Economic Regulation and the Federal System*. Toronto: University of Toronto Press.

Sell, S.K., and A. Prakash. 2004. "Using Ideas Strategically: The Contest between Business and NGO Networks in Intellectual Property Rights," *International Studies Quarterly* 48, no. 1: 143–75.

Shapiro, Robert Y., and Lawrence R. Jacobs. 1989. "The Relationship between Public Opinion and Public Policy: A Review," in S. Long, ed., *Political Behaviour Annual*. Boulder, CO: Westview Press.

Siaroff, Alan. 1999. "Corporatism in 24 Industrial Democracies: Meaning and Measurement," *European Journal of Political Research* 36: 175–205.

Smith, Martin J. 1993. *Pressure, Power and Policy: State Autonomy and Policy Networks in Britain and the United States*. Aldershot: Harvester Wheatsheaf.

Soroka, Stuart. 2002. *Agenda-Setting Dynamics in Canada*. Vancouver: University of British Columbia Press.

Speers, Kimberly. 2007. "The Invisible Public Service: Consultants and Public Policy in Canada," in Dobuzinskis et al. (2007: 220–31).

Spitzer, Robert J., ed. 1993. *Media and Public Policy*. Westport, Conn.: Praeger.

Stewart, John. 1974. *The Canadian House of Commons*. Montreal and Kingston: McGill-Queen's University Press.

Stoker, Robert P. 1989. "A Regime Framework for Implementation Analysis," *Policy Studies Review* 9, 1.

Stone, Diane A. 1996. Capturing the Political Imagination. London: Frank Cass.

———. 2002. "Introduction: Knowledge and Advocacy Networks," *Global Networks* 2: 1–12.

———. 2007. "Recycling Bins, Garbage Cans, or Think Tanks? Three Myths Regarding Policy Analysis Institutes," Public Administration 85, 2: 259–78.

———, Andrew Denham, and Mark Garnett. 1998. *Think Tanks across Nations: A Comparative Approach*. Manchester: Manchester University Press.

———. 2008. "Global Public Policy, Transnational Policy Communities, and Their Networks," *Policy Studies Journal* 36, no. 1: 19–38.

Surel, Yves. 2000. "The Role of Cognitive and Normative Frames in Policy-Making," *Journal of European Public Policy* 7, no. 4: 495–512.

Sutherland, Sharon L. 1993. "The Public Service and Policy Development," in M. Michael Atkinson, ed., *Governing Canada: Institutions and Public Policy*. Toronto: Harcourt Brace Jovanovich.

Swank, Duane. 2000. *Diminished Democracy? Global Capital, Political Institutions, and Policy Change in Developed Welfare States*. New York: Cambridge University Press.

Taylor, Andrew J. 1989. *Trade Unions and Politics: A Comparative Introduction*. Basingstoke: Macmillan.

Thacher, D., and M. Rein. 2004. "Managing Value Conflict in Public Policy," *Governance* 17, no. 4: 457–86.

t'Hart, Paul, and Ariadne Vromen. 2008. "A New Era for Think Tanks in Public Policy? International Trends, Australian Realities," *Australian Journal of Public Administration* 67, no. 2: 135–48.

Therborn, G. 1977. "The Rule of Capital and the Rise of Democracy," *New Left Review* 103.

Thomson, Robert. 2001. "The Programme to Policy Linkage: The Fulfilment of Election Pledges on Socio-Economic Policy in the Netherlands, 1986–1998," *European Journal of Political Research* 40: 171–97.

Timmermans, Arco, and Ivar Bleiklie. 1999. "Institutional Conditions for Policy Design: Types of Arenas and Rules of the Game," ECPR Joint Sessions of Workshops, Mannheim.

Torgerson, Douglas. 1996. "Power and Insight in Policy Discourse: Post-Positivism and Policy Discourse," in L. Dobuzinskis, M. Howlett, and D. Laycock, eds, *Policy Studies in Canada: The State of the Art*. Toronto: University of Toronto Press, 266–98.

UNCTAD, UN. 2007. "World Investment Report 2007: Transnational Corporations, Extractive Industries and Development." United Nations Conference on Trade and Development, Geneva: United Nations.

———. 2017. "World Investment Report 2017: Investment and the Digital Economy." United Nations Conference on Trade and Development, Geneva: United Nations.

Unger, Brigitte, and Frans van Waarden. 1995. "Introduction: An Interdisciplinary Approach to Convergence," in Unger and van Waarden, eds, *Convergence or Diversity? Internationalization and Economic Policy Response*. Aldershot: Avebury, 1–35.

van den Berg, Caspar, Michael Howlett, Andrea Migone, Michael Howard, Frida Pemer, and Helen M. Gunter. 2020. *Policy Consultancy in Comparative Perspective: Patterns, Nuances and Implications of the Contractor State*. Cambridge, UK; New York, NY: Cambridge University Press.

Verheijen, T. 1999. *Civil Service Systems in Central and Eastern Europe*. Cheltenham: Edward Elgar.

Walker, Jack L. 1977. "Setting the Agenda in the U.S. Senate: A Theory of Problem Selection," *British Journal of Political Science* 7: 423–45.

———. 1991. *Mobilizing Interest Groups in America: Patrons, Professions and Social Movements*. Ann Arbor: University of Michigan Press.

Walsh, James I. 1994. "Institutional Constraints and Domestic Choices: Economic Convergence and Exchange Rate Policy in France and Italy," *Political Studies* 42: 243–58.

Warwick, Paul V. 2000. "Policy Horizons in West European Parliamentary Systems," *European Journal of Political Research* 38: 37–61.

Weaver, R. Kent. 1988. *Automatic Government: The Politics of Indexation*. Washington: Brookings Institution.

———. 1989. "The Changing World of Think Tanks," *PS: Political Science and Politics* 22: 563–78.

———, and Bert A. Rockman, eds. 1993a. *Do Institutions Matter? Government Capabilities in the United States and Abroad*. Washington: Brookings Institution.

Weiss, Carol H. 1977a. *Using Social Research in Public Policy Making*. Lexington, MA: Lexington Books.

———. 1977b. "Research for Policy's Sake: The Enlightenment Function of Social Science Research," *Policy Analysis* 3, no. 4: 531–45.

Weiss, Linda. 1999. "Globalization and National Governance: Autonomy or Interdependence," *Review of International Studies* 25 (supp.): 59–88.

Whitley, Edgar A., Ian R. Hosein, Ian O. Angell, and Simon Davies. 2007. "Reflections on the Academic Policy Analysis Process and the UK Identity Cards Scheme," *The Information Society* 23: 51–8.

Wilensky, Harold L. 1975. *The Welfare State and Equality: Structural and Ideological Roots of Public Expenditures*. Berkeley: University of California Press.

Wilks, Stephen, and Maurice Wright. 1987. "Conclusion: Comparing Government–Industry Relations: States, Sectors, and Networks," in Wilks and Wright, eds, *Comparative Government–Industry Relations: Western Europe, the United States, and Japan*. Oxford: Clarendon Press, 274–313.

Wilson, Graham K. 1990a. *Business and Politics: A Comparative Introduction*, 2nd edn. London: Macmillan.

Woodward, Richard. 2004. "The Organisation for Economic Cooperation and Development," *New Political Economy* 9, no. 1: 113–27.

Woolley, Samuel C., and Philip N. Howard, eds. 2018. *Computational Propaganda: Political Parties, Politicians, and Political Manipulation on Social Media*. Reprint edition. New York, NY: Oxford University Press.

Wukich, Clayton, and Ines Mergel. 2016. "Reusing Social Media Information in Government," *Government Information Quarterly* 33: 305-312.

Young, Oran R. 1980. "International Regimes: Problems of Concept Formation," *World Politics* 32: 331–56.

Chapter 4 Sources

Aaron, H.J. 1967. "Social Security: International Comparison," in O. Eckstein, ed., *Studies in the Economics of Income Maintenance*. Washington: Brookings Institution, 13–49.

Ackrill, R., Kay, A., and Zahariadis, N. 2013. "Ambiguity, multiple streams, and EU policy," *Journal of European Public Policy* 20, no. 6: 871–887.

Adams, Greg D. 1997. "Abortion: Evidence of an Issue Evolution," *American Journal of Political Science* 41, no. 3: 718–37.

Adler, Emanuel, and Peter M. Haas. 1992. "Conclusion: Epistemic Communities, World Order, and the Creation of a Reflective Research Program," *International organization* 46, no. 1: 367–90.

Arts, B., Leroy, P., and Van Tatenhove, J. 2006. "Political modernization and policy arrangements: a framework for understanding environmental policy change," *Public Organization Review* 6, no. 2: 93–106.

Bachrach, Peter, and Morton S. Baratz. 1962. "Decisions and Non-decisions: An Analytical Framework," *American Political Science Review* 56, no. 2: 632–42.

———, and ———. 1970. *Power and Poverty: Theory and Practice*. New York: Oxford University Press.

Baumgartner, Frank R., and Bryan D. Jones. 1991. "Agenda Dynamics and Policy Subsystems," *Journal of Politics* 53, no. 4: 1044–74.

———, and ———. 1993. *Agendas and Instability in American Politics*. Chicago: University of Chicago Press.

———, and ———. 1994. "Attention, Boundary Effects, and Large-Scale Policy Change in Air Transportation Policy," in D.A. Rochefort and R.W. Cobb, eds, *The Politics of Problem Definition: Shaping the Policy Agenda*. Lawrence: University Press of Kansas.

Béland, Daniel. 2016. "Kingdon Reconsidered: Ideas, Interests and Institutions in

Comparative Policy Analysis," *Journal of Comparative Policy Analysis: Research and Practice* 18, no. 3 (May 26): 228–42. doi:10.1080/13876988.2015.1029770.

Beland, Daniel, and Michael Howlett. "How Solutions Chase Problems: Instrument Constituencies in the Policy Process," *Governance*, 2016.

Bennett, Colin J. 1991. "What Is Policy Convergence and What Causes It?" *British Journal of Political Science* 21, no. 2: 215–33.

Berger, Peter L., and Thomas Luckmann. 1966. *The Social Construction of Reality: A Treatise in the Sociology of Knowledge*. New York: Doubleday.

Biddle, J. C., and Koontz, T. M. 2014. "Goal Specificity: A Proxy Measure for Improvements in Environmental Outcomes in Collaborative Governance," *Journal of Environmental Management* 145: 268–76.

Birkland, Thomas A. 1997. *After Disaster: Agenda Setting, Public Policy and Focusing Events*. Washington: Georgetown University Press.

——. 1998. "Focusing Events, Mobilization, and Agenda Setting," *Journal of Public Policy* 18, no. 1: 53–74.

——, and Regina G Lawrence. 2009. "Media Framing and Policy Change After Columbine," *American Behavioral Scientist* 52, no. 10 (June 1): 1405–25. doi:10.1177/0002764209332555.

Bleich, Erik. 2002. "Integrating Ideas into Policy-Making Analysis: Frames and Race Policies in Britain and France," *Comparative Political Studies* 35, no. 9: 1054–76.

Boddy, Raford, and James Crotty. 1975. "Class Conflict and Macro-Policy: The Political Business Cycle," *Review of Radical Political Economics* 7, no. 1: 1–19.

Boin, R. Arjen, and Marc H.P. Otten. 1996. "Beyond the Crisis Window for Reform: Some Ramifications for Implementation," *Journal of Contingencies and Crisis Management* 4, no. 3: 149–61.

Bonafont, Laura Chaqués, Frank R. Baumgartner, and Anna Palau. 2015. *Agenda Dynamics in Spain*. London: Palgrave Macmillan.

Boswell, Christina. 2012. "How Information Scarcity Influences the Policy Agenda: Evidence from U.K. Immigration

Policy," *Governance* 25, no. 3: 367–389. doi:10.1111/j.1468–0491.2012.01570.x.

Braun, Dietmar. 1999. "Interests or Ideas? An Overview of Ideational Concepts in Public Policy Research," in D. Braun and A. Busch, eds, *Public Policy and Political Ideas*. Cheltenham: Edward Elgar, 11–29.

Cairney, P. 2012. *Understanding Public Policy*. Basingstoke, UK: Palgrave

——, and M.D. Jones. 2015. "Kingdon's Multiple Streams Approach: What Is the Empirical Impact of This Universal Theory?" *Policy Studies Journal*. doi:10.1111/psj.12111

——, and ——. 2016. "Kingdon's Multiple Streams Approach: What Is the Empirical Impact of This Universal Theory?" *Policy Studies Journal* 44, no. 1 (February 1): 37–58. doi:10.1111/psj.12111.

Cameron, David R. 1984. "Social Democracy, Corporatism, Labour Quiescence and the Representation of Economic Interest in Advanced Capitalist Society," in J.H. Goldthorpe, ed., *Order and Conflict in Contemporary Capitalism*. Oxford: Clarendon Press.

Campbell, John L. 1998. "Institutional Analysis and the Role of Ideas in Political Economy," *Theory and Society* 27, no. 5: 377–409.

Chadwick, Andrew. 2000. "Studying Political Ideas: A Public Political Discourse Approach," *Political Studies* 48, no. 2: 283–301.

Churchman, C. West. 1967. "Wicked Problems," *Management Science* 14, no. 4: B141–2.

Clark, B.T. 2004. "Agenda Setting and Issue Dynamics: Dam Breaching on the Lower Snake River," *Society and Natural Resources* 17: 599–609.

Cnossen, S. 2005. *Theory and Practice of Excise Taxation: Smoking, Drinking, Gambling, Polluting and Driving*. Oxford: Oxford University Press.

Cobb, Roger W., and Charles D. Elder. 1972. *Participation in American Politics: The Dynamics of Agenda-Building*. Boston: Allyn and Bacon.

——, and D.M. Primo. 2003. *The Plane Truth: Airline Crashes, the Media, and Transportation Policy*. Washington: Brookings Institution.

——, J.K. Ross, and M.H. Ross. 1976. "Agenda Building as a Comparative Political Process," *American Political Science Review* 70, no. 1: 126–38.

————, and Marc Howard Ross, eds. 1997a. *Cultural Strategies of Agenda Denial: Avoidance, Attack and Redefinition*. Lawrence: University Press of Kansas.

Colebatch, H. K. 2006. *Beyond the Policy Cycle: The Policy Process in Australia*. Crows Nest: Allen and Unwin.

Cook, F.L., et al. 1983. "Media and Agenda Setting: Effects on the Public, Interest Group Leaders, Policy Makers, and Policy," *Public Opinion Quarterly* 47, no. 1: 16–35.

Copeland, Paul, and Scott James. 2014. "Policy Windows, Ambiguity and Commission Entrepreneurship: Explaining the Relaunch of the European Union's Economic Reform Agenda," *Journal of European Public Policy* 21, no. 1 (January 2): 1–19. doi:10.1080/13501763.2013.800789.

Cutright, P. 1965. "Political Structure, Economic Development, and National Security Programs," *American Journal of Sociology* 70, no. 5: 537–50.

Daugbjerg, Carsten and A.B. Perdersen. 2004. "New Policy Ideas and Old Policy Networks: Implementing Green Taxation in Scandinavia," *Journal of Public Policy* 24, no. 2: 219–49.

————, and J. Studsgaard. 2005. "Issue Redefinition, Venue Change and Radical Agricultural Policy Reforms in Sweden and New Zealand," *Scandinavian Political Studies* 28, no. 2: 103–24.

Daw, Jamie R., Steven G. Morgan, Paige A. Thomson, and Michael R. Law. 2013. "Here Today, Gone Tomorrow: The Issue Attention Cycle and National Print Media Coverage of Prescription Drug Financing in Canada," *Health Policy* 110, no. 1 (April): 67–75. doi:10.1016/j.healthpol.2013.01.006.

Debnam, Geoffrey. 1975. "Non-decisions and Power: The Two Faces of Bachrach and Baratz," *American Political Science Review* 69, no. 3: 889–900.

Dery, David. 2000. "Agenda Setting and Problem Definition," *Policy Studies* 21, no. 1: 37–47.

Dion, Leon. 1973. "The Politics of Consultation," *Government and Opposition* 8, no. 3: 332–53.

Dodge, Martin, and Christopher Hood. 2002. "Pavlovian Policy Responses to Media Feeding Frenzies? Dangerous Drugs Regulation in Comparative Perspective," *Journal of Contingencies and Crisis Management* 10, no. 1: 1–13.

Dostal, J.M. 2004. "Campaigning on Expertise: How the OECD Framed Welfare and Labour Market Policies—and Why Success Could Trigger Failure," *Journal of European Public Policy* 11, no. 3: 440–60.

Dowding, Keith, Andrew Hindmoor, and Aaron Martin. 2015. "The Comparative Policy Agendas Project: Theory, Measurement and Findings," *Journal of Public Policy* FirstView (May): 1–23. doi:10.1017/S0143814X15000124.

————, Andrew Hindmoor, Richard Iles, and Peter John. 2010. "Policy Agendas in Australian Politics: The Governor-General's Speeches, 1945–2008," *Australian Journal of Political Science* 45, no. 4: 533. doi:10.1080/10361146.2010.517174.

Downs, Anthony. 1972. "Up and Down with Ecology—the "Issue-Attention Cycle," *The Public Interest* 28: 38–50.

Durr, Robert H. 1993. "What Moves Policy Sentiment?" *American Political Science Review* 87, no. 1: 158–72.

Dye, Thomas R. 1966. *Politics, Economics, and the Public: Policy Outcomes in the American States*. Chicago: Rand McNally.

Edelman, Murray. 1988. *Constructing the Political Spectacle*. Chicago: University of Chicago Press.

Elliott, Euel, and Andrew I.E. Ewoh. 2000. "The Evolution of an Issue: The Rise and Decline of Affirmative Action," *Policy Studies Reviews* 17, nos. 2 and 3: 212–37.

Erbring, Lutz, Edie N. Goldenberg, and Arthur H. Miller. 1980. "Front Page News and Real-World Cues: A New Look at Agenda-Setting by the Media," *American Journal of Political Science* 24, no. 1: 16–49.

Epp, Derek A., and Frank R. Baumgartner. "Complexity, Capacity, and Budget Punctuations," *Policy Studies Journal*, February 1, 2016. doi:10.1111/psj.12148.

Esping-Andersen, Gosta. 1985. "Power and Distributional Regimes," *Politics and Society* 14, no. 2: 223–56.

————, Gosta and Walter Korpi. 1984. "Social Policy as Class Politics in Post-War Capitalism: Scandinavia, Austria, and Germany," in J.H. Goldthorpe, ed., *Order and Conflict in Contemporary Capitalism*. Oxford: Clarendon Press.

Felstiner, W.L., Richard L. Abel, and Austin Sarat. 1980–1. "The Emergence and Transformation of Disputes: Naming, Blaming, Claiming," *Law and Society Review* 15, nos. 3 and 4: 631–54.

Fischer, F. 2003. *Reframing Public Policy: Discursive Politics and Deliberative Practices.* Oxford: Oxford University Press.

———, and John Forester, eds. 1993. *The Argumentative Turn in Policy Analysis and Planning.* Durham, NC: Duke University Press.

Flathman, Richard E. 1966. *The Public Interest: An Essay Concerning the Normative Discourse of Politics.* New York: Wiley.

Flemming, Roy B., B. Dan Wood, and John Bohte. 1999. "Attention to Issues in a System of Separated Powers: The Macrodynamics of American Policy Agendas," *Journal of Politics* 61, no. 1: 76–108.

Foot, David K. 1979. "Political Cycles, Economic Cycles and the Trend in Public Employment in Canada," in Meyer W. Bucovetsky, ed., *Studies in Public Employment and Compensation in Canada.* Toronto: Butterworths for Institute for Research on Public Policy, 65–80.

Foucault, Michel. 1972. "The Discourse on Language," in Foucault, ed., *The Archaeology of Knowledge.* New York: Pantheon.

Freeman, Jody. 1997. "Collaborative Governance in the Administrative State," *UCLA Law Review* 45, no. 1: 1–98.

French, M., and J. Phillips. 2004. "Windows and Barriers in Policy-Making: Food Poisoning in Britain, 1945–56," *Social History of Medicine* 17, no. 2: 269–84.

Frey, Bruno S. 1978. "Politico-Economic Models and Cycles," *Journal of Public Economics* 9: 203–20.

Frey, Frederick W. 1971. "Comment: On Issues and Non-issues in the Study of Power," *American Political Science Review* 65: 1081–1101.

George, Alexander L. 1969. "The "Operational Code": A Neglected Approach to the Study of Political Leaders and Decision-Making," *International Studies Quarterly* 13: 190–222.

Goffman, Erving. 1974. *Frame Analysis: An Essay on the Organization of Experience.* Cambridge, MA: Harvard University Press.

Goldstein, Judith, and Robert O. Keohane, eds. 1993b. "Ideas and Foreign Policy: An Analytical Framework," in Goldstein and Keohane (1993: 3–30).

Gough, C. and Shackley, S. 2001. "The Respectable Politics of Climate Change: The Epistemic Communities and NGOs," *International Affairs*, 77: 329–346.

Gough, Clair, Ian Taylor, and Simon Shackley. 2002. "Burying Carbon Under the Sea: An Initial Exploration of Public Opinions," *Energy & Environment* 13, no. 6: 883–900.

Graziano, Paolo R., and Marco Percoco. 2016. "Agenda Setting and the Political Economy of Fear: How Crime News Influences Voters' Beliefs," *International Political Science Review*, September 5, 192512116656947. doi:10.1177/0192512116656947.

Green-Pedersen, Christoffer. 2004. "The Dependent Variable Problem within the Study of Welfare State Retrenchment: Defining the Problem and Looking for Solutions," *Journal of Comparative Policy Analysis* 6, no. 1: 3–14.

———, and Peter B. Mortensen. 2010. "Who Sets the Agenda and Who Responds to It in the Danish Parliament? A New Model of Issue Competition and Agenda-Setting," *European Journal of Political Research* 49, no. 2 (March): 257–81. doi:10.1111/j.1475–6765.2009.01897.x.

Greenwood, Molly M., Mary E. Sorenson, and Benjamin R. Warner. 2016. "Ferguson on Facebook: Political Persuasion in a New Era of Media Effects," *Computers in Human Behavior* 57 (April): 1–10. doi:10.1016/j.chb.2015.12.003.

Haas, Peter M. 1989. "Do Regimes Matter? Epistemic Communities and Mediterranean Pollution Control," *International organization* 43, no. 3: 377–403.

Haas, Peter M. 1992. "Introduction: Epistemic Communities and International Policy Coordination," *International Organization* 46, no. 1: 1–36.

Haider-Markel, Donald P., and Mark R. Joslyn. 2001. "Gun Policy, Opinion, Tragedy and Blame Attribution: The Conditional Influence of Issue Frames," *Journal of Politics* 63, no. 2: 520–43.

Halpern, Daniel, and Jennifer Gibbs. 2013. "Social Media as a Catalyst for Online Deliberation? Exploring the Affordances of Facebook and Youtube For Political Expression," *Computers in Human Behavior* 29 no. 3: 1159–68.

Hammond, Thomas H. 1986. "Agenda Control, Organizational Structure, and Bureaucratic Politics," *American Journal of Political Science* 30, no. 2: 379–420.

Hancock, M. Donald. 1983. "Comparative Public Policy: An Assessment," in A.W. Finifter, ed., *Political Science: The State of the Discipline*. Washington: American Political Science Association, 283–308.

Hansford, T.G. 2004. "Lobbying Strategies, Venue Selection, and Organized Interest Involvement at the U.S. Supreme Court," *American Politics Research* 32, no. 2: 170–97.

Harring, Niklas, Sverker C. Jagers, and Johan Martinsson. 2011. "Explaining Ups and Downs in the Public's Environmental Concern in Sweden The Effects of Ecological Modernization, the Economy, and the Media," *Organization and Environment* 24, no. 4 (December 1): 388–403. doi:10.1177/1086026611420300.

Head, Brian, Michele Ferguson, Adrian Cherney, and Paul Boreham. 2014. "Are Policy-Makers Interested in Social Research? Exploring the Sources and Uses of Valued Information among Public Servants in Australia," *Policy and Society*, Contemporary Policy Work in Subnational States and NGOs, 33, no. 2 (June 2014): 89–101. doi:10.1016/j.polsoc.2014.04.004.

Heidenheimer, Arnold J., Hugh Heclo, and Carolyn Teich Adams, eds. 1975. *Comparative Public Policy: The Politics of Social Choice in Europe and America*. New York: St Martin's Press.

Herweg, N., Huss, C., and Zohlnhöfer, R. 2015. "Straightening the Three Streams: Theorising Extensions of the Multiple Streams Framework," *European Journal of Political Research*.

Hilgartner, Stephen, and Charles L. Bosk. 1981. "The Rise and Fall of Social Problems: A Public Arenas Model," *American Journal of Sociology* 94, no. 1: 53–78.

Hisschemoller, Matthijs, and Rob Hoppe. 1995. "Coping with Intractable Controversies: The Case for Problem Structuring in

Policy Design and Analysis," *Knowledge and Policy* 8, no. 4: 40–61.

Hofferbert, Richard I. 1974. *The Study of Public Policy*. Indianapolis: Bobbs-Merrill.

Hogwood, Brian W. 1992. *Ups and Downs: Is There an Issue-Attention Cycle in Britain?* Glasgow: Strathclyde Papers in Government and Politics no. 89.

Holzner, Burkart, and John H. Marx. 1979. *Knowledge Application: The Knowledge System in Society*. Wellesley, MA: Allyn and Bacon.

Howlett, M. 1997. "Issue-Attention and Punctuated Equilibria Frameworks Reconsidered: An Empirical Examination of the Dynamics of Agenda-Setting in Canada," *Canadian Journal of Political Science* 30, no. 1: 3–29.

———. 1997b. "Predictable and Unpredictable Policy Windows: Issue, Institutional and Exogenous Correlates of Canadian Federal Agenda-Setting," paper presented to the annual meeting of the Canadian Political Science Association, St John's, NL.

———. 1998. "Predictable and Unpredictable Policy Windows: Institutional and Exogenous Correlates of Canadian Federal Agenda-Setting," *Canadian Journal of Political Science/Revue Canadienne de Science Politique* 31, no. 3: 495–524.

———, and Janet S. Cuenca. 2016. "The Use of Indicators in Environmental Policy Appraisal: Lessons from the Design and Evolution of Water Security Policy Measures," *Journal of Environmental Policy & Planning* (July 19): 1–15. doi:10.1080/1523908X.2016.1207507.

———, Ramesh, M., and Perl, A. 2009. *Studying Public Policy: Policy Cycles & Policy Subsystems,* 3rd edn. Toronto: Oxford University Press.

———, McConnell, A. and Perl, A. 2015. "Streams and stages: Reconciling Kingdon and policy process theory," *European Journal of Political Research.* doi:10.1111/1475-6765.12064.

———, Allan McConnell, and Anthony Perl. 2016. "Moving Policy Theory Forward: Connecting Multiple Stream and Advocacy Coalition Frameworks to Policy Cycle Models of Analysis," *Australian*

Journal of Public Administration, March 1. doi:10.1111/1467–8500.12191.

Htun, Mala, and S. Laurel Weldon. 2012. "The Civic Origins of Progressive Policy Change: Combating Violence against Women in Global Perspective, 1975–2005," *American Political Science Review*, 106, no. 3: 548–69. doi:10.1017/S0003055412000226.

Jann, W. and Wegrich, K. 2007. In *Theories of the Policy Cycle*. Handbook of public policy analysis: theory, politics, and methods / edited by Frank Fischer, Gerald J. Miller, and Mara S. Sidney. New York: Routledge.

Jenson, Jane. 1991. "All the World's a Stage: Ideas about Political Space and Time," *Studies in Political Economy* 36: 43–72.

Jeon, Yongjoo, and Donald P. Haider-Markel. 2001. "Tracing Issue Definition and Policy Change: An Analysis of Disability Issue Images and Policy Response," *Policy Studies Journal* 29, no. 2: 215–31.

John, Peter, and Shaun Bevan. 2012. "What are Policy Punctuations? Large Changes in the Legislative Agenda of the UK Government, 1911–2008," *Policy Studies Journal* 40, no. 1: 89–108.

John, Peter, and Will Jennings. 2010. "Punctuations and Turning Points in British Politics: The Policy Agenda of the Queen's Speech, 1940–2005," *British Journal of Political Science* 40 no. 3: 561–86.

John, P., A. Bertelli, W. Jennings, and S. Bevan. 2013. *Policy Agendas in British Politics*. London: Springer.

———, and H. Margetts. 2003. "Policy Punctuations in the UK: Fluctuations and Equilibria in Central Government Expenditure Since 1951," *Public Administration* 81, no. 3: 411–32.

Johnson, Genevieve Fuji. 2007. "The Discourse of Democracy in Canadian Nuclear Waste Management Policy," *Policy Science* 40: 79–99.

Johnston, Richard. 1986. *Public Opinion and Public Policy in Canada: Questions of Confidence*. Toronto: University of Toronto Press.

Jones, Bryan D. 1994. *Reconceiving Decision-Making in Democratic Politics: Attention, Choice and Public Policy*. Chicago: University of Chicago Press.

———, and Frank R. Baumgartner. 2002. "Punctuations, Ideas and Public Policy," in *Policy Dynamics*, 293–306. Chicago: University of Chicago Press.

Jones, Bryan D., and Frank R. Baumgartner. 2005. *The Politics of Attention: How Government Prioritizes Problems*. Chicago: University of Chicago Press.

———, Frank R. Baumgartner, Christian Breunig, Christopher Wlezien, Stuart Soroka, Martial Foucault, Abel François, Christoffer Green-Pederson, Chris Koski, Peter John, Peter B. Mortensen, Frederic Varone, and Stefaan Walrave. 2009. "A General Empirical Law of Public Budgets: A Comparative Analysis," *American Journal of Political Science* 53, no. 4: 855–73.

Jordan, A. and Huitema, D. 2014. "Innovations in Climate Policy: The Politics of Invention, Diffusion, and Evaluation," *Environmental Politics* 23, no. 5: 715–734

Katzenstein, Peter J. 1985. *Small States in World Markets: Industrial Policy in Europe*. Ithaca, NY: Cornell University Press.

Keeler, John T.S. 1993. "Opening the Window for Reform: Mandates, Crises and Extraordinary Policy-Making," *Comparative Political Studies* 25, no. 4: 433–86.

Kerr, Clark. 1983. The Future of Industrial Societies: Convergence or Continuing Diversity? Cambridge, MA: Harvard University Press.

King, Anthony. 1973. "Ideas, Institutions and the Policies of Governments: A Comparative Analysis: Part III," *British Journal of Political Science* 3, no. 4: 409–23.

Kingdon, John W. 1984. *Agendas, Alternatives and Public Policies*. Boston: Little, Brown.

———. 2010. *Agendas, Alternatives and Public Policies*, 2nd edn. Boston: Longman.

Korpi, Walter, 1980. "Social Policy and Distributional Conflict in Capitalist Democracies," *West European Politics* 3: 296–316.

———. 1983. *The Democratic Class Struggle*. London: Routledge & Kegan Paul.

Knaggård, Å. 2015. "The Multiple Streams Framework and the Problem Broker," *European Journal of Political Research*.

Landry, R., M. Lamari, and N. Amara. 2003. "The Extent and Determinants of the Utilization of University Research in Government Agencies," *Public Administration Review*. 63, no. 2: 192–205.

Lehtonen, Markku. 2009. "Indicators as an Appraisal Technology: Framework for Analysing Policy Influence and Early Insights into Indicator Role in the UK Energy Sector." Paper presented at the ECPR Joint Sessions of Workshops.

———. 2013. "Indicators as a Tool for Policy Formulation." Paper prepared for the workshop on the role of analytical tools within the Policy Formulation Process, London, April 18–19, 2013.

———, Léa Sébastien, and Tom Bauler. 2016. "The Multiple Roles of Sustainability Indicators in Informational Governance: Between Intended Use and Unanticipated Influence," *Current Opinion in Environmental Sustainability, Sustainability Governance and Transformation* 18 (February 2016): 1–9. doi:10.1016/j.cosust.2015.05.009.

Levin, K., Cashore, B., Bernstein, S. and Auld, G., 2012. "Overcoming the tragedy of super wicked problems: constraining our future selves to ameliorate global climate change," *Policy Sciences* 45: 123–152.

Lewis-Beck, Michael S. 1988. *Economics and Elections: The Major Western Democracies.* Ann Arbor: University of Michigan Press.

Lober, Douglas J. 1997. "Explaining the Formation of Business–Environmentalist Collaborations: Collaborative Windows and the Paper Task Force," *Policy Sciences* 30: 1–24.

Locksley, Gareth. 1980. "The Political Business Cycle: Alternative Interpretations," in Paul Whiteley, ed., *Models of Political Economy.* London: Sage.

McBeth, Mark K., Elizabeth A. Shanahan, and Michael D. Jones. 2005. "The Science of Storytelling: Measuring Policy Briefs in Greater Yellowstone," *Society and Natural Resources* 18: 413–29.

McCallum, B. 1978. "The Political Business Cycle: An Empirical Test," *Southern Economic Journal* 44: 504–15.

McCool, Daniel. 1989. "Subgovernments and the Impact of Policy Fragmentation and Accommodation," *Policy Studies Review* 8, 2: 264–87.

———. 1998. "The Subsystem Family of Concepts: A Critique and a Proposal," *Political Research Quarterly* 51, no. 2: 551–70.

McRobbie, A., and S.L. Thornton. 1995. "Rethinking "Moral Panic" for Multi-Mediated Social Worlds," *British Journal of Sociology* 46, no. 4: 559–74.

Mann, C., and Simons, A. 2014. "Local Emergence and International Developments of Conservation Trading Systems: Innovation Dynamics and Related Problems," *Environmental Conservation,* 1–10.

Marsh, Ian. 2013. "Setting the Post War Australian Policy Agenda–Causes and Content," *Australian Journal of Public Administration* 72, no. 4: 473–480. doi:10.1111/1467–8500.12046.

Maurer, Andreas, and Roderick Parkes. 2007. "The Prospects for Policy-Change in EU Asylum Policy: Venues and Image at the European Level," *European Journal of Migration and Law* 9: 173–205.

May, Peter J, Joshua Sapotichne, and Samuel Workman. 2007. "Policy Disruption across Subsystems: Terrorism, Public Risks, and Homeland Security," paper presented at the American Political Science Association annual meeting.

Mazmanian, Daniel A., and Paul A. Sabatier. 1980. "A Multivariate Model of Public PolicyMaking," *American Journal of Political Science* 24, no. 3: 439–68.

Meijerink, S.; Huitema, D. 2010. "Policy Entrepreneurs and Change Strategies: Lessons from Sixteen Case Studies of Water Transitions Around the Globe," *Ecology and Society* 15: 21.

Mertha, Andrew C., and William R. Lowry. 2006. "Seminal Events and Policy Change in China, Australia and the United States," *Comparative Politics* 39, no. 1: 1–20.

Mintrom, Michael. 1997. "Policy Entrepreneurs and the Diffusion of Innovation," *American Journal of Political Science* 41, no. 3: 738–70.

———, and Phillipa Norman. 2009. "Policy Entrepreneurship and Policy Change," *Policy Studies Journal* 37, no. 4: 649–67.

———, and Norman, P. 2009. "Policy Entrepreneurship and Policy Change," *Policy Studies Journal* 37: 649–667

Mortensen, Peter B., and Henrik B. Seeberg. 2015. "Why Are Some Policy Agendas Larger than Others?" *Policy Studies Journal,* October 1. doi:10.1111/psj.12134.

Mukherjee, Ishani and Michael Howlett. 2014. "Who is a Stream? Epistemic Communities, Instrument Constituencies and Advocacy Coalitions in Public Policy-Making," *Politics and Governance* 3, no. 2: 65–75.

Muntigl, Peter. 2002. "Policy, Politics and Social Control: A Systemic Functional Linguistic Analysis of EU Employment Policy," *Text* 22, no. 3: 393–441.

Newig, Jens. 2004. "Public Attention, Political Action: The Example of Environmental Regulation," *Rationality and Society* 16, no. 2: 149–90.

Nohrstedt, D. 2005. "External Shocks and Policy Change: Three Mile Island and Swedish Nuclear Energy Policy," *Journal of European Public Policy* 12, no. 6: 1041–59.

Nordhaus, W. 1975. "The Political Business Cycle," *Review of Economic Studies* 42: 169–90.

Nordlinger, Eric A. 1981. *On the Autonomy of the Democratic State*. Cambridge, MA: Harvard University Press.

Parsons, W. 2004. "Not Just Steering but Weaving: Relevant Knowledge and the Craft of Building Policy Capacity and Coherence," *Australian Journal of Public Administration* 63, no. 1: 43–57.

Peters, B. G. 2005. "Conclusion: The Future of Instruments Research," in *Designing Government: From Instruments to Governance*, edited by P. Eliadis, M. Hill, and M. Howlett, 353–363. Montreal: McGill-Queen's University Press.

Pralle, S.B. 2003. "Venue Shopping, Political Strategy, and Policy Change: The Internationalization of Canadian Forest Advocacy," *Journal of Public Policy* 23, no. 3: 233–60.

Princen, Sebastiaan. 2007. "Agenda-Setting in the European Union: A Theoretical Exploration and Agenda for Research," *Journal of European Public Policy* 14, no. 1: 21–38.

———. *Agenda-Setting in the European Union*. Basingtoke: Palgrave/Macmillan, 2009.

Pritchard, David. 1992. "The News Media and Public Policy Agendas," in Kennamer (1992).

Pross, A. Paul. 1992. *Group Politics and Public Policy*. Toronto: Oxford University Press.

Pryor, F.L. 1968. *Public Expenditures in Communist and Capitalist Nations*. Homewood, IL: R.D. Irwin.

Pump, Barry. 2011. "Beyond Metaphors: New Research on Agendas in the Policy Process," *Policy Studies Journal* 39 (April): 1–12.

Rapport D. and A. Friend. 1979. "Towards a Comprehensive Framework for Environmenal Statistics: A Stress-Response Approach." Statistics Canada catalogue 11–510. Ministry of Supply and Services Canada, Ottawa.

Rittel, Horst W.J., and Melvin M. Webber. 1973. "Dilemmas in a General Theory of Planning," *Policy Sciences* 4: 155–69.

Roberts, Nancy C., and Paula J. King. 1991. "Policy Entrepreneurs: Their Activity Structure and Function in the Policy Process," *Journal of Public Administration Research and Theory* 1, no. 2: 147–75.

Rochefort, David A., and Roger W. Cobb. 1993. "Problem Definition, Agenda Access, and Policy Choice," *Policy Studies Journal* 21, no. 1: 56–71.

Rochefort, David A., and Roger W. Cobb. 1994. *The Politics of Problem Definition: Shaping the Policy Agenda*. Lawrence, KA: University Press of Kansas.

Rose, Naomi A., and E.C.M. Parsons. 2015. "'Back Off, Man, I'm a Scientist!' When Marine Conservation Science Meets Policy," *Ocean & Coastal Management* 115: 71–6.

Rosenbloom, David. 2008. "The Politics–Administration Dichotomy in US Historical Context," *Public Administration Review* 68, no. 1: 57–60.

Rudd, Murray A. 2014. "Scientists' Perspectives on Global Ocean Research Priorities," *Frontiers in Marine Science* 1: 36.

———. 2015. "Scientists' Framing of the Ocean Science–Policy Interface," *Global Environmental Change* 33: 44–60.

Russell Neuman, W., Lauren Guggenheim, S. Mo Jang, and Soo Young Bae. 2014. "The Dynamics of Public Attention: Agenda-Setting Theory Meets Big Data: Dynamics of Public Attention," *Journal of Communication* 64, no. 2 (April): 193–214. doi:10.1111/jcom.12088.

Sabatier, Paul A. 1987. "Knowledge, Policy-Oriented Learning, and Policy Change," *Knowledge: Creation, Diffusion, Utilization* 8, no. 4: 649–92.

———. 1988. "An Advocacy Coalition Framework of Policy Change and the Role of

Policy-Oriented Learning Therein," *Policy Sciences* 21, nos. 2 and 3: 129–68.

————. 2007. "The Need for Better Theories," in Sabatier P., ed., *Theories of the Policy Process.* Oxford: Westview Press, pp. 3–18.

Sabatier, PA, and Weible, C.M., eds. 2007. *Theories of the Policy Process.* Boulder: Westview Press.

Schaffrin, André, Sebastian Sewerin, and Sibylle Seubert. "The Innovativeness of National Policy Portfolios – Climate Policy Change in Austria, Germany, and the UK," *Environmental Politics* 23, no. 5 (September): 860–883. http://doi.org/10.1 080/09644016.2014.924206.

Schlager, E., and Blomquist W. 1996. "Emerging Political Theories of the Policy Process: Institutional Rational Choice, the Politics of Structural Choice, and Advocacy Coalitions," *Political Research Quarterly* 49 (September): 651–672.

Schmidt, Vivien A and C.M. Radaelli. 2005. "Policy Change and Discourses in Europe: Conceptual and Methodological Issues," in C.M. Radaelli and V.A. Schmidt *Policy Change and Discourse in Europe.* New York: Routledge.

Schneider, F., and Bruno S. Frey. 1988. "Politico-Economic Models of Macroeconomic Policy: A Review of the Empirical Evidence," in Thomas D. Willett, ed., *Political Business Cycles: The Political Economy of Money, Inflation and Unemployment.* Durham, NC: Duke University Press, 239–75.

Schon, Donald A., and Martin Rein. 1994. *Frame Reflection: Towards the Resolution of Intractable Policy Controversies.* New York: Basic Books.

Seeliger, R. 1996. "Conceptualizing and Researching Policy Convergence," *Policy Studies Journal* 24, no. 2: 287–310.

Sharkansky, Ira. 1971. "Constraints on Innovation in Policy Making: Economic Development and Political Routines," in Frank Marini, ed., *Toward a New Public Administration: The Minnowbrook Perspective.* Scranton, PA: Chandler.

Sharp, Elaine B. 1994a. "Paradoxes of National Anti-Drug Policymaking," in David A. Rochefort and Roger W. Cobb, eds, *The Politics of Problem Definition: Shaping the Policy Agenda.* Lawrence: University Press of Kansas, 98–116.

————. 1994b. "The Dynamics of Issue Expansion: Cases from Disability Rights and Fetal Research Controversy," *Journal of Politics* 56, no. 4: 919–39.

Sheingate, Adam D. 2000. "Agricultural Retrenchment Revisited: Issue Definition and Venue Change in the United States and European Union," *Governance* 13, no. 3: 335–63.

Simeon, Richard. 1976a. "Studying Public Policy," *Canadian Journal of Political Science* 9, no. 4: 548–80.

Simon, Herbert A. 1973. "The Structure of Ill Structured Problems," *Artificial Intelligence* 4: 181–201.

Skodvin, Tora, Anne Therese Gullberg, and Stine Aakre. 2010. "Target-Group Influence and Political Feasibility: The Case of Climate Policy Design in Europe," *Journal of European Public Policy* 17, no. 6: 854. doi:10.1080/13501763.201 0.486991.

Skok, James E. 1995. "Policy Issue Networks and the Public Policy Cycle: A Structural-Functional Framework for Public Administration," *Public Administration Review*: 325–332.

Smith, Richard A. 1979. "Decision Making and Non-Decision Making in Cities: Some Implications for Community Structural Research," *American Sociological Review* 44, no. 1: 147–61.

Snow, David A., and Robert D. Benford. 1992. "Master Frames and Cycles of Protest," in A.D. Morris and C.M. Mueller, eds, *Frontiers in Social Movement Theory.* New Haven: Yale University Press, 133–55.

Spector, Malcolm, and John I. Kitsuse. 1987. *Constructing Social Problems.* New York: Aldine de Gruyter.

Stark, Andrew. 1992. "'Political-Discourse' Analysis and the Debate over Canada's Lobbying Legislation," *Canadian Journal of Political Science* 25, no. 3: 513–34.

Steinberg, Marc W. 1998. "Tilting the Frame: Considerations on Collective Action Framing from a Discursive Turn," *Theory and Society* 27, no. 6: 845–72.

Stevenson, Randolph T. 2001. "The Economy and Policy Mood: A Fundamental Dynamic of Democratic Politics," *American Journal of Political Science* 45, no. 3: 620–33.

Stimson, James A. 1991. *Public Opinion in America: Moods, Cycles and Swings*. Boulder, CO: Westview Press.

———, Michael B. Mackuen, and Robert S. Erikson. 1995. "Dynamic Representation," *American Political Science Review* 89, no. 3: 543–65.

Stone, Deborah A. 1988. *Policy Paradox and Political Reason*. Glenview, IL: Scott, Foresman.

———. 1989. "Causal Stories and the Formation of Policy Agendas," *Political Science Quarterly* 104, no. 2: 281–300.

Stone, Deborah. 2002. *Policy Paradox: The Art of Political Decision Making*. New York: W. W. Norton & Co. Inc.

Studlar, D. T. *Tobacco Control: Comparative Politics in the United States and Canada*. Peterborough: Broadview Press, 2002.

Surel, Yves. 2000. "The Role of Cognitive and Normative Frames in Policy-Making," *Journal of European Public Policy* 7, no. 4: 495–512.

Suzuki, Motoshi. 1992. "Political Business Cycles in the Public Mind," *American Political Science Review* 86, no. 4: 989–96

Tepper, S.J. 2004. "Setting Agendas and Designing Alternatives: Policymaking and the Strategic Role of Meetings," *Review of Policy Research* 21, no. 4: 523–42.

Therborn, Goran. 1989. "States, Populations and Productivity: Towards a Political Theory of Welfare States," in Lassman, Peter, ed., *Politics and Social Theory*. London: Routledge, pp. 62–84.

Thompson, John B. 1990. *Ideology and Modern Culture: Critical Social Theory in the Era of Mass Communication*. Cambridge: Polity Press.

Tufte, Edward R. 1978. *Political Control of the Economy*. Princeton, NJ: Princeton University Press.

Tumber, H., and S.R. Waisbord. 2004. "Political Scandals and Media across Democracies, Volume I," *American Behavioural Scientist* 47, no. 8: 1031–9.

Turnhout, Esther, Matthijs Hisschemoller, and Herman Eijsackers. 2007. "Ecological Indicators: Between the Two Fires of Science and Policy," *Ecological Indicators* 7: 215–228.

Uusitalo, Hannu. 1984. "Comparative Research on the Determinants of the Welfare State: The State of the Art," *European Journal of Political Research* 12, no. 4: 403–22.

Van Assche, Tobias. 2011. "When Do New Issues Appear? Punctuations in the Belgian Executive Agenda," *Acta Politica* 47, no. 2 (December 30): 128–50. doi:10.1057/ap.2011.33.

Vliegenthart, Rens, Stefaan Walgrave, Frank R. Baumgartner, Shaun Bevan, Christian Breunig, Sylvain Brouard, Laura Chaqués Bonafont, et al. 2016. "Do the Media Set the Parliamentary Agenda? A Comparative Study in Seven Countries," *European Journal of Political Research*, February. doi:10.1111/1475–6765.12134.

Voss, Jan-Peter, and Arno Simons. 2014. "Instrument Constituencies and the Supply Side of Policy Innovation: The Social Life of Emissions Trading," *Environmental Politics* 23, no. 5: 735–54.

Walgrave, Stefaan, and Rens Vliegenthart. 2010. "Why Are Policy Agendas Punctuated? Friction and Cascading in Parliament and Mass Media in Belgium," *Journal of European Public Policy* 17, no. 8: 1147. doi:10.1080/13501763.2010.513 562

Weible, Christopher M., Paul A. Sabatier, Hank C. Jenkins-Smith, Daniel Nohrstedt, Adam Douglas Henry, and Peter DeLeon. 2011. "A Quarter Century of the Advocacy Coalition Framework: An Introduction to the Special Issue," *Policy Studies Journal* 39, no. 3: 349–60.

Weishaar, H. et al. 2015. "Best of Enemies: Using Social Network Analysis to Explore a Policy Network in European Smoke-Free Policy," *Social Science & Medicine*.

Weiss, C.H. 1977. "Research for Policy's Sake: The Enlightenment Function of Social Science Research," *Policy Analysis* 3, no. 4: 531–45.

———. 1986. "The Circuitry of Enlightenment: Diffusion of Social Science Research to Policymakers," *Knowledge: Creation, Diffusion, Utilization* 8, no. 2: 274–81.

Whiteman, David. 1985. "Reaffirming the Importance of Strategic Use: A Two-Dimensional Perspective on Policy Analysis in Congress," *Knowledge: Creation, Diffusion, Utilization* 6, no. 3: 203–24.

Wilensky, Harold L. 1975. *The Welfare State and Equality: Structural and Ideological Roots of Public Expenditures.* Berkeley: University of California Press.

Wu, Xun, M. Ramesh, Michael Howlett, and Scott A. Fritzen. 2017. *The Public Policy Primer: Managing the Policy Process.* London: Routledge.

Wukich, Clayton, and Ines Mergel. 2016. "Reusing Social Media Information in Government," *Government Information Quarterly.* doi:10.1016/j.giq.2016.01.011.

Yanow, Dvora. 1992. "Silences in Public Policy Discourse: Organizational and Policy Myths," *Journal of Public Administration Research and Theory* 2, no. 4: 399–423.

Yishai, Yael. 1993. "Public Ideas and Public Policy," *Comparative Politics* 25, no. 2: 207–28.

Zahariadis, N. 1995. *Markets, States, and Public Policy: Privatization in Britain and France.* Ann Arbor: University of Michigan Press.

———. 2007. "The Multiple Streams Framework: Structure, Limitations, Prospects," in Sabatier, P., ed. *Theories of the Policy Process.* Boulder, CO: Westview

———, and Christopher S. Allen. 1995. "Ideas, Networks, and Policy Streams: Privatization in Britain and Germany," *Policy Studies Review* 14, nos. 1 and 2: 71–98.

Zito, A.R. 2001. "Epistemic Communities, Collective Entrepreneurship and European Integration," *Journal of European Public Policy* 8, no. 4: 585–603.

Chapter 5 Sources

Aberbach, Joel D., and Bert A. Rockman. 1989. "On the Rise, Transformation, and Decline of Analysis in the US Government," *Governance* 2, no. 3: 293–314.

Adcroft, A., and R. Willis. 2005. "The (Un) Intended Outcome of Public Sector Performance Measurement," *International Journal of Public Sector Management* 18, no. 5: 386–400.

Adler, Robert S., and R. David Pittle. 1984. "Cajolery or Command: Are Education Campaigns an Adequate Substitute for Regulation," *Yale Journal on Regulation* 1: 159–93.

Advani, Asheesh, and Sandford Borins. 2001. "Managing Airports: A Test of the New Public Management," *International Public Management Journal* 4: 91–107.

AECOM. 2011. *Energy Demand Research Project: Final Analysis.* London: Ofgem. Available online: https://www.ofgem.gov.uk/ofgem-publications/59105/energy-demand-research-project-final-analysis.pdf

Ahroni, Yair. 1986. *Evolution and Management of State-Owned Enterprises.* Cambridge, MA: Ballinger.

Alford, John. 1998. "A Public Management Road Less Travelled: Clients as Co-producers of Public Services," Australian Journal of Public Administration 57, no. 4 (December 1): 128–37.

Alford, John. 2002. "Defining the Client in the Public Sector: A Social-Exchange Perspective," *Public Administration Review* 62, no. 3: 337–346.

Alcott, Hunt, 2011. "Social Norms and Energy Conservation," *Journal of Public Economics* 95 (9–10): 1082–95.

Amenta, Edwin and Carruthers, Bruce G. 1988. "The Formative Years of US Social Spending Policies: Theories of the Welfare State and the American States during the Great Depression," *American Sociological Review,* 53: 661–678.

Anderson, G. 1996. "The New Focus on the Policy Capacity of the Federal Government," *Canadian Public Administration* 39, no. 4: 469–88.

Anderson, James E., ed. 1976. *Economic Regulatory Policies.* Lexington, MA: Lexington Books.

Andrews, Richard. 1998. "Environmental Regulation and Business 'Self-Regulation,'" *Policy Sciences* 31: 177–97.

Armstrong, Jim, and Donald G. Lenihan. 1999. *From Controlling to Collaborating; When Governments Want to be Partners: A Report on the Collaborative Partnership Project.* Toronto: Institute of Public Administration of Canada New Directions, Number 3.

Ascher, Kate.1987. *The Politics of Privatisation: Contracting Out Public Services.* Basingstoke: Macmillan.

Ascher, William. 1986. "The Evolution of the Policy Sciences: Understanding the Rise and Avoiding the Fall," *Journal of Policy Analysis and Management* 5: 365–89.

Aucoin, Peter. 1997. "The Design of Public Organizations for the 21st Century: Why Bureaucracy Will Survive in Public

Management," *Canadian Public Administration* 40, no. 2: 290–306.

———. 2006. "Accountability and Coordination with Independent Foundations: A Canadian Case of Autonomization," in Tom Christensen and Per Laegreid, eds, *Autonomy and Regulation: Coping with Agencies in the Modern State*. Cheltenham: Edward Elgar, 110–33.

Averch, Harvey. 1990. *Private Markets and Public Interventions: A Primer for Policy Designers*. Pittsburgh: University of Pittsburgh Press

Ayres, Ian, Sophie Raseman, and Alice Shih. 2013. "Evidence from Two Large Field Experiments That Peer Comparison Feedback Can Reduce Residential Energy Usage," *The Journal of Law, Economics, and Organization* 29, no. 5: 992–1022.

Baksi, Soham, and Pinaki Bose. 2007. "Credence Goods, Efficient Labelling Policies, and Regulatory Enforcement," *Environmental and Resource Economics* 37: 411–30.

Balch, George I. 1980. "The Stick, the Carrot, and Other Strategies: A Theoretical Analysis of Governmental Intervention," *Law and Policy Quarterly* 2, no. 1: 35–60.

Balla, Steven J., and John R. Wright. 2001. "Interest Groups, Advisory Committees, and Congressional Control of the Bureaucracy," *American Journal of Political Science* 45, no. 4: 799–812.

Banting, Keith G. 1995. "The Social Policy Review: Policy-Making in a Semi-Sovereign Society," *Canadian Public Administration* 38, no. 2: 283–90

Barker, Anthony, and B. Guy Peters, eds. 1993. *The Politics of Expert Advice: Creating, Using and Manipulating Scientific Knowledge for Public Policy*. Pittsburgh: University of Pittsburgh Press.

Barr, Stewart, Andrew Gilg, and Gareth Shaw. 2011. "Citizens, Consumers and Sustainability: (Re)Framing Environmental Practice in an Age of Climate Change," *Global Environmental Change* 21, no. 4: 1224–33.

Bason, Christian. 2014. *Design for Policy*. New edition. Farnham, Surrey; Burlington, VT: Gower.

Beam, David A., and Timothy J. Conlan. 2002. "Grants," in Salamon (2002a: 340–80).

Beesley, M.E. 1992. *Privatization, Regulation and Deregulation*. New York: Routledge.

Béland, Daniel, and Alex Waddan. 2012. "The Obama Presidency and Health Insurance Reform: Assessing Continuity and Change," *Social Policy and Society* 11, no. 03: 319–330.

Beland, Daniel, and Michael Howlett. 2016. "How Solutions Chase Problems: Instrument Constituencies in the Policy Process," *Governance*.

———, and Alex Waddan. 2012. "The Obama Presidency and Health Insurance Reform: Assessing Continuity and Change," *Social Policy and Society* 11, no. 03: 319–330.

Bellehumeur, Robert. 1997. "Review: An Instrument of Change," *Optimum* 27, no. 1: 37–42.

Bemelmans-Videc, Marie-Louise, Ray C. Rist, and Evert Vedung, eds. 1998. *Carrots, Sticks and Sermons: Policy Instruments and Their Evaluation*. New Brunswick, NJ: Transaction.

Bendor, J., Kumar, S., and Siegel, D. A. 2009. "Satisficing: A 'Pretty Good' Heuristic," *The B.E. Journal of Theoretical Economics* 9, no. 1. doi:10.2202/1935–1704.1478.

Bennett, Colin J. 1990. "The Formation of a Canadian Privacy Policy: The Art and Craft of Lesson-Drawing," *Canadian Public Administration* 33, no. 4: 551–70

———. 1992a. *Regulating Privacy: Data Protection and Public Policy in Europe and the United States*. Ithaca, NY: Cornell University Press.

———. 1992b. "The International Regulation of Personal Data: From Epistemic Community to Policy Sector," paper presented at the annual meeting of the Canadian Political Science Association, Charlottetown, PEI.

Bennett, S., and M. McPhail. 1992. "Policy Process Perceptions of Senior Canadian Federal Civil Servants: A View of the State and Its Environment," *Canadian Public Administration* 35, no. 3: 299–316.

Bertelli, Anthony, and Sven E. Feldmann. 2007. "Strategic Appointments," *Journal of Public Administration Research and Theory* 17, no. 1: 19–38.

Bevir, M., and R. A. W. Rhodes. 2001. "Decentering Tradition: Interpreting British

Government," *Administration & Society* 33, no. 2: 107–32.

———, R. A. W. Rhodes, and P. Weller. 2003. "Traditions of Governance: Interpreting the Changing Role of the Public Sector," *Public Administration* 81, no. 1: 1–17.

Blomkamp, Emma. 2018. "The Promise of Co-Design for Public Policy: The Promise of Co-Design for Public Policy," *Australian Journal of Public Administration* 77, no. 4 (December): 729–43.

Bobrow, Davis B. 2006. "Policy Design: Ubiquitous, Necessary and Difficult," in B. Guy Peters and Jon Pierre, eds, *Handbook of Public Policy*. London: Sage, 75–96.

———, and John S. Dryzek. 1987. *Policy Analysis by Design*. Pittsburgh: University of Pittsburgh Press.

Bolleyer, Nicole, and Tanja A. Borzel. 2010. "Non-Hierarchical Policy Coordination in Multilevel Systems," *European Political Science Review* 2, no. 02: 157–185

Bolom, Jan-Tjeerd. 2000. "International Emissions Trading Under the Kyoto Protocol: Credit Trading," *Energy Policy* 29: 605–13.

Bos, Dieter. 1991. *Privatization: A Theoretical Treatment*. Oxford: Clarendon Press.

Bovaird, Tony. 2007. "Beyond Engagement and Participation: User And Community Coproduction of Public Services," *Public Administration Review* 67, no. 5: 846–60.

Bovens, Mark, and Paul t'Hart and B. Guy Peters. 2001. "Analysing Governance Success and Failure in Six European States," in Bovens, t'Hart, and Peters, eds, *Success and Failure in Public Governance: A Comparative Analysis*. Cheltenham: Edward Elgar, 12–32.

Bradford, Neil. 1999. "The Policy Influence of Economic Ideas: Interests, Institutions and Innovation in Canada," *Studies in Political Economy* 59: 17–60.

Brandsen, Taco, and Victor Pestoff. 2006. "Co-Production, the Third Sector and the Delivery of Public Services," *Public Management Review* 8 (December): 493–501.

Brint, Steven. 1990. "Rethinking the Policy Influence of Experts: From General Characterizations to Analysis of Variation," *Sociological Forum* 5, no. 3. Kluwer Academic Publishers-Plenum Publishers.

Brown, David S. 1955. "The Public Advisory Board as an Instrument of Government," *Public Administration Review* 15: 196–201.

———. 1972. "The Management of Advisory Committees: An Assignment for the '70's," Public Administration Review 32: 334–42.

Brown, Christina L., and Aradhna Krishna. 2004. "The Skeptical Shopper: A Metacognitive Account for the Effects of Default Options on Choice," *Journal of Consumer Research* 31, no. 3: 529–39.

Brown, Tim, and Jocelyn Wyatt. 2010. "Design Thinking for Social Innovation (SSIR)," *Stanford Social Innovation Review,* Winter.

Brunori, David. 1997. "Principle of Tax Policy and Targeted Tax Incentives," *State and Local Government Review* 29, no. 1: 50–61.

Bullock H., J. Mountford, and R. Stanley. 2001. *Better Policy-Making*. London: Centre for Management and Policy Studies, Cabinet Office, United Kingdom.

Cairns, Alan C. 1990a. "Reflections on Commission Research," in A.P. Pross, I. Christie, and J.A. Yogis, eds, *Commissions of Inquiry*. Toronto: Carswell, 87–110.

Camilleri, Adrian R., and Richard P. Larrick. 2014. "Metric and Scale Design as Choice Architecture Tools," *Journal of Public Policy & Marketing* 33, no. 1: 108–25.

Canadian Government. 1996. *Strengthening Our Policy Capacity. Report of the Task Force on Strengthening the Policy Capacity of the Federal Government.*

Cantor, Robin, Stuart Henry, and Steve Rayner. 1992. *Making Markets: An Interdisciplinary Perspective on Economic Exchange*. Westport, Conn.: Greenwood Press

Cashore, Benjamin, and Michael Howlett. 2007. "Punctuating Which Equilibrium? Understanding Thermostatic Policy Dynamics in Pacific Northwest Forestry," *American Journal of Political Science* 51, no. 3: 532–551.

Cardozo, Andrew. 1996. "Lion Taming: Downsizing the Opponents of Downsizing," in G. Swimmer, ed., *How Ottawa Spends 1996–97: Life Under the Knife*. Ottawa: Carleton University Press, 303–36.

Carlsson, Lars. 2000. "Policy Networks as Collective Action," *Policy Studies Journal* 28, no. 3: 502–22.

Carver, John. 2001. "A Theory of Governing the Public's Business: Redesigning the Jobs of Boards, Councils and Commissions," *Public Management Review* 3, no. 1: 53–72.

Cavaillès, Henri. 1946. *La route française: son histoire, sa fonction*. Paris: Librarie Armand Colin.

Chapman, Richard A. 1973. "Commissions in Policy-Making," in Chapman, ed., *The Role of Commissions in Policy-Making*. London: George Allen and Unwin, 174–88.

———. 2003. "A Policy Mix for Environmentally Sustainable Development—Learning from the Dutch Experience," *New Zealand Journal of Environmental Law* 7, no. 1: 29–51.

Chindarkar, Namrata, Michael Howlett, and M. Ramesh. 2017. "Conceptualizing Effective Social Policy Design: Design Spaces and Capacity Challenges," *Public Administration and Development* 37, no. 1: 3–14. doi:10.1002/pad.1789.

Christensen, Tom, and Per Laegreid, eds. 2003. "Coping with Complex Leadership Roles: The Problematic Redefinition of Government-Owned Enterprises," *Public Administration* 81, no. 4: 803–31.

Cialdini, Robert B. 2008. "Turning Persuasion from an Art Into a Science," in *Clashes of Knowledge*. Springer, Dordrecht, 199–209.

Clokie, Hugh McDowall, and J. William Robinson. 1969. *Royal Commissions of Inquiry: The Significance of Investigations in British Politics*. New York: Octagon Books.

Cnossen, S. 2005. *Theory and Practice of Excise Taxation: Smoking, Drinking, Gambling, Polluting and Driving*. Oxford: Oxford University Press.

Codagnone, Cristiano, Francesco Bogliacino, and Giuseppe Veltri. 2013. *Testing CO2/Car Labelling Options and Consumer Information. Final Report*. Brussels: European Commission.

Coglianese, Cary. 1997. "Assessing Consensus: The Promise and Performance of Negotiated Rulemaking," *Duke Law Journal* 46, no. 6: 1255–1349.

Cohen, Mark A., and V. Santhakumar. 2007. "Information Disclosure as Environmental Regulation: A Theoretical Analysis," *Environmental and Resource Economics* 37: 599–620.

Cohen, M. D., J. G. March, and J. P. Olsen. 1979. "People, Problems, Solutions and the Ambiguity of Relevance," in *Ambiguity and Choice in Organizations*, 24–37. Bergen: Universitetsforlaget.

Cohen, M., J. March, and J. Olsen. 1972. "A Garbage Can Framework of Organizational Choice," *Administrative Science Quarterly* 17, no. 1: 1–25.

Colebatch, H.K. *Policy*. Minneapolis: University of Minnesota Press, 1998.

Cook, D. 2002. "Consultation, for a Change? Engaging Users and Communities in the Policy Process," *Social Policy and Administration* 36, no. 5: 516–31.

Cordes, Joseph J. 2002. "Corrective Taxes, Charges and Tradable Permits," in Salamon (2002a: 255–81).

Datta, Saugato, Juan José Miranda, Laura Zoratto, Oscar Calvo-González, Matthew Darling, and Karina Lorenzana. 2015. *A Behavioral Approach to Water Conservation: Evidence from Costa Rica*. The World Bank.

Davies H.T.O., S.M. Nutley, and P.C. Smith, eds. 2000. *What Works? Evidence-based Policy and Practice in Public Services*. Bristol: The Policy Press.

Davis, G., P. Weller, E. Craswell, and S. Eggins. 1999. "What Drives Machinery of Government Change? Australia, Canada and the United Kingdom 1950–1997," *Public Administration* 77, no. 1: 7–50.

DeHoog, Ruth Hoogland, and Lester M. Salamon. 2002. "Purchase-of-Service Contracting," in Salamon (2002a: 319–39).

de la Mothe, John. 1996. "One Small Step in an Uncertain Direction: The Science and Technology Review and Public Administration in Canada," *Canadian Public Administration* 39, no. 3: 403–17.

de la Porte, Caroline, Phillipe Pochet, and Graham Room. 2001. "Social Benchmarking, Policy Making and New Governance in the EU," *Journal of European Social Policy* 11, no. 1: 291–307.

deLeon, Peter. 1988. "The Contextual Burdens of Policy Design," *Policy Studies Journal* 17, no. 2: 297–309. doi:10.1111/j.1541–0072.1988.tb00583.x.

———. 1992. "Policy Formulation: Where Ignorant Armies Clash by Night," *Policy Studies Review* 11, nos. 3 and 4: 389–405.

Delmas, Magali A., Miriam Fischlein, and Omar I. Asensio. 2013. "Information Strategies and Energy Conservation Behavior: A Meta-Analysis Of Experimental Studies from 1975 to 2012," *Energy Policy* 61: 729–39.

Del Río, Pablo. 2014. "On Evaluating Success in Complex Policy Mixes: The Case of Renewable Energy Support Schemes," *Policy Sciences*, 1–21. doi:10.1007/s11077-013-9189-7.

Del Río, Pablo. 2010. "Analysing the Interactions Between Renewable Energy Promotion and Energy Efficiency Support Schemes: The Impact of Different Instruments and Design Elements," *Energy Policy* 38, no. 9 (September): 4978–4989.

Department of Energy and Climate Change. 2014. *Evaluation of the DECC/John Lewis Energy Labeling Trial.* Available online: https://assets.publishing.service.gov.uk/government/uploads/system/uploads/attachment_data/file/350282/John_Lewis_trial_report_010914FINAL.pdf

Devas, N., S. Delay, and M. Hubbard. 2001. "Revenue Authorities: Are They the Right Vehicle for Improved Tax Administration?" *Public Administration and Development* 21, no. 3: 211–22.

Dery, D. 1984. *Problem Definition in Policy Analysis.* Lawrence: University of Kansas.

Dinner, I., E. J. Johnson, D. G. Goldstein, and K. Liu. 2011. "Partitioning default effects: Why people choose not to choose," *Journal of Experimental Psychology: Applied* 17, no. 4: 332–341.

Dobuzinskis, Laurent, M. Howlett, and D. Laycock. 2007. *Policy Analysis in Canada: The State of the Art.* Toronto: University of Toronto Press

Doern, G. Bruce. 1971. "The Role of Central Advisory Councils: The Science Council of Canada," in Doern and Aucoin (1971: 246–66).

Dolan, Paul, Antony Elliott, Robert Metcalfe, and Ivo Vlaev. 2012. "Influencing Financial Behavior: From Changing Minds to Changing Contexts," *Journal of Behavioral Finance* 13, no. 2: 126–42.

———, and Robert Metcalfe. 2012. "Measuring Subjective Wellbeing: Recommendations on Measures for Use by National Governments," *Journal of Social Policy* 41, no. 2: 409–27.

Dollery, Brian E., and Joe L. Wallis. 2003. *The Political Economy of the Voluntary Sector: A Reappraisal of the Comparative Institutional Advantage of Voluntary Organisations.* Cheltenham: Edward Elgar.

d'Ombrain, N. 1997. "Public Inquiries in Canada," *Canadian Public Administration* 40, no. 1: 86–107.

Donahue, John D. 1989. *The Privatization Decision: Public Ends, Private Means.* New York: Basic Books.

———, and Joseph S. Nye Jr., eds. 2001. *Governance and Bigger, Better Markets.* Washington: Brookings Institution.

———, and Richard J. Zeckhauser. 2006. "Public–Private Collaboration," in Michael Moran, Martin Rein, and Robert E. Goodin, eds, *The Oxford Handbook of Public Policy.* Oxford: Oxford University Press, 496–525.

Doremus, H. "A Policy Portfolio Approach to Biodiversity Protection on Private Lands," *Environmental Science & Policy* 6: 217–232.

Dryzek, J. 1983. "Don't Toss Coins in Garbage Cans: A Prologue to Policy Design," *Journal of Public Policy* 3, no. 4: 345–367.

———, and B. Ripley. 1988. "The Ambitions of Policy Design," *Policy Studies Review* 7, no. 4: 705–719.

Dunsire, Andrew. 1986. "A Cybernetic View of Guidance, Control and Evaluation in the Public Sector," in Franz-Xavier Kaufman, Giandomenico Majone, and Vincent Ostrom, eds, *Guidance, Control, and Evaluation in the Public Sector.* Berlin: Walter de Gruyter, 327–46.

———. 1993a. *Manipulating Social Tensions: Collaboration as an Alternative Mode of Government Intervention.* Koln: Max Plank Institute, 1993a.

Dyerson, Romano, and Frank Mueller. 1993. "Intervention by Outsiders: A Strategic Perspective on Government Industrial Policy," *Journal of Public Policy* 13, no. 1: 69–88.

Edelenbos, J., and E.-H. Klijn. 2006. "Managing Stakeholder Involvement in Decision Making: A Comparative Analysis of Six Interactive Processes in the Netherlands," *Journal of Public Administration Research and Theory* 16, no. 3: 417–46.

Eichbaum, Chris, and Richard Shaw. 2007. "Ministerial Advisers and the Politics of

Policy-Making: Bureaucratic Permanence and Popular Control," *The Australian Journal of Public Administration* 66, no. 4: 453–467.

Eijlander, P. 2005. "Possibilities and Constraints in the Use of Self-regulation and Co-Regulation in Legislative Policy: Experiences in the Netherlands—Lessons to Be Learned for the EU," *Electronic Journal of Comparative Law* 9, no. 1: 1–8.

Elliott, Chris, and Rodolphe Schlaepfer. 2001. "The Advocacy Coalition Framework: Application to the Policy Process for the Development of Forest Certification in Sweden," *Journal of European Public Policy* 8, no. 4: 642–61.

Elliott, Dominic, and Martina McGuinness. 2001. "Public Inquiry: Panacea or Placebo?" *Journal of Contingencies and Crisis Management* 10, no. 1: 14–25.

Esping-Andersen, G. 1990. *The Three Worlds of Welfare Capitalism.* Polity Press.

Falkner, G. 2000. "Policy Networks in a Multi-Level System: Convergence towards Moderate Diversity?" *West European Politics* 23, no. 4: 94–120.

Feldman, Martha. 1989. *Order Without Design: Information Production and Policy Making.* 1st ed. Palo Alto, CA: Stanford University Press.

Feldman, Ron J. 2002. "Government Insurance," in Salamon (2002a: 186–216).

Ferraro, Paul J., Juan Jose Miranda, and Michael K. Price. 2011. "The Persistence Of Treatment Effects with Norm-Based Policy Instruments: Evidence from a Randomized Environmental Policy Experiment," *American Economic Review* 101, no. 3: 318–22.

———, and Michael K. Price. 2013. "Using Nonpecuniary Strategies to Influence Behavior: Evidence from a Large-Scale Field Experiment," *Review of Economics and Statistics* 95, no. 1: 64–73.

Festinger, Leon. 1962. "Cognitive Dissonance," *Scientific American* 207.4: 93-106.

Finkle, Peter, et al. 1994. *Federal Government Relations with Interest Groups: A Reconsideration.* Ottawa: Privy Council Office.

Firestone, O.J. 1970. *The Public Persuader: Government Advertising.* Toronto: Methuen.

Flinders, Matthew V., and Hugh McConnel. 1999. "Diversity and Complexity: The QuangoContinuum," in Flinders and Martin J. Smith, eds, *Quangos, Accountability and Reform: The Politics of Quasi-Government.* Sheffield: Political Economy Research Centre, 17–39.

Flitner, D. 1986. *The Politics of Presidential Commissions.* New York: Transnational Publishers.

Flora, Peter and Arnold J. Heidenheimer, eds. 1981. *The Development of Welfare States in Europe and America.* New Brunswick: Transaction Books.

Forester, John. 1983. "What Analysts Do," in Dunn, William N., ed. *Values, Ethics and the Practice of Policy Analysis.* Lexington: Lexington Books, 47–62.

Franchino, Fabio, and Bjorn Hoyland. 2009. "Legislative Involvement in Parliamentary Systems: Opportunities, Conflict and Institutional Constraints," *American Political Science Review* 103, no. 4: 607–621.

Fukuyama, Francis. 2013. "What Is Governance?" *Governance.* doi:10.1111/gove.12035.

Gero, John S. 1990. "Design Prototypes: A Knowledge Representation Schema for Design," *Text.Serial.Journal,* December 15.

Gifford, Robert, and Louise A. Comeau. 2011. "Message Framing Influences Perceived Climate Change Competence, Engagement, And Behavioral Intentions," *Global Environmental Change* 21 no. 4: 1301–07.

Gilabert, Pablo and Holly Lawford-Smith, 2012. "Political Feasibility: A Conceptual Exploration," *Political Studies* 60, no. 4: 809–25.

Gill, Norman N. 1940. "Permanent Advisory Committees in the Federal Government," *Journal of Politics* 2: 411–25.

Gilmore, Thomas N., and James Krantz. 1991. "Innovation in the Public Sector: Dilemmas in the Use of Ad Hoc Processes," *Journal of Policy Analysis and Management* 10, no. 3: 455–68.

Givoni, Moshe. 2013. "Addressing Transport Policy Challenges through Policy-Packaging," *Transportation Research Part A: Policy and Practice.* doi:10.1016/j.tra.2013.10.012.

———, James Macmillen, David Banister, and Eran Feitelson. 2012. "From Policy

Measures to Policy Packages," *Transport Reviews*: 1–20. doi:10.1080/01441647.2012.744779.

Gleeson, Deborah H., David G. Legge, and Deirdre O'Neill. 2009. "Evaluating Health Policy Capacity: Learning from International and Australian Experience," *Australia and New Zealand Health Policy* 6, no. 1 (February 26)

——, David Legge, Deirdre O'Neill, and Monica Pfeffer. 2011. "Negotiating Tensions in Developing Organizational Policy Capacity: Comparative Lessons to Be Drawn," *Journal of Comparative Policy Analysis: Research and Practice* 13, no. 3 (June): 237–263.

Grabosky, P. 1995. "Counterproductive Regulation," *International Journal of the Sociology of Law* 23 (1995): 347–369.

Goldstein, Noah J., Robert B. Cialdini, and Vladas Griskevicius. 2008. "A Room With a Viewpoint: Using Social Norms to Motivate Environmental Conservation in Hotels," *Journal of consumer Research* 35, no. 3: 472–82.

Gregory, Robert, and Zsuzsanna Lonti. 2008. "Chasing Shadows? Performance Measurement of Policy Advice in New Zealand Government Departments," *Public Administration* 86, no. 3: 837–56.

Grimshaw, Damian, Steven Vincent, and Hugh Willmott. 2001. "New Control Modes and Emergent Organizational Forms: Private–Public Contracting in Public Administration," *Administrative Theory and Practice* 23, no. 3: 407–30.

Gunningham, Neil, Peter Grabosky, and Darren Sinclair. 1998. *Smart Regulation: Designing Environmental Policy*. Oxford: Clarendon Press.

——, and Joseph Rees. 1997. "Industry Self-Regulation: An Institutional Perspective," *Law and Policy* 19, no. 4: 363–414.

——, and Mike D. Young. 1997. "Toward Optimal Environmental Policy: The Case of Biodiversity Conservation," *Ecology Law Quarterly* 24: 243–98.

Guo, Chao. 2007. "When Government Becomes the Principal Philanthropist: The Effects of Public Funding on Patterns of Nonprofit Governance," *Public Administration Review* (May–June): 458–73.

Haider, Donald. 1989. "Grants as a Tool of Public Policy," in Salamon (1989a: 93–124).

Haider, H., Mcloughlin, C and Scott, Z. 2011. *Topic Guide on Communication and Governance, Second edition*. Birmingham, UK: Governance and Social Development Resource Centre. http://www.gsdrc.org/go/topic-guides/communication-and-governance/the-role-of-communication-in-governance-and-development.

Hajer, Maarten A. 2005. "Setting the Stage: A Dramaturgy of Policy Deliberation," *Administration and Society* 36, no. 6: 624–47.

Hall, J. W., J. J. Henreiques, A. J. Hickford, and R. J. Nicholls (eds). 2012. "A Fast Track Analysis of strategies for infrastructure provision in Great Britain: Technical Report," Environmental Change Institute, University of Oxford.

Hardisty, David J., Eric J. Johnson, and Elke U. Weber. 2010. "A Dirty Word or a Dirty World? Attribute Framing, Political Affiliation, and Query Theory," *Psychological Science* 21, no. 1: 86–92.

Haufler, Virginia. 2000. "Private Sector International Regimes," in R.A. Higgott and G.R.D. Underhill, eds, *Andreas Bieler*. London: Routledge, 121–37.

——. 2001. *A Public Role for the Private Sector: Industry Self-Regulation in a Global Economy*. Washington: Carnegie Endowment for International Peace.

Hawke, Gary Richard. 1993. *Improving Policy Advice*. Institute of Policy Studies, Victoria University of Wellington.

Heinrichs, Harald. 2005. "Advisory Systems in Pluralistic Knowledge Societies: A Criteria-Based Typology to Assess And Optimize Environmental Policy Advice," in *Democratization of Expertise?* Springer, Dordrecht, 41–61.

Hennicke, P. "Scenarios for a Robust Policy Mix: The Final Report of the German Study Commission on Sustainable Energy Supply," *Energy Policy* 32, no. 15 (October): 1673–1678.

Hertin, Julia, John Turnpenny, Andrew Jordan, Mans Nilsson, Duncan Russel, and Bjorn Nykvist. 2009. "Rationalising the Policy Mess? Ex Ante Policy Assessment and the Utilization of Knowledge in the Policy Process," *Environment and Planning A* 41: 1185–1200.

Hillier, Bill, and Adrian Leaman. 1974. "How is Design Possible: A Sketch for a Theory,"

DMG-DRS Journal: Design Research and Methods 8, no. 1: 40–50.

———, John Musgrave, and Pat O'Sullivan. 1972. "Knowledge and Design," in *Environmental Design: Research and Practice*, edited by William J. Mitchell, 29.3.1–29.3.14. Los Angeles: University of California-Los Angeles.

Hood, C. 1986. *The Tools of Government*. Chatham: Chatham House Publishers.

———. 2010. *The Blame Game: Spin, Bureaucracy and Self-Preservation in Government*. Princeton, NJ: Princeton University Press.

Hosseus, D., and L. A. Pal. 1997. "Anatomy of a Policy Area: The Case of Shipping," *Canadian Public Policy* 23, no. 4: 399–416.

Howard, Christopher. 1993. "The Hidden Side of the American Welfare States," *Political Science Quarterly* 108, no. 3: 403–36.

———. 1995. "Testing the Tools Approach: Tax Expenditures versus Direct Expenditures," *Public Administration Review* 55, no. 5: 439–47.

———. 1997. *The Hidden Welfare State: Tax Expenditures and Social Policy in the United States*. Princeton, NJ: Princeton University Press.

———. 2002. "Tax Expenditures," in Salamon (2002a: 410–44).

Howells, G. 2005. "The Potential and Limits of Consumer Empowerment by Information," *Journal of Law and Society* 32, no. 3: 349–70.

Howlett, Michael. 1990. "The Round Table Experience: Representation and Legitimacy in Canadian Environmental Policy Making," *Queen's Quarterly* 97, no. 4: 580–601.

———. 1999. "Federalism and Public Policy," in Bickerton, J. and A. Gagnon, eds. *Canadian Politics*, 3rd edn. Peterborough, ON: Broadview Press.

———. 2002. "Do Networks Matter? Linking Policy Network Structure to Policy Outcomes: Evidence from Four Canadian Policy Sectors, 1990–2000," *Canadian Journal of Political Science* 35, no. 2: 235–68.

———. 2005. "What Is a Policy Instrument? Policy Tools, Policy Mixes and Policy Implementation Styles," in Eliadis, P., M. Hill, and M. Howlett. *Designing Government: From Instruments to Governance*. Montreal: McGill-Queen's University Press, 31–50.

———. 2009a. "Governance Modes, Policy Regimes and Operational Plans: A Multi-Level Nested Model of Policy Instrument Choice and Policy Design," *Policy Sciences* 42: 73–89.

Howlett, Michael. 2014. "From the 'Old' to the 'New' Policy Design: Design Thinking beyond Markets and Collaborative Governance," *Policy Sciences* 47, no. 3 (September): 187–207.

———. 2015. "Policy Analytical Capacity: The Supply and Demand for Policy Analysis in Government," *Policy and Society*, Special Issue on The Dynamics of Policy Capacity, 34, no. 3: 173–82.

———, and Cashore, B. 2009. "The Dependent Variable Problem in the Study of Policy Change: Understanding Policy Change as a Methodological Problem," *Journal of Comparative Policy Analysis: Research and Practice* 11, no. 1: 33–46.

———, J. Kim, and P. Weaver. 2006. "Assessing Instrument Mixes Through Program- and Agency-Level Data: Methodological Issues in Contemporary Implementation Research," *Review of Policy Research* 23, no. 1: 129–151.

———, and E. Lindquist. 2004. "Policy Alaysis and Governance: Analytical and Policy Styles in Canada," *Journal of Comparative Policy Analysis* 6, no. 3: 225–249.

———, and ———. 2011. "Policy Analysis and Governance: Analytical and Policy Styles," in Howlett, M. *Designing Public Policies: Principles and Instruments*. New York: Routledge.

———, McConnell, A. and Perl, A. 2014. "Streams and Stages: Reconciling Kingdon and Policy Process Theory," *European Journal of Political Research* 54, no. 3: 419–434

———, and Ishani Mukherjee. 2014. "Policy Design and Non-Design: Towards a Spectrum of Policy Formulation Types," *Politics and Governance* 2, no. 2 (November 13): 57–71

———, eds. 2017. *Handbook of Policy Formulation*. Cheltenham: Edward Elgar.

———, and Joshua Newman. 2010. "Policy Analysis and Policy Work in Federal Systems: Policy Advice and Its Contribution to Evidence-Based Policy-Making in Multi-Level Governance Systems," *Policy and Society* 29, no. 1: 123–136.

———, and M. Ramesh. 1993. "Patterns of Policy Instrument Choice: Policy Styles, Policy Learning and the Privatization Experience," *Policy Studies Review* 12, 1: 3–24.

———Ramesh, M., and Perl, A. 2009. *Studying Public Policy: Policy Cycles and Policy Subsystems, Third Edition*. Toronto: Oxford University Press.

———, and Jeremy Rayner. 2007. "Design Principles for Policy Mixes: Cohesion and Coherence in 'New Governance Arrangements,'" *Policy and Society* 26, no. 4: 1–18.

———, and Rayner, J. 2013. Patching vs Packaging in Policy Formulation: Assessing Policy Portfolio Design. *Politics and Governance* 1, no. 2: 170–182.

Howlett, Michael, Ishani Mukherjee, and Jeremy Rayner. 2018. "Understanding Policy Designs Over Time: Layering, Stretching, Patching and Packaging." In *Routledge Handbook of Policy Design*, edited by Michael Howlett and Ishani Mukherjee, 136–144. New York: Routledge. doi:10.4324/9781351252928-9.

Hula, Richard C. 1988. "Using Markets to Implement Public Policy," in Hula, ed., *MarketBased Public Policy*. London: Macmillan, 3–18.

———, Cynthia Jackson-Elmoore, and Laura Reese. 2007. "Mixing God's Work and the Public Business: A Framework for the Analysis of Faith-Based Service Delivery," *Review of Policy Research* 24, no. 1: 67–89.

Iannuzzi, Alphonse. 2001. *Industry Self-Regulation and Voluntary Environmental Compliance*. Boca Raton, FL: Lewis Publishers.

Ikenberry, G. John. 1988. "Conclusion: An Institutional Approach to American Foreign Economic Policy," *International Organization* 42, no. 1: 219–43.

Jenson, Jane. 1994. "Commissioning Ideas: Representation and Royal Commissions," in S.D. Phillips, ed., *How Ottawa Spends 1994–95: Making Change*. Ottawa: Carleton University Press, 39–69.

Johnsen, A. 2005. "What Does 25 Years of Experience Tell Us about the State of Performance Measurement in Public Policy and Management?" *Public Money and Management* 25, no. 1: 9–17.

Johnson, Norman. 1987. *The Welfare State in Transition: The Theory and Practice of Welfare Pluralism*. Brighton, Sussex: Wheatsheaf Books.

Johnson, Eric J., and Daniel Goldstein. 2003. "Do Defaults Save Lives?" *Science* 302: 1338–39.

Jones, Charles O. 1984. *An Introduction to the Study of Public Policy*, 3rd edn. Monterey, CA: Brooks/Cole.

Jonsson, G., and I. Zakrisson. 2005. "Organizational Dilemmas in Voluntary Associations," *International Journal of Public Administration* 28: 849–56.

Jordan, A. Grant and William A. Maloney. 1998. "Manipulating Membership: Supply-Side Influences on Group Size," *British Journal of Political Science* 28, no. 2: 389–409.

———., D. Benson, A. Zito, and Wurzel R. 2012. "Environmental Policy: Governing by Multiple Policy Tools?" In *Constructing a Policy State? Policy Dynamics in the EU*, edited by J.J. Richardson. Oxford: Oxford University Press.

Jordan, Andrew, David Benson, Rudiger Wurzel, and Anthony Zito. 2011. "Policy Tools in Practice," in *Oxford Handbook of Climate Change and Society*, edited by J.S. Dryzek, R.B. Norgaard, and D. Schlosberg, 536–49. Oxford: Oxford University Press.

———, and John Turnpenny, eds. 2014. *The Tools of Policy Formulation: Actors, Capacities, Venues and Effects*. Cheltenham: Edward Elgar.

Junginger, Sabine. 2013. "Design and Innovation in the Public Sector: Matters of Design in policymaking and Policy Implementation," presented at 10th European Academy of Design Conference—Crafting the Future.

Justen, Andreas, Nils Fearnley, Moshe Givoni, and James Macmillen. 2013a. "A Process for Designing Policy Packaging: Ideals and Realities," *Transportation Research Part A: Policy and Practice* (2013a). doi:10.1016/j.tra.2013.10.016.

———, Jens Schippl, Barbara Lenz, and Torsten Fleischer. 2013b. "Assessment of Policies and Detection of Unintended Effects: Guiding Principles for the Consideration of Methods and Tools in Policy-Packaging," *Transportation Research*

Part A: Policy and Practice (2013b). doi:10.1016/j.tra.2013.10.015.

Kagel, John H., and Dan Levin. 2002. *Common Value Auctions and the Winner's Curse.* Princeton, NJ: Princeton University Press.

Kahneman, D. 2003. Maps of Bounded Rationality: Psychology for Behavioral Economics *American Economic Review* 93, no. 5: pp. 1449–1475.

———. 2013. *Thinking, Fast and Slow.* New York: Farrar, Strauss and Giroux.

———, and Amos Tversky. 1979. "Prospect Theory: An Analysis of Decision under Risk," *Econometrica* 47: 263–89.

Kallbekken, Steffen, and Hakon Sælen. 2011. "Public Acceptance for Environmental Taxes: Self-Interest, Environmental and Distributional Concerns," *Energy Policy,* 39, no. 5: 2966–2973.

Katzman, Martin T. 1988. "Societal Risk Management through the Insurance Market," in R.C. Hula, ed., *Market-Based Public Policy.* London: Macmillan, 21–42.

Kay, Adrian. 2011. "Evidence-Based Policy-Making: The Elusive Search for Rational Public Administration," *Australian Journal of Public Administration* 70, no. 3 (September 1): 236–45.

Kelman, Steven. 2002. "Contracting," in Salamon (2002a: 282–318).

Kernaghan, Kenneth. 1993. "Partnership and Public Administration: Conceptual and Practical Considerations," *Canadian Public Administration* 36, no. 1: 57–76.

Kerwin, Cornelius M. 1994. "The Elements of Rule-Making," in Rosenbloom and Schwartz (1994: 345–81).

———. 1999. *Rulemaking: How Government Agencies Write Law and Make Policy.* Washington: Congressional Quarterly Press.

Keyes, J.M. 1996. "Power Tools: The Form and Function of Legal Instruments for Government Action," *Canadian Journal of Administrative Law and Practice* 10: 133–174.

Kickert, Walter J.M. 2001. "Public Management of Hybrid Organizations: Governance of Quasi-Autonomous Executive Agencies," *International Public Management Journal* 4: 135–50.

Kirschen, E.S., et al. 1964. *Economic Policy in Our Time,* vol. 1—*General Theory.* Chicago: Rand McNally.

Kingdon, John W. 1984. *Agendas, Alternatives and Public Policies.* Boston: Little, Brown.

Knill, Christoph. 2001. "Private Governance across Multiple Arenas: European Interest Associations as Interface Actors," *Journal of European Public Policy* 8, no. 2: 227–46.

Knott, Jack H., and Diane McCarthy. 2007. "Policy Venture Capital: Foundations, Government Partnerships, and Child Care Programs," *Administration and Society* 39, no. 3: 319–53.

Kooiman, Jan. 2008. "Exploring the Concept of Governability," *Journal of Comparative Policy Analysis: Research and Practice* 10, no. 2: 171–90.

Koppell, J.G.S. 2003. *The Politics of Quasi-Government: Hybrid Organizations and the Dynamics of Bureaucratic Control.* Cambridge: Cambridge University Press.

Koppenjan, Joop, Mirjam Kars, and Haiko van der Voort. 2009. "Vertical Politics in Horizontal Policy Networks: Framework Settings as Coupling Arrangement," *Policy Studies Journal* 37, no. 4: 769–792.

Korpi, Walter. 1980. "Social Policy and Distributional Conflict in Capitalist Democracies," *West European Politics,* 3: 296–316.

Krause, Rachel Marie. 2011. "An Assessment of the Greenhouse Gas Reducing Activities Being Implemented in US Cities," *Local Environment* 16, no. 2: 193–211.

Kuhfuss, Laure, Raphaële Préget, Sophie Thoyer, Nick Hanley, Philippe Le Coent, and Mathieu Désolé. 2016. "Nudges, Social Norms, and Permanence in Agri-Environmental Schemes," *Land Economics* 92, no. 4: 641–55.

Kuttner, Robert. 1997. *Everything for Sale: The Virtues and Limits of Markets.* New York: Alfred A. Knopf.

Lane, Jan-Erik. 2001. "From Long-Term to Short-Term Contracting," *Public Administration* 79, no. 1: 29–48.

Lane, Wheaton. 1950. "The Early Highway in America," in Jean Labatut and Wheaton Lane, *Highways in Our National Life.* Princeton, NJ: Princeton University Press, 68–75.

Lee, Mordecai. 2001. "The Agency Spokesperson: Connecting Public Administration and the Media," *Public Administration Quarterly* 25, no. 1: 101–30.

Leeuw, Frans L. 1998. "The Carrot: Subsidies as a Tool of Government," in Bemelmans, Videc et al. (1998: 77–102).

Leplay, Solenn, and Sophie Thoyer. 2011. *Synergy Effects of International Policy Tools to Reduce Deforestation: a Cross-country Panel Data Analysis*. Working Paper. LAMETA, University of Montpellier. http://ideas.repec.org/p/lam/wpaper/11–01.html.

Le Grand, Julian and Ray Robinson, eds. 1984. *Privatization and the Welfare State*. London: George Allen and Unwin.

Leman, Christopher. 1989. "The Forgotten Fundamental: Successes and Excesses of Direct Government," in Salamon (1989a).

———. 2002. "Direct Government," in Salamon (2002a: 48–79).

Leutz, Walter N. 1999. "Five Laws for Integrating Medical and Social Services: Lessons from the United States and the United Kingdom," *The Milbank Quarterly* 77, no. 1 (January 1): 77–110.

Libecap, Gary D. 1986. "Deregulation as an Instrument in Industrial Policy: Comment," *Journal of Institutional and Theoretical Economics (JITE)/Zeitschrift für die gesamte Staatswissenschaft* 142, no. 1: 71–4.

Linder, Stephen H. 1999. "Coming to Terms with Public–Private Partnership," *American Behavioural Scientist* 43, no. 1: 35–51.

———, and B. G. Peters. 1988. "The Analysis of Design or the Design of Analysis?" *Policy Studies Review* 7, no. 4: 738–750.

Lindquist, E. 1998. "A Quarter Century of Canadian Think Tanks: Evolving Institutions, Conditions and Strategies," in *Think Tanks Across Nations: A Comparative Approach*, edited by D. Stone, A. Denham, and M. Garnett, 127–144. Manchester: Manchester University Press.

———. 1992. "Public Managers and Policy Communities: Learning to Meet New Challenges," *Canadian Public Administration* 35, no. 2: 127–59.

Lindvall, Johannes. 2009. "The Real but Limited Influence of Expert Ideas," *World Politics* 61, no. 4: 703–730.

Lourenço, Joana Sousa, Emanuele Ciriolo, Sara Rafael Almeida, and Xavier Troussard. 2016. "Behavioural Insights Applied to Policy: European Report 2016," Brussels: European Commission.

Lowi, Theodore J. 1985. "The State in Politics: The Relation between Policy and Administration," in R.G. Noll, ed., *Regulatory Policy and the Social Sciences*. Berkeley: University of California Press, 67–105.

Lowry, R.C. 1999. "Foundation Patronage toward Citizen Groups and Think Tanks: Who Gets Grants?" *Journal of Politics* 81, no. 3: 758–76.

Lund, Michael S. 1989. "Between Welfare and the Market: Loan Guarantees as a Policy Tool," in Salamon (1989a: 125–66).

Lunn, Pete. 2014. *Regulatory Policy and Behavioural Economics*. OECD Publishing.

MacAvoy, Paul, et al., eds. 1989. *Privatization and State-Owned Enterprises: Lessons from the United States, Great Britain, and Canada*. Boston: Kluwer.

MacRae, D., and D. Whittington. 1997. *Expert Advice for Policy Choice: Analysis and Discourse*. Washington DC: Georgetown University Press.

Majone, G. 1975. "On the Notion of Political Feasibility," *European Journal of Political Research* 3, no. 2: 259–274.

———. 1989. *Evidence, Argument, and Persuasion in the Policy Process*. New Haven: Yale University Press.

Maley, Maria. 2000. "Conceptualising Advisers' Policy Work: The Distinctive Policy Roles of Ministerial Advisers in the Keating Government, 1991–96," *Australian Journal of Political Science* 35, no. 3: 449–449.

Maloney, William A, Grant Jordan, and Andrew M. McLaughlin. 1994. "Interest Groups and Public Policy: The Insider/Outsider Model Revisited," *Journal of Public Policy* 14, no. 1: 17–38.

Mandell, Svante. 2008. "Optimal Mix of Emissions Taxes and Cap-and-Trade," *Journal of Environmental Economics and Management* 56: 131–140.

Mann, C., and Simons, A. 2014. "Local Emergence and International Developments of Conservation Trading Systems: Innovation Dynamics and Related Problems," *Environmental Conservation*: 1–10.

Maor, M. 2012. "Policy Overreaction," *Journal of Public Policy* 32, no. 3: 231–59.

March, James G., and Johan P. Olsen. 1996. "Institutional Perspectives on Political Institutions," *Governance* 9, no. 3: 247–64.

Marion, Justin, and Erich Muehlegger. 2007. *Measuring Illegal Activity and the Effects of Regulatory Innovation: A Study of Diesel Fuel Tax Evasion*. Cambridge, MA: John F. Kennedy School of Government Faculty Research Working Paper Series RWP07–026.

Maslove, Allan, ed. 1994. *Taxing and Spending: Issues of Process*. Toronto: University of Toronto Press.

May, P. 2003. "Policy Design and Implementation," in B. Guy Peters and Jon Pierre (eds), *Handbook of Public Administration* (pp. 223–233). Beverly Hills: Sage Publications.

Mayer, I., P. Bots, and E. van Daalen. 2004. "Perspectives on Policy Analysis: A Framework for Understanding and Design," *International Journal of Technology, Policy and Management* 4, no. 1: 169–191.

Mayntz, Renate. 1979. "Public Bureaucracies and Policy Implementation," *International Social Science Journal* 31, no. 4: 633–45.

McCubbins, Mathew D., Roger G. Noll, and Barry R. Weingast. 1987. "Administrative Procedures as Instruments of Political Control," *Journal of Law, Economics, and Organization* 3, no. 2: 243–77.

———, ———, and ———. 1989. "Structure and Process, Politics and Policy: Administrative Arrangements and the Political Control of Agencies," *Virginia Law Review* 75, no. 2: 431–482.

McDaniel, Paul R. 1989. "Tax Expenditures as Tools of Government Action," in Salamon (1989a).

McKenzie, Evan. 2006. "Emerging Trends in State Regulation of Private Communities in the U.S." *GeoJournal* 66, no. 1: 89–102. doi:10.1007.s10708-006-9019-y.

McKirnan, David J. 1980. "The Identification Of Deviance: A Conceptualization and Initial Test of a Model of Social Norms," *European Journal of Social Psychology* 10, no. 1: 75–93.

Merton, Robert K. 1948. "The Self-Fulfilling Prophecy," *Antioch Review* 8, 2: 193–210.

Milkman, Katherine L., Mary Carol Mazza, Lisa L. Shu, Chia-Jung Tsay, and Max H. Bazerman. 2012. "Policy Bundling to Overcome Loss Aversion: A Method for Improving Legislative Outcomes," *Organizational Behavior and Human Decision Processes* 117, no. 1 (January): 158–167.

Mitchell, K. 2001. "Transnationalism, Neo-Liberalism and the Rise of the Shadow State," *Economy and Society* 30, no. 2: 165–89.

Mitnick, Barry M. 1980. *The Political Economy of Regulation: Creating, Designing, and Removing Regulatory Forms*. New York: Columbia University Press.

Mizrahi, Shlomo. 2012. "Self-Provision of Public Services: Its Evolution and Impact," *Public Administration Review* 72, no. 2: 285–91.

Montpetit, Eric. 2002. "Policy Networks, Federal Arrangements, and the Development of Environmental Regulations: A Comparison of the Canadian and American Agricultural Sectors," *Governance* 15, no. 1: 1–20.

———. 2003. "Public Consultations in Policy Network Environments," *Canadian Public Policy* 29, no. 1: 95–110.

Moore, Don A., and Paul J. Healy. 2008. "The Trouble with Overconfidence," *Psychological Review* 115, no. 2: 502.

Moss, David A. 2002. *When All Else Fails: Government as the Ultimate Risk Manager*. Cambridge, MA: Harvard University Press.

Mucciaroni, G. 1992. "The Garbage Can Model And the Study of policymaking: A Critique," *Polity* 24, no. 3: 460–82.

Mukherjee, Ishani and Michael Howlett. 2015. "Who is a Stream? Epistemic Communities, Instrument Constituencies and Advocacy Coalitions in Public Policy-Making," *Politics and Governance* 3, no. 2: 65–75.

Mullainathan, Sendhil, and Eldar Shafir. 2013. *Scarcity: Why Having Too Little Means So Much*. New York: Henry Holt and Co.

Musolf, Lloyd D. 1989. "The Government Corporation Tool: Permutations and Possibilities," in Salamon (1989a: 231–52).

Myles, John. 1989. Old Age in the Welfare State: The Political Economy of Public Pensions. Lawrence, KA: University Press of Kansas.

Nelson, R. 1977. *The Moon and the Ghetto: An Assay on Public Policy Analysis*. Chicago: WW Norton.

Norberg-Bohm, V. 1999. "Stimulating "Green" Technological Innovation: An Analysis of Alternative Policy Mechanisms," *Policy Sciences* 32: 13–38.

Nownes, Anthony J. 1995. "The Other Exchange: Public Interest Groups, Patrons, and Benefits," *Social Science Quarterly* 76, no. 2: 381–401.

———, and Grant Neeley. 1996. "Toward an Explanation for Public Interest Group Formation and Proliferation: 'Seed Money,' Disturbances, Entrepreneurship, and Patronage," *Policy Studies Journal* 24, no. 1: 74–92.

Nutley, Sandra M., Isabel Walter, and Huw T. O. Davies. 2007. *Using Evidence: How Research Can Inform Public Services*. Bristol: Policy Press

O'Donoghue, Ted, and Matthew Rabin. 1999. "Doing It Now or Later," *American Economic Review* 89, no. 1: 103–124.

OECD, 2017. *Behavioural Insights and Public Policy Lessons from Around the World*. Paris: OECD.

Olsen, J.P. 2005. "Maybe It Is Time to Rediscover Bureaucracy," *Journal of Public Administration Research and Theory* 16, no. 1: 1–24.

Organization for Economic Co-operation and Development (OECD). 1993. *Managing with Market-Type Mechanisms*. Paris: OECD.

———. 2006. *The Political Economy of Environmentally Related Taxes*. Paris: OECD.

Osborne, Stephen P. 2006. "The New Public Governance?" *Public Management Review* 8, no. 3: 377–387.

Ostrom, Elinor. 1973. *Community Organization and the Provision of Police Services*. California: Sage Publications.

———. 1996. "Crossing the Great Divide: Coproduction, Synergy, and Development," *World Development* 24, no. 6: 1073–87.

Overbye, Einar. 1994. "Convergence in Policy Outcomes: Social Security Systems in Perspectives," *Journal of Public Policy*, 14, no. 2: 147–74.

Owens, Susan, and Tim Rayner. 1999. "'When Knowledge Matters': The Role and Influence of the Royal Commission on Environmental Pollution," *Journal of Environmental Policy and Planning* 1: 7–24.

Packwood, A. 2002. "Evidence-Based Policy: Rhetoric and Reality," *Social Policy & Society* 1, no. 3: 267–72.

Padberg, D.I. 1992. "Nutritional Labeling as a Policy Instrument," *American Journal of Agricultural Economics* 74, no. 5: 1208–13.

Page, Edward C. 2010. "Bureaucrats and expertise: Elucidating a problematic relationship in three tableaux and six jurisdictions," *Sociologie du Travail* 52, no. 2: 255–273.

Pal, Leslie A. 1992. *Public Policy Analysis: An Introduction*, 2nd edn. Scarborough, ON: Nelson.

———. 1993a. Interests of State: The Politics of Language, Multiculturalism, and Feminism in Canada. Montreal and Kingston: McGill-Queen's University Press.

Palier, Bruno. 2007. "Tracking the Evolution of a Single Instrument Can Reveal Profound Changes: The Case of Funded Pensions in France," *Governance* 20, no. 1: 85–107.

Papaioannou, H. Rush, and J. Bassant. 2006. "Performance Management: Benchmarking as a Policy-Making Tool: From the Private to the Public Sector," *Science and Public Policy* 33, no. 2: 91–102.

Parks, Roger B., Paula C. Baker, Larry Kiser, Ronald Oakerson, Elinor Ostrom, Vincent Ostrom, Stephen L. Percy, Martha B. Vandivort, Gordon P. Whitaker, and Rick Wilson. 1981. "Consumers as Coproducers Of Public Services: Some Economic and Institutional Considerations," *Policy Studies Journal* 9, no. 7: 1001–1011.

Parks, Roger B., Stephen D. Mastrofski, Christina DeJong, and M. Kevin Gray. 1999. "How Officers Spend Their Time With the Community," *Justice Quarterly* 16, no. 3: 483–518.

Pawson, R. 2002. "Evidence-Based Policy: In Search of a Method?" *Evaluation* 8, no. 2: 157–81.

Peled, A. 2002. "Why Style Matters: A Comparison of Two Administrative Reform Initiatives in the Israeli Public Sector, 1989–1998," *Journal of Public Administration Research and Theory* 12, no. 2: 217–40.

Perez-Batres, Luis A., Van V. Miller, and Michael J. Pisani. 2011. "Institutionalizing Sustainability: An Empirical Study of Corporate Registration and Commitment to the United Nations Global Compact Guidelines," *Journal of Cleaner Production* 19, no. 8: 843–51.

Perl, Anthony and James A. Dunn Jr. 1997. "Reinventing Amtrak: The Politics of

Survival," *Journal of Policy Analysis and Management* 16, no. 4: 598–614.

Pestoff, Victor. 2006. "Citizens and Co-Production of Welfare Services," *Public Management Review* 8 (December): 503–519.

Pestoff, Victor, and Taco Brandsen. 2009. "Public Governance and the Third Sector: Opportunities for Co-Production and Innovation?" Paper presented at the conference of the European Group of Public Administration, September 2–4, 2009, St. Julians, Malta. Available at: http://citeseerx.ist.psu.edu/viewdoc/download?doi=10.1.1.951.5418&rep=rep1&type=pdf

———, Taco Brandsen, and Bram Verschuere. 2012. *New Public Governance, the Third Sector and Co-Production*. New York: Routledge.

Peters, B. Guy. 1992b. "Government Reorganization: A Theoretical Analysis," *International Political Science Review* 13, no. 2: 199–218.

———. 1998. *Managing Horizontal Government: The Politics of Coordination*. Ottawa: Canadian Centre for Management Development.

———. 2005. "Conclusion: The Future of Instruments Research," in *Designing Government: From Instruments to Governance*, edited by P. Eliadis, M. Hill, and M. Howlett, 353–363. Montreal: McGill-Queen's University Press.

———, and Anthony Barker, eds. 1993. *Advising West European Governments: Inquiries, Expertise and Public Policy*. Edinburgh: Edinburgh University Press.

Phidd, Richard W. 1975. "The Economic Council of Canada: Its Establishment, Structure, and Role in the Canadian Policy-Making System 1963–74," *Canadian Public Administration* 18, no. 3: 428–73.

Phillips, Jim, Bruce Chapman, and David Stevens, eds. 2001. *Between State and Market: Essays on Charities, Law and Policy in Canada*. Toronto: University of Toronto Press.

Phillips, Susan D. 1991a. "How Ottawa Blends: Shifting Government Relationships with Interest Groups," in F. Abele, ed., *How Ottawa Spends 1991–92: The Politics of Fragmentation*. Ottawa: Carleton University Press, 183–228.

———, and Karine Levasseur. 2004. "The Snakes and Ladders of Accountability: Contradictions between Contracting and Collaboration for Canada's Voluntary Sector," *Canadian Public Administration* 47, no. 4: 451–74.

Pichert, Daniel, and Konstantinos V. Katsikopoulos. 2008. "Green Defaults: Information Presentation and Pro-Environmental Behaviour," *Journal of Environmental Psychology* 28, no. 1: 63–73.

Poocharoen, Ora-orn, and Bernard Ting. 2015. "Collaboration, Co-production, Networks: Convergence of Theories," *Public Management Review* 17, no. 4: 587–614.

Post, L. A., Salmon, T. and Raile, A., 2008, "Using Public Will to Secure Political Will," ch. 7 in *Governance Reform Under Real World Conditions*, eds. S. Odugbemi and T. Jacobson, Communication for Governance and Accountability Program, World Bank, Washington DC. http://www.gsdrc.org/go/display&type=Document&id=3710

Prentice, Susan. "Childcare, Co-Production and the Third Sector in Canada," *Public Management Review* 8, no. 4: 521–36.

Prince, Michael. 1983. *Policy Advice and Organizational Survival*. Aldershot: Gower.

Pross, A. Paul and Iain S. Stewart. 1993. "Lobbying, the Voluntary Sector and the Public Purse," in S.D. Phillips, ed., *How Ottawa Spends 1993–1994: A More Democratic Canada?* Ottawa: Carleton University Press, 109–42.

Putnam, Robert D. 1995a. "Bowling Alone: America's Declining Social Capital," *Journal of Democracy* 6, no. 1: 65–78.

———. 1995b. "Tuning In, Tuning Out: The Strange Disappearance of Social Capital in America," *PS: Political Science and Politics* (Dec.): 664–83.

———. 1996. *The Decline of Civil Society: How Come? So What?* Ottawa: Canadian Centre for Management Development.

———. 2000. *Bowling Alone: The Collapse and Revival of American Community*. New York: Simon and Schuster.

———. 2001. "Social Capital: Measurement and Consequences," *Isuma* 2, no. 1: 41–52.

Qualter, Terence H. 1985. *Opinion Control in the Democracies*. London: Macmillan.

Raboy, Marc. 1995. "Influencing Public Policy on Canadian Broadcasting," *Canadian Public Administration* 38, no. 3: 411–32.

Ramesh, M. 2008. "Healthcare Reforms in Thailand: Rethinking Conventional Wisdom," in Scott Fritzen and M Ramesh, eds, *Transforming Asian Governance*, Routledge. 2008.

Relyea, Harold C. 1977. "The Provision of Government Information: The Freedom of Information Act Experience," *Canadian Public Administration* 20, no. 2: 317–41.

Resodihardjo, S.L. 2006. "Wielding a Double-Edged Sword: The Use of Inquiries at Times of Crisis," *Journal of Contingencies and Crisis Management* 14, no. 4: 199–206.

Rich, A. 2004. *Think Tanks, Public Policy, and the Politics of Expertise*. New York: Cambridge University Press.

Riker, William H. 1983. "Political Theory and the Art of Heresthetics," in Ada W. Finifter, ed., *Political Science: The State of the Discipline*. Washington: American Political Science Association, 47–67.

———. 1986. *The Art of Political Manipulation*. New Haven: Yale University Press.

Rimlinger, G. V. 1971. *Welfare Policy and Industrialization in Europe, America and Russia*. New York: Wiley.

Rochet, C. 2004. "Rethinking the Management of Information in the Strategic Monitoring of Public Policies by Agencies," *Industrial Management & Data Systems* 104, no. 3: 201–08

Rosenbloom, David H. 2007. "Administrative Law and Regulation," in Jack Rabin, W. Bartley Hildreth, and Gerald J. Miller, eds, *Handbook of Public Administration*. London: CRC Taylor & Francis, 635–96.

Rotberg, Robert I. 2014. "Good Governance Means Performance and Results," *Governance*. doi:10.1111/gove.12084.

Sabatier, Paul A. 1975. "Social Movements and Regulatory Agencies: Toward a More Adequate—and Less Pessimistic—Theory of "Clientele Capture," *Policy Sciences* 6: 301–42.

———. 1977. "Regulatory Policy-Making: Toward a Framework of Analysis," *Natural Resources Journal* 17, no. 3: 415–60.

———, H. Jenkins-Smith, P.A. Sabatier, and H.C. Jenkins-Smith. 1993. "The Advocacy Coalition Framework: Assessment, Revisions, and Implications for Scholars and Practitioners," in *Policy Change and Learning: An Advocacy Coalition Approach*, 211–36. Boulder, CO: Westview.

Sager, Fritz, and Yvan Rielle. 2013. "Sorting through the Garbage Can: Under What Conditions Do Governments Adopt Policy Programs?" *Policy Sciences* 46, no. 1: 1–21. doi:10.1007/s11077–012–9165–7.

Salamon, Lester M. 1981. "Rethinking Public Management: Third-Party Government and the Changing Forms of Government Action," *Public Policy* 29, no. 3: 255–75.

———. 1987. "Of Market Failure, Voluntary Failure, and Third-Party Government," in Ostrander and Langton (1987).

Salamon, L.M.1989. "The Tools Approach: Basic Analytics," in *Beyond Privatization: The Tools of Government Action*, edited by L. S. Salamon and M.S. Lund, 23–50. Washington D.C.: Urban Institute, 1989.

———. 1995. *Partners in Public Service: Government-Nonprofit Relations in the Modern Welfare State*. Baltimore: Johns Hopkins University Press.

———. 2002. *The Tools of Government: A Guide to the New Governance*. New York: Oxford University Press.

———. 2002b. "Economic Regulation," in Salamon (2002a: 117–55).

———. 2002c. "The New Governance and the Tools of Public Action," in Salamon (2002a: 1–47).

———, and Michael S. Lund. 1989. "The Tools Approach: Basic Analytics," in Salamon (1989a: 23–50).

Salmon, Charles, ed. 1989a. *Information Campaigns: Managing the Process of Social Change*. Newberry Park, CA: Sage.

———. 1989b. "Campaigns for Social Improvement: An Overview of Values, Rationales, and Impacts," in Salmon (1989a: 1–32).

Sampson, Steven, 1991. "Is There an Anthropology of Socialism?" *Anthropology Today* 7, no. 5: 16–19

Sanderson, Ian. 2009. "Intelligent Policy Making for a Complex World: Pragmatism, Evidence and Learning," *Political Studies* 57: 699–719.

Schön, D. A. 1988. "Designing: Rules, Types and Words," *Design Studies 9*, no. 3: 181–190.

———. 1992. "Designing as Reflective Conversation with the Materials of a Design Situation," *Knowledge-Based Systems* 5, no. 1: 3–14.

Savoia, Antonio and Kunal Sen. 2014. "Measurement, Evolution, Determinants, and Consequences of State Capacity: A Review of Recent Research," *Journal of Economic Surveys*. doi:10.1111/joes.12065

Saward, Michael. 1990. "Cooption and Power: Who Gets What from Formal Incorporation," *Political Studies* 38: 588–602.

———. 1992. *Co-Optive Politics and State Legitimacy*. Aldershot: Dartmouth.

Schmitter, Phillipe C. 1977. "Modes of Interest Intermediation and Models of Societal Change in Western Europe," *Comparative Political Studies* 10, no. 1: 7–38.

———. 1985. "Neo-corporatism and the State," in W. Grant, ed., *The Political Economy of Corporatism*. London: Macmillan.

Sethi-Iyengar, Sheena, Gur Huberman, and Wei Jiang. 2004. "How Much Choice Is Too Much? Contributions to 401(K) Retirement Plans," *Pension Design and Structure: New Lessons from Behavioral Finance* 83: 84–87.

Shah, Anuj K., and Daniel M. Oppenheimer. 2008. "Heuristics Made Easy: An Effort-Reduction Framework," *Psychological Bulletin* 134, no. 2: 207.

Shalev, Michael. 1983. "The Social Democratic Model and Beyond: Two Generations of Comparative Research on the Welfare State," *Comparative Social Research*: 315–51.

Sheriff, Peta E. 1983. "State Theory, Social Science, and Governmental Commissions," *American Behavioural Scientist* 26, no. 5: 669–80.

Sidney, Mara S. 2007. "Policy Formulation: Design and Tools," in *Handbook of Public Policy Analysis: Theory, Politics and Methods*, edited by Frank Fischer, Gerald J. Miller, and Mara S. Sidney, 79–87. New Brunswick, N. J.: CRC Taylor & Francis.

Simon, Herbert A. 1955. "A Behavioral Model of Rational Choice," *Quarterly Journal of Economics* 69, no. 1: 99–118.

———. 1957a. *Administrative Behavior: A Study of Decision-Making Processes in Administrative Organization*, 2nd edn. New York: Macmillan.

Simon, Herbert A. 1976. *"From Substantive to Procedural Rationality"*: *25 Years of Economic Theory*. Boston, MA: Springer, 65–86.

Sinclair, Darren. 1997. "Self-Regulation versus Command and Control? Beyond False Dichotomies," *Law and Policy* 19, no. 4: 529–59.

Smith, Martin J., David Marsh, and David Richards. 1993. "Central Government Departments and the Policy Process," *Public Administration* 71 (Winter): 567–94.

Smith, Thomas B. 1977. "Advisory Committees in the Public Policy Process," *International Review of Administrative Sciences* 43, no. 2: 153–66.

Sproule-Jones, M. 1994. "User Fees," in A.M. Maslove, ed., *Taxes as Instruments of Public Policy*. Toronto: University of Toronto Press, 3–38.

Stanbury, W.T., and Jane Fulton. 1984. "Suasion as a Governing Instrument," in A. Maslove, ed., *How Ottawa Spends 1984: The New Agenda*. Toronto: James Lorimer.

Stanton, Thomas H. 2002. "Loans and Loan Guarantees," in Salamon (2002a: 381–409).

———, and Ronald C. Moe. 2002. "Government Corporations and Government-Sponsored Enterprises," in Salamon (2002a: 80–116).

Starr, Paul. 1989. "The Meaning of Privatization," in S.B. Kamerman and A.J. Kahn, eds, *Privatization and the Welfare State*. Princeton, NJ: Princeton University Press, 15–48.

———. 1990a. "The Limits of Privatization," in D.J. Gayle and J.N. Goodrich, eds, *Privatization and Deregulation in Global Perspective*. New York: Quorum Books.

Staub, Ervin. 1972. "Instigation to Goodness: The Role of Social Norms and Interpersonal Influence," *Journal of Social Issues* 28, no. 3: 131–150.

Stavins, Robert N. 2008. "A Meaningful US Cap-and-Trade System to Address Climate Change," *Harvard Environmental Law Review* 32: 293.

Steuerle, C. Eugene, and Eric C. Twombly. 2002. "Vouchers," in Salamon (2002a: 445–65).

Stewart, Jenny. 1993. "Rational Choice Theory, Public Policy and The Liberal State," *Policy Sciences* 26, no. 4: 317–330.

Stone, Diane. 2001. "Learning Lessons, Policy Transfer and The International Diffusion of Policy Ideas," *Centre for the Study of Globalisation And Regionalisation Working Paper* 69/01.

Studlar, Donley T. 2002. *Tobacco Control: Comparative Politics in the United States and Canada*. Peterborough, ON: Broadview Press.

Sunnevag, Kjell J. 2000. "Designing Auctions for Offshore Petroleum Lease Allocation," *Resources Policy* 26: 3–16.

Sunstein, Cass R. 2014. *Why Nudge?: The Politics of Libertarian Paternalism*. New Haven: Yale University Press.

——, and Lucia Reisch. 2013. "Green by Default," *Kyklos* 66, no. 3: 398–402.

——, and Lucia A. Reisch. 2016. "Behaviorally Green: Why, Which and When Defaults Can Help," *New Perspectives for Environmental Policies Through Behavioral Economics*. Springer, Cham, 161–94.

Teisman, G. 2000. "Models for research into decision-making processes: On phases, streams and decision-making rounds," *Public Administration* 1, no. 1.

Thaler, Richard H., and Cass R. Sunstein, 2008. *Nudge: Improving Decisions about Health, Wealth, and Happiness*. New Haven: Yale University Press.

Thissen, W.A.H., and P.G.J. Twaalfhoven. 2001. "Toward a Conceptual Structure for Evaluating Policy Analytic Activities," *European Journal of Operational Research* 129: 627–49.

Thomas, H.G. 2001. "Towards a New Higher Education Law in Lithuania: Reflections on the Process of Policy Formulation," *Higher Education Policy* 14, no. 3: 213–23.

Thompson, G.F. 2003. *Between Hierarchies and Markets: The Logic and Limits of Network Forms of Organization*. Oxford: Oxford University Press.

Tiernan, A., and Wanna, J. 2006. "Competence, Capacity, Capability: Towards Conceptual Clarity in the Discourse of Declining Policy Skills," presented at the Govnet International Conference, Australian National University. Canberra: ANU, 2006.

Townsend, R.E., J. McColl, and M.D. Young. 2006. "Design Principles for Individual Transferable Quotas," *Marine Policy* 30: 131–41.

Trebilcock, Michael J., et al. 1982. *The Choice of Governing Instrument*. Ottawa: Canadian Government Publication Centre.

——, and J.R.S. Prichard. 1983. "Crown Corporations: The Calculus of Instrument Choice," in *Crown Corporations in Canada: The Calculus of Instrument Choice*, 1–50. Toronto: Butterworths.

Tribe, L.H. 1972. "Policy Science: Analysis or Ideology?" *Philosophy and Public Affairs* 2, no. 1: 66–110.

Trischler, Jakob, Timo Dietrich, and Sharyn Rundle-Thiele. 2019. "Co-Design: From Expert- to User-Driven Ideas in Public Service Design," *Public Management Review* 21, no. 11: 1595–1619.

Tuohy, Caroline and A.D. Wolfson. 1978. "Self-Regulation: Who Qualifies?" in P. Slayton and M.J. Trebilcock, eds, *The Professions and Public Policy*. Toronto: University of Toronto Press, 111–22.

Tupper, Allan and G.B. Doern. 1981. "Public Corporations and Public Policy in Canada," in Tupper and Doern, eds, *Public Corporations and Public Policy in Canada*. Montreal: Institute for Research on Public Policy, 1–50.

Turnpenny, John, Claudio M. Radaelli, Andrew Jordan, and Klaus Jacob. 2009. "The Policy and Politics of Policy Appraisal: Emerging Trends and New Directions," *Journal of European Public Policy* 16, no. 4: 640–53.

Tversky, Amos, and Daniel Kahneman. 1974. "Judgment Under Uncertainty: Heuristics and Biases," *Science* 185, no. 4157: 1124–31.

Tversky, Amos, and Daniel Kahneman. 1981. "The Framing of Decisions and the Psychology of Choice," *Science* 211 (Jan.): 453–8.

Tversky, Amos, and Daniel Kahneman, eds. 2000. *Choices, Values, and Frames*. UK: Cambridge University Press.

Valkama, Pekka, and Stephen J. Bailey. 2001. "Vouchers as an Alternative Public Sector Funding System," *Public Policy and Administration* 16, 1: 32–58.

van de Kerkof, Marleen. 2006. "Making a Difference: On the Constraints of Consensus Building and the Relevance of Deliberation in Stakeholder Dialogues," *Policy Sciences* 39, 3: 279–99.

Vedung, Evert, and Frans C.J. van der Doelen. 1998. "The Sermon: Information Programs in the Public Policy Process— Choice, Effects and Evaluation," in Bemelmans-Videc et al. (1998: 103–28).

Verschuere, Bram. 2009. "The Role of Public Agencies in the Policy Making Process," *Public Policy and Administration* 24, no. 1: 23–46.

Voorberg, W.H., V.J.J.M. Bekkers, and L.G. Tummers. 2014. "A Systematic Review of Co-Creation and Co-Production: Embarking on the Social Innovation Journey," *Public Management Review* (June 30): 1–25.

Voss, Jan-Peter, and Arno Simons. 2014. "Instrument Constituencies and the Supply Side of Policy Innovation: The Social Life of Emissions Trading," *Environmental Politics* 23, no. 5: 735–54.

———, and Arno Simons. 2014. "Instrument Constituencies and the Supply Side of Policy Innovation: The Social Life of Emissions Trading," *Environmental Politics* 23, no. 5: 735–54.

Waller, Mike. 1992. "Evaluating Policy Advice," *Australian Journal of Public Administration* 51, no. 4: 440–49.

Walsh, Annmarie Hauck. 1978. *The Public's Business: The Politics and Practices of Government Corporations.* Cambridge, MA: MIT Press.

Warwick, Paul V. 2000. "Policy Horizons in West European Parliamentary Systems," *European Journal of Political Research* 38: 37–61.

Weaver, Kent. 2009. "If You Build It, Will They Come? Overcoming Unforeseen Obstacles to Program Effectiveness," The Tansley Lecture, presented at University of Saskatchewan, 2009.

———. 2009a. "If You Build It, Will They Come? Overcoming Unforeseen Obstacles to Program Effectiveness," The Tansley Lecture, presented at University of Saskatchewan, 2009.

———. 2009b. *Target Compliance: The Final Frontier of Policy Implementation.* Washington DC: Brookings Institution.

———. 2010. *But Will It Work?: Implementation Analysis to Improve Government Performance.* Washington DC: Brookings Institution. http://www.brookings.edu/research/papers/2010/02/implementation-analysis-weaver.

———. 2013. "Compliance Regimes and Barriers to Behavioral Change," *Governance.* doi:10.1111/gove.12032.

———. 2015. "Getting People to Behave: Research Lessons for Policy Makers," *Public Administration Review,* July 1. doi:10.1111/puar.12412.

Weber, Edward P., and Anne M. Khademian. 2008. "Wicked Problems, Knowledge Challenges and Collaborative Capacity Builders in Network Settings," *Public Administration Review* 68, no. 2: 334–349.

Weiss, Janet A. and Mary Tschirhart. 1994. "Public Information Campaigns as Policy Instruments," *Journal of Policy Analysis and Management* 13, no. 1: 82–119.

Wellstead, Adam M., Michael Howlett, and Jeremy Rayner. 2013a. "The Neglect of Governance in Forest Sector Vulnerability Assessments: Structural-Functionalism and 'Black Box' Problems in Climate Change Adaptation Planning," *Ecology and Society* 18, no. 3. doi:10.5751/ES–05685–180323.

Wellstead, Adam, Jeremy Rayner, and Michael Howlett. 2013b. "Beyond the Black Box: Forest Sector Vulnerability Assessments and Adaptation to Climate Change in North America," *Environmental Science & Policy.* doi:10.1016/j.envsci.2013.04.002.

Whitaker, Gordon P. 1980. "Coproduction: Citizen Participation in Service Delivery," *Public Administration Review:* 240–46.

Williams, A. M., and V. Balaz. 1999. "Privatisation in Central Europe: Different Legacies, Methods and Outcomes," *Environment and Planning C: Government and Policy* 17: 731–751.

Wilson, James Q. 1974. "The Politics of Regulation," in J.W. McKie, ed., *Social Responsibility and the Business Predicament.* Washington: Brookings Institution, 135–68.

Wintges, Rene. 2007. *Monitoring and Analysis of Policies and Public Financing Instruments Conducive to Higher Levels of R&D Investments: The "Policy Mix"*

Project—Case Study: The Netherlands. Maastricht: UNU-MERIT, 2007.

Woerdman, Edwin. 2000. "Organizing Emissions Trading: The Barrier of Domestic Permit Allocation," *Energy Policy* 28: 613–23.

Wollmann, Hellmut. 1989. "Policy Analysis in West Germany's Federal Government: A Case of Unfinished Governmental and Administrative Modernization?" *Governance* 2, no. 3: 233–266.

Wraith, R.E., and G.B. Lamb. 1971. *Public Inquiries as an Instrument of Government*. London: George Allen and Unwin.

Wu, Xun, M. Ramesh, and M. Howlett. 2015. "Policy Capacity: Conceptual Framework and Measures," *Policy & Society*, Fall 2015.

———, M. Ramesh, Michael Howlett, and Scott Fritzen. 2010. *The Public Policy Primer: Managing Public Policy*. London: Routledge.

Wuthnow, Robert, ed. 1991. *Between States and Markets: The Voluntary Sector in Comparative Perspective*. Princeton, NJ: Princeton University Press.

Yanow, Dvora. 1992. "Silences in Public Policy Discourse: Organizational and Policy Myths," *Journal of Public Administration Research and Theory* 2, no. 4: 399–423.

Yee, Albert S. 1996. "The Causal Effects of Ideas on Policies," *International Organizations* 50, no. 1: 69–108.

Yishai, Yael. 1993. "Public Ideas and Public Policy," *Comparative Politics* 25, no. 2: 207–28.

Young, L., and J. Everitt. 2004. *Advocacy Groups*. Vancouver: University of British Columbia Press.

Zarco-Jasso, Hugo. 2005. "Public–Private Partnerships: A Multidimensional Model for Contracting," *International Journal of Public Policy* 1, nos. 1 and 2: 22–40.

Zaval, Lisa, and James F.M. Cornwell. 2016. "Cognitive Biases, Non-Rational Judgments, and Public Perceptions of Climate Change," *Oxford Research Encyclopedia of Climate Science*. Oxford University Press.

Zeckhauser, Richard. 1981. "Preferred Policies When There Is a Concern for Probability of Adoption," *Journal of Environmental Economics and Management* 8: 215–37.

Chapter 6 Sources

Abelson, Donald E. 2007. "Any ideas? think tanks and policy analysis in Canada," in *Policy analysis in Canada: The State of the Art.*, eds L. Dobuzinskis, M. Howlett and D. Laycock, 298–310. Toronto: University of Toronto Press.

Aberbach, Joel D., Robert D. Putnam, and Bert A. Rockman. 1981. *Bureaucrats and Politicians in Western Democracies*. Cambridge, MA: Harvard University Press.

Agranoff, R., and Mete Yildiz. 2007. "Decision Making in Public Management Networks," in *Morçöl* (319–45).

Alexander, Ernest R. 1979. "The Design of Alternatives in Organizational Contexts: A Pilot Study," *Administrative Sciences Quarterly* 24: 382–404.

———. 1982. "Design in the Decision-Making Process," *Policy Sciences* 14: 279–92.

Allison, Graham. 1969. "Conceptual Models and the Cuban Missile Crisis," *American Political Science Review* 63: 689–718.

———. 1971. *Essence of Decision: Explaining the Cuban Missile Crisis*. Boston: Little, Brown.

———, and Morton H. Halperin. 1972. "Bureaucratic Politics: A Paradigm and Some Policy Implications," *World Politics* 24 (supp.): 40–79.

Anderson, Paul A. 1983. "Decision Making by Objection and the Cuban Missile Crisis," *Administrative Science Quarterly* 28: 201–22.

Ansell, Chris, and Alison Gash. 2008. "Collaborative Governance in Theory and Practice," *Journal of Public Administration Research and Theory* 18, no. 4 (October 1): 543–71.

Atkinson, Michael M., and William D. Coleman. 1989a. "Strong States and Weak States: Sectoral Policy Networks in Advanced Capitalist Economies," *British Journal of Political Science* 19, no. 1: 47–67.

Bachrach, Peter, and Morton S. Baratz. 1962. "Decisions and Non-decisions: An Analytical Framework," *American Political Science Review* 56, no. 2: 632–42.

———, and ———. 1970. *Power and Poverty: Theory and Practice*. New York: Oxford University Press.

———, and ———. 1975. "Power and Its Two Faces Revisited: A Reply to Geoffrey Debnam," *American Political Science Review* 69, no. 3: 900–7.

Bailey, J.J., and R.J. O'Connor. 1975. "Operationalizing Incrementalism: Measuring the Muddles," *Public Administration Review* 35: 60–6.

Baumgartner, F.R., and B.D. Jones. 2002. *Policy Dynamics.* Chicago: University of Chicago Press.

Beach, L.R., and T.R. Mitchell. 1978. "A Contingency Model for the Selection of Decision Strategies," *Academy of Management Review* 3, no. 3: 439–49.

Bellman, R.E., and L.A. Zadeh. 1970. "Decision-Making in a Fuzzy Environment," *Management Science* 17, 4: B141–64

Bendor, Jonathan. 1995. "A Model of Muddling Through," *American Political Science Review* 89, no. 4: 819–40.

———, and Thomas H. Hammond. 1992. "Re-Thinking Allison's Models," *American Political Science Review* 86, no. 2: 301–22.

Berridge, V. 2005. "Issue Network versus Producer Network? ASH, the Tobacco Products Research Trust and UK Smoking Policy," *Clio Medica* 75, no. 1: 101–24.

Berry, William T. 1990. "The Confusing Case of Budgetary Incrementalism: Too Many Meanings for a Single Concept," *Journal of Politics* 52: 167–96.

Blaikie, P. and H. Brookfield. 1987. *Land Degradation and Society.* London: Methuen & Co.

Boaz, Annette, Lesley Grayson, Ruth Levitt, and William Solesbury. 2008. "Does Evidence-Based Policy Work? Learning from the UK Experience," *Evidence & Policy* 4, no. 2: 233–253.

Boston, Jonathan. 1994. "Purchasing Policy Advice: The Limits of Contracting Out," *Governance* 7, no. 1: 1–30.

Boyer, B., and L. Cremieux. 1999. "The Anatomy of Association: NGOs and the Evolution of Swiss Climate and Biodiversity Policies," *International Negotiation* 4: 255–82.

Bozeman, Barry and S.K. Pandey. 2004. "Public Management Decision Making: Effect of Decision Content," *Public Administration Review* 64, no. 5: 553–65.

Braybrooke, David, and Charles Lindblom. 1963. *A Strategy of Decision: Policy Evaluation as a Social Process.* New York: Free Press of Glencoe.

Bressers, Hans A., and Laurence J. O'Toole. 1998. "The Selection of Policy Instruments: A Network-based

Perspective," *Journal of Public Policy* 18, no. 3: 213–39.

Brewer, Garry D and Peter deLeon. 1983. *The Foundations of Policy Analysis.* Homewood, NJ: Dorsey.

Brule, David J. 2008. "The Poliheuristic Research Program: An Assessment and Suggestions for Further Progress," *International Studies Review* 10, no. 2: 266–93.

Butler, David and Austin Ranney, eds. 1994. *Referendums Around the World: A Comparative Study of Practice and Theory.* Washington: American Enterprise Institute.

Carley, Michael. 1980. *Rational Techniques in Policy Analysis.* London: Heinemann Educational Books

Chari, R.S., and H. McMahon. 2003. "Reconsidering the Patterns of Organised Interests in Irish Policy Making," *Irish Political Studies* 18, no. 1: 27–50.

Cohen, M.D., J.G. March, and J.P. Olsen. 1979. "People, Problems, Solutions and the Ambiguity of Relevance," in *Ambiguity and Choice in Organizations,* 24–37. Bergen: Universitetsforlaget.

Cohen, M., J. March, and J. Olsen. 1972. "A Garbage Can Framework of Organizational Choice," *Administrative Science Quarterly* 17, no. 1: 1–25.

Colebatch, H. K. 2006. *Beyond the Policy Cycle: The Policy Process in Australia.* Crows Nest: Allen and Unwin.

Colebatch, H.K. and Beryl A. Radin. 2006. "Mapping the Work of Policy," in H. K. Colebatch, ed., *The Work of Policy: An International Survey.* New York: Rowman and Littlefield. 217–226.

Connaughton, B. 2010a. "Ireland," in C. Eichbaum and R. Shaw, eds, *Partisan Appointees and Public Servants: An International Analysis of the Role of the Political Adviser,* Aldershot: Edward Elgar, pp. 151–179.

Connaughton, Bernadette. 2010. "'Glorified Gofers, Policy Experts or Good Generalists': A Classification of the Roles of the Irish Ministerial Adviser," *Irish Political Studies* 25, no. 3: 347–369.

Conlisk, J. 1996. "Why Bounded Rationality?" *Journal of Economic Literature* 34: 669–700.

Cross, William. 2007. "Policy Study and Development in Canada's Political Parties," in *Policy Analysis in Canada: The State of the*

Art, edited by L. Dobuzinskis, M. Howlett, and D. Laycock, 233–242. Toronto: University of Toronto Press.

Dahl, Robert A and Charles E. Lindblom. 1953. *Politics, Economics and Welfare: Planning and Politico-economic Systems Resolved into Basic Social Processes*. New York: Harper and Row.

Davies, P. 2004. "Is Evidence-Based Government Possible?" 4th Annual Campbell Collaboration Colloquium, London. Jerry Lee Lecture 2004.

Day, P. and Klein, R., 1989. "Interpreting the Unexpected. The case of AIDS policy-making in Britain," *Journal of Public Policy* 9, 337–353.

Debnam, Geoffrey. 1975. "Non-decisions and Power: The Two Faces of Bachrach and Baratz," *American Political Science Review* 69, no. 3: 889–900.

de Bruijn, Johan A. and Ernst F. ten Heuvelhof. 2000. *Networks and Decision-Making*. Utrecht: Lemma Publishers.

deLeon, P. 1999. "The Missing Link Revisited: Contemporary Implementation Research," *Policy Studies Review* 16, no. 3: 311–338.

Desch, M. C. 2007/8. "America's Liberal Illiberalism. The Ideological Origins of Overreaction in U.S. Foreign Policy," *International Security* 32, no. 3: 7–43.

deVries, M. S. 2010. *The Importance of Neglect in Policy-Making*. Basingstoke: Palgrave Macmillan.

Drezner, Daniel W. 2000. "Ideas, Bureaucratic Politics, and the Crafting of Foreign Policy," *American Journal of Political Science* 44, no. 4: 733–49.

Driedger, S.M., and J. Eyles. 2003. "Charting Uncertainty in Science-Policy Discourses: The Construction of the Chlorinated Drinking-Water Issue and Cancer," *Environment and Planning C: Government and Policy* 21: 429–44.

Dror, Yehezkel. 1964. "Muddling Through—'Science' or Inertia," *Public Administration Review* 24, no. 3: 154–7.

———. 1968. *Public Policymaking Re-examined*. San Francisco: Chandler.

Dunn, D. 1997. *Politics and Administration at the Top: Lessons from Down Under*. Pittsburgh: University of Pittsburgh Press.

Edwards, Ward. 1954. "The Theory of Decision Making," *Psychological Bulletin* 51, no. 4: 380–417.

Eichbaum, Chris, and Richard Shaw. 2008. "Revisiting Politicization: Political Advisers and Public Servants in Westminster Systems," *Governance* 21, no. 3: 337–363.

Einhorn, Hillel J. 1982. "Learning from Experience and Suboptimal Rules in Decision Making," in D. Kahneman, P. Slovic, and A. Tversky, eds, *Judgement Under Uncertainty: Heuristics and Biases*. Cambridge: Cambridge University Press, 268–83.

———, and Robin M. Hogarth. 1986. "Decision Making under Ambiguity," *Journal of Business* 59, 4, part 2: S225–S251.

Elster, Jon. 1991. "The Possibility of Rational Politics," in D. Held, ed., *Political Theory Today*. Oxford: Polity.

Etzioni, Amitai. 1967. "Mixed-Scanning: A Third Approach to Decision-Making," *Public Administration Review* 27, no. 5: 385–92.

Fayol, Henri. 1949. *General and Industrial Management*. London: Pitman.

Fernandes, Ronald, and Herbert A. Simon. 1999. "A Study of How Individuals Solve Complex and Ill-Structured Problems," *Policy Sciences* 32: 225–45.

Forester, John. 1984. "Bounded Rationality and the Politics of Muddling Through," *Public Administration Review* 44, no. 1: 23–31.

———. 1989. *Planning in the Face of Power*. Berkeley: University of California Press.

Gains, Francesca, and Gerry Stoker. 2011. "Special Advisers and the Transmission of Ideas From The Policy Primeval Soup," *Policy & Politics* 39, no. 4: 485–98.

Gawthrop, Louis C. 1971. *Administrative Politics and Social Change*. New York: St. Martin's Press.

Genschel, Philipp, Achim Kemmerling, and Eric Seils. 2011. "Accelerating Downhill: How the EU Shapes Corporate Tax Competition in the Single Market," *JCMS: Journal of Common Market Studies* 49, no. 3: 585–606.

George, Alexander L. 1969. "The "Operational Code": A Neglected Approach to the Study of Political Leaders and Decision-Making," *International Studies Quarterly* 13: 190–222.

———. 1979. "The Causal Nexus between Cognitive Beliefs and Decision-Making Behaviour: The 'Operational Code' Belief System," in L.S. Falkowski, ed.,

Psychological Models in International Politics. Boulder, CO: Westview Press, 95–124.

———. 1980. *Presidential Decision-making in Foreign Policy: The Effective Use of Information and Advice*. Boulder, CO: Westview Press.

Geva-May, Iris, and Allan M. Maslove. 2007. "In between Trends: Developments of Public Policy Analysis and Policy Analysis Instruction in Canada, the United States and the European Union," in *Policy Analysis in Canada: The State of the Art*, edited by L. Dobuzinskis, M. Howlett and D. Laycock, 186–216. Toronto: University of Toronto Press.

Gill, Judith I., and Laura Saunders. 1992. "Toward a Definition of Policy Analysis," *New Directions for Institutional Research*, no. 76: 5–13.

Gortner, Harold, Julianne Mahler, and Jeanne Bell Nicholson. 1987. *Organization Theory: A Public Perspective*. Chicago: Dorsey Press.

Gow, J. I. and S.L. Sutherland. 2004. "Comparison of Canadian Masters Programs in Public Administration, Public Management and Public Policy," *Canadian Public Administration*. 47, no. 3: 379–405

Gulick, Luther H. 1937. "Notes on the Theory of Organization," in Gulick and Urwick *Notes on the Theory of Organization* (1937). New York, NY: Columbia University.

Gupta, J., X. Olsthoorn, and E. Rotenberg. 2003. "The Role of Scientific Uncertainty in Compliance with the Kyoto Protocol to the Climate Change Convention," *Environmental Science and Policy* 6: 475–86.

Haas, Mark L. 2001. "Prospect Theory and the Cuban Missile Crisis," *International Studies Quarterly* 45: 241–70.

Haas, Peter M. 1992. "Introduction: Epistemic Communities and International Policy Coordination," *International Organization* 46, no. 1: 1–36.

Hall, P. A. 1993. "Policy Paradigms, Social Learning and the State: The Case of Economic Policy Making in Britain," *Comparative Politics* 25, no. 3: 275–296.

Halligan, John, and John Marcus Power. 1992. *Political Management in the 1990s*. Oxford: Oxford University Press.

Hammersley, M. 2005. "Is the Evidence-Based Practice Movement Doing More Good Than Harm? Reflections on Iain Chalmers" Case for Research-Based Policy Making and Practice," *Evidence & Policy* 1, no. 1: 85–100.

Hammond, Thomas H. 1986. "Agenda Control, Organizational Structure, and Bureaucratic Politics," *American Journal of Political Science* 30, no. 2: 379–420.

———. 2003. "Veto Points, Policy Preferences, and Bureaucratic Autonomy in Democratic Systems," in G.A. Krause and K.J. Meier, eds, *Politics, Policy and Organizations: Frontiers in the Scientific Study of Bureaucracy*. Ann Arbor: University of Michigan Press, 73–103.

Hargrove, E.L. 1975. *The Missing Link: The Study of the Implementation of Social Policy*. Washington: Urban Institute.

Hawke, G. R. 1983. *Improving Policy Advice*. Wellington: Victoria University Institute of Policy Studies.

Hayes, Michael T. 2007. "Policy Making through Disjointed Incrementalism," in *Morçöl* 2007: 39–59.

Heikkila, Tanya and K.R. Isett. 2004. "Modeling Operational Decision Making in Public Organizations: An Integration of Two Institutional Theories," *American Review of Public Administration* 34, no. 1: 3–19.

Heller, William B., Andreas P. Kyriacou, and Oriol Roca-Sagalés. 2016. "Institutional Checks and Corruption: The Effect of Formal Agenda Access on Governance," *European Journal of Political Research* 55, no. 4 (November 1): 681–701. doi:10.1111/1475–6765.12155.

Hird, J. A. 2005. "Policy Analysis for What? The Effectiveness of Nonpartisan Policy Research Organizations," *Policy Studies Journal* 33, no. 1: 83–105.

Hisschemoller, Matthijs, and Rob Hoppe. 1995. "Coping with Intractable Controversies: The Case for Problem Structuring in Policy Design and Analysis," *Knowledge and Policy* 8, no. 4: 40–61.

Holzmann, Robert, M. Orenstein, and M. Rutkowski, eds. 2003. *Pension Reform in Europe: Process. and Progress*. Washington: World Bank.

Hood, Christopher. 1999. "The Garbage Can Model of Organization: Describing a Condition of Prescriptive Design Principle," in

M. Egeberg and P. Laegreid, eds, *Organizing Political Institutions: Essays for Johan P. Olsen*. Oslo: Scandinavian University Press, 59–78.

———. 2002. "The Risk Game and the Blame Game," *Government and Opposition* 37, no. 1: 15–54.

———, and H. Rothstein. 2001. "Risk Regulation under Pressure: Problem Solving or Blame Shifting?" *Administration and Society* 33, no. 1: 21–53.

Howard, S. Kenneth. 1971. "Analysis, Rationality, and Administrative Decision-Making," in F. Marini, ed., *Toward a New Public Administration: The Minnowbrook Perspective*. Scranton, PA: Chandler.

Howlett, Michael. 1986. "Acts of Commission and Acts of Omission: Legal-Historical Research and the Intentions of Government in a Federal State," *Canadian Journal of Political Science* 19: 363–71.

———. 1999. "Federalism and Public Policy," in J. Bickerton and A. Gagnon, eds, *Canadian Politics*, 3rd edn. Peterborough, ON: Broadview Press.

———. 2007. "Analyzing Multi-Actor, Multi-Round Public Policy Decision-Making Processes in Government: Findings from Five Canadian Cases," *Canadian Journal of Political Science* 40, no. 3: 659–84.

———, and M. Ramesh. 1998. "Policy Subsystem Configurations and Policy Change: Operationalizing the Postpositivist Analysis of the Politics of the Policy Process," *Policy Studies Journal* 26, no. 3: 466–82.

Howlett, Michael. 2009. "Government Communication as a Policy Tool: A Framework for Analysis," *The Canadian Political Science Review* 3, no. 2. June

Huitt, Ralph K. 1968. "Political Feasibility," in A. Ranney, ed., *Political Science and Public Policy*. Chicago: Markham Publishing, 263–76.

Innvaer, S., G. Vist, M. Trommald, and A. Oxman. 2002. "Health Policy-Makers' Perceptions of Their Use of Evidence: A Systematic Review," *Journal of Health Services Research and Policy* 7, no. 4: 239–45.

Jackson, Peter M. 2007. "Making Sense of Policy Advice," *Public Money & Management* 27, no. 4: 257–64.

Jann, Werner. 1991. "From Policy Analysis to Political Management? An Outside Look at Public Policy Training in the United States," in *Social Sciences and Modern States: National Experiences and Theoretical Crossroads*, edited by C.H.W. Peter Wagner, Bjorn Wittrock, Helmut Wollman, 110–30. Cambridge: Cambridge University Press.

Jennings, Bruce. 1987. "Interpretation and the Practice of Policy Analysis," in Fischer and Forester *Confronting Vlaues in Policy Analysis: The Politics of Criteria* (1987). Sage Publications.

Johnson, Genevieve. "The Discourse of Democracy in Canadian Nuclear Waste Management Policy," *Policy Sciences* 40: 79–99.

Jones, Bryan D. 2001. *Politics and the Architecture of Choice: Bounded Rationality and Governance*. Chicago: University of Chicago Press.

———. 2002. "Bounded Rationality and Public Policy: Herbert A. Simon and the Decisional Foundation of Collective Choice," *Policy Sciences* 35: 269–84.

Jones, B. D., H. F. Thomas III, and M. Wolfe. 2014. "Policy Bubbles," *Policy Studies Journal* 42, no. 1: 146–171.

———, James L. True, and Frank R. Baumgartner. 1997. "Does Incrementalism Stem from Political Consensus or from Institutional Gridlock?" *American Journal of Political Science* 41, no. 4: 1319–39.

Jordana, J., and D. Sancho. 2005. "Policy Networks and Market Opening: Telecommunications Liberalization in Spain," *European Journal of Political Research* 44: 519–46.

Kahneman, Daniel. 2003. Maps of Bounded Rationality: Psychology for Behavioral Economics *American Economic Review* 93, no. 5: pp. 1449–1475.

———and Amos Tversky. 1979. "Prospect Theory: An Analysis of Decision under Risk," *Econometrica* 47: 263–89.

Kanner, Michael D. 2005. "A Prospect Dynamic Model of Decision-Making," *Journal of Theoretical Politics* 17, no. 5: 3: 311–38.

Kasekende, Elizabeth, Charles Abuka, and Mare Sarr. 2016. "Extractive Industries and Corruption: Investigating the Effectiveness of EITI as a Scrutiny Mechanism," *Resources Policy* 48 (2016): 117–28. doi:10.1016/j.resourpol.2016.03.002.

Kekez, Anka, Michael Howlett, and M. Ramesh, eds. 2020. *Collaboration in Public Service Delivery: Promise and Pitfalls.* Cheltenham: Edward Elgar.

Kemmerling, Achim, and Kristin Makszin. 2018. "When Does Policy Diffusion Affect Policy Instability? Cases of Excessive Policy Volatility in Welfare Policies in East Central Europe," *Policy Experiments, Failures and Innovations: Beyond Accession in Central and Eastern Europe*: 26.

Kenis, Patrick. 1991. "The Pre-Conditions for Policy Networks: Some Findings from a Three Country Study on Industrial Re-Structuring," in Marin and Mayntz *Empirical evidence and theoretical considerations* (1991: 297–330).

Kepner, Charles H., and Benjamin B. Tregoe. 1965. *The Rational Manager: A Systematic Approach to Problem Solving and Decision Making.* New York: McGraw-Hill.

Klijn, Erik-Hans. 2001. "Rules as Institutional Context for Decision Making in Networks: The Approach to Postwar Housing Districts in Two Cities," *Administration and Society* 33, no. 2: 133–64.

——, and ——. 2000b. "Politicians and Interactive Decision Making: Institutional Spoilsports or Playmakers," *Public Administration* 78, no. 2: 365–87.

——, and ——. 2005. "Interactive Decision Making and Representative Democracy: Institutional Collisions and Solutions," *International Review of Administrative Sciences* 71, no. 4: 109–34.

——, and G.R. Teisman. 1991. "Effective Policymaking in a Multi-Actor Setting: Networks and Steering," in Roeland, t'Veld et al., eds, *Autopoiesis and Configuration Theory: New Approaches to Societal Steering*. Dordrecht: Kluwer, 99–111.

Knight, F.H., 1921. *Risk, Uncertainty, and Profit.* Boston, MA: Hart, Schaffner & Marx; Houghton Mifflin Company.

Krause, George A. 1997. "Policy Preference Formation and Subsystem Behaviour: The Case of Commercial Bank Regulation," *British Journal of Political Science* 27: 525–50.

Kriesi, Hanspeter, and Maya Jegen. 2001. "The Swiss Energy Policy Elite: The Actor Constellation of a Policy Domain in Transition," *European Journal of Political Research* 39: 251–87.

Kruse, R., E. Schwecke, and J. Heinsohn. 1991. *Uncertainty and Vagueness in Knowledge-Based Systems.* Berlin: Springer-Verlag.

Kwakkel, J.H., W.E. Walker, and V.A.W.J. Marchau. 2010. "Classifying and Communicating Uncertainties in Model-Based Policy Analysis," *International Journal of Technology, Policy and Management* 10, no. 4: 299–315.

Laforest, R., and M. Orsini. 2005. "Evidence-Based Engagement in the Voluntary Sector: Lessons from Canada," *Social Policy & Administration* 39, no. 5: 481–97.

Lempert, Robert J., Popper, Steven W., and Bankes, Steven C. 2003. *Shaping the Next One Hundred Years: New Methods for Quantitative, Long-Term Policy Analysis.* Santa Monica, CA: RAND

Levin, K., Cashore, B., Bernstein, S. and Auld, G. 2012. Overcoming the Tragedy of Super Wicked Problems: Constraining Our Future Selves to Ameliorate Global Climate Change," *Policy Sciences* 45: 123–152.

Levy, Jack S. 1997. "Prospect Theory and the Cognitive-Rational Debate," in N. Geva and A. Mintz, eds, *Decision-making on War and Peace: The Cognitive-Rational Debate*. Boulder, CO: Lynne Rienner, 33–50.

Ley-Borras, R. 2005. "A Decision Analysis Approach to Policy Issues: The NAFTA Case," *Review of Policy Research* 22, no. 5: 687–708.

Lindblom, Charles E. 1955. *Bargaining: The Hidden Hand in Government.* Los Angeles: Rand Corporation.

——. 1958. "Policy Analysis," *American Economic Review* 48, no. 3: 298–312.

——. 1959. "The Science of Muddling Through," *Public Administration Review* 19, no. 2: 79–88.

——. 1968. *The Policy-Making Process.* Englewood Cliffs, NJ: Prentice-Hall.

——. 1979. "Still Muddling, Not Yet Through," *Public Administration Review* 39, no. 6: 517–26.

——, and D.K. Cohen. 1979. *Usable Knowledge: Social Science and Social Problem Solving.* New Haven: Yale University Press.

Lindquist, Evert A. 1988. "What Do Decision Models Tell Us about Information Use?" *Knowledge in Society* 1, no. 2: 86–111.

Lustick, Ian. 1980. "Explaining the Variable Utility of Disjointed Incrementalism: Four Propositions," *American Political Science Review* 74, no. 2: 342–53.

Majone, Giandomenico. 1991. "Cross-National Sources of Regulatory Policymaking in Europe and the United States," *Journal of Public Policy* 11, no. 1: 79–106.

———. 1989. *Evidence, Argument, and Persuasion in the Policy Process*: New Haven: Yale University Press.

Maley, Maria. 2000. "Conceptualising Advisers' Policy Work: The Distinctive Policy Roles of Ministerial Advisers in the Keating Government, 1991–96," *Australian Journal of Political Science* 35, no. 3: 449–449.

———. 2011. "Strategic Links in a Cut-throat World: Rethinking the Role and Relationships of Australian Ministerial Staff," *Public Administration* 89, no. 4: 1469–1488. doi:10.1111/j .1467-9299.2011.01928.x.

Maor, M. 2012. "Policy Overreaction," *Journal of Public Policy* 32, no. 3: 231–59.

———. 2014a. "Policy Bubbles: Policy Overreaction and Positive Feedback," *Governance* 27, no. 3: 469–87.

———. 2014b. "Policy Persistence, Risk Estimation and Policy Underreaction," *Policy Sciences* 47(4), pp. 425–43.

March, James G. 1978. "Bounded Rationality, Ambiguity, and the Engineering of Choice," *Bell Journal of Economics* 9, no. 2: 587–608.

March, J.G. 1981. "Decision Making Perspective: Decisions in Organizations and Theories of Choice," in *Perspectives on Organization Design and Behaviour*, edited by A. H. van de Ven and W.F. Joyce. New York: Wiley.

———. 1994. *A Primer on Decision-Making: How Decisions Happen*. New York: Free Press.

———, and Johan P. Olsen. 1979a. *Ambiguity and Choice in Organizations*. Bergen: Universitetsforlaget.

———, and ———. 1979b. "Organizational Choice under Ambiguity," in March and Olsen (1979a).*Ambiguity and Choice in Organizations*. Bergen: Universitetsforlaget.

Markoff, John. 1975. "Governmental Bureaucratization: General Processes and an Anomalous Case," *Comparative Studies in Society and History* 17, no. 4: 479–503

Marsh, David, and R.A.W. Rhodes. 1992b. "Policy Communities and Issue Networks: Beyond Typology," in Marsh and Rhodes (1992a: 248–68).

Marsh, Michael, and James Tilley. 2010. "The Attribution of Credit and Blame to Governments and Its Impact on Vote Choice," *British Journal of Political Science* 40, no. 1: 115. doi:10.1017/ S0007123409990275.

Martin, John F. 1998. *Reorienting a Nation: Consultants and Australian Public Policy*. Aldershot: Ashgate.

Maule, A. John, and Ola Svenson. 1993. "Theoretical and Empirical Approaches to Behavioural Decision Making and Their Relations to Time Constraints," in Svenson and Maule, eds, *Time Pressure and Stress in Human Judgement and Decision Making*. New York: Plenum Press, 3–25.

McGann, J.G., and E.C. Johnson. 2005. *Comparative Think Tanks, Politics and Public Policy*. Cheltenham: Edward Elgar.

Meltsner, Arnold J. 1975. "Bureaucratic Policy Analysts," *Policy Analysis* 1, no. 1: 115–131.

Meltsner, Arnold J. 1976. *Policy Analysts in the Bureaucracy*. Berkeley: University of California Press.

Mendoza, Guillermo A., and William Sprouse. 1989. "Forest Planning and Decision Making under Fuzzy Environments: An Overview and Illustration," *Forest Science* 35, no. 2: 481–502.

Mintrom, M. 2003. *People Skills for Policy Analysts*. Washington, DC: Georgetown University Press.

Mintrom, Michael. 2007. "The Policy Analysis Movement," in *Policy Analysis in Canada: The State of the Art*, edited by L. Dobuzinskis, M. Howlett, and D. Laycock, 71–84. Toronto: University of Toronto Press.

Mintz, Alex. 2004. "How Do Leaders Make Decisions?" *Journal of Conflict Resolution* 48, no. 1: 3–13.

———. 2005. "Applied Decision Analysis: Utilizing Poliheuristic Theory to Explain and Predict Foreign Policy and National Security Decisions," *International Studies Perspectives* 6, no. 1: 94–8.

———, and Nehemia Geva. 1997. "The Poliheuristic Theory of Foreign Policy

Decision Making," in Geva and Mintz, eds, *Decision-Making in War and Peace: The CognitiveRational Debate*. Boulder, CO: Lynne Rienner.

———et al. 1997. "The Effect of Dynamic and Static Choice Sets on Political Decision Making: An Analysis Using the Decision Board Platform," *American Political Science Review* 91, no. 3: 553–66.

Mintzberg, Henry, Duru Raisinghani, and Andre Theoret. 1976. "The Structure of 'Unstructured' Decision Processes," *Administrative Science Quarterly* 21: 246–75.

Morçöl, Göktug, and Nadezda P. Ivanova. 2010. "Methods Taught in Public Policy Programs: Are Quantitative Methods Still Prevalent?" *Journal of Public Affairs Education* 16, no. 2: 255–77.

Morgan, M.G., and M. Henrion. 1990. *Uncertainty: A Guide to Dealing with Uncertainty in Quantitative Risk and Policy Analysis*. Cambridge: Cambridge University Press.

Mossberger, Karen. 2000. *The Politics of Ideas and the Spread of Enterprise Zones*. Washington: Georgetown University Press.

Mucciaroni, Gary. 1992. "The Garbage Can Model and the Study of Policy Making: A Critique," *Polity* 24, no. 3: 460–82.

Murray, Catherine. 2007. "The Media," in *Policy Analysis in Canada: The State of the Art*, edited by L. Dobuzinskis, M. Howlett, and D. Laycock, 286–297. Toronto: University of Toronto Press.

Mushkin, Selma J. 1977. "Policy Analysis in State and Community," *Public Administration Review* 37, no. 3 (June): 245–253.

Nice, D.C. 1987. "Incremental and Non-incremental Policy Responses: The States and the Railroads," *Polity* 20: 145–56.

Nilsson, Mans, Andrew Jordan, John Turnpenny, Julia Hertin, Bjorn Nykvist, and Duncan Russel. 2008. "The Use and Non-Use of Policy Appraisal Tools in Public Policy Making: An Analysis of Three European Countries and the European Union," *Policy Sciences* 41: 335–55.

OECD. 2011. *Ministerial Advisors: Role, Influence and Management*. OECD Publishing. DOI:10.1787/9789264124936-en

Oliviera, M. D., J. M. Magone, and J. A. Pereira. "Nondecision Making and Inertia in Portuguese Health Policy," *Journal of Health Politics, Policy and Law* 30, nos. 1–2: 211–230.

Oosterveer, P. 2002. "Reinventing Risk Politics: Reflexive Modernity and the European BSE Crisis," *Journal of Environmental Policy and Planning* 4: 215–29.

Ostrom, Elinor. 1999. "Institutional Rational Choice: An Assessment of the Institutional Analysis and Development Framework," in Sabatier (1999a: 35–71).

Ostrom, E. et al. 1999. "Revisiting the Commons: Local Lessons, Global Challenges," *Science* 284 (9 April): 278–282.

O'Sullivan, Deborah, and Barry Down. 2001. "Policy Decision-making Models in Practice: A Case Study of the Western Australian "Sentencing Acts," *Policy Studies Journal* 29, no. 1: 56–70.

Packwood, A. 2002. "Evidence-Based Policy: Rhetoric and Reality," *Social Policy & Society* 1, no. 3: 267–72.

Page, Edward C. 1985a. *Political Authority and Bureaucratic Power: A Comparative Analysis*. Brighton, Sussex: Wheatsheaf.

Pal, Leslie A. 1993b. "Advocacy Organizations and Legislative Politics: The Effects of the Charter of Rights and Freedoms on Interest Lobbying of Federal Legislation, 1989–1991," in F.L. Seidle, ed., *Equity and Community: The Charter, Interest Advocacy and Representation*. Montreal: Institute for Research on Public Policy, 119–57.

Pappi, Franz Urban, and Christian H.C.A. Henning. 1998. "Policy Networks: More Than a Metaphor," *Journal of Theoretical Politics* 10, no. 4: 553–75.

Pawson, R. 2002. "Evidence-Based Policy: In Search of a Method?" *Evaluation* 8, no. 2: 157–81.

Pawson, R., T. Greenhalgh, G. Harvey, and K. Walshe. 2005. "Realist Review— a New Method of Systematic Review Designed for Complex Policy Interventions," *Journal of Health Services Research Policy* 10, Supplement 1: S1:21-S1:34.

Payne, John W. 1982. "Contingent Decision Behaviour," *Psychological Bulletin* 92, no. 2: 382–402.

———, James R. Bettman, and Eric J. Johnson. 1988. "Adaptive Strategy Selection in Decision Making," *Journal of Experimental Psychology; Learning, Memory and Cognition* 14, no. 3: 534–52.

Perrow, Charles. 1984. *Normal Accidents: Living with High-Risk Technologies*. New York: Basic Books.

Pierson, Paul. 2000a. "Increasing Returns, Path Dependence, and the Study of Politics," *American Political Science Review* 94, no. 2: 251–67.

———. 2000b. "Not Just What, but When: Timing and Sequence in Political Processes," *Studies in American Political Development* 14: 72–92.

———. 2000c. "The Limits of Design: Explaining Institutional Origins and Change," *Governance* 13, no. 4: 475–99.

Pollock, P.H., S. A. Lilie, and M. E. Vittes. 1993. "Hard Issues, Core Values and Vertical Constraint: The Case of Nuclear Power," *British Journal of Political Science* 23, no. 1: 29–50.

Potoski, M. 1999. "Managing Uncertainty through Bureaucratic Design: Administrative Procedures and State Air Pollution Control Agencies," *Journal of Public Administration Research and Theory* 9, no. 4: 623–39.

Prince, Michael. 1983. *Policy Advice and Organizational Survival*. Aldershot: Gower.

Raab, Jorg, and Patrick Kenis. 2007. "Taking Stock of Policy Networks: Do They Matter?" in Frank Fischer, Gerlad J. Miller, and Mara S. Sidney, eds, *Handbook of Public Policy Analysis: Theory, Politics and Methods*. Boca Raton, FL: CRC Press, 187–200.

Radford, K.J. 1977. *Complex Decision Problems: An Integrated Strategy for Resolution*. Reston, Va: Reston Publishing Company.

Radin, B.A., and J.P. Boase. 2000. "Federalism, Political Structure, and Public Policy in the United States and Canada," *Journal of Comparative Policy Analysis* 2, no. 1: 65–90.

Rhodes, R.A.W and David Marsh. 1992. "New Directions in the Study of Policy Networks," *European Journal of Political Science* 21: 181–205.

Richardson, Jeremy J., A.G. Jordan, and R.H. Kimber. 1978. "Lobbying, Administrative Reform and Policy Styles: The Case of Land Drainage," *Political Studies* 26, no. 1: 47–64.

Rittel, Horst W.J., and Melvin M. Webber. 1973. "Dilemmas in a General Theory of Planning," *Policy Sciences* 4: 155–69.

Rochefort, David A., and Roger W. Cobb. 1993. "Problem Definition, Agenda Access, and Policy Choice," *Policy Studies Journal* 21, no. 1: 56–71.

Rochet, C. 2004. "Rethinking the Management of Information in the Strategic Monitoring of Public Policies by Agencies," *Industrial Management & Data Systems* 104, no. 3: 201–08.

Roe, Emory. 1990. *Taking Complexity Seriously: Policy Analysis, Triangulation and Sustainable Development*. Boston: Kluwer.

Ryan, Phil. 1995. 'Miniature Mila and Flying Geese: Government Advertising and Canadian Democracy', in S.D. Phillips, ed., *How Ottawa Spends 1995–96: Mid-Life Crises*. Ottawa: Carleton University Press, 263–86.

Sabatier, Paul A. 1988. "An Advocacy Coalition Framework of Policy Change and the Role of Policy-Oriented Learning Therein," *Policy Sciences* 21, nos. 2 and 3: 129–68.

Sager, Tore. 2001. "Manipulative Features of Planning Styles," *Environment and Planning A* 33: 765–91.

Sarpkaya, S. 1988. *Lobbying in Canada—Ways and Means*. Don Mills, ON: CCH Canadian.

Savas, E.S. 1977. *Alternatives for Delivering Public Services: Toward Improved Performance*. Boulder, CO: Westview Press.

Scharpf, Fritz W. 1991. "Political Institutions, Decision Styles, and Policy Choices," in R.M. Czada and A. Windhoff-Heritier, eds, *Political Choice: Institutions, Rules and the Limits of Rationality*. Frankfurt: Campus Verlag, 53–86.

Schmidt, Vivien A. 2001. "The Politics of Economic Adjustment in France and Britain: When Does Discourse Matter?" *Journal of European Public Policy* 8, no. 2: 247–64.

Sharkansky, Ira. 1997. *Policy Making in Israel: Routines for Simple Problems and Coping with the Complex*. Pittsburgh: University of Pittsburgh Press.

Simon, Herbert A. 1955. "A Behavioral Model of Rational Choice," *Quarterly Journal of Economics* 69, no. 1: 99–118

———. 1957b. *Models of Man, Social and Rational: Mathematical Essays on Rational Human Behavior in a Social Setting*. New York: Wiley.

———. 1973. "The Structure of Ill Structured Problems," *Artificial Intelligence* 4: 181–201.

Simon, H. A. 1991. "Bounded Rationality and Organizational Learning," *Organization Science* 2, no. 1: 125–134.

Slovic, P. 1992. "Perception of Risk: Reflections on the Psychometric Paradigm," in S. Krimsky and D. Golding, eds, *Social*

Theories of Risk, pp. 117–152. Westport, CT and London: Praeger.

Slovic, Paul, Baruch Fischoff, and Sarah Lichtenstein. 1977. "Behavioural Decision Theory," *Annual Review of Psychology* 28: 1–39.

———, ———, and ———. 1985. "Regulation of Risk: A Psychological Perspective," in R.G. Noll, ed., *Regulatory Policy and the Social Sciences.* Berkeley: University of California Press, 241–78.

Smith, Gilbert, and David May. 1980. "The Artificial Debate between Rationalist and Incrementalist Models of Decision-Making," *Policy and Politics* 8, no. 2: 147–61.

Smith, Richard A. 1979. "Decision Making and Non-Decision Making in Cities: Some Implications for Community Structural Research," *American Sociological Review* 44, no. 1: 147–61.

Smith, Thomas B. 1977. "Advisory Committees in the Public Policy Process," *International Review of Administrative Sciences* 43, no. 2: 153–66.

Speers, Kimberly. 2007. "The Invisible Public Service: Consultants and Public Policy in Canada," in *Policy analysis in Canada: The state of the art*, edited by L. Dobuzinskis, M. Howlett, and D. Laycock, 220–231. Toronto: University of Toronto Press.

Spranca, Mark, Elisa Minsk, and Jonathan Baron. 1991. "Omission and Commission in Judgement and Choice," *Journal of Experimental Social Psychology* 27: 76–105.

Stokman, F.N., and J. Berveling. 1998. "Predicting Outcomes of Decision-Making: Five Competing Models of Policy-Making," in M. Fennema, C. Van der Eijk, and H. Schijf, eds, *In Search of Structure: Essays in Social Science and Methodology.* Amsterdam: Het Spinhuis, 147–71.

Stone, D., and A. Denham, eds. 2004. *Think Tank Traditions: Policy Research and the Politics of Ideas.* Manchester: Manchester University Press.

Stritch, Andrew. 2007. "Business Associations and Policy Analysis in Canada," in *Policy Analysis in Canada: The State of the Art,* edited by L. Dobuzinskis, M. Howlett, and D. Laycock, 242–259. Toronto: University of Toronto Press.

Suedfeld, Peter, and Philip E. Tetlock. 1992. "Psychological Advice about Political Decision Making: Heuristics, Biases, and Cognitive Defects," in Suedfeld and Tetlock, eds, *Psychology and Social Policy.* New York: Hemisphere Publishing, 51–70.

Sulitzeanu-Kenan, R., and C. Hood. 2005. "Blame Avoidance with Adjectives? Motivation, Opportunity, Activity and Outcome," paper for ECPR Joint Sessions, Blame Avoidance and Blame Management Workshop 14–20 Apr., Granada, Spain.

Svenson, Ola. 1979. "Process Descriptions of Decision Making," *Organizational Behaviour and Human Performance* 23: 86–112.

Swanson, D., Barg S., Tyler S., Venema H., Tomar S., Bhadwal S., Nair S., Roy D., and Drexhage J., 2010. "Seven Tools for Creating Aadaptive Policies," *Technological Forecasting & Social Change* 77, no. 6: 924–939.

Taeihagh, A., Bañares-Alcántara, R. and Givoni, M. 2013. "A virtual environment for the formulation of policy packages," *Transportation Research Part A: Policy and Practice* 60: 53–68.

Teisman, Geert R. 2000. "Models for Research into Decision-Making Processes: On Phases, Streams and Decision-Making Rounds," *Public Administration* 78, no. 4: 937–56.

Tenbensel, T. 2004. "Does More Evidence Lead to Better Policy? The Implications of Explicit Priority Setting in New Zealand's Health Policy for Evidence-Based Policy," *Policy Studies* 25, no. 3: 190–207.

t'Hart, Paul, and Marieka Kleiboer. 1995. "Policy Controversies in the Negotiatory State," *Knowledge and Policy* 8, no. 4: 5–26.

Thomson, Robert, Frans N. Stokman, and Rene Torenvlied. 2003. "Models of Collective Decision Making: Introduction," *Rationality and Society* 15, no. 1: 5–14.

Timmermans, Arco. 2001. "Arenas as Institutional Sites for Policymaking: Patterns and Effects in Comparative Perspective," *Journal of Comparative Policy Analysis* 3: 311–37.

Torgerson, Douglas. 1986. "Between Knowledge and Politics: Three Faces of Policy Analysis," *Policy Sciences* 19, no. 1: 33–59.

Tosun, J. 2013. "How the EU Handles Uncertain Risks: Understanding the Role of the Precautionary Principle," *Journal of European Public Policy* 20, no. 10: 1517–1528.

Tsebelis, George. 2002. *Veto Players. How Political Institutions Work*. Princeton: Princeton University Press.

Tversky, Amos, and Daniel Kahneman. 1981. "The Framing of Decisions and the Psychology of Choice," *Science* 211 (Jan.): 453–8.

———, and ———. 1982. "Judgement under Uncertainty: Heuristics and Biases," in Kahneman, P. Slovic, and Tversky, eds, *Judgement under Uncertainty: Heuristics and Biases*. Cambridge: Cambridge University Press, 3–20.

———, and ———. 1986. "Rational Choice and the Framing of Decisions," *Journal of Business* 59, no. 4, part 2: S251–79.

Twight, C. 1991. "From Claiming Credit to Avoiding Blame: The Evolution of Congressional Strategy for Asbestos Management," *Journal of Public Policy* 11, no. 2: 153–86.

van Bueren, Ellen, Erik-Hans Klijn, and Joop Koppenjan. 2001. "Network Management as a Linking Mechanism in Complex Policy-Making and Implementation Processes: Analyzing Decision-Making and Learning for an Environmental Issue," paper for the Fifth International Research Symposium in Public Management, Barcelona, 9–11 Apr.

van der Eijk, Door C., and W.J.P. Kok. 1975. "Non-decisions Reconsidered," *Acta Politika* 10, no. 3: 277–301.

Vertzberger, Yaacov Y.I. 1998. *Risk Taking and Decision-making: Foreign Military Intervention Decisions*. Stanford, CA: Stanford University Press.

Voss, James F. 1998. "On the Representation of Problems: An Information-Processing Approach to Foreign Policy Decision Making," in D.A. Sylvan and J.F. Voss, eds, *Problem Representation in Foreign Policy Decision Making*. Cambridge: Cambridge University Press, 8–26.

———, and Timothy A. Post. 1988. "On the Solving of Ill-Structured Problems," in M.T.H. Chi, R. Glaser, and M.J. Farr, eds, *The Nature of Expertise*. Hillsdale, NJ: Lawrence Erlbaum Associates, 261–85.

Wagschal, Uwe. 1997. "Direct Democracy and Public Policy-Making," *Journal of Public Policy* 17, no. 2: 223–46.

Walker, W.E., and V.A.W.J. Marchau. 2004. "Dealing with Uncertainty in Policy Analysis and Policymaking," *Integrated Assessment* 4, no. 1: 1–4.

Walker W., V. Marchau, and D. Swanson. 2010. "Addressing deep uncertainties using adaptive policies," *Technological Forecasting & Social Change* 77, no. 6: Special Section 2.

Walker, W.E., Harremoes, P., Rotmans, J., van der Sluijs, J., van Asselt, M.B.A., Janssen, P., Krayer von Krauss, M.P., 2003. "Defining Uncertainty: A Conceptual Basis for Uncertainty Management in Model-Based Decision Support," *Integrated Assessment* 4, no. 1: 5–17.

Walker, W.E., Lempert, R.J. and Kwakkel, J.H. 2012. *Deep Uncertainty*. Delft: Delft University of Technology and RAND Santa Monica.

Wardekker, J.A., de Jong, A., Knoop J.M., van der Sluijs, J.P. 2010. "Operationalising a Resilience Approach to Adapting an Urban Delta to Uncertain Climate Changes," *Technological Forecasting & Social Change* 77: 987–998.

Weaver, R. Kent. 1986. "The Politics of Blame Avoidance," *Journal of Public Policy* 6, no. 4: 371–98.

Weaver, R. Kent and Bert A. Rockman. 1993b. "When and How Do Institutions Matter?" in Weaver and Rockman (1993a). Do Institutions Matter? Government Capabilities in the United States and Abroad. Washington: Brookings Institution.

Webber, David J. 1992. "The Distribution and Use of Policy Knowledge in the Policy Process," in W.N. Dunn and R.M. Kelly, eds, *Advances in Policy Studies Since 1950*. New Brunswick, NJ: Transaction.

Wedel, Janine R. 2012. "Rethinking Corruption in an Age of Ambiguity," *Annual Review of Law and Social Science* 8, no. 1 (December): 453–98. doi:10.1146/annurev.lawsocsci.093008.131558.

Weick, Karl E. 1976. "Educational Organizations as Loosely Coupled Systems," *Administrative Science Quarterly* 21: 1–19.

Weimer, David L., and Aidan R. Vining. *Policy Analysis: Concepts and Practice*. New Jersey: Prentice Hall, 1999.

Weiss, Andrew, and Edward Woodhouse. 1992. "Reframing Incrementalism: A

Constructive Response to Critics," *Policy Sciences* 25, no. 3: 255–73.

Weiss, Carol H. 1977b. "Research for Policy's Sake: The Enlightenment Function of Social Science Research," *Policy Analysis* 3, no. 4: 531–45.

———. 1980. "Knowledge Creep and Decision Accretion," *Knowledge: Creation, Diffusion, Utilization* 1, no. 3: 381–404.

Weiss, Janet A. 1982. "Coping with Complexity: An Experimental Study of Public Policy Decision-Making," *Journal of Policy Analysis and Management* 2, no. 1: 66–87.

Weyland, K. 2005. "Theories of Policy Diffusion—Lessons from Latin American Pension Reform," *World Politics* 57, no. 2: 262–95.

Whalen, Thomas. 1987. "Introduction to Decision-Making under Various Kinds of Uncertainty," in J. Kacprzyk and S.A. Orlovski, eds, *Optimization Models Using Fuzzy Sets and Possibility Theory*. Dordrecht: D. Reidel, 27–49.

Wildavsky, Aaron. 1962. "The Analysis of Issue-Contexts in the Study of Decision-Making," *Journal of Politics* 24, no. 4: 717–32.

Wildavsky, A.B. 1979. Speaking *Truth to Power: The Art and Craft of Policy Analysis*. Boston: Little-Brown.

Woll, Cornelia. 2007. "Leading the Dance? Power and Political Resources of Business Lobbyists," *Journal of Public Policy* 27, no. 1: 57–78.

Wollmann, Hellmut. 1989. "Policy Analysis in West Germany's Federal Government: A Case of Unfinished Governmental and Administrative Modernization?" *Governance* 2, no. 3: 233–266.

Wright, P. 1974. "The Harassed Decision Maker: Time Pressures, Distraction and the Use of Evidence," *Journal of Applied Psychology* 59, no. 5: 555–61.

Yates, J. Frank, and Lisa G. Zukowski. 1976. "Characterization of Ambiguity in Decision Making," *Behavioural Science* 21: 19–25.

Ye, Min. 2007. "Poliheuristic Theory, Bargaining, and Crisis Decision Making," *Foreign Policy Analysis* 3: 317–44.

Young, K., D. Ashby, A. Boaz, and L. Grayson. 2002. "Social Science and the Evidence-Based Policy Movement," *Social Policy and Society* 1, no. 3: 215–24.

———, D. Ashby, A. Boaz, and L. Grayson. 2002. "Social Science and the Evidence-Based Policy Movement," *Social Policy and Society* 1, no. 3: 215–24.

Zahariadis, N. and Christopher S. Allen. 1995. "Ideas, Networks, and Policy Streams: Privatization in Britain and Germany," *Policy Studies Review* 14, nos. 1 and 2: 71–98.

Zelditch, Morris, Jr., and Joan Butler Ford. 1994. "Uncertainty, Potential Power and Nondecisions," *Social Psychology Quarterly* 57, no. 1: 64–76.

———, William Harris, George M. Thomas, and Henry A. Walker. 1983. "Decisions, Nondecisions and Metadecisions," *Research in Social Movements, Conflict and Change* 5: 1–32.

Zijlstra, Gerrit Jan. 1978–9. "Networks in Public Policy: Nuclear Energy in the Netherlands," *Social Networks* 1: 359–89.

Zuckerman, Ezra W. 2012. "Construction, Concentration, and (Dis)Continuities in Social Valuations," *Annual Review of Sociology* 38: 223–245.

Chapter 7 Sources

Adler, Emanuel, and Peter M. Haas. 1992. "Conclusion: Epistemic Communities, World Order, and the Creation of a Reflective Research Program," *International organization* 46, no. 1: 367–90.

Advani, Asheesh, and Sandford Borins. 2001. "Managing Airports: A Test of the New Public Management," *International Public Management Journal* 4: 91–107.

Agranoff, R., and M. McGuire. 1999. "Managing in Network Settings," *Policy Studies Review* 16, no. 1: 18–41.

Alford, John. 2009. *Engaging Public Sector Clients: From Service-Delivery to Co-Production*. Basingstoke, UK and New York: Palgrave Macmillan.

Anderson, G. 1996. "The New Focus on the Policy Capacity of the Federal Government," *Canadian Public Administration* 39, no. 4: 469–88.

Araral, Eduardo. 2014. "Policy and Regulatory Design for Developing Countries: A Mechanism Design and Transaction Cost Approach," *Policy Sciences* 47, no. 3: 289–303.

Ariely, Dan. 2010. *Predictably Irrational, Revised and Expanded Edition: The Hidden*

Forces That Shape Our Decisions. New York: Harper Perennial.

Armstrong, Jim, and Donald G. Lenihan. 1999. *From Controlling to Collaborating; When Governments Want to be Partners: A Report on the Collaborative Partnership Project.* Toronto: Institute of Public Administration of Canada New Directions, Number 3.

Arts, B., Leroy, P., and van Tatenhove, J. 2006. "Political modernization and policy arrangements: a framework for understanding environmental policy change," *Public Organization Review* 6, no. 2: 93–106.

Atkinson, Michael M., and William D. Coleman. 1989. "Strong States and Weak States: Sectoral Policy Networks in Advanced Capitalist Economies," *British Journal of Political Science* 19, no. 1: 47–67.

Bache, I., and M. Flinders. 2004. *Multi-Level Governance.* New York: Oxford University Press.

Bakvis, Herman. 2000. "Rebuilding Policy Capacity in the Era of the Fiscal Dividend: A Report from Canada," *Governance* 13, no. 1: 71–103.

Balch, G.I. 1980. "The Stick, the Carrot, and Other Strategies: A Theoretical Analysis of Governmental Intervention," *Law and Policy Quarterly* 2, no. 1: 35–60.

Baldwin, Robert, and Martin Cave. 1999. *Understanding Regulation: Theory, Strategy and Practice.* Oxford: Oxford University Press.

Banfield, Edward. 1977. "Planning in Whose Interest?" in Neil Gilbert and Harry Spect, eds., *Planning for Social Welfare: Issues, Models, and Tasks,* Englewood Cliffs, NJ: Prentice Hall: p. 44.

Banks, Jeffrey S. 1995. "The Design of Institutions," in D.L. Weimer, ed., *Institutional Design.* Boston: Kluwer, 17–36.

Bardach, Eugene. 1977. The Implementation Game: What Happens after a Bill Becomes a Law. Cambridge, MA: MIT Press.

Barrett, S.M. 2004. "Implementation Studies: Time for a Revival? Personal Reflections on 20 Years of Implementation Studies," *Public Administration* 82, no. 2: 249–62.

Bason, Christian. 2013. "Engaging Citizens in Policy Innovation: Benefiting Public Policy from the Design Inputs Of Citizens And Stakeholders As 'Experts,', in Evert Lindquist, Sam Vincent and John Wanna, eds., *Putting Citizens First: Engagement in Policy and Service Delivery for the 21ˢᵗ Century.* Canberra: Australian National University E-Press, pp. 61–73.

Bason, Christian. 2014. *Design for Policy.* New edition. Farnham, Surrey; Burlington, VT: Gower.

Bator, Francis M. 1958. "The Anatomy of Market Failure," *Quarterly Journal of Economics* 72, no. 3: 351–79.

Becker, Selwyn W., and Fred O. Brownson. 1964. "What Price Ambiguity? Or the Role of Ambiguity in Decision-Making," *Journal of Political Economy* 72, no. 1 (February 1): 62–73.

Beland, Daniel. 2007. "Ideas and Institutional Change in Social Security: Conversion, Layering and Policy Drift," *Social Science Quarterly* 88, no. 1: 20–38.

———. 1992b. "The International Regulation of Personal Data: From Epistemic Community to Policy Sector," paper presented at the annual meeting of the Canadian Political Science Association, Charlottetown, PEI.

Bennett, Scott, and Margaret McPhail. 1992. "Policy Process Perceptions of Senior Canadian Federal Civil Servants: A View of the State and Its Environment," *Canadian Public Administration* 35, no. 3: 299–316.

Bernstein, Marver H. 1955. *Regulating Business by Independent Commission.* Princeton, NJ: Princeton University Press.

Biddle, J.C., and Koontz, T.M. 2014. "Goal Specificity: A Proxy Measure for Improvements in Environmental Outcomes in Collaborative Governance," *Journal of Environmental Management* 145: 268–76.

Blind, Peri K. 2006. *Building Trust in Government in the Twenty-First Century: Review of Literature and Emerging Issues.* UNDESA.

Bobrow, Davis B. 2006. "Policy Design: Ubiquitous, Necessary and Difficult," in B. Guy Peters and Jon Pierre, eds, *Handbook of Public Policy.* London: Sage, 75–96.

Bode, I. 2006. "Disorganized Welfare Mixes: Voluntary Agencies and New Governance Regimes in Western Europe," *Journal of European Social Policy* 16, no. 4: 346–359.

Bogart, W.A. 2002. *Consequences: The Impact of Law and Its Complexity*. Toronto: University of Toronto Press.

Bond, Alan, Angus Morrison-Saunders, Jill A. E. Gunn, Jenny Pope, and Francois Retief. 2015. "Managing Uncertainty, Ambiguity and Ignorance in Impact Assessment by Embedding Evolutionary Resilience, Participatory Modeling and Adaptive Management," *Journal of Environmental Management* 151 (March 15): 97–104. doi:10.1016/j.jenvman.2014.12.030.

Boonekamp, Piet G.M. 2006. "Actual Interaction Effects Between Policy Measures for Energy efficiency—A Qualitative Matrix Method and Quantitative Simulation Results for Households," *Energy* 31, no. 14 (November): 2848–2873. doi:10.1016/j.energy.2006.01.004.

Boswell, Christina. 2014. "The Double Life of Targets in Public Policy: Disciplining and Signaling in UK Asylum Policy," *Public Administration*, October 1.

Bovens, Mark, and Paul t'Hart. 1996. *Understanding Policy Fiascoes*. New Brunswick, NJ: Transaction.

Bozeman, Barry, ed. 1993. *Public Management: The State of the Art*. San Francisco: Jossey-Bass.

Braathen, Nils Axel. 2007. "Instrument Mixes for Environmental Policy: How Many Stones Should Be Used to Kill a Bird?" *International Review of Environmental and Resource Economics* 1, no. 2 (May 16): 185–235.

———, and E. Croci. 2005. "Environmental Agreements Used in Combination with Other Policy Tools," in *The Handbook of Environmental Voluntary Agreements Vol* 43, 335–364. Dodrecht: Springer.

Braithwaite, J., J. Walker, et al. 1987. "An Enforcement Taxonomy of Regulatory Agencies," *Law and Policy* 9, 3: 323–51.

Braithwaite, V.A., ed. 2003. *Taxing Democracy: Understanding Tax Avoidance and Evasion*. Aldershot, England; Burlington, VT: Ashgate Publishing Ltd.

Brandsen, Taco, and Victor Pestoff. 2006. "Co-Production: The Third Sector and the Delivery of Public Services," *Public Management Review* 8 (December): 493–501.

Bressers, Hans Th.A. 1998. "The Choice of Policy Instruments in Policy Networks," in Peters and Van Nispen (1998: 85–105), *Public Policy Instruments: Evaluating the Tools of Public Administration*. Edward Elgar Publishing.

———, and Laurence J. O'Toole. 1998. "The Selection of Policy Instruments: A Networkbased Perspective," *Journal of Public Policy* 18, no. 3: 213–39.

———, and ———. 2005. "Instrument Selection and Implementation in a Networked Context," in P. Eliadis, M. Hill, and M. Howlett, eds, *Designing Government: From Instruments to Governance*. Montreal and Kingston: McGill-Queen's University Press, 132–53.

Breyer, Stephen. 1979. "Analyzing Regulatory Failure: Mismatches, Less Restrictive Alternatives, and Reform," *Harvard Law Review* 92, no. 3: 549–609.

———. 1982. *Regulation and Its Reform*. Cambridge, MA: Harvard University Press.

Briassoulis, H. 2005. *Policy Integration for Complex Environmental Problems: The Example of Mediterranean Desertification*. Aldershot: Ashgate.

Brinkerhoff, D.W., and B.L. Crosby. 2002. *Managing Policy Reform: Concepts and Tools for Decision-Makers in Developing and Transitional Countries*. Bloomfield: Kumarian Press.

Brown, David S. 1955. "The Public Advisory Board as an Instrument of Government," *Public Administration Review* 15: 196–201.

———. 1972. "The Management of Advisory Committees: An Assignment for the '70's," *Public Administration Review* 32: 334–42.

Browne, William P. 1991. "Issue Niches and the Limits of Interest Group Influence," in Allan J. Cigler and Burdett A. Loomis, eds, *Interest Group Politics*. Washington: CQ Press, 345–70.

Bryson, John M., and Barbara C. Crosby. 1993. "Policy Planning and the Design and Use of Forums, Arenas, and Courts," in Bozeman (1993).

Buchanan, James. 1980. "Rent Seeking and Profit Seeking," in Buchanan et al. (1980), *Toward a Theory of the Rent-Seeking Society*. College Station: Texas A&M University Press.

Bullock H., Mountford J., and Stanley R. 2001. *Better Policy-Making*. London: Centre for Management and Policy Studies, Cabinet Office, United Kingdom.

Calvert, Randall L., Mathew D. McCubbins, and Barry R. Weingast. 1989. "A Theory of Political Control and Agency Discretion," *American Journal of Political Science* 33, no. 3: 588–611.

Canadian Government. 1996. *Strengthening Our Policy Capacity. Report of the Task Force on Strengthening the Policy Capacity of the Federal Government*.

Carter, Pam. 2012. "Policy as Palimpsest," *Policy & Politics* 40, no. 3: 423–443. doi:10.1332/030557312X626613.

Chandler, M.A. 1983. "The Politics of Public Enterprise," in Prichard (1983: 185–218) *Crown Corporations in Canda: The Calculus of Instrument Choice*. Toronto: Butterworths.

Christensen, Tom, and Per Laegreid. 2007. "Regulatory Agencies—The Challenges of Balancing Agency Autonomy and Political Control," *Governance* 20, no. 3: 499–520.

———, ———, and L. R. Wise. "Transforming Administrative Policy," *Public Administration* 80, no. 1: 153–179.

Churchman, C. West. 1967. "Wicked Problems," *Management Science* 14, no. 4: B141–2.

Coglianese, Cary. 1997. "Assessing Consensus: The Promise and Performance of Negotiated Rulemaking," *Duke Law Journal* 46, no. 6: 1255–1349.

Colebatch, Hal K. 2006. "What Work Makes Policy?" *Policy Sciences* 39, no. 4 (November 2006): 309–321.

Colebatch, Hal K., Robert Hoppe, and Mirko Noordegraaf, eds. 2011. *Working for Policy*. Amsterdam University Press.

Considine, Mark. 2012. "Thinking Outside the Box? Applying Design Theory to Public Policy," *Politics & Policy* 40, no. 4: 704–724. doi:10.1111/j.1747–1346.2012.00372.x.

Corner, Adam, and Alex Randall. 2011. "Selling Climate Change? The Limitations of Social Marketing as a Strategy for Climate Change Public Engagement," *Global Environmental Change* 21, no. 3 (August): 1005–14.

Cross, M. and Davis, K. 2015. "The Limits of Epistemic Communities: EU Security Agencies," *Politics and Governance* 3, no. 1: 90.

Cushman, Robert E. 1941. *The Independent Regulatory Commissions*. London: Oxford University Press.

Davis, Glyn. 2000. "Conclusion: Policy Capacity and the Future Of Governance," in Glyn Davis and Michael Keating, eds., The *Future of Governance*. St. Leonards, New South Wales: Allen Unwin.

deLeon, Peter. 1992. "Policy Formulation: Where Ignorant Armies Clash by Night," *Policy Studies Review* 11, nos. 3 and 4: 389–405.

———. 1999a. "The Missing Link Revisited: Contemporary Implementation Research," *Policy Studies Review* 16, nos. 3 and 4: 311–38.

Del Río, Pablo, Anxo Calvo Silvosa, and Guillermo Iglesias Gómez. 2011. "Policies and Design Elements for the Repowering of Wind Farms: A Qualitative Analysis of Different Options," *Energy Policy* 39, no. 4 (April): 1897–1908.

Dion, Leon. 1973. "The Politics of Consultation," *Government and Opposition* 8, no. 3: 332–53.

Doern, G. Bruce. 1981. *The Nature of Scientific and Technological Controversy in Federal Policy Formation*. Ottawa: Science Council of Canada.

———. 1998. "The Interplay among Regimes: Mapping Regulatory Institutions in the United Kingdom, the United States, and Canada," in Doern and Wilks (1998: 29–50). *Regulatory Institutions in North America*. Toronto: University of Toronto Press.

———, and R. W. Phidd. 1983. *Canadian Public Policy: Ideas, Structure, Process*. Toronto: Methuen.

———, and S. Wilks, eds. 1998. *Changing Regulatory Institutions in Britain and North America*. Toronto: University of Toronto Press.

Donovan, M.C. 2001. *Taking Aim: Target Populations and the Wars on AIDS and Drugs*. Washington: Georgetown University Press.

Duesberg, Stefanie, Áine Ní Dhubháin, and Deirdre O'Connor. 2014. "Assessing Policy Tools for Encouraging Farm Afforestation in Ireland," *Land Use Policy* 38 (May): 194–203.

Dye, Thomas R. 2001. *Top-Down Policymaking*. New York: Chatham House.

Economic Council of Canada. 1979. *Responsible Regulation: An Interim Report*. Ottawa: Supply and Services Canada.

Eliadis, P., M. Hill, and M. Howlett. 2005. *Designing Government: From Instruments to Governance*. Montreal and Kingston: McGill-Queen's University Press.

Ellig, Jerry, and Don Lavoie. 1995. "The Principle–Agent Relationship in Organizations," in P. Foss, ed., *Economic Approaches to Organizations and Institutions: An Introduction*. Aldershot: Dartmouth.

Elmore, Richard F. 1978. "Organizational Models of Social Program Implementation," *Public Policy* 26, no. 2: 185–228.

English, Linda M., and Matthew Skellern. 2005. "Public–Private Partnerships and Public Sector Management Reform: A Comparative Perspective," *International Journal of Public Policy* 1, nos. 1–2: 1–21.

Etienne, Julien. "Compliance Theory: A Goal Framing Approach," *Law & Policy* 33, no. 3 (July 1): 305–33.

Feeley, Malcolm. 1970. "Coercion and Compliance: A New Look at an Old Problem," *Law & Society Review* 4, no. 4 (May 1): 505–19.

Francis, John G. 1993. *The Politics of Regulation: A Comparative Perspective*. Oxford: Blackwell.

Freeman, Gary P. 1985. "National Styles and Policy Sectors: Explaining Structured Variation," *Journal of Public Policy* 5, no. 4: 467–96.

Freeman, Jody. 1997. "Collaborative Governance in the Administrative State," *UCLA Law Review* 45, no. 1: 1–98.

Fukuyama, Francis. 2013. "What Is Governance?" *Governance*. doi:10.1111/gove.12035.

Gall, Gerald L. 1983. *The Canadian Legal System*, 2nd edn. Toronto: Carswell.

Gaus, John M. 1931. "Notes on Administration," *American Political Science Review* 25, no. 1: 123–34.

Gevrek, Z. Eylem, and Ayse Uyduranoglu. 2015. "Public Preferences for Carbon Tax Attributes," *Ecological Economics* 118 (October): 186–97.

Ghosh, Atish R., Jonathan D. Ostry, and Marcos Chamon. 2015. "Two Targets, Two Instruments: Monetary and Exchange Rate Policies in Emerging Market Economies," *Journal of International Money and Finance*. Accessed May 8, 2015.

Ginsburg, N. 1992. *Divisions of Welfare: A Critical Introduction to Comparative Social Policy*. London: Sage.

Giuliani, Mark. 1999. "'Soft' Institutions for Hard Problems: Instituting Air Pollution Policies in Three Italian Regions," in W. Grant, A. Perl, and P. Knoepfel, eds, *The Politics of Improving Urban Air Quality*. Cheltenham: Edward Elgar, 31–51.

Gleeson, Deborah H., David G. Legge, and Deirdre O'Neill. 2009. "Evaluating Health Policy Capacity: Learning from International and Australian Experience," *Australia and New Zealand Health Policy* 6, no. 1 (February 26).

Goggin, Malcolm L., et al. 1990. *Implementation Theory and Practice: Toward a Third Generation*. Glenview, IL: Scott, Foresman/Little, Brown.

Gleeson, Deborah, David Legge, Deirdre O'Neill, and Monica Pfeffer. 2011. "Negotiating Tensions in Developing Organizational Policy Capacity: Comparative Lessons to Be Drawn," *Journal of Comparative Policy Analysis: Research and Practice* 13, no. 3 (June): 237–263.

Goodnow, Frank J. 1900. *Politics and Administration: A Study in Government*. New York: Russell and Russell.

Gough, C. and Shackley, S. 2001. "The Respectable Politics of Climate Change: The Epistemic Communities and NGOs," *International Affairs* 77: 329–346.

Grabosky, Peter N. 1995. "Using Non-Governmental Resources to Foster Regulatory Compliance," *Governance* 8, no. 4: 527–50.

Grabosky, P. 1995. "Counterproductive Regulation," *International Journal of the Sociology of Law* 23: 347–369.

Grima, A.P. 1985. "Participatory Rites: Integrating Public Involvement in Environmental Impact Assessment," in J.B.R. Whitney and V.W. Maclaren, eds, *Environmental Impact Assessment: The Canadian Experience*. Toronto: University of Toronto Institute for Environmental Studies, 33–51.

Grimshaw, Damian, Steven Vincent, and Hugh Willmott. 2001. "New Control Modes and Emergent Organizational Forms:

Private–Public Contracting in Public Administration," *Administrative Theory and Practice* 23, no. 3: 407–30.

Gunningham, Neil, Peter Grabosky, and Darren Sinclair. 1998. *Smart Regulation: Designing Environmental Policy.* Oxford: Clarendon Press.

Gunningham, Neil, and Darren Sinclair. 1999. "Regulatory Pluralism: Designing Policy Mixes for Environmental Protection," *Law and Policy* 21, no. 1: 49–76.

Haas, Peter M. 1992. "Introduction: Epistemic Communities and International Policy Coordination," *International Organization* 46, 1: no. 1–36.

Hacker, J.S. 2005. "Policy Drift: The Hidden Politics of US Welfare State Retrenchment," in *Beyond Continuity: Institutional Change in Advanced Political Economies*, edited by W. Streek and K. Thelen. Oxford: Oxford University Press, 40–82.

———. 2004. "Review Article: Dismantling the Health Care State? Political Institutions, Public Policies and the Comparative Politics of Health Reform," *British Journal of Political Science* 34: 693–724.

Hajer, M.A. 1997. *The Politics of Environmental Discourse: Ecologial Modernization and the Policy Process.* Oxford: Oxford University Press

———. 2005. "Setting the Stage: A Dramaturgy of Policy Deliberation," *Administration & Society* 36, no. 6: 624–647.

Hargrove, E.L. 1975. *The Missing Link: The Study of the Implementation of Social Policy.* Washington: Urban Institute.

Hawkins, Keith. 1984. *Environment and Enforcement: Regulation and the Social Definition of Pollution.* Oxford: Clarendon Press.

———, and John M. Thomas, eds. 1989a. *Making Regulatory Policy.* Pittsburgh: University of Pittsburgh Press.

———, and J.M. Thomas. 1989. "Making Policy in Regulatory Bureaucracies," in *Making Regulatory Policy*, edited by K. Hawkins and J.M. Thomas. Pittsburgh: University of Pittsburgh Press, 3–30.

Head, Brian W., and John Alford. 2013. "Wicked Problems: Implications for Public Policy and Management," *Administration & Society*, March 28. doi:10.1177/0095399713481601.

Heritier, Adrienne. 1997. "Policy-Making by Subterfuge: Interest Accommodation, Innovation and Substitute Democratic Legitimation in Europe—Perspectives from Distinctive Policy Areas," *Journal of European Public Policy* 4, no. 2: 171–89.

———. 1999. "Elements of Democratic Legitimation in Europe: An Alternative Perspective," *Journal of European Public Policy* 6, no. 2: 269–82.

Hill, M. and P. Hupe. 2002. *Implementing Public Policy: Governance in Theory and Practice.* London: Sage Publications.

Hill, Michael, and Peter L Hupe. 2009. *Implementing Public Policy: An Introduction to the Study of Operational Governance.* 2nd edn. Sage Publications Ltd.

Hisschemoller, Matthijs, and Rob Hoppe. 1995. "Coping with Intractable Controversies: The Case for Problem Structuring in Policy Design and Analysis," *Knowledge and Policy* 8, no. 4: 40–61.

Hjern, Benny. 1982. "Implementation Research—The Link Gone Missing," *Journal of Public Policy* 2, no. 3: 301–8.

Hodge, Graeme A., and Carsten Greve. 2007. "Public–Private Partnerships: An International Performance Review," *Public Administration Review* 67, no. 3: 545–58.

Hogwood, B., and Gunn, L. 1993. "Why 'perfect implementation' is unattainable," *The Policy Process: A reader,* 2: 217–25.

Holmberg, Sören, Bo Rothstein, and Naghmeh Nasiritousi. 2009. "Quality of Government: What You Get," *Annual Review of Political Science* 12: 135–161.

Hood, Christopher. 1983. "Using Bureaucracy Sparingly," *Public Administration* 61, no. 2: 197–208.

———. 1986. *The Tools of Government.* Chatham: Chatham House Publishers.

———. 1986b. "The Hidden Public Sector: The 'Quangocratization' of the World?" in Kaufman et al. (1986: 183–207). *Guidance, Control and Evaluation in the Public Sector.* Berlin and New York: deGruyter.

———. 1988. "Keeping the Centre Small: Explanation of Agency Type," *Political Studies* 36, no. 1: 30–46.

———. 2002. "Control, Bargains, and Cheating: The Politics of Public-Service Reform," *Journal of Public Administration Research and Theory* 12, no. 3: 309–332.

———. 2010. *The Blame Game: Spin, Bureaucracy, and Self-Preservation in Government*. Princeton University Press.

Hou, Yilin, and Gene Brewer. 2010. "Substitution and Supplementation Between Co-Functional Policy Tools: Evidence from State Budget Stabilization Practices," *Public Administration Review* 70, no. 6: 914–924.

Howlett, Michael. 1991. "Policy Instruments, Policy Styles, and Policy Implementation: National Approaches to Theories of Instrument Choice," *Policy Studies Journal* 19, no. 2: 1–21.

———. 2000. "Managing the "Hollow State": Procedural Policy Instruments and Modern Governance," *Canadian Public Administration* 43, no. 4: 412–31.

———. 2003. "Administrative Styles and the Limits of Administrative Reform: A Neo-Institutional Analysis of Administrative Culture," *Canadian Public Administration* 46, no. 4: 471–94.

———. 2005. "What Is a Policy Instrument? Policy Tools, Policy Mixes and Policy Implementation Styles," in *Designing Government: From Instruments to Governance*, edited by P. Eliadis, M. Hill, and M. Howlett, 31–50. Montreal: McGill-Queen's University Press.

———. 2009. "Government Communication as a Policy Tool: A Framework for Analysis," *The Canadian Political Science Review* 3: 2. June.

———. 2011. *Designing Public Policies: Principles and Instruments*. New York: Routledge.

———, and Ishani Muhkerjee. 2014. "Policy Design and Non-Design: Towards a Spectrum of Policy Formulation Types," *Politics and Governance* 2, no. 2 (November): 57–71.

———, and Jeremy Rayner. 1995. "Do Ideas Matter? Policy Subsystem Configurations and Policy Change in the Canadian Forest Sector," *Canadian Public Administration* 38, no. 3: 382–410.

———, and Richard M Walker. 2012. "Public Managers in the Policy Process: More Evidence on the Missing Variable?" *Policy Studies Journal* 40, no. 2 (May 1): 211–233.

———, Ramesh, M., and Perl, A. 2009. *Studying Public Policy: Policy Cycles and Policy Subsystems*. 3rd edn. Toronto: Oxford University Press.

Howse, Robert J., Robert S. Prichard, and Michael J. Trebilcock. 1990. "Smaller or Smarter Government?" *University of Toronto Law Journal* 40: 498–541.

Hutter, Bridget M., and P.K. Manning. 1990. "The Contexts of Regulation: The Impact upon Health and Safety Inspectorates in Britain," *Law and Policy* 12, no. 2: 103–36.

Ingraham, P. 1987. "Toward More Systematic Considerations of Policy Design," *Policy Studies Journal* 15, no. 4: 611–28.

Jarvis, D. S. L. 2011. "Theorising Risk and Uncertainty in International Relations: The Contributions of Frank Knight," *International Relations* 25, no. 3 (September 1): 296–312. doi:10.1177/0047117811415485.

Johansson, R., and K. Borell. 1999. "Central Steering and Local Networks: Old-Age Care in Sweden," *Public Administration* 77, 3: 585–98.

John, Peter, Graham Smith, and Gerry Stoker. 2009. "Nudge Nudge, Think Think: Two Strategies for Changing Civic Behaviour," *The Political Quarterly* 80, no. 3 (July 1): 361–70.

Jones, B.D., H.F. Thomas III, and M. Wolfe. 2014. "Policy Bubbles," *Policy Studies Journal* 42, no. 1: 146–171.

Junginger, Sabine. 2013. "Design and Innovation in the Public Sector: Matters of Design in policymaking and Policy Implementation," 10th European Academy of Design Conference—Crafting the Future.

Kagan, Robert A. 1994. "Regulatory Enforcement," in Rosenbloom and Schwartz (1994: 383–422), *Handbook of Regulation and Adminstrative Law*. New York: Dekker.

———. 1996. "The Political Construction of American Adversarial Legalism," in A. Ranney, ed., *Courts and the Political Process*. Berkeley, CA: Institute of Governmental Studies Press, 19–39.

———. 2001. *Adversarial Legalism: The American Way of Law*. Cambridge: Harvard University Press.

Kaine, Geoff, Helen Murdoch, Ruth Lourey, and Denise Bewsell. 2010. "A Framework for Understanding Individual Response to Regulation," *Food Policy* 35, no. 6 (December): 531–37.

Kay, Adrian. 2007. "Tense Layering and Synthetic Policy Paradigms: The Politics of

Health Insurance in Australia," *Australian Journal of Political Science* 42, no. 4: 579–591.

Kernaghan, Kenneth. 1993. "Partnership and Public Administration: Conceptual and Practical Considerations," *Canadian Public Administration* 36, no. 1: 57–76.

Kerwin, Cornelius M. 1994. "The Elements of Rule-Making," in Rosenbloom and Schwartz (1994: 345–81). *Handbook of Regulation and Adminstrative Law*. New York: Dekker

———. 1999. *Rulemaking: How Government Agencies Write Law and Make Policy*. Washington: Congressional Quarterly Press.

Keyes, J.M. 1996. "Power Tools: The Form and Function of Legal Instruments for Government Action," *Canadian Journal of Administrative Law and Practice* 10: 133–174.

King, David C., and Jack L. Walker. 1991. "An Ecology of Interest Groups in America," in Walker (1991: 57–73). *Mobilizing Interest Groups in America*. Ann Arbor: University of Michigan Press.

Kingdon, John W. *Agendas, Alternatives and Public Policies*, 2nd edn. Boston: Longman, 2011.

Kiss, Bernadett, Clara González Manchón, and Lena Neij. 2012. "The Role of Policy Tools in Supporting the Development of Mineral Wool Insulation in Germany, Sweden and the United Kingdom," *Journal of Cleaner Production*. Accessed December 29, 2012.

Kiviniemi, Markku. 1986. "Public Policies and Their Targets: A Typology of the Concept of Implementation," *International Social Science Journal* 38, 108: 251–66.

Klijn, Erik-Hans. 2002. "Governing Networks in the Hollow State: Contracting Out, Process Management, or a Combination of the Two?" *Public Management Review* 4, no. 2: 149–65.

Knaggård, Å. 2015. "The Multiple Streams Framework and the Problem Broker," *European Journal of Political Research* 54, no. 3: 450–465.

Knill, Christoph. 1999. "Explaining Cross-National Variance in Administrative Reform: Autonomous versus Instrumental Bureaucracies," *Journal of Public Policy* 19, no. 2: 113–39.

Koppell, J.G.S. 2003. *The Politics of Quasi-Government: Hybrid Organizations and the Dynamics of Bureaucratic Control*. Cambridge: Cambridge University Press.

Kuo, D. 2006. *Tempting Faith: An Inside Story of Political Seduction*. New York: Free Press.

Lange, Philipp et al. 2013. "Governing towards Sustainability—Conceptualizing Modes of Governance," *Journal of Environmental Policy and Planning* 15, no. 3: 403–425.

Laux, Jeanne Kirk, and Maureen Appel Molot. 1988. *State Capitalism: Public Enterprise in Canada*. Ithaca, NY: Cornell University Press.

Leggett, Will. 2014. "The Politics of Behaviour Change: Nudge, Neoliberalism and the State," *Policy & Politics* 42, no. 1: 3–19.

Lempert, R., S. Popper, and S. Bankes. 2002. "Confronting Surprise," *Social Science Computer Review* 20, no. 4: 420–40.

———, ———. and ———. 2003. *Shaping the Next One Hundred Years: New Methods for Quantitative, Long-Term Policy Analysis*. Santa Monica, CA: RAND.

Lester, James P., and Malcolm L. Goggin. 1998. "Back to the Future: The Rediscovery of Implementation Studies," *Policy Currents* 8, no. 3: 1–9.

———et al. 1987. "Public Policy Implementation: Evolution of the Field and Agenda for Future Research," *Policy Studies Review* 7: 200–16.

Leung, Wanda, Bram Noble, Jill Gunn, and Jochen A.G. Jaeger. 2015. "A Review of Uncertainty Research in Impact Assessment," *Environmental Impact Assessment Review* 50 (January): 116–23. doi:10.1016/j.eiar.2014.09.005.

Lichtenstein, Sarah and Paul Slovic. 2006. *The Construction of Preference*. Cambridge University Press.

Linder, Stephen H and B. Guy Peters. 1988. "The Analysis of Design or the Design of Analysis?" *Policy Studies Review* 7, no. 4: 738–50.

Lindquist, Evert A. 2006. "Organizing for Policy Implementation: The Emergence and Role of Implementation Units in Policy Design and Oversight," *Journal of Comparative Policy Analysis: Research and Practice* 8, no. 4: 311–24.

Ling, T. 2002. "Delivering Joined-Up Government in the UK: Dimensions, Issues and

Problems," *Public Administration* 80, no. 4: 615–642.

Lipsky, Michael. 1980. *Street-Level Bureaucracy: Dilemmas of the Individual in Public Services.* New York: Russell Sage Foundation.

Lowi, Theodore J. 1996. "Distribution, Regulation, Redistribution: The Functions of Government," in Randall B. Ripley (ed.), *Public Policies and Their Politics: Techniques of Government Control.* New York: W.W. Norton, pp. 27–40.

Lowndes, V. and Skelcher, C. 1998. "The Dynamics of Multi-Organizational Partnerships: An Analysis of Changing Modes of Governance," *Public Administration* 76: 313–333.

Maloney, William A. 2001. "Regulation in an Episodic Policy-Making Environment: The Water Industry in England and Wales," *Public Administration* 79, no. 3: 625–42.

Mandell, M.P. 2000. "A Revised Look at Management in Network Structures," *International Journal of Organizational Theory and Behavior* 3, nos. 1 and 2: 185–210.

March, J.G., and J.P. Olsen. 1989. *Rediscovering Institutions: The Organizational Basis of Politics.* New York: Free Press.

Matland, R.E. 1995. "Synthesizing the Implementation Literature: The Ambiguity-Conflict Model of Policy Implementation," *Journal of Public Administration Research and Theory* 5, no. 2: 145–74.

May, P. 2003. "Policy Design and Implementation," in B. Guy Peters and Jon Pierre, eds, *Handbook of Public Administration.* Beverly Hills: Sage Publications, pp. 223–233.

———. 2004. "Compliance Motivations: Affirmative and Negative Bases," *Law & Society Review* 38, no. 1: 41–68

Mayntz, Renate. 1979. "Public Bureaucracies and Policy Implementation," *International Social Science Journal* 31, no. 4: 633–45.

———. 1983. "The Conditions of Effective Public Policy: A New Challenge for Policy Analysis," *Policy and Politics* 11, no. 2: 123–43.

Mazmanian, Daniel A., and Paul A. Sabatier. 1983. *Implementation and Public Policy.* Glenview, IL: Scott, Foresman.

McCubbins, Arthur Lupia and Mathew D. 1994. "Learning from Oversight: Fire Alarms and Policy Patrols Reconstructed," *Journal of Law, Economics and Organization* 10, no. 1: 96–125.

McCubbins, Mathew D., Roger G. Noll, and Barry R. Weingast. 1987. "Administrative Procedures as Instruments of Political Control," *Journal of Law, Economics, and Organization* 3, no. 2: 243–77.

———, ———, and ———. 1989. "Structure and Process, Politics and Policy: Administrative Arrangements and the Political Control of Agencies," *Virginia Law Review* 75, no. 2: 431–82.

———, and Thomas Schwartz. 1984. "Congressional Oversight Overlooked: Policy Patrols versus Fire Alarms," *American Journal of Political Science* 28, 1: 165–79.

McGann, James G., Anna Viden, and Jillian Rafferty, eds. 2014. *How Think Tanks Shape Social Development Policies.* University of Pennsylvania Press.

McInerney, David, Robert Lempert, and Klaus Keller. 2012. "What Are Robust Strategies in the Face of Uncertain Climate Threshold Responses?" *Climatic Change* 112, nos. 3–4 (January 3): 547–68. doi:10.1007/s10584–011–0377–1.

McMullen, K., and G. Schellenberg. 2002. *Mapping the Non-Profit Sector.* Ottawa: Canadian Policy Research Networks.

Meier, Kenneth J., and David R. Morgan. 1982. "Citizen Compliance with Public Policy: The National Maximum Speed Law," *Western Political Quarterly* 35, no. 2: 258–73.

Meijers, E., and D. Stead. 2004. "Policy Integration: What Does It Mean and How Can It Be Achieved? A Multi-Disciplinary Review," paper presented at the Berlin Conference on the Human Dimensions of Global Environmental Change: Greening of Policies— Interlinkages and Policy Integration.

Milward, H. Brinton and Keith G. Provan. 1998. "Principles for Controlling Agents: The Political Economy of Network Structure," *Journal of Public Administration Research and Theory* 8, no. 2: 203–22.

Mitnick, Barry M. 1980. *The Political Economy of Regulation: Creating, Designing, and Removing Regulatory Forms.* New York: Columbia University Press.

Montgomery, John D. 2000. "Social Capital as a Policy Resource," *Policy Sciences* 33: 227–43.

Morgan, M.G., and M. Henrion. 1990. *Uncertainty: A Guide to Dealing with Uncertainty in Quantitative Risk and Policy Analysis.* Cambridge: Cambridge University Press.

Mulford, C. L., and A. Etzioni. 1978. "Why They Don't Even When They Ought to: Implications of Compliance Theory for Policymakers," in Policy Research, 47–62. Leiden: E.J. Brill.

Mulgan, Geoff. 2008. *The Art of Public Strategy: Mobilizing Power and Knowledge for the Common Good.* Oxford; New York: Oxford University Press.

Nair, Sreeja and Michael Howlett. 2015. "Scaling up of Policy Experiments and Pilots: A Qualitative Comparative Analysis and Lessons for the Water Sector," *Water Resources Management* 29, no. 14: 4945–4961.

Nielsen, Vibeke Lehmann, and Christine Parker. 2012. "Mixed Motives: Economic, Social, and Normative Motivations in Business Compliance," *Law & Policy* 34, no. 4: 428–62.

Nicholson-Crotty, S. 2005. "Bureaucratic Competition in the Policy Process," *Policy Studies Journal* 33, no. 3: 341–61.

Oliver, Adam. 2015. "Nudging, Shoving, and Budging: Behavioural Economic-Informed Policy," *Public Administration*, March 1.

Orren, Karen, and Stephen Skowronek. 1998–9. "Regimes and Regime Building in American Government: A Review of Literature on the 1940s," *Political Science Quarterly* 113, no. 4: 689–702.

O'Flynn, Janine. 2007. "From New Public Management to Public Value: Paradigmatic Change And Managerial Implications," *Australian Journal of Public Administration* 66, no. 3: 353–66.

OToole, Laurence J. 2000b. "Research on Policy Implementation: Assessment and Prospects," *Journal of Public Administration Research and Theory* 10, no. 2: 263–88.

———. 2004. "The Theory–Practice Issue in Policy Implementation Research," *Public Administration* 82, no. 2: 309–29.

Painter, M., and J. Pierre. 2005. *Challenges to State Policy Capacity: Global Trends and Comparative Perspectives.* London: Palgrave Macmillan.

Pal, L. A. 1993. *Interests of State: The Politics of Language, Multiculturalism, and Feminism in Canada.* Montreal, McGill-Queen's University Press.

Parsons, W. 2004. "Not Just Steering but Weaving: Relevant Knowledge and the Craft of Building Policy Capacity and Coherence," *Australian Journal of Public Administration* 63, no. 1: 43–57.

Pestoff, Victor. 2006. "Citizens and Co-Production of Welfare Services," *Public Management Review* 8 (December): 503–519.

Pestoff, Victor, and Taco Brandsen. 2009. *Co-Production: The Third Sector and the Delivery of Public Services.* New York: CRC Press.

Pestoff, Victor Alexis, Taco Brandsen, and Bram Verschuere. 2012. *New Public Governance, the Third Sector and Co-Production.* New York: Routledge.

———, Stephen P. Osborne, and Taco Brandsen. 2006. "Patterns of Co-Production in Public Services," *Public Management Review* 8 (December): 591–95.

Peters, B. Guy and F.K.M. Van Nispen, eds. 1998. *Public Policy Instruments: Evaluating the Tools of Public Administration.* New York: Edward Elgar.

Peters, B. G., and D. J. Savoie. 1996. "Managing Incoherence: The Coordination and Empowerment Conundrum," *Public Administration Review* 56, no. 3: 280–93.

Peters, B. Guy. 2013. "Toward Policy Coordination: Alternatives to Hierarchy," *Policy & Politics* 41, no. 4 (October 1): 569–84.

Phidd, Richard W. and G. Bruce Doern. 1983. *Canadian Public Policy: Ideas, Structures, Process.* Toronto: Methuen.

Phillips, Susan D. and Karine Levasseur. 2004. "The Snakes and Ladders of Accountability: Contradictions between Contracting and Collaboration for Canada's Voluntary Sector," *Canadian Public Administration* 47, no. 4: 451–74.

Pierson, Paul. 2000a. "Increasing Returns, Path Dependence, and the Study of Politics," *American Political Science Review* 94, no. 2: 251–67.

———. 2004. *Politics in Time: History, Institutions, and Social Analysis.* Princeton, NJ: Princeton University Press.

Posner, Richard A. 1974. "Theories of Economic Regulation," *Bell Journal of*

Economics and Management Science 5, no. 2: 335–58.

Pressman, J.L. and A.B. Wildavsky. 1973. *Implementation: How Great Expectations in Washington are Dashed in Oakland.* Berkeley, CA: University of California Press.

Ramesh, M., and Scott Fritzen, eds. 2009. *Transforming Asian Governance: Rethinking Assumptions, Challenging Practices.* London; New York: Routledge.

———, and Michael Howlett, eds. 2006. *Deregulation and Its Discontents: Rewriting the Rules in Asia.* Cheltenham: Edward Elgar.

Rayner, J., et al. 2001. "Privileging the Sub-Sector: Critical Sub-Sectors and Sectoral Relationships in Forest Policy-Making," *Forest Policy and Economics* 2, nos. 3 and 4: 319–32.

Reagan, Michael D. 1987. *Regulation: The Politics of Policy.* Boston: Little, Brown.

Rein, Martin, and Donald Schön. 1994. *Frame Reflection: Toward the Resolution of Intractable Policy Controversies.* New York: Basic Books.

Rhodes, R.A.W. 1997. *Understanding Governance: Policy Networks, Governance, Reflexivity and Accountability.* Buckingham, UK: Open University Press.

Richardson, Jeremy J., Gunnel Gustafsson, and Grant Jordan. 1982. "The Concept of Policy Style," in Richardson, ed., *Policy Styles in Western Europe.* London: George Allen and Unwin.

Rittel, Horst W.J., and Melvin M. Webber. 1973. "Dilemmas in a General Theory of Planning," *Policy Sciences* 4: 155–69.

Rodgers, Harrell R. 1975. *Coercion to Compliance, Or How Great Expectations in Washington Are Actually Realized at the Local Level, This Being the Saga of School Desegregation in the South as Told by Two Sympathetic Observers—Lessons on Getting Things Done.* Lexington Books.

Room, Graham. 2013. "Evidence for Agile Policy Makers: The Contribution of Transformative Realism," *Evidence & Policy: A Journal of Research, Debate and Practice* 9, no. 2 (May 24): 225–44. doi:10.1332/174426413X662653.

Rotberg, Robert I. 2014. "Good Governance Means Performance and Results," *Governance.* doi:10.1111/gove.12084.

Rothmayr, Christine, Uwe Serduelt, and Elisabeth Maurer. 1997. "Policy Instruments: An Analytical Category Revised," paper presented at the ECPR Joint Sessions Workshops, 27 Feb.–4 Mar., Bern.

Sabatier, Paul A. 1975. "Social Movements and Regulatory Agencies: Toward a More Adequate—and Less Pessimistic—Theory of 'Clientele Capture,'" *Policy Sciences* 6: 301–42.

Sabatier, P.A. 1991. "Toward Better Theories of the Policy Process," *PS: Political Science and Politics* 24, no. 2: 144–56.

———. 1986. "Top-Down and Bottom-Up Approaches to Implementation Research: A Critical Analysis and Suggested Synthesis," *Journal of Public Policy* 6: 21–48.

———, and D.A. Mazmanian. 1981. *Effective Policy Implementation.* Lexington, MA: Lexington Books.

———, and Weible, C.M., eds. 2007. *Theories of the Policy Process.* Boulder: Westview Press.

Salamon, Lester M. 1981. "Rethinking Public Management: Third-Party Government and the Changing Forms of Government Action," *Public Policy* 29, no. 3: 255–75.

Saward, Michael. 1990. "Cooption and Power: Who Gets What from Formal Incorporation," *Political Studies* 38: 588–602.

———. 1992. *Co-Optive Politics and State Legitimacy.* Aldershot: Dartmouth.

Schlager, Edella, and William Blomquist. 1996. "Emerging Political Theories of the Policy Process: Institutional Rational Choice, the Politics of Structural Choice, and Advocacy Coalitions," *Political Research Quarterly* 49 (September): 651–672.

Schneider, Anne, and Helen Ingram. 1990a. "Behavioural Assumptions of Policy Tools," *Journal of Politics* 52, no. 2: 510–29.

———, and ———. 1990b. "Policy Design: Elements, Premises and Strategies," in S.S. Nagel, ed., *Policy Theory and Policy Evaluation: Concepts, Knowledge, Causes and Norms.* New York: Greenwood, 77–102.

———, and ———. 1993. "Social Construction of Target Populations: Implications for Politics and Policy," *American Political Science Review* 87, no. 2: 334–47.

——, and ——. 1997. *Policy Design for Democracy*. Lawrence: University Press of Kansas.

——, and ——. 1994. "Social Constructions and Policy Design: Implications for Public Administration," *Research in Public Administration* 3: 137–173.

Schneider, A., and H. Ingram. 2005. *Deserving and Entitled: Social Constructions and Public Policy*. SUNY Series in Public Policy. Albany: State University of New York.

Scholz, John T. 1984. "Cooperation, Deterrence, and the Ecology of Regulatory Enforcement," *Law and Society Review* 18, no. 2: 179–224.

——. 1991. "Cooperative Regulatory Enforcement and the Politics of Administrative Effectiveness," *American Political Science Review* 85, no. 1: 115–36.

Schrader, S., Riggs, W.M. and Smith, R.P. 1993. "Choice over Uncertainty and Ambiguity in Technical Problem Solving," *Journal of Engineering and Technology Management* 10: 73–99.

Simon, Herbert A. 1973. "The Structure of Ill Structured Problems," *Artificial Intelligence* 4: 181–201.

Sinclair, Darren. 1997. "Self-Regulation versus Command and Control? Beyond False Dichotomies," *Law and Policy* 19, no. 4: 529–59.

Smith, Thomas B. 1977. "Advisory Committees in the Public Policy Process," *International Review of Administrative Sciences* 43, no. 2: 153–66.

Spicker, P. 2005. "Targeting, Residual Welfare and Related Concepts: Modes of Operation in Public Policy," *Public Administration* 83, no. 2: 345–65.

——. 2006. *Policy Analysis for Practice*. Bristol: Policy Press.

Stanton, Thomas H. 2002. "Loans and Loan Guarantees," in Salamon (2002a: 381–409).

Stavins, Robert N. 2001. *Lessons from the American Experiment with Market-Based Environmental Policies*. Washington: Resources for the Future.

Stead, D., H. Geerlings, and E. Meijers. 2004. *Policy Integration in Practice: The Integration of Land Use Planning, Transport and Environmental Policy-Making in Denmark, England and Germany*. Delft: Delft University Press.

Steg, Linda, Jan Willem Bolderdijk, Kees Keizer, and Goda Perlaviciute. 2014. "An Integrated Framework for Encouraging Pro-Environmental Behaviour: The Role of Values, Situational Factors and Goals," *Journal of Environmental Psychology* 38 (June): 104–15.

Stigler, George J. 1975. *The Citizen and the State: Essays on Regulation*. Chicago: University of Chicago Press.

Stirling, Andy. 2010. "Keep It Complex," *Nature* 468, no. 7327 (December 23): 1029–31. doi:10.1038/4681029a.

Stokey, Edith, and Richard Zeckhauser. 1978. *A Primer for Policy Analysis*. New York: Norton.

Stover, Robert V and Don W. Brown. 1975. "Understanding Compliance and Noncompliance with Law: The Contributions of Utility Theory" Social Science Quarterly 56, no. 3 (December 1): 363–75.

Streeck, W., and K. Thelen. 2005. "Institutional Changes in Advanced Political Economies," in *Beyond Continuity: Institutional Change in Advanced Political Economies*. Oxford: Oxford University Press.

Swanson, D., Barg S., Tyler S., Venema H., Tomar S., Bhadwal S., Nair S., Roy D., and Drexhage J., 2010. "Seven Tools for Creating Adaptive Policies," *Technological Forecasting & Social Change* 77, no. 6: 924–939.

Suchman, Mark C. 1995. "Managing Legitimacy: Strategic and Institutional Approaches," *Academy of Management Review* 20, no. 3: 571–610.

Talbert, Jeffrey C., Bryan D. Jones, and Frank R. Baumgartner. 1995. "Non-legislative Hearings and Policy Change in Congress," *American Journal of Political Science* 39, no. 2: 383–406.

Taylor, C.M., S.J.T. Pollard, A.J. Angus, and S.A. Rocks. 2013. "Better by Design: Rethinking Interventions for Better Environmental Regulation," *Science of The Total Environment* 447 (March 1): 488–99.

Thaler, Richard H., and Cass R. Sunstein. 2009. *Nudge: Improving Decisions About Health, Wealth, and Happiness*. Revised and Expanded edition. New York: Penguin Books.

——, ——, and John P. Balz. 2010. "Choice Architecture," SSRN Scholarly Paper. Rochester, NY: Social Science Research Network, April 2.

Thelen, Kathleen. 2003. "How Institutions Evolve: Insights from Comparative Historical Analysis," in *Comparative Historical Analysis in the Social Sciences*, edited by J. Mahoney and D. Rueschemeyer, 208–240. Cambridge: Cambridge University Press.

——. 2004. *How Institutions Evolve: The Economy of Skills in Germany, Britain, the United States and Japan*. Cambridge: Cambridge University Press.

Tiernan, A., and Wanna, J. 2006. "Competence, Capacity, Capability: Towards Conceptual Clarity in the Discourse of Declining Policy Skills," presented at the Govnet International Conference, Australian National University. Canberra: ANU.

Tinbergen, Jan. 1952. *On the Theory of Economic Policy*. North-Holland Pub. Co.

Treib, O., Bahr, H. and Falkner, G. 2007. "Modes of governance: Towards a Conceptual Clarification," *Journal of European Public Policy* 14: 1–20.

Trebilcock, Michael J., and Douglas G. Hartle. 1982. "The Choice of Governing Instrument," *International Review of Law and Economics* 2: 29–46.

Tribe, Laurence H. 1972. "Policy Science: Analysis or Ideology?" *Philosophy and Public Affairs* 2, no. 1: 66–110.

Tupper, Allan and G.B. Doern. 1981. "Public Corporations and Public Policy in Canada," in Tupper and Doern, eds, *Public Corporations and Public Policy in Canada*. Montreal: Institute for Research on Public Policy, 1–50.

Utton, M.A. 1986. *The Economics of Regulating Industry*. Oxford: Blackwell.

Van der Heijden, J. 2010. "A Short History of Studying Incremental Change. Does Explaining Institutional Change Provide Any New Explanations?" *Regulation and Governance* 4: 230–243.

——. 2013. "Different but Equally Plausible Narratives of Policy Transformation: A Plea for Theoretical Pluralism," *International Political Science Review* 34, no. 1: 57–73.

van Meter, D., and C. van Horn. 1975. "The Policy Implementation Process: A Conceptual Framework," *Administration and Society* 6, no. 4: 445–88.

van Tatenhove, Jan, Bas Arts, and Pieter Leroy. 2000. *Political Modernisation and the Environment*. Springer, Dordrecht. 35–51.

Varone, Frederic and Rejean Landry. 1997. "The Choice of Policy Tools: In Search of Deductive Theory," paper presented at the European Consortium for Political Research Joint Sessions, Bern, Switzerland, 27 Feb.–4 Mar.

Voss, Jan-Peter, and Arno Simons. 2014. "Instrument Constituencies and the Supply Side of Policy Innovation: The Social Life of Emissions Trading," *Environmental Politics* 23, no. 5: 735–54.

——, Dierk Bauknecht, and Rene Kemp, eds. 2006. *Reflexive Governance for Sustainable Development*. Cheltenham: Edward Elgar.

Walker W., Marchau V. and Swanson D. 2010. "Addressing deep uncertainties using adaptive policies," *Technological Forecasting & Social Change* 77, no. 6, Special Section 2.

Wardekker, J. Arjan, Arie de Jong, Joost M. Knoop, and Jeroen P. van der Sluijs. 2010. "Operationalising a Resilience Approach to Adapting an Urban Delta to Uncertain Climate Changes," *Technological Forecasting and Social Change* 77, no. 6 (July): 987–98. doi:10.1016/j.techfore.2009.11.005.

Weaver, R. Kent. 1986. "The Politics of Blame Avoidance," *Journal of Public Policy* 6, no. 4: 371–98.

——. 2009a. "If You Build It, Will They Come? Overcoming Unforeseen Obstacles to Program Effectiveness," The Tansley Lecture—University of Saskatchewan, 2009a.

——. 2009b. *Target Compliance: The Final Frontier of Policy Implementation*. Washington DC: Brookings Institution.

——. 2010. *But Will It Work?: Implementation Analysis to Improve Government Performance*. Washington DC: Brookings Institution. http://www.brookings.edu/research/papers/2010/02/implementation-analysis-weaver.

——. 2013. "Compliance Regimes and Barriers to Behavioral Change," *Governance*. doi:10.1111/gove.12032.

———. 2015. "Getting People to Behave: Research Lessons for Policy Makers," *Public Administration Review*, July 1. doi:10.1111/puar.12412.

Weber, M., Driessen, P.P., and Runhaar, H.A.C. 2011. "Environmental Noise Policy in the Netherlands: Drivers of and Barriers to Shifts from Government to Governance," *Journal of Environmental Policy and Planning* 13: 119–137.

Weimer, David L., and Aidan R. Vining. 1992. *Policy Analysis: Concepts and Practice*, 2nd edn. Englewood Cliffs, NJ: Prentice-Hall.

Weishaar, Heide, Amanda Amos, and Jeff Collin. 2015. "Best of Enemies: Using Social Network Analysis to Explore a Policy Network in European Smoke-Free Policy," *Social Science & Medicine* 133: 85–92.

Wilson, James Q. 1974. "The Politics of Regulation," in J.W. McKie, ed., *Social Responsibility and the Business Predicament*. Washington: Brookings Institution, 135–68.

Wilson, Woodrow. 1887. "The Study of Administration," *Political Science Quarterly* 2, no. 2: 197–222.

Winter, Søren C., and Peter J. May. 2001. "Motivation for Compliance with Environmental Regulations," *Journal of Policy Analysis and Management* 20, no. 4: 675–98.

Wolf, Charles, Jr. 1987. "Markets and Non-Market Failures: Comparison and Assessment," *Journal of Public Policy* 7, no. 1: 43–70.

Woodside, K. 1979. "Tax Incentives vs. Subsidies: Political Considerations in Governmental Choice," *Canadian Public Policy* 5, no. 2: 248–56.

Wu, Xun, M. Ramesh, Michael Howlett, and Scott Fritzen. 2010. *The Public Policy Primer: Managing Public Policy*. London: Routledge.

Wu, Xun, M. Ramesh, Michael Howlett, and Scott A. Fritzen. *The Public Policy Primer: Managing the Policy Process*. 2nd edn. New York: Routledge, 2017.

Ziller, J. 2005. "Public Law: A Tool for Modern Management, Not an Impediment to Reform," *International Review of Administrative Sciences* 71, no. 2: 267–77.

Zito, Anthony R. 2001. "Epistemic Communities, Collective Entrepreneurship and European Integration," *Journal of European Public Policy* 8:4, 585–603, DOI: 10.1080/13501760110064401

Chapter 8 Sources

Abelson, Donald E. 1996. *American Think Tanks and Their Role in U.S. Foreign Policy*. London: Macmillan.

———. 2002. *Do Think Tanks Matter? Assessing the Impact of Public Policy Institutes*. Montreal and Kingston: McGill-Queen's University Press.

———. 2007. "Any Ideas? Think Tanks and Policy Analysis in Canada," in Dobuzinskis et al. *Policy Analysis in Canada: The State of the Art* (298–310). Toronto: University of Toronto Press.

Abma, Tineke A, and Mirko Noordegraaf. 2003. "Public Managers amidst Ambiguity: Towards a Typology of Evaluative Practices in Public Management," *Evaluation* 9, no. 3: 285–306.

Abrahamson, Eric, and Gregory Fairchild. 1999. "Management Fashion, Lifecycles, Triggers, and Collective Learning Processes," *Administrative Science Quarterly* 44: 708–40.

Adair, John J., and Rex Simmons. 1988. "From Voucher Auditing to Junkyard Dogs: The Evolution of Federal Inspectors General," *Public Budgeting and Finance* 8, 2: 91–100.

Aldrich, Howard, and Diane Herker. 1977. "Boundary Spanning Roles and Organizational Structure," *Academy of Management Review* 2 (Apr.): 217–30.

Anderson, Charles W. 1979a. "The Place of Principles in Policy Analysis," *American Political Science Review* 73, no. 3: 711–23.

Anglund, Sandra M. 1999. "Policy Feedback: The Comparison Effect and Small Business Procurement Policy," *Policy Studies Journal* 27, no. 1: 11–27.

Ardila, Arturo and Gerhard Menckoff. 2002. "Transportation Policies in Bogota Columbia: Building a Transportation System for the People," in *Transportation Research Record* 1817: 130–36.

Argyris, Chris. 1992. *On Organizational Learning*. London: Blackwell.

————, and Donald A. Schon. 1978. *Organizational Learning: A Theory of Action Perspective*. Reading, MA: Addison-Wesley.

Aucoin, Peter. 1990. "Administrative Reform in Public Management: Paradigms, Principles, Paradoxes and Pendulums," *Governance* 3, no. 2: 115–37.

Bakvis, Herman. 1997. "Advising the Executive: Think Tanks, Consultants, Political Staff and Kitchen Cabinets," in P. Weller, H. Bakvis, and R.A.W. Rhodes, eds, *The Hollow Crown: Countervailing Trends in Core Executives*. New York: St Martin's Press, 84–125.

Banting, Keith G. 1995. "The Social Policy Review: Policy-Making in a Semi-Sovereign Society," *Canadian Public Administration* 38, no. 2: 283–90.

Bardach, Eugene. 1976. "Policy Termination as a Political Process," *Policy Sciences* 7, no. 2: 123–31.

Behn, Robert D. 1977. "How to Terminate a Public Policy: A Dozen Hints for the Wouldbe Terminator," *Policy Analysis* 4, no. 3: 393–414.

Bennett, Colin J. and Michael Howlett. 1991. "The Lessons of Learning: Reconciling Theories of Policy Learning and Policy Change," *Policy Sciences* 25, no. 3: 275–94.

Billings, Robert S., and Charles F. Hermann. 1998. "Problem Identification in Sequential Policy Decision-Making: The Re-representation of Problems," in D.A. Sylvan and J.F. Voss, eds, *Problem Representation in Foreign Policy Decision-Making*. Cambridge: Cambridge University Press, 53–79.

Boardman, A.E., D.H. Greenberg, A.R. Vining, and D.L. Weimer. 2001. *Cost-Benefit Analysis: Concepts and Practice*. Upper Saddle River, NJ: Prentice-Hall.

Bovens, Mark, and Paul t'Hart. 1995. "Frame Multiplicity and Policy Fiascoes: Limits to Explanation," *Knowledge and Policy* 8, 4: 61–83.

————, and ————. 1996. *Understanding Policy Fiascoes*. New Brunswick, NJ: Transaction.

————, ————, and B. Guy Peters. 2001. "Analysing Governance Success and Failure in Six European States," in Bovens, t'Hart, and Peters, eds, *Success and Failure in Public Governance: A Comparative Analysis*. Cheltenham: Edward Elgar, 12–32.

Brandstrom, A., and S. Kuipers. 2003. "From "Normal Incidents" to Political Crises: Understanding the Selective Politicization of Policy Failures," *Government and Opposition* 38, no. 3: 279–305.

Brewer, Garry D. and Peter deLeon. 1983. *The Foundations of Policy Analysis*. Homewood, NJ: Dorsey.

Busenberg, George J. 2000. "Innovation, Learning and Policy Evolution in Hazardous Systems," *American Behavioral Scientist* 44, no. 4: 679–91.

————. 2001. "Learning in Organizations and Public Policy," *Journal of Public Policy* 21, no. 2: 173–89.

————. 2004a. "Wildfire Management in the United States: The Evolution of a Policy Failure," *Review of Policy Research* 21, no. 2: 145–56.

————. 2004b. "Adaptive Policy Design for the Management of Wildfire Hazards," *American Behavioral Scientist* 48, no. 3: 314–26.

Cahill, Anthony G., and E. Sam Overman. 1990. "The Evolution of Rationality in Policy Analysis," in S.S. Nagel, ed., *Policy Theory and Policy Evaluation: Concepts, Knowledge, Causes, and Norms*. New York: Greenwood Press.

Cairney, Paul. 2016. *The Politics of Evidence-Based Policy Making*. Springer.

Cairns, Alan C. 1990a. "Reflections on Commission Research," in A.P. Pross, I. Christie, and J.A. Yogis, eds, *Commissions of Inquiry*. Toronto: Carswell, 87–110.

Canada, Auditor General. 1993. *Report of the Auditor General to the House of Commons*. Ottawa: Supply and Services Canada.

Canada, Treasury Board. 2012. *Theory-Based Approaches to Evaluation: Concepts and Practices*. Ottawa, Ontario: Treasury Board of Canada Secretariat. http://publications.gc.ca/pub?id=9.696088&sl=0.

Cardwell, Diane. 2008. "City Council Approves Fee to Drive Below 60th." *The New York Times*, April 1, sec. New York Region

Chelimsky, Eleanor. 1995. "Where We Stand Today in the Practice of Evaluation: Some Reflections," *Knowledge and Policy* 8, 3: 8–20.

Churchman, C. West. 1967. "Wicked Problems," *Management Science* 14, no. 4: B141–2.

Clokie, Hugh McDowall, and J. William Robinson. 1969. *Royal Commissions of Inquiry: The Significance of Investigations in British Politics*. New York: Octagon Books.

Cohen, G.A. 1978. *Karl Marx's Theory of History: A Defense*. Oxford: Clarendon Press

Cohen, Wesley M., and Daniel A. Levinthal. 1990. "Absorptive Capacity: A New Perspective on Learning and Innovation," *Administrative Science Quarterly* 35: 128–52.

Coleman, William D, Grace Skogstad, and Michael Atkinson. 1996. "Paradigm Shifts and Policy Networks: Cumulative Change in Agriculture," *Journal of Public Policy* 16, no. 3: 273–302

Craig, Peter. 2017. "Natural Experiments: An Overview of Methods, Approaches, and Contributions to Public Health Intervention Research," *Annual Review of Public Health* 38: 39–56. doi:10.1146/annurev-publhealth–031816–044327

Daniels, Mark R. 1997. *Terminating Public Programs: An American Political Paradox*. Armonk, NJ: M.E. Sharpe.

Davies, I. 1999. "Evaluation and Performance Management in Government," *Evaluation* 8, no. 2: 150–9.

Dean, Benjamin. 2017. "Natural and Quasi-Natural Experiments to Evaluate Cybersecurity Policies," *Columbia SIPA Journal of International Affairs*. https://jia.sipa.columbia.edu/natural-and-quasi-natural-experiments-evaluate-cybersecurity-policies

de la Mothe, John. 1996. "One Small Step in an Uncertain Direction: The Science and Technology Review and Public Administration in Canada," *Canadian Public Administration* 39, no. 3: 403–17.

de la Porte, Caroline, Phillipe Pochet, and Graham Room. 2001. "Social Benchmarking, Policy Making and New Governance in the EU," *Journal of European Social Policy* 11, no. 1: 291–307.

deLeon, Peter. 1978. "A Theory of Policy Termination," in J.V. May and A.B. Wildavsky, eds, *The Policy Cycle*. Beverly Hills, CA: Sage, 279–300.

———. 1983. "Policy Evaluation and Program Termination," *Policy Studies Review* 2, no. 4: 631–47.

———. 1997. *Democracy and the Policy Sciences*. Albany: State University of New York Press.

Dell, Gillian and Andrew McDevitt. 2018. *Exporting Corruption–Progress Report 2018: Assessing Enforcement of the OECD Anti-Bribery Convention*. Berlin: Transparency International.

Dent, Helen. 2002. "Consultants and the Public Service," *Australian Journal of Public Administration* 61, no. 1: 108–13

de Smith, S.A. 1973. *Judicial Review of Administrative Action*. London: Stevens and Son.

Dobell, Rodney, and David Zussman. 1981. "An Evaluation System for Government: If Politics Is Theatre, Then Evaluation Is (Mostly) Art," *Canadian Public Administration* 24, no. 3: 404–27.

Doern, G. Bruce. 1967. "The Role of Royal Commissions in the General Policy Process and in Federal–Provincial Relations," *Canadian Public Administration* 10, no. 4: 417–33.

Dye, Thomas R. 1972. *Understanding Public Policy*. Englewood Cliffs, NJ: Prentice-Hall.

Edley, Christopher F., Jr. 1990. *Administrative Law: Rethinking Judicial Control of Bureaucracy*. New Haven: Yale University Press.

Ellig, Jerry, and Don Lavoie. 1995. "The Principal–Agent Relationship in Organizations," in P. Foss, ed., *Economic Approaches to Organizations and Institutions: An Introduction*. Aldershot: Dartmouth.

Englehart, Kenneth G., and Michael J. Trebilcock. 1981. *Public Participation in the Regulatory Process: The Issue of Funding*. Ottawa: Economic Council of Canada.

Etheredge, Lloyd S. 1981. "Government Learning: An Overview," in S.L. Long, ed., *The Handbook of Political Behavior*. New York: Plenum.

———, and James Short. 1983. "Thinking about Government Learning," *Journal of Management Studies* 20, no. 1: 41–58.

Evaluation Cooperation Group. 2012. Good Practice Standards (GPS). Online at https://wpqr4.adb.org/LotusQuickr/ecg/PageLibrary48257B910010370B.nsf/h_9DF-721C00F70E93948257B9500303684/DFC7E13EBD11975B48257B-950034FE96/?OpenDocument

Fischer, F., and J. Forester. 1987. *Confronting Values in Policy Analysis: The Politics of Criteria*. Beverly Hills, CA: Sage.

Formaini, Robert. 1990. *The Myth of Scientific Public Policy*. New Brunswick, NJ: Transaction.

Franz, Marion J., John P. Bantle, Christine A. Beebe, John D. Brunzell, Jean-Louis Chiasson, Abhimanyu Garg, Lea Ann

Holzmeister, et al. 2002. "Evidence-Based Nutrition Principles and recommendations for the Treatment and Prevention of Diabetes and Related Complications," *Diabetes Care* 25, no. 1: 148-198.

Friedman, Lee S. 2002. *The Microeconomics of Public Policy Analysis*. Princeton, NJ: Princeton University Press.

Funnell, S.C. and Rogers, P. J. 2011. *Purposeful Program Theory: Effective Use of Theories of Change and Logic Models*. San Francisco: Jossey-Bass/Wiley.

Gerston, Larry N. 1997. *Public Policy Making: Process and Principles*. Armonk, NY: M.E. Sharpe.

Geva-May, Iris. 2001. "When the Motto is 'Till Death Do Us Part': The Conceptualization and the Craft of Termination in the Public Policy Cycle," *International Journal of Public Administration* 24, no. 3: 263–88.

———, and Aaron Wildavsky. 1997. *An Operational Approach to Policy Analysis: The Craft Prescriptions for Better Analysis*. Boston: Kluwer.

Good, D. 2003. *The Politics of Public Management: The HRDC Audit of Grants and Contributions*. Toronto: University of Toronto Press.

Gray, Pat, and Paul t'Hart. 1998. *Public Policy Disasters in Western Europe*. London: Routledge.

Greener, I. 2005. "The Potential of Path Dependence in Political Studies," *Politics* 25, no. 1: 62–72.

Grin, John, and Anne Loeber. 2007. "Theories of Policy Learning: Agency, Structure and Change," in Frank Fischer, Gerald D. Miller, and Mara S. Sidney, eds, *Handbook of Public Policy Analysis*. London: Taylor and Francis, 201–19.

Guay, Jennifer. 2018. "Evidence-Based Policymaking: Is There Room for Science in Politics?" *Apolitical*, March 7. https://apolitical.co/solution_article/evidence-based-policymaking-is-there-room-for-science-in-politics/

Guess, George M., and Paul G. Farnham. 2000. *Cases in Public Policy Analysis*. Washington: Georgetown University Press.

Gundel, S. 2005. "Towards a New Typology of Crises," *Journal of Contingencies and Crisis Management* 13, no. 3: 106–15.

Hall, Peter A. 1993. "Policy Paradigms, Social Learning and the State: The Case of Economic Policy Making in Britain," *Comparative Politics* 25, no. 3: 275–96.

Hammersley, M. 2005. "Is the Evidence-Based Practice Movement Doing More Good Than Harm? Reflections on Iain Chalmers' Case for Research-Based Policy Making and Practice," *Evidence and Policy* 1, no. 1: 85–100.

Hastak, Manoj, Michael B. Mazis, and Louis A. Morris. 2001. "The Role of Consumer Surveys in Public Policy Decision Making," *Journal of Public Policy and Marketing* 20, no. 2: 170–85.

Head, Brian W. 2008. "Three Lenses of Evidence-Based Policy," *Australian Journal of Public Administration* 67, no. 1: 1–11.

Hearn, S. and Buffardi, A.L. 2016. *What Is Impact?* A Methods Lab publication. London: Overseas Development Institute. https://www.odi.org/sites/odi.org.uk/files/resource-documents/10352.pdf

Heclo, Hugh. 1974. *Modern Social Politics in Britain and Sweden: From Relief to Income Maintenance*. New Haven: Yale University Press.

Hellstern, Gerd-Michael. 1986. "Assessing Evaluation Research," in Kaufman et al. (1986: 279–312).

Hirshleifer, J., Glazer, A., and Hirshleifer, D. 2005. *Price Theory and Applications: Decisions, Markets, and Information*. Cambridge University Press.

HM Treasury. 2003. The HM Treasury: Guidance Notes for Policy Evaluation and Analysis. Great Britain. Treasury. Government Social Research Unit. http://dera.ioe.ac.uk/10521/1/complete_Magenta_tcm6–8611.pdf

Hood, Christopher. 2002. "The Risk Game and the Blame Game," *Government and Opposition* 37, 1: 15–54.

———, and H. Rothstein. 2001. "Risk Regulation under Pressure: Problem Solving or Blame Shifting?" *Administration and Society* 33, 1: 21–53.

Howlett, Michael. 2007. "Analyzing Multi-Actor, Multi-Round Public Policy Decision-Making Processes in Government: Findings from Five Canadian Cases," *Canadian Journal of Political Science* 40, no. 3: 659–84.

Huber, George P. 1991. "Organization Learning: The Contributing Processes and the Literatures," *Organization Science* 2, no. 1: 88–115.

Humphries, Martha Anne, and Donald R. Songer. 1999. "Law and Politics in Judicial

Oversight of Federal Administrative Agencies," *Journal of Politics* 61, no. 1: 207–20.

Imas, Linda G. Morra and Ray Rist. 2009. *The Road to Results, Designing and Conducting Effective Development Evaluations.* Washington, DC: World Bank.

Independent Evaluation Group. 2013. *World Bank Group Impact Evaluations: Relevance and Effectiveness.* Washington, DC: World Bank.

Ingram, Helen M., and Dean E. Mann, eds. 1980a. *Why Policies Succeed or Fail.* Beverly Hills, CA: Sage.

——, and ——. 1980b. "Policy Failure: An Issue Deserving Analysis," in Ingram and Mann (1980a).

IOB. 2009. "Evaluation policy and guidelines for evaluations." Policy and Operations Evaluation Department, the Dutch Ministry of Foreign Affairs. https://www.oecd.org/dac/evaluation/iob-evaluation-policy-and-guidelines-for-evaluations.pdf

Jackson, Peter M. 2007. "Making Sense of Policy Advice," *Public Money and Management* 27, no. 4: 257–64.

Jacobson, Peter D., Elizabeth Selvin, and Scott D. Pomfret. 2001. "The Role of the Courts in Shaping Health Policy: An Empirical Analysis," *Journal of Law, Medicine and Ethics* 29: 278–89.

Jaffe, Louis L. 1965. *Judicial Control of Administrative Action.* Boston: Little, Brown.

——. 1969. *English and American Judges as Lawmakers.* Oxford: Clarendon.

Jordan, J.M., and S.L. Sutherland. 1979. "Assessing the Results of Public Expenditure: Program Evaluation in the Federal Government," *Canadian Public Administration* 22, no. 4: 581–609.

Judge, K. and Bauld, L. 2001. Strong theory, flexible methods: evaluating complex community-based initiatives. *Critical Public Health* 11, no. 1: 19–38.

Kaufman, Herbert. 1976. *Are Government Organizations Immortal?* Washington: Brookings Institution

Kay, Adrian. 2005. "A Critique of the Use of Path Dependency in Policy Studies," *Public Administration* 83, no. 3: 553–71.

Kernaghan, Kenneth, Brian Marson, and Sandford Borins. 2000. *The New Public Organization.* Toronto: Institute of Public Administration of Canada.

Kerr, Donna H. 1976. "The Logic of "Policy" and Successful Policies," *Policy Sciences* 7, no. 3: 351–63.

King, Anthony. 1981. "What Do Elections Decide?" in Butler et al. (1981).

Kirkpatrick, Susan E., James P. Lester, and Mark R. Peterson. 1999. "The Policy Termination Process: A Conceptual Framework and Application to Revenue Sharing," *Policy Studies Review* 16, no. 1: 209–36.

Ladi, Stella. 2005. *Globalisation, Policy Transfer and Policy Research Institutes.* Cheltenham: Edward Elgar.

Laforest, R., and M. Orsini. 2005. "Evidence-Based Engagement in the Voluntary Sector: Lessons from Canada," *Social Policy and Administration* 39, no. 5: 481–97.

Lane, Peter J., and Michael Lubatkin. 1998. "Relative Absorptive Capacity and Interorganizational Learning," *Strategic Management Journal* 19: 461–77.

Lapsley, Irvine, and Rosie Oldfield. 2001. "Transforming the Public Sector: Management Consultants as Agents of Change," *European Accounting Review* 10, no. 3: 523–43.

Leatherdale, Scott T. 2018. "Natural Experiment Methodology For Research: A Review of How Different Methods can Support Real-World Research," *International Journal of Social Research Methodology,* doi: 10.1080/13645579.2018.1488449.

Lehtonen, Markku. 2005. "OECD Environmental Performance Review Programme: Accountability (F)or Learning?" *Evaluation* 11, no. 2: 169–88.

——. 2006. "Deliberative Democracy, Participation, and OECD Peer Reviews of Environmental Policies," *American Journal of Evaluation* 27, no. 2: 185–200.

Levitt, Barbara, and James G. March. 1988. "Organizational Learning," *Annual Review of Sociology* 14: 319–40.

Levy, Roger. 2001. "EU Performance Management 1977–96: A Performance Indicators Analysis," *Public Administration* 79, no. 2: 423–44.

Lewis, David E. 2002. "The Politics of Agency Termination: Confronting the Myth of Agency Immortality," *Journal of Politics* 64, no. 1: 89–107.

Lewis J.M. 2003. "Evidence-Based Policy: A Technocratic Wish in a Political World," in V. Lin and B. Gibson, eds, *Evidence-Based Health Policy: Problems And Possibilities.* Melbourne: Oxford University Press, 250–259.

Lindquist, E. 1998. "A Quarter Century of Canadian Think Tanks: Evolving

Institutions, Conditions and Strategies," in *Think Tanks Across Nations: A Comparative Approach*, edited by D. Stone, A. Denham, and M. Garnett, 127–144. Manchester: Manchester University Press.

———. 2004. "Three Decades of Canadian Think Tanks: Evolving Institutions, Conditions and Strategies," in D. Stone and A. Denham, eds, *Think Tank Traditions: Policy Research and the Politics of Ideas*. Manchester: Manchester University Press, 264–80.

McCubbins, Arthur Lupia and Mathew D. 1994. "Learning from Oversight: Fire Alarms and Policy Patrols Reconstructed," *Journal of Law, Economics and Organization* 10, no. 1: 96–125.

———, and Thomas Schwartz. 1984. "Congressional Oversight Overlooked: Policy Patrols versus Fire Alarms," *American Journal of Political Science* 28, no. 1: 165–79.

McGann, James G. and E.C. Johnson. 2005. *Comparative Think Tanks, Politics and Public Policy*. Cheltenham: Edward Elgar.

McGraw, Kathleen M. 1990. "Avoiding Blame: An Experimental Investigation of Political Excuses and Justifications," *British Journal of Political Science* 20: 199–242

McLaughlin, Milbrey W. 1985. "Implementation Realities and Evaluation Design," in Shotland and Mark (1985).

Manzer, Ronald. 1984. "Policy Rationality and Policy Analysis: The Problem of the Choice of Criteria for Decision-making," in O.P. Dwivedi, ed., *Public Policy and Administrative Studies*. Guelph, ON: University of Guelph.

March, James G. and Johan P. Olsen. 1975. "The Uncertainty of the Past: Organizational Learning under Ambiguity," *European Journal of Political Research* 3: 147–71.

Martin, John F. 1998. *Reorienting a Nation: Consultants and Australian Public Policy*. Aldershot: Ashgate.

May, Peter J. 1992. "Policy Learning and Failure," *Journal of Public Policy* 12, no. 4: 331–54.

———. 1999. "Fostering Policy Learning: A Challenge for Public Administration," *International Review of Public Administration* 4, no. 1: 21–31.

Meltsner, Arnold J. 1976. *Policy Analysts in the Bureaucracy*. Berkeley: University of California Press.

Merton, Robert K. 1936. "The Unanticipated Consequences of Purposive Social Action," *American Sociological Review* 6, no. 1: 894–904.

Michael, E.J. 2006. *Public Policy: The Competitive Framework*. Melbourne: Oxford University Press.

Mintrom, Michael. 2007. "The Policy Analysis Movement," in Dobuzinskis et al. (2007: 71–84).

Mitchell, Ronald K., Bradley R. Age, and Donna J. Wood. 1997. "Toward a Theory of Stakeholder Identification and Salience: Defining the Principle of Who and What Really Counts," *Academy of Management Review* 22, no. 4: 853–86.

Molund, Stefan, and Göran Schill. 2004. *Looking Back, Moving Forward: SIDA Evaluation Manual*. SIDA.

Moran, M. 2001. "Not Steering but Drowning: Policy Catastrophes and the Regulatory State," *Political Quarterly* 72: 414–27.

Moseley, A., and S. Tierney. 2004. "Evidence-Based Practice in the Real World," *Evidence and Policy* 1, no. 1: 113–19.

Mucciaroni, Gary. 1990. *The Political Failure of Employment Policy, 1945–1982*. Pittsburgh: University of Pittsburgh Press.

Mulvale, Gillian, Julia Abelson, and Paula Goering. 2007. "Mental Health Service Delivery in Ontario, Canada: How Do Policy Legacies Shape Prospects for Reform?" *Health Economics, Policy and Law* 2: 363–89.

Nachmias, David. 1979. *Public Policy Evaluation: Approaches and Methods*. New York: St Martin's Press.

Neves, Claudia. 2008. "International Organisations and the Evaluation of Education Systems: A Critical Comparative Analysis," *European Journal of Vocational Training* 45, no. 3: 72–89.

OECD, 2002. OECD *Glossary of Key Terms in Evaluation and Results Based Management*. Development Assistance Committee. Paris.

Osborne, D., and E. Gaebler. 1992. Reinventing Government. Reading, MA: Addison Wesley.

Packwood, A. 2002. "Evidence-Based Policy: Rhetoric and Reality," *Social Policy and Society* 1, no. 3: 267–72.

Palumbo, Dennis J. 1987. *The Politics of Program Evaluation*. Beverly Hills, CA: Sage.

Pateman, Carole. 1970. *Participation and Democratic Theory*. Cambridge: Cambridge University Press.

Patton, Carl V., and David S. Sawicki. 1993. *Basic Methods of Policy Analysis and Planning*. Englewood Cliffs, NJ: Prentice-Hall.

Patton, M. Q. 1990. *Qualitative Evaluation and Research Methods*, 2nd ed. Thousand Oaks: Sage Publications.

Pawson, Ray. 2002. "Evidence-Based Policy: In Search of a Method?" *Evaluation* 8, no. 2: 157–81.

———. 2006. *Evidence-Based Policy: A Realist Perspective*. London: Sage.

Perl, Anthony and Donald J. White. 2002. "The Changing Role of Consultants in Canadian Policy Analysis," *Policy and Society* 21, no. 1: 49–73.

Perrow, Charles. 1984. *Normal Accidents: Living with High-Risk Technologies*. New York: Basic Books.

Peters, B. Guy. 1998. "The Experimenting Society and Policy Design," in William N. Dunn, ed., *The Experimenting Society: Essays in Honour of Donald T. Campbell*. New Brunswick, NJ: Transaction, 125–39.

———, and Anthony Barker, eds. 1993. *Advising West European Governments: Inquiries, Expertise and Public Policy*. Edinburgh: Edinburgh University Press.

Pierson, Paul. 1993. "When Effect Becomes Cause: Policy Feedback and Political Change," *World Politics* 45: 595–628.

———. 2000a. "Increasing Returns, Path Dependence, and the Study of Politics," *American Political Science Review* 94, no. 2: 251–67.

Pindyck, R. and D. Rubinfeld. 2018. *Microeconomics*. Toronto: Pearson.

Pollitt, C. 2001. "Clarifying Convergence: Striking Similarities and Durable Differences in Public Management Reform," *Public Management Review* 4, no. 1: 471–92.

Pressman, J.L., and A.B. Wildavsky. 1973. *Implementation: How Great Expectations in Washington are Dashed in Oakland*. Berkeley: University of California Press

Pressman, Jeffrey L., and Aaron B. Wildavsky. 1984. *Implementation: How Great Expectations in Washington Are Dashed in Oakland*, 3rd edn. Berkeley: University of California Press.

Reid, Timothy E. 1979. "The Failure of PPBS: Real Incentives for the 1980s," *Optimum* 10, no. 4: 23–37.

Ricci, David. 1993. *The Transformation of American Politics: The New Washington and the Rise of Think Tanks*. New Haven: Yale University Press.

Rich, A. 2004. *Think Tanks, Public Policy, and the Politics of Expertise*. New York: Cambridge University Press.

Rist, Ray C. 1994. "The Preconditions for Learning: Lessons from the Public Sector," in F.L. Leeuw, R.C. Rist, and R.C. Sonnischen, eds, *Can Governments Learn: Comparative Perspectives on Evaluation and Organizational Learning*. New Brunswick, NJ: Transaction.

Rogers, Harry. 1978. "Management Control in the Public Service," *Optimum* 9, no. 3: 14–28.

Rogers, Patricia J. and Carol H. Weiss. 2007. "Theory-Based Evaluation: Reflections Ten Years On: Theory-Based Evaluation: Past, Present, and Future," *New Directions for Evaluation* 114: 63–81.

Roots, R.I. 2004. "When Laws Backfire: Unintended Consequences of Public Policy," *American Behavioural Scientist* 47, no. 11: 1376–94.

Rose, Richard. 1988. "Comparative Policy Analysis: The Program Approach," in M. Dogan, ed., *Comparing Pluralist Democracies: Strains on Legitimacy*. Boulder, CO: Westview Press, 219–41.

———. 1991. "What Is Lesson-Drawing?" *Journal of Public Policy* 11, no. 1: 3–30.

Sabatier, Paul A. 1987. "Knowledge, Policy-Oriented Learning, and Policy Change," *Knowledge: Creation, Diffusion, Utilization* 8, no. 4: 649–92.

———. 1988. "An Advocacy Coalition Framework of Policy Change and the Role of Policy-Oriented Learning Therein," *Policy Sciences* 21, nos. 2 and 3: 129–68.

Saint-Martin, Denis. 1998. "The New Managerialism and the Policy Influence of Consultants in Government: An Historical-Institutionalist Analysis of Britain, Canada and France," *Governance* 11, no. 3: 319–56.

Salter, Liora. 1981. *Public Inquiries in Canada*. Ottawa: Science Council of Canada.

Sanderson, Ian. 2002a. "Evaluation, Policy Learning and Evidence-Based Policy-Making," *Public Administration* 80, no. 1: 1–22.

———. 2002b. "Making Sense of What Works: Evidence Based Policymaking as Instrumental Rationality?" *Public Policy and Administration* 17, no. 3: 61–75.

———. 2006. "Complexity, "Practical Rationality" and Evidence-Based Policy Making," *Policy and Politics* 34, no. 1: 115–32.

Scharpf, F.W. 1986. "Policy Failure and Institutional Reform: Why Should Form Follow Function?" *International Social Science Journal* 108: 179–190.

Schwab, Klaus. 2018. *The Global Competitiveness Report 2018*. Geneva: World Economic Forum. http://www3.weforum.org/docs/GCR2018/05FullReport/TheGlobalCompetitivenessReport2018.pdf

Schwartz, Bryan. 1997. "Public Inquiries," *Canadian Public Administration* 40, 1: 72–85.

Sieber, Sam D. 1981. *Fatal Remedies: The Ironies of Social Intervention*. New York: Plenum.

Simon, Herbert A. 1991. "Bounded Rationality and Organizational Learning," *Organization Science* 2, no. 1: 125–35.

Sinden, J.A., and D.J. Thampapillai. 1995. *Introduction to Benefit Cost Analysis*. Melbourne: Addison-Wesley Longman.

Snow, David A., and Robert D. Benford. 1992. "Master Frames and Cycles of Protest," in A.D. Morris and C.M. Mueller, eds, *Frontiers in Social Movement Theory*. New Haven: Yale University Press, 133–55.

Speers, Kimberly. 2007. "The Invisible Public Service: Consultants and Public Policy in Canada," in Dobuzinskis et al. (2007: 220–31).

Stone, Diane A. 2007. "Recycling Bins, Garbage Cans, or Think Tanks? Three Myths Regarding Policy Analysis Institutes," *Public Administration* 85, no. 2: 259–78.

Suchman, Edward A. 1967. *Evaluative Research: Principles and Practices in Public Service and Social Action Programs*. New York: Russell Sage Foundation.

———. 1979. *Social Sciences in Policy-Making*. Paris: OECD.

Swiss, James E. 1991. *Public Management Systems: Monitoring and Managing Government Performance*. Upper Saddle River, NJ: Prentice-Hall.

Tamuz, Michael. 2001. "Learning Disabilities for Regulators: The Perils of Organizational Learning in the Air Transportation Industry," *Administration and Society* 33, 3: 276–302.

Tenbensel, T. 2004. "Does More Evidence Lead to Better Policy? The Implications of Explicit Priority-Setting in New Zealand's Health Policy for Evidence-Based Policy," *Policy Studies* 25, no. 3: 190–207.

Triantafillou, Peter. 2007. "Benchmarking in the Public Sector: A Critical Conceptual Framework," *Public Administration* 85, no. 3: 829–46.

Twight, C. 1991. "From Claiming Credit to Avoiding Blame: The Evolution of Congressional Strategy for Asbestos Management," *Journal of Public Policy* 11, no. 2: 153–86.

UNCTAD. 2001. *World Investment Report 2001*. New York: United Nations.

U.S. Agency for International Development. 2016. *Strengthening Evidence-Based Development: Five Years of Better Practice at USAID 2011–2016*. Washington: USAID. https://www.usaid.gov/sites/default/files/documents/1870/Strengthening%20Evidence-Based%20Development%20-%20Five%20Years%20of%20Better%20Evaluation%20Practice%20at%20USAID.pdf

Vaughan, Diane. 1996. *The Challenger Launch Decision: Risky Technology, Culture and Deviance at NASA*. Chicago: University of Chicago Press.

Vedung, Evert. 2010. "Four Waves of Evaluation," *Evaluation* 16, no. 3: 263–277. DOI: 10.1177/1356389010372452

Wade, H.W.R. 1965. "Anglo-American Administrative Law: Some Reflections," *Law Quarterly Review* 81: 357–79.

———. 1966. "Anglo-American Administrative Law: More Reflections," *Law Quarterly Review* 82: 226–52.

Wagle, Udaya. 2000. "The Policy Science of Democracy: The Issues of Methodology and Citizen Participation," *Policy Sciences* 33: 207–23.

Weaver, R. Kent. 1986. "The Politics of Blame Avoidance," *Journal of Public Policy* 6, no. 4: 371–98.

———. 1988. *Automatic Government: The Politics of Indexation*. Washington: Brookings Institution.

———. 1989. "The Changing World of Think Tanks," *PS: Political Science and Politics* 22: 563–78.

Weiss, Carol H. 1977a. *Using Social Research in Public Policy Making*. Lexington, MA: Lexington Books.

Weiss, C. H. 1997. "Theory-Based Evaluation: Past, Present, and Future," *New Directions for Evaluation* 76: 41–55.

Weiss, Carol H. 1997. *Evaluation: Methods for Studying Programs and Policies*, 2nd edn. Upper Saddle River, NJ: Prentice Hall.

White, H., and S. Sabarwal. 2014. Quasi-experimental Design and Methods, Methodological Briefs: Impact Evaluation 8. UNICEF Office of Research, Florence. https://www.unicef-irc.org/KM/IE/img/downloads/Quasi-Experimental_Design_and_Methods_ENG.pdf

Wildavsky, Aaron. 1969. "Rescuing Policy Analysis from PPBS," *Public Administration Review* (Mar.–Apr.): 189–202.

Wilson, V. Seymour. 1971. "The Role of Royal Commissions and Task Forces," in Doern and Aucoin (1971: 113–29).

Wisler, Carl. 1996. "Evaluation and Auditing: Prospects for Convergence," New Directions for Evaluation 71: 1–71.

World Bank. 2019. *Doing Business 2019: Training for Reform*. Washington, DC: World Bank. http://www.doingbusiness.org/content/dam/doingBusiness/media/Annual-Reports/English/DB2019-report_print-version.pdf

Wraith, R.E., and G.B. Lamb. 1971. *Public Inquiries as an Instrument of Government*. London: George Allen and Unwin.

Zarkin, Michael J. 2008. "Organisational Learning in Novel Policy Situations: Two Cases of United States Communications Regulation," *Policy Studies* 29, no. 1: 87–100.

Chapter 9 Sources

Alink, Fleur, Arjen Boin, and Paul t'Hart. 2001. "Institutional Crises and Reforms in Policy Sectors: The Case of Asylum Policy in Europe," *Journal of European Public Policy* 8, no. 2: 286–306.

Anderson, James E. 1975. *Public Policy-Making*. New York: Praeger.

Arthur, W. Brian. 1989. "Competing Technologies, Increasing Returns, and Lock-In by Historical Events," *Economic Journal* 99: 116–31.

Bannink, Duco, and Marcel Hoogenboom. 2007. "Hidden Change: Disaggregation of Welfare Regimes for Greater Insight into Welfare State Change," *Journal of European Social Policy* 17, no. 1: 19–32.

Baumgartner, Frank R., and Bryan D. Jones. 1991. "Agenda Dynamics and Policy Subsystems," *Journal of Politics* 53, no. 4: 1044–74.

——, and ——. 1993. *Agendas and Instability in American Politics*. Chicago: University of Chicago Press.

Baumgartner, F. R., and B. D. Jones. 2002. *Policy Dynamics*. Chicago: University of Chicago Press.

Behn, Robert D. 1977. "How to Terminate a Public Policy: A Dozen Hints for the Wouldbe Terminator," *Policy Analysis* 4, no. 3: 393–414.

Bennet, Colin J. and Michael Howlett. 1991. "The Lessons of Learning: Reconciling Theories of Policy Learning and Policy Change," *Policy Sciences* 25, no. 3: 275–94.

Benz, A., and D. Furst. 2002. "Policy Learning in Regional Networks," *European Urban and Regional Studies* 9, no. 1: 21–35.

Bernstein, S., R.N. Lebow, J.G. Stein, and S. Weber. 2000. "God Gave Physics the Easy Problems: Adapting Social Science to an Unpredictable World," *European Journal of International Relations* 6, no. 1: 43–76.

Berry, William T. 1990. "The Confusing Case of Budgetary Incrementalism: Too Many Meanings for a Single Concept," *Journal of Politics* 52: 167–96.

Birkland, Thomas A. 2004. "'The World Changed Today': Agenda-Setting and Policy Change in the Wake of the September 11 Terrorist Attacks," *Review of Policy Research* 21, no. 2: 179–200.

Bleich, Erik. 2002. "Integrating Ideas into Policy-Making Analysis: Frames and Race Policies in Britain and France," *Comparative Political Studies* 35, no. 9: 1054–76.

——. 2006. "Institutional Continuity and Change: Norms, Lesson-Drawing, and the Introduction of Race-Conscious Measures in the 1976 British Race Relations Act," *Policy Studies* 27, no. 3: 219–34.

Brandstrom, A., and S. Kuipers. 2003. "From "Normal Incidents" to Political Crises: Understanding the Selective Politicization of Policy Failures," *Government and Opposition* 38, no. 3: 279–305.

Braun, Dietmar. 1999. "Interests or Ideas? An Overview of Ideational Concepts in Public Policy Research," in D. Braun and A. Busch, eds, *Public Policy and Political Ideas*. Cheltenham: Edward Elgar, 11–29.

Brewer, Garry D. 1974. "The Policy Sciences Emerge: To Nurture and Structure a Discipline," *Policy Sciences* 5, no. 3: 239–44.

Browne, William P. 1990. "Organized Interests and Their Issue Niches: A Search for Pluralism in a Policy Domain," *Journal of Politics* 52, no. 2: 477–509.

——. 1991. "Issue Niches and the Limits of Interest Group Influence," in Allan J. Cigler and Burdett A. Loomis, eds,

Interest Group Politics. Washington: CQ Press, 345–70.

Bundgaard, Ulrik, and Karsten Vrangbaek. 2007. "Reform by Coincidence? Explaining the Policy Process of Structural Reform in Denmark," *Scandinavian Political Studies* 30, no. 4: 491–520.

Campbell, John L. 1997. "Mechanisms of Evolutionary Change in Economic Governance: Interaction, Interpretation and Bricolage," in Lars Magnusson and Jan Ottosson, eds, *Evolutionary Economics and Path Dependence*. Cheltenham: Edward Elgar.

Capano, Giliberto. 2012. "Policy Dynamics and Change: The Never-Ending Puzzle," in *Routledge Handbook of Public Policy*, edited by Eduardo Araral, Scott Fritzen, Michael Howlett, M. Ramesh, and Xun Wu, 451–72. New York: Routledge.

Carlsson, Lars. 2017. "Policy Science at an Impasse: A Matter of Conceptual Stretching?" *Politics & Policy* 45, no. 2 (April 1): 148–68. doi:10.1111/polp.12196.

Cashore, Benjamin, and Michael Howlett. 2007. "Punctuating Which Equilibrium? Understanding Thermostatic Policy Dynamics in Pacific Northwest Forestry," *American Journal of Political Science* 51, no. 3.

Cerny, Philip G. 2001. "From 'Iron Triangles' to 'Golden Pentangles'? Globalizing the Policy Process," *Global Governance* 7: 397–410.

Cobb, Roger W. and D.M. Primo. 2003. *The Plane Truth: Airline Crashes, the Media, and Transportation Policy*. Washington: Brookings Institution.

Cook, Thomas D. 1985. "Postpositivist Critical Multiplism," in Shotland and Mark (1985).

Daniels, Mark R. 1997. *Terminating Public Programs: An American Political Paradox*. Armonk, NJ: M.E. Sharpe.

Daugbjerg, Carsten. 1997. "Policy Networks and Agricultural Policy Reforms: Explaining Deregulation in Sweden and Re-regulation in the European Community," *Governance* 10, no. 2: 123–42.

Davidson, A. 2004. "Dynamics without Change: Continuity of Canadian Health Policy," *Canadian Public Administration* 47, no. 3: 251–79.

Deeg, Richard. 2007. "Complementarity and Institutional Change in Capitalist Systems," *Journal of European Public Policy* 14, no. 4: 611–30.

de Jong, Martin, and Jurian Edelenbos. 2007. "An Insider's Look into Policy Transfer in Transnational Expert Networks," *European Planning Studies* 15, no. 5: 687–706.

deLeon, Peter. 1978. "A Theory of Policy Termination," in J.V. May and A.B. Wildavsky, eds, *The Policy Cycle*. Beverly Hills, CA: Sage, 279–300.

———. 1983. "Policy Evaluation and Program Termination," *Policy Studies Review* 2, no. 4: 631–47.

———, and Katie Kaufmanis. 2001. "Public Policy Theory: Will It Play in Peoria?" *Policy Currents* 10, 4: 9–13.

Dery, David. 1999. "Policy by the Way: When Policy is Incidental to Making Other Policies," *Journal of Public Policy* 18, no. 2: 163–76.

de Vries, M.S. 2000. "The Secret and Cost of Success: Institutional Change and Policy Change," in O. Van Heffen, W.J.M. Kickert, and J.J.A. Thomassen, eds, *Governance in Modern Society: Effects, Change and Formation of Government Institutions*. Dordrecht: Kluwer, 61–86.

———. 2005. "Generations of Interactive Policy-Making in the Netherlands," *International Review of Administrative Sciences* 71, no. 4: 577–91.

———. 2005b. "Changing Policy Views at the Local Level: The Effect of Age, Generations and Policy Periods in Five European Countries," *European Journal of Political Research* 44: 1–15.

Djelic, Marie-Laure, and Sigrid Quack. 2007. "Overcoming Path Dependency: Path Generation in Open Systems," *Theory and Society* 36: 161–86.

Dobrowolsky, Alexandra, and Denis Saint-Martin. 2005. "Agency, Actors and Change in a Child-Focused Future: "Path Dependency" Problematised," *Commonwealth and Comparative Politics* 43, no. 1: 1–33.

Doern, G. Bruce, L. Pal, and B.W. Tomlin, eds. 1996a. *Border Crossings: The Internationalization of Canadian Public Policy*. Toronto: Oxford University Press.

Dossey, Larry. "Agnotology: On the Varieties of Ignorance, Criminal Negligence, and Crimes Against Humanity," *EXPLORE: The Journal of Science and Healing* 10, no. 6 (November): 331–44. https://doi.org/10.1016/j.explore.2014.08.011.

Dudley, Geoffrey, Wayne Parsons, and Claudio M. Radaelli. 2000. "Symposium: Theories of the Policy Process," *Journal of European Public Policy* 7, no. 1: 122–40.

———, and Jeremy Richardson. 1998. "Arenas without Rules and the Policy Change Process: Outsider Groups and British Roads Policy," *Political Studies* 46: 727–47.

Duit, Andreas. 2007. "Path Dependency and Institutional Change: The Case of Industrial Emission Control in Sweden," *Public Administration* 85, no. 4: 1097–1118.

Eldredge, Niles, and Stephen Jay Gould. 1972. "Punctuated Equilibria: An Alternative to Phyletic Gradualism," in T.J.M. Schopf, ed., *Paleobiology*. San Francisco: Freeman, Cooper, 82–115.

Eliadis, P., M. Hill, and M. Howlett. 2005. *Designing Government: From Instruments to Governance*. Montreal and Kingston: McGill-Queen's University Press.

Epstein, Paul J. 1997. "Beyond Policy Community: French Agriculture and the GATT," *Journal of European Public Policy* 4, no. 3: 355–72.

Evers, A. 2005. "Mixed Welfare Systems and Hybrid Organizations: Changes in the Governance and Provision of Social Services," *International Journal of Public Administration* 28: 737–48.

———, and H. Wintersberger. 1990. *Shifts in the Welfare Mix: Their Impact on Work, Social Services and Welfare Policies*. Boulder, CO: Westview Press.

Falkenmark, M. 2004. "Towards Integrated Catchment Management: Opening the Paradigm Locks between Hydrology, Ecology and Policy-Making," *Water Resources Development* 20, no. 3: 275–82.

Flink, Carla M. 2017. "Rethinking Punctuated Equilibrium Theory: A Public Administration Approach to Budgetary Changes," *Policy Studies Journal* 45, no. 1: 101–20.

Frantz, J.E. 2002. "Political Resources for Policy Terminators," *Policy Studies Journal* 30, no. 1: 11–28.

Gehring, Thomas, and Sebastian Oberthur. 2000. "Exploring Regime Interaction: A Framework of Analysis," paper presented to the Final Conference of the EU-financed Concerted Action Programme on the Effectiveness of International Environmental Agreements and EU Legislation—Fridtjof Nansen Institute, Barcelona, 9–11 Nov. 2000.

Gersick, Connie J.G. 1991. "Revolutionary Change Theories: A Multilevel Exploration of the Punctuated Equilibrium Paradigm," *Academy of Management Review* 16, no. 1: 10–36.

Geva-May, Iris. 2001. "When the Motto is 'Till Death Do Us Part': The Conceptualization and the Craft of Termination in the Public Policy Cycle," *International Journal of Public Administration* 24, no. 3: 263–88.

———, and Aaron Wildavsky. 1997. *An Operational Approach to Policy Analysis: The Craft Prescriptions for Better Analysis*. Boston: Kluwer.

Gould, S. J. 2007. Punctuated Equilibrium. Cambridge, MA: Belknap Press.

———. and N. Eldredge. 1977. "Puncutated Equilibria: The Tempo and Mode of Evolutin Reconsidered," *Paleobiology* 3, no. 2: 115–151.

Grant, Wyn, and Anne MacNamara. 1995. "When Policy Communities Intersect: The Cases of Agriculture and Banking," *Political Studies* 43: 509–15.

Greenaway, John, Brian Salter, and Stella Hart. 2007. "How Policy Networks Can Damage Democratic Health: A Case Study in the Government of Governance," *Public Administration* 85, no. 3: 717–38.

Greener, I. 2002. "Understanding NHS Reform: The Policy-Transfer, Social Learning and Path Dependency Perspectives," *Governance* 15, no. 2: 161–83.

Greenwood, Molly M., Mary E. Sorenson, and Benjamin R. Warner. 2016. "Ferguson on Facebook: Political Persuasion in a New Era of Media Effects," *Computers in Human Behavior* 57 (April): 1–10. doi:10.1016/j.chb.2015.12.003.

Greer, Scott. 2008. "Choosing Paths in European Health Services Policy: A Political Analysis of a Critical Juncture," *Journal of European Social Policy* 18, no. 3: 219–31.

Gunningham, Neil, Peter Grabosky, and Darren Sinclair. 1998. *Smart Regulation: Designing Environmental Policy*. Oxford: Clarendon Press.

Hacker, Jacob S. 2004a. "Reform without Change, Change without Reform: The Politics of US Health Policy Reform in Comparative Perspective," in M.A. Levin and M. Shapiro, eds, *Transatlantic Policymaking in an Age of Austerity: Diversity and Drift*. Washington: Georgetown University Press, 13–63.

———. 2004b. "Review Article: Dismantling the Health Care State? Political Institutions, Public Policies and the Comparative Politics of Health Reform," *British Journal of Political Science* 34: 693–724.

Hall, Peter A., ed. 1989. *The Political Power of Economic Ideas: Keynesianism across Nations*. Princeton, NJ: Princeton University Press.

———. 1992. "The Change from Keynesianism to Monetarism: Institutional Analysis and British Economic Policy in the 1970s," in S. Steinmo et al., eds, *Structuring Politics: Historical Institutionalism in Comparative Analysis*. Cambridge: Cambridge University Press, 90–114.

———. 1993. "Policy Paradigms, Social Learning and the State: The Case of Economic Policy Making in Britain," *Comparative Politics* 25, no. 3: 275–96.

Hammond, Thomas H. and Jack H. Knott. 2000. "Public Management, Administrative Leadership and Policy Change," in J.L. Brudney, L.J. O'Toole, and H.G. Rainey, eds, *Advancing Public Management: New Developments in Theory, Methods and Practice*. Washington: Georgetown University Press, 49–74.

Haydu, Jeffrey. 1998. "Making Use of the Past: Time Periods as Cases to Compare and as Sequences of Problem Solving," *American Journal of Sociology* 104, no. 2: 339–71.

Hayes, Michael T. 1992. *Incrementalism and Public Policy*. New York: Longmans.

———. 2001. *The Limits of Policy Change: Incrementalism, Worldview and the Rule of Law*. Washington: Georgetown University Press.

Hays, Samuel P. 1959. *Conservation and the Gospel of Efficiency: The Progressive Conservation Movement 1890–1920*. Cambridge, MA: Harvard University Press.

———. 1987. *Beauty, Health and Permanence: Environmental Politics in the United States, 1955–1985*. New York: Cambridge University Press.

Heclo, Hugh. 1974. *Modern Social Politics in Britain and Sweden: From Relief to Income Maintenance*. New Haven: Yale University Press.

Heron, Tony, and Ben Richardson. 2008. "Path Dependency and the Politics of Liberalisation in the Textiles and Clothing Industry," *New Political Economy* 13, no. 1: 1–18.

Hilgartner, Stephen, and Charles L. Bosk. 1981. "The Rise and Fall of Social Problems: A Public Arenas Model," *American Journal of Sociology* 94, no. 1: 53–78.

Hoberg, George. 1998. "Distinguishing Learning from Other Sources of Policy Change: The Case of Forestry in the Pacific Northwest," paper presented to the annual meeting of the American Political Science Association, Boston.

———, and E. Morawaski. 1997. "Policy Change through Sector Intersection: Forest and Aboriginal Policy in Clayoquot Sound," *Canadian Public Administration* 40, no. 3: 387–414.

Holzner, Burkart, and John H. Marx. 1979. *Knowledge Application: The Knowledge System in Society*. Wellesley, MA: Allyn and Bacon.

Hong, Sounman, and Daniel Nadler. 2016. "The Unheavenly Chorus: Political Voices of Organized Interests on Social Media," *Policy & Internet* 8, no. 1 (March 1): 91–106. doi:10.1002/poi3.110.

Howlette, Michael and Benjamin Cashore. 2007. "Re-Visiting the New Orthodoxy of Policy Dynamics: The Dependent Variable and Re-Aggregation Problems in the Study of Policy Change," *Canadian Political cal Science Review* 1, no. 2: 50–62.

———, and ———. 1998. "Policy Subsystem Configurations and Policy Change: Operationalizing the Postpositivist Analysis of the Politics of the Policy Process," *Policy Studies Journal* 26, no. 3: 466–82.

———, and Jeremy Rayner. 1995. "Do Ideas Matter? Policy Subsystem Configurations and Policy Change in the Canadian Forest Sector," *Canadian Public Administration* 38, no. 3: 382–410.

———, and ———. 2006. "Understanding the Historical Turn in the Policy Sciences: A Critique of Stochastic, Narrative, Path Dependency and Process-Sequencing Models of Policy-Making over Time," *Policy Sciences* 39, no. 1: 1–18.

Jenkins-Smith, Hank C., Gilbert K. St. Clair, and Brian Woods. 1991. "Explaining Change in Policy Subsystems: Analysis of Coalition Stability and Defection over Time," *American Journal of Political Science* 35, no. 4: 851–80.

Jennings, Bruce. 1987. "Interpretation and the Practice of Policy Analysis," in Fischer and Forester (1987).

Jenson, Jane. 1989. "Paradigms and Political Discourse: Protective Legislation in France and the United States before

1914," *Canadian Journal of Political Science* 22, no. 2: 235–58.

John, Peter. 2003. "Is There Life after Policy Streams, Advocacy Coalitions and Punctuations: Using Evolutionary Theory to Explain Policy Change?" *Policy Studies Journal* 31, no. 4: 481–98.

Johnson, Thomas J., and Barbara K. Kaye. 2016. "Some Like It Lots: The Influence of Interactivity and Reliance on Credibility," *Computers in Human Behavior* 61 (August): 136–45. doi:10.1016/j .chb.2016.03.012.

Jones, Bryan D. and Frank R. Baumgartner. 2005. *The Politics of Attention: How Government Prioritizes Problems.* Chicago: University of Chicago Press. kakutani

Jones, Charles O. 1984. *An Introduction to the Study of Public Policy*, 3rd edn. Monterey, CA: Brooks/Cole.

Jordan, A. Grant. 1998. "Indirect Causes and Effects in Policy Change: Shell, Greenpeace and the Brent Spar," paper presented to the annual meeting of the American Political Science Association, Boston.

Kakutani, Michiko. 2018. *The Death of Truth: Notes on Falsehood in the Age of Trump.* New York: Tim Duggan Books.

Kaufman, Herbert. 1976. *Are Government Organizations Immortal?* Washington: Brookings Institution.

Kavanagh, Jennifer and Michael D. Rich. 2018. *Truth Decay: An Initial Exploration of the Diminishing Role of Facts and Analysis in American Public Life.* Santa Monica, California: RAND Corporation.

Kay, Adrian. 2005. "A Critique of the Use of Path Dependency in Policy Studies," *Public Administration* 83, no. 3: 553–71.

———. 2006. The Dynamics of Public Policy: Theory and Evidence. Cheltenham: Edward Elgar.

Kenis, Patrick. 1991. "The Pre-Conditions for Policy Networks: Some Findings from a Three Country Study on Industrial Re-Structuring," in Marin and Mayntz (1991: 297–330).

Kindleberger, C.P. 1996. *Manias, Panics and Crashes: A History of Financial Crises.* New York: John Wiley and Sons.

Kingdon, John W. 1984. *Agendas, Alternatives and Public Policies.* Boston: Little, Brown.

Knoepfel, Peter and Ingrid Kissling-Naf. 1998. "Social Learning in Policy Networks," *Policy and Politics* 26, no. 3: 343–67.

Kruger, Justin, and David Dunning. 1999. "Unskilled and Unaware of It: How Difficulties in Recognizing One's Own Incompetence Lead to Inflated Self-Assessments," *Journal of Personality and Social Psychology* 77, no. 6: 1121–34. doi:10.1037/0022–3514.77.6.1121.

Kubler, Daniel. 2001. "Understanding Policy Change with the Advocacy Coalition Framework: An Application to Swiss Drug Policy," *Journal of European Public Policy* 8, no. 4: 623–41.

Kuhner, Stefan. 2007. "Country-Level Comparisons of Welfare State Change Measures: Another Facet of the Dependent Variable Problem within the Comparative Analysis of the Welfare State," *Journal of European Social Policy* 17, no. 1: 5–18.

Lafferty, W.M., and E. Hovden. 2003. "Environmental Policy Integration: Towards an Analytical Framework," *Environmental Politics* 12, no. 3: 1–22.

Lasswell, Harold D. 1956. *The Decision Process: Seven Categories of Functional Analysis.* College Park: University of Maryland Press.

———. 1971. *A Pre-View of Policy Sciences.* New York: American Elsevier.

Legro, Jeffrey W. 2000. "The Transformation of Policy Ideas," *American Journal of Political Science* 44, no. 3: 419–32.

Lewis, David E. 2002. "The Politics of Agency Termination: Confronting the Myth of Agency Immortality," *Journal of Politics* 64, 1: 89–107.

Liefferink, Duncan. 2006. "The Dynamics of Policy Arrangements: Turning Round the Tetrahedron," in Bas Arts and Pieter Leroy, eds, *Institutional Dynamics in Environmental Governance.* Dordrecht: Springer, 45–68.

Lindblom, Charles E. 1959. "The Science of Muddling Through," *Public Administration Review* 19, no. 2: 79–88.

Linz, Juan J. 1978. "Crisis, Breakdown, and Re-equilibration," in Linz and A. Stepan, eds, *The Breakdown of Democratic Regimes.* Baltimore: Johns Hopkins University Press, 3–124.

Loughlin, J. 2004. "The 'Transformation' of Governance: New Directions in Policy and Politics," *Australian Journal of Politics and History* 50, no. 1: 8–22.

Lynggaard, Kennet. 2001. "The Study of Policy Change: Constructing an Analytical Strategy," paper presented at the ECPR

29th Joint Session Workshops, Grenoble, 6–11 Apr.

Lynn, Laurence E. 1999. "A Place at the Table: Policy Analysis, Its Postpositive Critics, and the Future of Practice," *Journal of Policy Analysis and Management* 18, no. 3: 411–24.

Macafee, Timothy. 2013. "Some of These Things Are Not like the Others: Examining Motivations and Political Predispositions among Political Facebook Activity," *Computers in Human Behavior* 29, no. 6 (November): 2766–75. doi:10.1016/j.chb.2013.07.019.

Mahoney, James. 2000. "Path Dependence in Historical Sociology," *Theory and Society* 29, no. 4: 507–48.

Marion, Russ. 1999. *The Edge of Organization: Chaos and Complexity Theories of Formal Social Systems*. London: Sage.

May, Peter J. 1992. "Policy Learning and Failure," *Journal of Public Policy* 12, no. 4: 331–54.

———, B.D. Jones, B.E. Beem, E.A. Neff-Sharum, and M.K. Poague. 2005. "Policy Coherence and Component-Driven Policymaking: Arctic Policy in Canada and the United States," *Policy Studies Journal* 33, no. 1: 37–63.

———, Joshua Sapotichne, and Samuel Workman. 2007. "Policy Disruption across Subsystems: Terrorism, Public Risks, and Homeland Security," paper presented at the American Political Science Association annual meeting.

McBeth, Mark K., Elizabeth A. Shanahan, Ruth J. Arnell, and Paul L. Hathaway. 2007. "The Intersection of Narrative Policy Analysis and Policy Change Theory," *Policy Studies Journal* 35, no. 1: 87–108.

McIntyre, Lee. 2018. *Post-truth*. Cambridge, Massachusetts: MIT Press.

Meijerink, S. 2005. "Understanding Policy Stability and Change. The Interplay of Advocacy Coalitions and Epistemic Communities, Windows of Opportunity and Dutch Coastal Flooding Policy 1945–2003," *Journal of European Public Policy* 12, no. 6: 1060–77.

Meijers, E., and D. Stead. 2004. "Policy Integration: What Does It Mean and How Can It Be Achieved? A Multi-Disciplinary Review," paper presented at the Berlin Conference on the Human Dimensions of Global Environmental Change: Greening of Policies—Interlinkages and Policy Integration.

Melo, M.A. 2004. "Institutional Choice and the Diffusion of Policy Paradigms: Brazil and the Second Wave of Pension Reform," *International Political Science Review* 25, no. 3: 320–41.

Menahem, Gila. 1998. "Policy Paradigms, Policy Networks and Water Policy in Israel," *Journal of Public Policy* 18, no. 3: 283–310.

———. 2001. "Water Policy in Israel 1948–2000: Policy Paradigms, Policy Networks and Public Policy," *Israel Affairs* 7, 4: 21–44.

Meyer, Alan D. 1982. "Adapting to Environmental Jolts," *Administrative Science Quarterly* 27: 515–37.

Mintrom, Michael. 2007. "The Policy Analysis Movement," in Dobuzinskis et al. (2007: 71–84).

Mortensen, Peter B. 2005. "Policy Punctuations in Danish Local Budgeting," *Public Administration* 83, 4: 931–50.

———. 2007. "Stability and Change in Public Policy: A Longitudinal Study of Comparative Subsystem Dynamics," *Policy Studies Journal* 35, no. 3: 373–94.

Motta, Matthew, Timothy Callaghan, and Steven Sylvester. 2018. "Knowing Less but Presuming More: Dunning-Kruger Effects and the Endorsement of Anti-Vaccine Policy Attitudes," *Social Science & Medicine* 211 (August): 274–81. doi:10.1016/j.socscimed.2018.06.032.

Nilsson, M. 2005. "Learning, Frames and Environmental Policy Integration: The Case of Swedish Energy Policy," *Environment and Planning* C 23: 207–26.

Nisbet, Robert. 1972. "Introduction: The Problem of Social Change," in Nisbet, ed., *Social Change*. New York: Harper and Row, 1–45.

Nunan, Fiona. 1999. "Policy Network Transformation: The Implementation of the EC Directive on Packaging and Packaging Waste," *Public Administration* 77, no. 3: 621–38.

Perl, Antony and James A. Dunn Jr. 2007. "Reframing Automobile Fuel Economy Policy in North America: The Politics of Punctuating a Policy Equilibrium," *Transport Reviews* 27, no. 1: 1–35.

Pierson, Paul. 1993. "When Effect Becomes Cause: Policy Feedback and Political Change," *World Politics* 45: 595–628.

———. 2000a. "Increasing Returns, Path Dependence, and the Study of Politics,"

American Political Science Review 94, no. 2: 251–67.

———. 2000c. "The Limits of Design: Explaining Institutional Origins and Change," *Governance* 13, no. 4: 475–99.

———. 2004. *Politics in Time: History, Institutions, and Social Analysis*. Princeton, NJ: Princeton University Press.

Pollock, Philip H., Stuart A. Lilie, and M. Elliot Vittes. 1989. "Hard Issues, Core Values and Vertical Constraint: The Case of Nuclear Power," *British Journal of Political Science* 23, no. 1: 29–50.

Polsby, Nelson W. 1984. *Political Innovation in America: The Politics of Policy Initiation*. New Haven: Yale University Press.

Proctor, Robert, and Londa Schiebinger, eds. 2008. *Agnotology: The Making and Unmaking of Ignorance*. Stanford, Calif: Stanford University Press.

Raphael, Dennis. 2008. "Shaping Public Policy and Population Health in the United States: Why Is the Public Health Community Missing in Action?" *International Journal of Health Services* 38, no. 1: 63–94.

Rayner, J., et al. 2001. "Privileging the Sub-Sector: Critical Sub-Sectors and Sectoral Relationships in Forest Policy-Making," *Forest Policy and Economics* 2, nos. 3 and 4: 319–32.

Reagan, Michael D. 1987. *Regulation: The Politics of Policy*. Boston: Little, Brown.

Rhodes, R.A.W. 1997a. *Understanding Governance: Policy Networks, Governance, Reflexivity, and Accountability*. Buckingham: Open University Press.

Richardson, Jeremy J. 1999. "Interest Groups, Multi-Arena Politics and Policy Change," in S.S. Nagel, ed., *The Policy Process*. Commack, NY: Nova Science, 65–100.

Robinson, Scott E. 2007. "Punctuated Equilibrium Models in Organizational Decision Making," in Morcöl (133–49).

———, and Flou'say Caver. 2006. "Punctuated Equilibrium and Congressional Budgeting," *Political Research Quarterly* 59, no. 1: 161–6.

———, ———, Kenneth J. Meier, and Laurence J. O'Toole Jr. 2007. "Explaining Policy Punctuations: Bureaucratization and Budget Change," *American Journal of Political Science* 51, no. 1: 140–50.

Roe, Emory. 1990. *Taking Complexity Seriously: Policy Analysis, Triangulation and Sustainable Development*. Boston: Kluwer.

———. 2000. "Poverty, Defense and the Environment: How Policy Optics, Policy Incompleteness, fastthinking.com, Equivalency Paradox, Deliberation Trap, Mailbox Dilemma, the Urban Ecosystem and the End of Problem Solving Recast Difficult Policy Issues," *Administration and Society* 31, no. 6: 687–725.

Rona-Tas, Akos. 1998. "Path Dependence and Capital Theory: Sociology of the Post-Communist Economic Transformation," *East European Politics and Societies* 12, no. 1: 107–31.

Rose, Richard. 1976. "Models of Change," in Rose, ed., *The Dynamics of Public Policy: A Comparative Analysis*. London: Sage, 7–33.

———. 1990. "Inheritance before Choice in Public Policy," *Journal of Theoretical Politics* 2, no. 3: 263–91.

Rosendal, G. Kristin. 2000. "Overlapping International Regimes: The Case of the Intergovernmental Forum on Forests (IFF) between Climate Change and Biodiversity," Oslo: Fridtjof Nansen Institute Paper. Online at: www.fni.no.

Ross, Fiona. 2007. "Questioning Path Dependency Theory: The Case of the British NHS," *Policy and Politics* 35, no. 4: 591–610.

Sabatier, Paul A. 1987. "Knowledge, Policy-Oriented Learning, and Policy Change," *Knowledge: Creation, Diffusion, Utilization* 8, no. 4: 649–92.

———. 1988. "An Advocacy Coalition Framework of Policy Change and the Role of Policy-Oriented Learning Therein," *Policy Sciences* 21, nos. 2 and 3: 129–68.

———, and Hank C. Jenkins-Smith, eds. 1993a. *Policy Change and Learning: An Advocacy Coalition Approach*. Boulder, CO: Westview Press.

Schaap, L., and M.J.W. van Twist. 1997. "The Dynamics of Closedness in Networks," in W.J.M. Kickert, E.-H. Klijn, and J.F.M. Koppenjan, eds, *Managing Complex Networks: Strategies for the Public Sector*. London: Sage, 62–78.

Schattschneider, E.E. 1935. *Politics, Pressures and the Tariff*. New York: Prentice-Hall.

Schon, Donald A., and Martin Rein. 1994. *Frame Reflection: Towards the Resolution of Intractable Policy Controversies*. New York: Basic Books.

Schrad, Mark Lawrence. 2007. "Constitutional Blemishes: American Alcohol Prohibition and Repeal as Policy Punctuation," *Policy Studies Journal* 35, no. 3: 437–63.

Scrase, J.I., and W.R. Sheate. 2002. "Integration and Integrated Approaches to Assessment: What Do They Mean for the Environment?" *Journal of Environmental Policy and Planning* 4, no. 1: 275–94.

Skogstad, Grace. 1998. "Ideas, Paradigms and Institutions: Agricultural Exceptionalism in the European Union and the United States," *Governance* 11, no. 4: 463–90.

Stead, D., and E. Meijers. 2004. "Policy Integration in Practice: Some Experiences of Integrating Transport, Land-Use Planning and Environmental Politics in Local Government," paper presented at the Berlin Conference on the Human Dimensions of Global Environmental Change: Greening of Policies—Interlinkages and Policy Integration.

Studlar, Donley T. 2007. "Ideas, Institutions and Diffusion: What Explains Tobacco Control Policy in Australia, Canada and New Zealand?" *Commonwealth and Comparative Politics* 45, no. 2: 164–84.

Thelen, Kathleen. 2003. "How Institutions Evolve: Insights from Comparative Historical Analysis," in J. Mahoney and D. Rueschemeyer, eds, *Comparative Historical Analysis in the Social Sciences*. Cambridge: Cambridge University Press, 208–40.

———. 2004. *How Institutions Evolve: The Political Economy of Skills in Germany, Britain, the United States and Japan*. Cambridge: Cambridge University Press.

Theocharis, Yannis, and Jan W. van Deth. 2018. "The Continuous Expansion of Citizen Participation: A New Taxonomy," *European Political Science Review* 10, no. 1 (February): 139–63. https://doi.org/10.1017/S1755773916000230.

Thomas, E.V. 2003. "Sustainable Development, Market Paradigms and Policy Integration," *Journal of Environmental Policy and Planning* 5, no. 2: 201–16.

Thomas, Gerald B. 1999. "External Shocks, Conflict and Learning as Interactive Sources of Change in U.S. Security Policy," *Journal of Public Policy* 19, no. 2: 209–31.

Torenvlied, Rene, and A. Akkerman. 2004. "Theory of 'Soft' Policy Implementation in Multilevel Systems with an Application to Social Partnership in the Netherlands," *Acta Politica* 39: 31–58.

True, James L., Bryan D. Jones, and Frank R. Baumgartner. 1999. "Punctuated-Equilibrium Theory: Explaining Stability and Change in American Policymaking," in Sabatier (1999a: 97–115).

Van Kersbergen, K., and F. Van Waarden. 2004. "'Governance' as a Bridge between Disciplines: Cross-Disciplinary Inspiration Regarding Shifts in Governance and Problems of Governability, Accountability and Legitimacy," *European Journal of Political Research* 43, no. 2: 143–72.

Vosoughi, Soroush, Deb Roy, and Sinan Aral. 2018. "The Spread of True and False News Online," in *Science* 359: 1146–1151.

Warnier, Jean-Pierre. 2013. "On Agnotology as Built-in Ignorance," *Africa Spectrum* 48, no. 1 (May 3): 113–16.

Weaver, R. Kent. 1988. *Automatic Government: The Politics of Indexation*. Washington: Brookings Institution.

Weir, Margaret. 1992. "Ideas and the Politics of Bounded Innovation," in Sven Steinmo, Kathleen Thelen, and Frank Longstreth, eds, *Structuring Politics: Historical Institutionalism in Comparative Analysis*. Cambridge: Cambridge University Press, 188–216.

Wilder, Matt, and Michael Howlett. 2014. "The Politics of Policy Anomalies: Bricolage and the Hermeneutics of Paradigms," *Critical Policy Studies* 8, no. 2: 183–202.

Wilsford, David. 1985. "The *Conjoncture* of Ideas and Interests," *Comparative Political Studies* 18, no. 3: 357–72.

———. 1994. "Path Dependency, or Why History Makes It Difficult but Not Impossible to Reform Health Care Systems in a Big Way," *Journal of Public Policy* 14, no. 3: 251–84.

Wilson, Carter A. 2000. "Policy Regimes and Policy Change," *Journal of Public Policy* 20, no. 3: 247–71.

Wollin, Andrew. 1999. "Punctuated Equilibrium: Reconciling Theory of Revolutionary and Incremental Change," *Systems Research and Behavioural Science* 16: 359–67.

Wood, R.S. 2006. "The Dynamics of Incrementalism: Subsystems, Politics and Public Lands," *Policy Studies Journal* 34, no. 1: 1–16.

Index